By the Same Author

Guy Gibson

Cheshire

The Biography of Leonard Cheshire
VC, OM

RICHARD MORRIS

VIKING

VIKING

Published by the Penguin Group
Penguin Books Ltd, 27 Wrights Lane, London w8 5tz, England
Penguin Putnam Inc., 375 Hudson Street, New York, New York 10014, USA
Penguin Books Australia Ltd, Ringwood, Victoria, Australia
Penguin Books Canada Ltd, 10 Alcorn Avenue, Toronto, Ontario, Canada m4v 3b2
Penguin Books (NZ) Ltd, Private Bag 102902, NSMC, Auckland, New Zealand

Penguin Books Ltd, Registered Offices: Harmondsworth, Middlesex, England

First published 2000
1 3 5 7 9 10 8 6 4 2

The author and publisher acknowledge with gratitude consent to publish extracts: Crecy Publishing for L.
Cheshire, *Bomber Pilot* and *Pathfinder*; HMSO for D. Richards and H. Saunders, *The Royal Air Force 1939–45*;
St Pauls Publishing for L. Cheshire and Fr Reginald Fuller, *Crossing the Finishing Line* and L. Cheshire, *Where is
God in All This?*; Greenhill Books Ltd for A. T. Harris, *Bomber Offensive*; Hamish Hamilton for A. Guinness, *My
Name Escapes Me*; Richard Cohen Books for K. Brownlow, *David Lean*; Random House UK for L. Cheshire,
The Face of Victory; Methuen for L. Cheshire, *The Light of Many Suns*; HarperCollins for L. Cheshire, *The Hidden
World*; the author for W. Russell, *New Lives for Old*.

Crown copyright material is reproduced with the permission of the Controller of
Her Majesty's Stationery Office.

While every effort has been made to obtain permission, the author and publishers would be pleased to
rectify any errors or omissions in future editions.

Set in 12/14.75 pt Monotype Bembo
Typeset by Rowland Phototypesetting Ltd,
Bury St Edmunds, Suffolk
Printed in Great Britain by Clays Ltd, St Ives plc

A CIP catalogue record for this book is available from the British Library

ISBN 0-670-86736-7

To the memory of Frank Long

The idea of a 'general resurrection', in which all those who perished before the fulfilment of history are brought back to participate in the final triumph, does justice to both the value of individual life, without which the fulfilment of history would be incomplete; and to the memory of the whole course of history, without which his life cannot be fulfilled.

Reinhold Niebuhr,
The Nature and Destiny of Man

We need a vision, a dream.
The vision should be the oneness, the essential and organic solidarity of the human family. The dream, that we each in our way make our personal contribution towards building unity and peace among us.

The only question is how.

Leonard Cheshire, *The Hidden World*

What matter if I be burnt up
As long as I light up His Face.

CONTENTS

LIST OF ILLUSTRATIONS

Photographic credits: Norman Boorer: 40, 41; Larry Curtis: 20, 22, 23; Colour Features: 35; *Flight*: 8; Hulton Getty: 31; Imperial War Museum: 11, 12, 13, 14, 25, 27, 30; Leonard Cheshire Archive: 1,

2, 3, 4 7, 9, 10, 15, 18, 21, 24, 26, 28, 29, 33, 34, 36, 37, 38, 39, 42–59; Ken McDonald: 16, 17; Sue Ryder: 60; Stowe School: 5, 6; *The Tatler*: 32; Times Newspapers Ltd: 19.

Preface and Acknowledgements

This book was written with a copy of June Mendoza's portrait of Leonard Cheshire propped to one side of my desk. For six years, there he has stood among the pencils, rubbers and paper clips. The stance – one hand on hip, head tilted – is informal yet not casual, the face serious but not solemn. The half-pursed lips suggest an imminent smile. Or the turning of an idea. Or some perplexity. Or – what? We do not know. As Bernard Malamud said, 'There is no life that can be recaptured wholly, as it was.'

Which is to say that all biography, like history, is ultimately a kind of fiction. To any protest that Leonard Cheshire was born in 1917 or that he won the VC, and that these are facts, the reply must be that facts alone do not amount to history or lives. There is history which is faithful to sources and history which isn't, but there is no objective or complete history. The past, like the present, is mediated by human minds, and every mind mediates it differently. In a world where there is little agreement about the interpretation of what is happening now, the likelihood of certainty about the past is small. All history is new. To agree this is not to downvalue history, nor to succumb to the kind of soggy relativism which Cheshire himself disliked. Truth is not denied by failure in the struggle to ascertain it.

So, while there is an abundance of information about Leonard Cheshire in what stands below, facts alone do not remake the man. The vast complexity of a human being cannot be caught by a few words. This book is not an authentic representation of *the* Leonard Cheshire. It is simply my portrait of a Leonard Cheshire. A 'definitive' study would imprison him.

Cheshire was a devout man, and quite early in the project I

became aware that I was working within a genre which hitherto I had assumed to be extinct – the saint's life, the *vita*. Saints intercede for humanity with God, and behind nearly every saint's cult there is a *vita*. A few, like Sulpicius Severus's Life of St Martin, were near-contemporary with their subjects. Others were written years or centuries later. Many are composite works, conflating material of different dates and provenances.

The *vita* was a genre for which there were templates. One common itinerary introduces a young person of good, sometimes high, birth, who progresses through an active secular youth, encounters God, embraces poverty, sometimes extreme hardship too, and exchanges materialism for spirituality. Miracles often follow. Antony and Benedict, for instance, were noblemen. Augustine and Francis were affluent and given to teenage roistering. Martin and Guthlac were warriors. The realization that Cheshire's life followed this pattern was a little unnerving. Was there a risk that, perhaps subconsciously, I would find myself writing to the template, or (perhaps more likely) avoiding it, to show that I had pulled no punches? I hope not. I have simply tried to describe what I found.

This is a book about Leonard Cheshire, not a history of the Leonard Cheshire Foundation or his other charities. To a degree, however, the story embraces a history of the foundation's origins, which were more complicated than some modern summaries allow and which puzzled Cheshire himself at the time, because he was uncertain how different areas of his work fitted together. Much of the thrill in researching the period 1945–60 lay in seeing, down the wrong end of history's telescope, just how much of it did fit.

In all kinds of ways Cheshire's was a strange life, and, because of its range, not an easy one about which to write. Although he was a public figure, ever ready to discuss his work and beliefs, he was emotionally guarded to the point at which colleagues who had worked with him closely for years sometimes felt that they did not really know him. Most who came into contact found him to be the warmest, most attractive person they ever met – a man for whom the phrase 'heart to heart' might have been invented, for he lived through the heart and caused others around him to do likewise.

When Cheshire talked to you, you might feel that you were the only person in the world with whom he wanted to be at that moment. This may well be because you were – a result of his belief that there is a smudge of Christ in everyone.

As for the guardedness, this is impossible to penetrate, and for the most part I have not tried. To have done so would have made aspects of the story heavily speculative, and while biographers' speculations may make good reading, in the absence of evidence they are not necessarily good biography. With so much else to explore, the fact that certain parts of the story are inaccessible is simply something to be accepted.

Having said this, I will speculate on one point. Whence did the guardedness come? My sense is that after his conversion there was not much about himself which he thought interesting or important. He knew there were some things at which he was good, but from 1947 when he turned completely to Christianity he saw himself less as an instigator than as a length of copper wire through which the charge of God's power might run. In the face of vast public admiration, he saw himself as unimportant. There are signs that some others hoped for more from him – confidence, affection, love – than they got, and because of that felt themselves to be at one remove from a warmth they longed to share. His given reason for that was that close friendships were unaffordable luxuries. All the time he had was husbanded for the work of God. Another feature of *vitae* is that their subjects were seldom comfortable people.

He met his last illness with a kind of gaiety. Having devoted most of his life to working with the sick and disabled he rejoiced to end it as one of them. The passage was not easy. The composer Béla Bartók said that one should die empty. Cheshire was not empty when he died – or, at any rate, he did not feel so. There were still things he wanted to do.

One of them was to write his autobiography. He often discussed it with Sue Ryder: a consummating work in which he would set out his faith. Millions would read it. The book was to be 'a project for Laundry', because he dreamed of a time when he could withdraw from public commitments and retire to Laundry Cottage, the family house in Hampshire, to write it. But writing did not come easily, and he worked himself so long and hard that when the time came, there was no time.

And yet, in a sense, he did write it. Down the years he wrote books and essays which collectively form an autobiographical collage. *Bomber Pilot* and *The Face of Victory* roughly span the period 1940–55. He regretted *Bomber Pilot, The Face of Victory* was the product of a long struggle and there are omissions from both for the modern biographer to make good. But the primary themes are there. Fragments of 'For Your Tomorrow', a book about ordinary people in war which was begun and abandoned in the 1960s, contain additional material. *The Light of Many Suns*, his account of the atomic bombing of Japan and its aftermath, links war and peace. *The Hidden World* is woven from memories and reflections. Near the end came *Where is God in All This?*, a set of extended interviews with Alenka Lawrence, while in the last two months of his life he struggled to spill out a series of reflections which in some respects take us closer to his spirituality than anything else he wrote. And he wrote a lot else. *Thoughts for the Future*, a filmed meditation about the evolution and structure of his work, anticipated aspects of modern management theory by several decades.

Cheshire was a great anticipator, with an uncanny instinct for the shape of things ahead. In 1945 he grasped the principle of deterrence in advance of the vocabulary which was later evolved to articulate it, and foresaw space exploration. In 1946 he defined the global village, and he was urging a version of 'small is beautiful' years before Schumacher made it fashionable. The idea of community-based rehabilitation was in his mind by 1955. He foresaw the tragedy in the Balkans.

About all these things, he wrote in articles, interviews, letters. At times, therefore, it has been possible to tell the story in Cheshire's own words. If they are not the words he would have used in a book of his own, they are often the words he used at the time. For someone who disliked paperwork his archive is good. From the mid-1940s he seldom threw anything away. Letters, postcards, telegrams, drafts of articles, ideas for books, even evanescent items like Christmas card lists, correspondence with removal firms, garage and tailors' bills – all were there.

Several factors explain this. His allergy to bureaucracy led him to recruit capable secretaries and assistants who compensated for it. Allied to that was his lifestyle. Between 1952, when he was diagnosed with advanced TB, and 1954 he was in Midhurst sanatorium. Here he learned to dictate letters, documents and messages on to tape. For six years thereafter he lived nowhere and was always moving to somewhere, usually in an old Bedford bus which he had converted to an office. Such itinerancy might be thought inimical to the survival of day-to-day records. In fact, it had the opposite effect. Incessant travel meant that to a large extent he communicated in letters and memos, which the secretariat preserved. From day to day, sometimes hour to hour, we can follow the evolution of his thinking, and others' reactions to it. For these central years I have as far as possible tried to let original voices speak.

Among the voices are all those that Andrew Boyle interviewed in 1954–5 when he was writing *No Passing Glory*. Few biographers can have enjoyed the privilege of complete access to the notes, correspondence and tapes of a predecessor, yet through the generosity of his widow, Eleanor Boyle, this is essentially what has happened here. Everything Cheshire said to Boyle was written down or dictated. Beyond this, Boyle retained a large body of personal material – photographs, correspondence, papers, accounts – which Cheshire gave to him in 1955. The answers to questions I would have asked of departed figures like Ralph Cochrane, Charles Whitworth or Maitland Wilson were thus miraculously available.

Many have helped, in many different ways: Geoff Almond, Eirene Andrews, Michael Barstow, Tom Bennett, Wilfrid Bickley, Terry Blatch, Norman Boorer, Eleanor Boyle, Mary Burns, the Hon. Mrs Nona Byrne, Harold Chapman, the late Christopher Cheshire, Susan Cheshire, Tom Chilton, Bill Chorley, Michael Cockram, Tony Dale, Colin Dobinson, Dr Renata Dwan, Larry Curtis, Pamela Farrell, Sir Christopher Foxley-Norris, Dr Noble Frankland, Fr. Reginald Fuller, Fay Gillon, Sir David and Lady Goodall, Judge Hilary Gosling, John Grimstone, Louis Gunter, Amy Haley, Ken Haley, Hugh Hanning, Glyn Hepworth, Frances Hopwood, Michael Hutchinson, Tony Iveson, Frances Jeram, Nikki King,

H. W. Kirtland, Bryne Knight, Edith Kup, E. Anne Layton, Paul Layton, Candida Lycett-Green, Lois Machin, Peter Mallender, Margaret Masters, Brian Matthews, Ken McDonald, R. J. R. McDougall, Douglas Mourton, Robert Owen, Albert Postma, Lord Puttnam, Sir Peter Ramsbotham, Ron Read, Paddy Reed, Brigadier John Regan, Kenric Rice, Peggy Roberts, G. Robson, Nickie Ross, Peter and Ethnea Rowley, Wilfrid Russell, the late David and Ann Shannon, Anthony Shillington, Carmel Short, Peggy Stead, Wally Sullivan, Laura Taylor, Ron Travers, Philip Tweedale, William Vernon, Kathy Vowles, Ted Wass, Alan Webb, Tom Wingham, G. E. Woods, Bob Worthington. I am indebted to all.

As regards institutions and their staff, my gratitude goes to Dr Sarah Bendall and Merton College library; to Sandra Amdor and Stowe School; Neil Young and the Imperial War Museum; the Old Lyme Historical Society, Connecticut; Academy of Motion Picture Arts and Sciences, Center for Motion Picture Study, Beverly Hills; Defense Visual Information Center, California; the Public Record Office; the Council for British Archaeology, who allowed me leave of absence to pursue research; and above all Jill Roberts, archivist of the Leonard Cheshire Archive at Staunton Harold, whose support throughout was a large blessing. Supportive, too, have been Jane, my wife, and Eva, my daughter, both of whom gave much help at Staunton Harold.

The chapters on 617 Squadron owe much to discussion with and help from Robert Owen (Official Historian, 617 Squadron Association), who also originated the maps and diagrams, and Tom Bennett. Michael Barstow, Robert Owen, Tom Bennett and Dr Noble Frankland read parts of the manuscript in draft, made many valuable suggestions and saved me from errors. Sue Ryder read it all although it should be explained that her views on the later chapters were interrupted by illness as the book was going to press. For encouragement, advice, criticism and support, and for the privilege of many hours of conversation, I give her my thanks.

Prologue

This is an ideal country for defence, and the devil to attack over. Imagine an immense mud-baked plain with scanty vegetation of burnt grass and partly bushes, here and there intersected by irrigation rills, and occasionally deep narrow canals about 6 ft deep, and you have Mesopotamia – anyway the Sinn area.[1]

It is 5 November 1916, and twenty-year-old Lt Edmund Leonard Barstow, always known as Leonard, is writing to his father, Lt Col. Thomas Anderson Adam Barstow, describing landscape in what today is the south-east corner of Iraq. At seventy-three Thomas looks back across a distinguished career in the 72nd Seaforth Highlanders, and memories of the second Afghan War. The Barstows have been an Army family since the eighteenth century. Today, all four of Thomas's sons are serving officers, three as members of Indian regiments. Leonard, his youngest, is on attachment to the 36th Sikhs. There are three daughters: Isabella Emily, Edith and Primrose. The girls are devoted to 'Lennie'.

Leonard's mother, Jane, is seventeen years younger than her husband. Fluent in French, Italian and German, she adores travel and continental life, and since 1904 the family has been living in Lausanne and Italy. This is partly because the cost of living is lower than in Britain, but mainly because Jane enjoys it. Thomas, by contrast, is less enamoured of Switzerland and gave the outbreak of war as his reason for returning to Edinburgh. The family's house at 32 India Street remains closed; he lives in the New Club.

Thomas is neither fully fit nor well off, and Leonard's letters show constant concern for him. Amid shelling by the Turks, Leonard is more concerned by news of his father's stomach trouble. Leonard has diverted much of his pay to his parents. He has sold his polo pony, given details of his bank account at Peshawar, and explained how his slender assets can be recovered in the event of his death.

Leonard's death is not improbable. Fighting is fierce. 'I wish they would bring some tanks out here,' he muses to his father five weeks later:

> they would do splendidly, ideal country for them, half a dozen at Sanagat would make Turco think a bit. The devils bombed one of our camps at Twin Canals between Sheikh Saad and Sinn Banks, killed and wounded 17 men, so our planes went over (6) and bombed their camps, and blew 7 tents to hell, to put it mildly . . .[2]

On the following day Leonard goes into action for the first time. His unit's objective is the town of Kut, situated beside the confluence of the rivers Hai and Tigris. Leonard's next letter, written on 23 December, describes extreme cold, heavy shelling and sleeplessness. After savage fighting on eight consecutive days, Kut remains in Turkish hands.

The weather breaks. At the end of the month Leonard tells his father: 'It has been raining cats and dogs since I last wrote, we have had a poor time of it without tents.' The rains make the ground impassable. At Christmas there are no parcels because the mail has 'completely broken down'. Carts are 'up their axles in mud' on unmetalled roads. The 'rotten railway' provided by army engineers is 'only light gauge, just lines laid on mud, no ballast or anything'. Overworked locomotives which run on it break down. By New Year's Eve the 36th Sikhs are on short rations, which Leonard and his colleagues augment by shooting wildfowl and wading into the marshes to catch mudfish by hitting them with sticks. Floods threaten. The Hai is in spate, 'as big as the Thames'. The Tigris rises by thirteen feet. Amid fire and flood there are occasional consolations. 'Your parcel containing shortbread and rock and handkerchiefs just arrived, ever so many thanks for them all, the h'chiefs are a godsend.'[3]

By 5 January Leonard's unit has advanced to the right bank of the River Hai, and from here he is intrigued to see a dogfight. 'By Jove,' he tells his father, 'an air fight of sorts is going on, the Turk

is hooking it, but has come round, the air is full of "Archibalds".'*
Leonard also notes heavy outgoing artillery fire. 'I wonder what it
all means?'

Leonard describes the assault to which this bombardment was a
prelude. Ordered to attack a fortified pocket in a meander of the
Tigris, they find Turkish trenches recently reinforced. Fighting is
'mainly hand to hand'. Some 1,400 yards of trenches are taken, of
which 400 yards are recaptured by a Turkish counter-attack, and
of these 100 yards are in their turn repossessed.

Leonard's accounts of fighting are interspersed with candid comments on morale, leadership, class and regimental rivalries. Pneu-
monia 'is bound to make its ravages soon', he reflects, when the rains
arrive, 'especially among the Sikh, who is very liable to it'. On the
other hand, the Sikhs have 'made themselves quite snug during the
rains, whereas the 1/4th Devons being absolutely without initiative
shivered in the rain'. Col. Orlando Gunning, the 36th's commanding
officer, who has been on active service 'without any decent rest'
since August 1914, is 'absolutely fed up with the whole show'.

By the last week in January Leonard's spirits are rising. Soon 'we
should have a fair chance of seeing what Kut looks like from the
inside – am tired of gazing at its walls – but the inside of it is mainly
ruins now'. Success in the air is heartening. 'Our planes went and
bombed Baghdad, dropped six 100 lb bombs on them, not a bad
effort.' The local Arab population, hitherto viewed warily, is now
less in evidence: 'The arabs are clearing off, one does not see so
many of them nowadays. The cavalry have raided them so often
and pinched all their grub that they are a trifle fed up.'

By late January the final assault on Kut is near.

Dear Pater, just a line before I go up into the trenches – 3 days' fighting for
Hai bridgehead defences; 4 Turkish counter-attacks, one succeeding but then
recountered. Artillery fire and trench mortars – By jove, we did bombard the
swine, I never saw such a show . . . Well my dear Pater, my turn has come at
last, and doubtless we shall 'hop it' tomorrow morning. The mess in the front
lines is appalling – bodies which will be stinking soon remaining unburied.[4]

---

* Slang for anti-aircraft fire.

Leonard is killed four days later. Beforehand, in the mud, among the putrefying corpses and haze of blowflies, awaiting his turn at last, had news of his sister Primrose's pregnancy reached him?

Immersed in the Army, the Barstows had taken 'a dim view' of Primrose's decision to marry a 'mere civilian' – a young law don called Geoffrey Chevalier Cheshire. Primrose, however, was not a Barstow for nothing and in the face of her intransigence her father had eventually given his blessing.

Geoffrey had shown his mettle by gaining a commission in the Cheshire Regiment at the outbreak of war, and had since transferred to the Royal Flying Corps. Whether membership of the new-fangled RFC made Geoffrey more or less suspect in Barstow eyes is unclear, but Primrose wrote regularly to her father with news of his son-in-law's progress. A few weeks previously she had recounted a remarkable adventure.

During the autumn of 1916 Geoffrey Cheshire was being trained for Balloon Observation work. On 16 November he volunteered to take part in a night flight to check the effectiveness of London's wartime lighting regulations. The balloon took off from Wandsworth soon after 6 p.m. with a crew of three. Drifting over London at 500 ft, Geoffrey quickly realized that their mission was futile. The capital's lights did indeed vary in intensity, but as Geoffrey recalled 'a delinquent light for all we could see, might be in Piccadilly or down Limehouse Way'. The reconnaissance was due to last an hour. Their pilot, a naval lieutenant, had more ambitious ideas. He refused to land, predicting that the wind would veer due south, carry them to Scotland and win them the record for the longest night flight made by a balloon.

Some time later, a near-collision with trees on unexpected high ground warned that the wind had not veered, and that it had risen. Peril now mingled with farce. Uncertain of their position, the three men attempted to ascertain it by shouting in unison 'What's the name of this place?' to people sighted below. When this was put to a cyclist on a lonely road somewhere in the Cotswolds Geoffrey recalled that 'the only effect was that he fell from his machine with a clearly audible crash'.

Swept by the gale north-west across the Midlands, Geoffrey was later astonished to recognize his home city of Chester. This placed them only ten miles from the coast. When Geoffrey pointed this out, the pilot 'without any hesitation pulled a complete panel out of the envelope'. Descending rapidly, the balloon hit the beach at Point of Ayr, forty yards short of the sea. The basket turned over and was dragged inverted. Geoffrey and the second crew member were shaken but unscathed. The pilot was less fortunate. His neck was broken, and he died.[5]

When told of this episode by his father, Leonard replied: 'Geoff seems to have had a very lucky escape, thank heavens it was no worse; probably cooled his ardour for flying considerably.' And now Leonard was gone. When Geoffrey and Primrose's first son is born later in the year they will bestow his name upon him: Leonard. A name to conjure with. Hermit, patron saint of the oppressed and marginalized, a dedication favoured by medieval travellers. To say it is the end and the beginning, for lives, too, are journeys. This Leonard's passage will be among the strangest of all.

PART ONE: TOKENS AND SIGNS, 1917–1940

1. Lines from Other Days

For Leonard Cheshire the family was a powerful image. In war the bomber crew was a kind of kin group. Peace demanded the conquest of 'all the things that disable our one human family'.[1] As a Catholic the Holy Family absorbed him. Of the Cheshire Homes, each 'is a family, so to speak'. He thought of the Cheshire Foundation as a global family.[2] Family was his subsoil.

Let us begin, then, with the Cheshires, whose heartland before the Great War lay in the county from which they took their name. Leonard's father, Geoffrey Chevalier Cheshire, was born in Chester on 27 June 1886, descending from a line which ran back through two generations of lawyers to a dynasty of gentleman landowners in the neighbourhood of Hartford, on the outskirts of Northwich. The family's fortunes during the nineteenth century oscillated between wealth and indigence. Geoffrey's grandfather Christopher, for instance, had been a man of 'unflagging perseverance and stainless character',[3] who from the 1840s built up a highly respected legal practice in Northwich and by hard work reversed ruinous losses which had been incurred by his father and younger brother in ill-advised speculation. Christopher's son Walter, by contrast, was 'one of the most successful escapists of all time', a self-absorbed obsessive whose main occupation was walking. He aimed to cover three thousand miles a year, and each night recorded the distance he had travelled, often going out again if his target had not been met. Subsidiary interests lay in racing, football and cricket – especially cricket – and the consumption of two bottles of whisky each week. Sport governed his reading (chiefly *Wisden* and *Ruff's Guide to the Turf*) and travel (an annual trip to London for Surrey fixtures at the Oval). His wants were correspondingly modest, ten shillings a week being sufficient for his whisky and a daily shave – 'a job he could not be bothered to do for himself'.

Luckily, Walter had a good wife, Clara Hatt-Cook of Hartford Hall, who was bright, companionable and resilient. She needed to be, for Walter's allergy to work soon undid all that his father had accomplished. Thereafter the family lived on £800 a year from the one public office that Walter retained: the registrarship of the County Court. Among other things the registrar was responsible for fines and money paid by litigants, tasks which Walter characteristically delegated to his chief clerk, who embezzled the funds. When the fraud was discovered the clerk drowned himself in the River Weaver, leaving a pile of folded clothes on the bank and a debt of £6,000 for which Walter was accountable. Clara stepped in. She sold their house, moved the family to more modest premises and took out a loan. Living expenses were cut, domestic servants reduced, holidays cancelled. Within four years the loan was repaid.

By a twist too strange for fiction the entire cycle then repeated itself. The new chief clerk exploited Walter's lassitude, once more there was a shortfall in public funds and again the clerk answered for it flinging himself into the River Weaver. For a second time Clara came to the rescue. House and furniture were sold. The family moved from one rented apartment to another, at various times living in Colwyn Bay, Chester and Buxton, whence Walter (who astonishingly still kept the Lord Chancellor's confidence) travelled back and forth to Northwich.

It was against this shifting, sometimes anxious background that young Geoffrey grew up. The second of three brothers, 'scraggy and frail' at birth, he defied an aunt's prediction that he would not outlive infancy by remaining hale for another ninety-two years. Clara's sacrifices ensured that his boyhood was healthy and well-adjusted, and that it followed the canonical path, a preparatory boarding school followed by public school, which would prepare him for a gentlemanly profession. The intended school was Shrewsbury, but when this became unaffordable he went instead to Denstone College, a school of Anglo-Catholic ethos for sons of poorer gentlefolk which had recently been planted on a draughty hilltop in north Staffordshire. Here Geoffrey passed 'four comparatively happy, though not very profitable, years on the classical side.'

Geoffrey left Denstone in 1905. Outwitting his father's efforts to steer him into a bank (an occupation which Walter discovered required no training and hence no further expense) he went to Oxford, entering Merton College to read law. After an idle first term he became industrious, obtaining a first class in the Final Honour School and then a lectureship at Aberystwyth; 1911 found him back in Oxford, tutoring pupils who included A. P. Herbert and C. R. Allen; in 1912 he was elected to a fellowship in law at Exeter College which he would hold for the next thirty-two years.

Geoffrey was tall, long-faced, with a dry sense of humour, and contentedly settled. He regulated his days by a self-devised routine that atoned for his father's apathy by allocating purpose to every hour: intellectual work from nine o'clock until one, an afternoon of tennis or golf, followed by study or writing from five until dinner at half past seven. He seldom worked after dinner, but spare time was invariably occupied. Reading absorbed him, especially Trollope; so did sport, walking and an enthusiasm for cars. The hundred guineas which accompanied the award of an Inns of Court Studentship in 1911 was used to buy a 'tin lizzie', a machine with an epicyclic gear and a tendency to stall on steep hills.

This takes us to 1913. That summer Geoffrey visited friends who lived across the road from his parents' house in Chester. With them was a visitor, Primrose Barstow. At twenty-four Primrose was much travelled, yet 'very British'. Geoffrey was drawn to her, and when at the summer's end they separated, Geoffrey to Oxford and Primrose to Italy, their friendship continued by letter. At Christmas Geoffrey travelled to Florence, and outside the entrance to the Ponte Vecchio, leaning over a wall above the River Arno, he asked her to marry him.

Primrose refused. Or, as Geoffrey later recalled, the proposal 'though not utterly repudiated, was not accepted'. Geoffrey was undeterred. The letters continued, and in the following summer they became engaged. On a hot August afternoon in 1914, amid London crowds gripped by war fever, we glimpse him pursuing Primrose across the city, imploring her to remain in England as she boarded a boat train to join her mother in Lausanne. Primrose returned in 1915, and they were married in November that year. Col. Barstow, by now resigned to the prospect of a civilian son-in-law, put his best face on it.

Geoffrey had meanwhile enlisted in the Army, and transferred to the Royal Flying Corps in 1916. Rejected for pilot training because of inadequate eyesight, he found himself assigned instead to artillery observation from kite balloons, making near-daily ascents to monitor and correct the fall of shells near Arras and Ypres. Tethered balloons filled with inflammable gas were vulnerable to gunfire from the ground and fighters in the air. On one occasion he watched helplessly as one balloon after another went down under the guns of a German fighter. Moments before his own balloon seemed likely to perish likewise, the aircraft was itself shot down. It was with deep relief, then, that in October 1917 he was ordered to return to England. Home on leave in Chester, he held his son for the first time. Leonard was seven weeks old; although he was christened Geoffrey Leonard, it was by his second name that he would always be known. Geoffrey senior passed the remaining months of the war in comparative safety, and in 1919 he returned to Oxford, now a 'city of ghosts', and resumed his career as a don.

An additional appointment as Exeter's domestic bursar lifted his income, and on the strength of this they bought a roomy house on the Woodstock Road. They were now reasonably well off, supported by a cook, a cleaner and a Swiss nanny to help care for Leonard and their second son, Christopher. Even so, Primrose remained compulsively thrifty. To save money she typed Geoffrey's manuscripts, bound his books, grew vegetables and knitted clothes. Downright in manner, self-sacrificial for her family, assiduous in churchgoing, averse to vulgarity, Primrose was also welcoming, open to fun and capable of roaring with laughter. A pianist who liked songs and singing, music and classical novels were among her recreations, even if household duties did not leave much time for them. Geoffrey called her Tops, perhaps because in his eyes she was.

Marriage had not yet moderated Primrose's zest for life abroad, and in 1921, while time remained before the boys reached school age, she took them to France. Here they lived for over a year, staying with Primrose's mother at Pau in the foothills of the Pyrénées, where Geoffrey joined them during vacations. The children returned bilingual. Their later aptitude for languages, Leonard's fondness for warm climates, perhaps even his subsequent affinity with nearby Lourdes, all drew from this experience.

Leonard and Christopher were normal, high-spirited children who climbed trees, occasionally got into trouble, and absorbed their father's passions for tennis and things mechanical. Leonard was given to moments of introspection which deepened as he grew older, but it was his open-heartedness, loyalty towards his parents, especially his mother, and underlying vigour which struck visitors and relatives. He also had a strong sense of pity. Oxford in the 1920s had its quota of beggars and limbless ex-servicemen who hobbled the streets or offered their caps from doorways. These people pierced him.[4]

In 1922 the family's income was further boosted by Geoffrey's election to a lectureship at All Souls, and from 1925 by royalties from his second book, *The Modern Law of Real Property*, which reinforced his growing reputation as a scholar. In this year Leonard was sent to the Dragon School, popular for the education of dons' children. At first he was considered small for his age and 'not terribly good at anything', but thereafter progressed happily enough.

Woodstock Road, Christopher recalled, became 'increasingly trafficky', and in 1929 Geoffrey and Primrose began to look for somewhere new to live. Their solution was not to buy a house but to build one. They chose a site at Cothill in Berkshire, twenty minutes' drive from Oxford, within easy walking distance of Frilford Heath golf course, and with sufficient land for tennis courts and a generous garden. For the design they turned to their friend T. Harold Hughes, a Glaswegian architect who had undertaken projects for the university. Hughes devised a building long in plan, with kitchen quarters at the centre, a roomy hall, two dining rooms (one small for informal family use, the other large), five bedrooms, a first-floor study for Geoffrey, three bathrooms and a garage to contain three cars. Thrifty and independent, they decided to build without a contractor. With advice from Exeter's Clerk of Works, Geoffrey purchased stone and timber, hired craftsmen, oversaw construction, and struggled – not entirely successfully – to outwit the suppliers and labourers who tried to fleece them. The project occupied the best part of a year, and the entire family took part in it.

For Leonard and Christopher, clambering about on scaffolding and roof trusses in summer evenings, these were golden days. In 1930 Leonard was in his thirteenth year, the openness of earlier childhood not yet outgrown, but now augmented by an emerging poise. The work was arduous, sometimes monotonous, but as the house took shape it generated a subdued excitement. Their effort and self-sufficiency had practical and unifying purpose, which put something in the place of nothing and exorcised the impermanencies of Geoffrey's childhood. They called the house Grey Walls. As the building weathered down, its mullioned windows, lanky chimneys and fabric of squared rubble recalled an older England.

Geoffrey's career continued to prosper. In 1933 he became a reader at All Souls and by now his third book, *Private International Law*, judged by many to be his best, was published. He stuck to the routine which balanced work and recreation. Out of term his mornings were put to writing, while afternoons were devoted to tennis, golf or gardening. The garden was a joint project and shared passion with Primrose. There was a gardener, but Primrose was the one with horticultural expertise, while Geoffrey was the labourer who under her direction laid paths and lawns, built pens for their geese, dug flowerbeds and felled or planted trees. Gardening and tennis played on the courts he laid with his own hands kept him fit. He retained his spare, wiry frame into old age.

Primrose, the boys, Grey Walls and the garden formed the hub of Geoffrey's life. When lectures, legal dinners or visits to his publishers took him to London he never tarried but hastened home. Family meals were taken together, and Grey Walls was enlivened by stimulating friends. An ardent Tory, impatient with obscurity in conversation or writing, traditional in outlook but capable of moving with the times, Geoffrey looked in others for loyalty, effort, mannerly behaviour, punctuality and care in the use of language. With Primrose, he had a knack of putting others at their ease. Such was their courtesy, indeed, that if anyone caused them annoyance or disappointment the transgressor seldom knew.

Although quietly spoken, Geoffrey tended to take the lead in mealtime conversation; and while Primrose was the more forthright, it was generally her husband who had the last word in matters of difference. Behind his understated manner lay a dry humour and inclination to mischief, witnessed in outrageous comments spoken in a softly expressionless way. More than one visiting scholar was befooled by the news that he was contemplating a legal textbook on *The Rights of Dogs*, and he assiduously fostered the legend – or was it? – that it was vital for him to seat himself in church early, lest the gardener's lips should touch the chalice before his own.[5]

Holidays were varied, numerous and often linked with sport. In the later 1920s the family rented a holiday home in Dorset, used by Hardy as the prototype for Tess's cottage in *Tess of the d'Urbervilles* and by Geoffrey as a base for golf tournaments. There were motoring expeditions into France, trips to Switzerland for skiing, skating and long Alpine walks. One Easter Geoffrey took them on a bicycling tour of Belgium, to see the trenches at Ypres and revisit places of his war service.

At Christmas they usually went to London for a few days, and there would be a ritual discussion about which three shows they would see. The outcome was invariably a thriller, a musical and a comedy. More serious drama was avoided. Shakespeare was considered obscure, opera too expensive. At home BBC radio comedies were favoured evening listening for Geoffrey and the boys, none of whom had much ear for the concerts of light classical music preferred by Primrose.[6]

Geoffrey's bursarial duties often took him out to Exeter College's estates and farms, where young Leonard's conversations with farmhands, molecatchers, mechanics and hedge-keepers foreshadowed his tendency to be 'chummy with unexpected people'.[7] In this the wider family itself provided considerable grounding. Beyond Grey Walls lay a constellation of relatives which twinkled with heroes, achievers, a few mavericks and eccentrics like the elderly aunt in Bristol who passed her days with binoculars trained on the Clifton suspension bridge in the hope of seeing a suicide.

Geoffrey was the second of three brothers. Christopher, the eldest, was an Anglican clergyman. Known as Uncle Kick, he was

tall, gentle and modest, with the same 'merry arresting eyes' as
Geoffrey. In later life Prebendary Cheshire was appointed chaplain
to the House of Commons. The boys loved him. They admired
Geoffrey's younger brother Humphrey too, though for different
reasons. Amiable, extravagant in youth, Humphrey was a racy
figure with a 'genius for getting into trouble of one sort or another'.
Expelled from university for a romantic misdemeanour, after wartime service in the Coldstream Guards he farmed sheep in the
Australian outback, came home to become a policeman, moved to
Canada, returned and eventually settled to a distinguished career
as a headmaster.

Then there were Walter's sisters, Geoffrey's aunts: Frances
(known as Aunt Frank) and Edith, who lived quietly according to
a strict routine which included an annual visit to Grey Walls. Frank
was rather scholarly; Edith, whose youth 'had not lacked romance',
was more practical and companionable. As for Walter himself,
following his career of sustained underachievement he had retired
to Brighton. When the boys visited their grandfather they found
him reclusive, stooped and only likely to appear at mealtimes, when
his conversation was limited to a grunted 'Where's the whisky?'
He died in 1924 and thus scarcely impinged on them, but Clara
lived on until 1945. The boys knew an annual ritual whereby their
grandmother would decline all invitations to spend Christmas at
Grey Walls, until a telephone call on Christmas Eve announced
that her plans had changed. A wait in fog or frost at Oxford station
would follow.[8]

Grey Walls also became a home base for the Barstows, many of
whom continued to live abroad or followed the peripatetic life
required by the Army and left pictures, items of furniture and
sometimes their children, for safekeeping with the Cheshires. A
few Barstow traits have already been glimpsed: loyalty, frugality,
punctiliousness, a fierce patriotism, resolution, devotion to the
Army and candour. The girls, like their mother, were strong-willed
and given to impulsiveness, although emotions were well guarded.
Socially, they tended towards clannishness. No one quite suited
them.[9]

Primrose's sister Edith had worked as a VAD in the Italian

mountains during the latter stages of the Great War, and in 1920 surprised everyone by marrying Gabriel Dichter, a Romanian journalist who worked in the oil industry. The Dichters settled happily in Paris, where their house at 81 Avenue des Villiers became a popular stopping place on trips to France. Despite her blunt, sometimes cutting manner Edith was indulgent towards the boys.[10]

If Edith was a favourite aunt, her elder brother Arthur was an admired uncle, who rose to the rank of major general between the wars. Arthur was to be shot by the Japanese as they overran Singapore in 1941. The generosity of his widow, Nancy, will have a large place in the story that follows.

There were other Barstows – Uncle Tommy, Uncle Jack – but Leonard was not much interested in family history. He looked ahead, as if in reaction to his father's affection for the past. Geoffrey Cheshire 'loved anything to do with pre-First World War Europe, cricket and trains. He would happily go to Crewe and spend a day there just watching the trains passing through.'[11] Crewe, whence lines led in all directions. A place to recollect childhood journeys with Clara, pre-war changes between Chester and Oxford, partings from Primrose or the anticipation in trips to join her. A stage in melancholy summer-end journeys back to school in Staffordshire. A place for memories of other days.

This was the milieu of Leonard's boyhood: secure, encouraging, disciplined but not unduly strict, materially comfortable but less than affluent, well-travelled, conservative, conventionally Anglican, academically high-aiming but culturally middlebrow, and tinged by nostalgia for the *belle époque*.

2. Stowe

By early 1931 Geoffrey Cheshire was having second thoughts about the next stage in Leonard's education. Leonard had earlier been entered for Marlborough, but with fees to find for two sons and limited means Dr Cheshire realized that Marlborough would be unaffordable unless Leonard obtained a scholarship: an eventuality which the Dragon School's headmaster, Mr A. E. Lynam, advised him to discount. Lynam counselled him instead to 'concentrate upon Stowe',[1] a school which had existed for only nine years but was already being talked about as the new Eton. On 21 May Lynam telephoned Stowe's headmaster to discuss the possibility of Leonard's entry. After the conversation, a letter:

The parents are both specially nice people . . . The boy is definitely not up to first-rate Scholarship form . . . but his progress in the last two years makes it apparent that he is one of those rather late developers, who is likely to come on exceedingly well later; and Joc [Lynam's son] has said to me more than once that he has been making a splendid show this term, and working very hard . . . Leonard is just the sort of boy whom I am sure you will regard as an ornament to Stowe, and as such I think he is worth capturing, even if he falls short of Scholarship form.[2]

Leonard did not fall short. On the following Tuesday he travelled up to London, sat the Common Entrance examination, and gained the tenth of ten scholarship places.

Stowe's success reflected the outlook and warmth of its founding headmaster, John Fergusson Roxburgh. Roxburgh and his school did much to orient Cheshire. It is worth pausing for a moment to consider what they stood for.

Public-school education in the aftermath of the Great War had changed little from the unvarying routine, Latin-centred curriculum and worship of games which Geoffrey Cheshire had experienced at Denstone in the 1890s.[3] Public schools still jailed emotions, stifled creativity and shored up class-consciousness by snobbish depreciation of science, modern languages and the arts.[4] Inertia and mawkish nostalgia had barricaded them against change. Roxburgh's project was to create a school where feeling for literature, nature and architecture might be aroused, science was taken seriously, and a poet and prop forward would feel on equal terms.[5] Roxburgh cherished individuality, and so saw to it that members of his school (he seldom referred to pupils as boys) had time in which to develop talents, read or explore their surroundings. He slackened, a little, two of the tightest clamps of repression – the petty tyrannies of the house system and obsession with sport[6] – and placed each boy under the guidance of a tutor who could foster his development aside from the influence of the housemaster.

Roxburgh's plan had a wider context. He believed that public schools were for the education of an elite, and that the elite had two functions. 'The first justification of an Aristocracy is that it shall give leadership and service. But the second is that it shall maintain a standard of culture and refinement to which other classes can look – and eventually rise.' Enlightenment was a matter of personal encounter which every boy had to make for himself. Beauty, however, was a pattern of discipline, and openness to beauty, Roxburgh believed, was the sun which ripened intellect. In his first headmaster's address Roxburgh vowed that 'Every boy who goes out from Stowe will know beauty when he sees it all the rest of his life.'[7] The school setting itself epitomized this aspiration. Stowe House is a noble eighteenth-century mansion, and the pleasure grounds in which it stands are bejewelled with obelisks, lakes, bridges, fountains, woodland and *temples d'amour*. In September 1931, a few days after his fourteenth birthday, Leonard was driven up the mile-long drive and delivered among them.

Roxburgh welcomed him. His greetings were legendary.

I remember when I had been at Stowe for only a few days I happened to meet J. F. somewhere about the school . . . He addressed me not merely by my

Christian name but by the diminutive form of it which was always used at home. There was not the slightest hesitation in his doing this. He already *knew who I was* . . .[8]

Roxburgh specialized in knowing who everyone was – and their nicknames, and their birthdays.[9] He could re-feel the desolation of boys new-parted from their families, and countered it by treating them as individuals in whom he was personally interested.

In the afternoon of my first day . . . a man walking through saw me, stopped, put both hands on my shoulders, and said, 'Good afternoon! What's your name?' I said, 'Dulley.' . . . He replied. 'Ah, yes, *David* Dulley,' in a rich, pleased, businesslike voice that suggested that I was the most distinguished member of a distinguished family, and that now I had arrived the school could really get going.[10]

Eleven years on we shall find Wing Commander Cheshire behaving in the same way. For the moment, however, he was a little homesick.

Stowe's houses were named after Whig lords. Leonard was placed in Chatham, and with another new boy called Jack Anderson he was introduced to his housemaster, Ivor Cross. Cross and Roxburgh were friends of long standing, although many boys saw them as opposites. Whereas Roxburgh was extrovert and attractive for his warmth, tolerance and humour, Cross was a deeply private man whose greatest strengths – sincerity, precision of intellect, a profound Christian faith – lay beneath his surface. Many boys did not see beyond this, finding him an old-fashioned disciplinarian who 'never found it easy to establish that essential rapport with pupils which good teachers express naturally'.[11] Life under the authoritarian rule of Ivor Cross is recalled as 'simple and tough'.[12]

Chatham stands apart from the main building, and its members were accordingly obliged to make daily treks to meals and Assembly, in all weathers, 'usually against the clock, to beat the clutches of the duty monitors'.[13] This inconvenience was offset by the special sense of community which detachment fostered, and by the superiority of Chatham's accommodation: 'No one else at Stowe . . . enjoyed the near certainty of a shared study, once the milestone of middle school and School Certificate had been reached and passed.'[14] Other advantages included proximity to Mr Moss's tuck shop, an inspiring prospect of the Octagon Lake and – for Cheshire – ready access to the tennis courts.

Stowe stirred Cheshire not simply because it was a new environment, much larger and more complicated than any he had lived in before, but also because it challenged him. Thus far he had been brought up in an orderly household by parents with settled views. Stowe faced him with new opinions, ideas and personalities, and the need to begin to make choices.

Years later Cheshire joked that he had secured a scholarship because his daring use of the word 'bloody' in a Common Entrance essay had caught the eye of T. H. White, Stowe's head of English.[15] There was more to it than that,* but the presence at Stowe of figures like Tim White illustrates Roxburgh's zeal for cultural breadth and his readiness to recruit men of opinions and tastes he did not always share. Works by post-Romantic artists usually baffled or pained him, but the masters who introduced boys to T. S. Eliot, D. H. Lawrence, Picasso or Stravinsky were given complete latitude, just as his own old-fashioned liberalism was not obtruded upon those who flirted with newer ideologies.

Leslie Huggins, the school's head of music, pioneered a programme which ran from sixteenth-century madrigals to new works by Vaughan Williams, Constant Lambert and Percy Grainger. Another with musical passions was Hugh Heckstall-Smith. Recruited by Roxburgh as a science tutor, Heckstall-Smith was as likely to galvanize young minds by introducing them to *Rheingold* or producing challenging facts about social deprivation in Birmingham as by his spellbinding lectures on atomic theory. His room reflected this range, and his disregard for convention: 'Books sat in piles on the floor, symphonic themes were chalked above the fireplace, and at one stage a boat was built in it. J. F. once surveyed the carnage awe-struck. "What superb disarray!" he murmured, and recoiled.'[16]

Then there was Tim White himself: novelist, poet, naturalist,

* Such a reaction would have been characteristic of White, but he did not join the school's staff until 1932.

horseman, hunter, artist, moralist, 'a sort of robust Harlequin, plunging from one activity to another'.[17] White's energy gusted through the school like a gale, banging its doors and rattling windows.

Tim was then I suppose in his late twenties and a fairly bohemian figure . . . He had an old open black Bentley and a red setter and among the boys enjoyed a reputation exciting, faintly discreditable and much envied on the strength of *Loved Helen* and *They Winter Abroad*, copies of which were eagerly sought after.[18]

During White's four years at Stowe he wrote four books and published seven, added shooting, fishing and flying to his accomplishments, produced plays, scourged arms manufacturers in 'Present Day' classes, and still found time to drink with friends into the small hours. It was said that White never gave punishments because boys were too absorbed by what he was saying to misbehave. For all his polytechnic span he was rigorous, demanding discipline in the use of language, and he was acerbic towards purveyors of second-hand opinions.

'Write an essay on anything you like,' he would say to an audience of boys whose short lives had been spent in being told what to do. What he wanted was sincerity. 'What does it *mean*?' he would say. 'If you don't know what it *means*' – his speech was full of emphases – 'how can you claim the right to say whether you like it or not?'[19]

Cheshire's official tutor was Patrick Hunter: a classicist, fastidious, capable and one of Roxburgh's principal lieutenants. Hunter's estimate of the lad has undertones of perplexity: 'His attitude to his studies is conscientious and certainly more than passive, but he cannot be called outstandingly bright at any subject. Quite clever, certainly above average, but really not remarkable.'[20] The hedging is curious. Good, but not so good; clever, 'but not remarkable'. Which? Or what? The prevailing view was that some latent vigour awaited arousal.

In July 1932, still only fourteen, Cheshire gained his School Certificate, with credits in English, Latin, Greek, French and Elementary Maths.[21] This took him into a form called The Twenty, 'which was for boys who were too clever to be with younger ones

and too young to be with older ones'.[22] The Twenty were taught
by Tim White, who found Cheshire 'charming' and 'a bit quizzical
or teasing'. White's efforts to transmit the basics of lucid writing
and good punctuation made their mark on Cheshire, who for ever
afterwards deployed commas and semicolons with the strictest care.

Much went on outside Stowe's classrooms. There were work-
shops for metalwork and joinery, study holidays abroad, trips to
the theatre. 'Stoics' (as members of the school knew themselves)
were introduced to industry, taken to factories, down coal mines.
Scholars and politicians came to lecture, musicians gave recitals.
For those who liked spectacle there were outdoor productions of
plays and operas – *Dido and Aeneas* in 1933; *Richard II* on the floodlit
steps of the Queen's Temple at the end of the 1935 summer term.
Societies thrived. The Vitruvians studied architecture; there was a
group for modern play-reading, another for modern music. The
Film Club's showings of new Hollywood talkies introduced boys
to what was then demurely called 'Western Electric accent', and
in Cheshire's later terms there were screenings of films by Eisenstein
and Leni Riefenstahl.

Cheshire, however, 'steered clear of all such bodies'.[23] Or nearly
all. He did join the Debating Society. The orators met in the long
library on Friday evenings, and one of the first debates he attended
was on the motion that 'This House would welcome a Nazi
Government'. The arguments give an inkling of views then circulat-
ing. Some declared Nazism to be an inevitable reaction to post-war
circumstances and argued that it would benefit internationalism by
cancelling war debts. Opponents viewed the Nazis as reactionary,
inimical to internationalism and dangerously anti-Semitic. The
motion was defeated, though narrowly.[24]

Politics loomed large in subsequent debates: 'This House sympa-
thizes with the hunger marchers'[25] (it did); or 'This House deplores
the Conservative policy of the national government' (motion
carried 28–19);[26] or 'That in the opinion of this House a Fascist
regime would be the best form of government for this country'.
To which the House agreed, by a large majority.[27] Much of this,
of course, was polemics. Provocative topics enabled adolescent
orators to exercise, and the House could cheerfully rally to the

Jarrow hunger-marchers in one week and Fascism in the next
without serious commitment to either.

There were, nevertheless, some real currents of ideology at
Stowe, and choppy water where they met. The choice was seen
less as between what we would now think of as right and left
than as between concepts of nationalism and internationalism. The
League of Nations was regarded by some as anti-patriotic and by
others as progressive. Keen interest was aroused, therefore, when
a branch of the League of Nations Club was formed in the autumn
of 1933, and Professor Gilbert Murray, chairman of the club's
executive, came to talk about it.

Murray spoke of the need for a new method of international
cooperation to renounce war as an instrument of national policy.
It was true, he said, that Japan had violated the covenant, and that
with Germany she had retired from the league. It was also true that
the United States and Russia had yet to be persuaded to join.
However, having listed most of the main protagonists in the forthcoming conflict, Murray emphasized that fifty-four other countries
were loyal to the convenant's spirit, and argued this as the source of
hope.[28] And that, roughly speaking, was where the sixteen-year-old
Cheshire stood: 'I belonged to a generation which in a hazy kind
of way recognized the debt it owed to those who had gone before,
but which rejected war as a means of solving differences between
nations and believed that war in Europe was a thing of the past.'[29]
He read widely about the Great War. The effects of conflict on
the individual engaged him:

There was a day at school when I had caught flu and, clutching my toothbrush
and pyjamas, was making my way slowly to the sanatorium, wondering if I could
manage a few hundred yards without help. Then the thought suddenly struck
me that were I a Tommy in the front line, far from having the prospect of a
comfortable bed, I would have to carry on as if nothing was wrong, ankle-deep
in mud . . . I realized a little shamefacedly that exploits such as these were not
for me.[30]

While most of Stowe's masters puzzled about Cheshire's apparently
unfulfilled capacity for learning, few seem to have noticed his
voracious reading or his capacity for empathy. Tim White was one

who did notice. Twenty years later he teased Andrew Boyle by professing not to remember which brother was which – Christopher had entered Chatham in 1934 – but the picture is clear:

. . . there were two of them – as far as I can remember one light and one [Cheese] dark haired . . . when setting the usual essay 'What did you do last holidays?' I implored the form not to give me the usual bunk . . . They all did give me the usual stuff – about camping at Aberystwyth or helping Daddy to build a dinghy – except *one* of these Cheeses (and the desolating thing is, I can't remember which) who wrote that he had gone to France and found a coffee-coloured girl, one year younger than himself, on the beach, a fact which he considered highly satisfactory, and so did I. I gave him an alpha plus for what was quite a sensuous (not sensual) and vivid piece of life appreciated. He or they always struck me as being nice, *feeling* . . . boys. It's so difficult to use words in the proper nuance . . . they had all the proper taste buds for eating Mars Bars or drinking fizzy lemonade or knowing that the sun was warm on their skins, like horses rolling in a field . . . He always did write me good essays after that – whichever of them it was . . . Correcting essays and schoolmastering was a melancholy pursuit, but I did manage to take a faint, genuine interest in this Cheese's. They were feeling essays, physically feeling, sands and summer seas and that. He was one of the few children of fourteen or so who could actually *tell* you that he liked to lie on his back in a hayfield, smelling clover and wondering what it would be like to fall upwards into the clouds. Not whimsy either.[31]

And here is Cheshire recalling Tim White, and the essay:

Yes, he was quite an influence on me. I don't quite know how. I remember . . . he got us to write an essay on something I'd seen happen . . . And he gave me very high marks indeed. He said I couldn't write at all – which was true – but in this case I'd written something very good indeed, because it was an eyewitness account . . . I didn't take in a great deal of poetry and so on. I didn't really understand it. I was very impressed by Tim White. I liked him very much, and learnt quite a bit from him.[32]

Cheshire had an eye, or ear, for the accent of different writers. White may have shown him a draft of *England Have My Bones*, or the notebooks upon which it was based, for in 1935 Cheshire was writing in a very White-like way in *The Stoic* about the layered meaning of English landscape and community.

White's recollection of 'an *appreciative* boy' who '*liked* being alive'[33] resonates with Cheshire's remembered teenage self. He had joined the OTC, finding it 'all quite fun'. One summer's afternoon he was introduced to the Lee Enfield .303 rifle. Ambling back from the range nursing a bruised shoulder from the recoil he sat down under a tree.

There must have been something special, even magical, about that moment . . . The spasmodic sound of firing that had accompanied me on my walk had ceased, I could hear faintly the shouted orders to unload, clean rifles and so on, and then there was silence. It was as if a profound peace had fallen upon the countryside. In a way I find difficult to describe, everything around me – the parkland, the blue sky, the varied scents of summer, the hum of a passing bee – conjured up an image of all that a young heart hopes for from life, of a future filled with nothing but happiness and promise.[34]

A dreamer, in search of a dream.

Stowe's surroundings invited interest in natural history. On summer Sundays Cheshire sometimes ventured into the green gloom of woodland to watch nesting birds, or to the margins of lakes among vigilant herons.[35] Patrick and Charles Ashton were pre-eminent among Chatham's naturalists, collectors of grass snakes and slow-worms, expert fishermen, and outstanding marksmen. Cheshire sometimes joined their expeditions, although he was a reluctant fisherman ('I didn't like picking up the fish') and 'a rotten shot. And very dangerous. Charles [Ashton] used to get livid about it I remember. But I used to enjoy it, very fond of it.'[36]

Patrick Ashton had a pet jackdaw which took to following him to Assembly. On one occasion the jackdaw arrived during prayers and drew delighted applause when it alighted on Ashton's shoulder. Afterwards Roxburgh dispatched a characteristic note: 'Ashton, kindly control your bird.'[37] Roxburgh's disciplinary methods, sometimes unorthodox, often witty,[38] braced pupils for future tests that could not be imagined. Ten springs on, Major Patrick Ashton was to be one of the first British officers to enter Belsen.

Cheshire was considerate to those around him and was well regarded, but some wondered if his poise guarded a shyness, perhaps even a vulnerability. At any rate, his self-sufficiency seems to have inhibited close friendships. There was, however, an exception. Jack Anderson, who had arrived on the same day in 1931, remembered as 'rock solid' and 'easy going',[39] was Cheshire's intimate. The two talked about everything under the sun, even contriving that their bath nights should coincide, to enable rambling conversations about the school, the world, their futures, while soaking in tepid water in adjacent cubicles. In the war ahead two Old Stoics will be awarded the Victoria Cross. One will be Cheshire. Jack Anderson will be the other.

Coincidence hovers around Cheshire wherever we find him, so it is no surprise either to learn that two other Chathamites were the sons of leading aircraft designers,* or that one of them would play a leading part in the development of a machine later described by Cheshire as 'the queen of wartime aircraft' – the Mosquito. For anyone interested – which at this point Cheshire wasn't – Stowe offered opportunities for flying. Geoffrey de Havilland occasionally visited in a Leopard Moth, landing on Bourbon Field and offering flights to curious boys. There were annual trips to Hendon, and the aviation society toured nearby RAF stations. Most beguiling of all might have been Tim White, who began taking flying lessons in 1934, and often invited a boy or two to ride in his open Bentley as he sped through country lanes to Sywell aerodrome on summer evenings. Years later White half convinced himself that he had introduced Cheshire to flying, and references to a boy nicknamed 'Cheese' in his book *England Have My Bones* have led others to think so too. However, as White teasingly explained:

I have just skipped through that narcissistic book . . . searching for references to 'Cheese', and I find, as suspected, that they are not to . . . Cheese at all. For some reason, in those days writers were terrified of libel, so one mixed up names of places and people. The 'Cheese' mentioned in *EHMB* was in fact . . . Pat Ashton. Also, as far as I can remember, he was 'Peter' . . . But it is possible that 'Peter' was Cheese. Surely one could not have used *two* names for one person? At least, I seem to have been flying with 'Peter'.[40]

* John de Havilland and Geoffrey Verdon-Roe. John de Havilland's elder brother Geoffrey (a member of Chatham in the 1920s) piloted the prototype of the de Havilland Mosquito on its maiden flight on 25 November 1940. John died in a mid-air collision in 1943.

But 'Peter' wasn't Cheshire either. Cheshire was adamant that he never flew with White.[41]

Aside from reading and natural history, Cheshire's main pursuit at Stowe was tennis. Schooled by his father on the courts at Grey Walls, he took the game seriously. A schoolfriend recalls: 'It wasn't until my last term, summer 1933, that Leonard "registered" . . . I was wrapped up in cricket & house and he was "on the way up" in tennis. We were both dedicated to success in our respective sports.'[42]

'*Dedicated to success*': Cheshire impressed that term as a member of Chatham's tennis pairs. In the following year he was a finalist in the Mornington Singles and was awarded School Colours. Spurred by Ivor Cross, Chatham in the early 1930s temporarily developed a culture of athleticism,[43] but in most games 'Leonard was not especially outstanding'.[44] In rugby he was 'gutsy' but 'not a natural', and it was his dogged will 'to put one foot after another' which sustained his cross-country running. He played golf until Christopher started to beat him. Resolution and a competitive streak, rather than natural ability, are the traits which gleam.

He read in Chapel, but expressed no interest in religion. He became a member of The Twelve, Stowe's elite club for emerging literary intellectuals, but showed no great enthusiasm for intellectualism. In the OTC he ended with the rank of sergeant, but engaged with the training 'more in the way boys play at soldiers than with any serious intent'.[45] By the summer of 1934 he was a House Monitor, and in his last two terms he was Head of House. When J. F. Roxburgh afterwards scoured his memory for portents of Cheshire's valour and stature, he found himself puzzled.

I have been thinking over your letter about Leonard Cheshire, but I have not found much to tell you in reply. As a schoolboy Leonard was very successful in the ordinary sense of the word – that is, he became Head of his House, a School Prefect, a member of the Sixth Form . . . and Captain of Lawn Tennis – but any first-rate boy can expect a career of that kind at his Public School, and I cannot remember that Leonard made more impression on his generation than several others did . . . I personally was much attached to him, and I felt for him not only affection but respect. There was something about him – was it perhaps a kind of moral dignity? – which made it inconceivable that he would think or do anything that was below top level. He knew how to make other people do the right thing too, and his courteous, even gentle, manner covered a pretty tough will, which made him a strong ruler in his house and an effective prefect in the school. But all this could be said of other boys who as men never became pre-eminent as Leonard did.[46]

The effects of Roxburgh and Stowe upon Cheshire were gradual rather than immediate, a process of slow release, and it was Roxburgh's humanity rather than Stowe's resplendence which made the more lasting impression. In October 1935 Roxburgh wrote to the Warden of Merton College, Oxford:

I expect you know already that Dr Cheshire, of Exeter, wants his elder son Leonard to go to Merton in October 1936 . . . Young Cheshire is an excellent boy. As a scholar he is tasteful and hard-working but not very gifted. None the less, being ambitious, he will probably want to compete in your Scholarship Exam this Christmas.[47]

'*Being ambitious . . .*'?

On 7 March 1936 Germany remilitarized the Rhineland. One of the last events of Stowe's spring term that year was a debate on the motion that 'This House would rather fight with than against Germany'. Of the 101 pupils present, seventy-three agreed.

Cheshire was looking forward to the summer term, and tennis. His father had other ideas. Roxburgh sometimes encouraged the parents of sixth formers who had gained university places to send them abroad for their last months. Dr Cheshire decided that a few months in Germany would be improving, and when Leonard came home for Easter he was told that he would not be returning to Stowe. Like a book unexpectedly snapped shut, Leonard's schooldays were over.

3. Oxford and Beyond

Cheshire went to Potsdam as a guest of the family of Ludwig von Reuter. Potsdam's wooded lakeland was attractive, and the von Reuters were hospitable. As a child Cheshire had learned to speak French without trace of English accent, and he relished the opportunity to gain command of German as well. Like his father he established a routine, passing most mornings alone in study or with a tutor, and afternoons playing tennis, cycling or swimming with von Reuter's three teenage sons. Sometimes they went dancing. There were visits to Berlin and other cities, and trips to watch motor racing at the Nürnberg Ring. Towards the end of his stay he travelled north to explore the Baltic island of Rügen, and entered a tennis tournament which he nearly won.

Von Reuter was a retired admiral, older than his wife, remembered as 'small and tubbyish' with silver hair, a penchant for little cigars, and a tendency to embark on prolix reminiscences about naval engagements in the Great War. Cheshire quite liked him, although he was startled by the stringent formality with which he ruled his sons (each of whom was named after a German warship) and staggered by von Reuter's social opinions.

Von Reuter had little time for the Nazis, but drew some of his views from the same poisoned well, considering only 5 per cent of humanity to be worthwhile. The rest, he assured Cheshire, were *Minderwertigen*, 'inferiors',[1] and war would be an efficient way to eliminate them.[2] Cheshire disagreed, strongly, although at this point he neither thought nor saw much of the Nazis.

By the summer's end Cheshire was 'speaking German practically like a native'.[3] Whilst aware that the Germans had 'an awful lot of tanks and so on – a bit more than we did', he was 'impressed by German thoroughness'[4] and socially at ease within a circle of tennis-playing friends. So readily, indeed, did he adapt to life in and around the von Reuters' household that when his parents arrived to take him home they found him reluctant to leave.[5] But his father's footsteps awaited, and in October 1936 he entered Merton College, Oxford, to read for a degree in jurisprudence.

What follows has been depicted as a sensational transformation. Leonard Cheshire's three years at Merton have acquired an awesome notoriety as a time of fast cars, reckless exploits, fantastic extravagance, mounting debts and shady associations. If this were the whole story then there would indeed be something to explain. However, although the legend of relentless gadding does owe something to reality, it owes not a little to the writings of Andrew Boyle and a great deal to the journalism of Russell Braddon. Revisitation of their sources suggests that they overdid it – in Boyle's case by selective accentuation of fact and in Braddon's by avoidance of much fact at all. In result their interpretation was circular, the notion of a dramatic personality change being demanded by the myth, and vice versa. The hedonistic, roistering Cheshire of the later 1930s was partly a construct of the 1950s.

The truth is that Cheshire passed through Oxford less in a blaze of rebellious individualism than as part of a genre. He became a model of what in his own eyes an undergraduate should be. Oxford in the 1930s contained many ex public schoolboys who breezed through the nine eight-week terms by supplementing what they already knew with a little work, put in some concentrated effort towards the end and left with second-class degrees. Along the way they climbed in and out of colleges after dark, drove about in second-hand cars, returned at speed from London nightclubs along deserted roads, invited each other to lunch or mulled claret, rioted in each other's rooms, argued at length about subjects they did not fully understand, and cocked a snook at university discipline by frequenting pubs. This was a kind of conformism.

Thus Cheshire did own a car,* but it was rather old. He also frequented dog tracks, telling Dr A. L. Rowse over lunch at Grey

* According to one friend, several.

Walls that he had found an invincible method of betting which would make him rich. Christopher considered that greyhound racing 'stopped his first', but if his father fretted 'because I didn't like the prospect of having him on my hands for the rest of time',[6] then plenty of parents have said as much, or worse, about student sons. Two of Cheshire's closest associates, Peter Lalor and Douglas Baxter, were indeed vigorous drinkers, but it emerges that Cheshire often tried to coax them *away* from alcohol, and that Jack Randle, his closest friend, was a devout churchgoer. Randle, whose room was on the same staircase, was a steadying influence. Uncannily, he too would win the Victoria Cross.

There were occasions when Cheshire did inane things, like drinking an entire bottle of whisky in one go to refute someone who said that it couldn't be done. The episode eluded Boyle, very possibly because Cheshire didn't remember it, nor lying down in the middle of Oxford's High Street shortly afterwards, nor much of the doctor's admonition on the following day.[7] Another adventure which seems to have escaped attention involved an intrusion into the grounds of the house of a very famous politician to invite one of his daughters out to dinner. Significantly, however, most of the really hair-raising stories concerned suicidal stunts about which he talked but which he never actually performed.[8] And alongside the twenty-one-year-old who did risk his skin to startle motorists by running in front of their cars on the Iffley Road, or whose plea of mitigation to a speeding charge earned the local newspaper headline 'Undergraduate Astonished that His Car Could Do 40 m.p.h.',[★] there was the thoughtful Cheshire who was recalled by one don's wife as the only undergraduate who offered to carry her shopping basket.

He kept up his tennis, playing for Merton and occasionally appearing in a sports shop in the Turl to try the balance of rackets he could not afford. Far from breaking with his father's pattern he

---

[★] The car belonged to his friend Peter Higgs. In mitigation Cheshire said that the vehicle was two years old and that he had never known it to exceed 35 m.p.h. Unimpressed. Oxford's magistrates fined him 10s. with 10s. costs, endorsed his licence and suspended it for one month. A further penalty was imposed for his driving Higgs's car without insurance.

followed it, working most mornings in his room or in the college library.[9] His tutor, F. M. Lawson, thought him 'a good student. Never wildly enthusiastic about jurisprudence, but intelligent and competent. He knew his own mark, and made it.' Lawson contested post-war rumours that he was a slacker. He 'kept up quite well . . . He wasn't the pure intellectual type. I was always satisfied with his work because he was a trier – without breaking his neck.'[10] When he graduated with a good second-class degree Lawson wasn't surprised.

Gestures of rebellion were part of the role, although 'I don't think I was brash in the sense of wanting to hurt other people. I saw myself more as self-assertive, extremely sure of my own opinions – and a little boastful. I didn't listen to the advice of Father and Mother. I would argue with people who were specialists in their fields and I liked creating a sensation.'[11] For some unknown reason he harboured a real animosity towards the college authorities. Contempt for Merton's dean and senior dons was still evident in seething letters to Douglas Baxter in 1940, perhaps because of his sense of injustice when they sent Peter Lalor down. Equally, among the dons there was a suspicion that whenever anything subversive was afoot Cheshire was likely to be at the bottom of it. He was an insurrectionist by proxy – 'the silent ringleader'.[12]

From the college's standpoint, one of Cheshire's most revolutionary characteristics lay in his friendships and easy alliances with porters, gardeners, scouts, bookies, barmen and others outside his class. Such relationships broke the conventions of social relations and marked him as dissident. One companion was Frank Hulbert, a hard-swearing college servant with whom he went ferreting, and for whose son he stood godparent in December 1938. There were bookies at the race tracks of Reading and Cowley with whom he imagined himself on good terms until their pitiless demands taught him otherwise.[13] Then there was 'Jig' Holloway, 'the sporting barber', landlord of the Chequers.[14] And Raymond Mays, founder of English Racing Automobiles, to whom for a time Cheshire loosely apprenticed himself. Portraits of Nuvollari and Caracialla, celebrated Grand Prix drivers, hung on Cheshire's walls. His driving was remarkable less for outright speed than for precision of handling, which enabled him to dart in and out of traffic. But his one outing

on the race track, at Donnington Park, ended prematurely. Legend
claims that he drove so fast that the engine seized. According to
Cheshire himself the car became undrivable when the gear lever
came off in his hand.

If ideology was alien, he did have an agenda. Cheshire later said
that his aims at Oxford were to 'drive a Bentley, dress in a Savile
Row suit, in short to make pots of money without too many
scruples how'.[15] The challenge lay more in the how than in the
scruples. The allowance of £200 a year he received from his parents
did not go far to sustain such an aim, and according to his mother
he was 'absolutely unable, at any time, to keep or save money'.
Nor did he have any clear idea about how he might accumulate it,
save perhaps to model himself on those who did.

Wealth appeared to be linked to celebrity, and for a time he
cultivated an appearance as The Saint, slicking back his hair and
flourishing a cigarette holder.[16] He worshipped Fred Astaire, and for
some months took tap dancing lessons in the hope of emulating him.[17]
Van Gogh and Gauguin intrigued him, not initially by their paintings
but through the individualism revealed in biographies. After reading
Lust for Life Cheshire recognized a Van Gogh print in an art shop
'purely from the description of who he was'. In 1939 he toyed with
the idea of flying the Atlantic from east to west in a Puss Moth. Like
many undergraduates he played jazz on his gramophone, and sat up
late arguing about religion, politics, literature or bawdier topics. He
argued about religion because he thought it pointless and despised
clericalism. His faith at this time was in himself: in the words of a
friend, 'survival of the fittest, weakest to the wall'.

All this has been considered difficult to reconcile with the steady
lad he had been at Stowe or the charismatic leader he would
become, still less with a man who would devote the greatest number
of his years to the work of God. This view, which is tantamount
to the theory that there were several Cheshires, ignores both the
context from which he was emerging and the fact that a considerable
number of medieval *Vitae* begin the same way. Already at Stowe
he knew that he was destined for something, the pre-echoes of a
vocation, but did not know what, nor did he yet possess the
specialized vocabulary with which to articulate it. To begin to find

out he had to explore, to try on guises. The masks of materialism, glamour and action fell nearest to hand, and it was these he tried on first.

I was mercenary; didn't have many scruples . . . No, better still I think I had two sides. I had the side that was industrious, and wanted to be honest and good and so on, and the other that was quite the opposite. So when it came to Oxford it was a question of which side was going to predominate. I think that largely depended upon what sort of people I came into contact with, influences, and I picked up with the people who spent a good deal of time drinking and so on and I suppose that tipped the scales. I still kept up a fair amount of work . . . it wasn't exactly a question of making money only I was after something spectacular. Something in the limelight. I always dreamed of being, so to speak, in the Centre Court.[18]

Many saw him as masked, a personality of concentric layers. His tutor considered him 'outstanding in this sense: though quiet and well-mannered and unassuming, he gave one the feeling that there was much more in reserve' – a view which echoes Patrick Hunter's earlier remark about 'latent vigour'. Few, if any, entered this hinterland. A girlfriend might have done so, and according to his brother there were a number,[19] at least one of whom horrified Primrose by wearing nail varnish. Andrew Boyle worked hard to identify them, but ascertained next to nothing about an inner Cheshire, or indeed about the girls themselves.[20] While Cheshire was generous and equable, rarely out of sorts or bad-tempered, usually natural and good-humoured, neatly dressed without being a dandy, often funny, given to ingenious devilry, 'attracted to attractive people',[21] good company and incurably optimistic, the social frontage concealed an unknown interior.

Years later, when Cheshire had become a household name, a few busybodies declared their disappointment at Andrew Boyle's failure to plumb the secret places of his mind. One of them was Lord Moran, who reviewed *No Passing Glory* for *The Sunday Times* and dismissed the early pages as tiresome, essentially because he was reacting to a catalogue of anecdotes which itself had missed the point.[22] Edith Stowell, a friend of the Cheshire family, wrote to set both critic and author straight:

To anyone who knew Cheshire when he was young there remains . . . an abiding impression of panache which may be the key to his elusiveness. Len Cheshire was not a vulgar seeker after notoriety . . . He was a young man whose unbounding nervous energy was translated into startling action. He did everything with an air, but there was at the same time a withdrawn quality about him, a secret self-sufficiency.[23]

'*Nervous energy*' A schoolfriend remembers him as 'highly strung'. Others mention his containment, although even those who imagined they knew him well could not guess what it was that was being contained.

There was another strand to Cheshire's undergraduate life. Late in his first term he entered the Oxford University Air Squadron, ostensibly to escape from the OTC, which he had joined with Jack Randle and discovered he did not like.

. . . as I was always looking for the spectacular, I thought, 'I'm not going to be an infantryman, I'll go for the cavalry', but because it was so rough and you had to run at the horse and somersault backwards off it, and the Sergeant shouted at you from start to finish, I decided it wasn't for me. Anyway I'm slightly afraid of horses, so I then went for the most sedentary thing I could find – an aeroplane.[24]

A family friend introduced him to Flt Lt J. N. Whitworth (Charles), a flying instructor with the University Air Squadron. The OUAS had its headquarters on Manor Road, where members attended evening lectures on the theory of flight, rigging, engines and air navigation, and joined in the squadron's social life of termly dinners and parties. Flying took place at Abingdon, not far from Grey Walls, where Cheshire had often seen the comings and goings of the squadron's frail-looking Avro Tutor biplanes. On a crisp morning early in February 1937 he was taken aloft and the view was reversed. From the Tutor's open cockpit he could look down into Grey Walls's garden, and into half a dozen shires: far beyond Oxford, across dark Wychwood and over the Cotswolds, south to the White Horse of Uffington tilted on the scarp of Berkshire's downs and east to the smudge of smoke which merged from five million London hearths.

Aeroplanes combined speed, technology and new sensations,

while in staider circles the Royal Air Force was still regarded as faintly disreputable, and thus worth belonging to for its outré exclusivity. Flying at someone else's expense was appealing, and Whitworth sensed that he would be good at it. Cheshire's visits to Abingdon were at first infrequent, but when he did turn up the successive exercises were both quickly mastered and remembered in the weeks that often lay between them.

After the end of Trinity term came the annual summer camp at Ford, under the Sussex Downs. Camp allowed for more concentrated tuition and practice. The weather that July was flawless, the students were accommodated under canvas and when they were not flying there were excursions to Calshot to view flying boats or to Southdean Sports Club for tennis. Ford is two miles from the sea, and in the evenings of hot days there was limitless swimming. It was all rather agreeable.

Less agreeable was Wg Cdr F. L. Hebbert, who took over as the OUAS's chief flying instructor in September 1937. Hebbert regarded Cheshire 'as a sort of ne'er-do-well . . . too undisciplined' and urged that he be expelled from the squadron. Whitworth countered by arguing that while Cheshire might not fit Hebbert's preconceptions of soundness, he had the makings of a better pilot than many who did.[25] Cheshire, meanwhile, had gone hitch-hiking in Ireland. While there he went into a Catholic church with a friend. As they looked around Cheshire was possessed by an unfamiliar feeling. He was impressed, but did not know why.[26]

Cheshire's undergraduate interest in politics and international affairs was small. Although Boyle depicts him baiting a pacifist speaker at a public meeting in St Giles, apparently in an effort to provoke a violent reaction which would contradict the message of the speech,[27] Cheshire could not corroborate the story because he did not recall it. British Fascism passed him by. 'I don't remember anything about Oswald Mosley and the Blackshirts,' he told Boyle, 'Just don't remember a thing. I'm sure politics meant nothing.'[28] Nonetheless, conversations at Manor Road, in Merton's junior common room and with friends like Jack Randle began to convince him that a war lay somewhere ahead. In 1937 he had little care for

the rights or wrongs of what such a war might be about. His concern
was simply to ensure that he had a prominent part in it. He enlisted
in the RAFVR.

In mid-June 1938 the OUAS travelled as usual to Ford for the
six-week summer camp. The squadron was split into two flights,
with elementary pupils flying Avro Tutors and more advanced
students, Cheshire now among them, concentrating on navigation
and instrument flying in an assortment of machines from the
Hart family. Sharp flints damaged their tyres, and the cadets
gained exercise by walking back and forth with orders to pick them
up.

They had not long returned to Oxford when international tension
began to rise. Since April Hitler had been indicating his intention
to occupy the Sudeten areas of Czechoslovakia, and in the second
week of September all the signs were that he was about to do so.
On 10 September RAF Abingdon was placed on an emergency
footing. Two weeks later events had become 'extremely grave'.
That Sunday all ranks were recalled from leave. Abingdon's resident
squadrons were ordered to readiness for service with an Advanced
Air Striking Force which would go to France. Cheshire watched
as aircraft were painted in war markings, and the station bustled in
a commotion of medical inspections, the issue of gas respirators
and active service documents, and preparations to evacuate the
married quarters. On 27 September war was considered certain,
and a station conference was held to prepare for the reception of
reservists.

Next day, Chamberlain proposed a last expedient. Abingdon
held its breath as negotiations began in Munich in the afternoon
of 29 September, and continued into the small hours of the 30th.
Later that day, as the station diarist put it: 'Following Mr Chamberlain's final visit to Herr Hitler and the Munich agreement the
political tension was greatly eased.'[29]

Abingdon relaxed, but only to a point. From now on the station's
aircraft were regularly dispersed on rotation to other aerodromes –
Shawbury, Benson, Boscombe Down – and in Cheshire's mind
war had become a matter not of if but when. Something else had
changed too. After Munich two things weighed with him. One

was a sense of moral repugnance: 'Unformed and immature though our judgement was, we felt a disquiet, a feeling of having betrayed a friendly nation, of not having lived up to the honour and sense of duty that had made Britain the great power she was.'[30] So there *were* rights and wrongs. And the other? 'I thought a lot about the coming war and Munich . . . but that was personally because I was interested in getting away from Oxford, and being let off work and getting on with it.'[31] Disappointed, he tried anyway, asking his father for leave to abandon his studies to join the RAF. Dr Cheshire refused, but agreed that his son could apply for a permanent commission under the RAF's direct-entry scheme. The arrangement would take effect immediately after he obtained his degree.

At the medical examination I was asked if I could read the exit sign over the door, made to do knees-up at the double for half a minute, then stretch my hands out to prove that they did not tremble unduly; and, everything apparently being satisfactory, I was passed. The interview board asked nothing much more difficult than, 'What games do you play?', and on being told rugger and tennis, indicated that I was in.[32]

Between March and June 1939 Cheshire reluctantly gave up flying to concentrate on his studies. After midsummer, final examinations over, the log book entries resume, now with almost frantic frequency. In late June and July he was taking off on training exercises two, three, sometimes four or five times a day.

Around him, or down at Lympne on summer camp, others were doing the same. Among them was Richard Hillary, a virile, sardonic, rather disruptive figure from Trinity at the end of his second year. Hillary's good looks would soon be seared by burning petrol, and his anguished book *The Last Enemy* would become one of the most moving of all warriors' attestations, striking 'some mysterious answering note in the British wartime mood'.[33] Absent just then, because he had been sent down, was Hillary's friend Noel Agazarian, 'Aga', a law student known to Cheshire, 'who combined intelligence, sporting ability and a disrespect for authority in about the same proportions as Hillary'.[34] Aga would soon be dead. Likewise doomed was another Trinity lawyer, H. M. Young, known as Melvin, a widely read man in whose company Cheshire sparkled.

Melvin Young would fly with Guy Gibson to the Ruhr dams in May 1943 and not return. Then there was Cheshire's brother Christopher, now very tall, fair-haired, popular, amiable. Christopher had followed him to Merton in 1937 and into the University Air Squadron. Ahead of him lay nearly four years in a German prison camp.

Their frustration during these sultry days lay in waiting, not knowing how far ahead the conflict lay. Weeks? Months? A year? At the end of July Hillary took himself away to France for a holiday, and Cheshire hitch-hiked to Paris on a budget of fifteen shillings, as usual because someone bet him that it couldn't be done.[35] When he returned in August the remaining days of the month were entirely devoted to flying. In two and a half hectic weeks he took off thirty times. There was night flying too, his first sight of Oxford bespangled by street lamps and the glimmer of farms and villages in the surrounding countryside.

Then the lights vanished. At the month's end his log book entries pause. Beneath, he wrote '*WAR*'.

The exultant moment had arrived: 'a heaven-sent release . . . a magic carpet on which to soar above the commonplace round of everyday life'.[36] War was uplifting in prospect because it offered an opportunity to harness and integrate all the aptitudes and potentials in himself which hitherto had been unapplied, and win approval for doing so. It was 'a turning point . . . because it gave me an outlet for my ambitions and energy . . . it diverted them into channels which were legalized excitement'.[37]

For a month he waited with mounting impatience, doing odd jobs at Grey Walls and clerical work for the RAFVR in Headington. Then a letter ordered him to join No. 14 Course at No. 9 Service Flying Training School, Hullavington, on 7 October. Where was Hullavington? In Wiltshire, not so far from home. Would he know anyone on the course? Yes, Melvin Young. What aircraft would they fly? Hawker Harts and Audaxes, with which he was familiar, or Avro Ansons, with which he wasn't.

Hullavington's business was flying training, which proceeded in three stages: initial, intermediate and advanced. The curriculum of the Initial Training Squadron centred on twenty-two separate exercises in aircraft handling and basic navigation. This work was intensive: between 10 October and mid-December Cheshire flew on almost every available day, completing the first stage of the course ten days before Christmas. Instructors rated his flying ability as Average.

All his training was flown on the Anson: an aircraft which was docile, dependable, achingly slow, with a hand-cranked undercarriage that did wonders for physical fitness – and twin-engined. He was destined to fly bombers. Memories differ as to whether this pleased him. According to Cheshire his first preference, like almost everyone else's, was for fighters, but a contemporary recalls that he chose to fly bombers. When asked why, Cheshire replied 'They'll hear about me.' A career as a bomber pilot was considered unenviable. Few wanted one. For that reason, Cheshire theorized, he would rise to prominence all the faster.[38]

After Christmas at Grey Walls Cheshire returned for the intermediate stage of the course. This was a syllabus of applied flying – rail and road reconnaissance, low-level bombing, photography, instrument flying – and more demanding. The weather was dreadful and progress slow. By mid-January No. 14 Course was already due for extension to compensate for weeks which had been lost. Worse followed: blizzards, days so cold that the Ansons' Cheetah engines refused to start, days when rain froze solid on the ground, and alternating spells of rain and snow which turned the aerodrome to a swamp.[39] When training resumed in March the remainder of the course was crammed into every available moment. At one point Cheshire flew six exercises on one day.

He passed with an overall mark of 84.3 per cent, a proficiency assessment of Average, and a prescient codicil from his instructors, as true in later life as it was then: 'If he can check his tendency to overconfidence should become Above the Average.'[40]

The entry in his Service Record tells more:

Ground subjects above average: attained 83% in intermediate exam and passed second. An average pilot who can be relied upon to do good work. Instrument flying exceptionally steady and accurate. Should make good leader with experience. Would have been granted 'Distinguished Pass' if allowed under war conditions.

On 6 April he was posted to No. 10 OTU at Abingdon,* and departed for a week's leave. Sunning himself on the lawn at Grey Walls, he felt troubled. In the hundred sorties he would fly during the next four years fear seldom disturbed him. But now, on the threshold, he did not know what to expect. He was frightened of being afraid.

No. 10 OTU was equipped with the Armstrong Whitworth Whitley, a strange, almost freakish-looking twin-engined aeroplane with a slender fuselage that tapered towards the twin rudders at the tail and deepened towards a slanting nose. The Whitley 'did everything nose-down'. Or as Sir Arthur Harris said: 'its design was so cock-eyed that it always flew in the most astonishing and unusual attitude with its tail right up behind its ears'.[41] However it flew, the Whitley was one of the few long-range bombers which Britain possessed. It was for such work that Cheshire now began to train.

He did so against a background of intensifying crisis. During his leave Germany had invaded Norway. When he flew his first exercise on 13 April, Bomber Command had dropped little more than leaflets on Germany and mines in her waters. On 10 May, the day he graduated to dual training by night, the Germans invaded Belgium and Holland. In the following week soldiers were rehearsing the defence of Abingdon itself. By 22 May, when Cheshire flew to Jurby in the Isle of Man for nine days' armament training,†[42] Guderian's tanks had passed through Abbéville and were turning north for Calais. When he returned to Abingdon the campaign in northern France was virtually finished. On 4 June, the day Cheshire completed his course, the last of 190,000 British and 140,000 French, Belgian and Polish troops were being evacuated from Dunkirk. Almost exactly a year before he had been starting his finals at Oxford, wondering if he would scrape a second. Now he was a

---

* Abingdon's Station Commander was then Grp Capt. Martin Massey, a veteran of the Great War. Shortly before a posting to the United States he opted to make 'one last trip' and was shot down. Massey was senior British officer at Stalag Luft III, Sagan, at the time of the Great Escape (March 1944) in which Christopher Cheshire was indirectly involved.
† Such training included dive- and stick-bombing, low-level attack and defence against fighters, and was Cheshire's first experience of the work which awaited him in action only two weeks later.

qualified bomber pilot, with a rating of flying ability which had risen to Exceptional. Tomorrow he would catch a train for Yorkshire, and war.

PART TWO: TO WAR, 1940–1943

4. Wonderful Life

On the eastern flank of the Yorkshire Wolds is Driffield, a market town of brick houses with wrinkled, red-tiled roofs, which in 1940 was busy with millers and corn merchants. The bomber station on its outskirts had opened in 1936, and bore the stamp of the day in the neo-Georgian facades of its accommodation and an arc of five hangars. Since 1938 the aerodrome had been home to two squadrons of Whitleys, Nos. 77 and 102. During air tests and stand-downs their crews could contemplate the neighbourhood to which they had been sent.

The Wolds are a realm of retrospection. Fickle seasonal streams, known locally as gypsies, flow in and out of their chalk foundations. Secluded dry valleys dream. Clumps of woodland shelter the higher isolated farms; elegant houses built by eighteenth-century land-owners occupy lusher corners. The emptier areas are eloquent. Patches of rumpled ground mark lost medieval hamlets, and the downlands are flecked with burial places seven times as old. By 1940 even recent, prosaic buildings had acquired a gentle poignancy. Lonely pre-war petrol stations and wayside art deco pubs evoked holidays and summer Sunday evenings when drowsy children were driven back from Scarborough and Filey to West Riding cities. But petrol was now rationed, the seaside was being wired and mined, the mansions had been requisitioned and roadblocks obstructed the highways.

Cheshire stepped into these surroundings on Wednesday 5 June. A branch-line train brought him to the town, and late in the afternoon he declared himself to a corporal at the guardroom beside RAF Driffield's main gate. It was hot, the air sweetened by hedgerow flowers, the atmosphere enervating. The evacuation of the BEF from Dunkirk had ended the day before, and Cheshire's life had been transformed in the space of eight hours: 'At breakfast I had been among people purely concerned with training . . . now at teatime I was to all intents and purposes in the front line.' Yet the atmosphere here was much as it had been at Abingdon: 'Life was just going on at a normal pace and in a normal way.'[1] In *Bomber Pilot*, a book begun in the present tense some eighteen months later, Cheshire looked back at himself in that week: 'I am still feeling my way; everything is new and interesting, even the smallest detail. Faces round about are strange; I feel rather self-conscious, almost apologetic – they are seasoned fighters, I am a new boy: at least, that is how I feel.'[2] The word 'feel' occurs three times, as if Tim White's urging voice was in his ear ('Yes, but what does it *feel* like? How can you describe it if you don't know what it *means*?').

Squadron membership had been fairly stable since before the war and some old hands grumbled at the sight of 'new bods'. 'Leonard Cheshire was our first university entrant and viewed with considerable suspicion . . . He was not one of us; he did not quite fit into the measured compartmentalized minds of the service at that time.'[3] Welcome or not, newcomers were needed. The tempo of the bombing war had quickened.[*] Losses had begun to rise, gaps were appearing in the duty rosters and the survivors – although they did not yet know it – would shortly be withdrawn from operations and sent for rest.

The Whitley had a crew of five.[†] Novice pilots were apprenticed to experienced captains before being given crews of their own, and next morning Cheshire was assigned to a crew. After lunch this was cancelled, and he was told to report instead to Plt Off. Frank

[*] 4 Group's first bombs had fallen in the sea near Borkum and Sylt in December 1939, in an attempt to prevent German seaplanes from mine-laying. Then followed patrols over the Frisian Islands, attacks on shipping and seaplane flare-paths, and 'Nickels' – leaflet operations which had ventured as far as Warsaw, Prague and Berlin. The first intended bombing of a land objective was the seaplane base at Hornum, on 19/20 March 1940. Attacks on Ruhr targets had begun in mid-May, three weeks before Cheshire's arrival.
[†] Pilot (captain), second pilot, navigator/bomb aimer, wireless operator and rear gunner. In June 1940 there was still some fluidity in roles, following earlier arrangements where the two pilots were also trained as navigators, the third crew member was designated as observer and the rear gunner was a second wireless operator.

Long, a regular officer who had been with 102 Squadron since before the war.★ Cheshire was already lucky. A few nights later the first crew failed to return.

Long was a New Zealander, and known as Lofty for his alpine stature. Strongly built, broad-shouldered, dark-haired and of unhurried manner, he was 'what we chose amongst ourselves to describe as a "character".' His juniors he treated as his equals and, as it appeared to us at the time, his seniors as something a little less.'[4] Long was meticulous in the preparation of his aircraft, vigilant when flying, calm at times of stress and gifted with a wry humour. As a mentor he was at once exacting and encouraging. Cheshire came to revere him, possibly even love him. Fifteen pages of *Bomber Pilot* dwell on the first hours of their acquaintance, and a quarter of the book deals with the six weeks of their partnership. All this was ahead. Long was on leave when Cheshire was put into his crew, but when he returned on the Saturday morning, Cheshire's schooling began.

Long quizzed him on the ways of the Whitley, testing his knowledge of the aeroplane's technicalities: crew drill, operational procedures, use of wireless, map-reading at night. 'I do not think there can have been a single piece of equipment or a single aspect of flying on which he failed to question me.'[5] At length he flicked Cheshire under the chin, smiled and led him out to the aircraft. 'There was the ground crew also, to each of whom Lofty introduced me individually, talking of their problems, and the background from which they came and explaining the importance of building up a personal relationship with them.'[6]

In the afternoon Long assembled the other members of his crew, and then took off for a cross-country to familiarize Cheshire with their procedures and assess his flying. The need to concentrate quelled Cheshire's apprehensions. But a worry still gnawed: when in action, would he make a fool of himself?[7]

Sunday morning, like the day before, dawned with a porcelain

★ On the night of 27/28 November 1939 Long was second pilot in a Whitley of 102 Squadron, captained by Fg Off. K. Gray, engaged on a Nickel sortie. While over the target their aeroplane was struck by lightning. Despite severe damage the two pilots nursed the aeroplane to a safe landing. Gray and Long were awarded immediate DFCs.

sky and a film of mist which was soon burnt away by the ascending
sun. After breakfast B Flight's pilots assembled in their crew room.
'The Flight Commander came in, tubby and jovial; just the opposite
of Lofty, but he scares you a bit. He read out roll-call . . . Then he
read the crew list for tonight – Rex, Frammy, Lofty. Yes, definitely
Lofty. What a wonderful sound, too! My heart leapt, and my face
must have shown it, for Lofty winked.'[8] During the morning they
checked their aircraft. By lunchtime the temperature was climbing
into the eighties. During the afternoon, on Long's advice, Cheshire
rested. Then a meal in the mess, and after that to station headquarters
for briefing.

For the past three weeks Bomber Command's effort had alternated between German oil plants and railway centres and tactical
objectives – chiefly road junctions, railways and bridges – in Belgium
and France. Both types of attack were intended to stem the onrush
of the panzers. Neither was doing so. Although the War Cabinet
had been assured that the bombing of oil refineries 'would unques-
tionably have the effect of retarding the land operations for which
the Germans required large quantities of petrol',[9] this was not
apparent to the French forces and two remaining British divisions
which were trying to hold them south of the Somme. The aircraft
being sent against oil plants were too few, and their bombing was
too inaccurate, to stifle production. In any case, Germany had
alternative sources of supply.

Bomber Command's efforts to provide close support by attacking
pinch-points in road and rail networks were similarly innocuous.
The cumbersome Whitleys were unsuitable for the work; they
were being deployed in penny packets, and their targets were
fugitive, often being selected on the basis of information which
was out of date by the time the aircraft arrived.

It was to such an objective that Cheshire was sent on his first
sortie. He listened intently to what the intelligence officer had to
say.

He talked briefly about the position of the battle front, about the German advance
and where they had reached, or, rather, where he thought they had reached,
because nobody seemed quite to know. On the large map on the wall was a red

line . . . it was supposed to represent the area behind which we could bomb; beyond it we would be bombing our own troops. He told us why we were doing this trip – it was Abbeville, the southern bridge. We were to help hold up the German advance by destroying their lines of communication. He made us feel the plight of such British troops as were left in France . . .[10]

The Operation Order issued that day reveals the baroque character and hopeless over-optimism of tactical planning at the time, with particular aircraft assigned to individual structures within the same target area. Long's primary was a road bridge at Abbeville East. Other crews were directed to bridges at St-Valéry, Pont-Remy and Picquiny. As alternatives they could bomb further listed targets, and in last resort 'any military objective north of five miles south of Somme'. In Long's Whitley the armourers had loaded four 500 lb and six 250 lb general-purpose bombs. The aircraft also carried twelve flares, which the Operation Order abstemiously reminded them were 'not to be wasted'.[11]

4 Group's operations in this period had something of the predictability of a scheduled air service. Take-off times were usually between nine o'clock and nine thirty in the evening, and routes followed pre-arranged corridors, each known by a different letter. On this occasion they were instructed to fly out and back along Corridor E, which ran via Abingdon and Hastings to northern France. Cheshire watched as Percy Brain, Long's navigator, laid off the track on the chart.

. . . amazingly neatly, too. I was most surprised and impressed . . . He measured off the distances and the bearings and filled in the log. Then we sorted out the navigational equipment and stowed it in the satchel. I never knew there would be so much stuff for what I imagined would be a simple operation. Maps, rulers, compass, dividers, CSC, pencils, rubber, penknife, code books, computer, plotter, Astro tables, watch sextant, planisphere, protractor, log book and Very cartridges.[12]

From briefing they moved to the crew room, where everyone changed. Here there was clamour. Towards half past eight, encumbered by flying clothing, flight bags, rations, thermos flasks, gear and parachutes, they climbed on to a lorry. The Whitleys were

scattered around the fringes of the aerodrome, and bystanders smiled
and waved as they were driven out to them.

At Whitley 'Q' they jumped down on to the grass. Here things
were calmer, less chatter, no more nervous laughter. The remaining
minutes were for final checks, the stowing of gear, talk with the
ground crew which was part business and part social, checking the
bomb-load chart and signing for the pins. A cigarette; mingled
scents of oily metal and summer grass. An awkward upward struggle
through the hatch. Settling in. Testing the intercom. Then:

Lofty opened the side window and shouted:
    'OK for starting up?'
    'OK, sir.'
    'Stand clear. Contact port engine.'
    'Contact.'

The engine stuttered, turned over once or twice, snorted oily
smoke and then caught with a clamour. Then the starboard engine.
More checks of equipment and controls, formal reports from each
member of the crew. Long waved away the chocks. Whitley 'Q'
began to move. 'We reached the down-wind side of the aerodrome
and looked at the time – two minutes to go. "N" and "P" were
there before us: they waited a few moments, and when they had
gone we turned into wind. Nothing coming; off we went.'[13] It
was twenty-one minutes past nine.

They circled while they climbed, the Wolds spreading in the
evening sunlight. Cheshire was in the front turret, looking down
at houses, wondering who lived in them and what they did, cars
parked outside a pub. 'I thought . . . of the evenings I had said,
"What the hell am I going to do to amuse myself tonight?" and it
occurred to me that you do not appreciate the simple things in life
until you suddenly realize you may never encounter them again.'[14]

After the first course was set on the compass Long invited
Cheshire to the controls. Cheshire wriggled back into the well
beside the pilot's seat, avoiding the hatch in the floor because
standing on it 'gave him a prickly feeling'. Changing places required
an agile manoeuvre which he had yet to master. They neared
Abingdon, and he strained for a glimpse of Grey Walls. 'I pictured

it in my mind: Father reading a book, Mother shutting the geese
up – she must be right down below this very minute – whistling
"Claire de Lune" and possibly wondering where I am . . .'[15] Exhaust
flames from the engines glowed brighter as the dusk deepened.

Lofty climbed down into the well and stood there with one foot on the step,
gazing out of the starboard window. Occasionally he made some remark, asked
me how I was getting on, and all the time he kept a close eye on the flying
panel. Now and then when he saw a beacon or landmark he went back to Percy
and plotted it on the chart . . . I asked Percy to dim his light; it reflected on the
perspex in front and I couldn't see out . . . I noticed the blackout: here and there
was an occasional twinkle; cars I could see, too, if they had their headlights on,
but nothing else. A few searchlights flickered on to us just long enough to see
what we were, and then switched off.[16]

Long took over as they crossed the Sussex coast. When the French
coastline neared Cheshire moved back into the well to allow Percy
Brain into the front turret to prepare for the bombing. Abbeville is
not far inland, and an expanding splash of orange fire indicated that
an attack was already in progress. Cheshire noticed specks of tracer,
fascinated by the leisurely way in which they appeared to rise. At first
the southern bridge eluded them. Brain released several flares, and
Long put the Whitley into a series of tight turns to gain a better view.
They found the bridge, but another Whitley bombed it during their
run up. Long went round again. After dropping two sticks of bombs
they went to look for the north bridge and Brain released the third
stick there. 'Percy came out of the front turret; he looked pleased.
Personally, I had not seen a thing; no bridge, no bombs. Lofty asked
me how I'd enjoyed it; I was disappointed in a way, but, if nothing
else, I felt happy from the infection of their high spirits.'[17] All around
in the countryside there were large fires burning.[18]

Back over the Channel Long returned the controls to Cheshire,
who skimmed the Whitley above a thickening sheet of cloud,
steering towards Yorkshire by a star that weakened in the summer
dawn. 'My mind was in a whirl. I needed time to piece everything
together; somehow it had not quite been what I expected; not
enough glamour, and too much to learn.'[19]

★

Next morning, Monday 10 June, Long and Cheshire were again on the crew list. Objectives for the evening were road and rail junctions and an enemy troop concentration near Poix. The weather was good when they took off at 20.20 but thereafter things didn't go so well. Everyone had been warned to take care lest Allied forces be bombed in error. Poix was masked by haze. Unable to locate anything they were supposed to attack, Long and Cheshire lugged the bombs back to Yorkshire.

102 Squadron, meanwhile, having previously known no 'Varsity pilots' at all, now gained two in one week. Melvin Young arrived. The company of a long-standing friend hoisted Cheshire's spirits yet higher, and provided support in the face of derisive comments about Oxford intellectuals. When some of Driffield's diehards pointed out that Cheshire's tailor had sewn his brevet too high above the left breast pocket of his tunic, he retorted in a matter-of-fact way that the space had been left on his instruction 'to make room for the VC, the DSO and the DFC'.[20]

Tuesday 11 June was a rest day for Long's crew. Cheshire was disappointed. The target was the Fiat works in Turin, and it appealed to him. So did the circumstances: Italy had just declared war on Britain and France, and the Operation Order urged crews to 'Press home attacks with vigour as first impressions will have a great influence.' But Long and Cheshire were in reserve when fifteen Whitleys of 77 and 102 Squadrons departed for the Channel Islands later in the day. They paused at Jersey airport to refuel, setting out again at 20.00. Few reached Italy.*

Cheshire wrote often to his parents. 'Going over again in a few moments,' he told them a week after his arrival. 'It's far better than slopping around doing nothing. And it really is grand fun.'[21] His gaiety was yet unaffected by awareness of the war's human consequences. While he was writing, the 51st (Highland) Division was being butchered at St-Valéry-en-Caux. Their efforts to hit a road junction at Aulnoye later that evening, and to interfere with enemy transport near Charleville on the next, did little to help them.

---

* A further twenty-one Whitleys of 10, 51 and 58 Squadrons proceeded via Guernsey airport. Severe storms and icing prevented many from clearing the Alps: of thirty-six aircraft dispatched only eleven bombed targets in Italy.

Cheshire settled into the rhythm, and on his next rest day he went to the seaside with Melvin Young while others prepared to attack marshalling yards. 'Don't worry about the news too much,' he told his parents on 15 June, writing between Scatter Scheme hops back and forth to Cottam, Driffield's satellite landing ground.* 'The French Army is in a tough spot; but it's still intact. The Germans have lost at least a million men and nearly 3,000 planes. I don't think they'll be able to keep it up much longer, and the railways behind the lines are just about bombed to hell.'[22] His assessment echoed the sanguine daily briefings provided by Driffield's intelligence officer. In fact, Luftwaffe aircraft losses were less than half this figure, and the Germans were already in Paris, where Aunt Edith was alarming her friends by snarling 'Bloody Boches!' at German soldiers in the streets.†

Before that day was out evidence of disaster stared them in the face. Towards evening a flight of Fairey Battles landed at Driffield. At breakfast time their crews had been part of the AASF in France. Ordered to withdraw at midday, they arrived in Yorkshire with the clothes in which they stood, while their forsaken ground crews trekked along clogged roads towards an Atlantic port.

Cheshire thrived on the immediacy. 'Life here still wonderful,' he wrote two days later, adding, 'although I haven't got very much to do at present.' 'At present' didn't mean that week or that day but *then and there*: the Air Staff's illusion that Bomber Command could throttle Germany's war effort by depriving it of oil remained unshaken, and he was waiting to take off to attack the synthetic oil plant at Gelsenkirchen-Buer.

More refugee Battles arrived the next day. Their crews told what had really been happening, and Cheshire's next letter home was a

* A precaution against pre-emptive air attack, whereby bombers were rotated between their home stations and satellite (sometimes more distant) airfields. Cottam, three miles north of Driffield, was brought into limited use for the dispersal of aircraft during June 1940.
† Edith and Gabriel Dichter attempted to leave France a few days later, but were stopped at St-Malo. They subsequently escaped into unoccupied France, made their way to Lisbon and thence to the United States. On return to Paris after its liberation they found the pictures and furniture in their home intact. The house had been occupied by German officers in their absence.

little more muted. There is more emphasis on 'us' and 'we', less 'I', and his earlier view of the war as a kind of recreational privilege is becoming moderated: 'Now we know where we stand, and thank God there is no one to let us down or betray us so we can fight in confidence.' This echoed mainstream feeling. After the quick surrenders of Holland and Belgium and the collapse of France there was a strong sense of betrayal by foreigners: 'It never occurred to them – it is only now becoming a commonplace – that the evacuation of the BEF had, in fact, left the French in the lurch.'[23] Cheshire continued: 'Jerry will come over here with his bombers and give us the same hell as the French, but I think we can take it. I only hope he tries invasion because that gives us the chance of beating him up.'[24]

The Germans visited Driffield that night. The attack was ineffectual. The few bombers that came were gulled by the station's Q Site – a nearby bombing decoy. 'No damage was caused except to the ground,' noted the station's diarist, who added smugly: 'One rabbit was killed.'[25] Long and Cheshire were over Germany at the time, where the failure of an engine obliged an early return.

The following evening was a night off, but on the next, Thursday 20 June, they took off into a drizzly twilight to attack the synthetic nitrogen plant and marshalling yards at Ludwigshaven-Oppau. Unable to locate either, Long and Cheshire went to Mannheim's marshalling yards instead, and it may have been here that Cheshire found the answer to a question which had troubled him since April. During his fifteen days at Driffield he had flown on five operations. Long's teaching had emphasized that the process of bombing was 'not difficult': there was a drill for everything, and anyone could do it if they mastered the drills.[26] In one respect, however, anyone could *not* do it. There was no drill for the conquest of fear. 'The only worry . . . was gunfire. Suppose I was frightened; suppose I found myself to be a coward and cried out for mercy! It could be. No one else did that, but then that is no help. It is difficult to imagine yourself being fired at and not feeling afraid.'[27] Earlier trips had not resolved this. Several of the French targets had been only lightly defended, and although he had seen anti-aircraft fire, it had not been close. Long had warned him that flak and searchlights were the principal dangers, and that they were lethal. Seen from a distance, however, coloured tracer, which glittered through the darkness, and the dilating, ragged yellow stars of heavy anti-aircraft explosions, formed a spectacle of 'fairylike beauty which attracted rather than repelled'.[28] So the question remained: when he met gunfire, how would he react?

Heavy flak announced itself with a growling roar, spattering lumps of metal which rattled through the skin of the fuselage. More shell bursts enclosed them in a pandemonium of 'crashes, groans and jerks'. Noise was the least of it. The blasts convulsed the Whitley in spasms, and the violence was accentuated by the shuddering twists, dives and climbs of Long's evasive flying.

Breath-snatched, what did he feel? Alarm – yes, but only fleetingly. After the first shock he discovered a piercing clarity of mind; a frigid awareness that it was 'personal – very personal', a matter of 'steel and gunpowder against flesh'; consciousness that any sense of protection from the enclosure of the cockpit was 'illusory, but reassuring'; and, as Long pushed the throttles wide for further stomach-sinking manoeuvres, a surge in his heart.

I understood suddenly the attraction, the priceless, gripping attraction, of night bombing. Without ack-ack these flights were just another cross-country . . . with ack-ack they were changed into something worth having; something that only war could give . . . I am afraid of many things, small, stupid things . . . and God knows I have suffered real, hopeless fear, but I am not afraid of ack-ack. It is nothing to be proud of. Fear is only the sum of the play of your imagination, and no two people's imagination plays the same way . . . No, unfortunately, it is nothing to be proud of, but it is something to cash in on.[29]

In time Cheshire would regret others' distortion of these words. Years later he would recall that he perceived danger 'only by the mind and the imagination, not by the bodily senses',[30] suggesting that his dread was less of fear than fear of fear, or panic. But for the moment he was exultant. Now he knew that he could play his part.

'Things are going well here, and I for one am thoroughly enjoying the war,' Cheshire told his parents before he took off for Mannheim. 'Mind you beat up any fifth columnists you can find: I fear the place is stiff with them, just as France was.'[31] It was a common view. In 1940 many airmen were more inclined to attribute the loss of a bomber to careless talk in the local pub than to German ability to notice Bomber Command's predilection for synthetic oil plants. The orthodoxy is interesting; uncritical acceptance of received opinion was seldom Cheshire's style. Only a few months before, indeed, he had been reprimanded for the dangerous speculation that some German propaganda might be factually accurate. Now, after two weeks' immersion in the ambience of the mess bar, his conformism temporarily exceeded that of some of the diehards. Young men who were studying instead of enlisting were for the time being 'cissys' and 'too scared to fight'.[32]

During the last week of June Cheshire did not operate. The Luftwaffe, on the other hand, were becoming increasingly active. Intruders began to probe the aerial defences of the east coast. On 30 June Driffield's Q Site again misled them, but four days later a Ju 88 slipped out of the clouds and bombed the aerodrome. More raiders came next day to attack the Chain Home station at Staxton Wold. The war was coming closer.

Although 1940's summer is remembered as a time of shimmering heat, Yorkshire's July was monotonously wet. Cheshire used days when they did not operate to study his craft. Frank Long taught him that flying a bomber at night was a matter of technique, and that learning was never finished.

. . . he kept drumming into my head the fundamental lesson of never thinking that you have mastered your job, of applying your whole heart and mind to the task of perfecting as far as is humanly possible the techniques of operational flying. He made me practise and re-practise, study and re-study, experiment and re-experiment. I had to sit in the cockpit blindfold and go through the different drills, sit in the rear turret, in the navigator's and the wireless operator's seat, and try and see life from their point of view.[33]

. . . I practised flying relaxed till I found it no more tiring than sitting down. I learned to fly on instruments till it was no more tiring than reading a book.[34]

I learned about engines, too: how to take care of them: their limitations and possibilities . . . For this I turned to the ground crews, and their anxiety to teach me was the greatest stimulus I could ever want.[35]

Airframe riggers, mechanics and electricians remember his eagerness, and gladly taught him *why* things worked (or, as might be, not). On air tests 'he appeared to be very meticulous as to the settings and set-up of the various equipment, and particularly the radio and intercom'. Contact with base was important for navigation and in emergencies, while crew cooperation hinged on communication. The Whitley's intercom connection with the rear turret was unreliable, but discussions with electricians showed where the problem lay and how it could be avoided. 'I've got a smashing second dicky,' Long told a friend. 'He's a better pilot than I am already.'

On the rare occasions when Cheshire was not in or near an aeroplane, his emerging reputation was as someone happy-go-lucky. 'He almost always had a half-humorous look on his face, he never seemed to worry.'[36] Here he is at dawn, walking back to camp after a night out in Scarborough, with twenty miles to go: 'The morning was gorgeous . . . I did not mind walking in the least: in fact, come to that, I did not mind whether I arrived back in time or not. If you are in the process of enjoying something, there is no point in spoiling it by worrying.'[37] A few minutes later he was given a lift back to Driffield by a girl in a sports car. He nicknamed her Scarlet. Years later Cheshire lived by the maxim that 'Today's troubles are enough for today.' He looked, but did not worry, ahead. 'It's a grand existence,' he told his parents. 'Nothing to worry about except getting up in time. Plenty of relaxation and enough excitement to keep you out of mischief. I'm afraid it's not so good for you just waiting. You mustn't worry because we don't here and I don't like to be worried when there's nothing to worry about. If we do get shot down, it's just too bad.'[38]

'Chesh is crackers,' said those who could not fathom his cryptic jokes, which were often simultaneously directed against himself and those around him, leaving others uncertain as to who was making fun of whom. Seniors marked his impishness and intelligence, and puzzled over apparent contradictions between modesty and self-advertisement, openness and containment, spontaneity and control. His inscrutability bred not one but a number of nicknames. 'Chesh' to some, 'Cheese' to most, yet others knew

him as 'Geoff'. Long alone called him 'Cheddar', and Cheshire in
his turn would devise names for his crew members which no one
else would use.

One of them was for Richard Rivaz, a newly arrived pilot officer
gunner. The mess was full, and Rivaz was asked to share a room.
Cheshire was sleeping in it.

He had scattered his clothes all over the place: some were on my bed, some
were on his bed, and some were on the floor. Also on my bed there was an
open suitcase, two tennis racquets, a squash racquet and his towel. I removed
the articles from my bed to the floor, making as little noise as I could . . . although
I need not have been so cautious as nothing other than a vigorous shaking will
awaken Leonard once he is asleep. I looked at his tunic, thrown carelessly over
the back of a chair . . .

Next morning Rivaz was roused by the buzzing of Cheshire's
electric razor. Looking up, he saw

a slight figure in brightly coloured pyjamas walking up and down the room
trailing a length of electric flex behind him and running the razor in a carefree
manner up and down his face. After a few moments I said 'Good morning' . . .
and was favoured with some sort of grunt in reply.[39]

Further questions elicited only further grunts. In following days
Rivaz saw 'this uncommunicative and, as I thought, strange person
several times . . . but never once did he show that he recognized
me'. Rivaz noticed that 'he seemed to know everybody, and that
most people called him Cheese'.

More trips followed: to the petroleum sheds at Emden on the
12th (leaving a fire visible seventy miles away); to Paderborn airfield
on the 14th. On the 19th they sought the oil plant at Gelsenkirchen-
Buer, but failed to find it and bombed an autobahn instead. Two
days later an aircraft factory at Kassel was the target, and strengthened
flak defences greeted them when they returned to it on the 23rd.
Thunder, rain and hail beset the squadron on its next operation,
to Mannheim and Hamm, when five of the nine crews taking part
brought their bombs back, one returned early and another did not
return at all. Only three found targets, Long and Cheshire among
them. The following trip was Cheshire's twentieth. It was to

Dusseldorf, and it was his last with Frank Long. He had served his apprenticeship.

Cheshire had developed a profound affection for his teacher.

. . . hardly any Captain that I ever knew would allow his Second Dicky into the driving seat whilst over the danger zone: thus when one was finally passed out and given a crew of one's own, one had no actual experience of handling the controls under fire. But Lofty was different: he would give me a clout – with his boot if he could possibly manage it – and bawl out at me to get into his seat and take over, usually with the addition of some comment as 'without making an ass of yourself, if you don't mind'. Then from the Second Pilot's position he would talk me into the target and back, not always perhaps in the most complimentary of tones, but in a way that gave me a confidence and experience that I could not possibly have otherwise gained. I must have been the only pilot in the squadron who was ever given such a start as this.[40]

Frank Long, patient and demanding, serious yet subversive, was perhaps Cheshire's ideal role model. Long had taught that 'Bombing is technical, a matter of knowledge and experience, not of setting your jaw and rushing in. And when you have the knowledge and the experience, the crux of the issue is crew cooperation.'[41]

So he set about getting to know his crew. Only six weeks before he had himself been freshman. Now he was tutor to a new second pilot. Desmond Coutts was tall, fair-haired and 'seemed to be in a permanent daydream'. Rivaz thought he looked 'more like a poet than a pilot'.[42] Cheshire got on well with Coutts, found him able and drilled him just as he had been drilled by Long. The wireless operator was Sgt Stokes, very experienced, fanatical about his equipment and considered the best on the squadron. Their first navigator was Sgt Howard, but after several weeks he was replaced by George Roberts, an amiable Welshman who continued to fly with Cheshire until the end of his first tour, and rejoined him in 1941. Sgt Pike was the rear gunner. From time to time places would be taken by others, but Stokie, Taffy and Desmond, as they knew one another, formed the nucleus of the companions with whom Cheshire flew and passed much of his time until early winter. He was devoted to them, and they to him.

Their first operation was on Saturday 10 August, when they took off at 21.05 as one of ten 102 Squadron aircraft which had been variously detailed to attack an oil storage depot at Frankfurt, the Hoechst explosives works and a power station at Cologne. 'The trip went off well. Terrible night. 60 mile an hour wind so we didn't find the target but anyway dropped the bombs on something in the Ruhr. We got caught in the searchlights at 3,000 feet, but weren't hit . . .' They had landed at 04.45: a long trip, the best part of eight hours. At debriefing the 'something' was reported as a factory near Osnabruck, and the bombing height rather higher than the 3,000 feet mentioned in the letter to his parents. His determination to hit targets often caused him to attack them from lower altitudes than those advised. His growing competence and versatility were also earning new responsibilities: 'Am squadron navigation officer for the time being – gives me more to do.'[43]

Next day he had a lot to do. 102 Squadron was ordered to prepare for an attack on the Caproni works in Milan. Previous Italian raids had used Jersey and Guernsey as advanced bases, but the Channel Islands were now in German hands and after lunch they flew instead to Harwell in Berkshire. At fourteen minutes past eight that evening Cheshire set forth. 'It was a very successful trip' he reported,

and we did a power of damage. There was bright moonlight all the way, or nearly all the way, and I've never seen anything so beautiful as the Alps – they stood out so clearly with their snow-covered tops, and down in the valleys were the villages and towns all lit up . . . it makes you laugh when you think that the Yanks pay thousands of dollars to see them and we get paid for it. Trip lasted nine and a half hours . . .[44]

On return they paused again at Harwell for interrogation and refuelling, telling of negligible opposition and 'enormous fires'. Back at Driffield congratulations on 'a grand show' awaited them from 4 Group's AOC, and the promise of a 'full group show' to wind up the moon period at the end of the week.

The Luftwaffe had other plans. Soon after breakfast next morning, Thursday 15 August, the first of some seventy Heinkel 111s began to take off from Stavanger in Norway. Supported by Me 110 long-range fighters, the force planned to make landfall on the Durham coast and then turn south to strike the bomber stations at

Dishforth and Linton-on-Ouse. A parallel attack was aimed at Driffield by fifty Ju 88s of KG30 from Ålborg in Denmark. In a further effort to divide defences, a third group of aircraft was dispatched from Norway towards Edinburgh, with instructions to turn back before it reached the coast. However, bungled navigation took the Heinkel force well to the north of its planned course over the North Sea and rendered the feint ineffectual. The approach of the Heinkels was observed by radar; fighters from Acklington, Drem and Catterick were ordered up to meet them, and at 12.45 Spitfires of 72 Squadron attacked the bombers thirty miles off the Northumberland coast. The formation began to break up. A flurry of engagements followed. Within thirty-five minutes eight Heinkels and seven Me 110s had been shot down.

Meanwhile the Ju 88s were approaching the Yorkshire coast. They too were detected by radar, harried over the sea by fighters and pursued inland. But on they came, and at twenty past one they reached Driffield. Cheshire tells us he was discussing Scarlet, his new girlfriend, with Desmond Coutts. Then: 'Air-raid siren. Nobody moved but I got up and walked towards the door: someone said "Cissy", and I said, "So what?" . . . Actually I only started to say it, because before I had finished there was the whine of a bomb, and in spite of my lead, I was not the first to the door.' Outside, Cheshire 'saw a bunch of them coming out of the sky. I didn't know anything could move so fast.'[45] The first bombs were exploding even as the air-raid siren sounded. Rivaz was in the mess writing a letter. 'I looked out of the window and saw people running to the shelters . . . The ante-room, which had been crowded a few seconds before, was almost empty, and the few remaining were rushing to the door . . . All other sounds were then promptly drowned by the largest explosion I had ever heard . . .' The next thing Rivaz knew 'I was lying on my face in the passage . . . covered with dust and choking and surrounded by broken glass and rubble. I got to my feet and saw through a cloud of smoke that the mess a few feet behind me was a complete ruin . . .'[46]

Cheshire, Desmond Coutts, Melvin Young and others ran to a shelter, which began to fill with injured servicemen and women, dust, smoke and the stink of cordite. A nearby hut caught fire, and

thousands of rounds of exploding ammunition within it began to
pop 'like peas being shelled'. John Grimstone, a radio mechanic,
was crouching

behind a hangar door (a very safe place) along with my 'oppo' LAC Bertrand
Ash, when he decided to leave the sanctuary of the hangar to release a 'works
and bricks' horse that had been abandoned on the tarmac by its driver. It was
rearing up in the shafts and making the most horrific sounds. Ash had only gone
a few yards when the horse suffered a direct hit from a bomb and Ash caught
shrapnel in his groin. He died the next morning.[47]

A parked Whitley exploded, taking two others with it. Bombs hit
four of Driffield's five hangars. As the attack proceeded a number
of the Ju 88s turned to engage the airfield's defences, skimming
low as they flew at the light anti-aircraft positions and fired into
them.

The raid subsided shortly after two o'clock. Rivaz went to look
at the hangars. 'They had been badly knocked about, and one was
on fire: the fire party were at work with their hoses amid a great
din of crackling and sizzling.'[48] In another, Rivaz saw the roof
dangling, and was bawled at for not wearing his tin hat:

'Do you want to get brained? . . . If you *want* something to do, go and help
move that Whitley; there's an unexploded bomb beside it . . .'[49]

Further on, men were digging frantically to recover colleagues who
had been buried in a trench shelter.

. . . orderlies were lifting a man – with his tunic, face and hair covered with
earth . . . I noticed that his legs were in an unnatural twisted position. Someone
was digging round another pair of legs: the body was still buried and the legs
obviously broken. I saw two more men crushed – with faces nearly the same
colour as their tunics – between sheets of corrugated iron: they were both dead.[50]

Cheshire told his parents that all the raiders had been shot down,[51]
and fifteen years later Andrew Boyle portrayed the incident as little
more than a nuisance raid:

. . . twenty German bombers repaid a few compliments by swooping down on
Driffield, killing a horse, a civilian, and four men, injuring twenty-nine more

of the two thousand people on the station, and damaging the hangars and a few aircraft . . .[52]

In fact the eventual death toll was fifteen, ten Whitleys had been destroyed and others damaged, four hangars were wrecked and just seven of the attackers had been shot down. Cheshire himself became less flippant about bombing: 'Don't hesitate to use the shelter if there are bombers overhead,' he warned his parents; 'all this "Oh well if I'm hit I'm hit, so what the hell" is all very well in theory but it's a bit different when the whole countryside comes tumbling round your ears.'[53]

The Luftwaffe's losses, while far smaller than Cheshire liked to think, nevertheless amounted to 14 per cent of the force dispatched. This was an unsustainable loss rate, and the Luftwaffe changed tactics. Four days later a solitary Ju 88 arrived after dark and dive-bombed the remaining intact hangar. KG30's campaign to demolish Driffield's buildings one by one resumed in the small hours of 25 August when more bombers delivered a succession of brief attacks which wrecked the sergeants' mess and ruptured water mains.[54] Their persistence paid off. Later that day the aerodrome was closed for repairs. Reconstruction took six months.

Evicted from Driffield, on 26 August 102 Squadron removed through drizzle to Leeming, between Northallerton and Bedale towards the north end of the Vale of York. Their stay here was brief, and tense. The day after their arrival six aircraft were ordered to stand by against possibility of invasion, and this readiness was held for three days.[55]

Cheshire believed that invasion was inevitable. 'There's going to be a lot of suffering and death in the next few weeks. I expect a simultaneous invasion of the whole of Gt Britain. Let them come.'[56] And as they waited, they were again uprooted. On Sunday 2 September

we got orders to stand by to move – where and why nobody knew. Anyway we started packing up. Early on Monday morning we had orders to move immediately to Prestwick and got off by 10.30. When we arrived we found everything was in a shambles – no hangars – no petrol, quarters or anything. But at least it was quiet. They've had two air-raid warnings since the war broke out, and no bombs at all.

Makeshift offices were established in tents and packing cases on the edge of the airfield. Cheshire thought the town 'rather fun, by the sea and the country is lovely, so are most of the girls, it's full of holidaymakers. The snag is that the job we're given is so dreadful – submarine spotting. Won't suit me at all.'[57] Impatient, he applied for transfer.

102 Squadron's remaining airworthy Whitleys were now attached to 15 Group Coastal Command. Their duty was convoy escort, and the depth charges with which they were armed were carried at the expense of fuel, and hence of range. One flight at a time was accordingly detached to Aldergrove in Northern Ireland, to allow greater radius of action. Cheshire thought Aldergrove 'a ghastly hole', although he admired the scenery, and for his twenty-third birthday his parents sent him money to buy a bicycle to explore it. 'You are a sweet pair,' he said in thanks, but

I don't think a bike will do me much good at present rate of mobility – although some people cart theirs around in the plane. So I don't yet know what to do with so much money, if I get into Belfast I shall buy a lot of things I need – the rest will stay put until I find a suitable use for it – it won't be frittered away on beer and cigarettes. Thanks also for your very sweet letters. I don't deserve any . . .[58]

Crews at Aldergrove were kept at readiness around the clock. When orders came to take off

we might have as little as a quarter of an hour to prepare. In other words, a quarter of an hour to draw our maps, report to Control, work out a flight plan and take off. It was not possible to do it all, so, since at any cost we had to be away on time, we went only with the bare essentials . . . and worked out the flight plan in the air. It was good practice in navigation and crew drill, but it made us bad-tempered.[59]

It was also important. Germany now controlled the continental coastline from the north of Norway to Bordeaux. Since July the French Atlantic ports had been used as bases for U-boats, and the 'wolf-pack' tactics pioneered by Karl Dönitz were becoming more effective. Convoys west of Ireland were now within reach of bombers stationed in Brittany, while a four-engined

Focke-Wulf FW 200C 'could take off from Brest or Bordeaux, fly round the British Isles to westward, land in Norway and make the return journey the next day'.[60] Britain was on the verge of being strangled.

Once airborne, a Whitley crew had to locate the convoy, make contact with the leading escort vessel and await instructions to be flashed by Aldis lamp. The usual task was to patrol an area some fifteen miles wide ahead of the convoy, as much for the morale of the merchant crews as to deter submarines or shadowing aircraft. Even doing this, however, could be perilous. One of Cheshire's colleagues recalls his first encounter with an incoming convoy:

... the Royal Navy had never seen a Whitley on Coastal Command at that time, and could not have been told because of radio silence, so seeing a large black aircraft converging on them [they] felt somewhat disconcerted and opened fire! We of course veered away and every time we approached the convoy we were fired on again, despite the fact that we were firing off the colours of the day, and the wireless operator was using the Aldis lamp giving the letters of the day. Eventually the firing stopped and we received a message by Aldis lamp from the leading destroyer, to the effect that we were to approach the convoy from the rear, descending to bridge height when passing the trailing destroyer, and continue through the convoy to the leading destroyer. This was to identify our markings. This we did, and what an eerie experience: as we passed the destroyers, every gun on board followed our movement.[61]

Cheshire flew his first patrol on 8 September, taking off late in the morning to shepherd the twenty-one ships and two escorts of Convoy OB210 up the Irish Sea. They found the convoy within half an hour, a few miles south-west of the Isle of Man, and bade farewell shortly before seven in the evening as the ships passed through the North Channel. The trip was uneventful, but long, and Cheshire was not alone in grumbling about the tedium and disorganization. Briefings were perfunctory, and '[we] didn't . . . receive any instruction in what we were supposed to be doing'.[62]

Atlantic patrols followed on 11 and 14 September, the latter to provide cover for the MV *Harpenden* which had been torpedoed but remained afloat. They found her west of Donegal Bay, under tow to the Clyde by two warships.[63] On the 17th, escort duty kept them aloft for eight hours; on the next day they were airborne for ten and a half: 'the destroyer signalled me that there was a boat with thirty men adrift so we stayed on till dark looking for it, but couldn't find it'.[64] Three more sorties followed, and when they returned to Prestwick for a few days' respite Cheshire found himself billeted with the local priest. Discontented as he was, however, he had been having second thoughts about his request for a posting: 'Getting away is a knotty problem. I could do it all right but it isn't very clever to ask for a change of squadron, you lose seniority – got to start all over again – and anyway it looks as though we will go back to our real job before very long – so I'm hanging on till they know just what they are going to do.'[65]

Convoy patrols were hazardous as well as tedious. Whitley engines did not take kindly to running close to the sea, ingesting spray and salt, and on 7 October Melvin Young's aircraft suffered engine trouble and was forced to ditch. The Whitley sank within five minutes. The crew managed to board their dinghy. After twenty-two hours they were rescued by a destroyer.

Cheshire, too, had a narrow escape. Two days previously he had been ordered to locate a convoy and had taken off in haste, ill-prepared, before Coutts could be found. The weather worsened and a signal ordered them to Prestwick. When they arrived the aerodrome was cloaked by thick cloud and unapproachable. Roberts urged Cheshire to go below the cloud for a pinpoint, and after some hesitation Cheshire complied, emerging at 400 feet to find that they were over a narrow loch with hills ascending to either side. Alarmed, Cheshire pushed the throttles wide and climbed steeply: 'All the time a creepy feeling, because it was impossible to tell which direction, if any, was out to sea and away from the hills.'[66] He described what followed:

. . . we were flying around in clouds and torrential rain for four hours without seeing a fly and couldn't get any results from the wireless. Eventually the trouble was solved and I landed in a howling storm with fifteen minutes fuel in hand. The joke was that they got hold of us on W/T, told us that everything was all right and we were over land and that we were to jump for it – but we hadn't got a parachute between us.[67]

When Cheshire entered the mess, red-eyed after nearly twelve and a half hours of continuous concentration, his flight commander 'didn't know whether to give him a terrific bollocking or a commendation. His independence of mind, skill and confidence in his own ability more than balanced the stupidity and sloppiness of getting into a scrape like that.'[68]

This was Cheshire's last sortie for Coastal Command. Four days later the squadron was ordered back to Yorkshire, and to a new airfield: Linton-on-Ouse, distantly overlooked by the White Horse of Kilburn and the Howardian Hills, in the Vale of York.

Linton was a permanent station of the expansion period, and thus popular for its centrally heated accommodation and proximity to the pubs and dance halls of York, if slightly less so for the fanaticism in enforcement of minor regulations. 'Discipline – saluting' intoned the daily orders:

The rider of a bicycle (pedal or motor) or the driver of a mechanical vehicle will not salute when the vehicle is in motion owing to the danger of taking his eyes off the road. When the vehicle is stationary he will salute by turning his head smartly towards the officer passing him, but will not remove his hand from the handlebar or steering wheel.[69]

One might hardly guess there was a war on, especially when the Ampleforth Beagles met outside the officers' mess. But there again one would: German intruders remained lethal visitors. As evenings lengthened Linton's blackout was ordered before lights were switched on in late afternoon,[70] and some aircraft were dispersed on rotation to a satellite landing ground.[71]

The night blitz had begun. Airmen returning from leave spoke of static water tanks on the sites of vanished buildings, Underground stations crammed with sleepers and town-hall clocks which told the times of explosions by the moments at which they had stopped. Men were summoned home to funerals. Children, lovers, mothers, grandparents in Glasgow, Birmingham, Derby or Liverpool were no longer safe.

Nor were German oil refineries and rolling stock safe from Cheshire. On 18 October he resumed his 'real job', and bombed the railway yards at Pretzsch; then Lünen, attacked from 3,000 ft at the cost of over a hundred holes in the aircraft, 'results not seen owing to searchlight glare'; then the oil refinery at Ruhland. It was in these weeks that his gifts of captaincy began to glow. 'After a raid we had a general discussion on the way things had gone, and I realized even then that Leonard was a cut above the other captains, more intelligent, more efficient, and more questioning and trying to find the answers.'[72] It had much to do with his determination. Cheshire noticed a tendency for colleagues to fall into two broad groups: those whose paramount urge was to find the target and destroy it, and those for whom anxiety about 'all the many things that might happen between take-off and landing dominated everything else'. He concluded that the worriers not only needed greater willpower, but were also at greater risk. Concentration kept other concerns at bay, and whereas a tenacious pilot would be likely to weigh up a crisis objectively, an anxious crew might overreact. George Roberts, his navigator, noticed this too.

The one [impression] that still lingers is the absolute faith he inspired . . . I flew with other captains, but it was only with him that I felt I was doing my job with real confidence; tackling a trip not just as another one, but with a direct interest in its result and success. It was such a temptation to drop the bombs as quickly as you could and get the hell out of the area. We felt we owed it to him to do our best, knowing that he would do the same for us (apart from the dreadful thought of those eyebrows meeting in a frown). With others, I felt it was a question of 'Will we get back?', not the right spirit I agree.[73]

Another strength lay in his ability to withstand the tensions of repeated passage from safety to danger and back again. On some evenings they were over Germany. For the rest of the time they lived in warm and relatively comfortable surroundings, ate decent food and slept in proper beds.[74] When not flying they might visit pubs or cinemas, walk a dog or go dancing in the De Grey Rooms in York. On 24 October Linton welcomed the London floor show *Paradise on Parade*. On the next evening members of the audience were under fire over Cuxhaven, Hamburg and Antwerp, and not all of them came back. There were some who found that continual readjustment was very hard to endure.[75]

Above all, he had assembled a happy, faithful crew. In late

October Coutts, Roberts, Stokes and Cheshire were still together, and Richard Rivaz had joined them in the rear turret. Tall, sparely built, in his early thirties and thus a good deal older than most aircrew, Rivaz was a self-effacing man with a kindly smile. A talented artist, it was weeks before Cheshire discovered that he was a Royal Academician. Off duty, Rivaz's indifference to bars and nightclubs was considered curious by younger spirits, as was his liking for farm labouring when on leave. He came to occupy a fatherly role.[76] He was also a good gunner – a talent which perhaps went with his artist's eye, and explains why senior captains later tried to poach him. In mid-October, however, Rivaz was still inexperienced. He had yet to find a place in a regular crew.

I had returned from leave . . . and the first person I saw when I got inside the mess was Leonard. 'I've got you in my crew,' he said.
  'Grand,' I replied. 'Thanks awfully . . .'
  'Don't thank me . . . you've not flown with me yet,' he said . . . and smiled. Leonard's smile is really beautiful; his mouth, instead of getting bigger, seems to get smaller, and his eyes shine. When he smiles he makes you feel glad; it is a smile meant for you . . . and you alone.[77]

And in the air, over Germany:

I began to feel rather lonely and cut off from the others, and wondered what was happening at the other end of the aeroplane . . . Almost as if he had been reading my thoughts Leonard said . . .
'How are you, Revs?' . . . Those four words bucked me up no end. I felt again that I was not the only person in the aeroplane, and once more felt part of the crew.[78]

These moments illuminate one of Cheshire's most powerful gifts: he made people feel better simply for being near him, and stirred desire for good because of it.

Rivaz and Cheshire gravitated towards one another, and wrote books which record their experiences from opposite ends of the same aeroplane. Their accounts of what happened on the night of 12/13 November are best read side by side.

They were briefed to attack the synthetic oil plant at Wesseling, near Cologne. Harold Chapman was in the first of 102 Squadron's Whitleys to take off. '. . . approaching the North Sea we found a bank of cloud, the base around 500 ft rising to around 17,000 ft; it was impossible to climb over the cloud, it would have been too costly in time and fuel, so we had no alternative but to press on through the cloud . . .' This proved hazardous, for there were icing layers at different heights. Over Germany they eventually broke cloud at 15,000 ft. '. . . the cloud then levelled out just below us at 12,000 ft with here and there tall thin columns of cloud rising about 500 ft from the main layer'. Conditions were not only difficult but eerie. Electricity 'zig-zagged along the front gun, the rear gunner reported the same from the trailing aerial and a blue bloom flashed along the wings'.

Cloud broke up as they neared the target. The moon-silvered Rhine and twin steeples of Cologne's cathedral were clearly visible. No searchlights or gunfire disturbed them, but as they descended to their bombing height fires appeared about five miles away. This was puzzling, as theirs should have been the first aircraft to attack. Suspecting a decoy, they continued their run-up. 'As soon as the first bomb dropped, all hell was let loose, hundreds of searchlights sprang up, and it seemed that hundreds of guns opened fire . . . light flak as well as heavy . . .'

In Cheshire's aircraft, meanwhile, an intercom fault had caused delay in pinpointing the target. By the time this was rectified 'Leonard was cursing some low cloud . . . like white fleece below us.'[79] Wesseling was obscured. The passivity of the defences seemed strange. Feeling uneasy, they turned for Cologne's marshalling yards instead. Then the barrage started, and found them.

A shell smashed through the front turret and out again, and exploded. Momentarily blinded, choked by smoke, for some seconds Cheshire lost his composure. The Whitley was sinking. A second shell burst behind the port wing, setting off a flare inside their flare chute: an instant of several million candlepower which knifed open the port side of the fuselage for a length of three and a half yards.

Cheshire gradually collected himself, levelled the aircraft, found that they had height in hand and that the engines still ran. Coutts appeared beside him in the well, looking down the fuselage and shouting 'Fire! The tank's on fire!' To which Cheshire replied 'Well, put it out then.'[80] He called Rivaz forward to help.

God, what a mess! The fuselage door had gone, and most of one side of the fuselage as well. Desmond was there, working like a maniac, with his blond hair shining in the light of the flames, and his eyes sparkling like brilliants: sweat was pouring from his face, and he was hurling flares, incendiaries and spare ammunition out of the gaping fuselage. I started to do the same . . . and he shouted at me to go back and get my parachute, as the aeroplane would probably break in two at any moment. 'Very probably,' I thought . . .[81]

In the cockpit Cheshire felt heat on his back.

I screwed my head round . . . Thick, black, oily smoke pouring out from beneath the petrol tank, and in the background red gashes of fire.[82]

Flak still engulfed them, but evasive action was not possible – the aircraft might break up. Cheshire wondered whether they should bale out, but found that 'the last thing I wanted to do was to get out and this in fact saved me because eventually the fire subsided'.[83] Rivaz and Coutts worked until the flames were gone. Then they crawled forward.

The wind and slipstream was whistling through the fuselage and tore at my clothing . . . Leonard was sitting at the controls, and turned round and smiled as I entered the cabin. Davy was sitting by his set fumbling with his morse key: his face was charred and black, and his clothing all burned.[84]

Davidson was the wireless operator. He had been standing beside the flare chute. His face was seared. For the moment he was blind. He was eighteen. This was his first trip.

Desmond had fetched the first-aid kit and covered Davy's face with the jelly used for burns. It was bitterly cold in the cabin, and for the next five hours we did all we could for Davy's comfort: I kept putting his fingers in my mouth and breathing hard on them to try and get them warm.[85]

With the fire out and some control regained, Cheshire's determination was restored. They dropped the bombs. Then the return.

... a nightmare ... with the five of us crammed in the cabin of the Whitley, hardly ever speaking, and wondering how far we should get. Leonard was sitting at the controls; he had taken his helmet off, but was still wearing his yellow skull cap, which looked grotesque in the half-light. Taffy was sitting at the navigation table grinning to himself most of the time ... Desmond, looking like a wild blond giant, was part of the time sitting beside Leonard and part of the time looking at Davy.[86]

No fighter found them, but fire and the freezing wind that blasted in through the shattered perspex had taken most of Roberts's maps. They reconstructed a course from memory. George Roberts: '... we believed him that we'd get back, although our eyes and reason told us otherwise. If ever an aircraft flew on faith and little else that one did.'[87]

At Linton-on-Ouse the first of 102 Squadron's Whitleys touched down at 06.35. Melvin Young returned ten minutes later. Others followed during the next hour. At debriefing Harold Chapman 'reported the dummy fires, the initial lack of searchlights and gunfire'. Afterwards, Wg Cdr Groom, 102 Squadron's CO, asked to see Chapman's aircraft. They counted 150 holes in it. Nearly half an hour had passed since the last aircraft landed. By now it was broad daylight. A little after eight o'clock: '... we heard in the distance the sound of Merlin engines. We scanned the sky but could not see an aircraft. The noise increased but we still could not see an aircraft. Then over the boundary hedge flopped a Whitley, which soon came to a stop.'[88] Chapman, Groom, the adjutant and others ran to the aeroplane. They were 'amazed that such a damaged aircraft could have flown'. Rivaz emerged first. Davidson was lifted into an ambulance. Unable to sleep, later in the day Rivaz, Coutts and Cheshire went into York. They visited Davidson, and then went to the cinema to see (in Cheshire's case for the sixth time) Fred Astaire in *Broadway Melody*.

The spectacle of Cheshire's Whitley had a sobering effect.

We went into one of the hangars and saw an aircraft that had also returned from this raid. The entire side had been blown out ... Up to now flying had been carefree, quite fun, but we were now beginning to realize what we had let ourselves in for. But human nature is very optimistic. We always think it is going to happen to someone else, but never to us.[89]

Two days later the squadron was transferred to Topcliffe, a few miles further north in the Vale of York, and three days after this Cheshire was sent on a course at the Blind Approach School at Watchfield, near Swindon in the Vale of the White Horse. This heralded greater changes. 'No news [*sic*] from this end,' he wrote to Douglas Baxter, '. . . have done 35 trips, am on a fortnight's special course at Watchfield. . . return to Yorkshire (TOPCLIFFE) at beginning December, and go off operations end of same month. [?] get a so-called rest, but actually have to get down to some really hard work . . .'⁹⁰

His letters to Baxter lapse into undergraduate chat: 'suppose you've cut down alcohol to ten pints per day – bloody good: keep it going and you may escape DTs yet'. It is easy to forget that only the year before he *was* an undergraduate; now, not many months later, he was a veteran bomber captain approaching his first retirement. More than this, on 23 November he was taken aside by Watchfield's CO, told that he had been awarded the DSO, and handed a telegram of congratulation from 4 Group's AOC which added 'you are the first junior officer in Bomber Command to be so decorated after fifteen months of war'.

No. 4 Course at Watchfield rehearsed the use of radio equipment to assist blind landings.★ He worked hard, practising first in the Link Trainer and then in Ansons.⁹¹ Off duty they were billeted in a large country house, but Watchfield was not far from Grey Walls and when he could Cheshire went home. He found his parents apprehensive. Christopher had completed his flying training and was about to embark on his first tour of bomber operations. The lives of both sons were now imperilled.

He went into Oxford. News of his DSO had been widely publicized, not least in the *Oxford Mail*, and Merton's dons, having earlier barred him from the college in reaction to a well-publicised practical joke, were now solicitous. Cheshire was stony. 'Dear Duggie' he wrote to Baxter, 'Saw Dean Jones – he said "I think we can lift the ban on you now" . . . suppose he thinks I'm a book –

★ The Lorenz system; imported from Philips of Eindhoven before the war, transmitted a dot/dash code, audible in the pilot's headphones, which varied according to the line of approach: hence the phrase 'on the beam'.

to be picked up and dropped at pleasure – asked me to a celebration at Merton – refused to go into the place.'[92]

Back at Topcliffe everything seemed mutable. In the space of a fortnight Wg Cdr Groom had been lost on an operation, and Melvin Young had survived another ditching, so acquiring his nickname 'Dinghy'. Stokes had gone. Rivaz was away on a course. Desmond Coutts had been made up to captain and was now flying with a crew of his own. Of the good companions of just a few weeks before only George Roberts remained. 'The loss took much of the joy of flying away; and I don't think we ever captured the same carefree teamwork.' Even the weather was depressing. Fog, rain, overcast. And mud.

No matter where you went or what you did, there was mud. Mother sent me a pair of vast rubbed-soled boots lined with sheepskin, and so life was a little easier. If we had operated from the aerodrome itself it would not have been so bad . . . Our aeroplanes were kept five miles away in an advanced landing-field . . . it transpired that a vehicle capable of dealing with the mud had yet to be designed, and past the gates, where the mud became slightly less deep, the only available accommodation was a derelict farmhouse devoid of heating and infested by rats. On the nights that we operated we dressed up in the hangars ready for forty degrees of frost and piled into the bus, sweating and panting. From where the bus left us we had to walk, carrying our equipment in the dark and through the mud, sometimes as much as half a mile. Not far really, but we had been brought up to a life of ease and sitting down. The only legitimate complaint was that the mud and water soaked our clothes, so that when we climbed into low temperature everything froze solid.[93]

During December he completed five more operations, the first in appalling conditions. At 11,000 feet the wings were glazed with ice, and 'inside the cabin it looked as though it had been snowing'. Their intended target was a power station at Mannheim, but defective instruments, 69 degrees of frost and an inch of ice on Roberts's navigation table eventually defeated them and they bombed Boulogne instead.[94] The Whitley was heavy to fly, and its unpredictable automatic pilot did little to alleviate tiredness during sorties to distant targets. A winter sortie to Berlin could last for ten or eleven hours and was a 'terrible ordeal'.[95] Cheshire was never heard to complain.

He went to Berlin on 15 December, but an attempted attack on the Tegel armament factory was frustrated by cloud and they diverted to other targets. At Mannheim, on the other hand, visited the next evening, Cheshire felt that they achieved real success. The raid was planned as a reprisal for the bombing of British cities in general and Coventry in particular. Over 130 aircraft took part – the largest force yet sent by Bomber Command to a single target. The aiming point, too, marked a change; instead of the customary factory, oil plant or railway yard it was the centre of the town itself. Cheshire described the result as 'literally a fire from end to end',[96] although in reality the bombing was scattered and the effects inconclusive.

Entirely conclusive, on the other hand, was the fate of the Whitley in which he had flown to Cologne. On 21 December the newly repaired aeroplane was standing at the edge of the aerodrome. Another Whitley was struggling to regain Topcliffe. Douglas Mourton was in it.

. . . one engine failed after we were thirty miles over the Dutch coast, so we turned around to return . . . We steadily lost height all the way back and Sergeant Rix was just able to pull the plane over the boundary hedge of our airfield. Unfortunately, on the other side there was a Whitley parked. We went right through the middle of it. We cut it in two.

Cheshire's DSO offered new opportunities for his humour. He went with friends to a party in the Majestic Hotel in Harrogate,

and the music was interrupted to announce: 'Ladies and Gentlemen. I have great pleasure to let you know that Flying Officer Leonard Cheshire is with us tonight. He has just been awarded the DSO for an act of bravery.' Chesh stood up, apparently surprised and embarrassed, acknowledging the ovation he received. One of the officers said, 'I wonder who told them?' to which Chesh replied, 'I did, you bloody fool.'[97]

In mid-December Cheshire told his parents: 'Don't know my future movements at all – whether I'll get leave over Xmas or what . . . so I wouldn't make any plans. After two or three more trips I shall cease operations.'[98] In the event there was a general stand-down over Christmas, and as nearly everyone else wanted to go home

Cheshire volunteered to stay at Topcliffe. Rising late on Christmas morning he ventured into the kitchens, noticed some mistletoe and pecked the cheek of a WAAF cook who happened to be underneath it. The moment coincided with the entry of the station commander, who ordered Cheshire out and awarded him fourteen days duty as orderly officer – a hard blow, for it excluded him from parties and celebrations.[99] A little luck, however, awaited him. On 27 December he flew his last operation with 102 Squadron, to attack the hangars at Merignac aerodrome in south-west France.[100] It was a long trip, and they were instructed to land at Abingdon on the way home. Poor weather detained them, and Cheshire enjoyed the next three days at Grey Walls.

From much that has been written about Leonard Cheshire's wartime career it would be easy to suppose that his operational flying was more or less unceasing. In fact, between 1940 and 1942 his operational duties were limited to episodes of months or even weeks at a time, interspersed between periods when he was – as he saw it – jailed by instructing, training or administration. Later on he found these non-operational periods irksome, but on this occasion he was pleased by the prospect of change. This was partly because he had been told that he would be flying the new four-engined Halifax, and partly too because his first tour had outrun its earlier magic. Towards midsummer he had arrived at Driffield knowing next to nothing; by the end of July he had flown twenty operations with Long; by November he headed a crew whose interdependence and mutual affection formed a landmark in his life – and within a few weeks more officialdom and chance had split them up. Passage of time led to promotion – he was now a flying officer (promotion was automatic after six months) – and growing experience brought nagging responsibilities. Life was becoming more complicated. He felt nostalgia for the fleeting period when a carefree life, trust and companionship in exhilarating danger had all been mingled.[101] Some of this he would taste again, but sensations are purest when they are new, and Cheshire's first tour was brushed by a vivid intensity which for ever afterwards eluded him. It was time to move on.

In the last days Cheshire still seemed 'a good sport, aways willing to join in anything that was going. When we had a great snowstorm he was to the forefront of the snowball fights and sliding on the ice, with Dinghy Young and Lofty.'[102] It snowed on New Year's Day. On the next evening Desmond Coutts, gentle Desmond whom he had taught, who had fought the fire and with whom he had shared so much, took off at sunset into a freezing sky, and disappeared.

5. Every Wise Man's Son

Coutts and his crew had been bound for Bremen. Around seven o'clock that evening Hans Hahn shot them down into the North Sea about thirty miles off Withernsea.* Cheshire obeyed Bomber Command's unwritten law that no fuss should be made and no emotion shown.[1] But after Desmond's end something changed.[2] In any case, it was time to go. On a Sunday late in January Cheshire said goodbye to Lofty Long, presented his log book for signature by Wg Cdr Cole (who rated his ability as 'exceptional') and set out for Linton-on-Ouse.

Topcliffe and Linton are only a few miles apart, and Cheshire's journey along ice-bound roads that grey afternoon might have taken half an hour. Technologically, he was covering a greater distance. 35 Squadron had been re-formed two months before with a remit to see the new four-engined Halifax into operational service.

Whitleys had been homely and simple, but here was a new atmosphere altogether: new equipment, new technique of flying and everything vastly more complicated. And so, as I had done once before, I threw myself into hibernation – to learn.[3]

There was a lot to learn.

We found that even cockpit drills did not follow the age-old mnemonics . . . It amazes me today that no one ever thought of printing the cockpit checks to carry in the aircraft . . . If the Germans had ever recovered a flyable Halifax, including the cockpit drills, it might have made it a little easier to fly.[4]

---

* Hahn was flying a Ju 88 of 3/NJG2. The bodies of Coutts and his crew were not found.

Aside from its greater size, capacity, sophistication and new crewing requirements, the Halifax I was being introduced in haste and was mechanically unready.* 'The Halifax seemed a dangerous aircraft, even before the Germans got at it.'[5] Nonetheless, Cheshire liked challenges, and he threw himself heart and mind into getting to know an aeroplane which, despite its faults, represented a large advance. Significantly, the Halifax always served him well, because he took the trouble to know it.

Progress towards operational readiness was nevertheless slow. At the end of January there were only five complete crews, few aircraft and not many days when the weather was good enough to fly them. Perhaps this was just as well, for some of the more tortuous aspects of the Halifax's engineering, like the byzantine fuel system,[6] were best mastered on the ground. 'Throughout the hours of this long hibernation there was time in abundance to meditate, and nothing but memories to live on.'[7]

There were compensations. Christopher had completed his training and was now stationed a dozen miles away at Dishforth, flying Whitleys with 78 Squadron. 'I saw him from time to time, once or twice for tea, but mostly in the evenings. He seemed to be his same smiling self: still flaxen hair and a young, fresh-coloured face. As usual the girls, and not he, seemed to be doing most of the chasing.'[8] Cheshire was rather proud of him, and a little sheltering. 'He was two years younger than I, and ever since the day that I had escorted him to school as a new boy I had felt a strong sense of responsibility for him. I had watched his progress through the various stages of flying training with some trepidation . . .'[9] Cheshire drew comfort from the fact that 78 Squadron was commanded by Charles Whitworth, his erstwhile Oxford flying instructor, now a wing commander.

Whitworth's reassuring presence exemplifies a strange aspect of

---

* In early Halifaxes a deficient hydraulic system led to difficulties with the undercarriage, while the forward-retracting tailwheel had a tendency to remain withdrawn on landing. On grass airfields, in the absence of appropriate jacks, this required ground crew to crawl under the fuselage and lift it while sandbags were piled beneath the tail. More seriously, the Halifax was found to be underpowered when fully loaded, and in certain circumstances it was unstable. See p. 106.

Cheshire's life, wherein figures met in one period have a tendency to reappear in others, often at timely moments. One such was Sqn Ldr J. B. Tait, who joined 35 Squadron as the commander of A Flight in late February.[10] Tait, like Cheshire, would emerge as one of Bomber Command's outstanding leaders. Their paths will be entwined. Another like this was Sgt George Holden, whose death in September 1943 would create the vacancy at the head of 617 Squadron which Cheshire eventually filled.

By early March 35 Squadron had expanded to ten crews, and new Halifaxes were being delivered every few days. On the night of 10/11 March the squadron flew its first operation, sending six crews to Le Havre as part of a force of fifteen.* Le Havre was always a prickly target and all the Halifaxes met flak. One suffered hydraulic failure as a result of battle damage and struggled back to Linton on three engines with an undercarriage leg dangling. Another, flown by Cheshire's flight commander, was mistakenly attacked by a British nightfighter and crashed in flames.[11]

Two days later came news which left Cheshire stunned. Frank Long had been shot down.† Dependable, warm, supremely competent Lofty. Lofty, who used to flick him under the chin and had taught him all he knew. Years later Cheshire wrote:

Whatever outward face I may have put on it, his loss affected me very deeply and the memory of what I owed him and of all that he stood for remained with me throughout the war. It may sound a peculiar thing to say, and certainly has no rational basis, but I came to think of Lofty as more or less indestructible. It was just, I suppose, that he was so strongly built, so physically fit, and so calm and competent, whatever the situation. Perhaps also there is some innate, subconscious need in man for the perfect model to which one can look up and from which to draw strength and inspiration. Or perhaps in times so uncertain, when even the immediate future was full of the unknown, one would clutch at any straw. At all events, with the night that Lofty failed to return the character of the war changed: I knew now that no one was immune and though

* This was the first Halifax operation of the war. Cheshire did not take part. The other aircraft involved were Blenheims.
† Flt Lt Long was killed on the night of 12/13 March 1941 in the course of an operation against Berlin. Hit by flak, his Whitley V crashed at Noord-Deuringen, Holland, at five minutes past midnight.

in the years that followed I was to meet others with perhaps even greater qualities and greater dedication than Lofty, to whom I also owe my own debt, never again would I look at someone and say, 'He at least will always come back.'[12]

His reaction at the time was more confrontational:

A struggle for existence in which the strongest survives is something I can well understand; in fact it is what I have always believed to be the essence of life. What I cannot understand is a struggle for existence in which survival hinges on luck.[13]

Here is the ideology – a kind of Darwinian materialism – which had served Cheshire since Oxford, and which Long's death had annihilated. If life was an anarchy how was it possible – *was* it possible – for luck to take sides? A world in which a bad pilot could fly unscathed through the heaviest barrage in the world, while 'a first-class pilot may fly straight into a shell that through faulty manufacture exploded 5,000 feet lower than it ought to have done' must be a world upside down. 'It isn't much comfort, though, is it?' wrote Cheshire, adding bleakly: 'I suppose that is the point.'[14] If Fortune existed he ought to be able to recognize her; if not, then what was left of his assumption that by personal effort it was possible to choose one's path: make money, become successful, be famous – survive?[15]

Provisionally, his suspicions pointed to a frigid chaos. Acceptance of nihilism, however, at least required that he ask whether the evidence for it was complete. He was, after all, a lawyer. The alternative, an unfathomable design, seemed unlikely, and in 1941 he dismissed it. Indeed, in months ahead his tendency to live for the moment would intensify. But if we seek a point of departure for Cheshire's search for universal meaning it is here, in the death of Frank Long.

It was in bleak times such as these that the clamped emotions of Bomber Command aircrew found release in gallows humour, occasional leaflet raids on neighbouring airfields, spontaneous 'beat-ups' in nearby pubs or a trip to the Half Moon in York, where it was said that the friendly landlord would cash a cheque for five pounds for any aircrew officer. The landlord claimed he had never had one bounce. 'He was either extremely lucky, or a real gentle-man.'[16] Monthly guest nights in the officers' mess were further occasions when formality and disorder were conjoined, an after-dinner riot itself being a kind of ceremony for the exorcism of feelings which at other times were strictly controlled. The presence of senior officers at the guest night held on 21 March did not inhibit 'the inauguration of a new skittle alley in the eaves of the E Wing' or prevent the 'phenomenal amount of damage done to mess property'.[17]

Cheshire had been assembling a crew. One day in late February George Roberts walked into the crew room: 'We fell into each other's arms.'[18] Pleas for the release of Stokes from his OTU were ignored, but Sgt Jackson − 'Jaco: five foot eleven, twelve stone; had boxed and played football for the RAF; knew no fear and could not find anything he did not know of the wireless set' − joined them instead. The Halifax carried two wireless operators, and the second, Sgt Gutteridge, was a happy man with a wide smile. Their flight engineer was Sgt Brown, willing, versatile and an ex-merchant seaman. Jerry Weldon, an experienced Whitley pilot, became second pilot. 'We settled down to get to know each other and in the course of two month's work and jollification, continually in each other's company, we emerged a team, as we thought, to be proud of.'[19]

It was 100 per cent activity all the time. Ideas bubbled forth, cars and scrapes followed in their wake. How often have I pictured that big Bentley, which was nothing but a monstrosity on wheels, tearing through quiet country lanes without lights and little brakes on a moonlight night, with arms and odd legs sticking out at odd angles and brushing the hedgerows rushing past, with howls from the back urging the laggard driver on and on. Why worry, Cheshire was at the wheel. Yes, we depended on him for our leisure even.[20]

One cold morning, Rivaz walked into the mess.[21] The story behind his arrival, like tragedy itself, was at once unhappy and elevated. On the night of 1/2 March he had been in a Whitley flown by Sqn Ldr C. E. E. Florigny on a sortie to Cologne. During the return they became lost, ran out of fuel and ditched off Cromer

in atrocious weather. Florigny drowned.⋆ The rest of the crew
passed half a night and a morning in an inverted, waterlogged
dinghy. Their survival owed much to Rivaz, who kept them awake
in such cold that when he tried to fire a Very light to attract the
attention of a searching aircraft his numb hands were unable to pull
the trigger.²² After his rescue Rivaz was invited to choose where
he wished to go. He chose 35 Squadron, and Cheshire. Cheshire,
Roberts and Rivaz looked for the warm magic which had bound
them during the previous autumn. But for reasons no one explained,
when Cheshire took off on his first Halifax operation, to Kiel on
15 April, Rivaz was forbidden to go.

This was Cheshire's first sortie since December 1940, and 35
Squadron's only operation that month. Another serious defect in
the Halifax's undercarriage had been found.²³ The Halifaxes were
not behaving themselves, and some aircrew were temporarily seconded to other duties while the teething troubles were tackled.

Of the pilots, two were to go to America for flying duties. We collected in the
adjutant's office to draw lots, and Willy, a burly New Zealander, and I won.
Somewhat sadly, but none the less optimistically, I said farewell to Revs and
Taffy and Jacko and Jerry and Brown and Hares,† spent a happy evening with
Christopher, and packed my bags.²⁴

So it was that on 4 May Fg Off. G. L. Cheshire and Plt Off. G. S.
Williams 'proceeded to Wilmslow to stand by for Atlantic Ferrying
Duties'.²⁵ Beforehand Cheshire won a promise that his crew would
be kept together and rested until his return. During his absence the
crew was split, Jackson, Hares, Gutteridge and Weldon were killed,
and George Roberts became a prisoner-of-war.

Cheshire and Williams were ordered to Montreal, headquarters
of the Atlantic Ferry Organization, to collect American aircraft and
deliver them to Britain. Cheshire went home to pick up some
civilian clothes. 'I . . . remember walking across the field to catch
the bus for Oxford en route for Bristol, from where the ship was
to sail, and shouting out to Mother and Father, "I'll come back

---

⋆ Sqn Ldr Florigny's brother, a member of 10 Squadron, was killed on the same evening.
† Hares was Cheshire's regular rear gunner in the early spring of 1941.

married!" What on earth prompted me to say it, heaven knows, for I only expected to be in Canada a few days.'[26]

They travelled on a small Norwegian cargo boat, in the company of earnest colleagues from Coastal Command, fluent in nautical jargon and practised navigators, who 'made a habit of breezing up to the captain and telling him where he was'.[27] It was a perilous journey. U-boats sank fifty-eight Allied ships that month.

In Montreal the Atlantic Ferry was swamped by an unexpected influx of pilots and navigators.[28] ATFERO 'knew not a thing about us – who we were or why we were there', and after several days of confusion they were put on indefinite standby, told to leave contact addresses and await instructions. Cheshire and Williams discussed what to do. New York had been Cheshire's boyhood Utopia, 'the city of swing music and film stars and fabulous wealth, which one could dream and read about but never expect to visit'.[29] They caught the night express for New York. 'A city full of secrets, and all of them new to me. For four days and four nights a riot. Cocktails, dances, drives through the city. Times Square on Broadway, Park Avenue, overhead railways . . . people who take you as you come, not as they come. And no sleep.'[30] After class-bound, rationed, bureaucratic, blacked-out Britain, America's openness, plenty, can-do spirit and colour induced a kind of delirium. Elated by Tommy Dorsey's band, animated by Madison Square Garden's 'hotcha' sessions, warmed by pro-British senti-ment, 'life was too good to waste time sleeping . . . but as it happened people had too much friendship to offer to let us sleep'.[31] And after four days of gregarious tumult: 'Peace, empty roads, occasionally a cream-coloured police car and now and then a dead skunk. Losing the way amid rocks and green trees.'[32]

He was in an open Cadillac on the road to Old Lyme in Connecti-cut. Its owner was a retired actress who had befriended him. Her name was Constance Binney.

The Binneys were affluent descendants of a line of New Eng-landers. There were two daughters, Faire and Constance,* upon

---

* Constance Binney was coy about her age. Most sources place her birth in 1900, but at least one puts it in 1896.

whose upbringing much had been lavished: dancing and elocution lessons, musical training and finishing schools in Connecticut and Paris. Both daughters aimed at careers in the theatre. Constance made her Broadway debut in 1918 as a dancer and understudy to Vivienne Segal in the musical *Oh Lady, Lady*. Her performance caught the attention of Maurice Tourneur, who cast both Constance and Faire in his film *The Sporting Life*. Tourneur thought Faire the more talented, and a disappointed Constance went back to the stage. In 1919, however, she reappeared on the screen as John Barrymore's leading lady in *The Test of Honor*. Subsequent success in the Broadway show *39 East* led to movie contracts with Realart and then Paramount.

Like a firework – momentarily impressive, but evanescent and soon forgotten – Constance Binney's film career flared and flickered out. A silent movie could be made in a few weeks, and during the next three years she appeared in eighteen of them, became runner-up to Mary Pickford for the title of 'America's sweetheart', and travelled to London to play in the British version of *A Bill of Divorcement*. After this – very little. Occasional stage appearances continued until the early 1930s, but by 1941 her celebrity lay well in the past. So did two husbands and two divorces. Constance Binney was extrovert, a little gaudy, wealthy and moved in a circle of world-famous friends.

In *Bomber Pilot*, begun six months later, Cheshire evoked the following days in a mosaic of things seen, heard or tasted: flickering fireflies, laughter, a telephone bell in the stillness of a hot afternoon, an ice-cold highball sipped in the shade of a tree, a plateful of salty clams.[33] The writing swelters with correlates of heat: the rasp of crickets, cool drinks, coloured butterflies, dark glasses, unshuttered windows. The atmosphere is at once motionless and charged.

Aunt Edith was in New York, noted the association and voiced her disapproval. So did Cheshire's parents, who sent cautionary cables. 'I might easily have given in to them,' wrote Cheshire; 'after all . . . defying people you have known all your life is quite a large break.'[34] And there again: 'I had an uncomfortable feeling in my heart that it was the wrong thing . . . But the future didn't count for much in those days and I was living in a kind of dreamland.'[35]

The young often assume that they are the first people in the world to have been faced with such difficult choices. Indifferent to Shakespeare, the twenty-three-year-old Cheshire probably didn't notice the well-worn path he was treading. '*What is love? 'Tis not hereafter; /Present mirth hath present laughter.*' An engagement notice appeared in the *New York Times*. Edith countered by contacting ATFERO, who recalled Cheshire to Montreal. Constance followed, Cheshire agonized. Departure was imminent. '*What's to come is still unsure. /In delay there lies no plenty . . .*' They were married at an impromptu ceremony on 15 July. 'If I hadn't', he explained in *Bomber Pilot*, 'I should have been too late, and now I should be . . . despising myself.'[36] '*Youth's a stuff will not endure.*'[37]

Six days later Cheshire took off from Montreal in a Lockheed Hudson. In the faces of the newly graduated navigator and wireless operator he glimpsed likenesses of himself a year before. They paused at Gander to refuel, and then headed east. There were 'icebergs below us and Northern Lights above us, but even at 10,000 feet it was warm enough to fly in shirtsleeves. We flew on and on: on through the daylight: on through the night and on to daylight once more.'[38] Ten hours later they crossed the Scottish coast, three miles south of track.

Back at Linton Rivaz took him aside. While he had been away the station commander and many colleagues had been killed during an attack on the aerodrome. At the end of June Tait had been awarded an immediate bar to his DSO following a daylight raid on Kiel in which the squadron had lost its first Halifax to enemy action. Three days later 35 Squadron's CO had been relieved of his command, and next morning Air Vice-Marshal Coningham, 4 Group's AOC, had visited to buttress morale.★

★ The calmly worded account of this episode in 35 Squadron's ORB does not wholly disguise a situation which appears to have bordered on crisis. Coningham spoke to 35 Squadron's aircrews and maintenance NCOs, expressing gratitude for their work in the face of great difficulties, the daylight attack on Kiel and technical failings of the Halifax I among them. He brought to notice 'his appreciation of the burden of responsibility which the commanding officer . . . has had to bear'. The 'strain has been such', concluded the squadron's diarist, that the AOC 'has ordered the CO to rest, and has been pleased to recommend that on his return to good health he is appointed to some duty, possibly to command a Halifax OTU, which his services have so well merited' (PRO AIR 27/379).

After Kiel, 35 Squadron's crews had fought their way back and forth to Magdeburg, Frankfurt, Leuna, Mannheim and twice to Hanover, in some cases to deliver the new 4,000 lb bomb: an 'ugly thing' which 'looked like an engine-boiler'.[39] Then there was the loss of Cheshire's crew. Only Rivaz was left, and for the time being even his companionship was denied: he had been poached by another captain.

Rivaz was down to fly on the day after Cheshire's return, when 35 Squadron was ordered to prepare for an unescorted daylight attack on the *Scharnhorst* at La Pallice. Despite a good deal of tragic evidence to the contrary, there were some in Bomber Command who continued to harbour a notion that small formations of heavy bombers could operate by day. Excluded, Cheshire watched as the Halifaxes of the nine chosen crews and transport aircraft carrying spares and maintenance staff departed into the warm evening for their advanced base at Stanton Harcourt.

The force set out soon after half past ten next morning, linking with six Halifaxes from 76 Squadron and proceeding in sections of three to the Lizard. The bombers kept to 1,000 feet on the first leg, which took them to a point 50 miles west of Ushant. Here they turned, climbing towards an intended bombing height of 19,000 feet. Unluckily, they were sighted by a German destroyer, which signalled ahead. The incoming force was greeted by flak from alerted defences, and a swarm of fighters. Within seconds one Halifax was descending in a slow, smoking spiral. The formation broke, and in the savage fight which followed five of the fifteen Halifaxes were shot down. Fighters pursued them far beyond the target. One Halifax was attacked twenty times, another ten and another nine. None that returned escaped damage. Four with dead and wounded landed at St Eval in Cornwall, others at Weston Zoyland and Stanton Harcourt. Despite the ferocious opposition the attack was considered a success: the *Scharnhorst* had been hit five times.* That night she fled to Brest, where repairs detained her for the next four months.

---

* Three strikes were from armour-piercing bombs which drilled through the ship without exploding.

Cheshire was told that he had been left out of the La Pallice operation because he was 'too inexperienced'.[40] He was now a flight lieutenant (promoted on 20 June 1941), and did not take kindly to the implication that he was out of touch or that he had been having an easy time. Nor was he pleased by cynical reactions to his marriage: 'On arriving back at the squadron the adjutant met me with the words: "Now it will be a rather different story, won't it? No more belly-aching to get into ops. No more applications for extension of tour. No more line-shooting about ops being the only life worth living . . ." '[41] Jolted, without discussion he accepted the new crew provided, and at 22.40 on the next evening, 'the night after we were crewed up, and before we had time to get used to ourselves', took off for Berlin.

This was the first in a concentrated campaign of nine operations which gave rise to a half-humorous rumour that Cheshire never slept because it wasted valuable bombing time. On 30/31 July Cheshire's crew went to Cologne, spending 50 minutes in search of the aiming point. Two nights later they returned to Berlin amid intense flak. Karlsruhe was attacked on the night of 5/6 August, leaving fires visible a hundred miles away. On the next night their attempt to bomb the Krupps works at Essen was defeated by industrial haze, but they settled instead for the oil refinery at Gelsenkirchen, achieving a spectacular direct hit on its hydrogen plant.

Cheshire's new crew were all NCOs, to whom he endeared himself by his unaffected courtesy and lack of formality. In 1940 many crew members had been pre-war regulars, but now rather more were drawn from peacetime occupations, and from many parts of the United Kingdom. The second pilot for most of the time was Peter Stead, a former veterinary student who found his captain 'kindness itself to a very young sergeant pilot'.[42] In place of Rivaz was Lou Martin, 'a wiry bus conductor from Tunbridge Wells, and therefore full of bright remarks at curious moments'. In the nose and second wireless operator was Sgt Crocker, an obliging Londoner with a background in the leather trade who 'always had a smile and a joke'. Gerry Henry, the navigator, was a friend of Roberts from Driffield days. Their flight engineer was Paddy

O'Kane from Londonderry, who spoke to everyone with the same easygoing assurance. The wireless operator, Jock Hill, came from Edinburgh, where his adoptive father worked on the docks. Quietly spoken, 'Jock was not an ever-smiling figure but not a dour Scot either. He was always ready to appreciate a joke . . . his grin when it came was a wide one.'[43] Hill and Cheshire became lifelong friends. Others 'tended to regard Chesh as perfect in all things, but Hill pointed out firmly if wryly that he wasn't a perfect pilot. "He's quite an ordinary pilot," he would argue. "I've flown with better. Sometimes he makes bloody awful landings, but he's a bloody good skipper." '[44] For the next two months they became very close, as accustomed to pile into Cheshire's ramshackle second-hand Bentley for a foray into York during a stand-down as into their Halifax on nights when they operated.

Christopher was now flying Halifaxes with 76 Squadron at Middleton St George. Cheshire was at once horrified and privately proud.[45] The fact that both Cheshire brothers were Halifax captains became a talking point in the newspapers. Until 12 August. On this evening an assorted force of Wellingtons, Stirlings, Manchesters and Halifaxes was ordered to Berlin. The briefing alarmed Cheshire. 'Bomber Command . . . had bungled the route, and sent us in to Berlin in a straight line between Wilhelmshaven and Bremen, which meant that all aircraft would be under fire from one side or the other, and those straying off track in great difficulty.'[46] Cheshire decided to ignore the briefed route, and tried to telephone Christopher to advise him to do the same. But he could not get through, and when Christopher took off on his twenty-fifth operation a little after half past nine that evening he was unaware of his brother's misgivings.

35 Squadron contributed five crews to the seventy which set forth. Only thirty-two bombed the city. Cheshire's terse record – 'Weather bad: intense searchlights and AA' – did scant justice to what happened. Amid fierce flak they circled the city for the best part of an hour, peering into filmy haze, the smoky trails of descending flares and the glare of searchlights in the quest for their aiming point. In the end the murk defeated them and they bombed at random.

Christopher never reached Berlin. Outbound over the North Sea, his flight engineer warned of excessive fuel consumption. They decided to divert to Hamburg. The defences remained lifeless during their approach, but opened up as the Halifax bombed. Abruptly lit by a conflux of searchlights, Christopher held the aircraft steady for the aiming-point photograph. The aircraft was hit, and hit again. The second explosion blew off the tail.

Christopher felt the controls go limp. Realizing he could do no more he ordered everyone out. The wireless operator, observer and second pilot jumped. Hearing nothing from the front and rear gunners,★ Christopher assumed them gone and left his seat, using precious seconds to fumble in the darkness for a parachute which at first he could not find. Making his way to the forward hatch he realized that another crew member was still behind him. It was Reg Wash, the flight engineer. Christopher stood aside to let him jump and then followed him out. The empty Halifax careered around them in the darkness, attracting more flak during its aimless descent. Then Christopher was flat on his back in a cow pasture, staring up into a sky in which his brother still flew. Picking himself up, he started to walk towards Holland. Shortly afterwards he was captured, and taken to the Luftwaffe HQ in Hamburg, where he found himself looking at a map of the city's anti-aircraft defences.[47]

Cheshire's return came close to calamity. Peter Stead, his second pilot:

We had an uneventful trip . . . until petrol began to get very short. We passed over Driffield and I think we all wanted to land there, but Cheshire was determined to get home. The port outer engine cut a few minutes later and it was a great relief to see the flare-path. We got a red as another aircraft was landing but we followed it in and one of the starboard engines cut.[48]

While taxiing, a third engine died. They could not even park the aircraft.

★ Sgt Woods (rear gunner) and Sgt Niven (front gunner) were already dead. Niven was on his first trip. Halifax crews at this date were often of mixed experience, and Sgt Eddie Gurmin (w/op) had already completed twenty-nine operations. He elected to continue flying with Christopher Cheshire and the observer/navigator (who was on his twenty-sixth operation) so that they could finish together. In a sense, they did.

Cheshire telephoned the ops room at Middleton St George. The reply was evasive. His heart sank. Confirmation came later in the morning. Cheshire called his parents. For months Primrose and Geoffrey had been troubled by the knowledge that both their sons were at risk. More recently they had been hurt by Cheshire's rejection of their pleas for caution over Constance, and in reaction to that Primrose had begun to dote the more on Christopher. Now it was for him to deepen their distress by saying that Christopher was missing and that no one had any idea what had happened to him. In due course they would be told whether he was in a prison camp or a grave. Unless he was burned. Or drowned. Or one of the thousands who were simply 'missing', gone, vanished, unfound, like Desmond. During weeks ahead there would be time enough for icy fantasies to breed. He was moved by their subdued dignity.

'Are you shaken?' inquired Cheshire's flight commander the next day. Cheshire replied that he was not so upset as to be unable to carry on.

'Good,' said the flight commander, who seems to have taken pleasure in provoking Cheshire, 'then you can be put on ops tonight.'[49]

The target was Magdeburg. They were held by a searchlight belt on their way in, and when they arrived the city was cloud-masked.

On ETA we felt certain of our position and therefore decided to come down and look for clearer air. The guns opened up, and in spite of the cloud, were exceptionally accurate. I feathered all four airscrews, switched the motors off, and turned through 180 degrees. It was a curious sensation watching a row of dead props over Germany, but none the less it fooled the defences completely: they continued firing way behind us along our previous course, and then finally stopped altogether.

Feathering the propellors to deceive the defences was a ploy of which Cheshire had heard talk in the mess bar. Peter Stead noted that during their air test earlier in the day

. . . we tried out a new idea – switching off all the engines – or rather feathering the airscrews until the engine stopped. This worked well but it took 1,500 ft to get them all going again; this we decided was too much but decided to try it that night and to 'cope' with more skill.[50]

The scheme was hazardous, and Cheshire's enthusiasm was not shared by the crew, who fell into apprehensive silence as air soughed over the wings. After a minute or two even Cheshire seems to have felt uneasy. 'At 9,000 feet,* for safety's sake, I tried to restart one engine, just to see if everything was in order, but everything was not in order: it refused to pick up.' Cheshire and O'Kane went to work with mounting urgency

but nothing very much happened. The engines turned over slowly and even fired for a brief moment, but that was all. At 7,000 feet the starboard outer started and of course the ack-ack opened up immediately. What we really wanted was the inboards, because they worked the generators, and the batteries could not last much longer under this strain.[51]

At 5,000 feet the starboard inner revived, but with bombs still on board the Halifax continued to sink. At 4,000 feet they jettisoned the bombs. Flak intensified; some crew members began to talk across one other on the intercom. The fourth engine 'got going just as a shell burst under the wing . . . The two combined to throw us into a tremendous turn of about 80 degrees.'[52] With the aircraft on its side, the gyros in the blind flying instruments toppled. Perhaps unaware that the last engine had restarted, Cheshire's effort to compensate by jamming the controls to starboard exacerbated the crisis. For the first time in his operational career he began to panic. Disorientated, the aircraft shuddering in an earthward spiral, he pronounced the Halifax ungovernable and ordered 'get your parachutes and jump'.[53]

The incredulity with which his command was received illuminates the unconditional faith which Cheshire inspired in those who flew with him. Hill could not believe his ears, and responded with words which have since been paraphrased in at least four different ways. The fragment 'you can do better than that' is common to them all. Stead went forward, picked up a parachute and returned to give it to Cheshire, but by this time Cheshire had grasped the

---

* According to Peter Stead, the second pilot, the attempted restart began at 6,000 ft. Risks 'were compounded by the fact that feathering all four propellors could have drained the batteries, and they might not have the strength to unfeather the critical port inner, from which they were recharged' (R. A. Read, 1995).

problem, throttled back the port engines and restored control.

The episode entered 4 Group's mythology.

The Halifax II at its best was a heavy aircraft and descended rapidly with any reduction of power. With all four engines feathered, it must have gone down like a brick. As for making a steep turn, the pilot must be crazy, or under extreme pressure . . . and at the end of every normal tactic of escape. The steep turn introduced the distinct risk of a spin, and a spinning Halifax was as close to making up the percentage figures for the night as you could get.[54]

Some thought the story so unlikely that a counter-legend started which denied that it had ever happened. One who knew better was 35 Squadon's CO, who took Cheshire aside and reprimanded him. By trying to be clever he had been reckless, imperilling his crew, himself and his aircraft. Cheshire did not cavil. It had been a peculiar week. He never did anything like this again.

The ninth and tenth operations, to Duisberg on 28/29 August and Berlin nine days later, were flown with as much zeal as all their predecessors. Over Duisberg they met savage flak and were pursued by a nightfighter. The trip to Berlin came close to Cheshire's idea of perfection. Rivaz, at last, was allowed to fly with him. The air was pellucid, flak slight and, after the flashes of their bombs were seen to either side of Unter den Linden, Cheshire flew across to Potsdam under the full moon, circling the lake for old time's sake, hoping for a glimpse of the von Reuters' house. When they touched down at Linton a little before half past three in the morning he was in good spirits.

'You are off ops.'

'What did you say?'

'You've been taken off ops.; you're through, finished, grounded.'[55]

He was told this at debriefing.

We sat down at the table, all seven of us, and the colonel asked us the usual routine questions. I looked around me at the six faces and thought: 'From now on I'm just another has-been, from now on I've got to sit in the background and live on memories, because never again will I be able to capture the companionship and confidence of men like these around me.' I shook them by the hand and walked out.[56]

The length of a bomber tour was defined mathematically, supposedly at a point which offered a realistic chance of survival.[57] Cheshire had now passed this point twice. Many aircrew were thankful to be 'taken off', but Cheshire likened it to 'someone kicking you in the pants and saying: "We've had enough of you, get out." '[58] Although he remained with 35 Squadron until early 1942, and continued to mingle with the boys who went to Brest, Stettin, Hamburg and the Altona marshalling yards, he was no longer fully within their brotherhood.

Gloomily he set about the dull tasks of ferrying Halifaxes from 24 MU at Ternhill and conveying senior officers from A to B. The retrieval of a Halifax from a ploughed field in Norfolk provided a diversion, and in mid-October he was promoted to squadron leader and made a flight commander. Leadership from the safety of Yorkshire, however, was a contradiction in terms.

Two events cheered him. One was a letter from Christopher: he was alive, unhurt and in a prisoner-of-war camp near Frankfurt. The news lifted a burden, for not only had Cheshire been deeply distressed by his brother's disappearance but he also felt in some way responsible for it.[59]

The other was the arrival of Constance. Since July he had been badgering the Foreign Office to obtain permission for her to come to England. Eventually she was given a passage on a troopship, and on 20 October he drove to Liverpool to meet her. In pouring rain he loaded trunkfuls of food and clothes into the car, 'and for a time there was the excitement of getting Constance installed in the expensive flat we had taken in Harrogate'.[60]

Constance aroused curiosity among Cheshire's colleagues and despondency within the family. 'Tell me about your wife,' Rivaz had asked when Cheshire returned from Montreal. 'You gave us a shock when it came out in the papers.' Cheshire had parried all such questions, advising those who asked them to wait until they met her.[61] Now they did, and if anything their puzzlement deepened. Geoffrey and Primrose took a deep dislike to Constance, seeing her as 'the opposite to everything we respected'. They dubbed her Jezabel, and a period of estrangement from their son ensued. Other relatives were unable to locate her cheerfully candid manner within the starched configuration of the English class system. Even kindly, Anglican Uncle Kick thought her a 'vulgar little woman'. Linton was abuzz with theories and lubricious rumours. 'Well, it's just what you'd have expected of Chesh', said one who supposed it to be some sort of recondite joke. Another speculated at the irresistibility of someone so completely American, 'a living caricature of Hollywood'. Yet others wondered if money was at the root of it. The pursuit of wealth, after all, had earlier been a stated goal, and several Oxford friends speculated that he had married to pay his debts. Christopher, too, had earlier formed the view that Constance Binney's affluence had been a factor.[62] It is true that Cheshire returned from the United States mysteriously better off than when he left, but he assured his parents that Constance's wealth was incidental: the marriage had nothing to do with money.[63]

In 1954, in the course of research for *No Passing Glory*, Andrew Boyle questioned many of Cheshire's relatives and wartime friends about Constance. Their verdicts left him puzzled, and he attempted to provoke an explanation from Cheshire by submitting a list of personal questions. Cheshire told him little, but amid much theorizing, and aside from the most obvious factor, about which Cheshire is least likely to have wished to talk, one statement was overlooked. It did not concern what 'he saw in her' – the question most asked at the time – but what she saw in him. In July 1941 Cheshire wrote to his parents: 'You probably don't know that under Constance's influence I have ceased to waste my life as I have done for the last twenty-three years, and that I now have an almost fantastic urge to seek out what talents I have and develop them until I can achieve a career that is worthwhile.'[64] In other words, Constance had recognized something that no one else thus far seems to have noticed. She saw that he was gifted.

The idea of Cheshire as anyone's protégé may seem odd: did not everyone acknowledge his self-assurance? Of course they did, but assurance and self-belief are not quite the same things, and for all his poise neither Cheshire nor anyone close to him yet knew what he was meant to *do*, let alone encouraged him to think that he might become good at it. At Oxford he had been a disappointment to his father, and his efforts to vault to fortune had stumbled. Aside from flying bombers – which one way or another was going to be a temporary occupation – his destiny was uncertain. Constance, by contrast, did not reproach him for his shortcomings but asserted his talents. For the first time, perhaps, someone took him seriously for what he was, rather than as others expected him to be, and asked nothing in return beyond his affection for as long as he wished to give it.[65] Where she thought his gifts lay we are not told, but her circle in New York had included composers – George Gershwin among them – film actors, screenwriters and authors. Within a few weeks of her arrival Cheshire embarked upon a book, and for more than a year afterwards he told others that he intended to become a writer.

Earlier in 1941 an officer called Paul Richey published a book about his experiences called *Fighter Pilot*. Cheshire decided to give a bomber pilot's viewpoint. Dusting off precepts taught by Tim White he wrote some sample sections, and early in December, armed with an introduction provided by Geoffrey Harmsworth, editor of *The Field* and an intelligence officer at Linton-on-Ouse, he took them to Mr W. T. Kimber of Hutchinson.

The trial passages were in contrasting styles. One of them struck Kimber as 'effusive and slightly jejune', but he was impressed by the 'unforced effect' of the others, thinking the 'plain but sharp narrative just right'. Kimber marked two passages he particularly liked and recommended them as models. If the whole book could be kept 'to the style and angle of these two extracts', he told Cheshire, 'I do not think you could go far wrong'.

Within a week Cheshire signed a contract with Hutchinson for *Bomber Pilot*. It is not clear whether anyone was available to advise him when he did so.* At any rate, either the confidence of inexperience or the publisher's willingness to take advantage of it are suggested in Cheshire's agreement to deliver a complete manuscript within thirty days.[66]

He began at furious speed, sending a first instalment almost by

* Cheshire appears to have signed the contract in innocence despite the presence of several unusual and unfavourable clauses. In 1942 Curtis Brown became his agents. When they examined the contract they advised him that 'In the circumstances . . . all we can do is to get our revenge when your next book comes along.'

return. Kimber was delighted. Aside from one or two phrases which suggested 'mannerisms made by Gertrude Stein and distributed by Ernest Hemingway', the general standard was admirable, 'miles ahead' of the original samples. Thereafter the work slowed and the January deadline was missed, though only narrowly. The first draft was under discussion between Kimber and Cheshire during February and March, and the *News Chronicle* asked to see passages with a view to serialization.

Revision took longer than the first writing. On 21 April Kimber wrote, with ill-disguised impatience, 'I wonder if you could speed up the delivery of the revised typescript? . . . I had hoped that by now it would be well in hand. Perhaps a little pressure from you would help a lot.' Perhaps Mr Kimber did not remember that there was a war on, that Cheshire had prior responsibilities, or indeed that since 16 February he had had a new job. He was now with 1652 Conversion Flight at RAF Marston Moor, 'for flying and instructional duties'.

6. Places You Might Not Come Back From

Marston Moor aerodrome opened in 1941 beside the village of Tockwith, about nine miles west of York.[1] Parts of it are still there, a scatter of concrete buildings and corrugated-iron-clad hangars. But while Marston resembled other bomber stations, its atmosphere was different. No one asked 'Are you on tonight?', and there was no hollow feeling in the stomach when you scanned crew lists on the noticeboard.[2]

Cheshire missed the tension, and disliked Marston's formality. Pilots who had been accustomed to do their cockpit drill while taxiing were now 'expected to be textbook minded'. Parades were frequent, and senior administrative officers were 'treated as if they were actually important people'.[3] Grounded by snow for much of February, he escaped to his writing, and a move to Linton-on-Wharfe, near Wetherby.

Constance . . . who had finally devised a means of compressing her outsize in wardrobes into the confines of a Harrogate flat – and her American sense of humour and fun into that of a wartime spa – was now confronted with a three-storey, barnlike country house, which even two pantechnicon loads of furniture could not succeed in filling, and the solitude of a partially evacuated country village. All in all, life was difficult and tedious.[4]

Life was also exacting, for a Halifax in inexperienced hands was a perilous machine. Difficult to taxi, it had an undercarriage-straining swing on take-off and called for special care on landing. The flap and bomb-door levers were easily confused, and novices who mistook a handle above the pilot's seat discovered 'yet another Handley Page design trick [. . .] the cockpit hood release'.[5] Fragile engine mountings meant that the radiators below the outer engines did not always withstand the vibration of repeated training landings. Consequently their pipes often burst and spewed out coolant. They had to be watched, 'as several aircraft had caught fire on, or shortly after take-off'.[6] Repeated landings caused 'tyre creep', whereby the inner tube and tyre inched around the rim of the wheel at each touchdown until the tyre burst. Alignment marks were painted on the wheel rims and tyres, and an engineer was posted at the runway end to watch each take-off and make sure that they were in line.

Then there were the twin rudders, so designed that at low speeds, using heavy foot force, it was possible to push them fully to one side; it was not easy to re-centre them. Many Halifaxes were lost as a result of this fault, known as 'rudder stall'.[7] Such crashes often followed the loss of an engine, because of the need to counteract the yaw which resulted from asymmetric power. Such an accident claimed one of Marston's aircraft in April, killing all nine men on board.[8]

Incessant flying caused wear and tear to the runways as well as to aircraft, and in late April the airfield was closed for ten days for runway repairs. During May contractors returned to lengthen two runways, only to halt the night-flying programme by cutting the cables of the airfield's lighting.

While Marston was shut an idea was forming in the mind of Bomber Command's new C-in-C, Air Chief Marshal Sir Arthur Harris. When Harris took command on 23 February 1942 his brief was 'to focus attacks on the morale of the enemy civil population, and, in particular, of the industrial workers'. During March and April he had begun to experiment with attacks which concentrated bombers in time and space, to engulf radar-controlled flak and fighters, and overwhelm a city's fire services.[9] The force inherited by Harris was nevertheless too small to do this on any scale, and his efforts to increase it were being sapped both by losses and by what he called the 'robbery' of trained crews by other commands. To make his case, Harris decided to gamble Bomber Command's reserves in an attack of unprecedented weight: a thousand aircraft against a single objective. 'The organization of such a force – about twice as great as any the Luftwaffe ever sent against this country – was no mean task in 1942. As the number of first-line aircraft in squadrons was quite inadequate, the training organization and conversion units had to make a very substantial contribution.'[10] The project was called 'Millennium'.

On 20 May Harris notified his group commanders of the plan. All leave was cancelled, and 4 Group was told to be prepare for operations on 28 May or the first suitable date thereafter. At Marston Moor training was suspended, and air and ground crews were told that operational serviceability would be required within forty-eight hours. Some of the worn-out Halifaxes were scarcely fit for a cross-country, let alone a trip to Germany, and maintenance staff were obliged to work day and night. During the next two days aircrew from other units began to arrive on attachment, and by teatime on 25 May there were eleven serviceable Halifaxes and thirteen crews captained by instructors. On 26 May the Operation Order was revised: crews should be ready from the following day. The weather forecast next morning was poor, however, and the operation was postponed. The delay enabled two more Halifaxes to be prepared. Conditions on the following day were still unfavourable, and remained so on the next. The crews waited.

During the morning of 30 May Harris conferred with his advisers. Conditions expected for airfields in England were good, and there would be a full moon. Germany's weather, on the other hand, looked unpromising. Thundery cloud covered much of the country, only one of the shortlisted targets might be cloud-free, and even this was doubtful. 'If I waited,' Harris reflected,

I might have to keep this very large force standing idle for some time, and I might lose the good weather over England: to land such a force in difficult weather would at that time have been to court disaster and for so many aircraft it was necessary to have a large number of bases free from cloud. But if I sent the force that night, the target might be cloud-covered, and the whole operation reduced to naught and our plan disclosed . . . it was a considerable risk.[11]

More than a third of his force was composed of instructors and trainees. Heavy losses among them would have a 'paralysing effect' on Bomber Command's future.[12] Harris made his decision. They would go to Cologne.

At noon the warning order signal was teletyped to 4 Group's

headquarters at Heslington Hall, whence the target code, 'Trout',★ was relayed to Yorkshire airfields. At six o'clock the crews made up of senior pupils, tour-expired navigators and instructors mustered for briefing.

Bombing was timed to begin at 00.50, led by experienced crews from 1 and 3 Groups in aircraft equipped with Gee – a recently introduced radio-based navigation aid – and would continue for ninety minutes. 4 Group's Whitleys and Halifaxes were scheduled to arrive during the second half of the attack, the slower Whitleys bombing in the second wave and the Halifaxes forming part of the third. To minimize the risk of collision each Halifax unit was allocated a ten-minute period within which to bomb and assigned to a 500-foot height band. 1652 HCU's appointed time came towards the raid's end. Their aiming point was the northernmost of three, north-west of the main railway station and the cathedral.[13]

After briefing the crews went to eat, and then waited – a listless time, when some tried to rest, others wrote letters, and moods veered between introspection, irritability and jittery facetiousness. Cheshire's custom was to find a quiet place and mentally rehearse the detail of what lay ahead: times, drills, codes, courses. For over nine months he had not been called upon to do this. Around 22.00 they began to change, and towards 23.00 emerged to climb into the trucks which took them out to their aircraft. Cheshire and his crew boarded Halifax E. Half an hour later the bombers began to ease forward into a noisy queue on the perimeter track.

Cheshire was first off from Marston Moor, at 23.44; the last left at eleven minutes past midnight. An hour since across Yorkshire, Lincolnshire and East Anglia a thousand others had been doing likewise, the din above one airfield merging with that of the next until the entire sky pulsated with the rumble of ascending bombers.

The outward route took them down to Suffolk, crossing the coast at Aldeburgh to a landfall on the far side of the North Sea at Ouddorp and thence direct to the target.[14] Of the twelve aircraft which set out from Marston Moor, eleven came back.[15] By the

★ Bomber Command's target codes were developed by Harris's deputy, AVM Robert Saundby, and reflected his enthusiasms as an amateur naturalist. Cities were designated by the names of fish.

time they returned 600 acres of Cologne had been ruined, 45,000 people were homeless, and over 5,000 were injured. At least 469 were dead.

Assembly of the Millennium armada had been arduous, and it made sense to relaunch it while it was still in being. The last day of May was a rest day for the crews, but on 1 June the teletypes again began to chatter, this time with orders for an attack on industrial Essen. Tactics were similar to those used at Cologne, but with results nowhere near as ruinous. Essen was almost always veiled by haze, and on this evening cloud masked it as well. Unable to focus, the force dissipated bombs across a wide area. Another of Marston's Halifaxes did not return.

Next day the Thousand force was disbanded, seconded aircrew returned to their home units and Marston's instructors were given forty-eight hours' leave. Cheshire used the time to visit Irene Josephy of the literary agents Curtis Brown in London. *Bomber Pilot* was finished, he had begun to produce short stories, and he had an idea for a film. By a nice coincidence its eventual title would be *48 Hours' Leave*.

Josephy suggested that he submit a written outline. Cheshire set to work, and within two days of returning to Yorkshire he wrote to her enclosing a new short story, and the outline for the film. This is how he described it:

The leading character is a Cockney Sergeant Air Gunner (Jack).
The leading girl is the youngest daughter of an eminently aristocratic and wealthy country family. She is very vivacious and, in the eyes of her parents, highly independable (sic) (Jill).
*   Jack hitch-hikes to town.*
*   Jill picks him up and takes him home for a drink. On the way he changes into civilian clothes. Jill's family are outraged . . . especially as they don't know who he is. They are giving a dinner party in the honour of a local young aristocrat who has just joined the Air Force as a commissioned rear gunner, and who is considered a suitable match for Jill. Jill compels her Father to invite Jack to stay for dinner: his costume − flannels, tweed coat and choker − is somewhat unusual, and the guests are horrified . . . When the 9 o'clock news announces the award of a high decoration to a rear gunner . . . they do not know that Jack is the man in question: they see him only as a Cockney bus conductor's son with a string*

of highly impertinent retorts, quite different to the dashing hero at the head of the table. After dinner they play cards: Jack, treated with the utmost suspicion but with Jill's encouragement, clears the table.

When the guests have gone, Jack and Jill set off secretly to London to spend Jack's winnings. They arrive at his home at daybreak, and the reception is very different. Jill for a day lives Jack's life: she sees the welcome he gets wherever he goes: she meets his friends – the ordinary man in the street: and she realizes that this welcome, more powerful than any dinner of honour, is not because of what he has done, but because of what he is to his friends.[16]

This improvises on a universal plot: the hindrances to a relationship between people of different backgrounds against the wishes of parents. There are also autobiographical elements. But there is more to it. Here is a first glimpse of Cheshire's lifelong preoccupation with the ordinary man in the street.

Cheshire did not say how the story would end, but in reply to Josephy's wish for a 'light and cheerful background' he argued that, whether or not the story was to be a comedy, there should be 'a more profound concluding twist'. Transformed by their experiences, where acquaintance, understanding and parting all came within a day, Jill and Jack might never have met again.

The proposal was passed to Joan Ling of Curtis Brown's drama department. Miss Ling agreed that 'there is a very good germ of an idea' but asked for 'a forty-eight-hours leave story, not twenty-four hours': the first signs of meddling.[17] Meanwhile, Curtis Brown sought to place the short story with the *New Yorker*; serialization of *Bomber Pilot* had begun in the *Sunday Graphic*; and Sir Arthur Harris was preparing to reconvene the Thousand force for an attack on Bremen.

The Millennium raid had lifted the political and public expectations of Bomber Command. Smaller attacks, hitherto the norm, now looked insignificant.[18] Harris was accordingly keen to see more mass attacks, and for a time he entertained the idea of reassembling the Thousand force several times each month.[19] Thus it was that on 21 June Marston Moor's instructors were warned that they would again be needed. Training ceased, eight Halifaxes and crews were made ready, and at a quarter to midnight on the evening of

25 June they set out for Bremen. As an experiment, Cheshire flew all the way in formation with two other aircraft.

The tactics of phased arrival, the bomber stream and the concentration used over Cologne were now established, although the bombing time was shortened, and different parts of the force were allocated to specific industrial objectives. Despite these refinements the raid was inconclusive. Cloud obscured the city, and while Cheshire found it many others did not. Losses, moreover, were high: 48 out of the 1,067 aircraft taking part were missing and 65 more were damaged. Over three times as many aircrew died as those killed on the ground. Nearly half of the RAF's dead were trainees.

This was the last of the thousand-bomber operations, although Harris kept some of the training units at readiness for several days more in the hope of revisiting Bremen. These intermittent standbys and stand-downs were disruptive – all personnel were confined to camp, leave was cancelled, passes suspended – and required ground staff to work through the night. Most Conversion Unit aircraft were worn out, and many items of equipment not carried during training had to be reinstalled when an operation was ordered, only to be removed afterwards.

Scarcely had routine been restored when training was re-interrupted. Marston's runways were again breaking up. Flying transferred to the nearby airfield at Rufforth, where within a week the runways there too were declared unfit.[20] Wearily, Cheshire led instructors, pupils and ground crews to Dalton, near Thirsk.[21]

On 25 July the unit was again ordered to prepare for an operation. This was not to be on the scale of Cologne or Bremen, but the force of 630 aircraft was much larger than any other dispatched that month, and a number of CU instructors were conscripted into it. Next day the operation was put off. On the 28th it was on again, only to be cancelled late in the evening. The same pattern of readiness, briefing and cancellation followed on 29 and 30 July. On the 30th the operation was called off as they were about to go out to the aircraft. Repeated cancellations were loathed, for there came a point when the tension and mental preparation were best sublimated by the operation itself. After three or four days of waiting, given a choice between the assurance of one more day of life and the trip itself, many would opt for the trip.

They at last got it over with on 31 July – or, more strictly, 1 August, for take-off began just after midnight. The target was Dusseldorf, and for Cheshire it was eventful. A jammed starter motor delayed their departure, and various difficulties caused them to return early.[22] Ten miles off the Dutch coast they were attacked by a fighter – apparently a Messerschmitt 210 – which Cheshire's gunners shot down in flames. It was unusual for a Halifax to get the better of a state-of-the-art nightfighter. After this life at Dalton seemed even less fulfilling than usual, especially as he was laid low with flu.

Throughout July's wanderings he had persevered with his writing. Following Joan Ling's advice he submitted an expanded film synopsis, now under the working title *48 Hours' Leave*. To judge from Ling's reactions it was developing as a farce.[23] In August Cheshire wrote the first scene and sent it to Ling, who replied 'go right ahead'.[24] Simultaneously, Irene Josephy said she 'enormously' liked a new story called 'The Face in the Sky',[25] and that the BBC was expressing interest in his writing. Could they see something? Ling suggested he rework a snippet of 'The Face in the Sky' into a play: nothing complete, 'the more tantalizing the better'.*[26]

The *New Yorker* liked his writing but said they had already published 'the John Strachey RAF pieces' and thought the genre too worn.[27] During the autumn Josephy continued to press Cheshire for the radio play, and then on 6 November wrote: 'Terrific news from New York: *Cosmopolitan* have bought 'The Face in the Sky' . . . you have broken into one of their big national magazines'.[28] Cheshire submitted another story, 'The Pact', and all three were sold to the *Sunday Graphic* in 1943. Others were sketched.

Would he have made a writer? On one level, of course, he did.

---

* He also wrote an article for the American magazine *Flying and Popular Aviation*. Commissioned via Flt Lt Roald Dahl, a member of the RAF Delegation in Washington, this became a temporary source of embarrassment. Dahl was unaware that Cheshire had an agent, while Cheshire's desire to be accommodating caused him to bypass Curtis Brown when he submitted it.

After the war he lived by journalism, and for the rest of his life he wrote for newspapers and periodicals. He also published four more books, worked on another and became an accomplished essayist. In most of his later output, however, he was writing because of what he wanted to say, rather than because he wanted to write. The question is whether he might have gone on to a career as an author of fiction.

There is not much music in his prose, but he had an ear for dialogue, an observant eye and a clear voice. His notebooks reveal his working. He was methodical, building up a story in layers upon a framework, rather as a sculptor might model clay around wire. He would begin by listing the phases of a plot in keywords: 'Adolescence. Incident. Advancement. Girl. Conflict. Culmination. Solution.' Characters were mapped, down to the invention of biographical details which would not actually be used.

The plots are mostly simple, their materials drawn from immediate surroundings, uneven in realization but displaying an instinct for form and a liking for cinematic devices. Imagery is sparse, sometimes jejune but occasionally striking. Like many writers he jotted down phrases or sentences which he invented or overheard, storing them for subsequent use. (Some of them give one pause: 'That's the only thing that gets a sensible reaction from you – pain.') His own experience is often transparent:

Then had come the war: he had joined up in the Air Force, not waiting to be called up. He thought he would enjoy it. At least he had some purpose, something to live for. His mind and his body seized their chance, and for the first time his character began to develop. In the course of his work he met men of all classes and of all types. He was no longer an actor: for once he had to stand on his merits and not on his money . . . War shuts off the past like a seal . . .

During the winter his output dwindled, and then ceased. 'I have been wondering about you a lot lately', Irene Josephy wrote to him on 31 March 1943, perhaps because his name and photograph had recently been in the newspapers. 'I take it you get no time for writing at all these days?' Indeed he did not. Since the previous August Cheshire had been a wing commander, the commanding officer of 76 Squadron, and had flown a third tour of operations.

76 Squadron had been Christopher's unit, and when Cheshire arrived at Middleton St George, near Darlington, on 5 August 1942 his first action was to search out the ground crew who had maintained his brother's aeroplane. He asked if they would do the same for him.

During August most of 76 Squadron's crews departed to the Middle East, leaving a small home echelon of five aircraft and fewer crews, which it fell to Cheshire to expand. His personal operations would be rationed. He had a quota of ten; and once they were flown his command would end. He accordingly ensured that each trip should count towards some further purpose. He returned from the first, to Mainz on 11 August, with a bull's-eye photograph of the aiming point which immediately set a standard.

The airfield was shared with 78 Squadron, commanded by Wg Cdr J. B. Tait, whom Cheshire had previously known at Linton-on-Ouse. To Linton they returned, as Middleton St George was to be handed over to the Canadians. Cheshire and Tait were contrasting figures. Cheshire had the rare gift of presence: 'When he entered an ante-room, without looking you knew he was there. When he spoke to groups, each member of his audience felt he was speaking to them.'[29] Tait was more reserved, 'dark and introvert, and a tough CO'. Strongly motivated, 'he was in RAF parlance a "press on" type, and he expected his crews to be the same'.[30] When Tait went round the squadron 'he would climb up on the servicing platforms, see for himself and tell the squadron engineering officer when the aircraft should be serviceable'.[31] Every squadron had an aircraft beset by minor faults. Such machines were avoided, but when Tait flew on ops 'the current hangar queen would be his for the night'.[32] In the mess he 'looked like a hawk that had touched down for a drink beside a pool somewhere, his head and eyes suddenly swivelling to lock on to someone talking to him'. The eyes could 'look through and beyond one'. Behind his unconcern for trivial chat lay a readiness to converse fluently upon a subject that interested him. 'I quickly discovered that with Willie you aren't talking on the surface . . . the conversation quickly takes the shape of a university seminar.'[33]

Cheshire and Tait were often to be seen in deep conversation on tactics, serviceability, morale. Together they strove to plan raids, bring on raw aircrew, administrate. Occasionally they slipped off the station to a pub in York, on one occasion ending the evening in a car crash which put Cheshire in hospital for several days. But off-duty hours were few. Running a bomber squadron could mean a twenty-hour day, sometimes with a raid at the end of it.

Linton itself flourished under the command of Grp Capt. John Whitley, who was friendly, humorous and widely liked. 'He was rarely in the mess, recognizing that it was the province of the squadron commanders, but everyone knew that the station master was getting in the odd trip.' From time to time an anonymous figure would turn up at dispersal and sit in as a second pilot, 'usually with a sprog crew'.[34] Eventually Whitley did this once too often and was shot down. He escaped into Spain and reappeared at Linton three weeks later.

Only once, it seems, did Whitley provoke discontent, when he was obliged to implement an Air Ministry reminder that aircrew sergeants should salute officers while at work on the station. This lasted for about a week: the aircrew who flew and so often died together, irrespective of rank, would have none of it. 'Neither did we mind the ground crews not saluting . . . particularly whilst on the job. They were all part of the team. It would have seemed stupid to have them drop their spanners . . . We had more serious things on our minds.'[35]

Cheshire's informality suited men and women whose shared experience had begun to dissolve many of the class barriers which had divided the pre-war Air Force.[36] For example:

A young wireless operator, who had arrived at Linton the previous day, was climbing into the truck for dispersals when he felt Cheshire's arm round his shoulder. 'Good luck, Wilson.' All the way to the aircraft, the w/op pondered . . . 'How the hell did the CO know my name?'[37]

Or:

'Hello, Read.' I did not know he knew my name. 'Hear you had a few problems tonight . . . Would you like to come and have a chat about it?' My first meeting with the nicest and most considerate squadron commander I ever met. It mattered not one iota that I was not in his squadron or his responsibility. I needed help and advice and he was ready to give it.[38]

His rapport with ground crews became legendary. 'He could get men to do anything. If he went into a billet on a Saturday morning, with airmen getting ready to go into York, and ask for eight volunteers, he'd get the lot.' He 'always believed he could learn more about the planes by talking to the ground staff than from "other personnel"'.[39] Mechanics on engine stands grew accustomed to Cheshire climbing up beside them to discuss what they were doing and why. On Christmas Day two radar mechanics were inspecting Gee equipment in a Halifax on a remote dispersal:

. . . it seemed a good idea to get some fresh air after a few drinks on Christmas Eve. We heard someone going through the plane but took no notice as we assumed it was another mechanic. It was in fact Wg Cdr Cheshire who wished us a very happy Christmas, had a few words with us and suggested we 'jack it in for the day and get back for Christmas dinner'. He did, in fact, go round the various dispersals on that Christmas morning and had a few words with everyone.[40]

After an arduous period of operations there was a squadron stand-down. With characteristic forethought, Cheshire sent instructions that a late breakfast be served to the ground staff next morning. An obdurate catering officer refused to vary normal routine until a personal visit by Cheshire changed his mind.

One of Cheshire's many morale-building steps was the inauguration of a monthly meeting in which all the aircrews would entertain all the ground crews. Another was 'The Plumbers' Meeting', a monthly conference attended by every member of the ground staff for discussion of their experiences, suggestions and complaints. A third was his realization that relaxation and humour were not alternatives to efficiency but prerequisites for it. In conversation with an airframe fitter he found that he was a jazz drummer. Were there other musicians on the station? Yes, there were. Could they form a dance band? Yes they could, calling themselves The Cheshire Cats and playing at monthly station dances.[41] If there was a run around the perimeter track Cheshire led it, if there was a cycling race, he was in it; if the squadron's football team was playing, he would cheer it; if the WAAFs of the accounts section put on a pantomime, he would thank them afterwards.

The effects of Cheshire's ubiquity, enthusiasm and encouragement were visible in 76 Squadron's maintenance record. At the end of November 1942, 4 Group noted: '76 Sqn deserve special credit. In 6 months operating only once has a turret failure caused a machine to return early. This points to very excellent maintenance and the armament staff of that Sqn deserve the highest praise.'[42] Looking back over February 1943, 4 Group's AOC, AVM Carr, congratulated the squadron for the 'consistently high level of serviceability maintained throughout the month'.[43] After this came congratulations from Harris himself.[44]

One day Flt Lt Ron Read of 78 Squadron found himself in a conversation about 'chop rates' with two of Linton's WAAF intelligence officers. Losses were then averaging 4 per cent per sortie. Read calculated that with thirty sorties to complete, the average crew had a minus 20 per cent chance of survival.

'Oh no,' the intelligence officers argued, 'it doesn't work like that. The statisticians say it starts from zero for every trip. So it's only ever 4 per cent.'

'If you only had to go once', Read replied, 'it would be 4 per cent, only as long as you don't go again . . . If you go again your percentage chance of the chop must go up. I've got to find a way to get on to someone else's percentage.' The discussion ended when Read said, 'If they'd find me a statistician who'd completed thirty sorties, I might believe it.'[45]

Read was right – it was a compound loss rate. Few operational Halifaxes lasted long enough to reach a major overhaul. When one did it attracted an awestruck entry in 4 Group's records: 'A Halifax II . . . is now on major inspection having flown all its time on ops. This is the first to do so in this Group. The S[tarboard]O[uter] engine has been there all the time and is still serviceable.'[46] The aircraft belonged to 76 Squadron.

Linton's senior intelligence officer saw in Cheshire 'a sense of duty greater than average. He was always on the lookout for new ways of getting more out of men and machines.'[47] Others wondered at his synchronous composure and energy: 'Among his many quali-

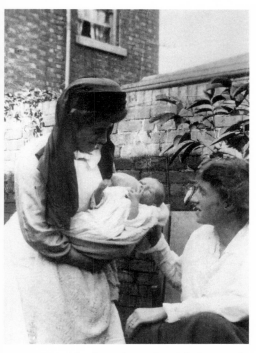

Primrose Cheshire (seated) with Leonard (held by his grandmother) shortly after his birth, September 1917

Primrose and Geoffrey Cheshire with Leonard, Christopher and grandmother Jane Barstow at Pau, 1921

Holiday in France, *c.* 1928

Leonard, *c.* 1929

Above left:
J. F. Roxburgh,
headmaster of Stowe

Above right:
T. H. White at
Stowe, *c.* 1935

Right:
Leonard, runner-up to the
local tennis champion at
Sellin, Rügen, Germany,
August 1936

Cheshire (signing book) with members of the Oxford University Air Squadron at Ford, Sussex, 1937

Merton College tennis team, 1938; Christopher stands at centre

Richard Rivaz ('Revs'), April 1941

Frank Long ('Lofty'), front right, with
Cheshire standing behind him, July 1940

Cheshire's Whitley at Topcliffe after returning from Cologne, 13 November 1940

Above: Handley Page Halifax Mk 1 ser. II of 76 Sqn, flown by Christopher over Whixley, N. Yorkshire, a few days before the aircraft's loss and his capture, August 1941.

Left: Christopher with his wireless operator Eddie Gurmin beside their Whitley at Dishforth, June 1941

Below: Cheshire in the saddle during a bicycle race, probably at Linton-on-Ouse, 1941

Marston Moor
aerodrome, 1943

Cheshire's railway
bungalow at Marston
Moor, 1943

Above: 12,000 lb high-capacity bomb, designed to destroy factories of relatively light construction, and to wreck plant and machinery

Left: Cheshire at Marston Moor, 1943

Wg Cdr Guy Gibson hands over to Sqn Ldr George Holden (sixth and fourth from right, respectively) on 2 August 1943 with five members of Gibson's crew, and ground staff. Gibson had just made his last flight as commander of 617 Squadron. Holden and four of the crew present were killed six weeks later

Above: 617 Squadron raid on La
Ricamerie needle bearing works,
St-Etienne, filmed from Cheshire's
Lancaster, 10/11 March 1944

Below: Flt Lt Ken Brown's aiming-point
photo of the Gnome-Rhône plant at
Limoges, revealing the accuracy of the
attack which followed Cheshire's
point-blank marking on the night of
8/9 February 1944

Above: Martin's battle-damaged P 'Popsie'
at Cagliari, Sardinia, following the attack
on the Antheor viaduct, 12/13 February
1944

ties was a contrast between outward calm and restless intelligence: you could always sense the ideas milling around inside his head.'[48] One of these ideas was to ascertain where the boundaries of the German fighter control 'boxes' were, and then to fox the controllers by changing height as aircraft passed from one box to another.[49] Another lay in the development of night cine photography, the better to analyse the progress of raids.[50]

Whence did the sense of duty come? In 1939 Cheshire had regarded the war as 'legalized excitement'. At some point since, perhaps in the six months between the death of Frank Long and Christopher's capture, he had begun to see it as something infinitely more serious.

On a morning when we were grounded by weather, another flight commander and I were in the Ops Room with the Ops officer when Leonard came in and joined us . . . he went and stood beside the wall map on which arcs of circles marked the various distances from Linton. Putting his finger on a small town in Germany just beyond the Dutch border, he said, 'Twelve of us, in formation, could go in there low and wipe the place out. Kill everyone!' . . . there was never any doubt on the station of his determination to kill Germans, caused partly, it was rumoured, by the fact that his younger brother had been shot down and was a prisoner.[51]

At 76 Squadron there was a joke about Cheshire: 'the moment he walks into a bar, you can see him starting to work out how much explosive it would need to knock it down'.[52] In fact, this wasn't a joke. He said as much himself. Anger and passion smoulder in this lecture he gave to factory workers in the autumn of 1942:

Being in the Air Force I occasionally go into a pub. Occasionally too I visit a factory, or stand in a bus queue, or listen to what my neighbours have to say in the local restaurant. These are about the only contacts I have with the outside world, because I never stay in the same place very long . . . However, in the course of these scattered . . . excursions I have seen some astonishing scenes. The women of ICI at Rawtenstall who work eight hours a day in the furnace room manipulating giant frames that even a man would find hard to lift. It's not so much that they do it, as that they have chosen to do it . . .

In Oxford, too, Frank Hulbert (see p. 25), who was wounded, gassed and decorated in the last war, who still coughs up the traces of mustard gas . . . who on 3 September 1939 left his job and at his own expense . . . [looked] for a recruiting officer who would wink at his age and health. He found one, and went through the London blitz with the balloon barrage, but in the end the mustard gas poisoning won and Frank was discharged. He is in a factory now. If you meet him, you will learn what fighting spirit *really* means.

In Camberwell, seventeen-year-old Lilian Latimer, who says: 'I have infantile paralysis in both legs, so as I cannot go to work I help Mother with the housework.' Mrs Prisett from Darlington, who lost her son – the last in the family – in a flying accident and said: 'The dead want us to keep smiling, to carry on and win the war, don't they? I have lost everything I have: I am crippled in both legs, but I still have a pair of hands. I shall find some war work.'

These are but a few. All over the country there are others like them. Land girls, nurses, firemen, lorry drivers . . . Unfortunately I haven't met them. I wish I had.

. . . As a nation we have not known the meaning of total war. We have not seen the enemy in our homes, and the courage and determination of the strong has been powerful enough to carry along the weak in its train . . . There is still the Harrogate businessman who oozes prosperity and good living and lack of worries, who has never heard a bomb or a shell, who said to me: 'Of course, you boys are too young to understand what war means. Do you realize that I've been losing £50 a week since it started?' Or the retired colonel from Wetherby who approached us with the remark: 'Can't you manage to have some consideration for other people? Just because you take off in the middle of the night, there's no need to wake the whole neighbourhood up.' Or the young man in Cambridge who, in a pub, boasted that he earned £8 a week and for the past month had managed to get away with screwing up only fourteen bolts a day. There are not many of these people, it is true. But none the less they exist. Until they wake up one day and find themselves looking into the wrong end of a gun . . .

For the rest, there is one thing I have noted that hurts a little. Most evenings people discuss the war. Sometimes they are interested in . . . tactics or strategy. But sometimes they are interested in neither. They wrap themselves in a mantle of gloom . . .

If these men and their crab-apple faces were to walk into the crew room down the passage from my office, if they were to come to meet the armourers who give up their afternoon off to load up a cargo of bombs in the right place or the ground crew who cancel their free evening to sit all night on a cold dispersal point waiting for their aircraft to come back, they ought to feel a twinge of conscience. If you could borrow their attention for a moment you might be able to conjure up in them a vision of the men who once frequented these hangars and crew rooms, but do so no more . . .

If the heart-aches have doubt on how we will win, what hope can those in Germany have? Here is a letter from one of them, my brother.

> For the King's birthday we all dressed ourselves up to the nines, and we looked, anyway for prisoners-of-war, exceedingly smart on parade. Tony Carr lent me his old tunic and I managed to smuggle myself out of the way as best I could. It was a lovely day, and for once we were all punctual. 8.30 a.m. is an early hour when time is our greatest enemy. I think the German officers were impressed as they marched on to the various parade grounds to count us. It was an orderly parade. By that I mean no one read books, no one talked, no one moved about and no one surreptitiously smoked. Normally we do all these things. The effect was so obviously noticed by all, and when the Germans dismissed us, we gave three of the heartiest cheers to His Majesty . . . the morning was a still one, and our cheers cut the atmosphere like the firing of a gun would during the two minutes' silence. This simple act was a tonic to us all and our morale went sky high and my bosom for once swelled with pride. When it was over, we changed back into our rags, and the day proceeded as all days do.

The British, then, still have the qualities that won them their victories in the past. Bombs and death can only serve to make them stronger. But may it not be forgotten that parasites, once tolerated, can breed uncommonly fast.[53]

The war was no longer any kind of excitement but a carnage. His effectiveness in mobilizing men and machines sprang from a longing to see it finished. Encouragement and example were his methods, not simply because they came naturally, but because he believed them more effective than despotism. People he saw under stress were sometimes invited to his room for a drink, or an evening listening to jazz from his wind-up gramophone. Towards any who failed without good reason, however, he gave short shrift.

On 2 October 1942 five crews were detailed for an attack on Krefeld. Just before take-off the hydraulic pumps in one aircraft were found to be unserviceable. The ground crew quickly made a repair, but the navigator 'firmly refused to enter the aircraft. By so doing the entire crew had to stand down.'[54] This may have been the occasion Cheshire recalled when a crew member

for some reason . . . made a scene and said he could not go on. He was a good lad and it was terribly distressing. I put him down as a member of my own crew to show I still trusted him. It was a risk, but it worked . . . This sort of treatment might have worked in other cases. I wish there had always been time for such understandings.[55]

Cheshire's normal response to LMF ('lack of moral fibre' – refusal to fly without good cause or cowardice in the face of the enemy) cases was swift and icy. The man would be locked in his room and expelled from the station within hours. 'You couldn't have a bloke saying he would not fly. The squadron commander's function was to keep the squadron operating.'

He was similarly uncompromising towards lapses in flying discipline and mishandling of equipment. Damaged aircraft were unavailable for operations and wasted the energies of ground staff. When a pilot clipped a tree during low-flying training Cheshire severely reprimanded him. When a Halifax's tailwheel collapsed after striking a water pipe which had been exposed by construction works, this was unforeseen and therefore forgivable. When a similar accident occurred, Cheshire punished it. Everyone had been warned. The second mishap was negligence.

Many Halifax accidents, however, were to do with deficiencies of the aircraft itself. A few days after his arrival one of 76 Squadron's aircraft spun into the ground near Thirsk.[56] Cheshire suspected a case of rudder overbalance. There had been others like it, and he embarked on a crusade to cure this and other weaknesses, making trips to AAEE Boscombe Down to take part in handling tests.

Cheshire considered the Halifax to be 'the most unmanageable four-engined aircraft in the service'.[57] During the war he never openly criticized the aeroplane or its builders, but afterwards he made his feelings known:

It . . . makes me angry the way the aircraft manufacturers lobbied politicians to keep useless aircraft in production. There was a particularly good example of this in Bomber Command, about which the least said the best perhaps, because it certainly caused unnecessary slaughter of crews and might well have led to some sensible refusals to fly. It was a disgrace . . .

4 Group squadrons embarked on some modifications themselves. The group's summary for October 1942 stated:

The vital urgency of doing everything humanly possible to improve Halifax performance is at last fully appreciated by everyone concerned and modifications are being incorporated as fast as possible both retrospectively and in production (Para. 101) . . . Probably the most effective of these is the shortening of the radiator shutters. This allows loaded aircraft to cruise at any altitude with the radiator shutters closed instead of open as in the past. This so reduces drag that an increase of 8 m.p.h. is obtained at the same power output.[58]

Another change was the removal of the 'elephant's ear' shrouds which covered the glowing exhaust pipes to either side of each engine. Cheshire argued that the shrouds caused turbulence in airflow and reduced performance. A decade later Sir Frederick Handley Page doubted that such changes had been made.[59] However, contemporary records confirm that by October 1942 many captains had begun to operate without exhaust shrouds and that losses had fallen in result.★[60]

Even the paint on a Halifax could slow it down. The matt finish added to friction in airflow, and the substitution of a semi-gloss finish was reckoned to add 5 m.p.h. to performance.[61] From around midwinter new Halifaxes were so coated as a matter of course; before this, Cheshire made sure that 76 Squadron repainted their aircraft themselves.

By December 1942 Handley Page were bringing forward modifications which embodied a number of ideas that had been improvised or tested under Cheshire's influence. A new close-fitting, light, aluminium exhaust shroud was developed which caused less drag and turbulence. Improvements were also made to the oil

---

★ 4 Group estimated that losses among Halifaxes which retained exhaust shrouds were of the order of 1 in 14, whereas losses for those without them were 1 in 25. Although Halifaxes without shrouds were more conspicuous to nightfighters, there was compensation in extra altitude and speed.

dilution system, and steps taken to counter the problem of rudder overbalance.

Towards the end of 1942 it was realized that the majority of attacks by radar-guided German nightfighters were being made from below:

... they tracked and overtook us from below where none of the gunners could see them. [Cheshire's] response was to cut a hole in the floor of the fuselage aft of the bomb bay and install a perspex blister. At the same time, and to improve the Halifax's performance, he had the mid-upper turret removed and the gap faired over. This added a few knots to the performance and transformed the mid-upper gunner into a mid-under sighter, lying prone to see what was happening underneath.[62]

At Cheshire's urging, 76 Squadron also exchanged weight for height and speed by stripping their Halifaxes of all expendable items, even down to the armour-plated door of the flight engineer's compartment.

In 1954 Andrew Boyle put criticisms of the Halifax to Sir Frederick Handley Page, who replied with slightly defensive dignity: 'I know nothing about pilots' complaints that the Halifax was "unwieldy". The Halifax control surfaces, etc., were the same at the end of the war as at the beginning. Some 6,000 odd Halifaxes were built *in toto*, and I cannot understand this complaint.'* Sir Frederick emphasized the value of modifications which came as a result of experience in service.[63] Or as a pilot at Linton put it: 'To help the illusion along, aircraft so modified were recoded from a Halifax II to a Halifax Mk2 Series 1 Special. Whatever they called it, it remained a lumbering under-powered sitting target.'[64]

Cheshire was becoming a public figure. In August 1942 he broadcast in the *Postcript* series for the BBC, and in October he wrote and broadcast a talk to evacuees in America.[65] The Air Ministry sent a war artist to paint his portrait; in January 1943 he addressed factory workers in London. The London lecture coincided with the publication of *Bomber Pilot*, which sold out its

---

* Sir Frederick was being a little disingenuous. The Halifax III, re-engined with the more powerful Hercules and with redesigned rudders, was a huge improvement on its predecessors. In some respects it was virtually a different aircraft.

first print of 10,000 copies in a month. The Air Ministry's Public Relations department told him: 'You are a very valuable person to Bomber Command,' adding ominously, 'perhaps more valuable on the ground at this stage than in the air over Germany.'[66]

Bomber Pilot was not so well received by aircrew.

It breached the 'line-shooting' code of the RAF, and he was regarded with some suspicion by many who read it, including most of my contemporaries. We couldn't accept that anyone who could break the code in such a way, obtaining considerable publicity while doing so, could still be a genuine, down-to-earth, ordinary operational pilot.[67]

Line-shooting was a serious offence. The style of the day was understatement,[68] and headlines like 'How I Conquered Fear' in the newspaper serialization[69] had made aircrew wince. Cheshire winced too, but the headlines were out of his hands.

And Constance? She was now living at Boston Spa, a few miles from Linton. On New Year's Day 1943 Cheshire wrote to his old friend Douglas Baxter:

I find married life very satisfying although I can't live out and don't see Constance very often. Why don't you try it? I've always thought you'd make an ideal husband. Especially if she had some ready cash . . . I'm heading strongly for my second half century of operations but fear the war may be over before I complete the circuit. I've been a wing commander these past five months: it's a drawback in that you are forced from time to time to set an example of behaviour. However, I find it possible now and then to overcome that obstacle, and on the whole enjoy myself pretty well.[70]

Opinions about Constance varied. Ken McDonald thought her 'a good sport' who played the piano in the mess and led the singing.[71] When Cheshire took her to Stowe, J. F. Roxburgh found her 'very nice and not at all the film-star type'.[72] Others were more guarded, or said the opposite. Admirers and sceptics alike agreed that neither Yorkshire's provincialism nor the limited amenities of bomber stations were to her liking. A WAAF who met her at a party formed the impression of someone 'out of her depth' who 'hated Britain in wartime'.[73] Cheshire never spoke harshly of her, but those who knew him sensed tensions.

At the end of February Carr warned Cheshire that his time was nearly up. Against all odds he had survived three tours of operations, and his leadership of 76 Squadron had been outstanding. But squadron command meant operational flying, and both for his own good and the greater good of Bomber Command this must now cease. A suitable posting would be found for him. Mainz, Karlsruhe, Duisburg, Krefeld, Genoa, Mannheim, Lorient, Berlin and Wilhelmshaven had been places from which he might not have returned. He now had to accept that it was he who would not be returning to them. His fighting war was over.

In March Cheshire went on leave, returning in early April when cold winds blew sand from surrounding fields into the aircraft engines and kept them on the ground. On 6 April there was a party in the airmen's mess. Cheshire 'went round and had a few words with everyone present'. Next morning he visited all the various sections and flights to say goodbye to all the mechanics. The adjutant wrote, a little wistfully, 'Wing Commander Cheshire left the squadron today on being posted as group captain to Marston Moor. What the squadron has lost Marston Moor will gain. It was under the direct and personal supervision of Gp Capt. Cheshire that the squadron became what it is today – one of the best in Bomber Command.'[74]

Gloom deepened when it became known that 76 Squadron was to be moved to Holme-on-Spalding Moor – 'the land of nod'. 'On reflection I see it was because we all missed Leonard on the flights and around the station, radiating that air of confidence.'[75]

During his leave he had gone back to Stowe. Numbers had fallen, the school's losses were rising. Elderly or inexperienced men were standing in for departed masters. But there was a happy meeting with J. F. Roxburgh, who jotted afterwards: 'He is now wing commander and permanently off operations. He could not have been nicer . . . Christopher reported by escaped friend to be well, happy and busy.'[76] So two Old Stoics, at any rate, seemed safe, even if one of them was in Stalag Luft 3.

Cheshire's appointment as the commander of Marston Moor caused a minor sensation: 'He's Bomber Station Chief at Twenty-five' ran one headline. He told his father: 'promoting anyone of my experience and years to the post was an entire innovation for the Air Force and only done after a great many exertions on the part of the AOC and a good deal of arguing into the bargain'. Cheshire was in the public eye again ten days later following announcement of the award of a bar to his DSO.

Marston Moor's base[77] commander was Air Commodore John Kirby, a slim, elegant, gentlemanly figure who was considered 'a skilled delegator, but nobody's fool'. Kirby's stately routine provided for two pink gins before lunch and a period of repose for an hour or so afterwards. He admired Cheshire's effectiveness.

Marston Moor's function as 4 Group's academy for new crews meant that there were tour-expired comrades from 76 Squadron among the instructors, and colleagues from Linton like Ken McDonald, who took command of 1652 Conversion Unit in April. Cheshire was thus in the company of friends at a familiar place where gifts of safety and seniority had been bestowed upon him. Nevertheless, he tells us that it was 'almost with a feeling of loneliness' that he reported for duty.[78] This was partly because the job itself was strange, and he was apprehensive about directing officers and senior NCOs who were older and more seasoned than himself.[79] It was also because a chapter in his life, perhaps the only vital chapter there would ever be, had closed. 'The work to be done, true enough, was no less important than that of the front-line squadron, but it *felt* less important. There was no visible enemy to fight, no emergencies to deal with; and once one has become accustomed to states of emergency, life without them becomes flat and dull.'

Not that training lacked incident. Between May and September 1943 serious flying accidents on and around the station averaged one every nine-and-a-half days. Aside from familiar risks posed by mishandling, undercarriage collapses and poor weather, Marston's instructors and ground staff still struggled to maintain the required output of new crews while training them in geriatric aeroplanes. '. . . all the Halifaxes . . . were really clapped out. In order to do cross-country training it was necessary to start at one end of a long line of Halifaxes and do pre-flight checks to try and find one that was "acceptable". None was ever fully serviceable and any one who wanted to go by the book would never have flown at all.'[80]

There were other pressures. The HCU course was based on a syllabus of forty hours; extra training was not allowed for in maintenance schedules and could only be accomplished if the ground crews worked longer hours. Beyond this, training was slowed by winter weather and there was a corresponding drive to increase output during the summer. April was 'always a tricky month', and the spring of 1943 was the most difficult of all. Cheshire had arrived at an exacting moment. 'Partly in order to make the best of a bad job, but partly also to find some outlet through which to let off steam, I embraced the cause of aircraft serviceability (about which I knew nothing, other than the fact that it governed the number of flying hours the station could do), and threw myself into it heart and soul.'[81] 'At first,' recalls Ken McDonald, 'the novelty of commanding a station was tangible. When Leonard invited me to accompany him on tours of the various sections he was alive with questions: "Why shouldn't we do it like this?" "How would it be if we tried going about it from another angle?" '[82] By now Cheshire had learned the 'importance of forethought, concentration on details, of letting every man know what was expected of him'.[83] He circulated a personal message to every member of the station which explained their common objective – 'to keep two aircraft from every flight in the air for ten hours a day, and to fly every available night-flying crew until they have finished' – and reminded them of many things which could obstruct it: 'a spare part that someone didn't order in time, a dirty room that spreads disease, a burst tyre from a stone on the runway, or a piece of grit in the glycol'.[84] Next:

On the side of the hangar there appeared a large red pointer, such as one sees on the wall of dilapidated churches, which gradually rose towards a zero mark representing a given number of hours flown per month. The idea was that as soon as the pointer reached the target, which was a 20 per cent increase on the previous average, the station closed down and everyone went on leave until the end of the month.[85]

The target was achieved.[86] Ironically, however, it was high leave returns, rather than the improvement in flying hours, that caught the eye of 4 Group's administrators. Panicked by the whiff of market doctrine in Cheshire's unorthodoxy, they ordered the scheme to be discontinued.

The idea of the red pointer might have been borrowed from the West Riding town of Ossett, where Cheshire was guest of honour at a Wings for Victory parade on 15 May, drawing loud applause when he mounted a ladder and set the indicator at £20,000.[87] His weekends were often now occupied by such appearances. The following Saturday found him at Abingdon, where the target was £200,000 – the cost of ten bombers.

Cheshire gave much the same speech on each occasion. He began by looking back across the three years of the strategic air offensive, tracing Bomber Command's expansion from the courageous but relatively ineffectual organization it had been in 1940 to a force which was now 'perhaps the biggest in the world'.

I have been asked why the RAF is doing what it is. People say 'Germany won't break up; you can't win the war that way.' That is not the point . . . Bomber Command's job is to help with all the other services . . . The war can only be won by the destruction of the enemy's equipment and his forces. Now it is possible for Bomber Command in one or two large-scale raids against a large factory to destroy perhaps as much equipment as could be destroyed by a whole army in a whole campaign . . . In order to keep this up we need two things. First we have to have crews. I am not an active pilot myself now, but I come from a part of the country where the crews work. I see them daily at work and can say that we . . . have the finest aircrews in the world, who will face anything, anywhere, in order to do their job, but they need aircraft and equipment . . .

There is the point at issue. More money means more equipment and more equipment means greater safety to the crews and a quicker end to the war.[88]

'A quicker end to the war.' By now Cheshire subscribed to von Moltke's dictum that 'The greatest kindness in war is to bring it to a speedy conclusion.' Neither factory visits nor the flaccid rhetoric of Ossett's MP (the climax of whose speech had been 'You cannot fly with the few, but you can buy with the many') seemed to match the urgency of this challenge. Cheshire's appearances before parades of Girl Guides, NFS members and Civil Defence volunteers exemplified his view that all contributions should be mutually valued.

By being there he was honouring *them*, just as by sending the station band to a village fête he was celebrating members of the wider community who played their part. Knowing this, however, did not dispel his ennui.[89]

Aside from running the station, Cheshire received an incessant flow of letters. Former colleagues kept in touch. Parents, wives and girlfriends of missing aircrew asked for news or reassurance. Relatives begged his help in tracing prisoners. Before their deaths or disappearances, scores, possibly hundreds, of young men had written home to say how good Cheshire had been to them. Afterwards their parents thanked him.[90] His popularity among NCOs and other ranks even brought entreaties to defend them at courts martial.

Demanding as all this was, Cheshire still had more spare time than he had known at Linton. He looked for diversions. One was the fortification of the airfield against assault by German paratroops,[91] followed by ground defence exercises in which at least one Commando unit which offhandedly volunteered to test their readiness found itself fought to a standstill. Another was taking bets on horses, 'quite profitable but not sufficiently so'.[92] A third was writing: he told a visiting journalist that this would be his post-war career.[93] And a fourth was to find somewhere interesting to live.

The quarters allocated to Marston Moor's CO were awash with damp. Constance installed herself in the Station Hotel in York while they looked for something better. Houses were available in nearby villages, but station commanders liked to live over the shop. In June Cheshire hit upon the idea of importing accommodation to the airfield. 'This consisted of a standard LNER carriage which had been shunted off at Cattal station and transported on a Queen Mary to a field of Dawson's Farm behind the Officers' Mess where it was installed on concrete blocks.' The carriage appealed to Cheshire's unconventional humour and tested his ingenuity. It tested Constance too, giving her 'sense of art and improvisation the biggest challenge she had yet faced'.[94]

Water was piped and a power cable and telephone line were passed to it from the Mess. One of the passenger doors was removed and a wooden annexe was built on to the resulting gap in the structure, partly to supply entrance steps and a conventional door, but also to house an Elsan. The interior of the carriage was stripped and divided into . . . a bedroom, a sitting room and a kitchen. However, the inside of a sealed door at the side of the sitting room was left untouched to display below the window the fading gold numeral 1 and, above the window, the warning of a five pound penalty for misuse of the emergency chain. Between the sitting room and the kitchen was a bathroom with a tiny tub. The kitchen was equipped with a two-burner and an insulated boiler . . . at the end was a curtained-off larder. Curved around the ménage on the side that faced the field was a fence strung with barbed wire to keep farmer Dawson's cows from bumping against the walls.[95]

Kirby noticed that Cheshire was intensely loyal to Constance, yet sensed some difficulty. Once, at a sergeants' party in a pub at Green Hammerton, Cheshire spoke to him about it.

During intervals from moving around the groups, chortling and standing them pints, L. said: 'I'm a bit worried about Constance. The family won't have anything to do with her now. It's getting me down a bit. What shall I do?'

Kirby recalled his reply:

'Presumably when you married her, you . . . wanted to make your life with her. It was your decision, not your family's, and I don't think their attitude should affect you . . .' It was all I could say. But he was grateful to have been able to confide in a friend and to be reassured. 'You know, that's exactly what I think and feel myself.' I felt there was much more to it than that, that he was probably realizing for the first time at close quarters what kind of life he had let himself in for, and the sort of woman he had to share it with.[96]

Kirby noticed that worries never affected his work, which was '100 per cent plus . . . his instructors thought the world of him because of his genuine personal interest in them and what they were doing. He often went up in Halifaxes to demonstrate training points for them.'[97] Some station commanders were remote, but Cheshire 'was often to be seen about the place . . . a constant reminder that Marston was very much a part of the offensive: the last stop before the squadron'. Other reminders lay in occasional sea searches for ditched aircrew, Bullseye sorties,★ and lectures on German interrogation methods which roughly one in eight of the trainees who attended them could expect to experience at first hand.

Yet while Cheshire worked to inspire others, he found it increasingly difficult to motivate himself. An officer in flying control was struck by his solitude,[98] and Cheshire remembered: 'we were so far out of it all, so utterly useless, frittering our time away on goodness only knows what'.[99]

'Frittering' in Cheshire's mind may have included the reception of parties of West Riding munitions workers, lord mayors, admirals and brigadiers who came to view the station's work. Another guest was AVM Donald Bennett, commander of 8 (PFF) Group, and in a quiet moment Cheshire asked if he would give him an operational post. Bennett replied that this would depend upon his flying – there would have to be a trial period. Cheshire bridled. 'Rather ungraciously, I suppose, I told him that if that was the case I would see if I could find anywhere else.'[100]

Bennett later disputed this, saying that it was 'obvious that he wasn't available' and that if the application had gone forward 'we'd have snapped him up'.[101] Exactly what was said we cannot know, but this was not the first time Bennett had passed Cheshire over. Wg Cdr T. G. Mahaddie, 8 Group's personnel officer, otherwise known as 'Bennett's horse-thief', recalled that Cheshire was the only person he had selected for Pathfinder training whom Bennett had vetoed. Moreover, Bennett had *previously* refused to accept Cheshire.† Mahaddie was never able to establish why.[102]

Cheshire's frustration deepened. In July a rumour reached him that Air Vice-Marshal Cochrane, AOC 5 Group, was seeking a successor for Guy Gibson as commander of 617 Squadron. Charles Whitworth was now the station commander at Scampton where

★ A graduation exercise which simulated operational conditions. Large numbers of searchlights were deployed at the targets, and crews taking part were liable to be 'attacked' by UK-based nightfighters.
† 35 Squadron was transferred into the Pathfinder Force at the time of PFF's formation in August 1942. The squadron command fell vacant when its CO was shot down a month later. According to Mahaddie, Bennett vetoed a proposal that Cheshire should take over.

617 Squadron was based. Cheshire flew to see him. Whitworth told him: 'No. I think you'd be too much for Cochrane to stomach. Too flighty . . . and opinionated – in a nice way, mind you. I know it's a nice way: I know you. But Cochrane doesn't, and won't perhaps want you. But apart from that, you're too late. George Holden's been given the squadron.'[103] Early in October, Cheshire went to see John Kirby and asked him to endorse a formal request to Carr that he should revert to operational flying. Six months before, Carr had gone to great trouble to secure Cheshire's appointment as a station commander. This was the first step in an itinerary of advancement – the staff course, senior command – which Cheshire now declined. Or as he put it to Douglas Baxter: 'I was a station commander, but had to tell them they could stuff the job as it was too bloody uninteresting and I got tired of being called Sir every minute of the day.'[104]

His refusal posed a problem. It was impossible for Carr to return him to operations within 4 Group, while his fretful state of mind seemed likely to undermine his performance in the job he had.[105] Carr consulted colleagues. Cochrane expressed interest. Guy Gibson had left 617 Squadron and his successor, George Holden, was dead. Cochrane invited Cheshire for interview. Contrary to Whitworth's fear that he would come across as opinionated, 'Cheshire spoke seldom, and then with an unwarranted diffidence. No false modesty.' Cochrane offered him the job.

Constance was furious. There was 'yet another (and unnecessary) period of danger and separation to come', and Cheshire had told her that he was going back to war because their railway carriage 'was too comfortable'.[106] There was a growing puritanism in his outlook,[107] and Constance was not the only person to whom he owed an explanation for it. He told his father:

. . . I have never felt that my duty lies in office work and I refused to accept the staff course. It would have ensured a comfortable and well-paid life for both Constance and me and, pleasant thought it would have been, I was not prepared to accept it. At the same time I volunteered to forfeit my rank in order to return to operations. I have just heard that this has been granted, and I am fortunate enough to be going to a job that can only be done by a volunteer . . .[108]

Geoffrey Cheshire replied with a passion which set Leonard back on his heels.

> Did I, he asked, seriously think that the few extra bombs I could drop myself, no matter how skilfully or courageously, would make any difference to the winning of the war? Could I not see that experience so hardly won was not one's own to scatter recklessly . . . but belonged to the country to dispose and command as she thought best? Hadn't I the wit to understand that to keep experience to oneself was to frustrate its purpose, it was to stultify its growth, to condemn it to perpetual stagnation? And come to that, wasn't I overestimating my own capabilities?[109]

Cheshire didn't argue. His reasons were emotional.

> . . . in a world so full of planning, is there not room for a little madness; or a place for the heart, not the intellect, to take charge? And does a bird just freed from captivity stop to listen to warnings? Does it worry at the thought of prowling cats or hovering hawks, or at the possible disappointment of those who used to gape and stare at it?[110]

For Ken McDonald, who moved into the vacant railway carriage, Cheshire's time at Marston had been 'a temporary challenge to his remarkable qualities, but also a forced suspension of his single-minded determination to do everything he could to beat the Nazis and end the war'.[111] Some detected a personal factor in this:

> I had the impression, and I wasn't the only one, that part of Chesh's motivation came from a burning desire to do as much as he could to speed up the war, in order to set his brother free. I think he felt impatient in 1943, with no sign of any invasion, that the RAF generally, and possibly himself in particular, must make all efforts to get it over with . . . I remember thinking this at the time I met him, when he was so demonstrably happy to be going to 617 . . .[112]

617 Squadron flew Lancasters, a type known in 4 Group as 'the *Daily Mirror* bomber' because Lancaster crews seemed to attract all the publicity. When Cochrane ordered him to attend a Lancaster conversion course he bridled,[113] thinking that he would pick up what he needed to know as he went along. But Cochrane insisted, and on 8 November Cheshire grudgingly presented himself to 1668 Conversion Unit at Balderton, near Newark, for three days of

tuition. Afterwards he described the experience as 'the saving of me'.[114] His instructor remembers him:

The Halifax was like a flying tank, less stable and forgiving than the Lanc which was a 'lady' – so tolerant and easy to fly. Of course, I was biased . . . I determined to be a good salesman and show off the Lanc so we threw it about – steep turns, stalling, corkscrewing and I believe we demonstrated flying with only three and two engines. As a matter of general practice we did our drills and this may be what he meant when saying 'it was the saving of him'.[115]

The drills. Know the drills. Learning is never finished. Lofty Long had said that.

PART THREE: LIGHTS AND FIRES, 1943–1944

7. Night Scenes

Leonard Cheshire's eight months in command of 617 Squadron form a special period, a life within a life. Enwrapped by his influence, 617 was not so much a unit as an evolving project in which each operation took some innovative step beyond the last. Legend remembers 617 as a select unit, a Lone Ranger of the skies licensed to fight a freelance war using Barnes Wallis's silver bullets. The squadron was indeed a *corps d'élite*,[1] and there were many occasions when it operated alone. But there was more to it than that. As time passed the squadron also worked in conjunction with other units, and pioneered techniques which passed into wider use. The story has sub-plots, while behind the scenes ran a mordant controversy between Cochrane and Bennett about Cheshire's methods, presided over by the Zeus-like figure of Harris.

A technical narrative runs in counterpoint with the battles. Cheshire was more or less continuously immersed in issues to do with weapons, electronics, mathematical analyses or the practicalities of engineering. The science fed the battle; in some respects it *was* the battle, and the nature of Cheshire's achievement cannot be understood without it. A given day could find him testing, training, discussing, administrating, organizing, caring and fighting. For eight months this was his life. For years afterwards, nothing compared with it.

617 Squadron had been formed at the end of March 1943 under the command of Wg Cdr Guy Gibson to attack the Ruhr dams. After eleven weeks of training the Möhne and Eder dams were breached on the night of 16/17 May at the cost of eight of the nineteen crews taking part. June and July were passed in high- and low-level training and occasional operations. Then Gibson went

abroad. His going left a void which his successor, Sqn Ldr George Holden, did not fill. Holden's incumbency was in any case brief: he perished on 15/16 September, a night of carnage when five out of eight crews were lost in a fruitless attempt to break the banks of the Dortmund–Ems canal.

Of twenty-one crews which had made up the squadron on the eve of the Dams Raid, just seven now remained.* The captain of one of them, Flt Lt H. B. Martin, known to all as Mick, was promoted to squadron leader and given temporary command. In following weeks the squadron reverted to training for high-altitude bombing, and the recruitment of new crews.

Martin was one of the war's outstanding bomber pilots. In the eyes of many in a position to judge he was pre-eminent. An Australian, 'thin, at times scraggy-looking',[2] Martin was frank, exacting, sometimes dissident, always operationally determined. He aroused keen loyalty among those who flew with him, and in his eyes gleamed a 'fierce look'.[3] His speciality was low flying, which he had mastered 'probably at some psychological cost to his crew who . . . had to get used to treetops, telephone posts and other objects more associated with fighting on land than in the air'.[4] Martin's aptitude for command was nevertheless suspect in the minds of certain Bomber Command patriarchs who could not quite come to terms with someone suspected to be (in the words of a friend) 'a bit of a larrikin'.[5]

The Dams Raid survivors formed a close-knit group. Newcomers found them aloof: even those with two or three tours behind them found it hard to enter their intimacy: 'It took them a while to find out that they couldn't do without new pilots.'[6] The inspirational Gibson, moreover, was still revered. Several of 617's founder pilots, like David Shannon, were Gibson's personal friends, and it was doubted if anyone could fill his shoes.† Except Martin.[7] Small wonder, then, that Cheshire's reception was cool. Copies of *Bomber*

---

* The surviving captains were Brown, Martin, McCarthy, Munro, Rice, Shannon and Townsend. Of the others, four had been killed and two posted. Townsend was posted out of the squadron in October 1943.

† Barnes Wallis described Gibson as a 'bundle of energy, more mercurial' and 'living on nerves', whereas Cheshire seemed 'cooler, and (showed) more interest'.

Pilot were left lying about, and the veterans eyed him with expressions ranging from suspicion to outright hostility.[8]

Not that on this day, 11 November, the old hands were overly interested in their new wing commander. They had other things in their minds. An operation had been ordered. The target was a nine-arched railway viaduct at Anthéor, near Cannes, on the Riviera route between France and Italy. Across it rumbled daily some 14,000 tons of war *matériel*. Although the viaduct had been attacked before, the railway still ran.

Anthéor was a difficult target. The viaduct's slenderness, curving path and location in the mouth of a ravine made it hard to identify and awkward to sight. Moreover, the Lancasters, each laden with a single 12,000 lb bomb, would be operating close to the limit of their range. The plan thus provided for them to continue across the Mediterranean to pause and refuel at Blida in north Africa.[9] Despite reasonably accurate bombing the attack was unsuccessful.

While the Anthéor force rested in north Africa, Cheshire settled down to take his bearings. He toured the technical sections and flights and introduced himself to ground staff. Beyond the airfield boundary there was new scenery. To the east spread a country of fen, gridded by banks and ditches holding water that reflected blue on bright days and grey in rain; to the north, chalky hills which reminded him of Driffield's wolds. Near Coningsby lay tracts of heathland and clumps of birch trees that late autumn had turned to the colour of mustard. Red-brick farmsteads and windmills made the area feel settled and busy, but there were some who some found the area remote, even outlandish.

It is not clear how much Cochrane had said about 617's intended future role. At this stage, indeed, it is uncertain how far Cochrane had clarified this for himself. Only a few weeks before the question had been whether 617 should be disbanded. Now the essence of it was that the squadron was being readied for precision attacks and, ultimately for a new weapon. Like the water-skipping mine, known as Upkeep, which the squadron had used against the Ruhr dams, its inventor was Barnes Wallis.

Wallis believed that the war could be won by 'pulling out the switches of German industrial power'. But how could this be done?

Germany's strong air defences meant that the RAF's bombing was largely nocturnal. During 1943 navigation and target-finding had been improved by radar aids, and by the Pathfinder Force, which could now lay route markers, lanes of flares and target indicators. Even so, Bomber Command remained more of a cudgel than a rapier; there were still many evenings when poor weather made it hard to locate a given city, let alone identify and hit a particular factory. Area bombing had been pursued less from choice than from the lack of it.

Nonetheless, there were those who argued that there *was* a choice. Analysts in the Ministry of Economic Warfare and USAAF[10] contended that Germany's ability to fight could be throttled by an offensive against selected sectors of German industry. Harris demurred. Industry-specific bombing, he argued, would be answered by a corresponding concentration of defences, while allowing the generality of Germany's transport and war production to flow and flourish unhindered. Nor could the continuity of a selective campaign be guaranteed. Proscribed industries would have to be attacked frequently, to prevent their recuperation, yet summer nights were too short for bombers to venture far into Germany. This would allow respite for repair, just as some targets would be protected by winter weather. German industry was in any case a hydra, sprouting new armament plants faster than the bomber offensive could lop them. Under the direction of Reich Minister Speer, who had at his disposal a vast force of impressed foreign labour, measures were in hand to disperse factories or hide them underground.

As for precision raids, Harris regarded them as an adjunct rather than as an alternative to area bombing. The lack of a routine method for undertaking them meant that each became a separate project which diverted men and aircraft from other operations. Thus far they had also tended to be costly in the lives of experienced crews, and their results rarely seemed to tally with MEW's optimistic forecasts.

For all these reasons, Harris considered that attacks on industrial towns as entities would accomplish more than fastidious selectivity, which his force was in any case unable to achieve. Sustained area bombing, he insisted, would slow down Germany's transport systems and economy as a whole – and the heavier it was the more *matériel* would be required for Germany's defence and so denied to other theatres. And there, as far as Bomber Command's C-in-C was concerned, the matter stood.

Until then. By late 1943 several of the obstacles to reliable target-finding were close to removal, and Wallis and Vickers Armstrong were developing their new bomb. Unlike conventional bombs which relied upon blast or fire, this emerging weapon was designed to bore down into the ground and detonate beneath its target. The ground, not air, would be the medium for pressure waves from the underground explosion, which would wrench a structure from below. The bomb was known as Tallboy. Tallboy required release from high altitude, to provide for its acceleration in a trans-sonic fall. It was being developed in three versions: Small, Medium and Large.*

Since Tallboy's effect relied upon propinquity, means had to be found of placing it exactly. In part this was answered by a remarkable device known as the Stabilizing Automatic Bomb Sight (SABS), a hand-built combination of precision optical instrument and calculator which was mounted on a platform in the Lancaster's nose. In practised hands SABS could deliver a bomb to within twenty or thirty yards from 20,000 feet, provided that the bomb aimer held the aiming point in the sight and that accurate data for certain variables were fed into it. These included the aircraft's airspeed (which would condition a bomb's trajectory in relation to wind velocity), the aircraft's speed over the ground, the exact release height and the outside air temperature.†

SABS demanded meticulous flying, flawless navigation and bomb aiming of the highest order. 617 had been rehearsing these arts for several months, and crews could now bomb from 13,000

* Development of Tallboy L, which became known as Grand Slam, was deferred at the end of 1943. Tallboy L eventually entered use in 1945.
† Height and temperature related to air density, and hence to the path described by the bomb. Temperature readings were influenced both by heat within the aircraft and friction caused by compression of the airflow outside. Thermometers were accordingly calibrated by airspeed, and 617 navigators used a formula to calculate air temperature from readings of two thermometers.

feet with results which ranged between 35 and 122 yards.[11] The
men themselves, however, had been selected for their zeal rather
than their patience. Cheshire found them 'fed up, browned off,
ready to mutiny if group didn't put an end to the bombing practices
and give them an operation'.[12] Tallboy was not yet ready, and at
this point it is unlikely that anyone at Coningsby knew about it.*

Aside from high-level bombing there were sporadic demands
for 617 to revert to the low-level role which had first made it
famous. The squadron retained fourteen Lancasters which had
been modified to carry Upkeep. Attacks on other dams were
contemplated by Cochrane and Harris. Although welcomed by 617
as a respite from SABS training, none of these episodes culminated in
an operation. Taken with other diversions they contributed to
a sense of listlessness. During Cheshire's first week one captain
transferred to another squadron: 617's inactivity had 'got him down'.

Cheshire found that 617 'had a discipline and an attitude of mind
towards senior officers all of its own. It also had a casualty rate all
of its own . . . when I went round the command looking for
volunteers for my crew, I met with a surprising lack of enthusiasm.'
Even Jock Hill refused: 'Pathfinders, yes; anything else, yes; but
617, no.'[13] Only one former colleague rejoined him: Reginald
Petch, who had flown as his rear gunner in 76 Squadron. Others

---

* Some of the pressure to ready Tallboy derived from an anticipated need to counter
the threat of long-range bombardment by Germany's emerging V-weapons. In July 1943
Harris had gathered his group commanders to report signs that Germany was developing
a ballistic missile. The A4 (= V-2) rocket was being built and tested at Peenemünde, on
the Baltic coast. Since 1942 work had also been in progress on the V-1 flying-bomb. For
a time intelligence reports about V-1 and V-2 were confused and conflated, but by late
August it was realized that two different weapons were under test. Development of the
V-weapons had been set back by a heavy raid on Peenemünde in August, but the threat
remained.
  There is no sign that Harris saw precision bombing with Tallboy as a substitute for
area attacks. He may, however, have seen it as a weapon which could *assist* the policy of
area bombing by removing the need to divert main-force aircraft to specialized targets.
Tallboy was seen as a means of attacking large bunker sites, once it became apparent that
they were connected with the V-weapon programme, and in July 1944 this prompted
Harris to call for the accelerated development of Tallboy Large. Writing to ACM Sir
Wilfred Freeman at MAP he said: 'Needless to say the matter is urgent, for as soon as
we can obtain this really "killing weapon" the sooner we can remove the threat to
London [i.e. from V-weapons], and so be free to get on with bombing targets of a more
profitable nature.'

were recruited. Pat Kelly of 49 Squadron, smallish, slim, with a large sense of humour,[14] became his navigator. Fg Off. Colin Keith Astbury, a lively Australian bomb-aimer, known as 'Aspro', was recruited from a Conversion unit at Winthorpe where he was instructing following a tour with 49 Squadron. Before he left, an air gunner called Wilfrid Bickley, a friendly Devonshire man with an infectious laugh and two tours behind him, jokingly told Astbury that if they were looking for anyone else he'd be available. Three days later Bickley was sent for and joined them as front gunner. Together they rehearsed on a near-daily basis, dropping practice bombs at the ranges at Epperstone and Wainfleet, and live weapons at Braid Fell.* Within a fortnight they achieved 85 yards error from 21,000 feet.

Laden with wine, fruit and several civilian passengers, the ten Lancasters which had paused in north Africa took off for England on 17 November. Only nine reached Coningsby; the tenth crashed into the sea off Portugal. The returned crews eyed their new leader afresh. Calmly spoken, a little gaunt, pensive but with a ready smile, he asked penetrating questions about what had gone wrong at Anthéor.

Flt Lt Bob Hay, Martin's bomb-aimer and 617's bombing leader, found that only four crews had identified and bombed the viaduct. Hay adduced several reasons for their failure: the edge of the target map fell awkwardly – an inconvenient break meant juggling maps in the target area; the hilly surroundings introduced difficulties, while similarities between adjacent bays on the coast had not been pointed out beforehand. The briefing itself had been hasty.[15] Cheshire thought that crews needed at least a day to study the route and target: 'I feel that any of the errors of bombing are chiefly attributable to the difficulty in picking out the aiming point.'[16] This touched the root of an issue to which no one seems to have given much thought. Training had concentrated on SABS technique, which required 'a bombing run that started twenty-five miles short

* Braid Fell, near Stranraer, was a building target operated under the auspices of the Ministry of Home Security to register the effects of bomb types upon structures and gather data for bomb development.

of the target and carried on steady as a rock, neither five feet up nor down, neither half a knot faster or slower'.[17] Maintaining such composure in battle would be demanding. In Cheshire's judgement, however, the main difference between rehearsal and battle was not to do with defences, but rather that on a bombing range the aiming point was distinct, whereas in combat it was usually obscure. Their task was to overcome 'the inherent obscurity of all aiming points and convert them into something as glaring as a practice target'.

Events would prove him right, although for the time being there were few events. As autumn turned to winter, 617 plugged away in its routine of training.[18] Tension rose once or twice when an operation was ordered, only to subside again as it was cancelled.[19] When poor weather grounded them Cheshire sometimes donned his greatcoat, turned up the collar and tramped the edge of the aerodrome, deep in thought.

December brought pelting squalls and hints of change; 8 December was a Wednesday, and on that morning Harris alerted his group commanders to intelligence that sites in northern France, henceforth to be known by the code name 'Crossbow,' were being prepared for the launching of long-range rockets or pilotless aircraft. Bomber Command would soon attack them.[20] Also on that Wednesday, Gp Capt. P. C. Pickard, the station commander of RAF Sculthorpe, home to Mosquitoes of No. 140 Wing of the 2nd Tactical Air Force, confirmed that he would visit Cheshire next day.[21] And in Coningsby's operations room a signal ordered the detachment of four crews to Tempsford for 'special duties'.

Tempsford lies before the Great North Road between Biggleswade and St Neots. In 1943 it was home to two squadrons which flew in support of SOE and the French Resistance. The four Lancasters departed at 11.00 next morning. Pickard arrived an hour later, and it has been conjectured that he came to advise on the impending operations for SOE.[22] Cheshire, however, had been told nothing about the special duties, and the signs are that Pickard came to discuss something else. Their conversation resumed on the following day, when Cheshire and Martin took a Lancaster for the twenty-minute hop across the Wash to Sculthorpe.

What were they talking about? Possibly two things. One was a scheme to drop presents of food and clothes into the compounds of Stalag Luft 3 – Christopher's camp, near Sagan in Poland – on Christmas morning. Christopher was ever in his thoughts, and his plan was for three Lancasters to fly out in darkness, arriving at dawn, and for Pickard's Mosquitoes to escort them home. The idea was dropped when it was pointed out that German guards would be unable to differentiate between containers of food and weapons.

The other issue then in Cheshire's mind was bombing accuracy. November's practice results had been only moderate and, as his comment about Anthéor shows, he had already begun to ask how an aiming point could be made distinct at night. The answer which emerged later was to denote the aiming point with a pyrotechnic marker, delivered point-blank from low level. Such marking called for a fast and agile aircraft, and in March 1944 two Mosquitoes were loaned to the squadron for the purpose. This runs ahead, but Pickard's wing flew Mosquito fighter-bombers, and it is possible that the discussions about bringing Christmas cheer to Stalag Luft 3 led to the germination of another idea. Nine days later Cheshire again flew to Sculthorpe, and on this occasion there is no doubt that he was fact-finding about the Mosquito. During the afternoon Pickard took him up in one.

Conventional marking was soon tested. On Monday 13 December Cochrane alerted Cheshire to forthcoming attacks on Crossbow sites in the Pas-de-Calais. Their first target would be a V-1 launch site at Flixecourt. After four weeks of training the prospect of action lifted spirits. Cheshire's first operational briefing intrigued them. He spoke calmly, almost conversationally, but yet was concise, factual and arresting. He was also inclusive, encouraging crews to put questions, express doubts and suggest amendments.

Two aspects of the raid lay outside their control. One was marking, which was to be provided by PFF Mosquitoes using Oboe to lay target indicators. The other was the weather. Frosty days condensed into foggy nights, and twice running the squadron chafed as the operation was postponed. But on the 16th nine crews took to the air at dusk, each Lancaster laden with one 12,000 lb bomb.[23]

When they returned soon after eight o'clock* Cochrane was waiting. First accounts seemed promising, but the detailed report was less encouraging. The PFF markers had missed the target by about 350 yards. Hence, while 617's bombs had fallen accurately around the point at which they had been aimed,[24] they had also fallen wide.[25] The Mosquito markers were nevertheless rather pleased with themselves, thinking their work to have been 'very accurate'.[26] By any conventional standard it was – a 350 yard error on an urban target would have been excellent. And here was the issue: if 617 exceeded the accuracy of those who marked for it, then their exactitude would count for nothing.

Flixecourt reinforced Cheshire's suspicion that Oboe marking would be too imprecise and mechanistic for 617's purposes. He was also unhappy about the target indicator. This was a standard cascading TI – a 250 lb bomb, which had been fused to burst on the ground (such TIs were often fused to burst in the air) and dissolve into a shower of candles, visible from above as semi-clustered crumbs of fire. The fires were evanescent, so relays of back-up markers were needed to sustain the aiming point. The result was much smoke, which obscured the view of crews who bombed late in the attack. Cheshire concluded that a more densely focused, longer-burning indicator would be better. What was needed, he told Cochrane, was a source of light, accurately placed, incapable of confusion with its own background, visible at considerable range and compact.

Cochrane pondered. Marking was the Pathfinders' business, and AVM Bennett would doubtless say that in such matters 8 Group knew best. Nonetheless, Cochrane was beginning to echo Cheshire's views. A week before Christmas he wrote to Harris about prospects for an attack on the Rothensee ship lift: a target on which the two men had long had their eye.[27] Success would demand a well-placed marker. Balloons and light flak would probably preclude marking from low level – which presumably implies that this was something now being talked about. 617 was also under strength. 'The supply of tour-expired crews,' he told Harris, 'has

---

* They were lucky to be back so early. This was 'Black Thursday', a night when low cloud prevented many main-force crews from regaining their home airfields. Thirty aircraft crashed or were abandoned on return, with the loss of some 154 lives.

not come up to expectations.' Cochrane proposed to draft in six more who had completed one tour or part of a second. Winter weather would not favour their training, but experience at Braid Fell and the concentration recently achieved at Flixecourt – albeit in the wrong place – suggested that an attack on Rothensee could succeed 'provided that the marking problem can be solved'.[28]

The marking problem. With so few SABS-trained crews available, and so many weeks required to train new ones, Cheshire could ill afford losses. On the first night of the December moon period, the four Lancasters at Tempsford had been dispatched to drop arms canisters to the French Resistance near Boulogne. Their crews had received no training for the work, and while going down low to look for pinpoints two of them were shot down. In the icy way which those who knew him recognized for anger, Cheshire demanded explanations. However, far from securing the return of the remaining crews, he was promptly ordered to supply two more.

On the night of 20/21 December eight of 617's home echelon flew to attack an armaments works near Liège. The marking method was the same as at Flixecourt, and the results no better. Only one Oboe Mosquito marked; the TI fell a quarter of a mile wide,[29] although the error turned out to be irrelevant because none of 617's bomb-aimers could see it anyway. After twenty-five minutes' fruitless searching Cheshire ordered his crews home. On the way back a crew was lost.[*] Cheshire wrote in his log book 'PFF failed again. Bombs brought back.'

Two nights later they tried and failed again. The target this time was a Crossbow site at Fréval, and there was to be a variation in the marking, with backing-up midway through the attack.[30] However, although the PFF Mosquitoes dropped yellow route markers and laid two red TIs on the target itself, 617's ten Lancasters never found their objective. The Mosquito markers loitered for nearly half an hour, wondering whether they were in the right place, and then went home.

Cheshire was frustrated. The list of problems seemed to lengthen

---

[*] The Lancaster of Flt Lt Geoffrey Rice DFC, one of the original members of the squadron and a veteran of the Dams Raid, was shot down by a nightfighter.

by the day. 8 Group's marking was unreliable. Perhaps they should lay markers for themselves – but if so, how? If they used SABS, then the marking attack would require prior illumination of the target area: how was this to be provided? Next, if crews aimed at the marker, what would happen if the marker were snuffed out by a bomb or hidden by smoke? Re-marking using SABS would take time, interrupt the attack and so add to dangers from awakened defences. And if a marker fell in the wrong place, how, from high level, would it be cancelled?

Perhaps to console himself, on 23 December Cheshire flew to visit old friends at Marston Moor. This may have been the occasion when he flew so low across the airfield that the station commander afterwards delivered a lecture on the foolhardiness of the display they had witnessed.

Christmas Eve was clear, with frost sparkling on the ground, ice in the ditches and the hollow tension of a standby. On Christmas Day, too, the mood was subdued. There was a rugby match in the afternoon and a dinner in the evening, but Bomber Command in wartime took no account of festivals and holidays. The war went on, and on Boxing Day HQ 5 Group was instructed on two points: the projected attack on the Rothensee ship lift would not now take place until March or April; and there would be a conference at High Wycombe early in January at which 'the policy of marking targets for No. 617 Squadron will be discussed'.[31]

Two days after Christmas Cheshire went on leave – his first days with Constance since early November. They went first to Thorpe Hall, near Louth, as guests of Geoffrey Harmsworth, and then to Grey Walls for New Year. In his absence there was an outburst of delirium. Everest was modelled with mess furniture, and those who conquered it left imprints of their feet, first dipped in jelly, on the ceiling.

Gp Capt. Evans Evans, Coningsby's station commander, jovially known around 5 Group as 'Evans squared', was meanwhile drafting a proposal for marking with SABS from 8,000 feet by the light of parachute flares released from a higher altitude by Pathfinder aircraft. The TIs aimed with SABS would be of three different colours. A controller would indicate by VHF radio which should be attacked.

A contingent of Mosquito fighter-bombers should be available to harry searchlights with cannon, and carry back-up TIs. Evans Evans explained that although Cheshire was on leave, the ideas in the paper were essentially his.[32] Certainly, new initiative was needed. On the following evening ten Lancasters returned to Flixecourt, and yet again the marking was imprecise.

New Year's Eve was marked by a strangely sedate party, and as 1943 turned to 1944 they toasted the formation of a new institution, 54 Base, consisting of Coningsby (the parent), and Woodhall Spa and Metheringham (the satellites), all whitened by new snow. Cheshire returned from leave, and on 4 January Evans Evans flew with him to Fréval, to see the problems for himself. Yet another variation was to be tried: running in low from an approach marker★ one PFF Mosquito would drop a red TI, to burst on impact, while two other Mosquitoes would drop air-bursting TIs with green and red candles which would cascade to ground.[33] In the event, Oboe was impeded by poor signals, there was an unexpectedly high tailwind, and when the first marker fell soon after seven o'clock in the evening it landed more than three miles from the target. Another was some 1,300 yards wide.[34] Evans Evans took the point.

Anthéor was still on 617's target list, and next day Cochrane drafted a memorandum about prerequisites for its destruction. This was a prescient document, which in key respects both anticipated the methodology which Cheshire successfully evolved in the following months, and demonstrates that much of the theoretical thinking had already taken place. Cochrane stressed a bomb-aimer's need to fix his eye on a single point during the run-up. At night, this meant a point of light. If Anthéor was attacked again,

it would have to be organized in advance and suitable means devised for placing a marker attached to a parachute which could be dropped from a very low height by an aircraft such as Mosquito. This problem also applies to other small targets where precision bombing is required . . . Given such a marker I have little doubt that No. 617 could, in conditions of an undisturbed bombing run, reproduce the pattern which they have consistently obtained in practice.

★ Such a marker, usually laid ten miles from a target, was common to most attacks in this period.

The problems, Cochrane assured Harris, could be solved 'if the necessary experimental work is taken in hand'.[35] The analysis was Cheshire's.

For the next few days there were no operations. Coningsby was overcrowded, and it was thought that security would be better served if 617 was on an airfield of its own.[36] The decision had therefore been taken to move the squadron to nearby Woodhall Spa. The aircraft were ferried across on 8 and 9 January, a flight of ten minutes and scarcely many more feet, so low was the ritual beat up* upon their going.

Woodhall Spa's ample villas, avenues and thickets of rhododendrons reminded John Betjeman of a fragment of Bournemouth stranded in Lincolnshire. Intended as a cosmopolitan spa, Woodhall feels unfinished, awaiting a prosperity that never came. South of the town lies the airfield, a typical wartime triangle of runways, some thirty concrete loop dispersal points, two corrugated-iron hangars, and a clump of temporary brick huts. Domestic sites were dispersed in surrounding countryside, which meant much cycling back and forth. Officers lived in the Petwood, a requisitioned mock-Tudor hotel set amid gracious gardens on Woodhall's northern edge.

Amenities were modest. Pubs like the Bluebell, in those days a one-room alehouse, stood near by, but a proper night out meant a fifteen-mile bus journey to Boston, where aircrew could be sure of music and dancing at the Gliderdrome until 11 p.m., Monday to Saturday. For movie-goers there was Woodhall's Kinema in the Woods or, as aircrew knew it, 'The Flicks in the Sticks', a rustic wooden picture-house which had started life as a cricket pavilion. Such gentle incongruities are still cherished by those who knew them then. When Cheshire was made a life peer in 1991, it was the name of Woodhall that he took.

The conference on marking policy convened at High Wycombe on the following Tuesday, 18 January. Air Marshal Saundby, Air Vice-Marshals Oxland and Bennett,† Gp Capt. Marwood Elton,‡

---

* RAF jargon for illicit or ultra-low flying over something or someone.
† AOC 8 (PFF) Group.
‡ Group Captain (Plans), HQ Bomber Command.

Cochrane and Cheshire were present, and their recorded purpose was to consider means of delivering an attack from high level on the Rothensee ship lift using Tallboy.[37] Such an attack, the meeting noted, would require the coordination of the forces to be employed – and, it might have been added, the cooperation of their commanders – both in training and for the operation itself.

The plan they agreed provided for location of the target by 8 Group aircraft using Oboe and H2S and plain illumination by a succession of flares. When the target was in sight, PFF would drop a line of markers across it, and the controller would use VHF radio to guide bombing at right angles to this line. This was a variation on the PFF's customary method of ground marking by sight. It was known as Newhaven, and the draft minutes record that 5 Group's representatives finally agreed that Newhaven (modified) stood the best chance of success. The minutes also say that Bennett promised the cooperation of 8 Group in prior training, 'provided this did not interfere with current operations.'

So much for the official record. Behind it lay a confrontation. Inevitably, much of the meeting centred on a review of 617's recent experience of PFF Crossbow marking. Cochrane explained that 8 Group's marking had been inadequate for 617's purposes, and introduced Cheshire's view that only low-level marking would provide the necessary precision. Bennett reached with hauteur. He did not believe that 617's results in practice could be so good as was claimed, and since he disputed them on grounds of ballistic impossibility it was obvious that the exactitude in marking which they demanded was unnecessary. Even if it was necessary, an approach at low level was not the way to do it. He knew what the view from an aircraft flying low and fast at night was like: the ground would flash past, and map-reading was impossible because everything would happen too quickly. It was also suicidally dangerous.

That was the technical argument. Other factors influenced Bennett's thinking. In contrast to his own group, which got on with the job with a calm and diligent professionalism, he saw 5 Group under Cochrane as unhealthily preoccupied with showmanship. He had a poor opinion of operations (like the Dams Raid) which required elaborate rehearsals that led to single performances, and he disliked the extravagant publicity which attended them. His own operational experience within the war stood in contrast to Cochrane's lack of it, while he regarded Cheshire's claims of bombing accuracy as 'naive and innocent'. As Harris remarked, Bennett 'could not suffer fools gladly, and by his own high standards there were many fools'.[38]

Cheshire was unabashed. In fact, he left the meeting feeling rather cheerful.

Bennett didn't believe in low-level flying at night. When it came to working out a means of marking for Tallboy, we had a meeting at Bomber Command . . . Bennett said that it was totally impossible to mark to an accuracy of 20 yards, and when we suggested that this should be done at low level he said that that kind of flying by night time was not practical and that he was not prepared to order his pilots to do it. So for the second time he did me a good turn, for the onus was then thrown on us.[39]

For his part, Bennett believed that he had been asked to address a trivial problem, and that he had done so. While privately derisive of 5 Group's wild ideas, his own certainties left him in no doubt that there was nothing more to say.

But there was. For one thing the meeting had ranged across a number of issues to do with marking, and new ideas had arisen. Among them was a suggestion from Marwood Elton that rocket projectiles fired from Mosquitoes might be used for target marking: a proposal which led to five months of research and experiment. For another, issues which had appeared settled were immediately reopened when the draft minutes began to circulate.

On 20 January a revised minute redefined 'Newhaven Modified' as involving the dropping of a PFF spotfire as a guide to the target's neighbourhood; flare illumination by H2S aircraft; and then a stick of four spotfires, now to be aimed visually by 617 using SABS. It was also suggested that a trial of this method against a Crossbow target would provide 'valuable data'.[40]

Next day Cochrane made more amendments, and suggested a radical alternative: marking by Mosquitoes from low level, which would require 'measures . . . to overcome the bounce of the target indicator on striking the ground'. He also recommended experiment with Highball, a smaller version of Upkeep intended for use against capital ships and adapted to contain an incendiary compound which would burn in water or on land. Cochrane's idea appears to have been to mark the ship lift by delivering a Highball marker along the canal. What Bennett made of this suggestion one hardly dares think; its interest here rests in the fact that Cochrane put it forward as an *alternative* to low-level marking, which in his mind had emerged as something to be entertained.[41]

On one point alone, it seems, was there accord between Cochrane and Bennett: the cascading type of marker which PFF had used hitherto was accepted as being too diffuse for 617's purposes. Henceforth they would adopt a more concentrated light source – a spotfire.

Of Woodhall and Cheshire, meanwhile, we catch kaleidoscopic glimpses. On 6 January, the arrival of a new captain – Hubert Knilans, an American from Wisconsin, now posted in from 619 Squadron, with fifty-three trips completed and a recent DSO. On the 7th and 8th Cheshire is in London. On the 9th, he is practising low-level bombing. Very low. 'Such a tall line of chimneys for making bricks . . . Getting so close. Closer . . . Not over the top, but in between, with a last-minute dip of the wing to slip through the gap.'[42] On the 10th, back to altitude for practice with SABS at Wainfleet – average error 9 yards. On the 16th, a frosty Sunday, the squadron's crew average falls to 72.5 yards.

A parcel arrives from Sqn Ldr Pat Moyna of Bomber Command's film unit. It contains three reels of priceless 16 mm Kodachrome, which it would be inadvisable to use 'except in sunny conditions'. Moyna hopes to meet Cheshire soon, 'and should you require any cooperation . . . please do not hesitate to get in touch with me'.[43] Cheshire does so. When Moyna appears later in the week he is told: 'He's flying now. He's always flying.' An hour later Moyna feels a tap on his shoulder, and turns to face Cheshire's irresistible smile. Cheshire is obviously busy, but he takes the time to walk Moyna round the airfield to explain what he wants: a filmed record of the squadron's evolving work. For some weeks, Moyna and his assistant become *de facto* members of the squadron.

The journalist Martha Gellhorn arrives, her impressions as colour to the monochrome of official records. By day trucks clank past, trailing bomb trolleys 'like great rust-coloured sausages'. Towards dusk the aircrews seem top-heavy in Mae Wests and jackets, their expressions 'tight and concentrated'. Navigation lights of their departing aircraft resemble 'slow-moving stars'. At debriefing she remarks lines marked under boys' eyes, and the murmur of low voices. Woodhall is a place where the visitor feels intrusive.

Cheshire's in-tray is piled with letters, forms and files. He works through them. More interested in results than formalities, he often bypasses official procedures and writes direct to aircraft companies and manufacturers of special equipment. The chamois leathers used for polishing perspex, for instance, have been obtained by his personal contact with the suppliers.[44]

On the 19th comes an order to prepare for another dams raid. The targets are in Italy: the Turano, the Salto and possibly the Bissorte.[45] Woodhall is electrified.

They rehearsed with Upkeep for a week. The plan called for the pre-positioning of the Lancasters in north Africa, and (in one case at least) a dive attack down to the 60 feet from which Upkeep had to be released. An area corresponding with the reservoir was marked out on the airfield, and in following days Lancasters plummeted out of the sky and roared across the aerodrome, their heights and speeds being checked by theodolite and stopwatch. Cheshire practised daily, on one occasion taking Moyna aloft for filming.

They also trained over the coast, where there was tragedy. Diving in from the Wash, Flt Lt O'Shaughnessy misjudged the pull-up over the shore. His Lancaster crashed on to Snettisham beach and caught fire. O'Shaughnessy and another crew member were killed.[46] Low flying also meant bird strikes: on one night three aircraft reported them. A gull or pheasant struck at several hundred miles an hour has much the same effect as a small boulder. A crew member's face was lacerated by shattered Plexiglas.

In the midst of the Upkeep training a Crossbow attack was ordered. The technique, 'Newhaven Modified', broadly followed the plan in the revised minutes of the meeting at High Wycombe. Three PFF Oboe Mosquitoes would drop markers to indicate the target's neighbourhood. Next, parachute flares would be released by 617's Lancasters, and by their light Cheshire would mark the aiming point with SABS from 8,000 feet, laying a stick of four ruby spotfires. Cheshire would then guide the bombing by VHF radio.[47] The target was a V-1 site at Hallencourt. The results seemed promising. The spotfires fell close enough for Cheshire to steer the bombing to inflict 'considerable damage'.[48]

After three more days the Italian dams raid was cancelled, and Newhaven Modified was repeated, this time at Fréval, a site which had previously eluded them.[49] Briefing was intensive, the crews being divided by profession for sectional instruction. Alongside Newhaven Modified something else was to be attempted.

Two weeks earlier it had been pointed out that the equipment of an Air Defence of Great Britain station — radar — could home an aircraft to within half a mile of any position within its range. Range would vary according to height, but a bomber at 20,000 feet could be tracked by a Type 16 radar on Beachy Head almost to Paris. V-weapon sites in northern France lay well inside this distance, and ADGB might in theory help a formation which attacked them, for instance by warning of the approach of night-fighters.[50] Such control, commonplace today, had never been tried. On this night they would test it.

Over the target they met a problem: there was much cloud, and the cloud base lay between 4,000 and 6,000 feet. Marking from above the cloud was not possible, while marking from below was hardly easier because the flares were drifting fast in a high wind and had spread. Nevertheless, with Martin's help the spotfires were laid from low level. 617's bombs followed, and reconnaissance on the following day revealed a cluster of seven satisfyingly large craters around the target.

In his log book Cheshire wrote 'L. L. marking. Very high wind. Successful with help of Micky.'[51] He was pleased, and for several reasons. In the first place the cloud had legitimized the experiment for which he and Martin had been yearning. Although Cochrane sympathized with their case for low-level marking, he had not previously allowed it. Fréval should have been marked with SABS from around 8,000 feet. To have done otherwise in good visibility would have been a breach of discipline, but departing from orders to overcome adverse conditions was initiative. And contrary to Bennett's gloomy prediction, it had worked. Bennett had imagined them trying to approach at low level, whereas the technique they had been quietly exploring in training used a shallow dive.

Cheshire was also heartened by the help from the Type 16 staff on Beachy Head. At the least, this lessened the threat from nightfighters. More fundamentally, on two successive operations 617 had both illuminated and marked the aiming point themselves. 8 Group's Oboe Mosquitoes had been needed only to lay TIs as a guide to the targets' neighbourhoods. So peripheral had they become that Cheshire was beginning to wonder if they were needed at all. Little by little he had been learning to shape 617's attacks while they were in progress. PFF's involvement had initially interfered with this, as 8 Group's Oboe Mosquitoes came and went like automata, as often as not scattering their lights and fires in the wrong places.

Our main point was that every attack should be coordinated and led by somebody so that somebody in charge could adapt himself, and the attack, to meet the circumstances. [The] point about Bomber Command was that everything was pre-set. You just had to go . . . everything had to be right. You couldn't possibly vary it. Well, obviously that's wrong. And it wasn't necessary . . . the whole of our technique was based on flexibility. Oboe generally is a very fine thing, but for our type of marking USELESS.[52]

While Cheshire himself was gaining confidence, the regime of incessant training interspersed with (in the main) inconclusive Crossbow sorties had led to mounting discontent among the crews. At the end of January Grp Capt. Peter Johnson, Woodhall Spa's station commander, warned Evans Evans:

Frankly I am unhappy about 617 Sqn and their commanding officer feels much more strongly than that. Several members of the squadron are applying for posting and others are considering it, which state of affairs is not conducive either to efficiency or discipline. They feel they are not being fully used, that they have given up their chances of advancement and useful work elsewhere . . .

Johnson stressed the need for operations which are 'difficult and important' where 'really high crew standard is vitally necessary' and which would 'materially affect the course of the war'. Without them, there could be a 'severe deterioration of morale and discipline'. Johnson asked if any Upkeep targets could be arranged during the forthcoming moon period. Would it be possible to apply recent tactics to other targets, deeper in enemy territory? The significance of recent targets was doubted − 'none of us here know anything about them at all' − and it was necessary to convince the crews 'that they are really vital'. Johnson concluded: 'at present everybody, especially the squadron commander and including I'm afraid myself feel we have tremendous possibilities but are not getting anywhere while time is slipping away from us'.[53]

Evans Evans relayed these concerns to 5 Group in a letter of which he pointedly said he would keep no copy. Evans said that although 617 was the most efficient bombing squadron in the command, its members felt that they could as well be at an OTU. Morale would be improved by more work on special targets. Perhaps Cochrane would give a talk to the squadron to explain the importance of its work? Perhaps, too, some Upkeep training might be allowed, to enable the squadron to retain its technique.[54]

Were things so bad? In fact the squadron *had* engaged in recent Upkeep training, and on the day that Evans Evans warned of sinking morale Cheshire told Douglas Baxter: 'I am now having the time of my life. Cost me £40 a month, but it's worth it.'[55] (It had indeed 'cost him': not only had he taken a drop in pay, but the Air Ministry's accounts department had recently noticed that although he had reverted to the rank of wing commander on 25 October 1943, he had continued to receive a group captain's pay until the end of November, and would he please therefore refund the overpayment of £25 5s. 8d.[56])

Whether by coincidence or as a result of Evans Evans's appeal, the following week saw developments which marked a turning point. On 2 February Cheshire summarized the results of their trials with red spotfires. They had found that the spotfires were not so bright as to obscure the sighting mark in the bombsight, they were small enough to fit the sighting point, their burning time of 15–20 minutes was adequate; and they did not sink into marshy ground. The main drawbacks were that in still air a spotfire could be obscured by its own smoke, and it was also liable to eclipse by bomb bursts.[57] But overall, it looked good. Next day Bomber Command allocated more Crossbow targets for bombing experiments by 617,[58] and Barnes Wallis – as if in answer to Johnson's plea – informed the Air Ministry of other dams which were likely to be vulnerable to Upkeep.*[59] Tallboy was still awaited, and not expected before March.[60]

On 7 February there was a bombing exercise, the significance of which became clear when the squadron was ordered to stand by for an operation.[61] The target was to be an aero-engine plant in Limoges which produced motors for the giant Me 323 transport aircraft. The factory stood in a built-up area and employed five hundred workers. Orders for the operation to proceed arrived next morning, and at 12.30 Cochrane telephoned Cheshire to warn him that safety of the workforce was a factor.†

They planned carefully. The force would consist of twelve Lancasters, two (flown by Cheshire and Martin) for marking, five bearing 12,000 lb HC bombs and the other five with loads of 1,000 lb bombs. The outward route ran via Beachy Head to Cabourg (under the watchful eye of their friends in ADGB) and thence direct to Limoges. Martin would drop a datum marker 25 miles north-east of the town, which the other bombers would orbit while marking proceeded. The factory was thought to be undefended, so marking would be from point-blank range using 30 lb incendiaries followed by red spotfires. The ten Lancasters would then be called in to bomb individually. Moyna would fly with Cheshire to film the raid, and during the day Cheshire's aircraft became festooned with cables, mountings and mirrors for the convenience of Moyna's cine cameras.

On arrival Cheshire made three low passes over the factory, his gunners firing into the air to warn the night shift. 'We were low, very low,' recalled Moyna. 'I'd never before had the feeling of having the target brought right under my nose, almost to pose for the cameras. Almost scraped the factory roof.' Then came the real

* Including the Tirso Dam, in Sardinia.
† Several authorities have reported Churchill's insistence that the bombing of Limoges should cost no French lives. In 1954 Cochrane disputed this.

marking approach, which was difficult because the factory stood in a valley and the run had to be made in a curve to avoid a pair of water towers and a chimney. Cheshire and Astbury could thus see little of the target until the final seconds. The incendiary markers went down at five minutes to midnight, Moyna filming their glittering bursts. Then the spotfire. Martin inspected the work and found it accurate. The waiting Lancasters were summoned one by one. Four of the five 12,000 lb bombs fell directly into the factory, each creating a fountain of debris. The fifth fell in the river, apparently because the spotfire became obscured by smoke. Martin re-marked, and four sticks of 1,000 lb bombs straddled it.

Limoges was a triumph. Bomber Command's night-raid report spoke of the 'extraordinary effect' of the 12,000 lb bombs and the 'crippling damage' caused. Air photographs obtained on 26 February showed that nearly half of the forty-eight bays of the machine shops had been completely destroyed, three were damaged and seventeen more had suffered roof displacement. The boiler and transformer houses were also damaged. Productive work at the factory came to an end save for the manufacture of certain components in smaller buildings.[62] And there had been no loss of life.

Portal sent his 'warmest congratulations'. Moyna's dramatic film was released for the newsreels,* and Bomber Command issued a list of targets for demolition by 617.[63] They included two more Crossbow sites, the John Cockerill works at Liège, an aero-engine factory at Woippy and the Michelin plant at Clermont-Ferrand. And Anthéor.

Limoges heralded a succession of pinpoint assaults on industrial targets. An aircraft factory at Albert was destroyed on 2 March. On the 10th they demolished a factory manufacturing components for gear boxes at St-Etienne-la-Ricamerie. On 16 March it was the Michelin works at Clermont-Ferrand. Three days later the Powderie Nationale at Bergerac vanished in a fifteen-second flash which lit up the Dordogne. On the following evening another

---

* The famous sequence of Cheshire's markers bursting on the factory roof had been filmed by a ventrally mounted mirror camera.

explosives works was bombed at Angoulême. Results were not always so good. Several operations were aborted on account of poor weather, and two attacks were disappointing. Overall, however, 617 had found its stride and its crews liked their employment. Unlike area bombing, 'you could see what you had done, and you knew why'.[64]

In the main, marking continued to rely upon SABS, but after Limoges Cheshire stepped up his campaign for low-level marking. Meanwhile, there were variations and experiments, and from mid-March they were often supported by aircraft from 106 Squadron which provided flare light as well as adding to the weight of bombs. More help was provided by their new allies at RAF Beachy Head, and Pat Moyna continued to chronicle 617's achievements on film. Before all this, however, four days after Limoges, they had returned to Anthéor.

Orders for 617's third attack on the Anthéor viaduct came through on the morning of 12 February.[65] Mindful of his earlier criticisms, Cheshire gave a preliminary briefing at noon. Ford, scene of his contented summers in the 1930s, was to be their advanced base, and in mid-afternoon they flew down to Sussex. A full briefing was given in early evening at which the marking plan was explained. This was an adaptation of the method they had used at Fréval – that is, Cheshire, with Martin as his deputy, would use SABS to lay a row of spotfires from 5,500 feet. The aircraft were operating close to the limit of their range, and since this would limit their tactical freedom Cheshire had requested that they continue to Sardinia, to ease pressure on fuel. Higher authority, however, had ruled this out. Towards ten o'clock the Lancasters began to leave.

At the target Cheshire and Martin found that they could see nothing of the viaduct from above 3,000 feet, and little other than light flak below. Disconcertingly, there was also heavy flak at unforeseen strength. Since SABS marking required a long unswerving approach these were not favourable conditions.

In a sky 'lit up like daylight'[66] Cheshire made the first run. Astbury could see little against the searchlights, and in the final minutes the opposition became so savage that Cheshire broke away. A run by Martin ended likewise. They changed tactics. In an effort to split the defences, Martin flew a mile or so out to sea while Cheshire made an approach. Again he was defeated.

The main force had now been loitering for the best part of half an hour. Time and fuel were running short, the mood was uneasy. Martin and Cheshire reversed roles, Cheshire now being the decoy. Martin found himself inland at about 4,000 feet, well placed for a run out of the hills and down the valley. The viaduct would be in silhouette against the sea, while his aircraft might merge into the dark background. Throttling back for stealth he followed the contours downwards. Cheshire, however, seems to have been too far away to attract the gunners, and as Martin drew closer the flak turned on him. Five hundred yards short Martin pushed the throttles forward to accelerate. A 20 mm shell punched through the nose. Ammunition in the front turret exploded. As Martin nursed the aircraft across the target and out over the Mediterranean, there were urgent voices in his headphones. The flight engineer was injured, the Lancaster was damaged and Bob Hay, the bomb-aimer, was silent. The markers were still aboard.

Shaken, Cheshire confronted the defences for a third time. Eventually he and his crew managed to place a row of spotfires within a hundred yards of the viaduct. Knowing that in the circumstances this was as good as they would get, he instructed the main force to make allowance and bomb accordingly. Several bombs fell within yards of the viaduct but none struck it. It had all been to no avail. At 01.35 Cheshire ordered them home.

While the main force headed north in worsening weather, Martin set course for Corsica. Flak and exploding ammunition had harmed the controls, cut wiring and punctured the hydraulics. Looking out, they saw trailing smoke. Fire was assumed, until it was realized that the 'smoke' was a mist raised from the sea by their propellors. They were that low.

The radio still worked. Corsica advised them to make for Cagliari, in Sardinia, where facilities were better. They signalled base in England, to report that they were still flying. Back in Morse came 'Kia ora'. Good luck.[67] Brakeless, they landed safely. But Bob Hay was dead.

At Ford there were complaints. There had been no target photos, they had been issued with an unsuitable type of flare, petrol had been insufficient to permit a change of tactics and intelligence briefing had underestimated the defences. Nor had misfortune finished with them. Ford was shrouded in cloud, and when Sqn Ldr Suggitt, one of the squadron's flight commanders, took off into the grey morning to return to Woodhall a misjudgement caused him to crash atop Waltham Down. The Lancaster burned.

Tom Lloyd, Woodhall's intelligence officer, and Flt Sgt John Pulford, Gibson's flight engineer on the Dams Raid, were among the dead. Suggitt had been dragged alive from the wreckage by a farmer but later he too died. Cheshire wrote to Lloyd's wife. Her husband's job had been on the ground; she had had no reason to fear his death. She replied in a letter that might have been in the script of *The Way to the Stars*. 'I would so much like to tell you how your letter has helped me; it was very kind of you to write, when I know how busy you are – I know the expression "perfect husband" has often been used, but Tommie was perfect – It comforts me to know he died with his boys.'[68] Except that it was a real letter.

Perhaps it was the weight of these events which lay behind the distant reception he gave to a new crew three days later. Looking spruce, they reported for interview in Cheshire's office where Fg Off. M. L. Hamilton, their captain, delivered a sharp salute. Without looking up, Cheshire said: 'Seventy yards. Come back when you can halve it'. They went off to look for a Lancaster and took Gibson's old aircraft, which Hamilton found 'clapped out'. Later, Cheshire accosted him and asked how the practice had gone. Before Hamilton could reply Cheshire told him: 'Thirty-six yards.' He already knew.[69]

Bombing accuracy was a kind of devotion. Training was incessant, and fierce peer pressure attended one's place on the squadron bombing ladder, on which everyone's averages were displayed. Bombs, Cheshire explained, were everyone's business. Air gunners did not fire at fighters – they defended bombs, just as flight engineers assisted in their carriage, navigators guided them or electricians made sure that they would release. On the day after Hamilton's arrival 5 Group's progress report noted that in training 617 was achieving average errors of 65 yards from 10,000 feet, adding that the squadron had now embarked on operations, with results 'almost as good as practice'.[70] If results were less than good, Cheshire 'could be forthright and scathing when the situation called for it'.[71]

Practice itself was not without risk. When they rehearsed marking under flares, Cheshire found his mind fixed 'not on the aiming point nor on the technique of the dive, but mainly on whether or not we were going to hit a flare – a collision that would almost certainly have been fatal'. When the method was used in action, on the other hand, the risk 'never crossed my mind'.[72] It was Cheshire's habit to fly all the time. 'If an op was cancelled I tried to take the crew up to do a little bit of night flying . . . and all the practice I possibly could in other ways with the auxiliary equipment. And I think that's axiomatic of everything in life – you've got to give it your whole heart, and keep in practice.' Or as Wilf Bickley remembers:

When there were no ops I'd sometimes be in the bar in the sergeants' mess, and there'd be a call telling me to go down to the flights at midnight or 01.00, and Leonard would take us off for low-level cross-country for several hours. That happened quite often. It was as if he couldn't sleep . . . The difference between 617 and some other squadrons was that 617 was keen on flying. They *liked* to fly, and when they went to war they knew what it was about.[73]

Demands on Cheshire's time were legion, and from one week to another he might seldom be seen. When Sgt Albert Hepworth arrived in February 1944 it was 'days and days' before he knew for certain that the slim, raincoated figure he occasionally saw prowling around the perimeter track, wearing no visible badges of rank, was in fact his CO. A salute was returned with a 'good morning' and a friendly smile.

Authority issued from this smile. He seldom raised his voice or gave an order twice, and only rarely gave direct commands once. He 'suggested' things rather than ordered them, and people did them as much because they were responding to him as a person as because an instruction had been given. With little time for himself he found endless time for others. 'He was like a welfare officer,' recalled Cochrane, 'only more natural.' His fondness for the ground

crews meant that battles were already half-won before he took off.
In briefings he inspired determination by explaining what a factory
made, what it was used for and why the war's end would be hastened
if the Germans were to be deprived of it. Outwardly he usually
seemed good-humoured, even gentle. Inside, 'there was steel'.[74]
Before raids he shut himself away for an hour or so to meditate on
what lay ahead. At other times silences signalled that his thoughts
were fixed on some problem – a condition which others knew not
to disturb. His calm was felt in battle. At dangerous moments voices
over the R/T tended to rise. When Cheshire spoke 'he could have
been boiling an egg'.[75]

> He was not shy, he was not reserved. On the other hand he was not gushing,
> alarmist or boastful. He had no side. He was cool, calm, sympathetic, he was
> impressive, he was patient with us and he was kind. He was also very learned in
> the art of bombing the enemy. But above all else to me, he was magnetic.[76]

Cheshire's pervasive influence was more remarkable for the fact
that socially he was retiring. 'He was not one of the roisterers'
crowd – he had too much to do.'[77] Occasionally he would join a
game of poker, where his deadpan manner and roguish humour
made him a dangerous adversary. But the sight of him at a party or
in a pub on a stand-down was unusual, and when he did join in
'He'd make a pint last all evening.'

His dog Simon, on the other hand, a large apricot poodle which
chewed shoes and caused havoc in his room, was very much in
evidence. Cheshire's frequent absences meant that Simon was often
left with WAAF orderlies at the Petwood, who walked him in the
grounds.

And Constance? In February she rented what Cheshire called 'a
charming little flat' in London. When he saw her locally it was
usually off the station, at Thorpe Hall, Skegness or in Lincoln. On
leaves in London they liked to frequent the Ritz, which as one friend
observed was 'Constance's natural environment'. At Woodhall few
knew her other than as someone cheerful who occasionally played
the mess piano.

A handful who came closer offer differing views. One senior
officer thought Constance 'an old cow', especially when her social

drinking went too far. Ann Shannon,* on the other hand, rather liked her, and noticed a tendency for others to mistake her American candour and democratic outlook for vulgarity. Her directness could be startling, as when she scandalized Lady Cochrane by striding up, without introduction, to launch into a risqué story. A year earlier Cheshire had found such episodes amusing; friends noticed that he was now beginning to react to them with embarrassment. But his loyalty to her remained, as, apparently, did his commitment to materialism. A puritan on the station, his Epicurean traits could still revive when he was off it. Yet to David Shannon,

> Leonard and Constance didn't look like married people at all . . . They were obviously attracted and fond of each other, and Cheshire found Constance exotic and rather intriguing, but they had nothing really in common. At that time she perfectly suited Leonard's phase of sophisticated luxury – highballs, witty banter and the Ritzy life . . . On duty she didn't see him and didn't know him. He was, off duty, the hero whose heroism was admirable, but rather remote, certainly not within her understanding.[78]

Heroism and hedonism. Constance sometimes talked of an unwritten book, to be called 'The Back of the Medal', its subject a relationship which remained uncomprehended by a wife until after the husband-hero's death.

By March David Shannon was due for rest. He had been flying operationally since June 1942. Australian politicians were keen to see the repatriation of their tour-expired aircrew, and there was pressure for Shannon's release. If he wished it, he could finish. There is poignancy in the thought of a twenty-one-year-old who could suddenly allow himself to imagine being old, or even twenty-two. Such was 617's sense of community that Shannon elected to stay.[79]

In Martin's case the relationship was different. After his return from Sardinia he went on leave. When he reappeared something had changed; his crew had been devoted to each other and Bob

* Formerly Ann Fowler, a WAAF in Intelligence Ops who married David Shannon in September 1943. At this date she was working at Dunholme Lodge. The Shannons and the Cheshires sometimes made a foursome at the White Hart at Lincoln.

Hay's death had altered that. After a few days more they split up and Martin departed.

Cheshire had relied heavily on Martin, both as a teacher and in battle. With his deputy gone, Cheshire turned more to Shannon, Munro and McCarthy, and a powerful sense of interdependence developed. Unshaded by Martin's prowess, and with more opportunities for responsibility, the senior captains flourished.* In an unspoken pact, they would finish together.

Early in March Cheshire and Woodhall's station commander, Gp Capt. Philpott, prepared a memorandum about development of the squadron's bombing. Sixty per cent of 617's bombs could now be expected to fall within 100 yards of the aiming point. However:

> The present method of marking is limited to one method. The Marker a/c is flown at 5–8,000 ft and marker is aimed by SABS MkIIA . . . This requires at least 15 min. from moment tgt is located to time marker is released. Local conditions vary, but it is exception rather than rule that marker is released before arrival of Main Force at tgt.

Ideally the main force should arrive *after* the target had been marked, proceed to bomb and depart. Loitering near a defended target was dangerous. It is interesting to notice that Bennett and Cheshire had reached opposite conclusions: Bennett dismissed low-level marking because he thought it unacceptably dangerous for those who did it; Cheshire repudiated high-level marking because its lengthy formality and risk of hiatus endangered those who waited for it. Moreover, Anthéor had suggested that the Germans were beginning to understand their method: defences would single out an individual aircraft during a marking approach, and seek both to blind it with searchlights and shoot it down.

Cheshire and Philpott arrived at three key points. First, the marker should mark the aiming point before the main force arrived. Second, alternative marking methods were needed, to give tactical freedom and allow an element of surprise. And third, they needed

---

* Shannon and McCarthy were recommended for promotion to (acting) squadron leader on 24 March, when they were placed in charge of A and C Flights. Munro was already a flight commander.

to eliminate the marker's long, steady run. Limoges had shown that all these requirements – promptitude, surprise, speed, flexibility, accuracy – could be met by marking from low level. Limoges, however, had been undefended, and low-level marking against a fortified target would not often be feasible in a Lancaster. For that they would need an aircraft which was smaller, faster and more agile. The memorandum concluded that 617 Squadron should be provided with two Mosquitoes, and that experiments should begin elsewhere to develop rocket projectile markers, to allow stand-off marking that would be safer still.[80]

Philpott submitted the paper to Air Commodore Sharp, who forwarded it to 5 Group on 16 March with his support. Two days later Cochrane commended the analysis to HQ Bomber Command, and endorsed the request for Mosquitoes.[81]

To Air Chief Marshal Harris a 'defended target' meant 'some-where in Germany', and his agreement to Cochrane's request on 26 March was given on condition that it was in Germany that the new method should be tried. Bomber Command's reply also noted that flares would be needed to light up the target area. This meant a flare-dropping force and a system for coordination between illuminators and markers. So, two Mk XVI Mosquitoes would be loaned to 617 Squadron. 617 would crew them. 5 Group should see to it that low-flying training by flare light began on the instant the aircraft arrived.[82]

This was not all. Harris wondered if such a low-level method might have another application. Would it be possible to deposit an initial marker on an aiming point in a town? If so, it could be used as a datum point for more intensive marking by the Pathfinder Force, upon which truly concentrated bombing would follow. The suggestion involved a strange mutation. Cheshire had handed Harris a rapier. Harris had touched it, and turned it back into a cudgel.

The Mosquitoes arrived on 26 March,[83] and Cheshire went straight to Coleby Grange to be taught the rudiments of flying them. Meanwhile, another memorandum on tactics was emerging from 54 Base. Entitled 'Conclusions of Recent Combined Ops by 617 and 106 Squadrons',[84] it epitomizes the continuum in which tactics emerged, were tried, polished or discarded.

Thus, aircraft from the two squadrons had been dropping both flares and bombs. Experience had taught that this dual role was distracting, and so a cause of avoidable inaccuracy. The remedy was specialization: 106 Squadron would drop flares, 617 Squadron would deal with marking and bombing.

Another issue lay in the colour of the markers. Hitherto they had used red spotfires, normally in salvos of three. On some occasions, however, the spotfires scattered, and on others more than one salvo was needed. Instructions given by VHF radio to explain which particular spotfire was correct were not made easier when all the spotfires were red. The answer lay in spotfires of at least three colours.

Then there was control. Until now Cheshire himself had been acting both as marker and controller, giving directions to the main force. Yet there were times when a spotfire visible to the marker was invisible from the altitude of the main force – for example, when it fell through the roof of a building. The remedy? A master of ceremonies for the main force, flying at their height and able to see what they saw, who would be in direct communication with the marker leader. Bombing involved people as well as equipment and techniques. The document finished ominously by noting that precision attacks were 'more likely to induce operational fatigue'.

On they went, and three days later Sharp reported that attacks on factory targets inside Germany could now be contemplated, provided that they took place on dark nights and that the targets lay outside the main defended areas. Elsewhere, other developments were in hand. One of them was research into rocket marking.[85] Another was the prospective operation against the Rothensee ship lift, which had occupied senior planners for months. Barnes Wallis had taken no part in these deliberations since late 1943, but it now dawned on him that they might be founded on a misapprehension. In March he wrote to Air Commodore Bufton, director of bombing operations at the Air Ministry, to point out that his support for an attack on the ship lift had always been based on the use of Tallboy L(arge). Yet development of Tallboy L had been suspended at the end of 1943, although it continued for Tallboy M, which many now simply called 'Tallboy'. Hence, a major attack was being planned on the assumption that Tallboy M would do a job originally intended for Tallboy L.[86]

One would like to think that Bufton, or (more daringly) even Saundby or Harris, saw a funny side to the farcical circumstances from which Wallis had delivered them. Probably not. But Wallis's letter had a galvanizing effect. For one thing it threw Tallboy M's future into the balance. The bomb was still unready, and if it was unlikely to destroy one of the main targets which everyone other than its designer had in mind for it, should it be proceeded with at all? On the other hand, 'another organization altogether had come upon the scene, presided over by a semi-fictitious figure: COSSAC, the Chief of Staff to a Supreme Allied Commander for Overlord'.[87] COSSAC was unwelcome to Harris, chiefly because he was about to appropriate his force and apply it to the disruption of French transport and communications – an employment which Harris regarded as a diversion from Bomber Command's proper purpose of ravaging German cities. However, COSSAC showed keen interest in Tallboy M. Could it be used against coastal defences? Coastal batteries? E-boat pens? Railway targets? Yes, said Wallis at a meeting with Solly Zuckermann, Sharp and Cheshire in the Air Ministry on 22 March, yes, it could. When would it be ready? Experiments with live weapons would begin in two to three weeks' time.[88]

This was heady stuff. Cheshire was present at the meeting, and perhaps for the first time he caught some sense of the quickening tempo and magnitude of events ahead: Overlord, the return to France, the beginning of the end of the war itself. Christopher's homecoming.

8. No Easy Run

On 4 April Cheshire reported that they were ready to begin operations with the Mosquito. An aircraft repair plant at Blagnac, near Toulouse, was selected for their début and was attacked on the next evening. Toulouse lay close to the limit of the Mosquito's range, so Cheshire flew down to refuel at Ford before setting off. Conditions were clear, and after two trial runs he released a pair of red spotfires into the centre of the main assembly shop. These were backed up by the deputy, and bombing followed. It had worked. Or so it seemed. (It was later found that although the roof of the main assembly shop had collapsed, the results overall were less destructive than was supposed at the time.)

In following days new crews were recruited, more crews were sent for initiation to the Mosquito and there were three raids against targets near Paris.★ Meanwhile, Tallboy's reality was approaching. The first live drop had taken place at Ashley Walk on 8 April. Nine days later Barnes Wallis told Cheshire:

You will by this time . . . have heard of the great success which has attended the dropping of one inert and two live Tallboy Ms. The live stores gave depths of penetration between 60 and 80 feet in gravel, sand and clay with excellent detonation. The films show that they are perfectly stable throughout their flight,

---

★ St-Cyr, a Luftwaffe depot near Versailles, on 10 April, marshalling yards at Juvisy, 18 April and marshalling yards at La Chapelle, 20 April. Whereas the attack on Toulouse involved low-level marking, the subsequent raid on St-Cyr seems to have been the first true use of a point-blank dive marking technique. La Chapelle inaugurated a system whereby all 54 Base's units operated together, with 83 and 97 Squadrons providing illumination for 617's (on later operations, 627's) marking. On 21 April 1944 the methodology for this approach was formally defined in a memorandum entitled 'No. 5 Group Target-Marking Procedure', AIR 14/868. Document 1a.

and I hope that we have therefore provided you with a new and effective weapon.[1]

Harris, meanwhile, had dropped a bombshell of his own. On 14 April he wrote to Portal: 'I am still today not satisfied that the institution of the PFF as a single entity has proved in the outcome to be either the right or the best solution.'[2] Never one to do things by halves, Harris decided to address the issues of illumination and marking not by tinkering with 617's establishment but by transplanting three squadrons from 8 Group into 5 Group. All would go to 54 Base: the Lancasters of 83 and 97 Squadrons to Coningsby, there to become 5 Group's flare force, and 627 Squadron, a Mosquito unit, to Woodhall Spa. In months ahead, 627 Squadron would become the inheritors and supreme practitioners of the methods which Cheshire and 617 had pioneered.

Bennett took this badly. A clue to his first feelings may lie in the fact that 97 Squadron's movement orders were cancelled three times before the unit transferred. The squadrons themselves resented it. It was some months before they became reconciled to citizenship in another group.

As far as we know, Cheshire was unaware of the friction which now developed between Cochrane and Bennett. Even if he did know, more pressing things claimed him. Harris's support had been conditional on testing their tactics in Germany. Eighteen days previously a 5 Group conference had been held to consider arrangements for such attacks. On that occasion 'special targets inside Germany' had been viewed as small towns or industrial sites with defences of fewer than eighty heavy guns. The first such raid took place on 22 April, and its target, Brunswick, broadly fulfilled these conditions.*[3] The second, for which Brunswick had been a

* The stated aim of this attack, 617's first low-level marking operation inside Germany, was 'to cause destruction to an enemy industrial centre'. A main force of 215 aircraft assisted by fifty-nine marking a/c of 54 Base took part. Tom Bennett recalls: 'We had an unblemished trip out, were approaching the Dummer See where a spurious German red TI ignited over it . . . The initial target flares went down early, when I still had a couple more minutes to ETA Brunswick, and from the angle at which we were to these flares I could see only open country illuminated beneath them . . . (The) other three Mossies were lured off to investigate but I told Gerry [Fawke] to carry on course. Then another salvo of flares went down ahead of us and we immediately identified the market square

rehearsal, did not, but rather took its cue from Harris's parting aside about the possibilities of point-blank marking within a city, to provide a datum for further marking and a massive attack. Like Mephistopheles, Harris called in his bargain. The target he wanted was Munich.

Munich, in the words of one 617 captain, was 'the kind of target you might not come back from'.[4] After Berlin it was the most heavily defended city in the Reich. It was also distant, close to the limit of a Mosquito's range and likely to expose all aircraft to flak and nightfighters. For 617, accustomed to the selective bombing of specialized targets, Munich was like a step back into main force days. Among some, at least, there was some sense of foreboding when the raid was ordered on the morning of 24 April.

The plan provided for 83 and 97 Squadrons to illuminate, four Mosquitoes flown by 617 crews to mark, 617 Lancasters to back up the marked aiming point with incendiaries and a main force of some 220 5 Group Lancasters to bomb. Cheshire would fly as marker leader, Shannon as deputy, with Kearns and Fawke as second and third deputies. To divide and confuse German defences, another attack was arranged for Karlsruhe and a spoof raid would be aimed at Milan.

The main force took off in daylight for a long haul, made longer by a detour across France. Cheshire and his companions left nearly two hours later, having first positioned themselves at Manston in Kent.

. . . we did not have an easy run . . . we were sent off before the arrival of the auxiliary drop-tanks, and without these, even allowing for take-off from the nearest point on the English coast, and assuming that we remained on track from start to finish and spent only two minutes on target, we couldn't hope for more than thirteen minutes' petrol on returning to base★. . . We lined the Mosquitoes

aiming point. Gerry dived and marked to such good effect that Chesh decided those spotfires did not need back-up and ordered to the Lancasters to commence bombing. Thus we were the first crew to "Mossie mark" a major German city . . .'
★ Tom Bennett, one of the Mosquito navigators, remembers: 'Certainly we were concerned that we would have to calculate from data collected en route just when the pilots *had* to leave the target in order to make a Manston landing feasible *and* impress on all pilots that they *had* to leave Munich when we said and not continue having a "look see". It was a serious time, but we all realized that it was make or break for our developed technique and we owed it to Chesh to see it through.'

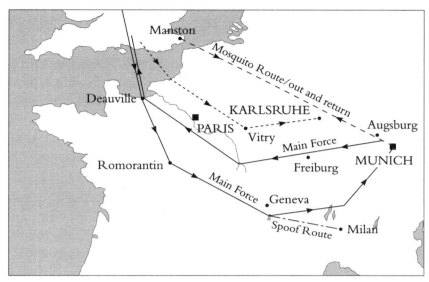

The raid on Munich: Bomber Command night operations
24/25 April 1944.

up on the downwind end of the runway, filled them to overflowing and took
off the moment the oil temperature needle began to move.[5]

Weather along the route was anticipated as poor, but although they
soon lost Gee the navigators kept them on course and schedule. A
clump of TIs had been dropped as a datum ten miles north-west
of the city. Here the Mosquitoes turned for the city together.

Munich's flak defences were already alert. What first struck the
markers were the searchlights. There were more than most had
ever seen, and in the midst of their conical, groping clumps of
white and blue shafts there were the orange flashes and smudges of
flak.

Cheshire and Kelly arrived as the first flares were descending.

In fact, as they ignited, I looked down and in a split second I saw my aiming
point immediately beneath us . . . Now the problem was that, to do a proper
run-in, I'd have to fly away, get into position and come back in, but I knew
that if I did that I risked losing it or maybe the flares might go out. On the other
hand, if I went straight in from where I was overhead, that meant a vertical dive,
and the two problems for that were, first that I'd exceed the safety-limit speed
of the aircraft and nobody was quite certain what would happen if I did that,

and secondly that if I released my markers in a vertical dive they might drop
through the forward bulkhead . . .[6]

Under the flarelight they had recognized the Theresienweise (a
kidney-shaped park) and the Nymphenburger Kanal, and sighted
the aiming point – a Gestapo building 150 yards east of the main
railway station. Without further ado Cheshire tilted the Mosquito
on to its wing-tip and went straight down from 5,000 feet. 'I just
knew I had to go.' Towards 1,500 feet he lifted the nose a little to
release two markers. 'OK, they didn't hit the forward bulkhead.'
The Mosquito's indicated speed touched 480 m.p.h., and the pull-
out was harsh. Cheshire normally flew aircraft well inside their
advised tolerances, but those who knew his flying remember that he
was prepared to exceed them in reaction to dangerous circumstances.[7] His climb out through the blizzard of light flak which clawed
for him over the city centre was such an occasion. Both he and Kelly
were disorientated when they emerged from it. 'I pulled up, but then
of course there were lights above me and lights below me and shells
bursting above me and so it was a very confusing situation. I didn't
really know if I was upside down or what I was doing, but I knew if
I just let go of the controls the aircraft would find her own level.'[8]
Things fell into place. Cheshire assessed the markers. They looked
accurate. He summoned Shannon, whose markers fell some 100 yards
from his own. Kearns followed, and his markers too were well-
placed. Fawke's markers failed to release. After this, 617's Lancasters
reinforced the spotfires with incendiaries. Munich's pyre had been
lit. The main force now put the city to the torch. High above, a 50
Squadron navigator was urged by a colleague to switch off his light,
draw back his black-out curtain and take a look.

He said that if I lived to be a hundred I would never see anything like this. I
looked out and beheld what seemed to be all the Guy Fawkes nights which had
ever taken place, rolled up into a minute. Tracer-fire from German fighters flew
across the picture, flak poured up from the ground in great loops and bombs
began to cascade down around the brilliant spotfires which had been placed on
top of Leonard Cheshire's original visually aimed marker.

And Cheshire?

As we ran in . . . his cool, collected and precise instructions came through our headphones with the kind of tone one might have expected from someone seated in a comfortable armchair telephoning from a drawing room.[9]

Such is the narrative from contemporary sources and the memories of those who were there. Here is the same episode through the eyes of AVM Donald Bennett:

Their master bomber went in low level in a Mosquito, with three others to back him up . . . He tried gallantly for nearly twenty minutes to get his markers on the correct aiming point, but in view of the difficulties of very fast flight very low over a built-up area he was unsuccessful. By this time his reserves had had to leave for home owing to shortage of fuel, and [he] was, therefore, forced in due course to call upon the PFF high-level master bomber to take over and mark the aiming point in accordance with the usual Newhaven procedure, which was done satisfactorily. From then on the raid was controlled by our master bomber with fairly good success. Incidentally, quite a number of aircraft were lost due to fighters whilst the PFF master bomber held them circling the target waiting for the low-level marker to do his stuff. In apparently [*sic*] criticizing this failure I make no reflection whatever on the very gallant attempt he made to do his job properly.[10]

How do we explain this? In the first place, Bennett was not there, and he was writing ten years later. In the second, his sources were not primary records, but mainly remembered reports (either direct or hearsay) from elements of 83 and 97 Squadrons who had remained in contact with their former group. These units had been at 54 Base for less than a fortnight, and some of their members may not yet have been completely familiar with the rationale behind the methods they were being asked to employ. It will, for instance, be remembered from the discussion of March (pp. 151–2) that a high-level master bomber was actually an *intended* participant, not someone who was called upon to step in. Hence the fact that Cheshire was not controlling the raid after the marking had been reinforced is neither here nor there – he was not meant to be. The statement that Cheshire's marking took twenty minutes is simply wrong,★ and the point about

★ Cheshire's markers fell at 01.41; the last of Kearns's, at 01.52. Recorded times of marking do, however, vary from source to source, and several minutes more should be added to allow for Fawke's unfulfilled attack.

main force losses is tendentious. There were losses – nine Lancasters – but there were losses on most raids, and as a percentage of the total of aircraft taking part the casualties on this evening were not exceptional: 3.5 per cent. One of the nine was from 617: the squadron's first operational loss since 20 December 1943.

An aspect which Bennett did not mention was the Mosquitoes' withdrawal. Cheshire and Kelly remained over the target until the last minutes that predicted fuel consumption would allow. All four Mosquitoes were engaged by defences which followed them for some 40 miles beyond the target. Back at Manston two hours later, none had sufficient petrol for more than twenty minutes' flying – a perilous margin. Manston's lighting was switched off just as Fawke was committed to the landing. Fawke's navigator saw a shower of sparks along the adjacent runway, remarking upon what looked like 'electrical trouble with the airfield lighting'. In fact, the 'sparks' were caused by cannon shells and bullets striking the runway. A German intruder was firing at them.[11]

The Lancasters flew more slowly: 'When we last saw it Munich was just one large bonfire and most of the searchlights in the target had doused.'[12] From the departing bombers, Munich's flames could be seen for a hundred miles.

Back from leave on 2 May, 617's aircrew were ordered to Wood-hall's briefing room. 617 were accustomed to tight security, but armed military police at the door and identity checks were unusual. The presence of Cochrane and Sharp confirmed that something exceptional was in the offing. Cochrane explained what it was.

Recent research had shown that falling Window – metallized strips – could produce the illusion of a mass of shipping on ship-watching radar. In the hours before the D-Day landings took place in Normandy, 617 Squadron would thus forge the radar signature of an invasion fleet approaching France between Boulogne and Le Havre. The hoax was to be the culmination of Operation Fortitude: an elaborate deception involving phantom units, dummy camps and contrived signals traffic which had been building up for months and was designed to delude the Germans about where the main weight of the invasion would fall. Fortitude called for a pair of frauds:

Operations Taxable and Glimmer. Taxable had been awarded to 617, Glimmer to 218 Squadron. There was, however, a snag. While the squadron was being asked to simulate a convoy advancing at 352 yards per minute, it was not clear how the underlying theory was to be realized in practice. Success would call for sustained flying and navigation of unprecedented precision, governed by data which in most cases were not yet available. Cochrane 'offered no guidance whatsoever at the initial meeting with the aircrew on 2 May, and neither did anybody else'.[13] This was work for navigators, and 617 Squadron's navigators went into conclave to consider how, or indeed if, it could be done.[14]

Fortitude and Taxable were supreme secrets, and to protect them 617 Squadron was withdrawn from operations until D-Day.[15] Within hours, however, this ruling was overturned. Bomber Command was now being aimed at tactical and transport targets in preparation for invasion, and on the next evening a raid was mounted by 1 and 5 Groups against a panzer establishment at Mailly-le-Camp. The attack was timed to open just before midnight, to catch soldiers returning to barracks in the open, in addition to wrecking the barracks themselves and impeding the care of tanks. The raid called for expert marking,[16] and Bomber Command reluctantly agreed that four 617 Mosquito crews should take part.

Cheshire coordinated the marking, which went well.[17] Tragically, however, VHF communication with the main force was drowned out by an American news broadcast, while the wireless set in the 83 Squadron master bomber's aircraft was off tune, negating efforts to give bombing orders by W/T. The delay meant re-marking, which led to more delay. While some 300 Lancasters orbited their holding point fifteen miles from the target, German nightfighters arrived among them. Under a brilliant three-quarter moon forty-two bombers were shot down.

When the raid eventually proceeded it was effective, but for most of those who took part it was terrifying, the more so because it was anticipated as an 'easy op'. Mailly was one of the few occasions when R/T discipline broke down and fear became palpable. In a sky filled with tracer and exploding aircraft, crews began to swear on air and talk across one another. Many assumed that the delay was being caused by 617's perfectionism. Some shouted at Cheshire himself. Next day there was resentful talk on bomber stations across Lincolnshire. Unaware of the disaster's cause, it was said that Cheshire's fastidiousness had cost lives.

After Mailly-le-Camp the ban on pre-Overlord operations held firm, and the search for solutions to Taxable's demands proceeded. Bomber Command needed to know of Taxable's viability within a fortnight. Dr Cockburn, a pioneer of the basic research, visited Woodhall Spa on 9 May to discuss progress. By now the navigators had evolved a methodology about which they were confident, and two days later Mr Charles Bellringer arrived from the Telecommunications Research Establishment at Defford, bringing with him calculations which combined Cockburn's work and the results of the squadron's trials. Quietly spoken and initially reserved, Bellringer went down well with the aircrew, who predictably rechristened him Ding Dong. Within a few days, an operational format had been worked out.

Each aircraft flew what can best be described as a series of 'spiralling elliptical-type circuits' of about seven minutes duration per orbit. These were two straight, reciprocal tracks, linked by a turn from one track to the other. The straight tracks were laid along two of the grid lines of the Gee navigational system, and the approach position of the head of the convoy was advanced by some 2,400 yards per orbit . . . the distance an invasion convoy would be expected to cover in the period of each circuit. 'Windowing' would take place *only* on the two straight legs . . . although the navigators were required to 'home' the pilots during the turn, to the exact point on the succeeding straight leg where 'Windowing' would recommence.[18]

There was, of course, more to it than this, not the least of it being that the orbits were to be flown by eight aircraft in formation, to give a breadth of 15 miles. Daily training led to much puzzlement among farmers and land girls as Lancasters cruised back and forth for up to two hours at a time in manoeuvres which were apparently as aimless as they were leisurely.

Bellringer arranged for a captured German coastal radar to be set up on Flamborough Head, and on 14 May some members of the squadron flew up to Driffield whence they were taken by bus to

Flamborough. Here 'the navigators took it in turns to group around the set, while a 617 Lancaster performed a series of circuits approaching the Yorkshire coast'. Much was learned, and Ding Dong declared himself pleased.

A host of related issues still demanded attention: the need for additional navigators, relief pilots, extra maintenance and servicing, extra Gee sets, a new Vernier scale which enabled Gee signal values to be interpreted to three decimal places, and security. How much the crews could be told to ensure success was left to Cheshire's discretion. Taxable also meant travel to meetings, more journeys to Flamborough and a succession of increasingly realistic exercises.[19]

As usual, Cheshire had more than one thing on his mind. Superimposed on Taxable were trials for the long-discussed rocket projectile target markers. Rockets with spotfire and incendiary heads were being tested on Salisbury Plain. Perhaps unsurprisingly, it was found that the rockets tended to bury their noses on impact, requiring the incendiary to be placed behind the motor.[20]

If rocket marking was no closer, Tallboy was almost in their hands. It made many new demands. A new weapon required new equipment – trolleys, cranes, tools – and new procedures. Moreover, such was Tallboy's sophistication that fractional refinements were being notified daily. On 27 May, for instance, attention was drawn to the fact that in a fall from 18,000 feet even the rotation of the earth would have an effect on Tallboy's accuracy – perhaps as much as ten yards – and that allowance should be made for it.[21] Taxable, moreover, was diverting them from high-level training. When the time came to deliver Tallboy, would they be in practice?

There were other pressures: 16 May was the anniversary of the Dams Raid, and four evenings later there was a station party to which Guy Gibson came as guest of honour. Cheshire and Gibson hardly knew one another, and Cheshire found it strange to see his friends gravitating back towards his predecessor. Despite everything which had happened since, Gibson, he felt, still in some sense *was* 617.[22] Perhaps to exorcise the spell, or any hangovers from the free beer, next day 'The Wingco took us on a route march in afternoon at breakneck pace. Feeling tired. Played Monopoly.'[23]

The greatest strain of all concerned the squadron's future. During

May, 617's status as a marking unit came under searching scrutiny. Cheshire wished the squadron to develop an autonomous capacity for marking, whereas others considered that all marking responsibility should now pass to 627 Squadron, which would work in tandem with the two former Pathfinder squadrons at Coningsby. The debate not only affected title to the Mosquitoes which Cheshire had struggled to acquire, but touched 617's very function and identity.[24]

Locally, Cheshire's staunchest ally was Woodhall's station commander, Gp Capt. Philpott. In some eyes Philpott suffered from a reputation as a diligent but abstracted man. In *The Face of Victory* Cheshire guyed Philpott's urge to discuss 617's poor showing on 5 Group's War Savings Ladder while he, Cheshire, was in the midst of a pre-operational crisis. On another occasion an operation was ordered after Cheshire had authorized a stand-down. While Cheshire tried to concentrate on teletypes and maps, Philpott paced about agitatedly, periodically saying, 'You know you shouldn't have done that, Leonard', to which Cheshire kept replying politely (without looking up) 'I know.' For others, Philpott's principal contribution to the war lay in his campaign to soften the brutalism of Woodhall's buildings with climbing plants and trellis work. Trellises appeared on huts, the parachute store, even the latrines. One day in the midst of a technical discussion Philpott's attention wandered. Staring out of the window he murmured, 'Nice piece of trellis out there.'[25]

Few knew that behind this whimsical front there stood an articulate ally who would brave the annoyance of superiors by sending them intrepid letters in Cheshire's support. Several such letters were written during May. One was to 54 Base's commander, Air Commodore Sharp, an abrasive, rather swaggering figure, one of the few towards whom Cheshire was ever known to show active dislike. Positioned as he was between Woodhall and 5 Group, Sharp nevertheless occupied an important interlocutory role. On 25 May Philpott warned Sharp of possible 'far-reaching effects on the morale and efficiency of No. 617 Squadron' if Cheshire's wish were to be denied, adding that these consequences 'would be out of all proportion to the small increase in aircraft establishment requested'. Philpott insisted that 617 needed a minimum of four Mosquitoes. He further pointed out that the squadron's success was in large measure due to the loyalty of its members and their faith in Cheshire. If 627 took over this role he predicted dissatisfaction, and an exodus of 617 crews.[26]

This was strong talk, although alongside the threat of exodus Cheshire spent much time in fielding offers from men who hoped to be part of an influx. 'I am fully aware that I am not at liberty to approach you on any service subject,' wrote a sergeant gunner, who languished among surplus aircrew at a Coastal Command OTU in Scotland, bemoaning a 'binding existence' among these 'bloody flying whales' – slang for the Short Sutherland – and offering his services. Another:

Even if I have to revert back to flying officer I don't mind.

Another:

I am an air gunner. I completed my second tour of operations on 20 December 1943 . . . I should very much appreciate any advice that you could give me as to the possibility of returning to active flying duties.[27]

Such letters had been arriving even in the days when 617 was regarded as a suicide squadron:

I wish to know if you have a vacancy for a wireless operator on the squadron . . . I have recently returned . . . after a walking tour on the Continent . . . I am now a 'spare body'. Therefore, if you have a vacancy, Sir, would you please inform me.[28]

Cheshire was on the lookout for seasoned aircrew who had been screened. 'I am forwarding the names of two experienced pilots who are extremely keen to return to operational duties on Mosquito aircraft', he wrote to Sharp on 20 May.[29] But with 627 Squadron now installed on the far side of the airfield, would 617 be needing Mosquito pilots for much longer?

On 29 May, a day when Woodhall sweltered, Sharp gave his own view. In general he supported Philpott. He agreed that it would be a mistake to undermine 617's 'traditional independent pioneering role'. To do so would be 'a tragedy'. On the question of the Mosquitoes he was less supportive, considering four desirable, three feasible and two operable. Sharp then launched into more radical speculations. Illumination might be provided by as few as five or six aircraft, bearing in mind a new type of flare just then coming into use. Or perhaps 617 could be converted into a specialized marker control squadron for 5 Group operations, composed, say, of twelve Mosquitoes and twelve Lancasters? Whatever the equation, Sharp cautioned against neglect of 'psychological and sentimental factors'.[30]

The argument about 617's future was but a footnote on the page of a larger altercation between Cochrane and Bennett. At the end of May Bennett implored Harris to return his three squadrons. His letter brimmed with reproach: 'Unfortunately, there is so much to be said on this subject that it is hard to condense it into a small space.' He reminded Harris that six weeks before 83, 97 and 627 Squadrons had been detached to 5 Group as an experiment. 'They complain that operational planning is so confused and so often left to the last minute that they are quite unable to give their best.' His unhappily exiled squadrons had to plan in the absence of anyone who understood their methods. The employment of 83 and 97 Squadrons simply as area illuminators was leading to loss of their skill, and hence a 'tremendous amount of difficulty and embarrassment'.

Bennett had nothing good to say about 617's marking, telling Harris that the method they 'purport' to use is shallow dive-bombing, which had been discredited in pre-war trials. Cochrane had told Bennett that he would 'shout the loudest in order to get what he wants', whereas Harris should surely judge what is 'right and wrong in actual fact and not merely on vague claims or loud assertions'. Results gave no justification for the continued alienation of his squadrons. Brunswick had been a failure, and while the raid on Munich had succeeded this was no thanks to Mosquito marking, which Bennett considered to have been a failure. Over France, traditional PFF methods had produced results no worse than those achieved by 617. If all this had occurred in peacetime, said Bennett, he would have resigned.[31]

Bennett ended by asking Harris not to regard his diatribe as sour grapes, a remarkable request, bearing in mind the allegation of 5

Group's incompetence, and an implication that Harris was blind to this because of his uncritical faith in – or favouritism towards – Cochrane. More fundamentally, in his passion Bennett had overlooked Harris's long-standing desire to see a variety of target-finding and marking methods, rather than the supremacy of a single system. The fact was that the bombing war was constantly evolving, and while in its early days 8 Group had been progressive, it was now Bennett himself who found it difficult to move with the times.

Paradoxically, something of this last point also applies to Cheshire. Although some of his finest tactical achievements still lay ahead, his greatest strategic contribution had already been made. Its result – a new kind of marking force at 54 Base and elsewhere[32] – had implications for 617 which at the time others may have seen more clearly than he did.

Taxable neared. One by one, refinements had been perfected. The navigators rejoiced in the work, although some others found the training repetitive, tiring, even a little disillusioning.[33] As May ended in sultry weather there was a sense of listlessness. Thursday 1 June saw more work to fit second Gee sets, and staff from RAE had joined them to help fit and calibrate Mk 8 automatic pilots. As trucks bearing Tallboys rumbled through the gates, monotonous but vital work proceeded on the packaging of Window bundles. During Taxable each aircraft would drop thirty-six packets of Window during each straight leg of every orbit. The Window signature had to gain in 'weight' as the aircraft made its run towards the coast, and then decrease during the reciprocal run.[34] Hence, the Window had to be graded (in eight different bundle sizes), to ensure that separate grades were released at different points in the orbit – a requirement which in turn meant that the parcels had to be stacked in the correct order, and that the deliverers and dispatchers must always know where they were in the sequence. This was assisted by a 'Windowing marshal' in each aircraft and a system of colour-coded lights which signalled the stages of each orbit.

They waited. On the Saturday there were refinements of SABS Tallboy settings, an athletics competition. On Sunday the mood tautened as Mosquitoes were painted with black and white D-Day stripes. Small arms and ammunition were issued, in case of retaliation by German commandos. Cheshire was aware of other anxieties, among them a worry that the Germans might reply to the invasion with chemical weapons.[35] Appropriately, with Taxable imminent, the film showing at the Kinema in the Woods was *The Great Impersonation*.

Next day crews were called to briefing. It was four years to the day since Plt Off. Cheshire had arrived at the gates of RAF Driffield, untried and uncertain, in the week of Dunkirk's evacuation. Tomorrow they would be going back.

9. Second to None

Briefing was simple – the method was so 'burned into our minds'. What was new was a chart which showed how Taxable fitted into Overlord's strategy. One deception bred another. Supper was non-operational – no bacon and eggs.

The first wave took off at dusk.[*] Cheshire, who had not taken much part in training because of other duties, flew as second pilot to Munro. Calibrating their altimeters by the Boston Stump, they flew out via Clacton (as usual being shot at by the Royal Navy) and then to a point off the Sussex coast where they settled to align with the vessels of a small surface fleet. This was in two flotillas, each consisting of three air-sea rescue launches, known as 'Moonshine Vessels', towing a balloon bearing a radar reflector, and six smaller boats. The Lancasters were established at their exact heights, speeds and mutual distance, and under a rising moon Taxable's ceremony began.

For two hours they flew, dropping Window bundles at fifteen-second intervals to form a fourteen-mile-wide curtain which edged towards Cap d'Antifer. Within the aircraft the calling out of times and turns became incantatory, amid surreal ornament which resulted from Window blown back into the fuselages.[1] Monotony veiled anxiety. The steadily manoeuvring aircraft were vulnerable to fighters, and early on the Lancasters were so stuffed with Window that movement within them was difficult. The second wave took over.

As time passed, as in the building of a tower of cards, the

[*] At 23.10. Double British Summer Time then applied: that is, two hours ahead of GMT.

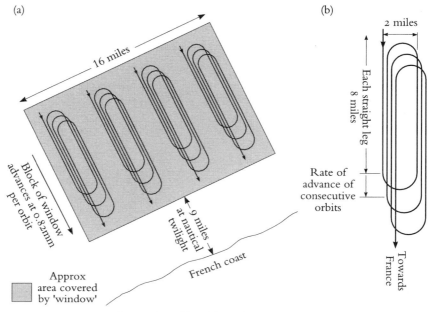

Operation Taxable, 5/6 June 1944.
(a) Subset of the operation showing the patterns traced by four aircraft
as they edged towards the French coast, releasing Window to simulate
the advance of an invasion fleet at about 7 knots. A following quartet
of aircraft, also discharging Window, provided 'depth' to the convoy as
it would register on German radar. Halfway through the operation all
eight aircraft were replaced by a second wave.
(b) Representation of the track of one aircraft, each orbit 8 miles long
and 2 miles wide, advancing at a rate of *c.* 0.82 nautical miles per orbit.
Window was dropped on straight legs only.

knowledge that error would spoil all caused tension to rise. But
nothing disturbed their office. By 04.00 it was growing light. The
crews turned for home; the phantom fleet dissolved. In the
grey dawn they marvelled at immense formations of aircraft, gliders
and ships heading for Normandy. It was a scene they had long
imagined.

Log books convey restrained jubilation. 'Special cooperation
with sea-borne forces. INVASION. Details secret,' wrote Flt Lt
Fearn. 'Tactical surprise to support the landing of troops on the
opening of the second front,' put Nick Ross. 'Certified that Sqn

Ldr Munro is still in possession of most of his faculties after completing the operation described on this page,' wrote Cheshire in Munro's log. In his own: 'Support of an assault carried out by combined services on the continent.' To a friend: 'They also serve who only sit and wait.'

Events now followed as if all the energies which had been bottled up during May's *longueur* were released in a tumble. Later in the day, while aircrew clustered round mess radios and armourers out on the fringes of the airfield sheltered from flying showers, Cochrane gave his verdict on their future. The squadron would retain its identity as a special duties unit '. . . trained to attack important objectives with types of bombs and other weapons not available to the main force. It will also continue to pioneer visual methods of marking targets.' Cochrane directed that 83 and 97 Squadrons would provide illumination for 617 when required, and would come under the 'general direction' of 617's commander when they did so. However, this meant that 617 would not receive the extra Mosquitoes. Instead, 627 Squadron's residence at 54 Base was to be made permanent,[2] and when Mosquitoes were needed it was hoped that they could be borrowed. These tidings were sweetened by news that Bomber Command had been asked to obtain a Mustang with long-range tanks. If it was practicable to mark with the fighter then this 'would help to overcome the shortage of Mosquitoes'.*[3]

Cochrane's decision balanced a rejection of greater independence for 617 with support for the more integrated deployment of 54 Base's varied resources, while retaining the essence of 617's pioneering tradition. The decision had Harris's endorsement, for Harris realized that Cheshire's ideas offered 'undreamed of accuracy, with fewer aircraft, less expenditure of effort and therefore greater economy'. For Bennett it came as a final snub. Not only had his pleas for the return of his squadrons gone unheeded, but the concept of a centralized Pathfinder force was now irretrievably eroded. Henceforth 54 Base's Lancasters and Mosquitoes might provide illumina-

---

* Two Mustang IIIs were delivered to Woodhall Spa on 22 June. Thereafter Cheshire used a Mustang for the remaining operations of his tour – to Siracourt (25 June), St Leu d'Esserent (4 July) and Mimoyecques (6 July).

tion and marking for 617 in particular or 5 Group as a whole; in either event, 8 Group had lost its monopoly.

June 7 dawned cloudy and wet, and there was a stand-down. The mood was buoyant,[4] and before crews left the station Cheshire convened the entire squadron to relay Harris's congratulations on the success of Glimmer and Taxable.

Late that afternoon, while 617's crews headed for Boston's pubs and dance halls, a lone PRU Mosquito was scrutinizing the railway between Niort and Saumur. This was a main line running from Bordeaux to the Normandy battle zone, and intelligence anticipated the imminent transport of German armour along it.

Overnight, Saumur itself was selected as the point at which the line should be cut. Here the railway enters a tunnel on sharply rising ground, emerges after two thirds of a mile on a steep bank above the Loire and proceeds on to a bridge. Two targets thus presented themselves: the bridge near the north-eastern mouth of the tunnel, and the south-western entrance of the tunnel itself. At twenty past eight next morning 5 Group's teletype rattled out instructions from High Wycombe: twenty-eight Lancasters and three Mosquitoes from 54 Base would attack Saumur that night.[5] 617's Lancasters would carry Tallboy.

This was the first operational use of Tallboy, and it was a tall order. Concentration on Taxable had left 617 out of practice in high-level bombing, while Tallboy's unfamiliarity posed unprecedented technical demands for the ground crews. Even the weather looked unpromising; the cloud base might be too low.

Problems or not, preparations went ahead through the day. While armourers sweated, sportsmen were recalled from a cricket match at Metheringham and Cheshire flew to RAE Farnborough for discussion on the elimination of SABS sighting errors, planning proceeded. Four 83 Squadron Lancasters using H2S would provide illumination for the Mosquitoes, which would lay red spotfires at the tunnel mouth. The Tallboys would be aimed here. Meanwhile, the illuminators would turn to attack the bridge with 1,000 lb bombs.

The first Lancaster roared off at 22.45. As usual, the faster Mosquitoes departed later, Cheshire leaving ahead of Shannon and

Fawke* to arrive over the target early. Conditions now looked fair. Illumination was more problematic. The target's H2S signature was poor, and flares were dispersed. Cheshire was nevertheless able to identify the tunnel mouth, and by 02.06 several red spotfires were glowing in the cutting within 45 yards of it. At 02.08 Cheshire ordered bombing to begin, and two minutes later the first Tallboy entered its fall.

Most of the Tallboys looked well laid. However, there was no wind, hanging smoke soon obscured the spotfires and some of the later bombs appeared to drop wide. One conscientious crew made seven runs in search of the aiming point before turning to attack the bridge instead.[6] Anxiously, they waited for the photos. Reconnaissance after daybreak showed that Tallboys had cut the line in at least two places. There was also a gaping crater above the tunnel. Harris told Cochrane:

I would like to congratulate you and all concerned in the splendid effort made yesterday in loading nineteen Tallboys at short notice. I can assure you that I fully appreciate what an enormous effort must have been made to load these heavy and unfamilar stores in so short a time, and I should like you to convey to all concerned my appreciation of their efforts.[7]

What the air photographs did not yet show was the effect of the bomb which had fallen over the tunnel. Loose earth within its crater disguised the fact that the bomb had bored through the chalk into the tunnel itself, causing collapse of the hill above.[8]

Saumur was only one of a number of railway targets to which Bomber Command reached out that night. At Alençon, Rennes, Fougères and other places there were assaults which cut lines and blocked the movement of German reinforcements. Four years before Lofty Long, Cheshire and a handful of others had been trying to do the same thing and had failed for want of strength and tactical discernment. Now, in a strange symmetry, they were succeeding.

On 12 June the flying bomb offensive began. Barnes Wallis

---

* Shannon and Fawke departed at 00.12 and 00.13, respectively. Cheshire's take-off time was logged as 23.23. It is possible that he flew from Bradwell Bay, having earlier flown down to top up his fuel to give more time to loiter over the target.

asked the Air Ministry for a scrambler, since 'It looks as though communication between us on targets connected with Tallboy will become more numerous in the near future.' It was not only flying bombs which prompted this request. Discussions were also in progress about U- and E-boat pens. Wallis had been reviewing his calculations on the susceptibility of such structures to Tallboy. Earlier in the year he had been confident that they would be vulnerable.[9] Now he was cautious. Nevertheless, the Admiralty were apprehensive about E-boats and the Chiefs of Staff had ruled that an experimental Tallboy attack should take place as soon as possible. Urgency was increased by the V-1 offensive, for it looked certain that Bomber Command would soon be diverted to counter it.[10]

Germany's *Schnellbootwaffe* was the one element of the German navy which could carry the fight to the Allies in the Channel. The latest E-boats were powered by Daimler Benz diesels which could sustain speeds up to 42 m.p.h. in battle. Highly manoeuvrable, equipped with radar and passive electronic detection devices, armed with torpedoes, mines and cannon, and with a low silhouette, E-boats were lethal adversaries.

E-boats were nocturnal. At Boulogne, Le Havre and Cherbourg they could be sheltered or serviced by day in massive bomb-resistant reinforced concrete hangars and defended by concentrations of light and heavy anti-aircraft artillery. Immediately after D-Day the bulk of the force had gravitated to Cherbourg and Boulogne, whence flotillas emerged each evening to stalk Allied shipping in the congested sea corridor between southern England and Normandy. Although comparatively few, E-boats in the hands of seasoned commanders were inflicting considerable harm on Allied shipping. Their threat, moreover, was expected to grow, as E-boats stationed as far away as the Baltic moved south to join the battle.

On 13 June the Allies saw an opportunity to eliminate this threat. Rudolf Petersen, commander of E-boat forces in the Channel, normally took care to disperse his flotillas between different bases and to vary their dispositions. Since D-Day, however, dispersal had been less easy. German communications between Cherbourg and the rest of France had been cut. By 10 June it was clear that the port had no future as an E-boat haven, and over the next three nights contingents of vessels escaped to Le Havre. On 12 June a number of boats were ordered to Boulogne, but for various reasons they had returned instead to Le Havre, where they were now joined by the refugees from Cherbourg. Hence, instead of being dispersed between several ports, three flotillas were temporarily crammed into one.[11] The Allies knew this, although it was not until just before nine o'clock on the morning of 14 June that the picture clarified. Air reconnaissance later in the day[12] confirmed that the tidal anchorage in the outer harbour was thronged with E-boats and other craft.

Admiral Ramsay, commander of Operation Neptune, telephoned Harris to request an attack before dusk. Harris agreed, albeit with reservations. Heavy bombers had not been used by day for more than a year. An escort of Spitfires was enlisted to drive off fighters.

The plan provided for two mass attacks. The first would begin at 22.35 (20.35 GMT) when bombs from 200 Lancasters of 1 Group were intended to shower the harbour as E-boats prepared to put to sea. Marking would be provided by Mosquitoes of 8 Group using Oboe. The second raid was timed to start an hour after nightfall (01.15 DBST), when a smaller force of Lancasters would augment earlier damage and disrupt the work of emergency services.[13]

617's part in these proceedings was carefully articulated. Five minutes before the arrival of the first main force, Mosquito markers – the customary trio of Fawke, Shannon and Cheshire – would lay red spotfires on the concrete pens, and twenty-two Tallboy-bearing Lancasters would attempt to demolish them. The volley of Tallboys required a clear view of the spotfires, so timing was critical.

The evening was sunny, and Cheshire, Shannon and Fawke watched the Lancasters leave before attending to their own final checks. The three took off an hour later, heading south in sunshine made warmer by the Plexiglas canopies of their cockpits. They flew in a vic formation, the navigators cheerfully exchanging signs. But behind the lightheartedness there was apprehension. German naval bases were among the riskiest of targets. A naval base in daylight, at low level, was one of the riskiest of all. While a first marking run might catch the defences off guard, the chances for anyone surviving a second or a third were slim.

By 22.25 Le Havre was in sight. At 22.29 Cheshire told Shannon and Fawke that he was 'going in'. The three Mosquitoes broke formation, Cheshire dipping downwards until he was skimming over the water at more than 400 knots. Circling two miles out, Shannon, Fawke and their navigators followed his progress, silently praying that their services would not be needed. For nearly a minute he was lost to sight. Then came the first glittering specks of tracer. Men who manned the light flak guns around the port were nervous of the loitering Mosquitoes, perhaps also distracted by the simultaneous approach of PFF aircraft at higher level, and as Cheshire raced towards them filaments of fire began to flay the air. Within half a minute the sky above the harbour was filled by a swirling tangle of glowing shells. From this, Cheshire emerged. Behind him red spotfires were glowing on the concrete pens.

From start to finish the marking had taken barely ninety seconds. The raid that followed occupied just twenty-one minutes. First fell the Tallboys. Seen from above their submarine explosions shivered the water in concentric rings. One Tallboy drilled through the roof of an E-boat pen and displaced its walls. Others lofted boats out of the water, jammed them against dock sides or simply smashed them. Devastation was widened by the main-force attacks which followed. By dawn there was scarcely a boat afloat, and of those that did float only one E-boat remained fit for sea. In the space of five hours the E-boat threat had been eliminated.

There is almost a monotony in some accounts of 617's remaining operations in June 1944, as one target after another appears to have been efficiently marked, pierced by a Tallboy and crossed off SHAEF's list. Original records give a different picture.[14] There were targets like Boulogne (more E-boat pens) which were acutely problematic. Several, like the great V-weapon blockhouses at Watten and Wizernes (visited on three occasions) called for rare tenacity. Some trips were flown at dawn, others by day – Cheshire in shirt sleeves, sweating in the sun under the perspex canopy of his Mustang★ – yet others at night. Some were not flown at all: 'Stand-by . . . feeling cheesed.' Behind the habitual composure of phrases like 'many fighters', 'one a/c badly damaged', 'believed red spots didn't ignite', 'adverse weather', 'fighters got into stream', lay exhaustion, strain and stabs of panic, and consolatory letters to parents and widows in their twenties. Even on the ground effort was unrelenting: Tallboy's ballistic perfection meant that the slightest delay in its release would cause it to fall wide, and throughout June there were difficulties with sluggish release slips.[15]

At 2.23 in the afternoon of Thursday 6 July Cheshire took off from Woodhall Spa to mark a site at Mimoyecques in northern France. The target was the third of Germany's V-weapons: a colossal gun, poised to fling shells 180 miles into London.† 617's visit left the weapon useless,[16] and so swift was the Mustang that by 4.25 Cheshire was back at Woodhall. In London that afternoon two representatives of the Jewish Agency met Anthony Eden, Britain's Foreign Secretary. They told him that Hungarian Jews were being deported to a camp in Silesia and gassed, and asked if the Allies could intervene – for example, by bombing the railway between Budapest and the place of the killings. Years later Cheshire asked himself, and others, the same question. It was a project he might have undertaken. The place was called Auschwitz-Birkenau.

For the time being, however, there would be no more projects. Next morning Cochrane told him that his command of 617 Squadron was over. Munro, Shannon, Ross and McCarthy would likewise be screened. The ruling was no surprise. Mimoyecques had been Cheshire's hundredth operation, while the three flight commanders had been flying with 617 since the Dams Raid.‡ Even so, while it seemed to one colleague that Cheshire accepted the decision with

---

★ Cheshire's unfamiliarity with pilot navigation prompted the navigators' union to serve him with a bogus memorandum headed 'Screening of operational navigator' which catalogued his crimes and recommended his disqualification.

† The V-3, otherwise known as Busy Lizzie, had a 150 metre barrel of 150 mm bore. Side chambers fed into the barrel on a herringbone pattern, to deliver additional propelling charges which fired a projectile at over 5,000 ft per second. Following 617's attack the V-3 was never used in anger.

‡ David Shannon had been flying on operations more or less continuously since June 1942.

good grace, according to Cochrane 'it broke his heart'. Argument with Cochrane, however, was seldom productive, and as the day passed protest gave way to an upsurge of playfulness as unacknowledged tensions fell away. By evening they were fooling about 'like children'. They had finished together.

Cochrane told Harris:

Dear C-in-C
I am writing to let you know that the 'old guard' of No. 617 Sqn have at last asked that they be given a rest and I have told them that they will be fitted into other jobs as soon as possible. I have realized for some time that a reconstruction of the squadron was inevitable and have made up numbers with younger blood and earmarked Tait as successor to Cheshire . . .[17]

Monty Philpott, Cheshire's steadfast ally, recommended him for a further decoration.

Since being awarded a second bar to his DSO early this year Wing Commander Cheshire has continued to lead his famous squadron on every one of its operations. Moreover, although the targets selected for attack have become of a far more hazardous nature, he has nevertheless further intensified the pioneer aspect of his brilliant leadership. As leader of each operation he has invariably retained his responsibility for the initial marking of the targets and he has now proved conclusively the efficacy of fast and manoeuvrable twin- and single-engine types of aircraft for this vitally important role.

Philpott went on to note Cheshire's 'complete disregard for his own personal safety', the 'unerring accuracy' of his marking of 'heavily defended targets such as Munich and Brunswick' and more recent daylight operations 'against precise targets in France'. Philpott rightly singled out the attack on Le Havre, observing that Cheshire had 'entirely ignored the extremely heavy ground defences'. In this instance alone many pilots have testified that he had only avoided destruction 'by a split second from the immense barrage which was entirely directed against his aircraft'. Philpott concluded, 'Wing Commander Cheshire's outstanding record as a squadron commander is in my opinion clearly far beyond mere words of praise and I therefore recommend him for the immediate award of a third bar to his DSO.'[18] A party was in prospect. Cochrane asked Harris if 'there was any possibility of your being able to find the time to come up. The squadron has maintained such a magnificent spirit throughout the whole of its history, in spite of heavy losses which it had earlier on, that I would like to give the old hands a suitable send-off and a visit, or even a message from you would be immensely appreciated.'[19] Harris sent a message.

Alteration and intensification of the operational set up ... have inevitably necessitated some modification of the constitution of the squadron. Now that the old lags depart to pastures new (and I hope, so well deserve, more peaceful) I take the opportunity to thank you all for your magnificent contribution to the war effort. 617 has fought famously and earned a place second to none amongst the fighting units of the Empire. The spirit which has fed the squadron since its inception will, of its own momentum, carry you forward throughout the times of great achievement which lie ahead in the day of victory.[20]

Cochrane read this out during the farewell dinner at the Petwood. Satterly and Sharp were there, and Mick Martin returned for it. The occasion had something of the ceremony of a pre-war guest night. There was also a mood of nostalgia, not just because so many were leaving but because all direct connection with the squadron's nativity was now gone.[21] Wallis was absent; always looking forwards rather than back, he was on his way to France to study Tallboy's effects.

The handover to Tait came next day. Cheshire wrote to Douglas Baxter: 'I'm leaving this job unfortunately in a week or so and have an invitation from the USAAF to visit them in the States, so I expect to be out of the country for some time ... Have at least passed my century.'[22] Harris vetoed the American trip. Guy Gibson had toured the United States the year before and there were many who considered that the experience had done him no good. While Harris pondered his future, Cheshire was entered for the month-long senior commanders' course at Cranwell.

He stayed on at Woodhall for a few days more, writing reports, letters, interviewing NCO aircrew under consideration for commissions. 'Wg Cdr Cheshire wished me goodbye and good luck,' noted one on the day he left. 'Everybody sorry. Know there will never be another like him.' On one of these last days there was a squadron lunch for him and the three flight commanders. Cheshire stood to make a short speech. After he finished there was an outbreak of clapping, whistling, shouting and table-banging which resounded for minutes. Cheshire dipped his head to disguise the tears. At last something had pierced him.

The Cranwell course began on 19 July. Five days later Harris told Cochrane: 'I have sent a personal signal to Peirse asking him if he can offer any suitable Gp Capt's post in staff, planning or command, and will let you know when I have a reply.' 'Peirse' was Air Chief Marshal Sir Richard Peirse, C-in-C Air Command, South-East Asia. Cheshire's new destiny was to be the war in Burma.

Constance's reaction is unrecorded, but the signs are that she did not take it well. Less than a year before she had, in Cheshire's words, 'gone off the deep end' when he announced his return to operations. Now, when virtually any safe job in the RAF could be his for the asking, he was going to confront the Japanese. His new post was ostensibly a staff job, but no one near him doubted his resolve to return to operations if he could. Indeed, a plan for doing so was already taking shape. Constance's response was to pack up and return to New York. Cheshire told his parents that 'all being well' she would join him in India, but this was self-delusion. She was, in fact, on the verge of a breakdown.

Cheshire readied himself for India. Simon the poodle was put in the hands of Kitty McQuillan, a friendly WAAF at Woodhall, and his search for another Alfa Romeo was discontinued.

Philpott's recommendation for a third bar to his DSO had meanwhile been gathering annotations as it passed from Philpott to Sharp to Cochrane, and finally to Harris. A few days after Cheshire finished at Cranwell he was summoned by Harris, who gently told him that he was being awarded the Victoria Cross. Uniquely, the 'Date of Act of Bravery' was given as 1940–44: four years of sustained courage, rather than any specific deed.

... he sent for me, from London. I wondered what an earth was going on ... he was very nice indeed. He told me I was getting the VC, and it was just before I went overseas, he was going to let me know. I was expecting ... I thought

I'd done something wrong. And he was very nice, and very fatherly and very friendly and I liked him very much.[23]

The source of the recommendation is unclear. It may have been Harris himself, for it had long been in his mind that the cumulative pressures upon bomber aircrew called for a special kind of fortitude which deserved decoration in itself. Eighteen months earlier he had upheld a recommendation for a bar to Guy Gibson's DSO on the grounds that any captain who had completed so many sorties 'is worth two DSOs if not a VC'. In Cheshire's case Harris ruled that a captain who had completed a hundred sorties was worth a VC rather than three DSOs.

But it might equally have come from Cochrane. Cochrane regarded Munich as a supreme moment for Cheshire, not because of his precision – Cochrane agreed that 627 Squadron later marked with greater accuracy – but because it was the apotheosis of an argument which he had pressed with his life as well as his intellect. 'There was only one VC in it because the entire original burden of proof was his. The unknown risk was his . . . Later we realized there was no [*sic*] danger in the method, but someone had to demonstrate it first. That someone was Cheshire.'[24]

The citation was published on 8 September. Whereas Philpott's original recommendation had placed emphasis on Le Havre, roughly half of the official citation centred upon the attack on Munich, which exemplified Cheshire's 'cold and calculated acceptance of risks'. What he did in the Munich operation, the citation concluded, 'was typical of the careful planning, brilliant execution and contempt for danger which has established for Wing Commander Cheshire a reputation second to none in Bomber Command'.

When 'second to none' was beamed through the prism of the Air Ministry's Public Relations Department it re-emerged as 'greatest of all'. *The Tatler* put his photograph on its cover, nonchalant and cool, and said that Cheshire was the 'greatest bomber pilot in the world'. 'The Greatest Bomber Pilot of Them All' was the headline in the *Evening Standard*. 'Ace of All Bombers Wins VC' sang the *Liverpool Daily Post*. He had his wish; there was hardly anyone in Britain who did not recognize him. Doorstepped by the press,

Primrose said, 'I didn't think it was possible for him to get any more decorations.' Grey Walls was busy, for by a strange concurrence the family gained two supreme honours within a week: Dr Cheshire was appointed to the University of Oxford's Vinerian Chair of Law.

Congratulations poured in: from Dobson at Avros, Frederick Handley Page, ACM Sir Douglas Evill, Carr and old friends in Yorkshire. Sir Archibald Sinclair acknowledged his 'background of devoted service, brilliant leadership and sustained achievement in the thick of the fighting throughout the war'. A 'Man in the Street 1914–1918' wrote on impulse to declare his jubilation.[25] At Stowe J. F. Roxburgh awarded a school holiday. On his last evening in England, Cheshire celebrated with friends in the Ritz.

Most of the letters reached him weeks later. On 10 September he boarded a Sunderland flying boat at Bournemouth for the first leg of the five-day journey to India. There was no farewell to his parents, and it was not until two months later that he heard of his father's Chair and wrote in belated congratulation.

One letter which caught up with him in Delhi was a generous handwritten note from Guy Gibson, now exiled to a staff job at Coningsby.

My Dear Leonard,

Just a line to congratulate you most heartily on your very well earned VC. It was a mighty fine effort and has received universal praise. More, it is a great show for 617. I don't know whether this will ever get [to] you but don't reply anyway as you will get a lot of these.

See you out there.

Yours Ever,

Guy Gibson[26]

'*See you out there.*' Gibson yearned to join the Japanese war himself. By the time Cheshire read his letter Gibson was charred and in a coffin.* Like Lofty Long, like Desmond Coutts, like Richard Hillary, 'Dinghy' Young, George Holden, Tommie Lloyd, Bob

---

* Wg Cdr Gibson and his navigator, Sqn Ldr J. B. Warwick, were killed late on the evening of 19 September while returning from a raid on Rheydt and München-Gladbach.

Hay, Jack Randle, Jack Anderson, like thousands of others in the pitiful, dragging procession, Guy Gibson was beyond all light, or fire.

PART FOUR: ONE OR TWO
VIOLENT SHOCKS, 1944–1945

10. Asia and Washington

After the adrenalin and comradeship of 617 there is a kind of stagnancy about the next period which caused Andrew Boyle to hurry past it.[1] Cheshire's service in India ended prematurely, while the life that followed in Washington involved 'going through files'. Administration does not make for stirring biography. Nor does silence. It was in this period that Cheshire recognized that his relationship with Constance had no future, and he was for ever afterwards mute about the circumstances. The phase nevertheless has interest, partly because some of its sources have not been previously examined, partly too because of its relationship with what came before and after, but above all because it sees the beginning of the end of his atheism.

Of course, when the Sunderland alighted at Karachi on 15 September 1944 neither Cheshire nor anyone else could have known that less than three months later he would be passing through in the opposite direction. He expected to be in Asia for months, possibly until the end of the war, and his few weeks there are best read as the opening fragment of an unfinished epic. His arrival cast a spell. A friend told him from England, 'It is really extraordinary how many people seem confident we shall do well in the air out there just on account of the fact that you are having a great deal to do with it.'

Since 1943 the air forces of South East Asia Command (SEAC) had been unified in one structure, Air Command South East Asia, staffed by officers of both the RAF and USAAF. ACSEA's RAF element had a tinge of Bomber Command in exile, and not a little of misfortune. At its head was Air Chief Marshal Sir Richard Peirse, who had been AOC-in-C Bomber Command until misgivings about his performance had led to his removal and the appointment of Harris.

Peirse's deputy was Major General George Stratemeyer, a lively and effective American who was also commander of Eastern Air Command, a component of ACSEA which flew in support of the reconquest of Burma. Within EAC were familiar figures like Air Marshal W. A. Coryton, Cochrane's predecessor, who had headed 5 Group until Harris fired him for disputing an order. Coryton now led the Third Tactical Air Force. Alongside him was Air Commodore F. J. W. Mellersh, commander of the Strategic Air Force. Stratemeyer's headquarters stood in a Calcutta suburb, and after several days of social whirl in Delhi it was here that Cheshire reported on temporary attachment on 19 September. In his first week he was 'given the gen'.

Burma was 'one of the world's most forbidding theatres of operation – seven hundred miles of virtually trackless, disease-infected, jungle-clad mountains, swamped for half the year by monsoon rains'.[2] Here there were no continuous fronts or lines, but rather a fluid intermingling of areas and positions possessed. The jungle's density bred tension as well as disease; ground changed hands in brutal fighting between men who could seldom see more than a few yards at a time. From above, the jungle appeared as a dull green froth, oceanic in its lack of landmarks. Only sluggish, yellow-brown winding rivers relieved the monotony.[3]

Overhead Beaufighters followed railways in search of enemy trains, Mitchells and Liberators flew to attack Japanese communications and drop mines in their waters, and a continuous train of Dakotas carried food, weapons, equipment and medicines to the men of General Slim's Fourteenth Army who slogged onward below. Air supply – which had been sustained through the torrential rains since July – was a phenomenon in its own right. On the airfield at Comilla Cheshire marvelled at the ceaseless traffic of Dakotas. Although Japanese aircraft were less in evidence, Allied casualties were high. Fire from the ground, weather and technical failures claimed thousands. Downed aircrew were seldom seen again. And for any, like Cheshire, who were repelled by slimy creatures, the Burmese jungle was not a good place to be.

Overall, Cheshire was told, the land battle was going well – or, at least, in the right direction. During the summer Sino-American forces had been pushing into north-east Burma, while Japan's grip upon Imphal and Kohima had been prised loose. Since July the Japanese Fifteenth Army had been retreating under British counter-attack and was now being pushed back across the River Chindwin. On the coastal plain, operations to repossess the island of Akyab and the Arakan were in prospect.

Cheshire went out to look for himself. He was a good listener – 'he drew you in' – and all kinds of people found themselves talking to him. His gift of making anyone feel that they mattered invited confidences and forthrightness. In a groaning Anson he shuttled from place to place to accumulate impressions, and presently arrived at fervent views on at least two issues.

One concerned maintenance and morale. General Slim's men knew themselves as 'The Forgotten Army': 'Rain, insects, heat and disease made life irksome enough, but the worst factor was the suspicion that everybody else in the war was better supplied, better equipped, better regarded at home and having a better time.'[4] To an extent this also applied to ACSEA, wherein many RAF units flew obsolescent aircraft, ground crews were exhausted and virtually everyone had lost weight as a result of dysentery, malaria or other disease.

Nothing here was new, and much of it was out of their hands. However, there was also an issue of standards. Cheshire was appalled not only by failures in India to protect specialized apparatus against the climate, but also by the slovenly way in which sensitive equipment was being packed in Britain before shipment. Automatic pilots, for instance, essential for long-range flying, became dysfunctional if carelessly or inexpertly handled.

Maintenance standards had long been a Cheshire speciality, and within days he began a crusade to improve them. He shared his concerns in correspondence with a friend at RAE Farnborough, who reflected that if equipment was being neglected then 'so are men and methods'. 'There is enough tragedy in the mere fact of men having to fight in such a muck-heap, but when one considers that in the past they have fought with the additional handicap of a muck-heap mentality at home and on the supply lines, it makes me believe that the air situation is in frightful peril . . .' In a later letter he added: 'There are a good many things which in my opinion have not been properly considered from the point of view of operating at your end, by the people at this end'; unless things are got right 'a good many brave men will needlessly lose their lives'.[5]

The second issue was bombing accuracy. Japanese communications were extremely extended.

About half the needs of the Japanese Army in Burma could be met by the products of the theatre in which it was operating, and the chief means whereby supplies were transported was provided by some 5,000 miles of railways. The most important . . . was the infamous railway linking Bangkok with Moulmein . . . It ran for 244 miles through thick jungles . . . round and sometimes over mountains, and along its length were no fewer than 688 bridges, spanning *chaungs*, rivers and ravines varying in breadth from 100 to 1,200 feet. This line alone received 2,700 tons of bombs . . . there were only a few large targets and the technique of the saturation raid could not in consequence be adopted. The bombers concentrated therefore on destroying bridges and obliterating tracks. Their greatest obstacle was . . . the vast distances they had to fly.[6]

Cheshire had just spent eight months perfecting methods for destroying small targets. In addition to breaking bridges, the same methods would be equally applicable to the strongly fortified, well-concealed positions with which the Japanese periodically held up Allied progress. Early in October he gathered his thoughts, put them in a paper entitled 'Employment of Heavy Bombers in the Far East'[7] and gave it to Air Commodore Mellersh. The paper recommended the formation of a small, specialized bombing force, equipped with Lancasters and flown by 'exceptionally highly skilled and highly trained aircrews'. Mellersh forwarded the paper to Brig. Gen. A. R. Luedecke, who told Stratemeyer:

. . . I consider the project to be extremely sound and I am convinced that he [Cheshire] himself is the right man to form and train such a force. He has for a long time been engaged in England on precisely this type of work. He is familiar with most of the up-to-date equipment, both British and American, and furthermore knows the scientists and research experts in the UK personally. In addition Gp Capt. Cheshire left behind in England a nucleus of the most experienced and talented crews of Bomber Command. These crews . . . are maintaining contact with Gp Capt. Cheshire and, I am told, repeatedly asked that they should be asked to come out to this theatre of war and serve once more under his command.[8]

In other words, Cheshire was seeking to re-create 617 Squadron for operations in Burma.

The idea was not entirely new. Nick Ross recalls conversations during the last days at Woodhall when it was dreamed that McCarthy, Shannon, Munro, Kearns and himself would go out to India and re-form the squadron.[9] A few days after submitting his paper Cheshire wrote to him: 'If ever I succeed in taking part in the war again, you will be just about the first person I shall send for.'[10]

And now the dream was becoming reality. Stratemeyer liked the idea, and in mid-October he sent the paper to Peirse. The following week Cheshire stayed with Peirse in Delhi, and there met SEAC's Commander-in-Chief, Lord Louis Mountbatten. Mountbatten, too, was impressed. He told Leigh-Mallory, SEAC's Air C-in-C designate:*

During my recent visit to Delhi I had a short talk with Gp Capt. G. L. Cheshire . . . who has recently come out to this theatre . . . He told me that he couldn't help observing the lower standard of skill and experience of the heavy bomber squadrons in Air Command, SEA compared with squadrons in Bomber Command. This naturally produces a lower standard of determination to fight through to the target. Peirse has . . . been aware for some time of this situation but it has not hitherto been possible to do much about it because of the low priority that this theatre has hitherto had when asking for assistance from other sources.

Mountbatten endorsed the plan for an elite bomber unit: 'What Peirse would like to do, therefore, is to be given the specialized aircrews and material to convert one of his squadrons into a specialized squadron on the lines of 617 in Bomber Command.'[11]

Peirse returned to London at the end of November and promoted

---

* Peirse's command was ending, following criticism which attended his elopement with the wife of General Sir Claude Auchinleck, C-in-C India.

the plan. On 1 December the Air Ministry agreed that the conversion of one heavy bomber squadron into a specialized unit akin to 617 Squadron should begin immediately.[12] Cheshire had made his case, and three days later he was posted to the RAF's headquarters in Burma to put it into practice. But he did not know this. He was no longer there.

On 18 November he had written to his parents:

Constance, I'm sad to say, is seriously ill in New York. I had a cable from her sister asking me to come over as soon as possible – it took nearly three weeks to arrive. Fortunately I work in an American Headquarters: General Stratemeyer cabled straight to Washington and got me an answer in twenty-four hours. He has also given me an air passage to New York and I shall go there as soon as I get RAF permission. They've been at least three days making their minds up already.[13]

The RAF first refused,[14] then relented. Five days later Cheshire was given permission to go to New York 'for a period not to exceed fourteen days'.[15]

Constance was in a nursing home. The nature of her illness is undisclosed, although when Andrew Boyle asked Cheshire about it his jotted record of the reply was 'C = mental case'.[16] In the book itself Boyle reported it as a 'severe nervous breakdown',[17] which in 1955 might have meant a number of things. Whatever it was, when Cheshire arrived the doctors 'were at pains to point out that the responsibility for her state of health was his alone'.[18] The corollary was that responsibility for her recovery must also be his. He had ignored Constance in 1943 when he had gone back to operations against her wishes; now he decided to stay and see her back to health.

The decision nevertheless troubled him. Aside from military discipline he had given his word to Stratemeyer that he would return. Happily, there was compassion in the system. His leave was first extended, and then three days before Christmas he was given a supernumerary appointment with the RAF delegation in Washington.[19] This regularized the matter and assuaged his guilt. On 15 January 1945 his residence was made permanent by an appointment as Group Captain (Plans), with responsibility for tactical and technical development within the British Joint Staff Mission.[20]

Merciful as all this was, 'I cannot help feeling uncomfortable at having left India for a comfortable and sedentary job.'[21] While the war continued his impulse was to be part of it, yet a letter from EAC in February stirred his conscience when it reproachfully mentioned help that 'we were badly in need of some time ago'.

Those who knew Cheshire in these days found him thinner, more tense, more strained than they could recall. He fell ill. On 22 January 1945 he was admitted to hospital in Pasadena. The cause is unrecorded, but he was in hospital for a week and convalescence took several weeks more. The episode heralded a pattern.

Back in Washington his work concerned planning for the integration of Bomber Command's Tiger Force with the Pacific strategic air offensive, and Operation Downfall – the invasion of Japan. Downfall's forecast casualties appalled him. By early June the minimum estimates of battle casualties in the projected amphibious assaults alone – Operations Olympic and Coronet★ – were being put at 193,000, and perhaps as high as a quarter of a million.

Alongside office duties he travelled and lectured on the theory and practice of precision bombing. It was the only subject about which he knew,[22] yet even in this field his experience was being overtaken. In May he submitted a paper to the air staff on long-range bombing against Japan. In one way this was his most lucid treatise. In another, it said little of which Air Ministry planners were not already aware. Ten months had passed and the bombing war, which, as he might have remembered, had evolved almost from week to week when he was part of it, had moved on. In the Air Ministry it was agreed that the views expressed were to be regarded 'purely as personal to Gp Capt. Cheshire' – a tactful way of implying that Gp Capt. Cheshire, now in Washington, was a little out of touch.[23]

★ Downfall would have involved two massive amphibious assaults: one on Kyushu (Operation Olympic, timetabled for 1 November), the other on Honshu (Coronet). The directive for Olympic was issued on 25 May 1945. US forecasts of casualties were 'not subject to accurate estimate', but a number of Truman's advisers forecast that Downfall would cost a minimum of 250,000 and possibly as many as 1,000,000 American casualties, with an equal number of Japanese. Meanwhile, between June 1944 and August 1945 the US strategic air offensive against Japan killed more than 240,000 Japanese and injured at least 300,000.

Washington. Constance had been discharged from the nursing home and was now with him. Cheshire gives a glimpse of his routine:

Summer 1945 . . . The doldrums. Not a breath of wind from any quarter. Not a ripple on the surface of the water. Not the remotest sign of hope . . . Get up at 8.15; breakfast 8.45; drive to the office of the British Joint Staff Mission – one-way traffic all the way in. Go through files until 12.30; lunch in the canteen; more files till 5; then get picked up on Constitution Avenue – one-way traffic all the way back. After that, house decorating, or move the furniture around, or go to a party, or just sit and talk.[24]

Harris had barred him from America lest he be seduced by flattery and luxurious living. The reality was a nine-to-five job and disillusion. Having fixed his stare on one object – fighting, to finish the war – for four and a half years, he began to blink, look away and daydream.

He reverted to thinking about himself, and his future. In March he travelled to the Bahamas, collecting literature and information with a view to pursuing a project discussed at Woodhall: the New Mayflower – a luxury hotel on a deserted island in the Caribbean. Simultaneously he was being courted by industrialists and businessmen, and his pre-war hankering for ambitious and remunerative projects began to revive. Seven years on, however, it was not simply wealth which attracted him. A stronger lure was to recapture the solidarity he had found in operational flying. On 6 March he wrote privately to a friend: 'I have recently become involved in a very large radio project backed by sufficient capital to compete with any existing concern.' The enterprise would require a 'highly efficient radar/radio section'. The business would be run 'by men who speak the same language that we used to speak at Woodhall Spa'.

He wrote another letter that day, which claimed that the capital available for this enterprise would be in millions, that it would be an Anglo-American conglomerate, and that its market would be worldwide. The company would need a chief executive. The individual Cheshire had in mind is not named on the carbon copy, but his parting sentence gives the game away: 'I hope that things go well with you and I am glad to see that Bomber Command is

functioning satisfactorily under your control.' Cheshire was offering
Harris a job.[25] He was beginning to lose his bearings.

Fighting and leadership had focused him, ousted his whimsicality
and self-interest. Now that he was not fighting or leading, both
resurfaced. Perhaps he should resume writing?[26] A literary-cum-
business proposition was put to him by a division of General Motors
in Michigan. Cheshire visited the plant in April, and was afterwards
asked if he would provide short stories and narratives of his war
experiences, for promotional purposes. Cheshire agreed, promising
to deliver the manuscripts by mid-August.[27]

With a stable address for the first time in months, letters began
to find him. Many were from parents or widows of dead aircrew.
'For nearly two years I have held off writing this letter,' began the
wife of one 76 Squadron member, imploring him for news of what
had happened when her husband had been shot down in 1942.[28]
There were dozens like this. Patiently, considerately, he did his
best.[29] Incongruously mingled with the echoes and ghosts were
irritating demands for decisions on his personal affairs in England.
Should his parents sell his old Bentley? Marston Moor was closing
down, he was told – what did he wish done with his railway
bungalow?[30]

Early in July he was called back to London. It was a brief visit,
less than a week, but it brought one part of his war to an end.
Christopher had come home. They met at the Ritz, and three days
of joyous celebration followed. Little by little Christopher unveiled
his life for the last four years; his part in preparations for the Great
Escape from Stalag Luft 3; the final weeks, when the Germans had
marched them west to escape the Red Army; the women in
bombed-out Lübeck who had threatened them; the bizarre experience of sitting in the blackness of a shelter during an Allied air raid,
listening to the dejected talk of a U-boat crew. And in the last days,
amid the rubble and chaos, a phrase in Goebbels's last broadcast:
'The Rhine will always run.'[31]

'It was late at night – the third in an almost non-stop celebration.'
Christopher had gone to bed; 'the original party had dwindled to
a mere three or four'. Cheshire was in the Vanity Fair, a Mayfair
nightclub. The conversation became noisy.

Then finally the most voluble of them all leant across the table at me and asked: 'How much do you know about God?'

She was a good-looking girl, whom I had met only twice before, a trifle worn perhaps from too many late nights and too much gin, but not the sort to fall for religion nor to lose her balance for more than a passing moment. So I answered in no uncertain terms . . . 'God is an inward conscience, personal to us all, that tells us what we ought to do and what we ought not; one thing to some of us, another to others. It's as simple as that, and if only people wouldn't go and confuse the issue by bringing religion into it, the world would be a lot better off.'

To which the girl replied: 'Absolute nonsense. God is a person. *A person.* And you know it just as well as I do.'

Cheshire was nonplussed. 'For I suddenly knew that what she had said was true.'[32] Possible implications flooded in – Sundays, churches, clericalism and its sing-song voices; for none of which he cared – and in the instant he determined not to accept them, 'anyway, not on the spur of the moment'.[33] But God was inescapable: not as a reality to be agreed to or that anyone had authenticated – simply as something, some*one* known.

Andrew Boyle's account of this episode was guarded, saying that Cheshire had 'claimed' that his interest in religion was 'momentarily awakened' during this brief leave.[34] What troubled Boyle was the date. He didn't believe it. Cheshire's absent-mindedness about times and place in his interviews was considerable, and Boyle became wary of uncorroborated dates. Here he is badgering Cheshire about it in 1954: 'I've asked you this before, Leonard, and I'm still not satisfied. Are you absolutely sure about that incident in the Mayfair when a strange woman contradicted you re the existence of God?' Everyone else Boyle had talked to had told him that it was most unlikely that Cheshire would have been thinking about religion in mid-1945. They had said a year later, perhaps, and Boyle told Cheshire, 'which I feel myself!' But Cheshire replied yes, he was sure that the occasion had been in July 1945.

Boyle remained sceptical, privately dating the episode to 1946. However, since his instinct and Cheshire's testimony were irreconcilable, he circumvented the problem in *No Passing Glory* by grudgingly accepting the date while reinterpreting the consequences.[35] History, with hindsight, has a tendency to seek meaning in events which were invisible to the participants as they approached them. Boyle was convinced that *something* in Cheshire's life must have been changed by the atomic bomb. Like almost everyone else he saw Nagasaki as Cheshire's Damascene moment. A conversation beforehand in a London bar was less of a story, although more (he might have reflected) in the tradition of the Gospels.

The original draft of *The Face of Victory* records a little more. The story is essentially the same, but some of its detail has a different accent. In this version the woman's Christian name is given, there is less noise, greater intimacy and the sense of an evening which 'had not been going too well'.

> I all but regretted that I had ever asked her out at all . . . I had embarked on the story of my life – anyway the matrimonial part: but what I had not bargained on was that Clare had her matrimonial problems too, and hardly had I got into my stride than she was telling me that she was in exactly the same boat and that the only answer was religion.[36]

This is probably as close as we shall come to the moment when Clare placed the Key of Promise in his hand, and his fingers closed on it.[37]

Back in Washington Cheshire was put on notice for a journey.[38] At first no great emphasis was placed on this – he was simply told that he would be going somewhere, and that he should be prepared to leave when the time came. On 11 July he told a colleague that he anticipated 'being on the move from the 21st of this month for a few weeks'. On 20 July he wrote about the sale of the railway bungalow, saying that he would be 'out of touch for some five or six weeks'.[39]

11. Potsdam and Tinian

I have a tent for a room and a camp bed to sleep on. The furniture, like everything else, is made out of wooden crates. The bathroom is a pipe in the open connected to a water tank: the tank itself is made out of salvaged bomb containers. There is no hot water and there is no batman to wake you up. Beside the coral path leading to the bathroom is a derelict Japanese foxhole. Beyond it by the sea is the graveyard of 1,100 marines who died in the battle for the island. On the other side, across a field of sugar cane, is a coral cliff about 100 ft high. It is covered in undergrowth and riddled with caves. There are still Japanese in those caves. Every now and then they come out and shoot someone.*[1]

He was on Tinian, an island in the Marianas in the western Pacific.

Two weeks earlier, a little before dawn on 16 July, the British physicist Professor Sir James Chadwick had been among 425 scientists, engineers and officials in reinforced shelters on a hill overlooking the desert at Alamogordo in New Mexico. The night had been cold, with lightning and gusting showers. The clocks turned 05.29. A standby flare traced a green arc. Chadwick looked through a piece of dark welder's glass. Forty-five more seconds passed. Then:

. . . an intense pinpoint of light which grew rapidly to a great ball. Looking sideways, I could see that the hills and desert around us were bathed in radiance, as if the sun had been turned on by a switch. The light began to diminish but, peeping round my dark glass, the ball of fire was still blindingly bright . . . The ball had then turned through orange to red and was surrounded by a purple luminosity. It was connected to the ground by a short grey stem, resembling a mushroom.[2]

★ Although Tinian was stormed by American troops in July 1944, several hundred Japanese remained at large on the island until the end of the war.

Mushroom cloud, fireball. New names for an altered world. The pinpoint of light had been hotter than the centre of the sun; the flash a brilliance which lit hills; the fireball an effulgent core surrounded by 'a reddening brightness with no definite boundary'. The ball ascended and darkened.

Chadwick was twenty miles away, so blast and sound followed. First, the air pressing hard against people and things; next a sharp clap, as if the sky had split; then a long rumbling, like 'wagons running around in the hills'. The glare shone in Albuquerque and Santa Fe.³ Some had an impression that the sun had risen and then set again.

The device had been exploded atop a hundred-foot steel tower. At Ground Zero – land immediately below the point of explosion – the desert was vitrified and the tower had evaporated. Half a mile from Ground Zero a strong steel frame had replicated the skeleton of a large urban building. Lacking walls against which blast could push and deeply anchored in concrete, no one expected it to be damaged. The explosion had uprooted the structure and torn it apart. One hundred and eighty miles away the shock's farthest ripples cracked windows. In this epiphany, atomic power seemed 'almost full grown at birth'.

The test carried the code name Trinity, and in Potsdam that Monday President Truman and Secretary of War Henry Stimson awaited news of it. The Allied leaders were gathering for their last conference. During the afternoon Truman toured Berlin, a city which Allied bombers had striven for three years to wreck. On his return a cable from the War Department told him that a weapon existed which could do more in less than a minute. Churchill was told by Stimson at noon★ the next day.

Some days before in Washington Cheshire had been summoned by Field Marshal Maitland Wilson, head of the British Joint Staff Mission.†

According to those who knew, the only other occasion on which an RAF officer below air rank had been sent for . . . was prior to his being cashiered . . .

★ Times given in this chapter are local to the places in which events occurred.
† Cheshire later placed this meeting on the morning of 17 July; however, Wilson was then in Potsdam.

I started off in an office staffed by some female secretaries and a lieutenant. From there I was ushered somewhat formally into another office where the ranks were considerably more senior. and finally with yet more formality into the Holy of Holies . . . the floor of which appeared to take several minutes to cross. Lord Maitland Wilson, whose proportions were of no mean size . . . unexpectedly rose from his chair and shook me warmly by the hand. He invited me to sit down and said that the Allies had invented an atom bomb.

Just like that.[4]

Did I know what an atomic bomb was? No, I hadn't the faintest idea. Neither, I suspected, did the field marshal, for he eyed me intently as he posed the question and relaxed visibly when he saw me shake my head.[5]

Wilson outlined something called the Manhattan Project – a colossal yet secret enterprise of science and engineering which had cost more than $2 billion. He explained that 'a determined effort was being made to persuade the Japanese to surrender, but if they refused the bomb would be dropped on a target in Japan'. The Manhattan team included British scientists. Chadwick had recommended that British observers should witness Manhattan's consummation, and Truman had agreed to Churchill's request that two should be present. One would be Dr William Penney, a mathematician who was already working for Manhattan. The other was Cheshire, whose task was to learn 'about the tactical aspects of using such a weapon, reach a conclusion about its future implications for air warfare and report back to the Prime Minister'.[6]

Cheshire next had an appointment with Manhattan's director, General Leslie Groves. Burly, tireless, quietly brusque, humourless and extremely effective, Groves 'ran the sprawling Manhattan Project as his personal fiefdom'.[7] Most of Manhattan's scientists loathed him, although Chadwick – himself 'retiring and sensitive'[8] – saw the merit of his single-minded drive, and by some attraction of opposites trust existed between them.

Groves was fanatically protective of Manhattan. Only those with a demonstrated need to know were allowed even the most rudimentary knowledge, and nothing which 'was not deemed relevant to their own narrowly defined concerns'.[9] Groves did everything he could to hold back cooperation with the United

Kingdom.[10] Divulging information to a stranger who was both inessential to Manhattan and British did not therefore come easily. Nonetheless, Groves told Cheshire something about Project Silverplate, the USAAF's companion programme for delivery of the bomb. A special unit, the 509th Composite Group, had been formed for the purpose, and it was to this that Cheshire would be attached.

This knowledge placed Cheshire in a category of privilege which is hard to exaggerate. Britain's Chiefs of Staff had not been consulted about use of the atomic bomb, and few in the War Cabinet even knew of its existence.* Cheshire could accordingly expect to be followed, overheard, and watched.

Carrying such a burden of confidentiality was a responsibility for which I was neither trained nor temperamentally suited, and as soon as I had seen General Groves I left for the anonymity of Los Angeles to mark time until called for the long flight to Tinian ... We were what was called 'processed' through the then principal gateway to the Pacific battle theatre, Hamilton Field near San Francisco ...[11]

At one moment he was exceptionally favoured; at the next he was ignored, isolated and 'transmuted, as it were ... into a parcel'.[12] He waited for six days. Events in Potsdam, Tokyo or Moscow might decide whether he would proceed.

Early in June the Japanese Cabinet had resolved to fight to the finish. Within the Cabinet, however, there was a peace faction, and on 12 July the Emperor and Prime Minister had authorized tentative diplomatic contact through the Soviet Union to ascertain if a formula could be found which would allow the war to end. Reports reaching the Americans through neutral embassies suggested that Japanese interest centred on the future of the imperial dynasty.

Hitherto, the Allies had insisted that Japan's surrender should be unconditional. An issue now for the Americans was whether

* Britain's agreement to use of the atomic bomb had already been given by Churchill. In April 1945 Wilson cabled that the weapon would soon be brought into US military planning, and asked for guidance on how Britain's position should be represented. He was told this was a military matter for the Prime Minister and Chiefs of Staff. In the event Churchill ratified the decision on 2 July without consulting either the Chiefs of Staff or the War Cabinet. A minute of the Combined Policy Committee on 4 July recorded Britain's concurrence.

'unconditional' should be moderated by an assurance about the position of the Emperor. This had already been discussed within the US Government and by the Combined Chiefs of Staff. It was not straightforward, for the peace party was in tension with a powerful section of Japan's military which remained 'blind to defeat'.[13] No one could anticipate which tendency would prevail.

Assessment of Japanese thinking was further complicated by the stance of the Soviet Union. On 17 July Stalin confirmed that the Soviet Union would honour an earlier undertaking to join the war against Japan. However, when Groves's full report on Trinity reached Truman, Soviet intervention began to seem inessential. Truman's reading of the report[14] left him transformed: in a subsequent discussion with Stalin 'He told the Russians just where they got on and off, and generally bossed the whole meeting.'[15] Churchill, too, 'was completely carried away'.[16] From 22 July the two leaders behaved as if they had drunk some potion which conferred invincibility. In place of Churchill's 'nightmare picture' of a 'a vast, indefinite butchery' was a vision 'of the end of the whole war in one or two violent shocks'.[17] All Truman now needed was the date when the bomb could be cast.

This information arrived in a cable from Groves on the 24th. An operation would become possible between 1 and 10 August. However, if this timetable was to apply, a prompt decision would be needed to allow for technical preparations. Truman saw this message next morning. Its implications coloured the emerging ultimatum to Japan.

When transmitted two days later the Potsdam Proclamation warned that the United States, Great Britain and China were 'poised to strike the final blows'. The Japanese people were invited to choose between 'self-willed militaristic advisers' and the 'path of reason'. The proclamation demanded unconditional surrender of all Japanese armed forces, but also guaranteed maintenance of Japan's economy, eventual participation in world trade and continued sovereignty over her four principal islands. 'The Japanese Government shall remove all obstacles to the revival and strengthening of democratic tendencies among the Japanese people. Freedom of speech, of religion and of thought, as well as respect for the fundamental human rights, shall be established.'[18] A distinction between polity and militarism was drawn. The alternative was 'complete and utter destruction'.

On 24 July, the day when these words were agreed, Cheshire's westward journey resumed.

... when finally seated at the start of our two-and-a-half day flight I found myself next to General Farrell, Commander of the Manhattan Project in the Marianas.* He was a friendly, sensitive man who, when not working on his files, spoke in terms I could understand about the technical aspects of the mission that lay ahead ...[19]

Farrell explained that Manhattan had produced two types of bomb. Code-named Little Boy and Fat Man, both worked by liberating the energy stored in atomic nuclei. Fat Man relied upon implosion: a 12 lb sphere of plutonium would be abruptly squeezed to super-criticality by the detonation of an envelope of explosive. It was a device of this type which had been tested at Alamogordo. Little Boy functioned by a gun mechanism which fired two subcritical masses of uranium 235 together.

Since Trinity had consumed the entire immediate supply of plutonium, the first atomic operation would employ a bomb of the Little Boy class. One part of the U_{235} mechanism was already on its way to Tinian aboard a cruiser, the USS *Indianapolis*; the other would be delivered by air in four or five days' time. The factor controlling Fat Man's use was the time needed to replenish plutonium. A date around 6 August was anticipated.

They travelled in a C54 transport of the 509th's communications flight, an aircraft classified as a 'Green Hornet'. Green Hornets enjoyed fabulous privileges. When landing, taking off or refuelling they took absolute priority, and senior officers who were accustomed to demand seats in half-empty aircraft were blithely turned aside by junior Green Hornet captains. At one moment anonymous, at the next called as witness to an epoch, Cheshire 'began to swing erratically between a feeling of inadequacy and a misplaced sense of self-importance'.[20]

---

* Brigadier General Thomas Farrell was deputy director of the Manhattan Project.

While Cheshire's mind raced, Truman looked again at the list of places chosen for atomic attack. One of them was Kyoto, a city of some million inhabitants which had been selected for its industry and size. Groves was eager to strike Kyoto because it was big enough 'to ensure that the damage from the bomb would run out within the city' and so testify to the extent of the weapon's destructive power. On the other hand Kyoto was Japan's ancient capital, a city of immense religious, historical and cultural significance. Stimson had protested. General Arnold, Commander of the Army Air Forces, voiced similar reservations. Truman pondered, and agreed that Kyoto should be spared. Three days later he wrote in his journal:

This weapon is to be used against Japan between now and August 10th. I have told the Sec. of War, Mr Stimson, to use it so that military objectives and soldiers and sailors are the target and not women and children. Even if the Japs are savages, ruthless, merciless and fanatic, we, as leader of the world for the common welfare cannot drop this terrible bomb on the old Capitol [sic] or the new. He & I are in accord. The target will be a purely military one . . .[21]

In May 1945 the Americans had hesitated about how the bomb should be used. A warning or a demonstration firing had been entertained, but both were considered to have drawbacks. A warning would increase difficulties of delivering the bomb if the Japanese fought on, and might also prompt them to assemble Allied prisoners of war as hostages. An exhibition was dismissed on the grounds that if the bomb failed to go off a flop would be counterproductive. Paucity of fissionable material posed a further problem. In May this had been estimated as sufficient for no more than three weapons. Since one would be required for test, a demonstration would leave only one available for immediate use if Japan refused to surrender.

On 1 June Truman's advisers had recommended that the weapon be used at the earliest opportunity, and without a warning that might betray its nature. They also recommended that 'while the bombs should not concentrate on civilian areas, they should seek to make as profound a psychological impression as possible. The most desirable target would be a vital war plant employing a large number of workers and closely surrounded by workers' houses.'[22]

This conclusion was just then large in Truman's mind, for the formal instruction to drop the bomb had been handed to General Carl Spaatz, Commanding General, US Army Strategic Air Force, earlier that day – 25 July. The directive ordered delivery of the first weapon as soon as weather allowed after about 3 August 1945.[23]

The C54 bearing Farrell and Cheshire droned westward under starshine. Their calendar had already turned to 26 July, and when the aircraft alighted at Guam after dawn the two men were invited to breakfast with General Curtis LeMay, commander of the Twentieth Air Force. LeMay's behaviour struck Cheshire as odd: 'he did not seem very pleased to see me . . . I had a feeling that something was wrong.'[24] Still puzzled by LeMay's mien, Cheshire boarded a C47 for the ninety-minute flight to Tinian.

Twelve miles long and never more than five miles wide, Tinian was a place of strong colours: emerald splashes of vegetation, flaxen sand, dark coral and a cobalt ocean. Descending between puffy clouds Cheshire caught his first glimpse of North Field: a rectangular airfield two miles long, which resembled a giant's gaming board plonked down across the island. Four parallel runways striped the board's length; taxiways gridded it into sixteen boxes, each enclosing ten silvery counters which resolved as B-29s. Beyond the airfield sprawled a megalopolis of prefabricated huts, new-made roads and files of tents. Twenty thousand American servicemen and a handful of women lived there.

Tinian was the apotheosis of strategic bombing, and for someone who despised ease in pursuit of war there was no better place to be. North Field could launch B-29s four at a time, each quartet at 45-second intervals, 200 in under an hour, and amid its tropical humidity, mud and fungal infections 'nowhere were to be seen the extra comforts that we had come to associate with American forces in Europe'.[25] The building of runways, roads and buildings fell to the Seabees, a cadre of colourful can-do individuals whose excavators gouged coral and trucks bounced to and fro with ceaseless urgency. Seabees appeared capable of making anything from anything: the 509th's Officers' Club was run up from plywood, canvas and mosquito netting, furnished from recycled crates, and looked out on rows of huts. Cheshire had a tent for his lodging, and 'the bathroom was just a stand-pipe which emitted either warm or very hot water, according to the height of the sun'.[26] He savoured the austerity and thrived in the industrious atmosphere.

A place of motion, Tinian was also a fulcrum against which distant powers turned. When Cheshire turned in their equilibrium had changed. During the day Churchill and Attlee had flown back to London for declaration of the polls. Britain had a new government. Late that afternoon Churchill had resigned, and Clement Attlee was returning to Potsdam as Prime Minister.

Attlee was unaware that he had an emissary on Tinian. Indeed, he knew next to nothing about the atomic bomb, and by the time he did the decision to use it was two days old. Only Japan's acceptance of the Potsdam Proclamation, broadcast a few hours before, could reverse that.

Privately, Truman and Stimson had allowed seven days for reply. Japan's answer came in three. Kantaro Suzuki, Japan's Prime Minister, announced that his government intended to disregard it. Suzuki's statement looked unequivocal, and from the Americans' perspective that was that. But behind it something more complicated lay concealed. Suzuki and a number of his colleagues were in fact minded to give qualified acceptance to the proclamation as a basis for negotiation. Sadly, they were unaware that their preferred diplomatic path through Moscow was blocked by the Soviet decision to attack them and that negotiation was not on offer. The Potsdam Proclamation said exactly that, although in several respects it left room for miscalculations, the position of the Emperor was not mentioned (although an explicit guarantee on this point had been advised by Joseph C. Grew, the former US ambassador to Japan), the threat of 'final blows'[27] was not elaborated and it contained no deadline other than the Churchillian 'We shall brook no delay'.[28]

Truman and Churchill had known, as Suzuki (and for that matter, until just then, Attlee) did not, that means for the proclamation's instant enforcement were now to hand. Although the ultimatum spoke truth when it warned that the penalty for rejection would be immediate, catastrophic and decisive, Tokyo was a place where words had become flaccid after four years of martial rhetoric. The warning could in any case be interpreted as a statement of what was already happening or as a reference to impending invasion.

Unaware that nothing in the proclamation was exaggerated, Japan's leaders imagined that its terms could be bettered and that time remained for their improvement. Over 10,000 people would be killed for each of the sixteen days it would take them to recognize that they were wrong.

12. Centreboard

Cheshire's feelings flickered between euphoria and self-doubt. Inner agitation was increased by rumours that Japan was about to surrender. 'Far from causing us to hope that the attacks would be postponed, it only served to aggravate our obsession to see the bombs explode.'[1]

During a conversation with Tibbets about the fact that the bomb made another world war impossible, I had impulsively suggested that if by some extraordinary chance the Japanese suddenly surrendered, some kind of demonstration drop ought to be arranged so that people would know just what it meant. He took me to task for it. But it was one of those things you say under stress and do not really mean.[2]

Lt Col. Paul Warfield Tibbets was the 509th's commander and one of America's most accomplished bomber pilots. Stocky, dark haired and thirty years old, behind him lay combat in Europe and a period test-flying the B-29 in days when many saw the Superfortress's teething troubles as more life-threatening than operational flying. Tibbets's impatience with failure or obstructionism led some to think him 'difficult', but more were aware of his alert concern for efficiency and an inscrutable courtesy. Few knew anything about his disciplinarian family background, or that the forenames of his doting mother were Enola Gay. Nor did many members of the 509th know the real reason for their training.

The 509th Composite Group was 'Composite' because in addition to its bombers it combined other elements so as to be self-sufficient in communications and supply. Transport was provided by C54s drawn from a troop carrier squadron. The operational component consisted of fifteen B-29 crews of the 393rd Heavy

Bombardment Squadron. Alongside the fliers was a thirty-seven-strong scientific colony drawn from the Manhattan laboratory at Los Alamos.

The 393rd's aircrew had arrived at the beginning of July. Before that their home had been Wendover Field, a dusty place on the Utah/Nevada border which was 'only' 125 miles from Salt Lake City. Solitude and security went together, and Wendover had been as detested by the crews as it was 'perfect' in the eyes of Tibbets.

An atomic strike would be known by the code name Centreboard, and seven B-29s would take part in it. One would be a spare, stationed at Iwo Jima, roughly midway between Tinian and Japan. Three would fly ahead to assess weather. The remaining three would go to the condemned city: one to drop the bomb, another for high-speed photography, the third bearing instruments to measure the weapon's effects.

The bombing altitude was to be between 20,000 and 31,000 feet, 'primarily . . . to prevent self-destruction'. Synchronization of the bombsight dictated that the axis of approach should involve no more than five degrees of drift and that the run should be of at least eight minutes' duration. Although B-29s were fitted with ground-scanning radar, the drop would be visual, for accuracy 'with such an expensive weapon'.[3] Here lay a problem. Japan's prevailing August weather is cloudy, and a given city could be anticipated as cloud-free perhaps only one day in five. Since this would restrict operations, it was decided to send aircraft to each of three possible targets an hour in advance. Their reports would be radioed to the commander of the bomb-carrying aircraft, who would make his choice in mid-air.

In line with the decision 'to make as profound a psychological impression as possible', Groves and others wished to maximize blast by detonating the bomb about 1,800 feet above the target. The drawback of an air burst lay in the limited time it left for the dropping aircraft to escape. For this, a special manoeuvre had been evolved. The aircraft would make its bombing run upwind to the point of release, then turn sharply, dive and retreat downwind. About 45 seconds would intervene between the release of the bomb and detonation. No one knew what would happen when the shock wave overtook it, but calculations suggested that the aircraft might cover as many as ten miles before that happened, and then be subject to an acceleration of 2G. The B-29 was designed with a safety factor of 4G, so 'it seemed that a sufficient margin of safety had been provided'.[4]

When Cheshire asked about flak he was told that Japanese heavy anti-aircraft defences were generally weak. Fighters posed more risk, especially during an unswerving upwind bombing run when air speed would be set at 200 m.p.h. – slower than a Zero (a Japanese Fighter plane). Tibbets had concluded that both flak and fighters would best be countered by sacrificing the B-29s' fuselage turrets and armour for height and speed.

A more insidious worry lay in the possibility that a security lapse might have given the Japanese enough information to attempt to detonate a bomb by radio before it was dropped, conceivably before take-off. Groves and Farrell took this threat seriously, and equipment was provided on Tinian and in the aircraft to scan relevant frequencies for signs of it.

What were the targets? US planners had urged an unequivocal display of the bomb's power. This meant a large target – a city. It also meant an intact city. There were two reasons for this. One was to assist analysis of the bomb's effect. The other was economy of use.

These criteria posed a tragic problem. Few places still met them. In June LeMay's staff had produced a list of places to be destroyed by 1 October: 'Thirty large and small cities, all to go.'[5] By the end of July most of them had already gone.[6] The Silverplate list was thus short – four names – although the cities on it had been shortlisted three months before and, like healthy beasts set apart for sacrifice, reserved from conventional attack.

Hiroshima headed the list, being the largest city in the Japanese homeland (except Kyoto) which remained undamaged, and a place of military industry. The other three were places of 'secondary industrial importance'. Kokura, about half Hiroshima's size, was earmarked because its arsenal manufactured light automatic weapons, anti-aircraft and anti-tank guns. Kokura also made combat vehicles, and was believed to produce poison gas. Niigata was included because of its oil, metalworking, transport and light industry.

Kyoto's replacement qualified for its shipbuilding, harbour, Mitsubishi plants and steelworks. The town occupied a 'very limited, amphitheatre-like site, extending from reclaimed land along the waterfront to the lower slopes of surrounding hills'. Over a quarter of a million people lived in Nagasaki.

Cheshire shared his tent with William Penney, who 'looked physically fit and strong', and was quietly welcoming. Penney was struck by Cheshire's lean, almost starved, physique, and a little startled by his earnest commitment to the industry of aerial bombing.[7] This tells us something about Cheshire, for at Los Alamos the combination of Penney's sunny countenance and dispassionate attitude to Allied bombing had led a colleague to dub him. 'The Smiling Killer'. Penney's bespectacled face did indeed break into a grin at almost any opportunity, and his gentle manner made a strange contrast with the violence latent in his scholarship. The two men took to one another.

Penney had been a member of the British contingent at Los Alamos since June 1944, when Chadwick recruited him for his knowledge of the effects of explosives. His mathematical skill had assisted calculations of blast, shock waves, bomb damage, the planning of Trinity, the selection of targets and tactics for dropping the bomb. Penney had also helped to design Fat Man, his contribution centring on the geometry and dynamics of the explosive charges which sheathed the plutonium core.

Cheshire was taken to the 509th's technical site, which lay in a barbed-wire enclosure near Tinian's north shore. Inside a Nissen hut 'filled with a disorderly array of tools, manuals and instruments of various kinds, and with a perfectly ordinary-looking man bending over a bench', assembly of Fat Man was in progress. The worker was Luis Alvarez, the physicist in charge.

He straightened up and without much formality began explaining the basic functions of the gadgetry . . . little of which I grasped despite his obvious efforts to keep it simple. Then for no particular reason he walked across to a yellow box lying on the floor and casually kicked it open with his foot. Inside I saw what appeared to be metallic sphere about the size of a football . . . it did not strike me as anything very special . . . until Alvarez said: 'That's the atom.' I must have looked startled, for he told me not to worry; it was perfectly harmless and I was quite free to touch it if I wanted, provided I wore a pair of gloves . . . Disbelief that the new monster bomb we had brought into being could be lying haphazardly on the floor . . . was followed by a sense of awe. Then I pulled myself together, accepted the gloves that Alvarez offered me and touched it. The sensation was rather like that of the first time you touch a live snake: you recoil from what you know will feel slimy and repulsive, and then to your surprise find that it is warmish, almost friendly . . . Hitherto the bomb had conjured images of devastating, unimaginable power . . . But now I had seen it cut down to size . . . True, there was a potentially lethal side to it: but equally an inert side that left it totally subservient to man's will.[8]

Fat Man bomb casings were large, plump and orange-striped, and so known as Pumpkins. To accustom the Japanese to incursions by small groups of high-flying B-29s Tibbets decided that it would be profitable for his crews to raid enemy targets using Pumpkins containing conventional explosive. On 20 July ten aircraft had flown Pumpkin missions to four Japanese towns. By 29 July the total of such sorties had risen to thirty-eight, with no losses.

Accidents were a different matter. On 29 July a Pumpkin flopped out of a bomb bay during take-off, bringing the aircraft to a grinding halt. Take-off accidents at North Field were not uncommon, and the risk of a consequential detonation was worrying. To avoid this, plans were changed to enable final arming of Little Boy after it was airborne. In the case of the plutonium bomb, however, no such adjustment was possible: the aircraft with Fat Man in its belly would take off with the bomb live.

Tinian's main force units operated almost nightly. Knowing nothing of the 509th's purpose, unimpressed by the Pumpkin sorties, jealous of the privileged Green Hornets, they taunted the 509th's aircrew for idleness and flung rocks into their compound. Even Cheshire caught the force of their sneers.[9]

July 29 brought a new worry. Penney pointed to signs that the Americans 'were not planning to take us with them'. Cheshire knew from talking to Tibbets that space was not a problem. If there was a veto, its source must be elsewhere. He went to see Farrell, who hitherto had been entirely helpful. Farrell's 'evasive' reaction confirmed that a difficulty existed. LeMay's frigidity three days before now made sense. Cheshire flew to Guam to see him.*

He said firmly that there was no room for either of us; in any case he couldn't see why we needed to be there, for we would receive a full written report and could ask to see any documentation we wanted. I replied that the 509th thought there was room, and asked on whose authority an order given by Churchill and approved by the President of the United States was being countermanded. He neither moved, nor offered an explanation, nor even smiled.[10]

Little time remained for Penney and Cheshire to unravel a problem they did not entirely understand. The Field Order for the first atomic strike was issued at 15.00 on 2 August. All that held Tibbets now was the weather. Spaatz arrived. In April 1944 Spaatz had visited Woodhall Spa. Then he had been friendly. He was convivial now, until Cheshire broached their exclusion. Spaatz then

looked very uncomfortable . . . it was quite clear to us that somewhere there was a policy directive to say that we were to be kept out of it at all costs . . . they said there was a ruling from Truman, that nobody could go on the raid without being authorized by Truman himself . . . they said they couldn't get his signature now, which indeed they couldn't. There was only about two days to go.[11]

After lunch on Saturday 4 August the 509th's briefing hut was placed under armed guard, its windows curtained and seven crews were summoned. A grim-faced Cheshire and Penney joined them at 2.45, seating themselves behind members of the scientific detachment. LeMay had just reconfirmed their exclusion.[12] At the briefing's end, Tibbets gave a short address.

The colonel began by saying that whatever any of us, including himself, had done before was small potatoes compared to what we were going to do now

* Boyle gave 4 August as the date of foreclosure (1955, p. 257). In *The Light of Many Suns* Cheshire dated the arousal of Penney's suspicions to 1 August. According to his log book, Cheshire flew to Guam on 29 July.

... this raid ... he said – and all the other bigwigs nodded when he said it – would shorten the war by at least six months. And you got the feeling that he really thought this bomb would end the war, period.[13]

Preparations continued on the Sunday. Monitoring of the bomb's detonator frequency revealed no signs of Japanese activity. In mid-afternoon Little Boy was hoisted on to a trolley, shrouded under canvas and taken from the technical site 'like a military funeral cortège'.[14] At half past three the bomb was winched up into Tibbets's aircraft. Early in the evening the Los Alamos team was ordered to move to another part of the island in case of a take-off accident. Realizing the futility of this instruction, the scientists stayed where they were.

A little before midnight the crews of the weather aircraft assembled for final briefing, followed by members of the strike force who arrived for a brief address by Tibbets. Weather prospects looked good, with near cloud-free conditions on the route, and cloud over Japan expected to clear at dawn. The meeting was concluded by a prayer, composed for the occasion by the 509th's chaplain; 6 August was the Feast of the Transfiguration.

A little before half past one in the morning the three weather aircraft took off simultaneously on parallel runways, each bound for a different city: Nagasaki, Kokura and Hiroshima. The standby aircraft left for Iwo Jima.

The remaining crews had meanwhile been driven out to their aircraft. During the day Tibbets's B29 had been named *Enola Gay*. She was now surrounded by lights, cameramen, journalists and a throng of senior officers and officials. For a time Tibbets's crew patiently obeyed demands for posed pictures and interviews. Then Tibbets shepherded them aboard, and the time for concentration began.

Enola Gay took off at 02.45, her companions, *The Great Artiste* and *No. 91*, two and three minutes later. After dawn the first of the weather aircraft reported less than 3/10 cloud over Hiroshima. Tibbets arrived above the city at 08.15, and before another minute was out Hiroshima was gone, and worse than gone.

★

Who stopped Cheshire and Penney from participating? Wilson thought that the opposition came from the USAAF.[15] Cheshire supposed it was LeMay.★ The balance of evidence, however, points to Groves. Spaatz told Cheshire that the veto was 'a Washington ruling',[16] and just as Groves had conceded and facilitated the request that Cheshire should join Penney on Tinian, so he was also placed to ensure that they went no further.[17] He had several reasons for doing so.

The ostensible reason for Groves's interference lay in a two-year-old War Department directive which forbade persons with knowledge of Manhattan from flying over enemy-held territory. On the eve of the first atomic strike this had led to an absurd situation whereby several people essential to its undertaking (including Tibbets) were disallowed from taking part because they already knew what it was about. When the problem was brought to Groves's attention

I immediately secured War Department authority to disregard the prohibition for both civilian and military personnel concerned with Centreboard . . . provided their flights were essential. It was provided further that they had to be specifically authorized by me or by General Farrell in the case of personnel not permanently assigned to the 509th Group . . . These authorizations had to be specifically contained in official written orders. Without such waivers we would have been seriously handicapped, not only in the bomb-carrying plane, but in the instrument plane and observation plane as well.[18]

By explaining how several people were enabled to go to Hiroshima, Groves also describes the means whereby Penney and Cheshire had been obstructed. Knowledge of the means, however, does not explain the motive. In Penney's case there may have been an unwillingness to put him at risk. Penney had originally been sent to Tinian not as a British observer but as a member of the Los Alamos group. Within that group there already were designated observers. If Penney went too there was a possibility that as many

★ According to the official historian it was the 'local commander' who prevented Penney and Cheshire from joining the attack on Hiroshima. Since Tibbets appears to have raised no objection, this presumably applies either to Farrell (who was acting directly on behalf of Groves) or LeMay (Gowing, 1964, p. 380).

as three of Manhattan's senior scientists could be killed or captured. Groves was prepared to sign waivers only for those whose flights were essential. From an American standpoint Penney's participation was not only inessential but conceivably counterproductive.

As for Cheshire, as far as Groves was concerned he was not relevant to Centreboard at all. Britain's wishes were neither here nor there. Centreboard was an American operation. Indeed, Groves had resolved that the first use of the atomic bomb should be an all-American occasion. When all else is said, Cheshire and Penney were prevented from going to Hiroshima not because they were inessential, or too important to lose, but because they were British.

Helpless in the face of invisible opposition, Cheshire and Penney marched into the Signals Office and sent a cable to Field Marshal Wilson.* They anticipated – correctly – that their message would be read by the American authorities, probably by Groves himself. By forcing discussion between Wilson and Groves 'we were pretty certain that something would happen'.[19]

Word of 'a new bomb' did not reach Tokyo until the early evening of 6 August, some three hours after Tibbets had brought *Enola Gay* to a safe homecoming. He and his crew emerged to face a flock of vehicles, hundreds of jubilant men and General Spaatz bearing a Distinguished Service Cross with which Tibbets was immediately invested. Amid the late-afternoon party which flowed with free beer and the entertainment which followed – a movie, *It's a Pleasure* (in technicolour) – Cheshire and Penney were subdued. 'We felt frustrated and rather flat. Emotionally and mentally it was a tense and perplexing time. On the one hand there were so many technical details to get one's head round: on the other there was the bewildering fact of the bomb.'[20]

Cheshire did not allow disappointment to override his professionalism. His notes to the British Joint Staff Mission, submitted twelve days later, were telling:

To my surprise the operation was executed as planned, the bomb being dropped within one minute of zero hour with both the observation plane and the photographic plane in the correct position. On the explosion of the bomb the

* According to Margaret Gowing (1964, p. 380) the appeal was to Chadwick.

two leading aircraft had turned on a reciprocal course and were thus free of danger, while the photographic aeroplane was flying directly towards the target at a distance of some 25 miles. Two severe shock waves were felt which all aircraft interpreted as flak and consequently started taking evasive action. The scientific observations were successfully made and after watching the spectacle for a short time the aircraft returned to base. No defences of any sort were encountered.[21]

'To my surprise . . . evasive action . . . No defences of any sort . . .' Privately, Cheshire did not think too much of Centreboard's organization. Tibbets was obviously good, and Cheshire was on close terms with several seasoned captains. Overall, however, the unit seemed to lack the experience, cohesion and discipline he had known in 617. If the job had been given to him it would, perhaps, have been done differently. But now it was done. Worn out by tension and a flight which had lasted more than half a day, some Centreboard aircrew were ready to sleep. Others lay awake.

Late on 6 August Truman issued a new warning.* As the next day passed reports reaching the General Staff in Tokyo gave an increasingly terrible picture. By 8 August they knew with tolerable certainty that Hiroshima had been obliterated by an atomic weapon.† Togo, Japan's Foreign Minister, informed the Emperor and advised surrender. Others quibbled. Some doubted whether the United States would have been able to build more than one bomb, and until the day's end – when the Soviet Union's declaration of war disabused them – the pathetic faith in Moscow still lingered. A decision on whether to stop or fight on required a meeting of the Supreme Council. A meeting was called on 8 August, but military leaders were 'too busy' to attend and the conference was not convened until the morning of 9 August. Thus were remaining hours squandered.

---

* Issued after 19.15 Eastern War Time, 'It was to spare the Japanese people from utter destruction that the ultimatum of 26 July was issued at Potsdam . . . If they do not now accept our terms, they may expect a rain of ruin from the air, the like of which has never been seen on this earth . . .'
† The USAAF had readied leaflets which confirmed to the Japanese that an atomic bomb had been dropped, urged an end to resistance and warned 'Evacuate your cities' – but did not begin to deliver them until 9 August.

Truman, Stimson and Groves had all expected some reaction in the aftermath of Hiroshima – presumably either surrender or a statement of defiance. Instead, there was nothing. Like a boxer stunned by a colossal punch, Japan swayed in a bewildered silence. Unanswered, the United States again raised its fist.

Spaatz had been ordered to continue Centreboard operations until 'otherwise instructed'. Reasonable weather was predicted for 9 August, but thereafter conditions were expected to deteriorate. Fat Man was ready. They would go again.

The Field Order for Centreboard strike 16 was issued from LeMay's headquarters on Guam at eight o'clock on the morning of 8 August. Kokura arsenal and city would be the primary target. In most respects the format of the operation would follow that of 6 August, save that on this occasion there were only two potential targets. The other was Nagasaki.

Tibbets flew to Guam for a press conference. In discussion with LeMay he announced that Major Charles Sweeney would lead the second strike. Sweeney had flown the instrument aircraft to Hiroshima and was thus fully familiar with operational procedures. Among the other crews, however, there would be some new faces.* Tibbets had decided to broaden participation. The instrument aircraft would be commanded by Capt. Frederick Bock, and the photographic aircraft was to be in the hands of Capt. James Hopkins. Hopkins's appointment was strange; as the 509th's operations officer he led no regular crew. Cheshire and Penney watched and waited. Again, it seemed, they were to be sidelined.

In Washington, the signal had 'started a bit of a flap'.[22] Wilson (or Chadwick?) appealed to Groves, who was doubtless awaiting

---

* Last-minute switches of personnel and aircraft have been a source of endless historical confusion. For those who care about such things, the line-up for Centreboard 16 was as follows. *Bock's Car* (call sign Victor 77), usually captained by Capt. Frederick Bock, was on this occasion flown by Maj. Charles Sweeney, with the crew of *The Great Artiste* (Victor 89). *The Great Artiste*'s captain, Charles Albury, flew as Sweeney's co-pilot in *Bock's Car*, while Capt. Bock flew *The Great Artiste* (which was fitted as the instrument aircraft and had flown to Hiroshima) with his own crew. *Big Stink* (Victor 90) normally flown by Capt. Herman Zahn, was commanded by Capt. James Hopkins, who led the crew of *Necessary Evil* (Victor 91). Call signs of other aircraft involved were Victor 88 (weather scout, Kokura) and Victor 95 (weather scout, Nagasaki), with *Full House* (Victor 83) as the standby aircraft at Iwo Jima.

the call. Although the decision lay in Groves's own gift he appears to have consulted Stimson, perhaps to weigh the political implications.[23] At length, Groves relented. Penney and Cheshire could go. The signal reached Tinian just after lunch. In London that morning the UK Chief of Staff received a salutory cable from the Joint Staff Mission on the subject of collaboration with the US 'in the field of research and development for defence purposes'.

2 You may have seen Embassy to FO tel[egrams] . . . of 14th and 16th July reporting serious restrictions now being imposed by the Americans in certain fields in the exchange of technical information . . . [concerning the disclosure of information to representatives of UK Command being contrary to US policy]

3 There are other indications of a closing down on the American side. We feel therefore that it is now urgent that this matter should be raised on the highest level and would suggest that you press for the earliest possible action . . . The Supply Council* concur.[24]

After two and a half years of Anglo-American collaboration, the atomic relationship was close to breakdown. Within a few weeks the 'A' in A bomb would come 'to symbolize not only "atomic" but also "American"'.[25]

The afternoon was hot and airless. As with the first, so the last: on that sweltering June afternoon at Driffield five years before, Lofty Long had advised Cheshire to rest. Cheshire tried to do that now, but the glare permeating his tent made sleep impossible. The main briefing began in early evening. Cheshire found it 'interminable'; he detected no great tension, although 'it was a momentous occasion'; he actually felt that this was the war's end.

Others were more highly strung. For one thing a Fat Man could not be — as 509th armourers put it — 'safed' before take-off. For another, fighters were now considered a danger. Japanese defences, earlier lulled by the Pumpkin stories, could now be expected to pay them more attention.

Once again Chaplain Downey prayed for the safety of the crews and an early return of peace. He read the prayer with great depth of feeling and, though I

* Chadwick's secretariat in Washington was part of the British Central Scientific Office, which in turn was attached to the British Supply Council.

cannot say why, for I believed that what we were about to do would end the war, and I had come to believe, too, that prayer is necessary, I was taken a little by surprise.[26]

Briefing was followed by a gargantuan meal for anyone who cared to eat it. After midnight they changed into their light green overalls and climbed aboard trucks which took them out to the aircraft. The two weather scouts departed. Crews of the strike force stood under floodlights for photographers and cine-cameras. Spaatz, Farrell and Tibbets circulated. Sweeney was distracted, for a fault had been found in *Bock's Car*'s fuel system: 600 gallons of petrol would be unavailable. His flight engineer calculated that with extreme care the trip would still be possible. Tibbets and Sweeney conferred; Sweeney decided to go.

The B-29 was a pressurized aircraft, with crew accommodation in fore and aft compartments which were linked by a narrow tunnel, faintly like the waist of a wasp. For several hours Cheshire and Penney sat in the soundproofed rear compartment with little to do other than doze. The night was clear except for intermittent squalls. Hopkins climbed to 39,000 feet to clear the turbulence, and after a time the three B-29s were parted. This need not matter – the flight plan provided for a rendezvous over one end of the island of Yakushima. The sun rose behind them and they rode the dawn.

Towards seven o'clock Hopkins invited Cheshire forward. The morning was bright and clear. As they neared Yakushima Cheshire became puzzled, for instead of descending to the height which had been briefed for the tryst with *Bock's Car* and *The Great Artiste*, Hopkins remained at 39,000 feet. More perplexingly still, he embarked on a series of lengthy dog legs around the island.* 'It

---

* In his report, submitted on 18 August 1945, Cheshire stated: 'On arrival at the rendezvous point the three aircraft failed to make contact, which did not surprise me in the least, since instead of orbiting Yakushima in a tight circle, they flew around in dog legs some 40 miles long at varying heights. There being no adequate arrangements in the event of contact not being made and the leader not being willing to break radio silence although there was no conceivable reason why he should not, the three aircraft continued to orbit for an hour and ten minutes.' In subsequent accounts Cheshire paid tribute to Sweeney's handling of the operation.

struck me as an extraordinary thing to do, and I would have queried it but for the fact that he had just invited me forward into the cockpit. I was the only one there other than the crew and felt too privileged to do anything other than thank him.'[27] Nine thousand feet below Sweeney and Bock had made contact. Radio silence forbade questions or explanations, so they continued to circle in the hope that Hopkins would appear. But of Victor 90 there was no sign. After forty minutes Sweeney signalled to Bock by rocking the wings of his aircraft, and together they turned for Kokura.

Hopkins eventually did likewise, though not before Cheshire had persuaded him that the others had probably already departed and talked him out of a desire to turn back. Hopkins now became slightly defensive, seeking to justify his manoeuvres by the need to keep his VIP passengers beyond the reach of danger.

A voice announced that the enemy coast was in sight. Hopkins suggested that Cheshire should go down into the glazed nose. The view from here was outstanding. Cheshire had never seen Japan, and its appearance brought an unexpected stab of nostalgia: 'My first sight of the Kyushu coast gave me a shock. It looked for all the world like the coast of Cornwall.'[28]

It was at this point I had my moment of revulsion . . . Here we were two and a half times higher than I had ever been before, sitting in shirtsleeves and comfortably warm. Hardly ever had I done a trip without flak of some kind . . . but here there was none: perhaps three or four bursts . . . Around me the others were quietly sitting, just getting on with their job as men and women do the world over, at desks, in the kitchen . . . There were other things that bothered me, too. I hadn't liked the practice sorties . . . they were necessary, of course . . . but they had the effect of making the Japanese think that there was nothing particularly sinister in this kind of formation at this height . . . it felt unfair.[29]

Unchivalrous or not, by now Sweeney had received reports from the two weather aircraft. Kokura was generally clear, with 3/10 low cloud. Nagasaki, too, was reported as unobscured. Kokura was the primary. Sweeney decided to attack it.

When *Bock's Car* arrived above Kokura conditions had changed. The city was masked by industrial haze, and by smoke drifting from Yawata, which had been bombed the night before. Sweeney made three runs, but on each occasion his bombardier was unable to see the target. The delay over Yakushima had cost them time and fuel, and each abortive run over Kokura used fifteen minutes' more petrol. Puffs of flak began to stain the sky; Sweeney's radio counter-measures officer reported activity on Japanese fighter control frequencies. Fighters were climbing towards them. Frustrated, Sweeney turned for Nagasaki.

Hopkins, meanwhile, had arrived in the vicinity, but he was still 9,000 feet too high and according to Cheshire he 'proceeded to fly around the approaches of Kokura wondering what we should do'.[30] Hopkins saw nothing of Sweeney's persevering efforts but he did notice the flak and began to take evasive action. Cheshire saw it too, and thought it innocuous. Although he never said so publicly, it is clear that Cheshire had come to consider Hopkins as overwrought.

The cumulative delays had placed *Bock's Car* at risk; there was a real possibility that fuel would run out. To economize Sweeney took *Bock's Car* straight across Kyushu. He also broke radio silence, to alert air–sea rescue in case he had to ditch, and in a final effort to re-establish contact with Hopkins.

When Sweeney reached Nagasaki ground visibility had worsened. A trial run found the city overcast, and with no time left in which to wait for improvement Frederick Ashworth, the weaponeer,★ reluctantly ordered that a second and final run be guided by H2S. This was in absolute contravention of the order to bomb visually, but in the circumstances Sweeney and Ashworth were agreed that they had no choice.

Sweeney turned upwind. Nagasaki's defences began to react, but the flak was 'very meagre and inaccurate'. Twenty seconds before the release point Beahan, the bombardier, interrupted to report that the cloud had parted. He could recognize part of the city. The area in view was a mile and a half from the intended aiming point, but this was close enough. In the last seconds Beahan directed the attack by eye.

Then Fat Man was falling.

★ Ashworth was operations officer, a military member of the Los Alamos team and an atomic weapons specialist.

Sweeney wheeled *Bock's Car* through a hundred and fifty degrees, dipped her nose, opened the throttles and fled downwind.★

Yosjitaka Kawamoto, a thirteen-year-old schoolboy, was in a classroom in a Nagasaki suburb. Glancing out of the window he noticed the silvery glint of an aeroplane.

Five hundred miles away in Tokyo a meeting of the Supreme Council was in progress.

Sweeney's crew braced themselves for the shock wave.

At 11.01 Victor 90 was eighty miles away.[31] For some time Hopkins's crew had been wearing their dark glasses. The late morning sun seemed dim. Edgy as ever, Hopkins was talking about going home.

A speck of brilliance swelled into a bubble of searing light.

'Suddenly,' recalled Cheshire, 'it was there.'

'Quite what warned us I am not certain – I think perhaps a fleeting flash – but we all seemed to know as if by instinct.'[32]

In the classroom air was compressed to a hammer which hit young Kawamoto with the force of 20 tonnes per square metre.

When Cheshire turned to face it, the fireball had already risen several thousand feet. Dust and smoke rocketed heavenward, blooming like some 'large piece of silk that had been compressed and then was suddenly released, just expanding and unwrapping and unrolling'.

Kawamoto's immediate injuries were teeth knocked out and a gashed arm. With thousands of others he was lucky: the bomb had detonated towards the suburbs, where an arc of hills sheltered parts of Nagasaki from the worst of the blast.†

In *The Great Artiste* a crew member made notes:

After explosion large white smoke ring formed, red ball of fire covering 1/2 of area. The column of smoke formed 1/2 mile wide, funnelling upward, bottom dark brown in colour, centre amber colour, top white. Column rose to 50,000

★ After the attack Major Sweeney made for Okinawa where he landed *Bock's Car* safely, albeit with scarcely enough fuel to park the aircraft.
† According to Groves the bomb was aimed about one and a half miles from the correct aiming point. In his report to the British Joint Staff Mission Cheshire stated, 'I had an excellent view of the ground and could see that the centre of the impact was some four miles north-east of the aiming point and that the city proper was untouched.'

feet, rising to 30,000 feet in one and one half to two minutes. Many small bright fires observed. Considerable smoke observed 175 miles from the area. Five shock waves felt.★

From Victor 90 it seemed that a measureless presence had joined them in the sky. Coaxed by Cheshire, Hopkins flew closer. Cheshire was bewitched by the symmetry of the ascending cloud. He sketched it. At its base was a boiling blackness; above, a turbulent stem of smoke, ash and dust which had an 'evil kind of luminous quality', not white, the 'colour of sulphur'.[33]

Even a miss by several miles had taken nearly half the city. '*The greatest kindness in war is to bring it to a speedy conclusion.*' Did that apply here? Commingled within the seething cloud were vaporized metals, steam from boiled-out canals, carbonized trees, particles of factories and roasted homes, and the soot of 40,000 souls.

★ At Hiroshima the *Enola Gay* had experienced two violent shock waves, one direct from the explosion, the other reflected from the ground. Both were actually visible, appearing as expanding rings, presumably the result of water vapour condensing in the compression. At Nagasaki four of the five shock waves felt by *The Great Artiste* resulted from multiple reflections from the hilly terrain.

13. Smitten Cities

A cypher telegram from Chadwick was handed to Clement Attlee on Tuesday 18 September: 'Group Capt. Cheshire, who was one of our observers in the Pacific and who took part in the Nagasaki Operation, will be in London from Monday, Sept. 17th. You can reach him care of the Ritz Hotel, if you wish to have a first-hand account of his experiences and observations.'[1] The message was annotated 'Do you wish to see him?' Attlee jotted, 'Yes', although much of what Cheshire might have to report was already splashed across that day's edition of the *News Chronicle*.

Atomic energy is a stern reality and is not in the realm of religion or magic. It is a staging post along the road of scientific knowledge and is not a secret locked in the bowels of the earth which may either be uncovered or hidden at the will of man.

Scientific knowledge is the property of the world and not of nations. It is not a physical possession like territory, and therefore cannot be denied or withheld except by denying the right to carry out research. Its progress cannot be halted any more than the development of industry or medicine can be halted.

. . . atomic energy will very shortly cease to be the exclusive property of England and America. We do not possess the power to withhold it . . . Today it carries the absolute power of victory because, so far as we know, no one else possesses it. Tomorrow, however, when the whole world possesses it, it will not by itself carry the power of victory any more than high explosive did a year ago.[2]

This bears the stamp of Chadwick, and anticipated an argument which Attlee was about to put to Truman. Whether it was written with official encouragement we do not know, but either way the article reflected his new fixation with nuclear physics. Before leaving America Cheshire had told the *Washington Mail* of his decision to devote the rest of his life to atomic research. Some day, he assured the reporter, humanity would use atomic energy safely, 'as it now controls fire'.[3] After returning from Tinian he had campaigned frantically to quit Washington – 'anything, any price, just to get out of America back to England and on with the plan of world peace'.[4] And when he succeeded, and said goodbye to Constance, there was no plan for them to meet again.

So, within three months the war had ended, he had confronted his own nihilism, glimpsed the apocalypse, realized that atomic science had 'drawn a line across history'[5] and conceded that his marriage had no future. It had all been, as he put it, 'a bit much'.

RAF doctors ordered him to St Luke's psychiatric hospital at Muswell Hill for rest and observation, wrote 'affective disorder' on his notes and jotted 'discharge'. Whether he wanted one or not, his career in the air force was finished. Other patients at St Luke's saw him as wan, thin and quietly unassuming. His interior state, however, was anything but quiet, and since he was free to come and go, Muswell Hill became a clearing house for correspondence and invitations to pick up old threads. One thread led back to writing, and his former agents, Curtis Brown. This was timely, as several journalists had the impression that they had secured sole rights to his atomic experiences. 'The whole thing seems to be an extraordinary tangle,' wrote the irritated editor of the *Daily Express*. Curtis Brown's first task was to disembarrass him.

The *Sunday Graphic* won. On 29 September the paper's editor, Reginald Simpson, confirmed an invitation to write a weekly column. Upon discharge from Muswell Hill Cheshire temporarily installed himself in the Mayfair Hotel while Curtis Brown advised on how he should organize his work. First, his weekly column – suggested rate of £35 plus £15 expenses, in addition to a retainer, leaving the agents to sell articles for republication in the Dominions. Second, he should begin his memoirs, with an eye to the American market (which would require a gushy title like 'Praise be Old Glory', or 'Thanks America', or 'America Went In to Bat'). Third, a book about civil aviation. And what about a lecture tour? He would need an office and a secretary, and he might like to form a company to handle the business side of his writing.

Cheshire had ideas of his own. One was a book for children. Another was the story of 617 Squadron, for which he had five albums of material.[6] Curtis Brown liked the idea of the children's book, but doubted the market for 617. One wonders if they remembered that when Paul Brickhill's best-selling *The Dam Busters* appeared.

Cheshire himself was news – what he did, where he went, his views, his plans and above all what he had to say about the bomb. In November he told an audience in Manchester that the ending of war was now 'a biological necessity'. The nation could bury itself far underground, abandon Britain and disperse, or rule out war. Bigger bombs were certain. The rational choice was not difficult.

The *Daily Telegraph* reported this the following day, when he was back in London to receive his VC from the King. Primrose travelled up for the investiture, and perhaps repeated his father's offer to pay for him to take a year's holiday anywhere in the world.[7] A second medical board[8] had diagnosed 'psychoneurosis', and insisted that he relinquish his commission with effect from 22 January 1946. Thereafter he would be placed on the retired list, retaining the rank of group captain. In the meantime he was told to proceed on sick leave, and that complete rest 'was the only hope'.[9]

Many assumed that it was Nagasaki which emptied him. In fact, as he kept pointing out, it was the war as a whole. Like Britain herself, he had been fighting or training for fighting since 1939. He was losing weight before he left England in 1944, and friends had worried about his haggard appearance in Washington. Nagasaki was not a turning point but a culmination, a shattering chord at the end of a long, dissonant symphony. As he told Primrose, 'I have no trade but killing . . . That's what they taught me to do for six years. I've had enough.' He was wrung out, while relief that the carnage was finished mingled with yearning for the emotional unity which battle had bestowed. War's exigencies had kept his calm surface and whirling interior energy in concord; in their absence, action, thought and feeling were flying apart, like gear wheels that turn but no longer work together.

Part of Cheshire's creativity sprang from a compulsive restlessness and a tendency to seek ways of improving on conventional wisdom. So perhaps it is no surprise that he turned down his parents' offer, disregarded the doctors and became an ever more public figure. Pathé Pictures arranged to interview him. He lectured widely and alongside his journalism he broadcast for the BBC, giving talks and making celebrity appearances.[10]

Behind all this lay a compulsion to spread the atomic insights with which, it seemed, he had been entrusted. His inaugural column for the *Sunday Graphic* addressed the future of the bomb,[11] and in two radio talks he tried to encapsulate the meaning of Nagasaki in words which ordinary listeners would understand. The first talk, transmitted on 21 December, described what he had seen. The ascent of the monstrous cloud to 60,000 feet, a towering jack-in-the-box, implied that 'some horrible form of life' was being vented, a rearing, animate malignancy. This was at odds with his experience on Tinian, when Fat Man's plutonium core had been subordinate to human will.

The subject of the second broadcast, on 4 February 1946, was the significance of what had happened. Nagasaki had been, in the poetic sense, awful: 'In plain language . . . we are faced either with the end of this country or the end of war.' To end war, 'each one of us must play our part . . . it is not a responsibility we can shelve nor one that we can say belongs exclusively to the government'.

'Each one of us must play our part . . .' The Labour government was putting up the scaffolding for its modern social service state to care for the individual.[12] While Christian socialism and philanthropy had done much to inspire this new Jerusalem, a quantum of materialism lay at its base and there was paternalism in its method. Cheshire began to contemplate a different principle, whereby progress towards the unity of mankind might grow from personal effort. This was no grand assertion of human powers, but a pre-echo of his concept of history: movement towards the realization of higher possibilities through the gradual elimination of injustice by a myriad small, practical actions, each taken according to individual means and opportunities. February 1946 was a time when others saw Cheshire (and Cheshire saw himself) as exhausted and aimless. Hindsight sees dormant seeds of purpose awaiting germination.

Cheshire's discharge from the RAF came two weeks before this broadcast. The RAF had been his life, and one wonders if the parting touched him. His own request for release and the medical board's ruling had, so to speak, crossed in the post.[13] However he reacted, the exit of Britain's most celebrated bomber pilot caused a public stir. The *Evening Standard* asked if it was true that he was retiring because of illness. He told the *Star* that he might seek a new education and then a job in one of the sciences, probably physics. The law was 'no earthly use now'.[14]

Nuclear physics, space travel and peace seemed linked. During his interview with Cheshire, the Prime Minister asked if he had any specific proposal to make. Cheshire replied that nuclear war would be unsurvivable, but that the world could be held at peace, for its own good, by the threat of 'sheer, unanswerable force'. Since a time would come when any nation could build an atomic weapon, deterrence would inhere not in the number or size of nuclear weapons, but in an ability to guarantee their delivery. Delivery systems would take many forms, but the most important would work through the medium of space. The solution was thus to stop thinking in terms of conventional aircraft and rockets and for Britain, at all costs, to initiate its own space programme.[15] At the mention of space Attlee 'took his pipe out of his mouth, settled down a shade deeper into his chair and steered the conversation on to generalities'.[16]

Professor Margaret Gowing, the official historian of Britain's part in the development of the atomic bomb, might have had this scene in mind when she wrote of the state of government thinking after Hiroshima:

It is certainly arguable that the attention given to the political problems of the atomic bomb was too cursory and that it was unfortunate that it was regarded largely as a military weapon. But unprecedented imagination and power of understanding were required of gravely overburdened statesmen.[17]

Cheshire *did* see beyond the bomb as a military weapon[18] – he saw so far, that what he described was greeted by incredulity and by men in white coats who politely ushered him out into Civvy Street.

Civvy Street. Few cars ran in it, chiefly for want of petrol, and ordinary people were drably dressed: women with a uniformity dictated by rationing, men often in the trilby hat and demob suit which were badges of recent service. Beset by shortages and bordered with queues, Civvy Street's sooty urban frontages were still gapped by bombs.[19] One of the few unrationed commodities in 1945 was grit from bomb-loosened mortar; on windy days there was a tendency for everyone to walk with bowed heads, eyes averted.

While Civvy Street was materially drear, hopes were high and there were blessings to count. No rockets or bombs fell out of the sky, a telegram could be opened without dread and for those with means or ingenuity shortages could be circumvented. Cheshire's journalism and other pursuits promised unprecedented income, and having spent £225 on new clothes from Savile Row[20] he set out to establish himself in style.

By the end of the year I had taken a three-storeyed house in Kensington Gardens, engaged a cook and a butler – and, of course, a char . . . Get woken up at eight with tea; struggle out of bed at nineish, tea untouched; partake of breakfast when strong enough to do so; discuss the domestic arrangements with the staff, and order lunch and dinner; start on a little correspondence and consider when to get down to the next *Sunday Graphic* article; drive down in the Bentley (acquired on a banker's overdraft guaranteed by Father) to the Mayfair – or possibly the Antelope – to take stock of the situation and settle a plan of campaign for the day. Decide at the last minute to stay on; ring up and cancel lunch. After a frustrating visit to the City in search of financial backing, return to the Mayfair for a breather, extend the duration of the visit on the off-chance of a useful contact, ring up and cancel dinner. Gravitate to one or other of the nightclubs, sit the session out; garage the Bentley and walk up Church Street approximately at milk-delivery time, think up a suitable apology to the staff, and decide to get down to things in earnest after breakfast. Occasionally, but only very occasionally, stay in for tea or supper and read a book on religion.[21]

While this catches an aimlessness which gnawed at Cheshire's spirit, it does scant justice to his diligence. Far from drifting into lie-a-bed languor, his routine was actually rather industrious. Alongside work for the *Graphic* he was hatching ideas for books, projects, broadcasts and business propositions, while from outside came invitations to lecture, to be interviewed, to accept consultancies, to join committees and boards.

He equivocated about journalism, and went to Godfrey Winn for advice. Winn opened the door to someone 'shy and diffident, delicate-looking, with very thin wrists', who 'did not know exactly what he wanted'.[22] Disenchantment with Fleet Street came early. 'Young Leonard bitterly complained that when he wrote articles for the general press on things that really mattered they paid him, but didn't print them. The editors wanted tripe on how he felt when dropping bombs, which does not interest him.'

Aeronautics did still interest him. He told Sir Roy Dobson of A. V. Roe that he wanted to boost the British aircraft industry.[23] Gaumont-British signed him as their aviation adviser for newsreels and short films.[24] He toyed with the idea of starting an air charter service, used his newspaper column to discuss supersonic flight,[25] enthused about the RAF's Gloster Meteor jets[26] and in October 1946 acquired a Mosquito to become 'the world's first flying reporter'.[27]

Supersonic technology presaged travel into space. Space was his dream-world, for it was there that he thought he saw the key to peace. And since peace was the overriding aim, all those preoccupations which to others looked disjointed[28] – like the bomb, science, global harmony, the role of the individual, interplanetary travel, Christianity – appeared to Cheshire himself as interdependent. He laboured hard to explain this. Among his manuscripts is a sketch for an article (perhaps one of those which Reginald Simpson refused to print) in which he predicted – correctly – that manned space flight would be a reality within twenty years. And after that?

... we shall have access to the moon and the planets ... Mankind has concerned itself with the universe for only one part of the 100,000 years that it has existed, and everything we know is the result of indirect and not direct observation. From the point of view of science the gateway will be open to an unbounded store of knowledge.

If people went to another part of the universe and looked back at the earth as a distant speck, they would learn 'something of the purpose and destiny of human life'.[29] Visionary stuff, and nothing so vividly captures Cheshire's inner commotion as what was on the back of the page: a note about possible whisky exports to a New York liquor dealer. While dreaming the future he was drafting cables such as 'Have immediately available unlimited quantities French Brandy and Champagne. Competitive prices. Can I go ahead.' The answer was no, and none of the other fanciful ventures with which he flirted fared better. His business life became a junkyard of abandoned projects.

Cheshire's entrepreneurial strengths lay on a narrow front. He was a leader rather than a manager, and while inventive and persuasive he displayed little of the merciless streak needed for the hard sell nor (at this time) the realism to recognize what was practicable.[30] He could also be impulsive, too trustful for his own good, and yet, at times, intransigent.

Something of all these traits, and of his flair for landing himself in unorthodox scrapes, can be seen in a deal which backfired over his Bentley. Anticipating (wrongly) the forthcoming gift of a Cadillac,[31] he offered the Bentley to a property developer called Ken Rowley in part exchange for two flats in Great Cumberland Place. Rowley paid a deposit on the car, which he handed to his son before completion on the property. Cheshire then discovered that the flats would not be ready for six months. He repossessed the car. Finding it damaged, he told Rowley that he would decide how much of the deposit would be refunded when the car was sold and the damage repaired. Rowley now disputed the facts, claiming the car to have been in 'terrible shape' when he received it, and contesting its year of manufacture. By late June, as Cheshire's solicitor wearily explained, the affair was emerging as 'one of those cases where ordinary common sense does not tie up with the law'. Since there was nothing in writing about the transaction '. . . the difficulty is, that if the property in the car passed to Rowley, he has damaged his own car, whereas, if the car was merely lent to him, he damaged your car'.[32] This argument smouldered until February 1947.[33]

Requests to talk about his war experiences arrived daily, and at first – perhaps because he felt a compulsion, a *duty* to explain the significance of the bomb – he was not good at declining them.

More often than was good for him he tramped Britain, talking to youth groups, Rotary clubs, schools, guides, village institutes. One lecture was in Oxford, and an undergraduate called Tony Benn, lately released from the RAF, went along to the University Air Squadron building in Manor Road to hear it. On the walls were pictures of past members, 'hardly more than one in six still alive'. The CO entered 'and asked us not to drop our cigarette ends on the floor, then he introduced Cheshire'. Cheshire gave a factual account of preparations for the atomic attacks, and described the raid on Nagasaki. Then:

Cheshire said quite plainly he did not want to discuss the ethics of the thing but he sobered everyone up by putting to us . . . the facts. If we have another war it will mean the end of our physical civilization, for man might survive but buildings can't. He spoke quietly and slowly. 'Realize this, that if these bombs are ever going to be used there is not much point in anything that you are doing now.'

He was quite remote and above us and no doubt the whole world seemed as unreal to him as he to it.[34]

Yet it was all too real. There was nothing remote about the people who wrote to tell him about their hopes and disappointments. Scores of letters came from wartime associates – fitters, aircrew, batmen, cooks – from all over the world. A lot ended 'God bless you'. A good few asked for references or testimonials, which he painstakingly provided. Some, not many, wrote to tell of their deliverance, describing last moments in burning, tumbling aircraft in the company of others who died.[35]

Britain Victorious subsumed another nation in shock. He became a proxy for dead sons whose smiles stared out of picture frames in the cool front rooms of suburban semis, and a counsellor to heartbroken parents. 'To both of us, even if you are too busy to reply to this letter, you will always be our dear boy's revered "Wing-Co".'[36] Some found consolation in spiritualism, and wrote to relay messages from Lofty and Desmond.[37] Wherever he looked, there were ghosts.

The other day I visited an aerodrome where I had once been stationed and which is now empty.

The only sign of life, apart from a few sheep and an occasional farmhand, was a handful of men packing up such RAF equipment as still remained.

In the crew room

The door, which never used to close properly, had a broken hinge and was creaking back and forth in the breeze. The window frames were rusty and no longer fitted, and when there was a gust of wind they rattled.

I walked across the room, sat down on the bench at the far end, where the CO used to stand, and lit a cigarette. On the wall to my right were a few stained and torn posters; one of them, with the aid of pictures, explained the procedure for landing in the sea and manning the dinghy.

As I looked at it my mind drifted back . . .

The first person he saw, in the corner on the left, on a freezing evening five years before, was Dick Rivaz. He remembered Revs's gentle dignity; how he had sucked Davy's charred fingers to keep them warm on the way back from Cologne; his ordeal after the ditching, when his frozen fingers could not fire a flare. Surely such life could be channelled to good purpose in peace as well as war? If so, this would 'enable them to carry on from where the Rivazs and all the others like him left off'.[38]

'All the others' included a boy he called Ginger. Across Britain there were empty bedrooms kept aired in the hope that one day, some day, boys posted 'Missing' might walk in. Cheshire was inundated by letters from girls and mothers who thought they recognized Ginger's description. But Ginger was dead. So was Revs. His father read the article and wrote to tell him.[39] What, oh what, had it all been for?

So many letters were tinged by despondency. There was something disconcertingly nonchalant about the way in which peace had been resumed. 'We are apt to forget that the changeover from War to Peace is just as fundamental as is the changeover from Peace to War. In 1939 those of us who were not in the armed forces knew nothing about the business of war . . . Today we are in much the same situation, only the other way round.'[40]

Men who only months before had been taking vast decisions were returning to mundane jobs. For a time Cheshire proposed

'Commandos for Peace', a scheme whereby former servicemen could divert their energies into scientific tasks in dangerous or inhospitable places.[41] Some had returned to no job at all, which led him to think about training. 'If the government was able to take accountants and draughtsmen and turn them into pilots and gunners, I am unable to see why they cannot reverse the process.'[42] More to the point, where was the specialized instruction in new skills which post-war Britain would need? 'Before the war Great Britain was still trying to revive the old staples. After it, she relied on new developing industries. Electricity, motor cars, iron and steel, machine tools, nylons and chemicals were all set for expansion . . . The very spirit of the nation had changed. No one in 1945 wanted to go back to 1939.'[43]

Unwillingness to go back, however, did not define a way forward. Politically, Cheshire was equivocal, at one moment calling for strategic measures and at the next reproaching the government for curtailing individual choice.[44] The source of his concurrent aversion to and desire for intervention lay in a distinction between direction and leadership. 'To achieve something great,' he told *Sunday Graphic* readers, 'involves in one way or another overcoming unequal odds, which means that men must go beyond the normal call of duty. Ideals are not sufficient, because . . . we need to see our cause embodied in an individual, and therefore we look to leadership.' However:

Today, for the first time in our history, we seem to have thrown leadership overboard, and we prefer a committee or a council.

These may be a safeguard against mistakes, but they are little else. A committee cannot lead: it can only give orders. It can never be in front for others to follow and, therefore, it cannot inspire. It relies on logic and efficiency, and disregards human emotions.

It sees men and women not as separate human individuals but as names, and it cannot influence them beyond their normal capacity for work. It thinks in terms of mass organization and not of individuality, thereby it builds not a team but a machine.[45]

Cheshire thus favoured organized action, but wished it to stem from native enterprise rather than regulation. 'Under Mr Attlee's guidance,' he told a colleague, 'our future is a little restricted.'[46]

In any case, training and employment were but symptoms of what Cheshire regarded as the inmost need: a unifying cause to reawaken selflessness. He shared R. H. Tawney's view that 'war is not the reversal of the habits and ideals we cultivate in peace. It is their concentration by a whole nation with all resources on an end as to which a whole nation can agree.' He also understood the corollary: 'If we are to end the horrors of war, we must first end the horror of peace.'[47] However, the main influence on his thinking at this time was not Tawney but a seventy-three-year-old jurist and Fellow of All Souls College, Oxford, called Lionel Curtis.

Sometime in the autumn of 1945 Cheshire read Curtis's book *World War – Its Cause and Cure*. The book impressed him. So did Curtis's record of action. While working for the London County Council in the 1890s he had sometimes adopted the life of a tramp, begging for food and sleeping in workhouses, the better to understand the problems of London's underclass. He next enlisted as a private soldier to fight in South Africa, emerging from the ranks to assist Lord Milner in shaping the Union of South Africa. Later still he helped to draft the Irish constitution, and in the 1930s it was Curtis who expounded the concept of the Commonwealth.[48]

Curtis recalled: 'He came to see me about what he felt was really important, which is to get a move on among ex-servicemen for winning the peace . . . He very sensibly went on to say that it was no use preaching a faith to ex-servicemen until they had something to live on.'[49] Desire to 'get a move on' was a characteristic of both men. Curtis had a 'burning zeal for causes' that functioned through a Cheshire-like self-abandonment 'which pressed into service the best energies of his friends whether they would or no, and without thought of recognition either of his efforts or theirs'.[50] Curtis attracted disciples – T. E. Lawrence had been another – and for a time he became Cheshire's mentor.

In mid-March Cheshire used his column in the *Sunday Graphic* to call for systematic training, predicting an exodus of disillusioned citizens if it was not provided.[51] Headlined 'A Raw Deal?', this struck a chord. 'Johnny' of Coventry, ex-army, picked up his pen that Sunday and began:

Sir. I read your article in the *Sunday Graphic* this morning. In my own words
'It's a disgrace to come back to this' after six and a half years away from home.
Before the war I was comfortable, butcher in a shop and driving a van for a
Cooperative firm. I come back and the answer is 'I cannot sack a man of sixty-two
can I?' . . . we went in at the roughest and came out of it a sight rougher. I'm
not one, but thousands of us think the country stinks.

Another:

I am not surprised to hear about so many ex-servicemen wanting to emigrate.
And if I did not have a wife and seven schoolchildren, I would go myself. This
country was never no good for servicemen.[52]

On 31 March he challenged the many who had written to join him
to do the job themselves. Together they could find a derelict airfield
and upon it establish a classless colony in which training, prosperity
and fulfilment would result from united effort and mutual support – a
solution to depend 'not on the government's pleasure or on someone
else's goodwill, but on you yourself'. Who would come with him?[53]

The idea went back at least to the autumn of 1945, and perhaps
to the quixotic plans which had been discussed at Woodhall Spa
in 1944, but the signs are that it had received no detailed attention
before the appearance of 'A Raw Deal?' on 17 March. Two days
later Curtis told Lord Perry (an authority on land settlement): 'his
idea is to begin with a land settlement scheme, first in this country
and then in the Dominions'.[54] Sir Malcolm Stewart, who had
succeeded in settlement schemes after 1919 and (in his words)
'generally speaking . . . failed' as a commissioner for the revival of
depressed areas in the 1930s, was identified as another potential
guru. Curtis also recommended approaches to Lady Macrobert,
who had offered land to ex-servicemen,[55] and several bankers.[56]
Reactions were muted, and of little help.[57]

Cheshire's scheme was nourished by two ideas: first, that it would
be possible to identify the cause of the individual with that of the
community, and second, that such a community could combine
cooperative effort with private enterprise and the acceptance of
competent and authoritative leadership. Friends and relatives shook
their heads. David Shannon told him that the idea was make-

believe,[58] and there were heated exchanges with Christopher, whose experiences as a prisoner-of-war had left him sceptical of artificial communities.[59]

Cheshire went ahead anyway. Hundreds thanked him: 'I do not think I have ever been so deeply moved as I have by their letters.'[60] On 14 April there was a public meeting. Cheshire wrote about it.

A few of us, some one hundred families in all, met last Sunday and discussed a plan . . .

We will take over a disused aerodrome or any other suitable estate and move into it. Our first task will be to make ourselves self-supporting, for least of all do we want to live on charity . . . whatever we lack in skill or resources we will make up for by hard work and unity.

Therefore we will farm and cultivate the land and carry out any productive industry that lies within our power.

When that is done we will create an organization to train those who need it in their own particular trade. We will use our pooled endeavours and knowledge not to make our personal fortunes but to help each and every member to set himself up in life to his best possible advantage.

The experience of war has taught us that there are qualities and talents in man, which in everyday life are never given a chance . . .

We do not by this mean to discuss the relative merits of collectivism or individualism, and above all we abhor Communism. We wish to live within and respect the framework of public government, and equally we wish to make ourselves useful members of society . . .

Our purpose is not to produce a closed community in which to spend the rest of our days. Instead, we intend to create a base, open to anyone of any class . . . from which . . . we may go out into the world, equipped to lead our own lives . . .

In the space of only six years, 1940 has been forgotten. Strength is once more measured in terms of guns, efficiency and dollars; the weak are still at the mercy of the strong, and we are already on the way towards another war.

If this trend is ever to stop, we shall have to go back in our minds to the time when we confounded the judgement of the world . . . Our greatness lay in our unity of purpose and our unselfishness . . . This spirit, which we all miss so much today . . . is nothing more or less than one of the basic principles of Christianity – the Second Commandment.[61]

The article sparked a quarrel with the *Sunday Graphic*'s editor. It appears that Cheshire's preoccupation with one subject was not what he wanted.[62] This escalated into a dispute about Cheshire's contract, into which Curtis Brown stepped to urge 'that you do not deal with this but refer Mr Simpson to us'.[63]

For a time, however, Cheshire was incapable of dealing with anyone. An attack of mumps felled him, and for several weeks he was confined to bed. Lionel Curtis cautioned against resuming work before he was fully fit: 'You at any rate should realize what a bad policy it is to go on running with one of the engines out of action.'[64] Curtis maintained his lookout for potential sources of know-how, but all led nowhere.

On 19 May, in St Phillip's Hall, Victoria, the association mooted by Cheshire came into being. The idea of acquiring an aerodrome was abandoned because it would take too long and cost too much. However, a property near Market Harborough in Leicestershire was on offer, rent-free for the first year. This was Gumley Hall: a house with forty-five bedrooms, outbuildings, a market garden and grounds for pigs and poultry. Up to 2,000 acres of land would become available for agriculture within eighteen months. The meeting resolved that 'The offer of Gumley Hall should be accepted with all attendant risks and an immediate start be made.'[65] On 3 June, less than five weeks after Cheshire's proposal, the first colonists arrived in their new-found land.

The association called itself 'Vade in Pacem' (VIP). Before we track its fortunes it is worth looking back to the context from which it sprang. Cheshire's 'Raw Deal?' article in mid-March had ranged far beyond training and domestic self-improvement. His vision was global, embracing Britain's relationship with the Empire, the role of Britain, America and the Dominions as agents of enlightenment, and 'the appalling urgency of the issue that lies ahead' – the bomb.

If these different aspects look like a disorderly heap, in Cheshire's thought they cohered. His aim was peace. Movement towards peace could result from individual actions, for if individuals at home combined to form one colony, this would be a nucleus for expansion into an international family. The cumulative witness of that network

would be a source of transforming influence. 'I can see no final
solution to the problems of the world, except by establishing a
Christian fellowship of mankind . . . the forces of good – both
active and passive – must be mobilized and encouraged to fight the
forces of evil . . . I consider it to be the duty of every one of us to
contribute something towards this cause.'[66]

His urgency reflected outside events. On 5 March Churchill had
delivered his Iron Curtain speech at Fulton. A few days later the
BBC contacted Cheshire about forthcoming atomic tests in the
Pacific. They were unsure if foreign correpondents would be
permitted, but might he be attending in some official capacity? If
so, perhaps he could act on the BBC's behalf?[67] *Another atomic
explosion.* Whether the pioneers who contemplated Gumley Hall's
dripping gutters and dodgy wiring realized that Cheshire saw their
repair as the first, fractional steps towards global fraternity we do
not know. But that was the plan.

VIP was ardent democracy with a military tinge. People were
'personnel', trades and crafts were grouped under 'sections', and
the president was anticipated as a retired regular officer. Beyond
the president there was to be an 'HQ Unit' to implement strategy,
administer intercolonial discipline, supply financial and technical
advice, plant new colonies, run training programmes and be a
vehicle for central sales, purchasing and publicity. Above this would
stand VIP's sovereign body – a general council. Fine-sounding as
this was, it didn't yet exist.

VIP's executive committee met to review progress on 28 June.
They noted achievement in the market garden, livestock (concentrating initially on poultry, rabbits and mice) and woodcraft, but
hopes were stronger than results. The greater part of the site
remained overgrown, and since they had started late in the season
the garden's forecast yield was unlikely to be attained until the
following year.[68] The stock of rabbits (eight) was not yet commer-
cially viable. However, they were buoyed up by plans. One colonist
outlined a scheme for training guard dogs, gun dogs and sheepdogs
'when there are facilities' (including, presumably, sheep). Other
ideas included beekeeping, bootmaking, cricket bats, crockery
painting, a flower service, instrument repairing, kayak making,

laundry, plastics, printing, surgical bootmaking and the manufacture of toys.

Ideas came free. To realize them they needed skills, capital and expertise in marketing, to ascertain the demand, say, for kayaks in Market Harborough. It was their hope 'to foster the individual craftsman and smallholder who otherwise cannot compete with mass production and is dying out'. This would provide diversity of opportunity and so suit individuals. It pre-echoed small-is-beautiful by two decades and sustainability theory by nearly five. But in the absence of training it was difficult to begin to specialize. Training cost money, yet they had virtually no capital. Which was where they came in.

Also against them were the demands of officialdom. The Ministry of Food demanded a residential Catering Licence and Canteen Licence. Egg ration coupons were needed to obtain feed for their hens. The market garden required a Market Garden Licence, and their proposed stall in Leicester market called for a Retail Licence.

Not that they had much to sell, and what little they had was difficult to deliver because transport posed a 'serious situation'. A member offered the use of his car. Administration and finance were rickety. The colony's secretary left. Members were warned that VIP's economy would not permit the drawing of wages in cash for some considerable time. Discord ensued, factions formed. Before June was out Gumley saw its first expulsion.[69] Cheshire told Lionel Curtis: 'We have had a great many difficulties, particularly in the matter of personalities. It is now obvious that a high percentage of members came here after their own ends. These, however, are no longer with us.'[70]

While sinking himself body and soul into VIP, Cheshire's public life and journalism continued concurrently. Having mended fences with Reginald Simpson he carried on writing for the *Sunday Graphic*, and when it suited them the government continued to beg his services. The Ministry of Information asked him to write something 'warm and personal' about Guy Gibson's *Enemy Coast Ahead* for their periodical *British Ally*, explaining that Cheshire's name was 'perhaps the best-known of the RAF to the Russians'.[71] An insouciant official invited him to give lectures to airmen on the 'advantages

of continuing in the RAF'.[72] From Gumley Hall he fielded requests
for his presence at exhibitions, celebrity luncheons, carnivals, flower
shows, company press days, village halls, churches and youth rallies.
The BBC asked for more scripts. News of his emerging Christian
commitment attracted an approach from Moral Rearmament. 'I
entirely agree with the general principles you lay down,' Cheshire
replied, 'but entirely disagree on the subject of MRA. I hold no
brief for it, and consider it a perversion of Christianity.'[73] He
declined an invitation to know more about Christian Science, and
replied politely to the fanatic who wrote 'OBEY HIS WORD'
in very large letters.

'I had counted upon you to step into my shoes,' confided a
disappointed secretary of the Royal Air Force Association when
Cheshire resigned from the association's executive, pleading pressure of work.[74] The secretary added: 'I am afraid my faith in human
nature has suffered too many setbacks, often from the people I have
most helped in life, that I am eager to be convinced that you will
succeed with your colony.'[75]

Cheshire was eager too. In August he wrote that the colony was
'thriving', an indisputable success. The misfits had gone. They were
poised to expand, with plans for new colonies, a holiday and rest
camp, a training centre – even an air charter service to increase
income and assist international fellowship.[76] But, as usual, most of
this was fantasy. VIP's finances remained precarious, its business
prospects poor and the membership disunited. They had 'set out
to create a spirit rather than an enterprise', but there had to be
effective enterprise to provide a context for the spirit. Both were
lacking.

Early in September Cheshire announced the formation of a
second colony, thirty miles from Market Harborough.[77] This was
premature – it came to nothing – but around the same time he
wrote to his Aunt Nancy, the widow of General Barstow, who
had died in the defence of Singapore, to sound her out as an investor
in VIP. She replied: 'At the moment I am afraid we are not in a
position to invest money, as we have still not finished paying death
duties on my father's estate . . . Once we sell this place however
(and at the moment I don't see much prospect of selling!) we will

certainly remember your loan which you are floating.'[78] 'This place' was Le (pronounced 'Lee') Court, a Victorian mansion and estate at Liss in Hampshire. The news that it was for sale sparked Cheshire's interest. Within a month Aunt Nancy offered it to him at a reduced price, to which his father generously volunteered to contribute 10 per cent as the deposit.

Cheshire's solicitor implored him to think again. VIP had £110 in the bank and liabilities of around £1,000, yet here he was seeking to buy the Liss estate for £25,000 plus £3,142 for stock. Cheshire and VIP were 'riding for the most imperial crash in the not very distant future'.[79] Cheshire replied by buying two Mosquitoes.[80] The *Sunday Graphic* helped by sponsoring one of them, thus making him 'Britain's first flying reporter', but their insurance – a hefty £750 – added to mounting commitments.

Spectators thought these steps outlandish, but as usual their rationales interlocked. Cheshire was convinced that VIP would soon spread abroad, to Holland, Australia or South America, and by daily radio conferences and fast air contact they could become one community in several places. His explanation to *Sunday Graphic* readers at the end of October anticipated the Global Village.

. . . the modern aeroplane has made the world a much smaller place than most of us realize. I want to acclimatize my mind to thinking globally, and not purely nationally . . . I think it is an essential part of modern education.

. . . I grow more certain that . . . the ideal world is to be found in the behaviour and example of the ordinary man who lives close to nature, and occupies himself with the problems of day-to-day existence: that it is not to be found in the capitals of the world, or in economics, or in the mere exposition of political doctrines.

The ordinary man has no axe to grind . . . and therefore he is on common ground whatever his nationality or politics.

The day that he makes his own direct contact with his counterpart in other countries, the day that he begins to join forces in common insistence on world unity, then perhaps we shall have peace.[81]

So, the Mosquito was not a gimmick – it had 'a crucial part to play'. It also triggered another cascade of heartbreaking letters.

My husband has been in America for fourteen months. On any of your trips to New York could you take my son and I. We would come just in the clothes we have, no luggage. Please help me.[82]

Or:

I am an ex-WAAF and wish to get to America, my fiancé an ex-soldier is seriously ill owing to war wounds. I have no possibility in getting the money to go by boat or plane, would you consider taking me as a passenger in your plane.[83]

Or:

. . . is there any chance of you taking me with you . . . ? During my brief two-year stay in the army, the only place I got to was Scotland, and I did not get much chance of learning anything there . . .[84]

So many sadnesses.

In November VIP's new launch at Le Court was national news. Cheshire blessed Aunt Nancy, who had handed back part of the purchase price as an interest-free loan. And since he was now a flying reporter he took the Mosquito for its first journalistic sortie. He went to Germany.

Cheshire had not seen the effects of Allied bombing at close quarters before. His account in the *Sunday Graphic* was muted, a succession of anthropological observations (about the Allied occupation as well as the Germans) and descriptions of smitten cities where starving families lived in holes burrowed into rubble. He was puzzled. 'You might well suppose that [the Germans] . . . would throw everything they have into their common cause and pull together; but they do not. Their creed has become a question of each man for himself, and few of them will raise a hand to help a neighbour who is in trouble . . . They no longer believe in National Socialism, but equally they no longer believe in anything else.' Only two weeks before he had celebrated world unity through the example of ordinary people. In Germany, he was forced to re-examine that idea.[85]

Back in England, fifty-three men, women and children, 'pioneers of Britain's most astonishing post-war experiment in living', had transferred to Le Court.[86] Cheshire spoke of growth: 'Three hundred Dutchmen are about to launch a colony in Holland. I am in touch with men and women interested in this idea in Australia and Ecuador, and I am negotiating for land in both countries.' A reporter came from the *Evening Standard*.[87] *Radio Newsreel* broadcast a feature.[88] The Press Association asked if his flight to South America would involve an attempt on the world record. His bank manager asked about his overdraft.[89]

Cheshire fell ill, retired to bed and stayed there for several weeks. He was becoming ever more prone to phases of collapse which stilled him for weeks at a time. Perhaps not coincidentally, around him lapped a rising tide of strains and worries as the consequences of one ill-judged choice after another returned to find him out.

In early December he was due to return to Germany for a lecture tour, but his health was not mended and the trip was put back. Some colonists were uneasy. Cheshire's idealism was the adhesive which held them together. When he was away there was friction, and they were thus apprehensive about his plan for a two-month world tour, due to start in January. Would it not be prudent to see Le Court soundly established first?

As far as Cheshire was concerned, it was. On 15 December he assured Barclays Bank in Oxford that No. 1 Colony at Liss 'is now on a very secure footing', with backing from a syndicate of businessmen, viable plans for agriculture and a capable management. Next day he departed for Germany and Berlin, via Holland, where Prince Bernhardt had offered a house for the use of VIP.

Berlin, where East and West met. In Berlin,

filled with spoils and loot of four victorious armies, and surrounded by the utmost extremes of luxury and privation, there was a sense of tension, a surge of inner turmoil . . . Whether one drove to a diplomatic reception or hitch-hiked to a NAAFI dance, one could be sure to find something to suit one's taste – from the Caspian, caviar: from Scotland, whisky: from the Rhineland, wine: from Denmark, cheese: from France, dancing girls: from America, the stars of swing and rhythm; from all the world, something.[90]

At some point that Christmas he fell to his knees. 'O my God, I desire, yet I desire not. I am weak, yet I long to be strong. Grant me Thy strength.'[91]

In Berlin[92] he again fell ill, entered hospital and did not emerge for nearly a month. The pause allowed for meditation on Christian teaching. He was becoming puzzled by the relativism of much that passed for theology.[93] As for VIP, the association was like blotting paper, soaking up all he could give.

I've never known a man who has been so loved – or so hated . . . You see lots of VIP ladies were admiring him very much, then hated him just as much as they'd admired . . . they admired the schoolboy and overlooked the man inside, the man with the job to do . . . It led to bitterness. They didn't see the serious side, didn't believe in his ideals or ideas, just admired his looks, his manners, his clothes, his humour, didn't want to make sacrifices or work hard for VIP – it wasn't VIP that mattered at all, only meals, rooms, being 'first' with GC.[94]

The German lecture tour revived nostalgia for the ready-made values of the RAF.[95] Perhaps he could rejoin?

Cheshire returned to England on 3 February 1947. Most of Britain was inert, buried under snow in temperatures which locked rivers and trapped trains. Since Le Court had no mains electricity VIP scarcely noticed the power cuts until their generator failed. But water froze in the taps and the coal merchant 'had long since given up the unequal struggle of supplying the household on credit'.[96]

Ruinous quarrels had broken out in his absence. He postponed his international trip, pleading the work to be done in the colony. 'It is not that I mind the work but that if I do not do it the whole enterprise may collapse. We are burdened with a number of people who do not pull their weight and who form a somewhat disruptive element.'[97] In parallel, he asked to re-enter the RAF – a request turned down on the grounds that he was unfit for service.

Dispirited and tired, Cheshire nevertheless knuckled down to restore Le Court's affairs. By the end of March he was guardedly optimistic.[98] A new farm manager was appointed. Finding the greenhouses neglected and seedlings for the coming season killed by frost, he reroofed the greenhouses, discovering as he did that among the colonists were 'too many parasites and unorganized individualists'.

Cheshire had plans for a pioneer school to help plant colonies in the Dominions, and he was optimistic that the RAF Benevolent Fund would provide financial help. He had also once again lost his bearings.

Apart from VIP I am not quite certain what to do. It doesn't of course leave me much time over but what there is I would like to use constructively. I have been invited to join Churchill's United Europe Committee but don't yet know whether to do so. I am not quite certain whether they are likely to achieve anything . . .[99]

Illness returned in late March, and again a month later. His doctor ordered six months' rest. Cheshire had other ideas. A journalist from the *Evening Standard* noticed his quiet voice and eloquent hands as he described plans for VIP's international expansion.[100] On 13 May the *Evening News* announced, 'in a week's time Group Captain G. L. Cheshire, VC, will take off from Abingdon in his private Mosquito on a 5,800-mile trip to British Columbia. His mission is to establish his first overseas VIP. . . settlement, on the lines of the two self-supporting colonies he has founded in England.' Fifty colonists, said the *News*, were ready to go. In reality, they weren't. Cheshire was on the verge of serious collapse. Problem after problem had piled up, and his dwindling energy was being consumed by financial and personal worries. He could not afford the Mosquitoes[101] and sold one.[102] Work to the other produced a crippling bill. In February he had suffered two contradictory rebuffs: as a result of his annual medical board his disability pension had been cancelled, yet his application to rejoin the RAF had been rejected on the ground that he was unfit for service. In April he appealed to his bank manager: 'I have just had this . . . and I haven't the faintest idea what to do about it. Could you possibly help me?'[103] 'This' was a surtax demand from the Inland Revenue for the financial year 1945/46.

His parents stepped in. Too frail to resist them, on 21 May he left as a passenger for Canada, to live as a guest of Hugh Embling, an Anglican bishop and friend of Cheshire's father who had retired to New Denver in the west of British Columbia. For six months Cheshire walked in forests, climbed, swam, read, talked theology, recovered his appetite and worked as a woodcutter.

Back at Le Court the resourceful farm manager raised crops of
peas, tomatoes, cauliflowers, sprouts and cabbages. He reckoned
that VIP's horticultural endeavours could earn £1,500–2,000 a
year: 'It could have worked.' The pea crop alone ought to have
raised £800–900. Yet when the time came to harvest the peas
much of the crop went to waste because nobody could be troubled
to pick it. 'They were always too busy . . . Too many bosses – too
few willing hands . . . Roomful of clerks, doing nothing.' At the
end of November VIP sent a cable demanding Cheshire's return.
Le Court was on the rocks. At a general meeting VIP was formally
pronounced a failure.[104] GC was 'impulsive – he had too much
faith in others, expected his own high standards of loyalty and vision
and integrity of purpose. [He] rarely got it . . . This exaggerated
trust in others let him down and the others down, and he never
learnt from his mistakes.' Cheshire's personal liabilities approached
£20,000. He sold the estate. By April's end only the house, its
immediate grounds and a handful of colonists were left. Day after day
he tramped Hampshire's lanes and footpaths, sometimes imagining
himself as a mendicant friar. In the circumstances, this was not
difficult.

In May he attended the Congress of Europe at The Hague as a
delegate of the United Europe Movement, and was depressed by
its 'naked and unashamed agnosticism'.[105] In June he wondered
whether to go to the Soviet Union, provoke his own arrest and so
gain entry to a concentration camp where he could evangelize. He
fought a losing battle against the weeds which invaded Le Court's
gardens. Then Arthur joined him.

Arthur Dykes had been a member of VIP, although Cheshire
scarcely remembered him. He was fifty, and for some time he had
been ill, most recently in Petersfield Hospital, where he lay dying
of liver cancer. The hospital could do nothing for him and were
keen to reclaim his bed. He should have been discharged to home,
but as he had no home other than Le Court, that is where he
went.[106] Following a crash course in the basics of nursing, Cheshire
looked after him. He fed him, made his bed, washed his pyjamas
and sheets, helped him to the lavatory. Sometimes they sat talking.
Or not talking. For hours at a time Cheshire sat wordlessly holding

his hand or supporting his head. They lived mainly on vegetables foraged from what was left of the kitchen garden, and Arthur's weekly pension, and as the days passed the washing was not for the squeamish. Arthur Dykes was a Catholic, so occasionally they talked about religion. At other times they discussed Le Court. The house was haggard, requiring all kinds of work which Cheshire could not afford. To avert bankruptcy he had a plan to split it into flats.

By early August Arthur seemed weightless and was turning to the colour of parchment. On the 19th he had a seizure and lapsed into unconsciousness. That evening Cheshire summoned Petersfield's Catholic priest, Father Clarke, who lit candles, anointed Arthur's head, hands and feet, with prayers for each anointing, and prayed the Lord 'forgive you all those sins which you have committed'. Arthur Dykes's soul went forth upon its journey in the early minutes of 20 August.

Cheshire described the events of that night in *The Face of Victory*. No embroidery of his account can add to it. But there is something else, a pattern in the longer flow of events.

By the end of 1945, as if in a dark folk tale, Cheshire had been granted his four wishes. He was universally admired, driving a Bentley, wearing Savile Row suits and had access to wealth. Then, having gained what he imagined he wanted most, he found it joyless, and one by one the wishes were reversed. Within two years 'he was down to the last shilling, the last chair, and those who had praised him most deserted him first'.

There is a strange symmetry about this progress from clamour to calm, wealth to ruin, and gregariousness to the most fundamental of all relationships – one person caring for another. Yet who was caring for whom? Cheshire had already noted the importance of small, practical actions, each taken according to individual means and opportunities. Here he was unexpectedly living this out. The symmetry becomes yet stranger when we look ahead, and a few days behind. Even before Arthur's dying, Cheshire was caring for a second arrival.

Most of what he had attempted since the war had been ram-shackle, but chosen. Through reason and compassion he had struggled to implement the Second Commandment. It had nearly crushed him. There was nothing planned about Arthur, yet through him Cheshire found himself contemplating the First Commandment. Three years before Clare had given him the Key of Promise. Arthur's gift was the understanding of how it could be turned.

14. Le Court

The day before Arthur's funeral Cheshire wrote to a new acquaintance:

My dear Rae,

A letter in haste to tell you that Arthur died in the early hours of Friday morning. He had a sudden relapse after lunch on Thursday, suffered a certain amount of pain and lapsed into final unconsciousness at 6.30 p.m. At 10.30 Fr Clarke came up to administer the last Sacraments, and we prayed for him to the best of our ability. At 12.20 he stopped breathing . . . It was a merciful end and we have much to be thankful for.

Thank you so much for the book, which I am reading with the greatest interest . . .

Yours very sincerely in Our Lord. GC[1]

'Rae' was Harry Rae, who hoped to launch an employment scheme for disabled Welsh quarry workers.[2] 'The book' was *One Lord, One Faith*, by Monsignor Vernon Johnson. Rae had lent it to Cheshire, who with other things on his mind had put it to one side. In the hour after Arthur's death Cheshire foraged for a cigarette, and the book turned up again.

I now picked it up and idly looked through it, devoutly wishing that it would turn itself into a packet of cigarettes. According to the title-page it was an explanation of the author's conversion to Catholicism . . . Better than a ghost story in the circumstances, but that was about the best one could say.[3]

Nonetheless, Cheshire began to read. A paragraph caught his eye.

The supreme reason [for my conversion] was that I could not resist the claim of the Catholic Church to be the one true Church founded by Our Lord Jesus

Christ to guard and teach the truth . . . She alone possesses the authority and unity necessary for such a Divine vocation.

'Truth' . . . 'authority' . . . 'unity': the words stirred him.

Another word in his thoughts was grace, the power of God operating within man. A few weeks before he had a made a promise.

It was early June, but not very warm, so we lit a coal fire, this looked very cheerful as we came in the room supporting Arthur, and he seemed very pleased indeed. Needless to say, the nursing he received at my inexperienced hands was very rough and ready. Nevertheless, he soon settled down to this new life and I was much surprised at the change that came over him. I think he felt that he was wanted.

I was so struck by this that I began to wonder if there weren't others in his position, dying and unwanted. I also decided that I would not go out of my way to find them, but would merely leave things to take their course. If they came my way, I would accept them; if they didn't, I would turn my mind to something else.[4]

Arthur listened. He looked almost excited.

'But are you prepared to accept anyone who turns up, no matter who they are – I mean assuming they are genuine, of course? . . . can you in good conscience turn round and refuse a patient just because he's too difficult or you're too busy? . . . And that goes for the helpers, too – everything in fact. If you're going to leave the initiative to God, you'll have to be consistent. Is that what you intend?'[5]

Cheshire said yes, that was what he intended.

A day or two later the Marchioness of Cholmondeley turned up bearing a hamper of food. She had recently met Cheshire in London, and he had told her about Arthur. A vanload of furniture followed. She told Cheshire: 'Le Court has succeeded in making one old man happy without exactly giving him *luxury*, and I don't see why it shouldn't do the same for many others, too. I wouldn't let anyone on earth talk you out of it.'[6]

There were, of course, plenty of people who tried to talk him out of it. Cheshire's father begged him to reconsider. So did Primrose, but neither parent made any more difference than the Anglican clergyman from Lambeth Palace, whose advice that

Cheshire should abstain from helping others in order to attend to his own soul struck him as oddly unchristian.[7] Health officials looked at the house and shook their heads. Le Court's external woodwork, long starved of paint, was in decay. Most of the eighty-odd windows 'were huge, had broken their sashes and were permanently either jammed shut or wedged open'. The lofty chimneys were clogged with soot and jackdaws' nests. Parquet floors 'were black and glutinous from successive layers of dirt, polish, more dirt and more polish'.[8] Parts of the fabric were no longer weatherproof, and ominous cracks had begun to appear. On rainy days water trickled down the wallpaper, nourishing colourful displays of fungi. Outside there were two and half acres of grass to mow, and huge flower and vegetable gardens which in the 1930s had absorbed the energies of over twenty men. Cheshire managed to keep two of them on, selling the vegetables and flowers in Alton.

No staff, no money, no experience, no proper premises. The drawbacks seemed conclusive. Against them, on the other hand, stood the authentic witness of Arthur's joy.[9] In any case, Cheshire was not rejecting anyone's advice. All he had resolved to do was to clear his mind of preconceived plans. Jesus said to Nicodemus, 'The wind bloweth where it listeth.'[10] Cheshire was simply waiting to see from which quarter it blew.

A few days later he received a telephone call from the porter of the block of flats in Kensington where Aunt Edith lived.

It appears my aunt had very strong views on the irresponsibilty of what I was doing and had voiced these in no uncertain terms to the porter! He, as it happened, had a grandmother-in-law who was bedridden and in a poor state of health. She was ninety-three and her husband had recently had a stroke and had been taken to hospital. He now asked me to take the old lady in, saying that she hadn't been looked after for months. I said that I would be delighted, and the following day she turned up in an ambulance and a very striking hat.[11]

Alf Willmot, a TB sufferer, came on the day of Arthur's funeral. 'I have three cases in already, two more on the way,' Cheshire told Rae nine weeks later. 'Also I have fairly active support, or at least interest, from the TB authorities.'[12] The wind was rising.

In another paragraph in that letter, Cheshire declared 'I am seriously considering becoming a Catholic.' His life hitherto had been akin to the search of a darkened mansion for a room which he would recognize as his. For a decade he had wandered its passageways, trying the handles of different doors. Some had been locked. Others opened, in a few cases rather too easily, and he had entered the rooms beyond. But none was right and sooner or later the quest was resumed.

What had foxed him most recently was the conditioning of his own background. When the reality of God became inescapable in 1945 he instinctively turned to the Established Church, because Anglicanism, like standing up for the National Anthem, was part of the furniture of his upbringing.[13] Yet Anglican teaching left him flummoxed. It struck him as inconsistent, even casuistical. Initially he ascribed this to his own ignorance, but as his understanding improved the contradictions multiplied. One cleric counselled confession, another scorned it. He received varying advice about his broken marriage. Disagreement even extended to definition of the Church itself. The Reformation understands that we are 'saved in hope', that faith is held inside history and looks forward to a completion of life which lies beyond human comprehension. This troubled him, for if aeronautics was governed by non-negotiable laws of flight, how much more certainty ought to attach to a Church which mediates the Word of God? And yet, apparently, there was no such certainty.[14]

In the days after Arthur's death he met the Catholic reply. Yes, God alone is infallible, and Christ is God, and the Church is the living continuity of Christ. 'Going, therefore, teach ye all nations, teaching them to observe all things whatsoever I have commanded you . . . He who hears you, hears me. He who despises you, despises me.' The Church is not an antitype of Christ; it *is* Christ, an extension of the Incarnation. No ifs or buts.

Anglicans had told him that deification of the Church was spiritually dangerous: the Church was subject to the laws of historical reality and thus it could not escape the ambiguities of historical existence. In their view there was only one certainty: God is love, and all that matters is to love Him, and our neighbour in Him. To which Cheshire later answered:

True enough, love is all that matters. But one cannot love what one does not know . . . To argue that it does not much matter what one believes about God, as long as one loves Him, is not love at all, it is to destroy the very foundation upon which love alone can exist. No love without knowledge; no knowledge without certainty of truth; no certainty of truth without infallibility; no infallibility unless the Church be Divinely founded and Divinely maintained.[15]

Catholicism transcended time, regarding history's enterprise as susceptible to completion and recognizing grace as a prerequisite power for the fulfilment of life.

Here, at last, he found the explicit structure which placed the individual in an ascertainable relationship with the universal. Truth, unity, authority became his watchwords. By November he was undergoing instruction.

Some were puzzled, or saw Catholicism as another craze. Father Clarke, Petersfield's Roman Catholic priest, wondered about this, and tested Cheshire by parrying his pleas for instruction with encouragement to study Anglican critique of Catholic teaching. He also inadvertently tested Cheshire's willpower by offering him cigarettes. Not for the first time, Cheshire had decided to give up smoking, but 'Fr Clarke was just no help at all.'[16] A few wartime associates felt sorry because they imagined that Chesh had fled to religion because he had lost his self-reliance. Others saw Catholicism as a kind of pious Fifth Column, and reproached him for treason. But on he pressed, and on Christmas Eve, 1948, after a morning cutting firewood and cleaning floors at Le Court, he changed, drove into Petersfield under a weak winter sun, and entered the church.

I, Geoffrey Leonard Cheshire, holding in my hand God's holy gospels, and enlightened by divine grace, publicly declare that I accept the Faith which is taught by the Catholic, Apostolic and Roman Church. I believe that Church to be the one true Church which Jesus Christ set up here on earth; to which I make my submission with all my heart.

Years later he looked back at himself on that day.

Christmas 1948 is the one that stands out . . . It was the Christmas that I was received into the Church, and the first Christmas at Le Court, where my work amongst disabled people began. We were living more or less hand to mouth, not really knowing where the money could come from to pay the weekly bills. There were twelve heavily disabled people in the house, some of them old and approaching the end of their life, and only one resident full-time helper other than myself. From one source or another we had managed to find a small present for everyone, but it looked as if there would be nothing special for Christmas dinner, until at the last moment, and completely out of the blue, a hamper arrived from Canada. It came from the Canadian ex-members of the Dambusters who – I don't know how – had heard something about Le Court and wanted to say Happy Christmas.

The combination of this, of having been received into the Church earlier in the day and of preparing myself for my first Midnight Mass, gave me a sense of wonder that I had never felt before.[17]

'An empty book,' wrote Thomas Traherne, 'is like an infant's soul, in which anything may be written. It is capable of all things, but containeth nothing.' Standing outside Le Court's entrance, gazing up at strange stars in that December night, Cheshire was newborn.

Rumours about 'what was going on' led Prebendary Cheshire – Uncle Kick – to see for himself. When they came to Granny Haynes's room his uncle asked: 'Who looks after her?' Cheshire replied, 'I do, of course.'

'No, I mean, who washes her and dresses her?'

'I do.'

Granny was, as they say, 'a character':

. . . she'd been a district nurse when she was young and was perpetually telling me that I was doing everything in the wrong way . . . And she was stone deaf . . . When she didn't want to hear something, she didn't hear it, no matter how hard you shouted and when you said something that had nothing to do with her in a whisper, you could be sure she picked it up. But we ended up with quite an affectionate relationship. One day she suddenly flung her arms round my neck, kissed me and said, 'I love a young man.' And I said, 'I love an old lady!'[18]

Le Court filled with the disabled, the unwanted, the helpless. The TB authorities sent TB patients. From a local council house

Reconnaissance of the Saumur railway tunnel, following 617 Squadron's attack on the night of 8/9 June 1944; one Tallboy has penetrated the tunnel itself

Reinforced concrete boat hangar at Le Havre, fractured by Tallboy during the attack on 14 June 1944

Tallboy falling from the Lancaster captained by Fg Off. Willsher towards a V-1 storage site at Siracourt, 25 June 1944

Cheshire flying a Mustang III during his last sortie of the European war, 6 July 1944

Opposite: Wreckage of part of the 150 metre barrel of a V-3 ultra-long-range gun, or 'Busy Lizzie'. The lateral tubes were for additional propelling charges, successively fired to increase acceleration of the projectile to over 5,000 ft per second

Above: Mimoyecques, where the rectangular outline of the 18 ft thick concrete slab which sheltered V–3s is visible left of centre. Amid the profligacy of earlier bombardment are the larger craters of Tallboy, three of which put the structure beyond repair

Right: Wg Cdr James Tait, Cheshire's former 4 Group colleague and successor as OC 617 Squadron

Opposite, top: Cheshire and Constance Binney, September 1944

Opposite, bottom: Primrose and Geoffrey Cheshire at Grey Walls, September 1944

Left: Cheshire in Washington, summer 1945

Bottom: Preliminary briefing for the atomic bombing of Hiroshima, held in a locked hut on the afternoon of 4 August 1945. Col. Tibbets (with pipe) sits in the second row. Behind him is Maj. Charles Sweeney (white vest), leader of the attack on Nagasaki

Opposite, top: Civvy Street: members of 617 Squadron at a Bomber Command reunion in 1947. Cheshire is flanked by Gerry Witherick (second from left) and Mick Martin (centre, bottle in pocket). Larry Curtis and Geoff Rice stand right and second from right

Opposite, bottom: Le Court

Above: Cheshire and his father with Mosquito G-ART, March 1947

Right: Frances Jeram and Primrose Cheshire, *c*. 1949

Below: VIP kennels at Le Court, 1947

came an elderly lady dying of cancer; from their own village of Empshott 'a bedridden widow partially out of her mind, covered with bedsores and incontinent'. Ted French was a Post Office cable layer, 'in plaster from the waist upwards with his right arm fixed rigidly above his shoulder'. New visitors were often startled by this dramatic salute.

To keep the wolf from the door we sold the flowers, the holly, even the best of the vegetables. To supply the missing brooms, cutlery and other items of daily household use, we scoured the surrounding dustbins and dumps – often with surprising results. To make up for the absence of staff, we parcelled out the housework among the patients, no one excluded . . . To avoid the cost of fitting bells we grouped those who needed help at night into adjoining rooms and I slept on the floor outside the door . . . Yet . . . in spite even of the perpetual disorganization that seemed to reign, no one appeared any the worse. Almost, one would be tempted to suppose, the better for it, the stronger even in body for having discovered that they were needed and that someone depended on them.[19]

Le Court attracted helpers. One of the first was Frances Jeram, a qualified almoner, who early in 1949 was working in the Portsmouth chest clinic. Word had reached her about 'some sort of wing commander out near Liss', and one day in March she and a friend resolved to pay him a call.

Cheshire looked diminutive. 'We were ushered down a stone-flagged passage into a room containing bare trestle tables, set with just about a knife and fork each'. With great courtesy Cheshire ladled out portions of a hotpot which contained 'just about any-thing', while Jeram's friend asked probing questions. Jeram was struck by the atmosphere of solidarity. After supper she walked with Cheshire in the garden. How did he collect the fees for the convalescent patients? 'I don't know. There aren't any fees.' Patients handed over their pensions, and that was it. Jeram explained that fees for some of the patients could be claimed from the National Assistance Board. A few days later she returned, and then wrote.

On my drive back I was thinking about your old ladies and the possibility of getting some money out of the NAB for them, and I wondered if it would be of any help to you if I came over now and again and dealt with any problems of this sort for you – as a sort of visiting almoner . . . I am also a trained shorthand typist, a VAD and can do all the normal things like cooking and washing up . . . You must forgive me for suggesting myself like this – but Le Court gives one the feeling that one must take one's coat off and join in . . .[20]

Cheshire wrote back like a shot.

That was a real bit of unexpected luck, and exactly what we need. I've been considering what I could do to get help in the almoner department. Also shorthand would be invaluable. Patients seem to be pouring in these last few days. I shall have to buy another house![21]

Frances Jeram took to putting in evenings at Le Court on her way home after work. 'Somehow I just got involved.' Cheshire soon began to rely on the fact that she had.

Could you manage Tuesday, instead of Monday? I shan't be back. Also I'm afraid I shan't be in until 7 p.m. Tuesday. There's a lot of work piling up. I'll leave some of it on the office desk, in case you get in before me.

. . . Also I'm taking in an old boy of sixty-five with amputated leg. He's ex-Army and ex-butler and will help with vegetables. He can pay £3 p.wk. We've got the answer from Mrs Laurie: it will do till Tuesday.

Life here is busy . . .[22]

A week later Cheshire invited Jeram to leave her job and work at Le Court.

Yes please I would love to come and do the job . . . I feel very proud indeed that you have asked me to take part in the work that you're doing because I think it is something that really counts – not only for the practical help it gives but in its great influence for good. I am very doubtful as to whether I possess the qualities needed for the role I am to take, but at any rate I can promise you I shall be in it heart and soul.[23]

Next:

Olive Selkirk has just taken over as sister in charge. There's been the usual opposition to authority and I am anxious to stand by her for a few days. She's making a wonderful improvement to the place, and it's a merciful thing that she turned up. The nursing department was getting in a bit of a mess . . .[24]

Sister Olive was herself a victim of TB. She directed the nursing
from her bed. Later in June:

I have just got a deputy to sister, a friend of hers, Sister Roberts. Fully fit, very
strong, a definite sense of vocation . . . She gives a month's notice tomorrow.[25]

Later that month Professor Cheshire resigned his Chair at Oxford,
put Grey Walls on the market and moved to Laundry Cottage, a
house on what was left of the Le Court estate. Having failed to talk
their son out of his latest hare-brained scheme, Cheshire's parents
decided to settle near by, so as to keep an eye on him. The
relinquishment of Grey Walls, for so long the centre of family life,
came as a surprise to Christopher.[26] Geoffrey and Primrose had
large parts to play in what lay ahead.

    Local authorities began to place patients, and more live-in helpers
presented themselves. One of them was Bill Roberts, who had just
completed his National Service. 'What would you like me to
do?' 'Anything,' replied Cheshire cheerfully. There was a kind of
pioneering bravery. The house was cold and uncomfortable, several
helpers slept on mattresses on the floor, food was limited and cooked
on paraffin stoves. Financially they lived from day to day. Cheshire
reassured them, laughed with them, charmed blankets, beds and
towels from Hampshire's gentry. Local tradespeople who had
become disenchanted with Le Court in the days of VIP now
reappeared bearing bags of flour or sacks of coal.[27] Cheshire welcomed new patients when they arrived, and sat with them for
hours, sometimes days, upon their dying. 'At this time,' recalls
Frances Jeram, 'it wouldn't have worked without him. GC was
their captain. He provided the inspiration.'[28]

    The best-adjusted communities have their collective mood
swings, and there were occasions when Cheshire misjudged them.
One day he declared that patients and staff would no longer eat
together, since by reorganizing the dining room they could make
space for more beds. By custom, everyone mobile at Le Court
ate together. The next meal was taken in complete silence. This
continued until Cheshire acknowledged that he had overstepped
the mark and backed down.

    Tensions sprang from other sources. On several occasions

Cheshire fired people with a chilly abruptness. The victims tended to be those who came between Cheshire and his conception of what Le Court was about, and some thought him ruthless because of it. A better explanation is found in Cheshire's linear cast of mind. When he saw to the heart of an issue he instinctively moved to address it by the shortest route. The fact that this could cause hurt was something he did not always apprehend until later.

Conversely, there were others whom Cheshire retained whose dismissal would have been popular. Just as it was a rule never to refuse anyone in genuine need of help, so he would not turn away anyone who wished to serve. This led to the presence of several helpers 'with problems of their own', while his idealism attracted nurses and others who were either personally drawn to him or hoped to bask in his reflected glory. 'It was a relief,' Jeram recalls, 'if GC asked for advice.'

Cheshire's relationship with Le Court was complicated and evolving, simultaneously submissive and possessive, conscious of the need for greater organization yet nostalgic for the spontaneity of the first days. Cross-woven with these oppositions were influences which derived from his religious and personal life, his health and from the outside world.

For over a year Cheshire did his best to avoid publicity. Incessant press interest in VIP had been akin to the repeated pulling up of a plant to examine its roots for signs of growth. He was anxious to screen Le Court's new family from this kind of scrutiny, and until the autumn of 1949 he did so. Then the press discovered the new story. 'What's happened to Group Captain Geoffrey Cheshire?' asked the *Standard* on 9 September, scooping a larger item which ran in the *News Chronicle* on the following day. The effect was startling. Gifts of clothes, furniture and cash poured in. The reaction was magnified when other newspapers recycled the story, first at home, then abroad. After months of poverty Le Court's bank balance rocketed to £1,200. The *News Chronicle* published a follow-up story on Christmas Eve, when piles of food parcels from Australia and Canada fleetingly made Le Court almost a place of luxury. Gone, it seemed, were the days when Cheshire would contemplate Le Court's empty cashbox with his cheery catchphrase

'God will provide' and a cheque or anonymous gift a day or two later would suggest that He had.

One paragraph in the *News Chronicle*'s article on 24 December had a familiar ring.

We should have heard more about Cheshire before but he has been ill.

He has been scrubbing, painting, carpentering in this mansion that he bought with his last money, nursing, feeding, washing the helpless and scheming to meet the bills (because you don't necessarily have to pay to enter the sanctuary at Le Court) and finally he collapsed.

But, he told me yesterday, he is back at work and he is better now.[29]

But he wasn't. The collapses had returned.

Cheshire's chronic ill health may have been abetted by his new enthusiasm for asceticism. During the middle months of 1949 he fasted often, resisted Frances Jeram's ever more ingenious strategies to feed him, restricted his sleep to five hours a night and divided his wakefulness between sustained hard work and long hours of prayer in Le Court's chapel. Perhaps he had been reading the lives of the Desert Fathers, or the Life of St Cuthbert; at any rate, when Father Clarke coaxed him into a short holiday on Skye he found Cheshire sizing up the eremitical possibilities of a rocky offshore islet, and scolded him for doing so. Feats of asceticism could form a kind of excess; they bred a competitive spirit, which led to pride – which was a sin. Moreover, reliance on Providence was all very well – but who was Cheshire to say whether a particular unexpected cheque was Providential? Intuition and chance had brought Le Court into being. Now that it flourished, Cheshire should consider that intellect, normality and common-sense were also God-given: why should such gifts not be applied to putting Le Court on a sound and permanent footing?

For six weeks early in 1950 Cheshire was again in bed with something that resembled perpetual flu. Around the same time in 1947 he had lost his bearings, and something similar now recurred. Most of the money raised by the appeal through the *News Chronicle* had been put towards the resurfacing of Le Court's long drive, which in winter had become a near-impassable quagmire for cars, to say nothing of wheelchairs. The overall financial position was deteriorating and by late winter debts totalled some £1,500. One morning he confided to Frances Jeram that 'St Teresa had come to him in the night', directing that Le Court be given up and placed in the hands of the National Health Service.[30] There followed a bizarre argument wherein Jeram (an Anglican) found herself defending Cheshire's original conception against Cheshire himself, and possibly against St Teresa.[31] Jeram's counter-argument, that Le Court's special spirit was its most precious asset, which would not withstand formalistic bureaucracy, eventually swayed him. There was in any case a third path along which they had already begun to move: the appointment of a management committee to oversee day-to-day affairs, and trustees to govern strategy. Inevitably this would diminish his personal control, but this would be balanced by Le Court's gain in stability. If Le Court mattered so much to those who belonged to it, and it obviously did, then surely Cheshire's obligation was to see that it was established in a way which guaranteed its continuity.

Cheshire understood this, but the transition was emotionally exacting. Le Court's family belonged to him, and he to it: a relationship that was possibly more intense than any he had yet experienced. He wrote again to Jeram the following month:

The only comfort is that difficulties are the one true testing ground both for people and for institutions, and I know that after Easter when I get back, it will be quite clear what course to take . . . From the beginning there have been so many turnings we might have taken, so many inexplicable developments about which we had no option, that it's difficult to pick out the pattern.[32]

From this time the financial crisis eased.[33]

He was writing from Solesmes, a small town in the Department of Sarthe in northern France. Solesmes centres on a Benedictine abbey.

Solesmes is a real tonic . . . I have always liked and wanted solitude, but solitude pure and simple brings many dangers in itself. Fortunately here there are the offices to keep one steady and set the day in its right proportion. Other than the little maid and the Father doorkeeper at the Abbey I don't speak to a soul. Yet the day seems to fly. I get up at 8.15, go to Terce and High Mass 10.00 to 11.30, lunch 12.30, walks all the afternoon. Nones and Vespers at 5 p.m. to 6 and Compline 8.45 to 9.15. Sunday I start with Matins, followed by Lauds and Low Mass 5.15 to 8. The routine continues with Prime and ends at 9, when we have breakfast, having got up at 4. How would you like to do that every day for the rest of your life![34]

It was a question he was beginning to ask himself.

Solesmes was discovered through Hélène. He had been introduced to her the previous November while staying with Aunt Edith and Uncle Gabriel in Paris, having been shooed out of Le Court by his parents and doctor with orders to go away and convalesce. In Paris, free of all responsibilities for the first time in over a year, he relaxed. One day Hélène came to lunch. Dark-haired, attractive, in her early thirties, she was working as a secretary. The meeting, Hélène recalls, was 'like a mutual clap of thunder'. She was startled by his 'hypnotic eyes'. Cheshire offered to drive her home, and thereby discover where she lived. They saw much of each other in following days. Cheshire told her of the difficulties he had faced after the war, the despair of VIP when 'nothing was working'. Now he prayed often, seeking guidance on the direction he should travel. The journey, it seemed, had led to Hélène. For some while he wrote to her every day.

In the New Year Cheshire again fell ill, and Hélène travelled across to nurse him and give a hand at Le Court. She stayed in Laundry Cottage, where Geoffrey and Primrose became devoted to her. Hélène's family lived near Le Mans, and after his sojourns at Solesmes Cheshire often stayed with them. One brother was a priest, another was a missionary in China. A strong Catholic family.[35]

If Hélène was much in his thoughts, so, again, were flying and war. Father Clarke's campaign to coax Cheshire towards a steadier existence had led to the suggestion that he take an outside job. There need be no parting from Le Court, but equally there was no reason why he should be there for every minute of every day. Sir Charles Symonds gave Cheshire a check-up in January 1950 and made much the same point. Sir Ralph Cochrane put him in touch with Barnes Wallis, 617's armourer of old, now head of Vickers' Research Department at Weybridge. Early in May

Cheshire presented himself for interview. Wallis, a little reluctantly, offered him a job.

The survival of Le Court was bound up with the survival of Britain. NATO was now in existence and, as he had prophesied, the Soviet Union had tested an atomic bomb. On 25 June North Korean troops crossed the 38th parallel into South Korea. On the 27th the UN Security Council urged members to repel the invasion. Next day Seoul fell to the Communists, and British warships in the Far East were placed at the disposal of the UN. On 29 June Cheshire wrote to Frances Jeram:

I once told you . . . that I would never leave Le Court except for war. When I was suddenly asked to take this job on it was clear that the authorities considered war as a not entirely remote possibility . . . This thought has long been at the back of my mind and I have felt a sense of urgency to get Le Court ready for any such eventuality . . .

He added:

I am only sad to think that our old team which bore the first brunt is breaking up . . . Whatever our . . . mistakes may have been, I can't frankly see how we could have got under way except in the way we did.[36]

15. Near England's End

Barnes Wallis, like Leonard Cheshire, was a patriot. Both men had a Victorian faith in Britain's global role,[1] which Wallis ascribed to geography.[2] His 'life-long passion for long-range flight at the highest speed that the technology of the time offered'[3] was essentially political, because he saw it as the key to Britain's economic future and safety. Designers of tea clipper sailing ships had been similarly motivated, and like them Wallis searched for shapes that would minimize resistance to motion.

Anticipating the Soviet Union as the post-war threat,[4] from as early as August 1945 Wallis was sketching ideas for long-range supersonic aircraft which could travel non-stop from Europe to Australia in a return journey time of a few hours. Flying at heights of 60,000 or 70,000 feet, such aircraft would connect the Empire, while their military derivatives would defend the United Kingdom by guarding her airspace and providing the means to strike Soviet industry in the event of war.

By 1950 Wallis was engaged upon several mutually informing experimental projects which led towards this goal. One, known as Heyday, was for a submarine which could travel underwater at speeds far higher than any previously attained. Another was an aeroplane based upon the revolutionary principle of variable geometry.* In both Wallis was searching for a low-drag shape which would deliver laminar flow – that is, constant streamlines of water or air with little or no turbulence.

---

* This idea eventually found its way into swing-wing aircraft like the F-111 and the Panavia Tornado. These designs, however, were unrefined approximations to Wallis's original concept, which envisaged wings not only of variable sweep but which would also move independently at different angles of incidence.

Wallis saw two initial applications for variable-sweep aircraft. One was a short-range interceptor, being pioneered in a project called Wild Goose. The other was a tailless supersonic airliner known as Swallow.*[5] Wild Goose† was a small pilotless aircraft, in effect a rocket-launched glider. It was unmanned partly because Wallis entertained the eventual interceptor as pilotless, but also because he was unwilling to risk lives in gathering experimental data.‡ Instead he opted for a graduated programme of experiment, first using small gliders and then tests in a free-flight wind-tunnel which led to trials with Wild Goose itself.

Cheshire was in formidable company. Wallis's research department included the mathematician Elsa Hoare; Herbert Jeffree, a physicist who concentrated on Wild Goose's instrumentation; Cecil Hayes, who worked as technician and aerodynamicist; and Norman Boorer, the chief designer. For a few weeks Cheshire worked in the technical office at Brooklands, doing his best to absorb the theory behind Wild Goose. Boorer was struck by the sparkle in his eyes, Wallis by the prodigality of his ideas.[6]

Wild Goose required many accessories. The absence of a test pilot called for remote flight-control systems, telemetric equipment, a rocket-propelled launch trolley, a track to run it on and a mechanism for the aircraft's automatic release. All of these had to be designed, built and tested, and Brooklands was a place where all kinds of contributory improvisations flourished under Wallis's direction. Even the 'cold motor' rockets (fuelled by hydrogen peroxide) were, so to speak, home-made, and covetous eyes were cast on the nearby London–Bournemouth railway line as a place to trial the launch trolley. Some of the early trolley experiments

---

* Both projects were funded by the Ministry of Supply. Early enthusiasm waned, however, and Swallow eventually fell victim to an inconstancy which became the hallmark of government influence on British aeronautical research in the 1950s.

† So called because the outline of a goose had influenced its configuration. A dead Canada goose was brought into the drawing office at Brooklands, where Wallis spread it out and traced round it, making calculations about its aerodynamic properties. Wallis's search for efficient shapes often looked to nature for underlying principles. His work on Heyday included study of the dolphin, while the concept of a tailless aerodyne owed some debt to the study of birds, as well as to Wallis's earlier experience with airships.

‡ A pilot-flown version of Wild Goose, the Heston JC-9, was considered, and went some distance in construction before being abandoned.

were carried out at the Royal Aeronautical Establishment's airfield at Thurleigh, near Bedford. From here Cheshire flew in July and August, calibrating avionics for the supersonic age in a biplane.

Security and safety demanded that Wild Goose itself be tested somewhere remote. For this the Ministry of Supply selected Predannack, a Cornish wartime airfield which had been unused since 1946. The site occupies a plateau on the Lizard peninsula, where black marshy pools are cupped by peat, hedges have been sculpted by Atlantic gales and trees lean in slanting poses. Mullion, a fishing village, and the hamlet of Ruan Major are the nearest places. In this solitude, a mile or two short of England's southernmost point, Cheshire's task was to establish Vickers's new outstation.

He moved down to Predannack in October 1950. Essential buildings were refurbished and a small resident team of technicians and a cook/housekeeper was installed. This population rose when flight trials or specialist work were in progress. Contact with Weybridge, nearly three hundred miles distant, was normally by the Paddington–Truro sleeper, but the round trip could be made in a day in the elderly de Havilland Dominie which became the project's air taxi. Cheshire himself had the use of a civilian registered Spitfire, in which he occasionally let off steam. He savoured the isolation. Hélène came down for a week. Together they looked around, visited Land's End and one day stopped in front of a white cottage near Mullion with a 'to let' sign. The White Cottage was small and furnished with monastic severity,[7] but it did have a telephone.

Mrs Jeram tells me that you telephoned her. I have just been posted down here and for a while am pretty tied up. Should I telephone or write you when I am likely to be nearer London? It's a bit difficult to anticipate my movements at the moment. I am not too clear from Mrs Jeram what you wanted.[8]

He was replying to a message from Andrew Boyle, a journalist on the *Catholic Herald* who wanted an interview about the relationship between faith and war.[9] Boyle was also curious about Le Court. On 24 October Cheshire wrote to him again.

Is there any chance of your coming here? It's peaceful and I have time . . .

I realize that, living in a physical world, force must play a part, but only a secondary part. To disobey any of God's moral laws is, at its lowest level, suicide and condemns you to failure. Deliberate area bombing involving civilians is murder, with the inevitable consequences to the perpetrators. Bombing soldiers is different: somehow it's part of the game and you know what you are asking for when you join up. Also we have a right and duty to defend our country – but only within the limits of God's laws.

At least that is what I think. Knowing that the beaten powers propose[d] to area bomb I contemplated trying to say what I think, but decided to keep quiet. I am only recently a Catholic – two years – and over-impulsive.

Converted is the right word. I was an out and out heathen. I'm not very keen on Le Court being written up except in its own right. To sell what you have and give to the poor looks very good on paper, but in fact it counts for very little. As you know better than I, it's giving up yourself that counts. And I never did that. I shouldn't like to give the impression that I did . . .[10]

Boyle visited. They sat up late talking about liturgy, celebrity fund-raising, strategic bombing and other discrepant topics which only Cheshire could unite.[11] It was the start of a lifelong relationship.

By now, it will be clear, Catholicism was the heart and sum of Cheshire's being. His faith was not an adjunct to other things – it was the centre from which other things sprang or to which they had to be related. Boyle's questions about the morality of war challenged him to re-confront the relationship between belief and bombing. He did so in an essay called 'The Catholic Bomber Pilot', composed during November evenings. 'I have written the enclosed draft,' he told Boyle, 'thinking that I might turn it into an article.'[12] Here are extracts:

My profession was to destroy, and therefore to shrink from doing so was a contradiction in terms. Carried a few stages further, I can well see how even the gas chamber becomes a possibility.

It may be argued that this trend is the consequence of absence of Grace and not of the work itself . . . I draw a sharp distinction between fighting an armed force and attacking non-combatants, regarding the former as lawful and the latter as an outright violation of our natures, so that Grace cannot exist in the man who participates.

I have always enjoyed the thought of battle, and my conversion has not changed me . . . If there has to be a war, fighting comes to me as a natural and even wholesome activity, but only so far as it applies to the opposing armed forces.

From the beginning of life until the end, we are at war in one form or another: at war with the world, at war with our own baser instincts, at war with the seductions of the world. War as such does not strike me as intrinsically evil, but rather as the inevitable consequence of the Fall and, under certain circumstances, as a necessary instrument of our salvation. In short I can well conceive that for a man in a state of Grace battle may become both a prayer and a means of giving Glory to God.

However:

When war extends to the civilian population . . . it changes its character completely, and I cannot conceive that any man engaged on mass indiscriminate bombing could supernaturalize his actions as I know he can when he is fighting a pitched battle. It is on these grounds that I account for the moral blight that descended upon us at the time of Nagasaki.

Cheshire had clarified his thinking on two points: the risk of insidious gradualism; and (a familiar theme) the responsibility of the individual.

My object is to make it clear that, given the will, one can set whatever limit one chooses to its application . . . This freedom of choice, by its very existence, involves every one of us in a share of responsibility for the outcome. We shall not be able to plead that it was not our concern . . . the disorders of the world are due to the fact that we are such bad Catholics, that we have failed to reflect the light that one needs to find his way. The responsibility is first and foremost ours . . .

A companion essay gave more context. He called it simply 'The Atom Bomb'.[13]

In point of fact the atom bomb did not influence the war one way or the other, for politically speaking the war was already over. What is more this was known to the Allies at the time . . . The argument that Hiroshima and Nagasaki were justifiable on the grounds they saved more lives than they destroyed is therefore invalid . . .

This belief that 'Hiroshima was a crime because it was unnecessary' was only temporarily held; his mature view was that the atomic bombings did shorten the war. The greater interest here lies in the corollary, that the crime had '*automatically involved us in a penalty, which will have to be paid in full*'. He was thinking of the fate of the soul. Cheshire believed in the existence of moral laws which operate identically to the laws of nature. To ignore such laws would be disastrous. Had he ignored them? Indiscriminate killing was both immoral and inessential to effective warfare. Wars are won, as Barnes Wallis reminded him, not by generalized slaughter but by cutting off an enemy's power. Civilian lives unavoidably lost in the course of attacks on an enemy's coal, oil, gas and hydro-electricity[14] could be accounted for in the final reckoning. Random mass bombing could not.

As in all things . . . it is the first step that counts. The choice we are presented with is seldom all or nothing: we are merely asked to make one small concession, and being human we generally make it. We say that we will go so far, but no further, that this is the one exception, justified by unusual circumstances, and so imperceptibly the process repeats itself. Familiarity and pressure of danger combine to obscure our vision of where we were heading. The moral law has been broken . . . And so from innocent beginnings we arrive at Nagasaki. Without, so far as we know, ever having had to make a decision at all, we have assented to the doctrine of supremacy by force. We have turned to fighting Communism with her own weapons, and therefore we have lost not only our only hope of peace, but our own souls as well.[15]

Such were his meditations as winter closed in and Atlantic storms smacked against the cliffs.

Before Wild Goose flew it was necessary to lay the launch track, and to refine the release mechanism which would enable the aircraft to rise free from its cradle when the rocket-driven trolley reached the required speed. Once airborne, Wild Goose was to be guided by two pilots – each with separate responsibilities for control in different planes – from control rigs set apart to give contrasting fields of view. For all of this, Cheshire had oversight. It was, however, the work of God rather than the work of Vickers which gripped him more, and his knack of drawing others into it is nicely illustrated in his correspondence with Andrew Boyle. Christmas and Le Court, for instance.

Mrs Jeram wonders what chance there is of finding a man to come down and help her with the festivities, sort of generally playing the fool and you know what. Last year we had two undergraduates . . . Do you have any ideas?[16]

Or a motor mechanic who had been adopted by Arthur Dykes,

and now in a sense has been adopted by me . . . He is impulsive and never really settles down. Because of some row, his children are not being educated at a Catholic school. His wife isn't a Catholic, though sometimes is on the point of becoming one. If they could settle down, she might make it. The main point is to find reasonable accommodation . . .[17]

There were a lot of nudges like this.

Boyle's article describing Le Court as 'unique in the land – a haven for homeless and helpless sick where the atmosphere radiates peace and happiness'[18] – appeared on the front page of the *Catholic Herald* three days before Christmas. Cheshire was then at Solesmes, going on to visit Hélène. Their affection had grown. Eighteen months before Father Clarke had advised:

Haven't you heard that sanctity consists not in doing the extraordinary, but in doing the ordinary extraordinarily well? . . . Don't you think that it would be better to settle down and marry? Marriage, after all, is the normal state for those who aren't priests or religious. You are free to do so, for the Church doesn't recognize divorce, and, in Her sight, your own marriage was null and void, for Constance had a husband before you married her; you may never go back to her. So think it over.[19]

He had been thinking it over. Joining the Wild Goose project was part of the result.[20] Hélène was another part. Friends were told that they planned to marry in the early summer of 1951, and she was looking forward to settling into the White Cottage: 'I dreamt of it for a long time.' In America, proceedings for a divorce from Constance were put in hand.[21] In January he flew the Spitfire up to Lincolnshire to see John Kirby, his old base commander of Marston Moor days. Kirby found him 'radiant, happy as a sandboy, full of his marriage to Hélène'.[22]

Unless the radiance stemmed from something else. While tramping Predannack's perimeter he had paused to examine an empty building, 'neglected for some five years, its metal window frames long since rusted by salt-laden gale-force winds which blow during the winter . . . cows had broken in . . . There was no mains electricity, no sewerage facilities, and no water . . .'.[23] In other words, it was ideal. All over Britain, he knew, there were homeless, disadvantaged or sick people who lacked proper accommodation. One of them, indeed, a former naval diver 'who was being evicted from one boarding house after another because he was an epileptic, and whom Le Court had turned down for fear of injury to the other residents', had just joined him in the White Cottage. Another was a member of Predannack's canteen staff who had fallen ill with no one to care for her, and on Cheshire's instruction had been moved to his own quarters until she recovered. Here was a building that no one needed. It was repairable. Why not repair it? He wrote to Boyle on 2 February:

Michael Gibson, the ex frogman, has arrived and is hard at work on the building. He hasn't had a fit yet. The change has done him good. He's only twenty-five and very impressive. The local officials are doing their utmost to find a way in which I can get the building officially. There's no water or sanitation for miles and it's in a terrible state, but it's basically very suitable. It's great fun. Do you know any strong men who don't know what to do with themselves?[24]

Strong men, and women, turned up. Colleagues from Vickers, airfield staff and local people came to paint, scrub, rewire, oil hinges and lay bricks. 'He somehow gave you a feeling that you were really doing yourself a favour by helping him.' News of the project was made public in mid-March, and reported by Boyle in the *Catholic Herald*:

Announcing the news himself at a meeting in the Catholic Hall at St Ives, Cornwall, Group Captain Cheshire told a large audience of his plan to found a 'Second Liss' in a disused building . . . [The] main reason for this new extension of his voluntary, part-time undertaking is the constant stream of applicants to Liss . . . for unwanted invalids whose relatives are either dead or no longer willing and able to look after them. Since the Hampshire centre became a fully state-recognized institution, it has not been possible to accommodate all those who sought admittance.

No stickler for red tape, but bound by the rules as much as by his own workaday preoccupation, as a secret research expert on a West-country airfield, Cheshire decided – if need be – 'to begin all over again'.

With his genius for 'making something out of nothing', and his characteristic energy, he now proposes to convert a derelict hut . . . into the first wing of the 'Second Liss'.

Catholics in the audience . . . heard him proclaim his trust in St Teresa of Lisieux, to whom the new hospital will be dedicated . . .[25]

Cheshire first came across Teresa in *One Lord, One Faith*, the book he had begun to read after Arthur Dykes's death. Then, she had meant little. Now he knew her to be an obscure girl who had taken the veil and then led such an unassuming existence that her superiors 'hardly knew what to say by way of formal tribute when she died of TB still in her twenties'. Teresa concentrated on what was practical and attainable from day to day. She was Cheshire's pattern.

News of the Second Liss did not go down too well at the First Liss, where finances remained shaky.[26] If it was a struggle to fund one home associated with Cheshire, how much harder would it be with two?

Unperturbed, Cheshire returned to Solesmes at Easter, then to Hélène's family home. A knee injury had left her temporarily disabled, and because of that they decided to postpone the wedding until late summer.[27] This left Cheshire feeling strangely thankful. Perhaps he needed more time in which to give St Teresa's his undivided attention?

At Predannack, local people brought food, utensils, furniture and bedding. When a lady asked what they needed most, and was told that it was sheets, twenty sets were delivered on the next day. The Royal Navy sent a machine to dig a hole for the septic tank. Two Australian nurses turned up, one of whom had been raised in the outback and cheerfully proclaimed St Teresa's a 'home from home'. The first patient, a partially paralysed elderly man, arrived on 2 May.[28] More followed. Since serious cases would come to

Predannack, Cheshire theorized that Le Court and St Teresa's would complement one another.[29]

A few onlookers were critical or nonplussed. Some muttered that St Teresa's was a place which attracted 'anybody who couldn't get in anywhere else', which of course was exactly the point. Others complained about the dysfunctional drains. One nurse considered the buildings to be 'completely and utterly unsuitable'. One day she found herself next to Barnes Wallis in the canteen lunch queue. 'What do you do?' he asked. The nurse said she worked at St Teresa's. 'Ah,' said Wallis, 'odd, that.' The subject continued to turn in his mind, for a few minutes later he returned and asked, 'But is it *right?*'[30]

Perhaps this was an early conversation, for Boyle's notes of his interview with Wallis show the scientist to have been much moved by Cheshire's work. Wallis quite often called at St Teresa's where he was moved by the special kind of happiness that glowed there. Wallis also visited Cheshire at the White Cottage, accepted an invitation to join him in prayer in the room he had converted to an oratory and found himself surprised by his own lack of inhibition when he did. Wallis was struck by the way in which resources for Cheshire's work seemed to arrive out of nowhere. In 1944 the two men had corresponded about probability theory.[31] Wallis now began to reflect that when things happened twice this was co-incidence; when they repeated they were minor miracles. As for the drains, one day two hefty RAF men turned up and began to lay them properly.

Publicity prompted more pleas for help. Some concerned the terminally ill, and within a week of St Teresa's opening Cheshire's mind was surging towards a 'new home I propose to start building in the beautiful site next to Ruan Major church'. The church itself was a ruin. 'If I can get the church too, which is not impossible, then the way will be clear for a real home for the dying.'[32]

It is easy to see why some assumed that he had lost interest in Le Court. Le Court was at a different stage of development, no longer requiring the impulsive self-surrender with which Cheshire started things, and arguably benefiting from his distance. He visited when he could. One early July morning some of Le Court's residents sighted a gleaming speck which raced towards them above Hampshire's woodland. The dot rapidly resolved into Cheshire's Spitfire, which overflew the house so low that Frances Jeram was convinced that it passed between the chimneys. This outburst of high spirits preceded a colourful fund-raising fête which drew over a thousand visitors. The weather was flawless, the event was opened by Ted Kavanagh, creator of ITMA, and residents performed scenes from *A Midsummer Night's Dream*.[33] Le Court was becoming known.

July 1951 was the month in which Frances Jeram published a short article that summarized Le Court's original aims.[34]

There were two main objects. The first, to take in those who had nowhere else to go and were not provided for by the state, asking in return only what they could afford to pay, and refusing no deserving case; the other, that Le Court should be a home in the best sense of the word, that this small community should be a family, and to this end both old and young, male and female, of all denominations and suffering from a variety of complaints, were accepted. Thus all were encouraged to give a hand in the running of the home, and to help each other, the young and the less disabled waiting on the older and more helpless members.

Not many people read *The Almoner*, the journal in which this appeared, but one who did showed it to her father, Sir George Dyson. Dyson was a composer, and head of the Royal Academy of Music. He was also vice-chairman of the United Kingdom Carnegie Trust. In October he invited Jeram to see him.

They met at the academy, Dyson seated beside a colossal grand piano. 'It's a little bit out of the ordinary for our trustees,' he told her, 'but if we could help, what would you need?' Jeram thought rapidly. Le Court in winter was the first thing that came to mind. 'Central heating.' She said this with diffidence, for central heating would be expensive – maybe as much as £300–400. Dyson smiled. 'We're thinking of something more than that.'

Cheshire reacted to this with studied nonchalance, perhaps because he sensed something grandiose and contrary to the example of St Teresa, or because large grants usually came with strings attached. When Dyson and two fellow-trustees came to visit, however, there was instant rapport. After lunch they walked in the grounds. Dyson asked him where, if funds were available, he would put a new purpose-built home. The question did not seem to surprise him. Cheshire pointed to an area of ground. 'Over there.' A charitable trust to which Le Court could be conveyed was now in prospect. After further discussion the Carnegie Trustees pledged support for a new Le Court in which spaces, levels and layout would be designed with the needs of the badly disabled specifically in mind. From being £500 in debt, Le Court was being offered a grant of £65,000.

Early in September Cheshire wrote to Boyle:

I have a large programme for building chapels. Building isn't the right word. I have the structures: they need converting and fitting out. I have no scruples about appealing for money when it's for a Catholic church or chapel, and I wonder if the *CH* [*Catholic Herald*] could help me. All I want is for people to send me their unwanted wool. It fetches 4s. a lb and to complete the programme up to next summer I need nearly £5,000. I shan't get it, but it's what I'd like. If I did get it, it wouldn't be wasted, because every structure that gets converted into a Catholic church is symbolic of the coming reconversion of England.

If the *CH* could start me off in a salvage drive, I could probably find enough well-wishers to keep it rolling and bring us the money we need.

For your private information the marriage is off. I think that I shall end by getting Ruan Major church, though it will probably take a few years: I hope to open the 3rd home on Oct 3rd. I shall probably give my job up . . .[35]

There is a lot in this letter. Almost too much: the reconversion of a nation, a campaign of church-building, another home, leaving Vickers and, incidentally, a cancelled marriage.

What had happened? Since May 1951, if not sooner, Cheshire's thinking had been subject to accelerating change. 'I shall probably give my job up . . .' To do what? Repeated visits to Solesmes and the cold hours in his oratory had caused him to ask if he had a monastic vocation. To be a soldier of Christ was to be in the front line, the place of action. Even if he didn't do that, the demands of Le Court, St Teresa's and whatever might follow, not to mention the mending of England's faith, could leave little or nothing of him for a wife, or a family. During the summer he had come to think that Father Clarke's advice had been wrong. Hélène had no place in whatever lay ahead. Having realized this, he simply told her, writing an 'incredible letter to break off [the] marriage, as if he would be "frustrated to hell" if he did not'.

To Hélène, this seemed unfathomable. She half suspected Father Clarke to be behind the declaration but, as she neither knew him nor possessed his address, she was unable to write to seek an explanation he could not in any case have given. Helpless and desolated, she fled to Spain. It took her two years to recover. Half a century later she reflected: 'I think it was Providence. I understand now . . . [that] he was tugged between God, humanitarian work and love', but was so generous 'that he never talked about all these dilemmas so as not to trouble me and, perhaps, he hoped to be able to reconcile everything'.

As 1951 neared its end, Cheshire turned towards an eremitical existence in which he neglected to eat regularly and passed hours on his knees. He seemed ever thinner, and those who knew him well began to notice a sharp, dry cough. He gave up smoking, but the cough persisted. So did his equable manner. There was no pious solemnity about him; rather, when he talked of faith it was in the unforced tones that others might use to discuss football. Nevertheless, the relationship between the different strands in his life was becoming tangled. For instance, was St Teresa's to be a kind of religious community, or was it something else?

Whatever it was, it flourished. By November there were twelve patients, with space for eight more in prospect, a staff of two nurses, a cook, a cleaner and a lady warden. Sisters from a nearby religious community gave help, and every Wednesday a party from the Royal Naval Air Station at Culdrose arrived to give the regular staff an afternoon off. Local people lent a hand, and there were more applications for places than the home could deal with.[36]

As at Le Court, the common sharing made for a special kind of *esprit*. The home brought together young and old, living and dying, hope and humour, faith and doubt. As Christmas neared they were given a huge tree, and made papier-mâché figures for a life-size crib in a half-ruined building to which all processed by lantern-light in a storm. On Christmas Eve forty carol singers arrived, handing

over the £30 they had raised. On Christmas Day Cheshire appeared
dressed as a chef to carve the turkey, and after the patients had been
served roles were reversed and patients served the staff. At the end
of 1951 the warden, Eirene Andrews, wrote to a friend about a
'perfectly wonderful Christmas – the first one I've ever met that
had the real spirit of goodwill and joyfulness'.

By midwinter Cheshire had all but resolved to offer himself for
the priesthood. By March 1952 he was looking forward to the
disciplined anonymity of a Cistercian community in Brittany, and
preparing to order his affairs to make this possible. In between he
had founded a third home.

The new home lay in dilapidated RAF hutting about three
quarters of a mile from St Teresa's. Although conceived as an
annexe to St Teresa's, the satellite soon acquired an identity of its
own. Cheshire called it Holy Cross, and it was intended as a
rehabilitation centre for ex-servicemen and women who were
'physically fit but mentally maladjusted by reason of wartime strain'.
Locally, this was not entirely popular. Holy Cross housed such
people as the schizophrenic former bomber pilot with shoulder-
length hair, flowing beard and open sandals whose striking appearance and quiet wandering earned the cruel sobriquet 'Creeping
Jesus'. Nevertheless, Holy Cross made progress, and that it did had
much to do with the growing influence of Shelagh Howe.

Shelagh Howe was a highly capable major in the WRAC, and
a member of a committed Catholic family living in Mullion. Frances
Jeram recalls:

She was divorced . . . My personal contact with her was when I was invited
down to St Teresa's at the very early stage, I suppose so that I could report back
to Le Court. S. H. met me at the station and drove me to the family house
where I stayed the night. They were very kind and hospitable, but *absolutely
bowled over* by G. C. [i.e. Leonard] and were ready to do anything to help.[37]

Shelagh Howe was also, in Cheshire's words, someone of 'forceful
personality',[38] and among the staff at St Teresa's there were some
who thought her 'rather too keen on G. C.'.[39]

Back at Liss, meanwhile, Le Court's affairs were again in flux,
in one sense almost literally. 'There are signs [that] Le Court's

foundations are cracking due to an underground stream.'⁴⁰ In the longer term this hardly mattered, but the Carnegie project had yet to start and it might be touch and go whether the new home would be ready before the old one fell down. A more immediate problem lay in Frances Jeram's resignation. The new managing body was about to come into being, and Jeram saw her work as done. On 10 January Cheshire wrote his thanks. Farewells are usually about individuals, but this one turned into a homily on Christian unity. Jeram was an Anglican, and Cheshire seems to have been concerned, perhaps even distressed, by the underlying division between them.

After three years as a Catholic I acknowledge humbly that so far as the Reformation aimed at purifying and dephariseeing the Roman Church it was right, and that we still have a lot to learn from you in the sense of living by the spirit and not by the letter . . . you on your side must try and realize that if Christ did not in fact establish an infallible, apostolic Catholic Church which really holds the keys of Heaven and wields power over sin and death, then the Apostles, the early Fathers and 1,900 years of Saints have all been deceived and are proved wrong. The first step must necessarily come from us, and I most devoutly hope that it will come before too long.⁴¹

Up on the airfield the time for Wild Goose's flight trials neared. Yet St Teresa's and Holy Cross demanded all his time. In March, with 'a mixture of regret and embarrassment', he asked Barnes Wallis to release him. He told Boyle:

All here goes well, I having left my job last weekend. I have started a third home for people who have problems other than physical ones, where I am temporarily living. It is a happy family and we are making strides . . .

On Good Friday . . . we are having a procession with a full-sized cross between the two homes, involving a quarter of a mile or more of the main road. A great many people are coming, some from quite far afield, including nuns, religious and the clergy . . . I have a realistic, and truly God-forsaken looking, Calvary, and also a sepulchre. We shall be making the Stations of the Cross . . . All this has arisen out of the spontaneous life-sized crib which I had at Christmas, and which attracted a lot of local interest . . .

I have two other specific homes in mind down here but it is a little premature to discuss them. On Easter Monday I go to Solesmes for three weeks . . .⁴²

While Cheshire was away Wild Goose flew. Wallis and his colleagues, and some at St Teresa's, watched as the aircraft lifted from the launch trolley and soared. For some seconds all went well, but inexperience in control coupled with blustery conditions led to a misjudgement and the aircraft crashed. Even so, Wild Goose was airborne long enough for Wallis to know that the concept was viable. In the following months it flew regularly.

Back from Solesmes in May, Cheshire laboured for his patients while Wild Goose circled them. During the summer he turned increasingly to outdoor evangelism, working with the Catholic Missionary Society in Cornish market squares and villages.

Where now? Perhaps he was back in the darkened mansion, trying the handles of more doors. At any rate, when, on 20 August, a door did swing open, he knew what it meant. On the previous afternoon he had given an open-air talk in Helston with Father Ripley, a CMS priest. On the way home he collapsed. Next morning Father Ripley found him no better and drove him to St Michael's Hospital at Hayle.[43] Another priest, Father Delaney, joined them.

I was present . . . when the Polish resident medical officer broke him the news that the X-ray revealed a large cavity in his lung. To Cheshire this must have been the worst news he had ever been told in his crowded and adventurous career – it might mean death in a short time or permanent incapacity, and it certainly meant a long period of inactivity and the separation from the work so urgent, and so dear to his heart . . . He did not wince: he did not complain: neither did he, by folded hands and bowed head, signify his acceptance of what the old Irishwoman, mixing her adjectives, called 'the *unscrupulous* Providence of God'.

He just gave the typical, broad Cheshire GRIN, and almost laughed out loud.[44]

Cheshire was laughing at the towelling around the doctor's head. It looked faintly ridiculous.

Shelagh Howe was away on duty. She took the news badly, seeing it as a grotesque reversal. Cheshire replied: 'Far from going wrong everything is going very well . . . far better than I ever dared hope. What you are overlooking is that Christ conquered the world by the folly and humiliation of the Cross. "*I have chosen the foolish things of the world to confound the wise.*" '[45] A week later Cheshire was transferred to the King Edward VIII sanatorium at Midhurst, Sussex. Shortly after that the Ministry of Supply cancelled Wild Goose.

The day of Cheshire's diagnosis, 20 August, was the fourth anniversary of the death of Arthur Dykes.

PART SIX: ALL OR NOTHING, 1952–1955

16. Contemplation and Action

Midhurst, 12 October 1952. To Shelagh Howe
They say that I'll be through here in 5–8 months. It's pouring with rain. I'm worried about the birds on the balcony collecting their breadcrumbs with no shelter at all.

In fact, he was to be in Midhurst for over two years. Forecast dates of release were put back in a disheartening cycle of lifted hopes and postponements. Less of him would leave than entered. In a succession of operations, surgeons removed most of one lung and several ribs.

. . . Cheshire underwent the severest operation known in the treatment of his illness. But in the convalescent periods . . . he embarked upon an enormous timetable of study which ignored the inevitably distracting sanatorium day routine, with its bells and hot drinks and chatty visits from walking patients.

Cheshire's room . . . vibrated with quiet purpose. He read St Thomas Aquinas (in Latin). He studied textbooks about the Church's attitude in abstruse medical problems; he studied the Scriptures. [To other patients] he would expound, in his undidactic manner, his view that suffering must be seen as a participation in Christ's Passion, otherwise it is hideous, meaningless nonsense.[1]

Midhurst influenced his way of working. Instead of doing things himself, much had now to be entrusted to helpers who were briefed by letter. The result is the first richly documented period of his life, when one can follow issues, projects, even his moods, from day to day.

Cheshire's methods of delegation were strange. Twenty years later he said, 'Delegation isn't abrogation, you give somebody a

job to do but hold him to account for it and if he doesn't do it
properly tell him or remove him.'[2] This was not how it seemed in
1952.

> Leonard draws voluntary helpers like a magnet, but he never bothers about
> sorting them into categories, or assessing their abilities. He employs the direct
> and time-saving course of just seeing how they 'get on'. It sometimes works,
> but it's also sometimes pretty agonizing for the other helpers, or for those who
> do not 'get on' at all. If anyone complains to him about the chaos created by a
> non-getter-on, he merely remarks gently, 'I know – but I'm not a very good
> judge of character, I just have to accept anyone who comes along with a genuine
> offer of help – and hope for the best.' He will then replace the defaulter with
> someone even less likely to 'get on'. It is a failing of always thinking the best of
> everyone . . .[3]

The element of chance was increased by his reluctance to share the
totality of an idea with those being asked to implement it. He had
a theory about this.

> If we stick to the principle of parcelling out the business in bits and acting as
> though each particular bit is all that remains to be done, I don't think we will
> have too much difficulty. The fatal mistake in all undertakings of this kind is to
> frighten off possible helpers by asking too much of them. For today, today's
> troubles are enough.[4]

It is a question how far the theory may have been a rationalization
of his natural guardedness. Whatever it was, helpers often found
themselves at cross-purposes because of it, sometimes in ways which
cost patience and time.[5] But then, for the foreseeable future, time
was all he had.

For several years Cheshire had tried to labour for God through
simple, unspectacular tasks. Like the work of a coral colony, however, the cumulative result of individual tiny efforts can be large.
His supreme desire was the unity of Christendom, for which the
restoration of England as a Catholic nation was a precondition.
Faith, he knew from experience, turned on what went on in
individual hearts. Change would come from individuals outwards,
and this led him to seek ways of reaching ordinary people, on their
terms. Care of the sick and dispossessed formed part of that. So did

the continued running of Le Court, St Teresa's and now Holy Cross.

History sees the homes as Cheshire's main endeavour, and their family unity as continuous. In fact, the homes formed only part of his work, their early development was piecemeal and their genealogy complicated. Hence, while the trust which held Le Court was non-denominational, Cheshire did not yet accept this as the prevailing model. On the contrary, he longed to establish projects under Catholic direction, and only gradually came to accept that his path led elsewhere. Finding the path was complicated by the fact that he was a voyager, in spirit akin to the peregrinating monks of the seventh century who abandoned homely warmth to cast themselves adrift before the winds of Providence. Alongside the issue of how, if at all, his different projects might be articulated, there was thus also the matter of how a life of personal instability might relate to their collective permanence.

Cheshire fixed his mind on these subjects and one by one addressed them. First was the question of a monastic vocation. Did he have one? 'It was the Cistercians that most appealed to me and whom I would have liked to have joined, partly because they are absolute in their standpoint and partly because I liked very much their balance of life with the harmony between mental life, prayer and very hard physical work.'[6] Perfectionism or action? On 22 November, St Cecilia's Day, he chose action. It is important not to oversimplify the decision. Cheshire did not so much eschew the cloister in favour of the world as embrace the world in the spirit of the cloister. To all intents and purposes he became a kind of lay monk, and within a year he would adopt a life not far from mendicancy. For a short time he even practised calligraphy, with a goose quill pen, in the idiom of old scriptoria. This might have given us the Midhurst Gospels, but more pressing things occupied him. In many of them he relied upon Shelagh Howe, who became his envoy and, perforce, troubleshooter at Predannack.

Her office was at Lower Felpham and later . . . near Didcot, Berkshire. In spite of working five days in her very responsible job in her office (she was in charge of the packaging of everything used by the Army) every Friday evening Shelagh

travelled on the overnight train to Cornwall. No sleeper, just sitting up five a
side. She stayed with her mother at their home in Mullion House, Mullion,
each weekend, travelling back overnight on Sunday.[7]

Following the incident when Cheshire's part-time secretary emptied a suitcase of unanswered mail on his bed, Howe also handled
much of his correspondence. She became a good friend of Primrose,
the two often comparing notes about Leonard, and what his mother
called the 'mad, wild schemes'.

At the end of February 1953 Cheshire underwent a major
operation.

16–20 March 1953. Primrose Cheshire to Shelagh Howe
Sir Geoffrey Todd [the consultant in charge of Cheshire's case] says he is so
plucky and a model patient and was greatly helping himself and so we must be
comforted but I get so distressed when I see the dear boy looking so ill and being
so uncomplaining and patient. We shall go again on Monday. It's quite useless
ringing up. The reply is always 'quite comfortable', and heaven knows that's the
last thing he is.[8]

A second operation left him immobile and in great pain. A life-sized
reproduction of the Holy Face from the Shroud of Turin had been
put on the wall at the foot of his bed.

And there, for a full month, I did little but lie and look at it . . . in front of me
was no face such as artists depict . . . but one that stood in a class of its own, one
that bore the unmistakable stamp of authenticity – the face of the dead Christ,
not painted by an artist's hand, but imprinted by some mysterious process of
natural photography . . . Here was a face . . . which had plumbed to the very
depths of the mystery of suffering and death. As I gazed at it I felt impelled to
inquire into its origin, and as I inquired I felt impelled not so much to go on
looking (though that I certainly did), as to get up and act.

For here before my eyes was the Face of Victory . . .[9]

On their next visit Primrose and Geoffrey were 'completely
shocked'. Leonard was bleeding from his wound, running a temperature of 102 degrees and very sick.[10] He was suffering from
anaemia. Primrose confided to Shelagh Howe, who was then down
at Mullion, that news from Cornwall is 'the one thing that interests

him', adding wistfully 'Le Court doesn't now.' He was coughing a lot. 'Talking only makes him worse.'[11] In April Cheshire told Andrew Boyle: 'Have had a rough ride since the 2nd op and haven't been able to cope with anything. Coming out into the clear now though. Slowly.' By late May he was again seriously ill. The operation wound had become infected.

At Easter he had prepared a message for friends in Cornwall. In the fifth and sixth centuries Christianity in Cornwall had preceded the conversion of the English. In a world where West stood against East, capital against labour, and where 'we Christians ourselves are divided', was it 'too much to hope that it may now once more fall to Cornwall to point the way to England?'

Cheshire's parents had yet to come to terms with their son's faith, and were alarmed not only by his physical condition but also by what Geoffrey dryly described as his 'new Messiah complex'.

24 May 1953. Primrose Cheshire to Shelagh Howe

I also want to tell you how much I appreciate your efforts to distract L.'s mind from this almost 'religious mania' he has got. It's *so* narrowing and bad for him to concentrate entirely on one subject and makes him boring to others. If only he would listen to good music as you suggest or read some of the classics . . . [we] are more than grateful to you for putting ideas in his head and do so wish he would adopt them. Music is just the most wonderful help in the world. How people live without it I don't know . . .[12]

There might have been music, in his head. One of the patients at St Teresa's was Lenny Dipsell, a man in his twenties who since childhood had been immobilized by Still's disease. Before coming to Predannack he had languished in a geriatric hospital. Cheshire had often talked to him about that. 'The impression I was left with was of the vigour and hope of youth reaching out to the future, but seeing nothing but the very old and dying, like a man alone and without help in a fearful and desolate wilderness.'[13] Lenny liked music. He teamed up with another patient, Enid Bottomley, who was a pianist. Together they rehearsed, and decided to put on a show in local village halls. Their first concert was at Ruan Major. The curtains parted to reveal Enid sitting in a wheelchair at the piano, while Lenny resembled a warped plank of wood which had been propped at an angle, with 'two hands more or less together below his chin'.[14] The audience, many of them tough fishermen, were shocked into silence. In this stillness, the plank began to sing, a young, clear voice singing 'Beneath the lights of home'.

Predannack was not going so well. Originally seen as one home in two places, the running of St Teresa's and Holy Cross was vested in a temporary committee.[15] 'Inevitably this led to trouble: for once St Teresa's had settled down and been taken over by a committee the ex-gaolbirds, social misfits and schizophrenics who found their home at nearby Holy Cross were not acceptable as neighbours of the more conventional St Teresa's.'[16] St Teresa's financial administration was rickety, there were complaints about a member of staff and the monthly terms upon which the buildings were rented from the Air Ministry discouraged expenditure on repair or investment.

Then, like a genie, a benefactor appeared. At the end of June Mr Cecil Tilson Chowne, the executor of the estate of a devout Catholic, offered Cheshire £1,750 – sufficient to buy the land on which St Teresa's stood and the freehold of a nearby farmhouse for Holy Cross, plus tenure of its land and buildings. The only condition was that the money be applied to strictly Catholic purposes, which would require the formation of a new, canonically Catholic, charitable trust. Cheshire welcomed the condition. Pending formation of the trust he withdrew Holy Cross from the temporary committee's jurisdiction[17] and asked Shelagh Howe to make an offer of £1,350 for the farm.

Even as this plan was put in hand, another emerged. Cheshire told Howe, 'My ideas are clear now about the future . . . I want to make an all-out effort – do or die – to reach the average man.'

I am going to hand everything I have to the new trust and receive back only the minimum and necessary expenses. I'll work with two types of helper . . . Part-time – who earn in their jobs and help in their spare time. Full-time – who come in on the same basis as myself. I am taking the necessary steps to get the legal [?] drawn up – and shall in due course notify the people concerned – but only those.[18]

The renunciation of wealth heralded a new basis for his work. So too did the idea that full-time help should be vocational, in effect a grade of Christian ministry.[19]

Cheshire assumed that the 'new trust' would be the same trust as the body which was being formed to handle the funds received via Cecil Chowne. Chowne was an elderly man, well-intended but devoted to detail, and when he heard about the new plan he objected that it involved an 'abrupt change of outlook'.[20] Cheshire accordingly decided to establish *two* trusts: one to comply with Chowne's stipulation, the other with a deed that could cover future Catholic homes and mission activity. The first was to be known as the St Helena Trust (after the name of the farm they hoped to buy),[21] the second as the Cheshire St Cecilia's Charitable Trust.

In September Cheshire told Howe:

I would like you to take on responsibility for Holy Cross, the farm and future Cornwall talks. Instead of Peter,★ Mrs Murray and . . . [the prospective warden] dealing with me could they deal with you? Would you think this over and let me know before the 25th?

I've today been offered a magnificent house in between Manchester and Liverpool [Hulton Hall]. Gives me something to think over anyway.[22]

Chowne, meanwhile, had been under the impression that the Catholic trust already existed, and when he discovered that it didn't, he objected.[23] Cheshire returned £1,500 to him pending resolution of the muddle,[24] but instructed his solicitors to continue with the farm purchase[25] with a bridging loan from Shelagh Howe.

Complications multiplied. The farm had a tenant who had yet to leave, and imperfect accounting at St Teresa's prevented constitution of the new trust until it was cleared up.[26] This blocked repayment of Shelagh Howe's loan, Cheshire's request to the warden of Holy Cross to re-audit St Teresa's accounts was badly received,[27] while the need to account for the £250 outstanding from Chowne's original payment revealed that £100 of it had gone to the wrong trust. The prospect of two new trusts[28] was confusing, for there were now potentially three charities with which Cheshire was connected,† and not everyone understood which was which.

★ Peter Meade, warden of Holy Cross at this time.
† The existing Cheshire Foundation Homes for the Sick and the emerging Cheshire St Cecilia's and St Helena's Trusts. By November 1953 Cheshire was beginning to refer to St Helena's alternatively as the 'Missionary Trust'.

Cheshire himself had evolving conceptions of what each trust was for, and there was fluidity between them. Bewilderment deepens when we find that neither of the new bodies was ever completely formed, while *another* trust, the Mission for the Relief of Suffering, was established for purposes which derived from the projects that were stillborn. But this runs ahead. Let us return to watch other events through the eyes of some who took part.

Back in early summer a seven-year-old boy called Richard Worthington wrote to Cheshire. For weeks there was no reply. Then:

[He] wrote in the friendliest way possible. He said that he was very sorry about the delay, but he'd had an operation and wasn't allowed to write. He went on to say that he had been so pleased to get Richard's letter . . . and there was a lot more. It was the kind of letter which we know now to be typical, but at the time we were very touched.[29]

Peggy and Bob Worthington, Richard's parents, became regular visitors at Midhurst.

By August Cheshire had been released from the surgical wing, was allowed to sit outside and told friends he expected to be discharged by Christmas.

2 September 1953. Primrose Cheshire to Shelagh Howe
But you know an active mind is hard to squash especially as he cannot use his body . . . The boy seems so keen and interested in his ideas. It's difficult to decry them, don't you agree? It's Leonard all over – always on with the next. It's you I'm unhappy about – you have so much to put up with . . . I often wonder if he appreciates the hours of work you and others have done.[30]

This was his plan, 'do or die', to take the Word of God to people in the street.

It seemed he had bought a bus, which was now being fitted out not far away from the sanatorium, and in which he intended to show films as a background to talks given on the tape recorder. It was to operate in London.[31]

The vehicle was refurbished by technicians mysteriously 'loaned' by the Army. 'Isn't the bus lovely?' he asked Shelagh Howe. The Worthingtons agreed.

[It] was painted a dark blue throughout and on the sides were small gold insignia, an M. surmounted by a crown and encircled by seven stars. The M, Leonard told us, represented the Virgin Mary, and the seven stars the seven mysteries . . . The inside . . . had been stripped of all the seats and the windows were curtained in a heavy grey material, joined in one long strip so that they could be pulled across all the windows in one movement. At the back was a built-in table, and behind this the cinema screen, which unrolled from the ceiling when in use.[32]

A few days later the bus cropped up again.

Operation Bus was still technically nothing to do with us and Leonard hadn't asked our aid in any way. Then one day he announced with some satisfaction that the bus was at last ready and was going up to London the following week . . . We were having tea when he mentioned this, and we had finished and were about to leave when he remarked quite casually that it was a bit of a nuisance but they hadn't been able to find a garage for it in town. Bob immediately rose to this, and said he would see what he could do.

'Oh, will you?' said Leonard in apparent surprise, and looking very pleased, said, 'Thank you very much.'

Bob Worthington located a lock-up garage in America Street.

After the triumph of this find nothing more was heard for a few days. Then Bob had a call from a complete stranger. The bus . . . had now been delivered to the park . . . There was a note for the driver . . . Bob asked who the driver might be. In some surprise the stranger replied . . . that he'd been asked to deliver the bus and then phone Bob, and that was all he knew about it . . . Bob rang Leonard a couple of days later. He asked him gently if he would like him to drive the bus temporarily.

'Oh, thank you very much,' said Leonard, 'would you do that?'[33]

Cheshire mapped out 'Bus Movements', military-style, and on 25 November he wrote to Father Reginald Fuller, the rector of the parish in which the 'Mobile Missionary Unit' would begin its work. The 25th was a Wednesday. He hoped to start on the Saturday – the first vespers of Advent – and asked if this would be permissible. Father Fuller,[34] who also happened to be the editor of *Scripture*, said that it would. Cheshire replied that he would welcome criticism: 'I am feeling my way.'[35]

So was Bob Worthington. All he had been asked to do was to make contact with someone called Shelagh, who sounded a bit intimidating.

On the Saturday following . . . Bob went up to London . . . to see what was cooking with Shelagh and the bus. When she turned up shortly after he got there, he found the conclusions he'd jumped to about her were all wrong . . . She was a major in the WRAC and she had got leave especially to help Leonard launch his baby on its career . . . She is a very nice person with the same driving energy which Bob has, but again, like Bob, she sometimes gets the bit between her teeth.[36]

To fix listeners' attention during the talks Cheshire had the idea of fish in a tank. Bob Worthington took the bus to collect the aquarium, relishing the deference from other road users. He returned with frogs. 'Fish [he] had been told at the fish shop, couldn't possibly travel in a tank in a moving vehicle . . . Frogs, on the other hand, were apparently very tough.'

The site chosen for the launching of this fantastic venture was in a cul-de-sac off Piccadilly. It was completely deserted and there was no sign of Shelagh, who had stampeded off again in the afternoon to go ahead of the bus to make final arrangements for tapping the power.[37]

Next day Cheshire sifted discouraging reports. Bob Worthington had been stunned by an electric shock; shoppers had declined to enter; and having begun with too few helpers the vehicle became crowded by too many. But they persevered. Ways were found to attract passers-by for the minute or two needed to listen to one of Cheshire's talks. Before long Worthington was taking the bus out three times a week, and a plan was hatched for a second bus, to function as a mobile canteen and pick up trade from the first.[38]

As Christmas neared Cheshire decided to replace the frogs with a crib. The Worthingtons built a crib. Then Leonard 'broke out with one of his more spectacular brainstorms'. Sanatorium patients built a stable.

The most surprising of all the Christmas cribs seen in London was a *live* crib that stood until four o'clock on Christmas morning near Leicester Square, in the heart of London's night life. The human figures were not real but the shepherds had two live lambs . . . inside the 'stable' which was fashioned out of an old thirty-two-seater bus . . . The bus is used as a travelling mission. All during Advent it has been moving through the Eltham and Tottenham areas and people have been able to hear an Advent meditation by Cheshire . . .[39]

Behind this lay episodes which at various times involved the RSPCA, a calf at large in the Worthingtons' garden and police intervention when Shelagh Howe's invitation to a man to enter the bus was misinterpreted. Yet, in its way, the project was working. By January several thousand people had heard one of the messages.

In parallel, Cheshire was thinking about a biography.[40] Andrew Boyle (who now worked for the BBC) told him this would be premature, and his father said 'Wait thirty years.' At first Cheshire agreed. Then he changed his mind, apparently for two reasons. One was a hunch that such a book would advance Catholicism because his wartime record would attract people who would not ordinarily read about Christianity. The other lay in a likelihood that such a book would be written anyway. The early 1950s saw a spate of warrior biographies and sooner or later someone would write about Cheshire. Publishers had already shown interest. Among them were Evans Brothers Ltd, who recognized that a Cheshire biography would make a strong sequel to their best-selling *The Dam Busters*. Cheshire reasoned that it would be better to take the initiative, while Boyle's status as a friend, a writer and a Catholic made him a natural choice as author.

1 December 1953. Andrew Boyle to Professor Cheshire
Partly because we now know one another unusually well, and have been loosely linked in forwarding the Le Court and St Teresa's experiments, Leonard has agreed that I should make a start on his biography . . . Naturally, I need much material, especially in regard to his early years . . . and I need even more the guidance and comments of you and Mrs Cheshire. This is, in a sense, the most difficult and important period of all to unfold and assess without falling into the snares of sentimentality or the false foreshadowing of Leonard's greatness as a man. With your cooperation, I am sure I can get it right.

. . . My sole aim is to write a book a little worthy of Leonard, surely one of the exceptional spirits of any age.[41]

A few weeks before Evans Bros. had told Boyle that 'Mr Cheshire
has agreed in principle that we will publish his biography', and
offered to pay Boyle for twelve weeks' research.[42] Boyle declined,
explaining to Cheshire that contracts were a matter for negotiation
between publisher and author, rather than publisher and subject,
and telling Evans that their proposals would mean 'surrendering to
you the raw material of the Cheshire story, leaving you free to
commission someone else to write the book'.

Evans persisted. Cheshire told Boyle: 'Evans have written in
effect repeating their original suggestion to you. I've answered
asking for certain clarification and in effect stalling. I think the best
thing is for you to collect the material independently and then to
agree.'[43] Evans continued to seek Cheshire's authority to override
Boyle, rather tactlessly suggesting that if Boyle did the spadework
they might 'bring in a more experienced writer' to produce the
final version.[44] Once again Cheshire appeared to acquiesce, and
once again Boyle declared his 'unalterable intention' to write the
book on his own.[45] Boyle got to work, and there, for the time
being, the matter rested.

Cheshire's days filled with plans. Early in January 1954 he asked
Shelagh Howe to join the search for a London headquarters, ideally
a house with self-contained accommodation 'and room for two
buses'.[46]

Formation of the St Helena's Trust had stalled. In its place
emerged yet another plan, whereby Chowne's donation would
pass to the Roman Catholic Diocese of Plymouth, the diocese
would buy the farm and then lease it back to Holy Cross.[47] Again,
however, there were complications. The farm still had a sitting
tenant, the diocese declined to proceed until he was gone and
Cheshire had meanwhile reverted to thinking about Holy Cross as
a headquarters for the mission as well as a home for 'all kinds of
social misfits'.[48] A dispute broke out over money which belonged
to Holy Cross but which remained in the hands of the St Teresa's
committee.[49]

Bob Worthington reported to Father Fuller on Operation Bus.
Cheshire's recorded talks – collectively titled 'Seven Minutes':

seven sixty-second stories (one for each day of the week) to make a 'complete picture of Britain's ancient and traditional faith. The world needs Britain: Britain needs the faith. The Faith needs you' – were going down well.[50] The talks were aimed at ordinary people, and Cheshire wondered if there were ways of improving their delivery. Perhaps there should be music – Gregorian chant?[51] Different tableaux were built by patients at the sanatorium. At Easter they installed a sepulchre, and for some weeks the bus had a resident pair of fantail pigeons. He bought another bus, confessing to Howe[52] that to do so he had borrowed £100 of the money earmarked for the deposit on St Helen's Farm.[53] Howe came to the rescue.

Boyle's book was going well.

Midhurst, 20 February 1954. To Andrew Boyle

. . . I am astounded at all the work you have put in and the ground you have covered. So are Mother and Father and they are both very pleased that it is you who are tackling the job . . .

They now give me June as the earliest date and I am temporarily back in bed pending some treatment. All goes very well, however, and life is very pleasant . . .[54]

Briefly, they considered two books. 'The idea of my writing a complementary *might* be a good one,' Cheshire told him, 'but on more mature thought it would be too much for me.'[55] There were greater priorities. 'These cases,' he said, waving his hand towards a cupboard – one of the ones filled with papers – 'have been on my mind for a long time.'[56] The papers were letters from old people who were chronically sick and uncared for. Hulton Hall had fallen through: the trustees-designate of the St Cecilia's Trust had rejected it.

'I've had to accept their decision,' he told us in a rare informative mood, 'as I'm not on the spot to do the thing myself . . . It's put me in a very awkward position . . . because not only was the house offered to me, but also £500 . . . to go towards renovating it, and I wrote and accepted. Now I've got to write again and refuse.' It was obvious . . . that he was bitterly disappointed . . . It was the first hint of how his inactivity was forcing him to bow to the opinion of others . . .[57]

Midhurst, 24 February 1954. To Father Fuller

I very urgently need a new home to accommodate a number of old and incurably sick people. I have, I think, the possibility of a house in the London district – but no money or furnishings. Also I am short of helpers. The home is to be Catholic and to provide a HQ for the bus.[58]

A house was found in St John's Wood.

[It] couldn't have been more unsuitable either for the bus headquarters or for elderly people to live in. It was on three floors, had a steep flight of steps up to the front door, no garage space and before anything at all could happen, a fire escape costing £4,000 had to be installed. However, Leonard, whose judgement seemed to have gone quite haywire in his anxiety to get some kind of Home going, told them to go ahead.[59]

Peggy Worthington began to look at houses near her home in Chislehurst.

St Teresa's was now vested in The Cheshire Foundation Homes for the Sick, the trust set up for Le Court in 1952. The proposed leaseback arrangement for St Helena's Farm had foundered, and in another switch of plan Cheshire asked the foundation to accept Holy Cross as well. The foundation refused. Cheshire's commitments to the bus campaign★ were such that he felt he must abandon purchase of the farm. However, he wondered if by any chance Shelagh Howe wanted it?[60] Howe bought the farm. Primrose hoped she would not regret it,[61] and was not alone in considering three homes and two buses to be quite enough.[62]

As predicted, other writers were becoming interested in Cheshire. One was gathering material for a book on *Christianity in Action*.[63] Cheshire passed the inquiry to Boyle 'for purposes of coordination', adding '*Picture Post* are running Russell Braddon's articles – six I think.' Russell Braddon? Boyle felt a stab of concern. So much for coordination. He asked for clarification.

★ At Easter Cheshire published a booklet, *The Holy Face: an Account of the Oldest Photograph in the World*, and began to consider the bus as a means of conveying the Shroud's message.

Midhurst, 17 April 1954. To Andrew Boyle (transcript)

Yes, well, Braddon. When he asked me whether I would agree to him doing some articles if he could find a publisher, I said yes on condition that he didn't consider a book . . . *Picture Post* then commissioned him to do it . . . I can't refuse to see the press . . . although I'm not keen on articles and don't take any steps to get any, if any paper comes along and asks to interview me I can't possibly refuse to see them. Also Fleet Street is a fairly competitive game, it's always one up against another, one has to take things as they come as I understand it . . . But I will undertake that no one else with my cooperation writes a book.[64]

In fact, Braddon *was* writing a book. Evans Bros. had invited him to expand the *Picture Post* articles into a biography. Boyle did not yet know this, and on 30 April 1954 he accepted an offer from Collins to publish his own book.[65]

Next day, Cheshire was released from Midhurst for forty-eight hours.

17. Lourdes and Bromley

Peggy Worthington found a house in Bromley which could hold eighteen patients. Cheshire was sceptical, but when Father Fuller pronounced it 'marvellous' Cheshire agreed, borrowed the deposit and raised the balance by a bank loan. On Saturday 1 May, the day he started his leave, he signed the deeds and went to Chislehurst as the Worthingtons' guest.

A few weeks before Peggy had asked when he expected to leave Midhurst. His reply was unexpectedly fierce. 'Never, at this rate – unless I just decide to leave with this thing still in.'

'This thing' was a tube which had been left in his side after his last operation nearly six months before. He had told us that fluid formed . . . above his partially collapsed lung . . . As far as I knew the tube would have to remain . . . until the fluid ceased to drain; he was then to have a further operation to close the cavity and if this was successful . . . he would be able to leave . . .[1]

During the evening the Worthingtons said that one day they would like to take him to Lourdes.

'That sounds very nice, Bob,' he said, turning on all his very considerable charm. 'Yes, very nice indeed – I should like that. Don't you think it would be a good idea to go there by bus? We could convert the bus . . . into an ambulance to take stretchers, then we could take some of the patients from the homes with us.'

Next morning Cheshire steered conversation back to Lourdes.

'You see, I've got seventy-two hours leave due to me – I was only going to take forty-eight of it this weekend, but I can extend it without having to get permission from the San. If we went to Lourdes this afternoon, we could be back before my leave is up. It's a wonderful opportunity.'[2]

In the space of two hours the Worthingtons chartered an aircraft, sent a taxi to collect Cheshire's passport and telephoned Father Fuller, who rearranged his duties. At 3.00 p.m. Bob Worthington, Father Fuller and Cheshire took off from Croydon Airport.[3] They returned the next evening. Peggy expected to find Cheshire worn out, but he 'pranced out of the airport as lively as a kitten'. After Lourdes, he was revitalized.[4]

The first instalment of Braddon's 'life story' appeared in *Picture Post*. The introduction catches the flavour.

Britain's greatest bomber ace, who turned to religion after seeing the atom bomb destroy a city, at last tells the full story of his life. In a hospital bed where, for eighteen months, he has been fighting tuberculosis and planning a great religious crusade, he has found time to talk – and to talk frankly and fearlessly. At his bedside, with tape recorder and notebook, sat the author of another best-selling war story, *The Naked Island*. In this series of articles, specially written for *Picture Post*, he relates vividly the conversion of a killer to a crusader.[5]

The killer–turned–crusader set Boyle back on his heels.

Midhurst, 13 May 1954. To Andrew Boyle[6]

In the last few days I have been approached by magazines, newspapers, publishers . . . American *Time* are now doing their own independent series. Consequently, I think it is of some urgency that you should get a rapid move on with the Book . . . [I] have a certain moral obligation to Collins [*sic*, = Evans] who approached me very insistently some while ago . . . Although I will continue to give you every opportunity and far more than I will give anyone else, you will realize . . . that it is impossible for me to refuse to answer the various questions that so many people are asking me.

Picture Post. . . are being bombarded by various publishers to print their series of articles in a short book form, and they have approached me for my reactions. My answer to Russell Braddon is that for at least a reasonable period, I will not give anyone else the same facilities as I am giving you. However, since the material is now in the public domain . . . I agree to his publishing in book form on the following conditions:

1 That a specific mention is made of the full-length and definitive book that you are preparing . . .

2 That his book does not claim to be a full-length biography.

I wonder if you could very kindly let me have your full and frank views on the whole subject . . . ?

Boyle was upset,[7] and he was not the only one to be alarmed by Braddon's articles. T. H. White told him:

I am finding this fellow's life of Cheshire in *Picture Post* so distasteful . . . that I have had to write to Cheese to find out about you. Please don't be cross about this. After all, at present we are discussing him behind his back, and I want his go-ahead before going on with it . . . until he assures me that there is a certain amount of dignity about your treatment I would rather not be mixed up in turning a real honey into a sort of popinjay.[8]

While Boyle simmered, Cheshire asked if Father Fuller would be his spiritual director. In the past, he explained, he had relied on the parish priest wherever he happened to be, and on Francis Grimshaw, the Bishop of Plymouth. Direction might 'make all the difference if I were strongly tempted to follow my own head'.[9] Father Fuller was struck by the imperturbable way in which Cheshire accepted criticism. Fuller was also intrigued by the contrast between Cheshire's 'hair-raising ideas' and the 'quiet, unemotional voice' in which he put them.[10]

Something similar might be said of Father Fuller, whose theological rigour, sensitive clemency and twinkling eye belie an openness to the audacious ways of Grace which could be every bit as breathtaking as Cheshire's. This made them a formidable pair. Living dangerously, doing the unexpected or unpopular thing, came easier to Cheshire if there was an external source of validation.

Meanwhile:

Midhurst, 17 May 1954. To Andrew Boyle[11]
I have discussed the whole thing with my Father and the picture is much clearer. I have no legal right at all to prevent RB writing a book . . .

I have been in touch with Braddon . . . He never thought of a book and never thought I would agree. I have told him that he may turn what material he already has into a book, provided he makes it clear that it is not claimed to be a full biography and provided he points to your book as the completion of his. He is more than willing to do this . . .

I know this isn't exactly what you hoped, and for that reason I am sorry. But I feel that it is the proper course for me to take under the circumstances.

18 May 1954. Andrew Boyle to Cheshire[12]

. . . One implication of your conditional permission to Braden [*sic*] . . . is that the interest of Collins . . . will be greatly weakened. I've no doubt at all about Braden, but it won't rest with him . . . Your conditions will be lost in the welter of publicity; and it's extremely doubtful if any publisher will feel himself bound by such conditions. That's why the book is as good as dead already – in the eyes of the person who matters, the man who has taken the financial risk of putting it on the market . . . there are conventions in these things which prevent the publishing world from becoming just a jungle. I'm afraid I'm depressed beyond words and am quite unsure what the next move is.

Maybe Collins's attitude on Thursday will tell me whether I should drop out or go on.

See you then.

Cheshire was thinking about something else. He asked the Worthingtons to Midhurst.

Leonard hardly ever asked anyone to go and see him unless he had some ulterior motive . . . Schemes and ideas were his life and he had no room left for what one might call 'idle friendships'.[13]

He had been thinking, he told us, as if we didn't know, about the best way to get people to Lourdes, and he wanted Bob to find out the cost of chartering a fairly large plane – seating up to twenty – and discover if it would be practicable to use it for a weekend flight. Bob had been expecting something like this, and seeing no harm in it, agreed to do so. Then Leonard, after lulling us into a false sense of security . . . staggered both of us by announcing blandly that he would like the first flight to go on the last weekend of May.

This allowed eleven days to find an aircraft, pilgrims to fill it and accommodation. Bob Worthington said this might be difficult.

He might as well have talked to the wall. Not that Leonard is unreasonable, far from it. It is just that he seems to be irresistible when he has set his heart on something. He didn't argue . . . he just said, 'Yes, I see, perhaps you are right', and he got out a diary and began, rather wistfully, looking up weekends in June. He remarked that it was a pity about the last weekend in May, because it was rather a good date – something to do with being Marian Year, I believe he said . . . and when Leonard went on to say that if May really was out of the question, any weekend in June would do, and what did Bob suggest, Bob was almost beaten – he said resignedly, 'Well, Leonard, let's find out whether we can get a plane first, what it would cost and so on, and then decide on a date after that.'

Leonard put down his diary, smiled at him and said, 'Thank you, Bob, that's a good idea, we'll leave it like that, shall we and see what happens.'[14]

Peggy Worthington found nothing available between a ten-seater Dove and a thirty-one seater Dakota. Cheshire 'thought the Dove too small . . . and didn't I think we could fill the Dakota by the end of the month?' He suggested she enlist the help of Father Fuller and Shelagh Howe.[15]

Peggy Worthington telephoned Father Fuller, who replied, ' "Oh dear", in the kind of way people are apt to do when they first hear of one of Leonard's ideas. But as he too seemed to find our "problem child" irresistible, he went on to say, "Well, I suppose we'll have to do something about it. I'll do some inquiring around . . ." ' Then she called Shelagh Howe, 'who fairly screamed down the phone that she could get *heaps* of people, would *certainly* go herself and didn't foresee any difficulty at all in filling the plane'.[16]

Cheshire explained that he was arranging monthly weekend pilgrimages, the fit on behalf of the sick, to ask some remission from their sufferings, or to offer part of their suffering for the salvation of the world.[17] He drafted a leaflet (bearing Father Fuller's name and address),[18] and asked for an intercom in the aircraft to enable the priest in charge to answer pilgrims' questions and lead prayers in flight.[19] Peggy Worthington reported that unless the Dakota took off full, the figures wouldn't balance. Cheshire pressed on anyway, and such was his 'strange influence' that the air charter firm agreed to credit.[20] When the Dakota took off for Lourdes on 29 May, it was not full.

While the pilgrims were gone Cheshire reflected on the rival biographies.[21] He told Geoffrey Harmsworth that Boyle's was the 'more serious undertaking', though 'whether it will appeal to the man in the street I can't tell'. '*The man in the street.*' So that was it.

St Cecilia's, the new home in Bromley, was to be vested in the new St Cecilia's Trust. The trust was still being formed, and Cheshire was fizzing with ideas about what it might do.

Midhurst, 1 June 1954. To Father Fuller[22]
Is it right to concentrate on the Holy Shroud and Lourdes? I would like (1) To consolidate the position so far reached by continuing with (*a*) the bus (*b*) the monthly pilgrimages; (2) To consider operating a mobile film unit in London showing films of Lourdes; (3) To consider an ambulance air lift to Lourdes for those too sick to stand the train journey. To this end I would like to mobilize the men I flew with in the dambusters . . . Apart from getting the invalids there, it gets non-Catholics actively cooperating in a Catholic work of charity. Sir Ralph Cochrane, my ex-AOC has offered to help. He is a Scotch [*sic*] Presbyterian.

Cheshire bridled when Shelagh Howe told him that he should calm down.

Midhurst, 4 June 1954. To Shelagh Howe[23]
It is no use telling me to relax and then hammering away at your new point of view. I do what I have to do and what I consider God sends me to do and then relax. Actually by far the central strain is standing up to the advice of my friends . . . Let us all get on with our own share calmly and trustfully correcting each other where necessary but briefly.

You mustn't lose sight of the main message of Lourdes. Prayer and penance. I am not suffering and I am getting cured. Our mission is for those who aren't being cured and are really suffering.

Another operation was due, and there were things to settle beforehand. Cheshire had been told that St Teresa's was going downhill. 'The place looked shoddy, not dirty . . . but not quite clean, and more important, unhappy.' Holy Cross remained an orphan project. £100 was needed to meet the shortfall on Lourdes, and there was a small loan to repay for the balance of purchase money for St Cecilia's. He wrote to Shelagh Howe, who obliged with a cheque for £125.

Primrose met Sir Geoffrey Todd after the operation and found him 'most unhappy'. There had been complications.[24] Cheshire nevertheless seemed serene and lucid, and brought Father Fuller up to date with two more projects which related to his hopes for an English counter-Reformation.

One was the draft for a new Rule or society for laypeople – that is, a pattern of religious discipline in the everyday world. Behind this lay two ideas: 'restoration of the Holy Family of Nazareth to its rightful and proper place in the world in general and one's own country in particular'; and 'salvation of our neighbour'. On the first:

> The basic trouble with Protestantism is that it has taken Our Lord out of his context. If Our Lord is to return to these shores, then His Mother must be brought back first. So, I imagine, must be Saint Joseph.

How would it work?

> Means: individually (strive for personal sanctification, each according to his own need and capacity), and collectively (work as team, with what resources we have). Daily sacrifices, offered up for the common intention.

Troubles were to be transfigured, like grit clothed by pearl. Beyond lay an immense project: the raising of Walsingham to a pre-eminent place as the Nazareth of England.[25]

July. Preparations were in hand for Le Court's annual fête. Alan Finch, the ebullient warden who averaged a seventeen-hour working day, told Boyle that he had asked the publicity manager of the *Standard* if he would bring the Windmill Girls ('whom I have laid on, and *personally selected*!') in his helicopter.[26] At Predannack, too, things were on the move. The foundation's trustees authorized Lady St Levan, a lively, formidable and influential Cornish figure, to establish a new local committee to manage St Teresa's, 'with a view to its removal as soon as possible to a more suitable place'.[27]

Cheshire had never set out to found a family of homes which would be organizationally integrated. Just then, indeed, his aim was exactly the opposite: 'The last thing I want is a chain of houses all under one trust, because then there would be an impossible load on the trustees and also a danger of bureaucracy.'[28] The Cheshire Foundation had initially been set up simply as the legal entity in which Le Court could be vested.[29] More recently, St Teresa's had passed into the foundation's hands. But that was it. The new home at Bromley, which had opened at the end of July, would have a trust of its own.

Cheshire enlisted Sir Cuthbert Fitzherbert, vice-chairman of Barclays Bank, to chair the emerging body.[30] However, there was already a local management committee, and the trustees-designate and local volunteers quickly found themselves at loggerheads. The nub of the problem lay in a perception that the trust was dictating a policy which put finance before patients.[31] Local people, who thus far had done the work, could not understand this. Fitzherbert and the other founding trustees had been chosen by Cheshire. Presumably, therefore, the new policy had his approval. Yet it contradicted what he himself had taught. The initiative in estab- lishing St Cecilia's had sprung entirely from volunteers who with their hearts, paintbrushes, jumble sales and time had animated the spirit of an idea – *Cheshire's* idea – which Cheshire's own placemen now appeared to be reversing.[32]

Worthington wrote to Cheshire, who did not reply – because just then he was under the surgeon's knife. Worthington next wrote to a trustee, pointing out that vigorous local campaigning had attracted gifts of equipment and money,[33] that the Inland Revenue had agreed to accept the home as a charity, that the home's eligibility for local authority grants was recognized and that it was substantially occupied and essentially debt-free. All this had been achieved without any 'business atmosphere'. Worthington was involved because he had been convinced by the rightness of Cheshire's ideas. Yet the spirit of the project was now threatened, and Father Fuller, who had been instrumental in helping to set up St Cecilia's, was excluded from the new trust.[34]

Correspondence in following days reveals the extraordinary extent to which the protagonists were at cross-purposes. The rising St Cecilia's Cheshire Trust was a high-powered body,[35] to which Cheshire had hitherto subordinated himself to such an extent that he had been insufficiently explicit in indicating his wish that Father Fuller should belong to it. By 17 August this was remedied.

Worthington accepted that the muddle had resulted from honest intentions, but continued to think that both Fitzherbert and Cheshire had 'acted without regard or thought for friends', although if 'Leonard is the saint, it is not for people like me to argue with him'. He told Father Fuller: 'I still want Lourdes, the home and the bus to be great successes, but oddly enough not because they are Leonard's but because I am sure they are good things in themselves.'[36] Cheshire would have been the first to agree. But then:

Leonard never discussed details about anything with anyone. Everything was left in an extraordinary dreamlike state of unreality, and unless one happened to be the person trying to put his scheme into operation, it appeared to spring into being in some miraculous way quite remote from human agency. Whether this reticence was due to natural secretiveness, or because he was just plain bored with practical details, was difficult to tell, but it was a fact that even if one was the person entrusted with launching a new venture, he would still not discuss really freely what one might consider to be very necessary details . . . I stress this extremely odd side of character because it is the one thing . . . which caused so many misunderstandings and hurt to his helpers. People felt let down and abandoned, simply because something had been left unsaid or unexplained . . .[37]

Before following the St Cecilia's story to its denouement we may ask how much Cheshire was actually thinking about it. Throughout these days many other issues jostled in his thoughts. For example: **The Shroud.** Two more publications were in prospect,[38] and he was entering discussions with the playwright R. C. Sherriff[39] about the possibility of a film. Cheshire had also begun to wonder how his own work related to that of the Confraternity of the Holy Shroud, a guild[40] which coordinated efforts to spread knowledge of the subject.[41] 'Do I transfer my activities to the guild, or do I continue under the Mission for the Relief of Suffering? If I continue as I am, what is the relationship of the Mission to the Guild?'[42]
The buses. The original vehicle had passed from Bob Worthington's care to that of a new committee.[43] Part of the reason was to lighten Worthington's load, although no one had thought to explain this to Worthington.[44]
The biography. Boyle was trying out possible titles. 'Straight is the Way?' 'The Pillar of Cloud'? 'Stairway to the Stars'? 'Out of the Blue'? What did he think?
Predannack. Lady St Levan planned to build St Teresa's anew on

a new site. In this event he would like the old building to be made over to Holy Cross.[45]

The Lourdes airlift. There were problems.[46]

The Mission. This now had an address: 7a Pitt's Head Mews, off Park Lane, where Philomena Loneragan, a new helper introduced by Russell Braddon, had rented a room.

England's Nazareth. On Sunday 12 August, the Feast of the Assumption, Cheshire told Father Fuller that he had asked a former wing commander (Vincent Byrne), a former fighter pilot, now a 'real-estate pro, also a Catholic', to start bidding for the Walsingham estate on his behalf. He had told him to work on the 'assumption that the money is forthcoming – and said that that is my worry, not his'. For the estate Cheshire reckoned on needing £100,000. He had a source in mind – Cecil Tilson Chowne – and asked Father Fuller to sound out Mrs Chowne.[47]

Angmering. Angmering? A fifth home was in prospect. The 'real-estate pro' handling the Walsingham negotiations was now thinking of founding one in Sussex.

St Cecilia's.[48]

So, he was busy.

Midhurst, 13 September 1954. To Father Fuller[49]

Bob [Worthington] came to visit . . . He feels very strongly about everything . . . It is clear to me . . . that I must be at fault somewhere, or at any rate that the situation is symptomatic of my shortcomings. When Bob has seen you I would be most grateful if you would assess things as objectively as possible – i.e. without regard to possible hurt to my feelings.

Cheshire now made the astounding confession that he had given Fitzherbert a free hand only because he, Cheshire, had assumed that Father Fuller 'strongly favoured him' as Chairman. Having discovered that he and his spiritual director were both, after all, of one mind, their path became gloriously obvious.

Fitzherbert wrote to Father Fuller, enclosing a copy of a letter he was sending to Cheshire and asking that it be read 'very calmly'. Fitzherbert was 'very disturbed' to hear of the Angmering venture. His willingness to chair the trustees of St Cecilia's had been conditional upon an undertaking from Cheshire that this should be, for the time being,

the limit of your activities in this line . . . Homes of the size of St Cecilia's are uneconomic units. The unavoidable overheads are of a nature and degree which can and should carry greater numbers . . . it is a thoroughly unsound conception to visualize a lot of homes dotted about the country whether they be independent of each other or whether they be part of a group.

. . . If I may say so the vital question of where the money is to be raised is entirely omitted from any of your outlined schemes . . . not only is it tempting Providence too far to give no consideration whatever to this aspect, but it is imposing an impossible burden and responsibility on those many people of goodwill whose help you enlist.

Fitzherbert accepted the commitment to Angmering, but demanded an assurance that there would be no more homes for the time being, warning that he would veto signature of the trust deed unless this were forthcoming.

This was the crunch. Cheshire replied on the following day. Far from being upset, 'your letter was very welcome and I have enjoyed reading it . . . you have put the case fairly and nicely'. He recognized Fitzherbert's argument, which had been 'raised against me all along the line', and did not dispute it in principle.

However, I do dispute it as applicable to my homes. Ever since the beginning I have maintained that my only chance of succeeding was to be perpetually short of money. If I had my own choice I would like to end each day not knowing how to manage for the next. Then I would be thrown entirely into the arms of Providence and would ultimately learn to refer everything to God.

With money in the bank Cheshire was free to lay plans with 'nothing to stop me'; 'I have learnt from experience – that always leads to trouble. When I have no money I can only do what Providence permits.' He did not wish to impose this on anyone else – 'I merely say that for me personally there is no alternative.'

Cheshire apologized for not having explained this before. As for the big grant-giving bodies (Fitzherbert was just then negotiating with the Nuffield Foundation) he preferred not to accept money that would be accompanied by too many restrictions. Nor did he agree that the family basis for the homes was unsound. 'Now . . . that you face me with all or nothing, I am forced to hold out. I couldn't in conscience renounce the right of deciding whether or not to open a new home.' Cheshire sent a draft of this to Father Fuller, saying, 'I only want to do God's will and He often asks things of us that seem to destroy everything we have set out to do. If therefore you think I should agree to Fitzherbert's request, I will gladly do so.' Father Fuller forwarded the letter unaltered, with a note:

I don't think there is much for me to add beyond saying that I am not prepared to persuade Leonard to change his mind. His heart would not be in it if I did. I feel in a dilemma because your way is so clearly a reasonable one; yet I see clearly now that it is not and could not really be Leonard's way . . . We are putting you in a difficult position especially in view of all the kindness you have shown.

Fitzherbert replied that Cheshire's letter had come as a relief – the air was clear, 'indeed very clear'. The way in which the issue had developed was also unregretted for, if it had taken longer, they would not now be looking 'a clear-cut situation fully in the face'. Fitzherbert said that if there was something he could do to help he would 'be happy and proud to do it' – but he could not accept 'trusteeship of the nature which is now envisaged'.

During these days Cheshire experienced something akin to the film of an explosion run backwards: things previously apart flew together. Cheshire reflected on a suggestion from his father that 'all homes, present and future, should come under one trust, to avoid confusion in the public mind. Although I couldn't agree to this in its entirety, I wonder whether perhaps I should confine myself to two organizations only – the Foundation and the Mission for the Relief of Suffering.' Under the former would come all homes that wished to run on conventional financial lines. While the central foundation would take no part in running individual homes, it would own their premises, act as a guardian and define relations with and between individual homes. Such a structure 'could easily provide for a Catholic management, if necessary'. This was tentative, but if the St Cecilia's trustees were in doubt about carrying on, the Foundation Home Trust might be an alternative.[50] Here is the concept of a *family* of homes which lies behind the

Leonard Cheshire Foundation as we now know it – and which Sir
Cuthbert Fitzherbert had dismissed as 'thoroughly unsound'.

Just then, however, it was Walsingham which preoccupied
Cheshire more:

> The idea is to hand the shrine to the Bishop, separate the mansion and surrounds
> for a home for dying TB. . . convert the friary into a hostel, and place the rest
> of the estate under a trust, to be run on strictly business lines, with the profits
> applied to such Catholic purposes as the trustees think fit. The interrelationship
> of these various undertakings could easily be worked out, so as to avoid confusing
> charity with business.
>
> Could it perhaps be that everything has been leading up to this? – a financier,
> a leading man in the city, a quantity surveyor, a member of the nobility . . . and
> yourself to represent the Church?[51]

The only problem was a lack of trustees to handle such an ambitious
project. But there again, the trustee body being formed for
St Cecilia's was a group of just such standing. Apparently oblivious
to the signs of its imminent dissolution, Cheshire left it to Father
Fuller to decide whether to raise this at the next meeting. 'One
way or another it will become quite clear what to do.' It was.

30 September 1954. Father Fuller to Cheshire[52]
Fitzherbert resigned and everyone else then resigned. The beautiful volume
bound in blue leather and titled in gold *The St Cecilia Cheshire Trust* looked a
trifle forlorn. Fitzherbert obviously feels upset, whatever he says . . .

When the St Cecilia's business was over, Father Fuller put Cheshire's
proposal on Walsingham. Fitzherbert listened with 'ill-concealed
impatience', commenting as the meeting broke up: 'The immediate
problem is not whether Cheshire can find £100,000 for Walsingham, but where matron's salary for next week is coming from.'

Hitherto Fitzherbert seems to have seen Father Fuller as a
restraining influence. Now the penny dropped, with a resounding
clang. On 8 October the banker told the priest: 'It has become
increasingly clear to me . . . that you are the one individual who is
in a key position and on whom I am, therefore, afraid the greatest
responsibility lies.' When it came to issue between himself and
Leonard, it was to Fuller that the final decision was referred. Since

Fuller was unprepared to tell Leonard 'to accept a measure of common-sense practice', Leonard was being allowed to follow his inclinations 'unfettered by any worldly consideration at all'.

. . . I am appalled at the responsibility which you have accepted and the consequences which almost inevitably flow therefrom. The practical consequence of what has happened, short of some intervention of Providence, on which, as we know Leonard relies entirely, is that in a few weeks St Cecilia's will be unable to pay the bills or wages. Over and above this the bank has, at my instigation, found the whole of the purchase price of the house as a temporary measure, and this in turn must be faced . . . Leonard refers everything to you and resigns all right to make a decision himself. I must say that from his point of view this seems to be too easy.[52a]

Cheshire was obsessed with Walsingham, seeing St Cecilia's as the lesser issue. History reverses that view. In 1997 Father Fuller reflected, 'Fitzherbert was determined to get Leonard to change his mind. If Leonard *had* changed his mind, I don't think the Cheshire Homes would ever have existed in the numbers we now have, if at all.'[53] In October 1954 the only person who could have changed Cheshire's mind was Father Fuller, who did not try. Nor did he discourage another project.

I have an obvious opportunity of starting a home in Kodaikanal, S. India – by proxy. The idea has been in my mind for some while and the man concerned has flown over twice in the last year to see me. He is a convert. I have dictated the letter authorizing him to make a preliminary start . . . But I won't dispatch it until I get a card saying I may. If you feel I mustn't, then I won't send it.[54]

Publication of Russell Braddon's *Cheshire VC* was imminent. After seeing an advance copy Boyle drafted a terse complaint which he invited Cheshire to sign.

October 1954 (n.d.). Draft letter from Group Captain Cheshire to Evans
I have just seen a copy of Russell Braddon's book about me in which the following phrases occur:

'. . . for practically every word in it is his'

'Leonard Cheshire granted me endless bedside interviews'

'. . . for his revision of this completed work, I am grateful'.

As you well know each of these phrases is so exaggerated as to be a misrepresentation of the truth. I must therefore insist that they be withdrawn from the book before publication.

I look forward to receiving from you, through my lawyer, an immediate assurance to this effect.[55]

Cheshire refused to sign. Boyle persisted, reminding him of his promise to disown any extravagant claims in Braddon's book and drafting a letter of protest to *The Bookseller*. Again, Cheshire declined.[56] Boyle wrote resignedly to Geoffrey Harmsworth: 'there's little enough I or Collins or anyone else can do to stop them. Leonard seems happy enough about it all, since he has long ago convinced himself that there is room for two books about himself.' Collins were 'badly let down'.[57]

Cheshire VC came out early in November. Castigated by Boyle as a 'nauseating portrait', as 'full of errors as blue cheese with veins', and 'breezily inaccurate',[58] it became an immediate best-seller.

Cheshire was back in the news. The BBC invited him to broadcast to the nation on Christmas Day, in the hour before the Queen's Message.[59] Hutchinsons remembered that they still had the rights to *Bomber Pilot*, and asked if they could reissue it as a paperback.[60] The *Observer* sent a feature writer down to Midhurst, who described the 'violent contrast in environment, from the heroic war activity to the quiet but intense life in the sanatorium, as external'.

It is not paralleled interiorly by a violent contrast between the Cheshire of today and the Cheshire of ten years ago. It is only necessary to be in his company for five minutes to realize that there is a thread of continuity and purpose, provided by an interest in meaningful human life, as first experienced in wartime comradeship, combined with a ruthless, practical logicality in expanding and developing it . . .

In his physical personality he gives an impression of forces balanced − of authority, with his piercing eyes and resonant, almost nasal bass voice, and of charity. His smile is often accompanied by a high falsetto laugh . . .

In everything Cheshire does there is a curious sense of tuning in to a preordained pattern. He seems to move from one practical goal to another: only then, because he is also an intellectual, does he concern himself with theoretical justification . . .[61]

Boyle's portrait was about two thirds finished. He told a friend:

There are two Cheshires, Cheshire the Myth and Cheshire the Man, and I'm concerned with the second. It's not likely to be terribly edifying even in the final phase of the homes and so-called 100% Christianity. I've passed well beyond the shiny folds of the myth and what I've discovered about the man behind them is highly interesting, diverting and amusing, but not altogether lovable.[62]

Yet in spite of the tensions, they remained on good terms.

Midhurst, 29 November 1954. To Andrew Boyle[63]
Dear Andrew,

How are you getting on and what do you want? I leave Dec. 8th. One week's retreat – out of reach – then Laundry Cottage* Dec. 14th. Once I get there I could give you a tape – or a visit, whichever you prefer.

I have found some old photographs – you might like them.

Hutchinsons are now reprinting *Bomber Pilot* – that is a blow. Altho it means I shall have to face up to writing its sequel . . .

With love to all the family, and please say a prayer for me.

30 November 1954. Andrew Boyle to Cheshire[64]
Glad you're leaving Midhurst at last. What a relief that must be. Please give yourself a chance to recuperate: you owe it to others . . .

Sorry Hutchinsons are to reprint *Bomber Pilot*. Why not write a preface? I think somehow you'll survive the shock.

The book is going as well as can be expected . . . Hope to finish the MS by February when I'd like you to see it. Don't imagine you'll be all that flattered by it, but feel you have the right to check points of fact and taste . . .

Midhurst, 27 November 1954. To Father Fuller[65]
My A'bp [Francis Grimshaw] has said 'don't occupy yourself with projects too much for six months . . . Consolidate!' I think I had better not push Walsingham any further for the time [being]. We have drawn a complete blank.

My leaving date is Dec. 8th. Isn't that a lovely day?

* A cottage at Le Court, by this time the home of Cheshire's parents.

18. Closely Observed

Cheshire came out of Midhurst like an uncoiling spring. Although still under medical supervision, required to rest daily and follow a special diet, his energy resembled that of a cyclone rather than a convalescent. Calm yet in motion, serious yet smiling, he knew what to do.

The new synthesis shone in his Christmas message for the *Catholic Herald*. The key to world peace lay not in nuclear force but in the suffering of the East. Peace was 'a question of harmony between East and West', and since the East was unable to deal with its afflictions it was up to the West to go to their help. If his own life could be transformed by caring for Arthur Dykes, 'then I don't see why it cannot equally happen to a whole Empire'. Shroud, homes, bomb, suffering, unity in faith, all connected. Next Christmas he would be penniless in India. For this one, a little before three o'clock on Christmas Day Primrose and Geoffrey listened as Leonard spoke to the nation. What a distance their boy had travelled.[1]

Cheshire's many projects now swirled in the corridor of 7 Pitt's Head Mews which had become the mission's headquarters. Here worked the sunnily capable Philomena Loneragan, an Australian who had turned aside from a European holiday to join the work. In January 1955 there was a lot of work.

The autobiography now had a provisional title, 'The Search', and the assistance of a ghost writer, Asgier Scott.[2]

Nested within the Mission for the Relief of Suffering lay plans for a Mission to Make Known the Holy Shroud, with three 'mobile demonstration units' (that is, buses: Cheshire had a penchant for official-sounding titles), a postal bureau for inquiries, and another bureau which offered lectures and a reference library. Discussions continued with R. C. Sherriff about a film, which might be called 'The Fifth Gospel'.

Plans for Walsingham were dormant, awaiting opportunity.

Weekend pilgrimages to Lourdes would resume. Cheshire hoped to introduce an air ambulance service.

The Rule for the association had reached a fourth draft.[3] It was now called The Holy Family Association, 'a proposed rule of life for ordinary people in the face of the atom bomb'.[4]

A home was planned near Cochin in India.

St Cecilia's was settling down after a stormy spell, about which Cheshire gently remarked that it seemed 'a little drastic to lose *all* the staff in one go'.[5] Down at Angmering there was now a steering committee, a house had been purchased in East Preston and the home had been given a name: St Bridget's. More homes were in prospect. Cheshire knew of advanced incurable TB sufferers who had nowhere to go.

15 January 1955

Now as to the TB. Things have moved quite fast; I have found a very nice house seven miles south of Bedford which has been given to me as a gift. I am moving up there on the 31st January to open it up and the first two patients arrive 3/4 days later.[6]

This was Ampthill, described by Primrose as the 'most unsuitable house imaginable'. But then, Primrose had not yet seen Staunton Harold.

Ampthill, 19 February, 1955. To Father Fuller[7]

I have been offered Staunton Harold which is a very large seventy-roomed house near Derby. The Historic Buildings Council would be willing to contribute something like £50,000 towards its repair, etc. There is a long story attached to this offer in which Teresa seems to have played a part . . . Could I very kindly know what you think about it?[8]

Staunton Harold is arcadia in Leicestershire: a great house, a church,[9] a lake, within Georgian parkland. In January 1955 the mansion looked doomed. Requisitioned from Lord Ferrers during the war, it had been returned to him as an incipient ruin. When Lord Ferrers died in 1954 the main house was sold to a demolition contractor.

Cheshire went to look. It had been snowing. Meltwater trickled through holes in the roof. Nearly £16,000 was needed simply to ransom the structure from demolition. The deadline was near. He walked across to the church and saw an inscription above the door. The church had been built during the Commonwealth '*when all thinges Sacred were throughout ye nation Either demolisht or profaned*'. The work celebrated '*the best things in ye worst times*'.

It was cold, too, on the grey February afternoon when he met a kindred spirit. A mutual friend suggested that he should invite someone called Sue Ryder to see Ampthill. The name rang no bells, for Cheshire did not watch television and seldom read newspapers. The unawareness was mutual. After a wartime career in the hermetic world of SOE Sue Ryder's life had been devoted to relief work among victims of Nazi atrocities, among the dispossessed, the sick and imprisoned. She had never heard of Leonard Cheshire. Her drive from Cavendish in Suffolk took her past Tempsford, prompting memories of other journeys, when SOE-trained agents were flown to France.

Ampthill Park's main gate was locked. Persevering, she found a way in, to be greeted by Cheshire in a room adjoining the kitchen. She had imagined someone much older. Their talk was hesitant. Sue Ryder outlined her work, and the principle of the Sue Ryder Foundation as a living memorial to the victims and opponents of tyranny. The cost of this, Cheshire thought, was written in her face. For her part, Ryder was impressed by Ampthill, asking a lot of questions. In several ways they were leading parallel lives. Both worked for the relief of suffering. Sue Ryder had established a small international foundation, lived a frugal existence and was looking at large houses with a view to providing care for the sick and disabled. Like Cheshire, her smile could light a room. In faith, she had been raised a high Anglo-Catholic. Although she declined a cup of tea, they agreed to meet again.

Even Father Fuller was shaken by Staunton. 'I can't imagine how the running of it can be financed.' But there again, perhaps he could. Several weeks before a stranger had walked into Pitt's Head Mews and asked if there was anything he could do. When Phil

Loneragan replied brightly that a loan of £1,000 would help, the visitor wrote out a cheque for £1,000. The same man had since moved to Ampthill to help ready the house for its first patients. Things like that simply happened when Cheshire was around, and recent months had seen an upsurge of them. Father Fuller concluded: 'I daresay it can be considered.'[10] Cheshire had also written to Archbishop Grimshaw.[11] 'I feel so big an undertaking ought to go for his approval.'

Ampthill, 1 March 1955. To Father Fuller[12]
I've just seen the Archbishop.

1 He has confirmed your direction of me.
2 He does not want the homes given a Catholic constitution. Carry on as before.
3 He is putting the homes and Mission on the agenda for the Bishops [*sic*] meeting after Easter. I asked whether I should not be 'controlled'. He said: No. Remain a non-Catholic organization. Rome wouldn't understand the set-up.
4 He likes the Staunton idea – so I shall go ahead – will keep you in touch. There being only a leasehold, I wonder if we couldn't have it under the Mission?

Such a simple note, it marked an epoch. Although the Cheshire Foundation Homes for the Sick was a non-denominational body, Cheshire had not yet accepted this as the prevailing model. Until this point he had continued to hope that future homes would be of Catholic complexion.[13] Grimshaw now counselled otherwise. The homes had awakened support from people of all religions and none. Their governance should reflect that. To this, Cheshire submitted.

So, all he had to do now was raise £16,000 before the end of March. Anticipating that something would happen if Providence willed it, he travelled to London for a script conference on the Shroud film, and told Father Fuller about the article he had just written for the *Daily Sketch*.

The *Sketch* was a tabloid, read by ordinary people. 'I Saw The Face of Christ' appeared on 7 March. It filled two pages, contrasting the force of a nuclear bomb with something immeasurably stronger.

The atom bomb, I was quite certain, was going to alter the course of history . . .
With the passing of time it sank back into its true perspective. I realized that it
was just another bomb . . . The Holy Face, on the other hand, worked in the
opposite direction. At first it looked just like another picture. But with the
passing of time . . . I recognized that here at last might lie the secret to world
peace.[14]

'Holy Shroud going ahead in leaps and bounds' he told Shelagh
Howe.[15] '*Picture Post* are running five-page Holy Week feature.'[16]
Woolworth's, where ordinary people shopped, volunteered to
make an Easter display in some London stores.[17] A new helper,
Dan Griffiths, a devotee of the Shroud, was enlisted to establish a
'Holy Shroud Inquiry Centre' in Nottingham and handle the deluge
of correspondence.

A stranger appeared on Shelagh Howe's doorstep, offering an
untidy parcel whence protruded some woolly garments.[18] Inside,
wrapped in an old cardigan, was a sugar carton. Three days later the
Queen Mother visited Le Court.[19] Cheshire stood at the entrance,
grasping the sugar carton while greeting guests. The carton contained
five hundred pound notes. They came from an old lady in Balham.
When her husband died after the Great War she had put his pension
in the savings bank. This was half of it. Six months later she gave the
other half. At the other extreme, a property developer on the
St Bridget's committee contributed £10,000. By 25 March enough
had been raised to make a successful offer for Staunton Harold.

These were jubilant days.[20] 'Hundreds of people came . . . Some
of them took on one room, others another; organizations such as
Rotary, the Round Table, Toc H, and so on, each took a room.'[21]
Villagers presented furniture, food and building materials. Some of
Sue Ryder's helpers came up to work. Midland firms loaned men
and equipment. Tradespeople gave goods. Margot Mason gave her
career. Mason had been the Ferrers's secretary, who helped out

more and more, until finally Lady Ferrers suggested that, as there wasn't now a
great deal for her to do with the family, and as Leonard seemed to be in a
desperate state of muddle, Margot had better choose whether to stay with them
or throw her lot in with Leonard. She made her choice, and ever since she hasn't
had time to be either glad or regretful.[22]

Cheshire lived in perpetual motion.

He has a bus which is fitted up as an office-cum-rest room, complete with bed, wash-basin and filing cabinets. In this he travels constantly, from Home to Home, and all over the country on his various engagements, taking rest periods – which he still has to observe wherever he is – on the bed en route.[23]

'Margot will know.' 'Margot will do something about it.' Cheshire relied heavily on Margot Mason, whom Frances Jeram described as 'one of the most normal people I ever met in that set-up. To say some-one is a normal person in that sort of context is high praise from me!'[24]

Boyle called his book *No Passing Glory*. He finished it in late March.[25] Getting the manuscript to Cheshire wasn't easy, as no one was ever quite sure where he was. The delay was worrying, as Boyle was being pressed for delivery, and Cheshire's reaction to the opening, which he had already seen, had been disconcerting. 'I suppose I did give the impression that I wasn't interested in the early chapters – so sorry. It isn't quite true. But originally I was thinking purely of a conversion story – & then we got a little out of step.'[26] Boyle was astonished.[27]

. . . there was never any question . . . of this being purely an account of your conversion. Even when Evans were in the field, sixteen months ago, the question was a *biography*. . . I think you'll find that in any case I've done justice to the conversion theme and the post-conversion period. It's as accurate as I can make it . . . please remember me in your prayers. Write soon.

Cheshire didn't write. He was voyaging in the bus.

6 April 1955. Andrew Boyle to Cheshire[28]
As you don't seem to have had my letter, please ignore it when you finally do get it. . . . This supersedes it . . . I've no doubt you'll want to suggest alterations here and there, and I hope you'll find time in the next fortnight to make a note of them. If you'd be happier to discuss it rather than write, I'll come to Cornwall for a couple of days if necessary. The time factor is important. Typesetting is due to begin on 1 May.

Cheshire sent his views. The chapters on his upbringing and the war were 'done well and substantially accurate'. However, whereas in the first half Boyle had said little about personal motives or faults, in the second he indulged in much psychological speculation. Cheshire argued that the same critical standpoint should apply throughout. He was disappointed that so little had been said about the homes. The concluding chapters also contained a number of 'misstatements', and Boyle had cast doubt on the authenticity of the Shroud. If this was to be the official biography, some rewriting would be needed.[29]

Events now took a risky turn. On 5 May Cheshire received a letter from George Greenfield, a principal partner of the literary agents John Farquharson. Greenfield was Russell Braddon's agent, and he had just heard (from Philomena Loneragan, who was a friend of Braddon) that 'the Boyle book and in particular . . . the latter part of it does not meet with your approval'. Greenfield understood that Cheshire was embarking upon a negotiation which was potentially difficult and wondered if Cheshire would find it helpful for him to act on his behalf. To do so, however, he would need to see Boyle's manuscript.[30] Mercifully, Cheshire was circumspect. For the moment he preferred to leave the matter in abeyance, pending a response from Collins about his 'complaints'.[31]

In fact, Cheshire's specified corrections were few, and only to two of them did Boyle react with any sense of reproach. In mid-May he told Cheshire that several key documents which affected the conversion sequence had 'come at last'. If he had been told about them in the first place, 'it would have saved a lot of avoidable work and fretting'. As for the Shroud, Boyle confessed to many faults, but 'heresy-making isn't one. I've already taken steps by sending my script out to be vetted. If I'm wrong, I'll stand corrected.'[32]

Accuracy mattered, but as usual other things were happening which concerned Cheshire more. During May there were problems at Ampthill, another Shroud project was in prospect[33] and new plans for Walsingham were stirring. For the tenth anniversary of VE day he made a television broadcast and gave newspaper interviews. Holy Cross remained problematic.[34] India lay ahead. The deadline for his own book was approaching.

It is a question, too, how far Cheshire was actually interested in Boyle's book. He had agreed to it in the hope that it would widen interest in Catholicism, but now doubted whether it would have this effect. Moreover, most of *No Passing Glory* was about his pre-Catholic history, and for Cheshire this was a remote region. Over and over again his replies to Boyle's questions on the Midhurst tapes had said, 'I'm sorry Andrew, but I don't remember'. Only the future was improvable.

Boyle had set out to avoid 'sentimental piety', and parts of his portrait were disconcertingly frank. There is no sign that Cheshire shrank from discussion of his weaknesses, although he may have regretted that the young, pagan Cheshire who had sworn, gambled and drunk, and upon whom the older Cheshire had turned his back, emerged rather well, while the Christian was severely tested. An amalgam of disappointment, humility and self-abasement explains the tone of Cheshire's reaction and, paradoxically, his sense of relief when Boyle stood his ground.

7 Pitt's Head Mews, 14 May 1955. To Andrew Boyle[35]
I can't tell you how pleased I am to receive your letter, and thank you so much for all it says. It is quite true that there have been a few misunderstandings between us. If I had been more sensible no doubt they could have been avoided . . . We can discuss all this when I see you on Wednesday . . .

They met for an amicable lunch, and discussed the book and the possibility of turning it into a film.[36]

On Wednesday 11 May a letter arrived at the Holy Shroud Inquiry Centre from Mrs Veronica Woollam. It concerned her ten-year-old daughter Josephine, who was afflicted by osteomyelitis in the hip and leg, and had an abscess on one lung. Josie had been in and out of hospital for five years. Her doctor had pronounced her 'incurable'. On the previous Friday she had received the last rites. 'I am writing to ask you if my daughter Josephine could be blessed with the relic of the Holy Shroud.'

Dan Griffiths replied that no relic of the Shroud was available, but enclosed a photograph. He also drove over to Staunton to show Mrs Woollam's letter to Cheshire. When Mrs Woollam wrote to thank Griffiths for the photograph, she reported that Josie had 'immediately felt better' on seeing it. Her doctor 'could not believe his eyes when he saw Josephine sat in a wheelchair on Friday'.[37] Cheshire pondered. He was about to go to Scotland and would be on the move for some days. However, he asked to be kept informed.

Margot Mason drove him north. They stopped at RAF Rufforth where his 35 Squadron wireless operator Jock Hill now served as a squadron leader. Cheshire hoped to recruit Hill for the mission to India. They paused again at the Catholic seminary at Ushaw in County Durham: a 'wonderful reception . . . everyone thrilled'.[38] On 30 May they arrived in Kingussie, staying at the Grampian Sanatorium and inspecting a house with an eye to its suitability as a home.

On 31 May Josie Woollam was allowed home from hospital.

Behind Cheshire's work lay several informal networks which he was assiduous in cultivating. One consisted of members of the Catholic aristocracy. Known to Margot Mason and Phil Loneragan as 'the Hons', they provided support, money, connections, occasionally their redundant houses. Lord and Lady Lothian were among these allies, and Cheshire now turned south to stay with them at their home near Jedburgh. Then back to Staunton, on to Oxford to lecture to the Newman Society and down to Devon for the consecration of the new Bishop of Plymouth. On 15 June he rendezvoused with the bus at Templewood. Two days later the bus was near Stroud. The Woollams lived near Stroud. He called to see them. Josie Woollam stated her belief that if she could touch the Shroud she would walk again. This decided him. 'Better get on with it and go.'

Next day Cheshire asked Archbishop Grimshaw if it would be permissible to take Josie Woollam on pilgrimage to Turin. He also mentioned the idea to Sir Anthony Tichbourne, with whom he discussed a forthcoming celebrity cricket match in support of the Cheshire Foundation. Sir Anthony telephoned the rector of the English College in Rome, who cautioned that the project would be difficult. The Holy Shroud was owned by the royal house of Italy. King Umberto, Italy's former monarch, now lived in Lisbon. The King's consent would be needed. Other permissions would be required and were unlikely to be forthcoming.

Far from being deterred, Cheshire sparkled with optimism. 'Leonard is quite wonderful,' Primrose wrote to Shelagh Howe next day. 'He blew in yesterday for an hour and looks so well. Played his game of tennis.'[39] As the bus headed for London he asked Phil Loneragan to organize air tickets for Lisbon, Rome and Turin, and wrote to Sir Geoffrey Todd at Midhurst: 'I have ten days free and would like to go to the south of France and northern Italy, travelling by air in a pressurized plane . . . Would this be all right or would you like me to come for a check-up first?'[40]

Cheshire told the Worthingtons about the plan.

It appeared, on the face of it, to be quite mad and impracticable . . . but it was Leonard at his best, being guided by a faith which had to be respected. He'd given no thought to the frightful complications of going off alone with a ten-year-old child who was unable to do anything for herself. I don't think he wanted to think about them and we certainly didn't try to point them out that day. The only thing we did ask him was why he didn't take someone with him, but he said he couldn't afford the two fares.[41]

With two days to go, Sir Geoffrey Todd forbade Cheshire to fly. Phil Loneragan worked frantically to produce a revised itinerary by rail. Since the Lisbon train passed through Spain, it was realized that they would now need visas.

Towards mid-morning on Thursday 30 June various helpers converged breathlessly upon Victoria Station: one in a taxi from the Spanish Embassy, another with money, a third bearing tickets, a fourth with luggage which had earlier been mislaid. At eleven o'clock the boat train pulled out, and the two companions disappeared on their strange journey.

Paris in the rush hour, an eleven-hour wait on the Spanish border, stifling heat, mis-timetabled trains which did not connect: it was not an easy journey. Josie weighed about three stone. Her left leg was twisted and useless. She could wash and dress herself, but not walk. King Umberto was sympathetic, although it was explained that rights of exposition of the Shroud were now vested in the cardinal in Turin. Cheshire nevertheless felt encouraged. The two pilgrims reached Turin on Wednesday 6 July. Five priests and a layman welcomed them at the station, and 'an astonished cardinal' made arrangements for a ceremony on the following afternoon.

Cheshire telephoned John Wilding, the mission's administrator, to say that permission to view the Shroud had been obtained, and would he, therefore, collect together any friends who would be willing to support Josie, and bring them out to Turin.

Two things moved Leonard to make this arrangement – one was that he felt that if the Shroud was to be exposed after all these years, then as many people as possible should take advantage of the chance to see it, the other was that he wished as many people as possible to be present to add their prayers to his and Josie's.[42]

Within a day, friends were contacted, an aircraft chartered. Unfortunately, the aircraft was diverted to Nice, and when Cheshire and Josie entered the cathedral at 4.15 on the next afternoon the friends had not arrived.[43]

Josephine was taken to a sacristy and changed into a dress of lace and white satin. She also put on new shoes, in which she hoped to walk out of the cathedral. They proceeded to the Chapel of the Holy Shroud. The triple locks of the safe were turned to produce a long embroidered casket. Josphine touched it. Could it be opened? The seven seals were cut, revealing a roll of red silk secured by more seals. This was placed on Josephine's lap, then against her leg, while two priests knelt in prayer to either side. Would it be possible to remove the cover? No. But Josephine was invited to put her hand inside, in contact with the Shroud. At the end, a deep silence.

Josie changed back into her ordinary clothes. The shoes were packed away.

A week later Francis Grimshaw wrote:

Somehow I was not surprised when the miracle did not happen. It would have been tantamount to the seal of God's authority set upon the relic; and my feeling is that this will not happen until human minds have had the opportunity that God always seems to give them of reaching either a clear conclusion or an impasse . . . which cannot be solved without a sign from heaven.

But the fact that you were able to get so easily what has not been conceded to others in centuries is to me a sign that the project was blessed, and it will not surprise me if the little patient does not get better from now on, slowly and perhaps not completely. We shall see.[44]

On Saturday 9 July England sweltered. Cheshire travelled to Le Court for the annual fête, arriving late, looking tired. Phil Loneragan, who had flown back from Milan earlier in the morning, went with him to run a stall. 'He was suffering badly from the effects of the constant journeyings over the last ten days, and could neither eat nor sleep properly.' After the fête he insisted on returning to London for a series of engagements. One was with the benefactor who had helped to establish Ampthill. This man was dying. Cheshire kept vigil through the night. Next day Margot Mason ordered him into her car and drove him to the Worthingtons' home at Chislehurst. Here he collapsed.

The Worthingtons' doctor found no serious problem, but advised bed and several days' complete rest. Margot Mason worked near by, seldom emerging save at mealtimes and for an hour or two each evening when Bob Worthington played tennis with her in the overpowering heat.

Collins had embarked upon trade advertising for *No Passing Glory* which mentioned the book's 'full and authentic' status. Cheshire protested that he had not yet seen corrected proofs and that until he had, it could not be said that the book had his approval.[45] Cheshire added that for two weeks following their meeting in May Boyle had done nothing to satisfy his requests for alterations. Cheshire copied the letter to Boyle. 'The enclosed speaks for itself. I have no doubt there is some explanation.'

William Collins replied immediately. All requested changes had been incorporated. Page proofs had been dispatched; if they contained anything with which Cheshire was unhappy, he had only to say and he – Collins – would attend to it personally.[46]

Boyle was more blunt.

18 July 1955. Andrew Boyle to Cheshire[47]

I know nothing about Collins's advertising. It does not come within my province. No doubt, as you say, there is some explanation. No doubt they will give it to you.

When we met . . . in May . . . The two points you still wanted to see were:

(*a*) the conversion sequence, which you have since read and approved; and (*b*) the Shroud passage which, at your request. I sent to Archbishop Grimshaw. You have also seen his letter approving of what I wrote.

Perhaps when you're next in London you could let me know so that we may meet. I think I owe you a lunch.

On the hottest day of the year, sitting in the shade of a pine tree, Peggy Worthington broached

the chaos which seemed to reign in most of his enterprises, and asked him why he did things the hard way. I can't remember his exact words but the gist of them was 'If things went too well, people would say – "that fellow Cheshire is a pretty good organizer, he doesn't need any help." It wouldn't do at all.' He may have been joking, but my mind went back to the morning I'd said that Leonard liked things done in a muddly way, and I accepted this as a genuine expression of how he felt.

The proofs arrived. Cheshire's comments mostly concerned passages in the Prologue and Epilogue. While Boyle had been at pains to note the existence of 'a mythical and a real Cheshire . . . he cannot involve me in agreeing that his version is correct and all others mythical'. Cheshire had contested Boyle's original summing up, which suggested that by 'condoning half-truths' Cheshire himself bore some responsibility for the 'slightly phoney legend' which now surrounded him. Cheshire countered by refuting the story of a 'spiritual awakening over Nagasaki'. This was a 'myth' about which he had 'always protested strongly', suspecting Boyle as its 'chief propagator and I think probably originator'. When Cheshire had mentioned this before, Boyle's reply had been: 'You may say what you like Leonard, but I am sticking to my story.'

And since Cheshire was sticking to his, Collins adroitly rewrote the blurb on the book's dustjacket. 'Many inaccuracies which until now have been accepted with the Cheshire legend are summarily disposed of. The most notable is the romantic assumption that his last wartime mission to Nagasaki . . . marked the decisive spiritual turning point of his life.'

A third complaint was that in discussion of his faith Boyle had 'overplayed the question of signs'. Cheshire agreed that this was a frailty, but 'I do not knowingly depend on signs'. As for the claim that he courted press attention, he disputed it.[48] Ironically, his absence from the scene had just that day become a subject of journalistic speculation. Even by doing nothing Cheshire attracted publicity.

A week after vanishing from public view, Cheshire was beginning to feel better. He embarked on an account of the pilgrimage to Turin, and prepared to leave the Chislehurst sanctuary. Peggy Worthington helped him pack. 'It didn't take long, because he had virtually nothing to pack.' 'Soon Margot was backing her little car out of the drive, and then they were gone. The house was unbearably quiet without the crashing of the typewriter or the murmur of someone, apparently talking to themselves.'[49]

Boyle made the final changes.

Staunton Harold, 22 July 1955. To Andrew Boyle[50]
Thank you very much for having made the corrections. I approve them all and now all should be plain sailing. Congratulations on the book. Apart from one or two things which you probably gather I feel could have been differently emphasized, I think it is very good and I am sure it will prove a credit to you. Anyway, I hope most sincerely it will be a great success.

Staunton sounds like 'rush hour in Hong Kong', Phil Loneragan wrote to Margot Mason. 'I can hardly wait to see thirty-five able-bodied men hard at work.' The Worthingtons visited next day.

Margot was sitting at a desk surrounded by the usual junk. There was no electricity . . . and the Dictaphone had to be run off a battery. This ran out of current while we were there, and Margot had to finish some of the typing sitting on the doorstep with the transformer and Dictaphone hitched to our car battery.

. . . All the floors, up and down, were stone flagged and in many of the rooms they sagged in the middle . . . as though about to crash to the rooms beneath. Barty (the first matron, a lovely person) said they weren't really dangerous, and were gradually being propped up again from below. Everywhere there were hordes of people painting and doing repairs . . . Apart from the leaking roof . . . the whole place seemed to be riddled with dry rot but no one offered to worry about this . . . 'There's only one bathroom and lavatory in the place,' said Barty cheerfully as she took us down yet another long corridor, 'and even that's out of order today.'

Then the kitchen:

They were having a lot of trouble with the modern heat-storage cooker . . . It
kept going out, and on one occasion a half-cooked chicken had to be whipped
out of the oven and finished off in a field oven hastily constructed by some of
the helpers.

And the former dining room:

I asked Barty how she was looking forward to winter. Margot, who had been
there often in the old days, said that they frequently dined in fur coats.[51]

Cheshire finished the account of the pilgrimage to the Shroud,
begun a few days before. The editor of *Woman's Illustrated* described
it as 'the most wonderful story that has ever come into this office'.[52]
George Greenfield★ agreed. It would make a 'good short book'.

Books. Delivery of 'The Search' was nearly due, yet little had
been written. The ghost-writing arrangement with Asgier Scott had
foundered. Cheshire had since recruited another helper, Reginald
Simpson, editor of the *Sunday Graphic* back in 1945. They met on
the morning of 28 July and signed a contract whereby Simpson
undertook to write Cheshire's life story, in the first person, on his
behalf, and to deliver the manuscript by 30 September. This was
hopelessly unrealistic – in the event, this book took another four
years – but Cheshire commended the first instalment: 'First rate.
Marvellous.'[53]

During August he recorded a broadcast for *The Week's Good
Cause*,[54] visited Lady Cholmondeley (an ally known as 'Mum
Chum'), drove to Lourdes with the Worthingtons, and then went
to Predannack, whence he wrote to Simpson about 'The Search'.
Again, progress seemed good. On 31 August he was at Ampthill,
announcing a 'Home Rescue Unit' – a typically progressive scheme
whereby volunteers could respond to emergency requests for domi-
ciliary care for the elderly, housebound or dying who wished to
stay in their own homes. Next day, 1 September, he dismissed
Reginald Simpson. In his bones, he knew that it wasn't working.[55]

★ Following Greenfield's approach in May, his position as Cheshire's literary agent had
been confirmed.

Simpson was furious. Thus far Cheshire had expressed only 'pleasure and delight' at his work, yet now he said the opposite. He threatened to sue.[56] George Greenfield, who had been away at the time of Simpson's dismissal, counselled Cheshire to 'weigh up possibilities and face facts'.[57] The dispute smouldered on into early October, when it was settled by a payment which Greenfield regarded as reasonable and Cheshire considered horrifyingly large.

Cheshire told Hutchinsons that he had been having 'a little bit of difficulty' over 'The Search', but that he had written something else. He enclosed the Turin manuscript. A new date was negotiated for the autobiography, and Hutchinsons offered a fresh contract for a book which might be titled 'Mission to the Holy Shroud'.

The mission to India was only weeks away. It was not yet clear how they would travel, or who would go. Amid continuing uncertainty, Cheshire travelled to Dublin, to Lisieux on retreat, promoted Wardour Castle, a Palladian house in Wiltshire, as a centre for discharged prisoners and went again to Walsingham.

He went to Walsingham with Shelagh Howe, who had kept Holy Cross going through the year while Cheshire had pursued other plans, with other people, in other places. She was devoted to him and his work: 'Yes, Walsingham was a success because it was simple and sincere — as you said it has brought us all together. Don't you realize Leonard, it could always be like that, if only you would let it be . . . There is *so* much I could do for you if only you would let one.'[58]

Primrose wrote consolingly. Leonard's interests were 'so widespread that we don't begin to know the half of them and as you know he only lets drop bits and pieces when he feels like it. I know he shuts himself away completely but he always did. I quite agree if he would only share with someone.'[59]

At that moment he did share something. Despite the perplexity of a local landowner ('Will somebody please tell Group Captain Cheshire that Walsingham is not for sale?') he sustained the vision of a pilgrimage centre commanding the entrance to the old priory, and suggested that Shelagh Howe should run it. Howe was rhapsodic. 'I can't think of anything else', she told him. 'Walsingham is the most exciting and wonderful prospect I have ever dreamed of. You are a pet to have thought of me.'

Cheshire's relationship with Shelagh Howe was of fluctuating intensity. A few days later it had cooled again, or it seemed so to Howe. Primrose tried to reassure her.

September 1955 (n.d.). Primrose Cheshire to Shelagh Howe
I'm terribly sorry you feel he has been 'peeved' with you but I somehow think you are wrong. He talked away happily about you and told me he knew unwittingly that he had upset you over several things and was extremely sorry. But you know he never bears a grudge against one for long? I think the more he frets about the more he worries . . . you know he isn't one to get his troubles off his chest. I don't think he has had undue admiration of late. He seems just the same lad he always was and I think few of us would remain untouched or changed if we had the sort of 'glamorous' life he has. I really always marvel at him and wonder whatever *I* should have been like in his shoes. I personally am all for this going to India. A beautiful place in the hills, and it will change his outlook and I hope do his health no end of good . . . I hope he will settle for some weeks if not months.

Assuming, of course, that they could get to India. There was no money.

Then, uncannily, money arrived. 'Mafeking has been relieved by Russie's royalties cheque,' announced Phil Loneragan.[60] Russell Braddon had given £400. A TV broadcast from Le Court was followed by nearly £2,000 in donations. Hutchinson's reprint of *Bomber Pilot* – regretted by Cheshire the year before – yielded £1,512. In the same week Andrew Boyle pledged a substantial part of his £400 advance on *No Passing Glory*.

With just over three weeks to go, Jock Hill produced a formal plan for the 'Cheshire Mission to India'. Departing on 2 November, the first stage would be from Dunkirk to Istanbul; the second from Istanbul to Kuwait; the third by sea to Bombay; and the fourth from Bombay to Kodai Kanal. Preparations would need to take account of the need for fuel, maps and charts, passports and visas, international driving permits, spares, tools, medical arrangements, customs carnets, vaccinations.[61] Their vehicles would be one of the Cheshire buses, a lorry and trailer, and there was talk of a light aircraft. Roy Sugden, short, slightly built, with a large moustache, was to be the principal driver, assisted by Sidney Whissen. Apart from Cheshire and Margot Mason, other members of the expedition would be Jock Hill, a doctor from Belgium and a nursing orderly from Palestine.[62] The men would sleep in the vehicles, the ladies in hotels, where there were hotels.

This was a lot to organize in three weeks. Little of it happened. The doctor and nurse never materialized. Jock Hill's secondment was blocked,[63] and when Cheshire was told that he could after all fly to Bombay he elected to do so. The rest of the party would now go by sea, with the vehicles as deck cargo.[64] There was no lorry and no aircraft, although late in October they accepted the offer of a tropicalized Land Rover at a discount.

No Passing Glory was published on 17 October. Andrew Boyle invited Cheshire to a private launch party at William Collins's house. Old friends were there: Taffy Roberts, Jock Hill, Micky Martin, David Shannon, Danny Walker, Charles Whitworth, John Kirby, the Cochranes. Valediction was in the air.

One factor which influenced Cheshire's determination to go to India was his concern to see the English homes put on a permanent footing. This required the destruction of the personality cult which attended everything he did. Only by his absence would individual homes discover self-reliance. On 25 October, for instance, a member of the Ampthill committee wrote:

. . . dear Leonard tell me before you go:

Who is to take charge of getting those repairs finished?

Who will administer any funds?

Who is left by you in charge of the whole affair? Is it your Father? John Wilding seems very young and inexperienced to have the whole burden on his shoulders. *Where* are the central funds? Who receives and keeps account of the money that comes in? *Is it for the Mission*? Who administers it?

You cannot go away leaving all this in doubt. It is your duty to make it clear . . .[65]

But he could, and he didn't.

Cheshire metabolized such stresses. He accepted with joy the trials of a day – irritation, disappointment, tiredness, failure, imposition from another, criticism – using them as prompts to prayer for the relief of someone's distress at their moment of death. Awkward helpers, relentless work, perpetual homelessness and Reginald Simpson's reproaches were assimilated in a vocation towards the dying, 'in whom we see a reflection of the Holy Face'. By these means, every minute in every day became a matter of life and death. Small wonder that he had no time for trivia, or that others were drawn to him like moths to a flame.

Before going to the airport he wrote to Father Fuller. '. . . I will found no more homes off my own bat in England. Henceforth all new foundations must go through the trust. The important thing seems to me now the building of an organic organization which will hold everything together and be capable of expansion.' He mused about friends and work. 'India coming strong . . . I get to Bombay tomorrow lunchtime and stay four days with the Cardinal before going south. I'm cleared for flying pressurized. Love to puss.'

And then he was gone.

PART SEVEN: INDIA,
1955–1959

19. Touch and Go

Margot Mason, Roy Sugden and Sidney Whissen began their voyage aboard the SS *Itria* three days later. There was a sense of being forsaken among well-wishers on the oily, crate-strewn quay that November afternoon.[1]

I felt this was truly the end of a chapter . . . Up to the moment of Leonard actually disappearing I think many people felt that he might never go at all. It was such a short time since he had left the sanatorium; it was almost as if he couldn't get away quickly enough. There was so much for him to do in this country, much he had left unfinished in a way . . .[2]

Cheshire was due back for three months from the following April, but many said that he had gone for good.

Where were they going, and what to do? On the way to the docks Margot Mason reported 'vague talk of everyone shooting off in the bus either for the home up in the Kodai Hills or to some unspecified site for a new one. Presumably Leonard would meet them, providing he remembered . . . Margot said she didn't think about the future – it was the best way.'[3]

While the *Itria* steamed east, Cheshire went to reconnoitre the house in the Nilgiri Hills which had been offered two years before. Finding it unsuitable,[4] he turned, so to speak, to Plan B, which assumed that land would be cheap and that they'd be able to build a home around themselves while using the bus as a base. He travelled up to Bombay to meet the *Itria*, and began to look around. Land prices were astronomic. Worse, when the *Itria* docked on 3 December the bus and their Land Rover were impounded by Indian Customs.[5] By this stroke they were immobilized, deprived of their accommodation and thrust into debt.[6]

'Overnight, we became three men and one woman in a great hurry, knowing that if we didn't find what we were looking for quickly – a piece of land without the requirement of any immediate down-payment – we were sunk.'[7] Christmas parcels made them feel homesick. Christopher wrote to say that his marriage was breaking up.[8] With less than £100 between them, the mission teetered on the edge of collapse.

Cheshire had one letter of introduction in Bombay. It was to Nina Carney, wife of the manager of the Burmah-Shell Oil Refineries. The Carneys introduced Cheshire to the owner of an acre and a half of a small hilltop in the jungle near Vinayala seventeen miles outside the city. Cheshire offered to buy it, promising to pay when he could. A building contractor donated a three-room prefabricated hut, which they called Bethlehem House, because it was assembled at Christmas. The site was attractive and peaceful, although it lay over a mile from the nearest road and was devoid of amenities. No sanitation, no electricity, no water. Everyone said that water was never found on hilltops – except during the monsoon, when they were warned that the track would become a quagmire.[9] Still, it was a start, and, as before, poverty became an asset.[10]

At first we bemoaned the loss of the Land Rover . . . but soon we discovered that we were almost better off without it, for those who have very little and are forced to fetch and carry on their own backs and dig trenches with their own hands are more readily taken to be poor, and thus more easily obtain help.[11]

Or as Francis Grimshaw reflected: 'St Paul thought nothing of a couple of years in jail . . . it is possible to pray with recollection when the whirlwind, where God is not, dies down.' A man with advanced cancer arrived, and they took him in.

Margot Mason remained in Bombay, trying to retrieve the vehicles. Early in January a message reached her from someone called Wilfrid Russell, an English businessman who had worked in India for twenty-one years.[12] Russell was married to an Indian, and a few days previously his sister-in-law had shown him letters which mentioned Cheshire's problems. One was signed by Nehru's Minister of Health, who wondered if Russell's sister-in-law could help.

Russell took Margot Mason to lunch at the Taj hotel, a welcome change from the austerity of the hostel in which she was staying. Russell was struck by her 'cheerfulness and a gay informal courage'. She was, however, less philosophical than Cheshire.[13] The vehicles had been sitting at the docks for five weeks, and their ransom now exceeded £1,000.

Soon afterwards Russell ran into an old wartime friend, Sobruto Mukerjee, now a marshal of the Indian Air Force. Together they went to see the chairman of the Port Trust and the Collector of Customs.* The air marshal asked for the release of the vehicles, and wrote a note guaranteeing the duty.[14] The bus and Land Rover were released next day.

Margot Mason and Russell drove out to Bethlehem House. It stood on Salsette Island, an area which had been invaded by urban development but yet retained a rural heart. At Andheri they turned off the crowded main road and crossed the railway line.

We crawled through the jungle along a bullock track. Clouds of red dust rose from the wheels as we slithered over potholes and cart ruts, and past village ponds, stagnant and filthy, but serene in the winter sunlight, until we turned off the track up a steep rise, past another board with its cheerful arrow, and emerged through a thicket into a clearing. There was an open space among the jungle trees. In the centre was an asbestos cement hut . . . I wondered what Cheshire would be like. Then, as we rounded the corner of the hut, I saw him for the first time. He was wearing grey flannels and an open-necked shirt, and was walking along the veranda of the hut carrying a bowl of water. He grinned, and said with deep seriousness:

'Hello, Dopey,† we hadn't seen you for so long we thought you had gone back to England.' He seldom spoke in the first person singular . . .

'I must finish doing Pop. Go into the office. I'll be with you in a minute.'

He disappeared with bandages and hot water into the first compartment of the hut. We sat down on soapboxes in the third room at the far end. There was a table, a recording machine, a shelf of books on theology, boxes full of medical

---

* There are two versions of this story, although in upshot they are essentially the same. According to Cheshire (*HW*, pp.47–8) it was he who went to visit the Chief of the Air Staff, in Delhi.

† Several helpers were nicknamed after characters in the film *Snow White and the Seven Dwarfs*.

stores and a jumble of papers and oddments which reminded me of an RAF Flight Commander's office . . .

Then Cheshire came in. Again there was the broad grin. Again I was struck by his slight build. He seemed to float through the air. I had read somewhere of his illness. He looked fit enough now. Margot Mason introduced us. He looked me straight in the eye and the playfulness disappeared for a moment.

'I can't thank you enough about what you did about the bus and Land Rover.' Then the grin again. 'Has Dopey told you what we're trying to do?'

Cheshire explained:

'Most people think it's a bit crazy to take in patients before you have the roof on. I always think it's best to get your feet in the door, then it's easier to let the rest of your body in. We've got four patients here now, and this hut was only finished the other day. An Indian contractor gave us the materials and built it free, and he has promised to put up a second one alongside, if we can get the materials.'

'Have you got them yet?' I asked.

'Not yet; but I expect they will turn up sometime. When they do we can bring nurses in. Then we can move on somewhere else and start a new home.'

I had never come across anything like this in my life, even in India, where the strangest things can happen . . . I had assumed that Cheshire in his jungle would be working for some time, probably a year or more, on getting one home going. The idea that he was already planning to move on elsewhere, when he seemed to be at the very beginning of his project, took my breath away.[15]

Shortly afterwards well-wishers delivered materials for the second hut.

Russell introduced Cheshire to Morarji Desai, the Chief Minister of Bombay State, whose efficiency and asceticism earned him the reputation of 'a sort of Hindu Oliver Cromwell'.[16] They met in Bombay's new secretariat building, an encounter of simplicities, with Desai in his homespun *khaddar* and Cheshire in a plain light suit. Cheshire outlined his plans, explaining that to achieve anything lasting you must start from small beginnings, and build outwards; that the way to contribute towards the peace of the world is to bring peace into your own surroundings, into someone else's life − first, of course, into your own.[17] Desai replied by speaking of Gandhi and renunciation. On this note of consonance, the conversation itself a little step, they parted. On the way out Cheshire challenged Russell to a race down the stairs. Russell charged down five flights. At the bottom he found himself alone. Cheshire stepped out of the lift, 'roaring with laughter'.[18]

Although Cheshire never seemed to have any money he was 'the most mobile man in the country'.[19] Later in February he was successively in New Delhi, Calcutta and Serampore. His spreading network included government ministers, churchmen, industrialists, members of princely families, generals. In all these meetings it was his rule never to ask for help, for to do so might forestall the designs of Providence. Before February was out a house had been offered for a second home.[20]

Cheshire was in India because he believed that the key to world peace lay in action to confront third-world suffering. Justice, he reasoned, is a prerequisite for peace,[21] and helping the East was a matter of justice, not charity.[22] And it was a matter for individuals. There were other influences – a hope that India's dearth would help to clarify God's will, and the fostering of local self-reliance among homes in England[23] – but justice was at the root of it, and he would have gone for that alone.

Coincidentally, his absence might also downplay the personality cult which was being boosted by *No Passing Glory*. Cheshire's father congratulated Boyle on 'a magnificent piece of work,' which had 'overcome difficulties with which the book teemed, and without omitting what may be called the less edifying episodes'.[24] Primrose was initially more squeamish, telling Shelagh Howe: 'I have to read [the] Boyle Book . . . I somehow have a dread of reading all the part of his life that is his and not the public's. I hate that it should have been published but I suppose his bad must go with the good.'[25] But by the time she finished it Primrose had partly changed her mind, and wrote to Boyle to say so. While the book contained much which 'very naturally I wish could have been left unsaid', it was a 'most moving and thrilling account . . . your insight into Leonard's character is amazing. You stress the lonely man, which I feel most deeply he is, and vulnerable.'[26]

Primrose was not the only one to acknowledge Boyle's acuity. Shelagh Howe winced at it, thinking the truth 'a little too ruthless' and likely to undermine the confidence of those who supported his work.[27] But this was a minority view. Most said the opposite. Bob Worthington, for instance, who had had misgivings while Boyle was writing, now thought the book 'a masterpiece and so fair to L. . . . I am sorry if in the past I thought, quite wrongly, that you might harm L.'s work.'[28] Barnes Wallis told Boyle: 'The analysis of Cheshire's complex and many-sided character must have been a fearful problem, but I think that you have contrived to present to your readers something of the spiritual source from which he draws his amazing strength.'[29] Many wrote like this, some to Cheshire himself:

Andrew Boyle has done you a great service . . . One would have to be completely insensitive to enjoy this literary 'vivisection' without some shrinking: and that you have, so candidly and simply, accepted this, will make you esteemed and better understood by many who cared less for 'the Cheshire Legend'.[30]

Cheshire wasn't so sure. It wasn't the candidness he minded, nor esteem that he wanted. The Legend was becoming a nuisance. What he wanted was for public attention to shift to the work,[31] although just then much of the English work looked shaky. Le Court and St Teresa's were secure, but other homes were struggling and reproachful.[32] Cheshire remained phlegmatic. 'They can't be much good, can they,' he said to Russell, 'if they have to have me around all the time?'[33] In due course his faith in their self-reliance would be vindicated, but at the start of 1956 it looked a matter of touch and go whether some would survive at all.

He was closer than they thought. Every day he set aside time to visit each home in his mind's eye and pray for its members, and letters described their progress.[34] Phil Loneragan wrote often, sometimes every two or three days. Late in November she visited Cornwall. 'I really think that St Teresa's is "me favourite",' she wrote on return to Pitt's Head Mews. 'They are all so happy and interested in everything, especially news of you.' She had stayed in the 'small hotel in Mullion and slept in "the white woman's burden", golly, it was freezing!'[35] The atmosphere of the work was in her letters, and when Cheshire opened them he breathed it.

Loneragan was a phenomenon. Young, effervescent, attractive, industrious and capable, she had 'a flair for getting on with the world at large',[36] accepted no salary and quietly paid many of the early secretarial expenses out of her own pocket.[37] She dealt with much of Cheshire's mail and forwarded the rest to wherever he was, made and remade travel arrangements, fielded inquiries and governed his diary. So much would be handled by any good social secretary, but Loneragan was more than that. She was a confidante, Cheshire's proxy in London and one of the few to whom he would delegate. She shared his unconditional faith in Providence, and like him could remain optimistic when others became demoralized. When Cheshire called her to India within days of his own arrival, she replied at once, saying, 'Yes, of course I'll come out to Bombay and help set up Pitt's Head Mews (2)', as if he was asking for no more than a cup of tea. But this plan, like all the others, was soon changed.

After a trustees' meeting in late January 1956, the foundation's treasurer, Sir Archibald Jamieson, wrote:

My principal object . . . is to tell you how much I like and admire young Wilding [the foundation's secretary], and to tell you – in my opinion – that all of us who are in any way concerned with your homes should be most grateful for the self-sacrificing way in which he has shouldered the burden during the last few months. This burden has, in fact, become too heavy for him, and under doctor's orders, he is going away for two, or – I hope – three weeks.[38]

A little ominously, Jamieson added: 'your father is going to write to you about Holy Cross'. Geoffrey did so.

Pots, my dear lad, I'm delighted to hear that you are well and happy, and more delighted than I can describe that you have cut out Australia.* Too great a tax on your energy. On the other hand, I should deprecate a too hasty return to India, for, having established so many homes in England, your first responsibility is to them and there is no doubt that with you absent public support and interest tend to wane.

Trustee meeting last night. All merry and bright except for Holy Cross, the main facts about which you know. But it is causing confusion and a deal of

---

* Cheshire had planned to go to Australia on a fund-raising tour in 1957.

resentment to the loyal people of Cornwall. The fundamental factor is old St Levan and her splendid committee were persuaded to come in and make such a splendid success of what was very obviously and seriously wilting on the distinct understanding by you that Teresa's is the one and only home in Cornwall . . . the mere existence of HC is bound to cause confusion . . . Lady St L. quoted a letter to some Catholic paper in which the writer described how she had raised money for HC, 'one of the Cheshire Homes'. St Levan & Co naturally regard this sort of thing as a breach of faith and as Cornwall is not rich enough to support two homes the trustees were much perturbed and asked me to tell you that in their opinion HC should be closed down *temporarily* until you return . . . I stressed and they appreciated that HC is very near to your heart . . .[39]

It was near to Shelagh Howe's heart too. The Army saw Howe as a high-flier, yet more than once she had put Cheshire's work before her career, and she had funded Holy Cross from her own pocket.[40] Primrose wrote in consolation:

My dear Shelagh

. . . I feel your loyalty to Leonard is taking you into deep waters indeed, and you've had *so* much worry on his account . . . I'm so worried about you trying to carry on . . . all to keep Leonard [happy]. Poor dear Shelagh, I hope you are not heartbroken . . . I *do* want you to know how I admire you for tackling the things done and how worried I am for your sake. Don't struggle any more.[41]

A few days later Cheshire was told of unrest at St Bridget's;[42] St Uriel's, the recently launched home for mentally handicapped children near Stroud was also in difficulties.[43] Phil Loneragan advised that the house occupied by St Uriel's was 'unsuitable in every way', and that they should close it. Cheshire agreed.[44]

Cheshire's absence exposed fundamental differences between the Mission for the Relief of Suffering and the Cheshire Foundation. The foundation was governed by an independent trustee body, its affairs were systematically documented, it was non-denominational and its purposes were constitutionally limited to care of chronic sick.[45] The mission, by contrast (described by Wilfrid Russell as a tenuous bank account into which Phil Loneragan paid any money that was handed to Cheshire without instruction as to how it should be spent), was an extension of Cheshire's faith and a medium for spontaneous innovation. Ex-prisoners, for instance, had been begging his help for years, and he yearned to see homes in which various kinds of maverick or maladjusted people could be rehabilitated by helping to care for the sick. The idea of tackling two different kinds of problem by putting one at the service of the other was typically creative. As Holy Cross had shown, it was also unpopular, while the foundation's refusal to allow Cheshire's name to be associated with other types of home restricted his ability to tackle newly identified kinds of need. As he put it later, 'my only hope of doing other things in this period – like the gaolbirds, for instance – was by working entirely on my own anonymously without any organization or official support, and that obviously wouldn't last'.[46] Nor did it leave so many records. Mission schemes could be launched, changed or dropped on the basis of a conversation, and this has left only a fragmentary picture of what they were.[47]

While the mission and the trust moved along separate paths, several of their dramatis personae worked on behalf of both. Among them was John Wilding, the foundation's conscientious secretary, who with Loneragan was also co-responsible for the mission. Wilding's workload had brought him close to a breakdown.[48] Loneragan was also becoming worried about his expenses. There was no question of dishonesty. The issue lay rather in the hint of an infringement of the tacit convention of extreme frugality by which Cheshire's closest followers were mutually bound. This was sad, for in hindsight the problem can be seen to have been partly of Cheshire's making. In the hectic days before India Cheshire had said a lot of things to a lot of people, and his directions to Loneragan and Wilding had left room for uncertainty about where the boundary between their responsibilities lay.[49] More incertitude resulted from the existence of two mission accounts, at different banks, which left neither Wilding nor Loneragan with a complete picture of the mission's financial position.[50] Sink or swim. They were finding out.

On 17 February George Greenfield cabled good news to India: the *Sunday Despatch* was offering £1,000 for serial rights to the 'Josie book'.[51] Hutchinsons promised publication of the hardback in the spring, which linked with another project now forming in Cheshire's mind: a pilgrimage to Rome and an audience with the Holy Father.

The Holy Shroud brought Cheshire and the mission into frequent contact with Miss Vera Barclay, UK steward of copyright in Shroud photographs. A devout Catholic, punctilious and touchy, Miss Barclay had been collaborating with Cheshire since the days of the first mission bus. She viewed his work with mixed feelings, combining admiration for his faith with despair about his aptitude for organization. Most of her complaints centred on Dan Griffiths, to whom Cheshire had committed the mission's 'Holy Shroud Inquiry Centre'. With Cheshire abroad Griffiths was too much involved for her liking. She lamented to Father Fuller:

Strange that a man so unsuitable should have been put so completely in control. Leonard has indeed left us to hold the baby – and some baby! I heard from him this morning. He says there is no more question of his going to Australia, and he means to carry on quietly in India. (I doubt if he means to return at Easter.) It seems a good solution for him – if only he will be content with small results.[52]

Her latest grievance concerned the over-hurried, 'almost Cheshire-like', and consequently flawed proposals for a trust in which oversight of matters relating to the Holy Shroud in the UK could be vested. The formation of such a trust was something for which Miss Barclay yearned, partly to relieve her of responsibilities for which she felt unsuited, and partly to remove the Shroud from the ambit of Cheshire's Mission for the Relief of Suffering.

I hope you agree with me that such a trust must not be a Cheshire affair, but that the mission must be one of the various groups that uses it and supports it, on an equality with the others. I feel that Leonard's dictatorship, and his incalculable choppings and changes of plans and 'personnel' are too risky. And the Mission's finances are too precarious.[53]

Cheshire appeared to Vera Barclay as a bundle of paradoxes, lucid yet a sower of confusion, an autocrat who had nevertheless delegated everything by walking away from it. He mystified her, and she grimaced at his service jargon, where colleagues were 'personnel'.

Cheshire remained equable, his mind on the more immediate needs of Bombay's destitute. Jimmy Carney sent a steamroller to tar the approach to Bethlehem House, giving all-weather access, and a team lugged a 10,000 gallon tank on to the site to collect monsoon run-off from the roofs. Cheshire was also thinking about the pilgrimage. 'Now, about Rome!' he wrote to Loneragan in March, before going into a fortnight's retreat. What about chartering an aircraft? They could fly out on 30 April, spend the next three days in Rome, leave for Turin early on the morning of the 4th and be back in London late that evening. He hoped to present a copy of *Pilgrimage to the Shroud* and a concise account of the homes[54] to the Holy Father.

The *New Statesman* had just scolded the *Sunday Despatch* for publishing a hangman's memoirs, and Miss Barclay feared that the *Despatch*'s forthcoming serialization of Josie's story would attract secularist attacks. Things were already 'bad enough without the precious picture itself being involved'. She was aghast at the possibility that Catholics might boost the *Despatch*'s circulation. In her view, Cheshire shouldn't be writing for 'this terrible paper' at all. It would all be grist to the *New Statesman*'s atheistic mill.

After publication, Miss Barclay let rip.

[Cheshire] has taken the great risk of leaving the matter in the hands of a non-Catholic agent, without, apparently, the check that consultation with Catholic Authority would have constituted.* The Shroud absolutely demands this . . . He has now let it down very badly indeed by this serial: though even the book would have done that. It is most unsuitable. Apart from the seeking of a miracle, and the anticlimax of the end of the story; and the suppression of the fact that the pilgrimage received that extraordinary check, the treatment of the little child who trusted him is in the worst possible taste, and against charity. He gives away intimate spiritual details, and makes fun of very private physical ones. And there is also the opportunity for the Enemy to exploit the ever-renewed argument against religion, of the permitted suffering of the innocent.

And so on. There was some backlash, one editor jeering that Cheshire had been hoodwinked by 'the biggest hoax since Pilt-

---

* In fact, Cheshire had submitted the entire manuscript to Catholic Authority.

down', but this appeared in an esoteric journal,[55] which hardly anyone – probably not even the Enemy himself – would have read. One wonders if the tumultuous Miss Barclay ever reflected on the Gospel accounts of a mission aimed at drunkards, whores, doubters and outcasts, as well as the intellectual faithful. We leave her with the thought that if the *Sunday Despatch* had circulated in first-century Galilee, Jesus might have written for it.

April neared, Cheshire was coming back.[56] On 9 April Phil Loneragan collected him from Heathrow and drove him down to Laundry Cottage.[57]

New things were happening, inspiring things. Several years before, the committee of St Teresa's had set about raising funds to replace the draughty old buildings at Predannack. With local help, labour and public contributions totalling £10,000 this work was finished. It stood at Newtown Longrock, near Penzance, and it had just opened.[58] April 20 was Family Day at St Teresa's, a moment for the renewal of old friendships and celebration of the home's rebirth.

Four days later Cheshire was guest of honour at a dinner in Halifax, where a group of local people had combined to establish another home. This would be White Windows at Sowerby Bridge. A few miles away in the Vale of York, not far from Cheshire's wartime bomber station at Linton-on-Ouse, others had begun to convert Alne Hall. Before going to India Cheshire had vowed to play no further personal part in founding homes in Britain. Six months later new homes were springing up unbidden.

He was back for fourteen weeks, and as usual packed more into them than others thought wise. Aside from visiting all the homes and ricocheting between fund-raising and lecture engagements[59] he made a flying pilgrimage to Lisieux,[60] another to Lourdes, went to Rome,[61] the Channel Islands and Turin, called on Josie Woollam, George Greenfield, his publishers, Father Fuller, the Boyles, attended a trustees' meeting, tried to resolve a dispute at St Cecilia's,[62] took part in a VC service in Westminster Abbey[63] and a parade before the Queen.

While in the Channel Islands he found T. H. White living on Alderney and enlisted his help to set up a new home.[64] Of his former pupil White said: 'he has all the characteristics necessary for a saint – obstinacy, fanaticism, charm'.[65]

Following his media shyness earlier in the year Cheshire had a new rule of thumb which his conscience found acceptable: 'Do not seek publicity but let publicity come to you.' It did so with a vengeance on 18 July, when Australia's visiting Test cricketers held a fund-raising ball at the Savoy.[66] Phil Loneragan wrote merrily to Margot Mason:

All flat out for the Ball tonight, Leonard is doing an exhibition of the 'Kangaroo Hop'[67] with Belita, she's a skater or dancer or something, he's gone off to rehearse with her this afternoon . . . this I shall really enjoy, for he swears he hasn't been on a dance floor for ten years, and I can well believe it! I'll write you all the dirt in detail after it's all over![68]

A reporter watched them practise. ' "I haven't danced since 1945," he said, and no one doubted it.'[69] Heralded by the headline 'Just Dig This Crazy VC, You Creeps',[70] Cheshire and Belita danced in front of seven hundred people, an ordeal softened by a boost to the foundation's funds. Next day he scribbled a note to Andrew Boyle. 'Just to say Godbless before leaving. So sorry you couldn't make the ball . . . Packing up. See you next spring.'

Eight or nine months in Asia, three or four in Europe. For four years, this was to be the pattern.

20. Gateway

Bethlehem House had endured 'many ups and downs' in Cheshire's absence. The main problem was money. A committee meeting was held in the shade of a mango tree to address this. Nina Carney suggested that they put on a pantomime and charge people to see it. The show was duly mounted in the garden of a Parsee lady on Malabar Hill. Everything – script, costumes, music – was home-made. The performance was greeted with such acclaim that it had to be thrice repeated, and Bethlehem House received a cheque for the equivalent of £3,000 as a result.[1] Three nurses from an order of Spanish nuns were invited in to staff it.

Even before the sisters arrived, the missioners had moved on. Their next project was in Dehra Dun, to which Margot Mason, Sidney Whissen, Roy Sugden and a newly arrived helper set off by road early in August. Hardships at Bethlehem House had toughened them, but nonetheless it was a considerable journey, the best part of a thousand miles north through Indore, Gwalior and Delhi. The few rupees they had went mostly on petrol and repairs for the Land Rover. Occasionally they slept in the open, amid the pulsing rasp of cicadas. Around them on their way were flies, gleeful children, fruit bats, feral dogs sifting rubbish, kites circling Parsee towers of silence, underfed buffalo patiently trekking out in the early morning light to begin a new day's work, gaudy lorries on dusty roads, frantic markets, grace, dignity and destitution.

Dehra Dun stands on a shelf at the foot of the Himalayas. It is a city with Raj roots, home to the Survey of India, the Indian Military Academy and the Forest Research Institute, a pleasant place where the wealthy send their children to elite schools and to which they retire when they grow old. Between the furnace heat of summer and a short winter there are times when the ground is aglow with shrubs and flowers. Beyond, the Himalayas rise like a wall, coloured anew from hour to hour by different lights and weathers. At night, the lamps in distant high-perched villages form speckled clusters which float in the sky. There is vast beauty here, and mingled with the beauty there is poverty.

The house to which they went was Govind Bhavan at 16 Pritnam Road. It wasn't really a house at all, rather a small nineteenth-century maharajah's palace which had been donated by the Princess of Nabha and now stood empty save for large colonies of bees and hornets which hung menacingly from its lofty ceilings. The palace suffered from what modern jargon calls a maintenance deficit. That is to say, it needed a lot of work, which demanded money, which as usual they did not have.

Money. Cheshire sounded George Greenfield on the possibility of an advance of £1,000 from Hutchinsons against future royalties from his unfinished autobiography. Greenfield was doubtful, but said that two authors for whom he acted would be willing to advance the money.[2] Whether Cheshire accepted this offer we do not know, but a few weeks later Greenfield landed a contract with the American firm McGraw-Hill Rock for US sales of *Pilgrimage to the Shroud*. McGraw-Hill offered a $1,500 advance, followed by royalties, and an option on 'The Search'. As often before, help arrived out of a clear sky.

We might wonder if Cheshire was beginning to take such preternatural episodes for granted, or if his imperturbability while awaiting them signified an immunity against the doubts which gnaw at the rest of us. His faith does indeed look secure against doubt. Faith, however, brings no freedom from feeling, unless it be a certitude of the kind which borders chilly fanaticism. Cheshire's faith was not like that at all, being more akin to the trust of a child in dialogue with a searching intellect. Many problematic decisions he referred back to Providence, which acquitted him of worry about them until the time came, while his ability to split big issues into small pieces enabled him to tackle each moiety at a time without becoming demoralized by problems he could not immediately solve. 'For today, today's troubles are enough.' Even so, as 1957 passed,

Cheshire became affected by a hazy sense of unease. The year ended, indeed, in a kind of personal crisis.

Among his papers, a note.

THE OBJECTIVE. . . To take those that are unwanted, and to make them wanted. Not to say to them: 'Now just lie back and be comfortably sick for the rest of your life', but to give them a purpose to live for, to give them the means of rising above their infirmity, to turn them into active members of the family, active helpers in the work that still has so far to go, so many countries to reach . . .[3]

That was the plan, and he saw India as the gateway to its working. 'India is a halfway house. It's Eastern but it's built on a British foundation.' From India, he said, 'we have an entrée really all over the world'.

Until now Cheshire had taken a personal part in everything. Hereafter the plan begins to pass into other hands, becoming a series of chain reactions in different parts of the world, each response generating others which multiplied in their turn. During the next three years a new Cheshire Home opened somewhere on average every three months. They did not, of course, begin of their own accord. The key lay in people, growing numbers of people who turned aside from whatever they had been doing to offer their hearts, gifts, time, talents, in some cases lives, to advance the work. So much was good, but as his shareholding, so to speak, became diluted, so his voice in policy was reduced. He was not inherently possessive, he had been through the process before, and his faith told him that Providence would work through others as well as himself. Nevertheless, it was around this that his doubts knotted. If something decided by someone else at first looked wrong, yet in its out-turn might be seen as right, how, in his heart, was he to know?

Inevitably, in this upwelling of enterprises and relationships it becomes difficult to braid even the main threads into a coherent narrative, or even, with Cheshire, to see what the main threads might be. There is simply too much going on. One solution would be to refocus on the bigger picture, the principal trends and steps taken. Let us do that.

News of what we were doing began to spread. The Catholic Archbishops of
Calcutta and Madras invited me to visit them and each in turn gave us a large
house. From a remote town of south India the widow of a Tamil civil servant
wrote offering her services, as did a senior Army officer in Babina. The former
had never undertaken any public work of any kind – I don't think she had even
used a telephone – and yet within eighteen months she had started our first
home for leprosy. The latter, General Virendra Singh, set about collecting funds
and was later to take charge of the whole Indian operation. My part, in those
early days, was to spend as much time as I could with each of the little groups,
helping to raise public support and interest, sharing the task of organizing life
within the home, and searching for suitable buildings.[4]

Thus, by mid-1957 five homes had opened. The fourth, at Vrishanti
House, near Vellor, was the one for burnt-out lepers. The fifth,
for disabled children, was at Jamshedpur, 150 miles west of Calcutta.
As in Britain, each was run by a local committee, while serving
them all was a central charitable trust under the able chairmanship
of Col. Leslie Sawhny. Alongside the trustees was a general council
which Cheshire already wanted to scrap, saying that he preferred
a single trustee body. This aside, key players among the trustees
included Brigadier Virendra Singh, and Larry Donnelly, chief
engineer with the firm Babcock and Wilcox, who had worked in
India since 1948. Donnelly was Calcutta-based, a Catholic, energetic
and a supporter of the work of Mother Teresa. He became the
managing trustee. Also temporarily at hand was Phil Loneragan,
who had come out to establish an administrative nucleus in Calcutta
while some of the first wave of missioners went home. Margot
Mason was now back in England, presiding at Pitt's Head Mews.

Wilfrid Russell was back in England, too, and at Cheshire's
suggestion he was appointed a trustee. One of his first tasks was to
bring about the closure of Holy Cross.[5] Perhaps Russell had a
flair for tricky assignments, for he was next asked to oversee the
winding-up of Wardour Castle. Andrew Boyle sent his condolences
about this to Cheshire.

You must admit it was a white elephant to cope with: too big and too antique
for a home, unless you'd been there to improvise and keep it going in spite of
everything. One of the handicaps is finding anyone capable (as you are) of

persevering all the better when things are at their worst. It's a rare gift of Providence; but it seems difficult to canalize and makes the creation of a rule binding on others something of an impossibility.[6]

Boyle's supposition that Cheshire's gifts lay beyond codification wasn't entirely true. Cheshire was again at work on his autobiography★ – or, at least, George Greenfield hoped he was and in thinking about how to write it he was beginning to analyse the chemistry of his activities: what worked and what didn't, and why.

For the time being, however, the book was a sideshow. The work took precedence. As ever, help and helpers arrived from all quarters, ranging from the 2s.6d. book of stamps given by a destitute pensioner to the talents of a thirty-year-old French count whose business career in Indochina, Manila and Brazil had been preceded by abscondment from a New York school and service as a commando. In March 1957 discussions with the Indian government flowered into the gift of a building on the outskirts of Delhi. This would become their sixth home.

So, the work was taking shape. It was even beginning to display familiar characteristics, such as tension between a central trust and local committees, or the syndrome of well-intended helpers who gave contradictory instructions. The Cheshire Homes India also now had addresses in Bombay and Calcutta, whence the founder wrote prodigious numbers of letters to friends, and between which their replies were forever being forwarded by Phil Loneragan. As in England, Cheshire was incessantly on the move, and not only inside India. His next target was Singapore, and by the end of 1957 a home would be opened there as well.

In tracing things out broadly, years at a time, we should not overlook simplicities and moments. Like everyone else Cheshire had an interior existence, and just occasionally we sense longing, or an aching memory. Asides in letters recall Father Fuller's cat curled beside the gas fire on a December night, or Cornish weather. 'I miss St Teresa's and keep picturing in my mind all of you against

---

★ In December 1956 Cheshire told at least one friend that the book was finished. If it was, however, the draft seems to have been withdrawn, as the first chapters of what eventually became *The Face of Victory* did not reach Greenfield until the end of 1957.

the background of, I suppose, gales and rain.' Out of the blue, a letter arrived from Hélène. She was now married.

He wrote to Father Fuller.

When I last saw you I said that I felt that I ought to circulate more in the world, even if need be at the expense of some of my daily devotions. But on second thoughts I'm not very happy about that & withdraw it. England was getting a little more hectic than I could really manage, and on the next visit (spring) I think that I will try and keep a bit more in the background. Even here I get so many invitations to dinner, drinks etc. that if I once accept it becomes an avalanche. Another thing that I find an embarrassment is invitations to talk. I get them here by the 100s, particularly from Priests and the Missionaries. The subject is always: my work or my experiences, neither of which I feel the least inclination to speak about, and I refuse unless absolutely forced to accept. Have you any guidance to give me?[7]

Early in 1957 Cheshire went to Singapore. A cousin of his, Pam Hickley, lived there, and in the British business community and RAF presence lay the makings of a start-up network for a new home. Cheshire had long set his heart on working in China, and Singapore was a step closer to that. On a short visit in 1956 amid civil unrest – independence was approaching – Cheshire was given a British military escort to visit RAF Changi. Nearby he happened upon a roofless building, formerly the Jungle Survival School. A committee was now being formed, and fund-raising was in progress.

In London, the foundation had been told to quit Pitt's Head Mews. An ideal building stood near by in Market Mews, but the lease seemed unaffordable. Around the same time, Hovenden House, a mansion near Spalding in Lincolnshire, was offered to the foundation on preferential terms.[8] But this, likewise, seemed beyond their reach. Shortly afterwards Cheshire returned to Britain for his annual visit. Amid the usual punishing round of lectures, interviews, guest-of-honour appearances[9] and visits to homes existing[10] and projected,[11] he met John Handscomb, manager of the Bishopsgate branch of the Westminster Bank. Asking nothing, Cheshire told him about the foundation's recent work. In reply, Handscomb offered an overdraft of up to £18,000. Hovenden House was bought, and the foundation moved to No. 7 Market Mews, which would be its home for the next twenty-two years.

In Singapore, the building at Changi seemed out of reach – the UK government's asking-price was exorbitant – until the incoming Singapore government bought the site and gave it to the local committee on an indefinite lease for a nominal rent. RAF volunteers, Rotary and a flood of other helpers embarked on its repair and conversion. In parts of Asia the colour red symbolizes joy. The local committee organized a fund-raising ball, with a red feather as its emblem. A red feather would become the badge of the Cheshire Homes.

During the first two weeks of November Cheshire toured all but one of the Indian homes. On the 15th he wrote to Andrew Boyle. Some of the Indian trustees believed that a book written in simple language might be a good idea. As always, it should be for 'the ordinary man in the street' – nothing intellectual, and as little as possible about Cheshire himself: 'I must come in purely incidentally.'[12] Could he explore this idea with Cheshire's father, who would be coming out to India in December.

On this day he was in Jamshedpur, to which Larry Donnelly had driven him for a meeting to consider future policy of the Indian homes.[13] Donnelly had business in Durgapur, so Cheshire used the time to visit a local hospital. Here he met an industrial accident victim, a young man of perhaps twenty, whose eyes fixed him. He was paralysed from the waist down, and catheterized. The hospital could do no more for him, and he was about to be sent home.

Cheshire had come across comparable cases before. He knew that if the lad could be taken into a home like, say, Le Court, much could be done – he could be taught how to handle a wheelchair, given confidence to rejoin the world, find a job, marry. His was no lost cause, unless premature discharge led to infection. In his home village, where the water supply was unprotected and there would be no one to supervise sterilization of his catheter, the chances of that were high.

Cheshire told the doctor who guided him that there was an outside chance that he might find a home where the young man could stay awhile. When the doctor passed this news on, the expression in the boy's eyes changed 'in a way which I do not think I will ever forget'.

That evening, Cheshire pre-empted the agenda of the Jamshed-pur committee by asking if they would take the young man into their home. The committee said no, they wouldn't. Their home was for mentally handicapped children, it was not ready and it lacked the right facilities. This patient would be outside its remit.

'At that time,' Cheshire wrote later, 'I was more surprised than hurt or offended. It just seemed incomprehensible that a committee as well-intentioned and understanding as this one should be unwilling, at very little extra trouble to themselves, to save the life of a boy who had suffered an accident of a kind that was liable to happen any day in their own steelworks at Jamshedpur.' On the other hand, in following days he accepted that it wasn't so simple. Indeed, from the committee's point of view the decision was understandable. But that didn't help the boy, and Cheshire did everything he could think of to find a home that would accept him. After several weeks, he succeeded. When he went to look for the boy, he was dead.[14]

On 5 December Cheshire was in Calcutta, writing letters all day. In the evening, after supper, he wrote to Father Fuller, enclosing a second letter to Archbishop Grimshaw.

The continuous public engagements have not done me much good spiritually and I fear that I have gradually been taking a more and more materialistic view of things – or rather viewing everything from a human standpoint instead of in the light of the Faith. Instead of concerning myself with organizing and so on I would like to concentrate on some more practical and manual work and try to do it in a spiritual manner and with a right intention. Above all I would like to come in contact with the sick again and some of the dirty work. I don't feel I can go on any more exhorting others to carry on and saying how well they have been doing.[14a]

As usual, he asked for Father Fuller's views; then he turned to describing his experience of the Holy Land, where he had paused on his way back from England. There were 'too many English in Jerusalem to get any peace', but Bethlehem was 'truly extraordinary: I shall never forget it. Particularly down on the Shepherds' Field – and field of Ruth – in the moonlight, looking up at Bethlehem.'

In the bus he kept a picture of Lourdes, 'reminding me of that day the three of us went'.

Many things were now running together.

The boy. His pleading look had been 'at me, . . . something new was being asked of me', yet the organization he himself had brought into being had been unwilling to answer. How could he exercise some measure of independent action[15] in the face of trustees who, for the best of reasons, considered that his autonomy should be curbed?

Helpers. November's tour had kept him thinking. What might be needed was a new kind of organization, 'a teaching and training body aimed at providing overseas founders and helpers with the information and experience they need to start their own homes' – something to nurture pioneer spirit and transcend the interests of individual nations.

Himself. He had been saying to others that the focus must be on the homes, not himself, yet here he was also saying that he must have freedom to act as his conscience spoke, possibly against the wishes of the trustees, and to reject his appointed role in favour of a return to the grass roots. How was it possible to be simultaneously self-effacing and assertive?

The truth is that I was in an unhappy state of knowing that something had to be done, unable to identify what and where, and convinced that whatever it was must be done today and not put off until tomorrow.

About its importance and its general direction you are absolutely certain, but as to specifics – what, how or where? – you are lost. You leap first here, then there, only to find that you are running along a blind alley. Your friends and family consider that you have become disoriented, or perhaps even worse. They urge caution. They advise concentration. They suggest a holiday.[16]

Except that this time, they didn't. When Primrose and Geoffrey flew into Bombay on 13 December, they embarked on one of happiest times of all their lives. Travelling from place to place, Geoffrey was fêted by Indian lawyers who had read his books. They met Leonard's friends, visited the homes, immersed themselves in the spirit of the work. And all the while, they talked.

At about this stage in my inner questioning my mother and father came out to India to visit the homes, and helped more than anyone else to clarify my thinking and at least reduce the options that were open to me. By the end of their visit I knew that what I wanted to do was to start a home in India for which I would be responsible . . . with the blessing and approval of the trustees, but not part of the Indian foundation.

This home would specialize, but in one respect it would be absolutely open: no one in ultimate need would be turned away from it. It would be an international centre. Cheshire's first thought was to put it at Jamshedpur, where he told friends that he expected to be for most of the year. The idea transformed all other troubles, anxieties and yearnings into positives.

All, that is, save one. Larry Donnelly and the local committee did not like it. On or around 19 February, Cheshire packed his bag and left Jamshedpur. There had been a collision of wills, and he was going into a kind of voluntary exile at Dehra Dun.

His parents were back in England, exhausted after their tour, Primrose none too well, but both happy. They had become ardent supporters, and missed a son with whom they had just passed the longest uninterrupted time since his youth. On 22 February Primrose wrote: 'Darling Pots. I can't tell you how sad we are at leaving you, & alone to fight your battles with that bully Larry. I hate to think of all you've been through with him. I wonder if it is best that he should keep on. You'll never have any peace.'[17] After hearing from Geoffrey, the UK trustees gave approval to the idea of a Cheshire Homes International Unit which would provide machinery for the overseas expansion of the homes, be a channel of communication between the existing trusts and perpetuate the spirit and vitality of the work of the foundation.

In following days Cheshire's father wrote several times more about 'this Larry business', suspecting the friction to be a result of petty jealousy and finding his son's sudden removal to Dehra Dun 'all very surprising'. Geoffrey had reservations about Dehra Dun. The best spot for the international unit would surely be in the Lebanon, where the Gulbenkian Foundation was 'keen to spend money' and Margot Mason had recently been on reconnaissance. If the right place could be found they should set it up there, though not to the exclusion of India.[18] 'We miss you terribly and are constantly harking back to the happy times we had together.'

Cheshire told Father Fuller about the new plan.

This doesn't prevent me visiting the other foundations at regular intervals, but it does mean that I will circulate much less and devote myself to building up this home on a firm foundation. If we want to start up in other countries, many of which have written to us, we would bring the personnel out here for training and briefing, and then send them out.

As regards the location of this unit, our first idea was the Lebanon, but we finally decided on India, partly because we are already established and known, partly because of the great keenness of the Indian helpers, and even authorities, to have it here and partly because of the political instability of the Middle East.

He added a postscript which combined self-criticism with an anonymously worded account of the tensions with Larry Donnelly.

From a personal point of view I feel the need to get away from the social life involved in perpetually visiting the various homes and their helpers, and to settle down to a more natural and constructive routine. Without some routine I find that one's resolutions gradually disappear and one loses sight of the ultimate objective. Moreover there are so many countries that I would like to visit, and could, with a view to starting homes, that the only solution seems to be to stay put in one home and see that as far as possible it fulfils all its obligations and meets all demands made upon it in an adequate manner and for the right motive. Then perhaps the expansion will come about by itself in God's good time.

From time to time we come across someone who, having outstanding business ability, throws himself wholeheartedly into the work and then feels that he should be given a completely free hand to administer the homes and myself too. The terms usually are: either let me handle it and let me show you how you ought to work, or I'll resign. There is usually a good deal of sense in what he says, but also a good deal of materialism; i.e. we must build up the funds, etc. before thinking of more patients (even though they are in great need). This sort of situation always causes me a slightly uneasy conscience, because I wonder whether I oughtn't to let him have his way – both for the good of my soul and that of his – i.e. trusting that by submitting to him, he will gradually spiritualize his outlook. I don't want to resist Grace – if it is Grace that makes me uneasy – and I should be glad of any advice for the future.[19]

Cheshire's underlying hope was for a project which synthesized the spirit of Le Court's earliest days with the practical experience gained since. During March he told his parents that he was going to do this come what may. He had written to Larry 'saying that I consider he acted in an arbitrary and unconstitutional manner, that his policy of encouraging homes not to admit difficult patients is contrary to the principles of the foundation, and that if he wishes to continue as managing trustee he must agree to my setting up the IU where and how I like and must refer to me all patients which the homes fail to admit'.[20]

On 19 March Cheshire's father replied that he'd still prefer to see his son settled in the more salubrious climate of Beirut, but agreeing that the 'immediate duty is to keep your word and set up CHIU in India'. Geoffrey was less certain about a project behind the Iron Curtain, about which his son has suddenly started to talk. And 'who on earth is SUE?'[21]

21. Raphael

Sue Ryder was born on 3 July 1923 in the West Riding city of Leeds. Her father, Charles Foster Ryder, was a gentleman landowner with estates in Yorkshire and East Anglia, and until the early 1930s the family's residence alternated between homes at Scarcroft, near Leeds, and The Hall at Great Thurlow in Suffolk. Susan was the last-born in a large family. Charles Ryder's first wife died leaving five children. In 1911 he married Mabel Sims, the daughter of an Anglican clergyman, and in quick succession came three sons, John, Michael and Stephen. A fourth child died in infancy, followed six years later by Susan, who, being much the youngest, spent a good deal of time with her parents.

Mabel was a warm-hearted mother who read aloud to her children, wrote them stories, invented games, played songs for them to sing and encouraged their interests. Musical, outgoing and gifted with an infectious, often self-deprecating, sense of humour, she also possessed an empathetic instinct for the moods of others which enabled her to form close relationships on apparently scant acquaintance. A tireless worker for scores of causes, she was one of life's givers.

Susan's father looks on first sight to be more reticent, even a little austere. Conservative in dress, simple in tastes, small in appetite, by now in middle age, he nevertheless remained an intrepid horseman and ardent walker, who began his days with a cold bath and fitness exercises, passed long hours touring his farms, and whose remedy for a child's cold was to dispatch the sufferer for a walk. There was, however, a good deal more to Charles Ryder than exertion and agriculture. At Cambridge he had gained a degree in mathematics, and his deepest interests lay in history and reading.

Novels, plays and poetry lay about the house, and there were Saturday afternoon excursions to museums or bookshops which became so engrossing that the browsers were sometimes unaware that the staff were about to leave. Quiet and reserved, Charles Ryder yet presided over a house which was thronged with visitors. From the age of eight, when Susan joined her parents for meals, she heard table talk which ranged across the arts, architecture, social policy and the latest novels of Aldous Huxley or H. G. Wells. Charles Ryder took a keen interest in international affairs, championed the liberties of small nations, and recognized the evils of Nazism well ahead of His Majesty's Government or *The Times*.

Susan was educated at home until the age of nine, and then sent to prep school and on to Benenden. At school she was considered buoyant, a hard worker and energetic games player – a good all-rounder, yet not so good as to be beyond mischief and practical jokes. In the holidays there were large, attractive gardens in which to play, and beyond them horses to ride, woods to ramble, fields to camp in, hedgerows along which to go blackberrying, and in August everyone would lend a hand in harvest. There were shadows, too, like the black tie worn by her father since the day a son had been killed in France,* or the disconcerting figure who toured local roads on a bicycle, cursing all he passed. Shell-shocked, he had 'no other occupation than bicycling on through the four seasons of the year'.[1]

Far from confining their daughter to conventionally feminine pursuits, the Ryders encouraged her immersion in practical skills. Although the household was served by a large staff – all of whom were daily mustered for family prayers – the children were expected to learn their tasks, so that rare spare moments were occupied by washing, ironing or scrubbing floors. Outside, pocket money was earned by selling eggs from her hens, and from the age of eight she lent a hand in the dairy, scrubbing its flagstones, dispensing milk to villagers, butter-making, assisting the delivery of calves and building up a small Jersey herd of her own. In the carpenter's shop

* William Harold Ryder, Susan's youngest half-brother, had been in the Royal Flying Corps. He died near Arras, conceivably under the eyes of Geoffrey Cheshire, whose observation balloon was moored nearby.

she learned about woodworking. When riding the estate with her father and his architect she was taught about buildings. In the farmyard she was licensed to bargain with scrap dealers over prices for obsolete machinery. By her mid-teens Susan Ryder was becoming as well acquainted with a tractor's gearbox as with irregular French verbs. Her career, when she thought about it, seemed to lie in the direction of medicine.

Towards the end of her time at Benenden she was also becoming politicized, not in any party sense, but with a clear awareness that something was badly wrong in Europe and that drastic action would be needed to put it right. A Jewish escapee from Italy joined the school. Susan wrote to her mother:

> She's in my dormie, and tells me in graphic detail about the arrests, suspicions and the Fascists. Her family only just got out in time, thousands were left. Many won't realize or believe the fate which awaits them. Equally, the majority of people don't understand the full horror of what is happening and being planned. Afterwards they'll say it's exaggerated or could have been averted. If one didn't believe in God and justice in the next world, one might despair.[2]

The roots of this faith are worth digging for. They might be mistaken for what today is imagined as the conventional furniture of an upper-middle-class upbringing. Mabel Ryder was on the high Anglo-Catholic wing of the Church of England, inheriting a Tractarian concern for social reform and a sense of responsibility for doing something to bring it about. From Scarcroft she put in large effort on hospital and school boards to better appalling conditions in Leeds. Behind Thurlow's beauty lay poverty, which she confronted. Her expeditions into Leeds slums, or along Suffolk lanes bearing baskets of food, clothes or presents were not ritual gestures of charity, but drew from a sense of reciprocal responsibility – a belief that all, according to their means, had a care for all others as individuals. Tramps who arrived on the doorstep were not given money and sent away, but invited in for a meal, a bath, if necessary a bed. The servants were paid little, but were well fed and housed, treated with as much courtesy as would be due to anyone else and cared for by the family when they retired. During the Depression, when agricultural bankruptcies and evictions became endemic,

Charles Ryder did what he could to shield his tenants from hardship, giving help he could ill afford and enlarging his own debts in the process. The slump eventually hit him like everyone else, and in the early 1930s the family was forced to give up the house at Scarcroft and removed permanently to Great Thurlow.

The fact that the Ryders operated within a class system in which they were locally prominent did not predispose them to imagine that the system was in balance, or that extra beneficence on their part was necessary to keep it so. Rather, it meant that there was more for them to do. Overcrowding, poor public health and poverty were things to be attacked to enable the individuals who suffered them to live lives of their own choosing. Support could take less discernible forms. A conversation with a hedgekeeper might be as edifying as a chat with the lord lieutenant, and among the infirm it was often companionship and time which counted for most. Mabel Ryder, one suspects, would have got on well with J. F. Roxburgh, who believed that the task of an elite was not to defend a dimwitted establishment but to serve, and eventually to eliminate itself by creating the cultural and economic conditions in which everyone belonged to it. Meanwhile, everyone mattered.

This, then, is where Sue Ryder came from: a family which mingled affection with discipline, sense and sensibility, scholarship and practicality, and put selflessness before self. Her own account of those years is dotted with fleeting sensualities and remembered feelings – simple things like the taste of a hot cross bun on Good Friday, the smells of horses and beeswax, lilies in a humid conservatory, the pent-up expectancy of Advent, the excitement of the annual train journey to Suffolk, farmhands singing in air clear of other noise, the prickle of corn stalks, the fun of dancing. Another life now overwrote them.

Sixteen in September 1939 and too young to enlist in anything, she went to work as a nurse in a local hospital. In 1940, soon after her seventeenth birthday, she joined the First Aid Nursing Yeomanry, whence after initial training she was posted to an address in Baker Street, London. Beyond its doors, 'the familiar, ordinary world was left behind, and I never returned to it'.[3] It was the headquarters of the Special Operations Executive, the clandestine organization responsible for subversion and sabotage in occupied Europe.

Separation was at first physical. Social contact with anyone near SOE stations was forbidden, and leave was so heavily restricted that in the next five years she saw Thurlow for no more than a few days. She worked chiefly amongst Polish units, assisting in the sending forth of agents she seldom saw again. The aircrew who flew them might be there to smile at her the next morning, the following week, perhaps even the following month. But sooner or later they too usually vanished. In 1942 her father died. In 1943 she was sent abroad, first to north Africa, then into Italy, where the front-line killing was close enough to take friends around her. And at the war's end, she found herself in hell.

One of many stupefying aspects of the Nazi era is that the German language was calmly used to devise, run and diligently record its irreparable evils while the languages of the Allies were unable to accommodate the results. Facts were soon clear enough, but their sense lay beyond words. If what had happened in the heart of a single child at Theresienstadt or engulfed by quicklime in a Warsaw sewer was unimaginable, how could language conduct thought or feeling for six million? Perhaps it was frustration rather than vengeance which caused American soldiers who arrived at one camp to beat the guards' heads into slush, for nothing existed in the most polluted recesses of English to cope with what they found, or fit it into any known system of cause or effect. The liberators, it seemed to some, were themselves condemned to a kind of helplessness. As newsreels ran in Bournemouth, unfamiliar names like Sobivor, Treblinka and Mauthausen soaked into the language like stains, and supposedly healthy words like 'enlightenment' and 'culture' were found to be infected. Like some asteroid bowling in from space and knocking the earth into a new and juddering cycle, a mere twelve years of virtuoso, state-run depravity had barged into history and twisted time.[4]

In the aftermath was a twenty-two-year-old Susan Ryder, working first as a member of the Amis Volontaires Français amid devastated areas of Normandy, then in prisons and hospitals with other international relief units in central Europe, later still on her own.

'Aftermath' might imply that it was over, but not so. Many of those who had survived one barbarism now found that they had done so only to be delivered into another. Among the liberators was the Soviet Union, led by Uncle Joe, who compounded the impossibility by killing millions more following their enforced repatriation. In and around Germany itself, post-war chaos left thousands without shelter and famished, trekking to the wind's four quarters or stranded up to half a continent away from a home that might no longer exist. Bewildered survivors of concentration camps and forced labour were at large in the countryside, foraging for food and raiding farms. Some developed entrepreneurial skills in the black market. Girls sold themselves. A few hunted down their former persecutors and killed them. Even those who steered clear of crime often did so only by finding temporary asylum in drink, which being usually home-made and based on some industrial alcohol could leave them self-blinded, or worse.

The Allied forces of occupation dealt brusquely with dis-obedience. Fairly minor infractions could earn two or three years' imprisonment. For armed robbery or for being in the unlawful possession of firearms, sentences varying from ten to thirty years were passed. The normal penalty for a reprisal killing was death.

Among these people Sue Ryder worked. They were 'The Boys'. She drove thousands of miles a year to visit them, challenged their indictments, pored over legal texts and pleaded for them in courts, sat with them around their night-fires amid the rubble of shattered cities, brought them books and food, pestered Allied officers for the commutation of their sentences, found new homes for them in other parts of the world, smuggled victims from zone to zone and pleaded their cause to anyone who would listen. As time passed, aspects of the problem worsened. In 1948 the French, British and American authorities restored judicial and penal powers to the Germans. 'Thus, the Boys were handed back, as far as they were concerned, to their old enemies, and it seemed that the Allies had deserted them.'[5]

For each Boy Sue Ryder adopted, she kept a record. By 1950 there were 1,400 of them. For as long as they remained in prison she continued to visit them, in the process not infrequently finding herself being asked to calm prisons on the point of insurrection, very frequently withstanding the boorishness or threats of German officials and former members of the SS, and once or twice herself being accused of espionage. Strangely, the only things which really alarmed her during these years were guard dogs. Alsatians made her nervous. In 1952 she established the first home for the Boys, in Bad Neuheim, replaced a little later – with help from a small group of German supporters – by another at Grossburgwedel. Other homes and projects followed. This sketches but a little of her work, or the range of those it touched.

Small wonder, therefore, that on the cold, grey February day when she had walked into the room adjoining Ampthill's kitchen, Leonard Cheshire thought she looked a little tired.

By now Sue Ryder was assisted by volunteers scattered across England, with others in Germany. Mabel Ryder played no small part, supplying food and money, and raising support. As the labour grew, the time came to give it more explicit shape. With the help of a small legacy, 'credit from the bank and much optimism', in 1953 a charitable foundation was formed. The body needed a base. After failing to find one anywhere else, in 1953 Sue Ryder bought the house in Cavendish to which her mother had moved in 1946, co-locating the foundation's headquarters and a home.[6]

Exactly where, how and when Sue Ryder and Leonard Cheshire began to think seriously about unifying their efforts is unclear. The high-pitched note of surprise in Geoffrey Cheshire's letter early in 1958 shows that until then Cheshire's parents had been unaware of her, although the plans which tumbled out in following weeks attest to lengthy gestation.

Since their first meeting in 1955, the two had kept in touch, Cheshire visiting Cavendish, Sue Ryder taking carloads of survivors to help at Staunton Harold. Although their two charities differed in scope, there were concordances. Both had begun as spontaneous individual responses to immediate need, both were concerned with the relief of suffering, each laid paramount emphasis upon personal, voluntary sacrifice and each had been fuelled by a Christian impulse.

During 1957 Sue Ryder visited India. It was on this journey, touring the country in the heat with Cheshire by bus and train that they really got to know each other. Until now Cheshire had been an emotional solitary. Since the separation from Constance there had been no intimate friendships other than with Hélène, who had discovered that she did not really know him. In matters of instinctive feeling he was an underground river. Even his mother did not know where it flowed. As for Sue Ryder, her later adolescence and twenties had been committed to the war and to countering its suffering. There had been a number of intense, wartime platonic friendships, but almost all of those with whom they formed had died or disappeared.

As individuals, therefore, Sue Ryder and Leonard Cheshire had hardly counted to themselves, until now, when the work which brought them into coalition introduced them to each other as people. The unprecedented closeness allowed each to confide in the other, a new blessing, and by March 1958 the keel-blocks of a number of projects had been laid down. While Geoffrey Cheshire puzzled over a reference to someone called Sue, and Primrose looked forward to the end of Lent, because 'I know full well you are "doing without" too much',[7] the first of them stood poised atop the Ryder–Cheshire slipway. In April Sue Ryder travelled to Poland to see if permission could be found for a new series of homes for the incurably sick.

Geoffrey voiced reservations. He hated opposing anything that Leonard was trying to do, but it appeared to him that the kind of scheme which the Polish government might accept would not be a Cheshire Home 'as we understand it', but 'a large unwieldy, impersonal institution'. Lady St Levan was yet more strongly opposed, believing that they were being 'used as a cat's-paw'. Geoffrey agreed that 'something should be done' behind the Iron Curtain, but considered that a 'quite separate organization' should be formed to do it.

As Sue Ryder appeared on the scene, Phil Loneragan left it. After four years of devoted work she had returned to Australia, breaking her journey in Singapore to do what she could (work had faltered, there were personality clashes) and missing her own welcome party in result. 'I was told that I would have enjoyed it, had I been there.' A cable and letter from Cheshire awaited her, for which she thanked him, 'and especially the nice things they contained which I don't deserve at all, but which gave me a very nice warm feeling just the same'.[8]

Cheshire replied happily. Singapore was 'coming out right' since the appearance on the scene of Alan Green, 'ex-RAF, now in business'. As for Dehra Dun, the nucleus of the international centre was being set up as an adjunct of the existing home at 16 Pritnam Road, where student helpers and patients were labouring hard. 'We are building a sluice and bathroom upstairs . . . putting in water-borne sanitation throughout the house . . . Practically all the patients do something, such as scraping off old paint, peeling the vegetables, digging soak pits, sifting rubble for the builders and so on'. There had been no recent news from Jamshedpur; although he had heard that Lesley Reardon – an Australian nurse who had become the highly effective and well-liked head of the home – was not too well.[9]

Cheshire was none too well either, having fallen victim to a serious attack of dysentery. Loneragan wrote to cheer him up.[10] As usual the letter was chatty. Unusually, there was a note of sadness. After four years working with Cheshire, she no longer seemed to fit in anywhere else. Her letter crossed with another from Cheshire, breathless with news about headway. There was also a tragedy. Lesley Reardon had died from tubercular meningitis.

Cheshire's illness lingered, and towards the end of June he returned to London for treatment at the School of Tropical Medicine. However unwell he felt, his spirits soared. The international centre had just received an endorsement.

A few years ago, Group Captain Leonard Cheshire came to see me in Delhi. I had heard of him previously and all the fine work he had done for the relief of suffering. I was happy to meet him. Since then he has expanded his work in India and now intends to make Dehra Dun the international headquarters of the Cheshire Homes. I am very glad to learn of this and I wish him every success.

The Cheshire Homes have set an example of unostentatious but effective work for the relief of suffering without much fuss, advertisement or expense. They are a remarkable example of what can be done by earnestness and enthusiasm. Most of us are apt to think nowadays of big schemes of hospitals, medical services and the like, which cost a great deal and tend to lose the personal touch. The big schemes may still be necessary for governments to undertake. But the type of work that Group Captain Cheshire has been doing with such great success seems to me essentially of even greater importance than these big schemes. Of course the two are not in conflict and help each other. He has shown how limited resources can be made to go a long way. Even more so, he has given an example of the human approach.

I would like to express my admiration for the work he is doing and, more especially, the spirit in which this is undertaken. He deserves every help.

Jawaharlal Nehru

22 June 1958

Unexpectedly finding himself back at Market Mews, Cheshire threw himself into fund-raising. Of late he had become more uncompromising in business matters, dismissing requests from newspaper editors unless they upped their fees – 'there is immense suffering out here'[11] – and embarking on Frances Jeram-like negotiations for the abatement of municipal charges and taxes. Sue Ryder may have helped to reinforce his self-denial. At any rate, for the new work at Pritnam Road, which initially centred upon a group of children who were too handicapped to fit in elsewhere, he went to extraordinary lengths to keep down costs. 'He would think twice before taking a bus to the city. I am ashamed to say that in all my years in India I have never ridden in a bus in a town, and I know very few Englishmen or women who have either.'[12]

It may have been the bus travel which sealed Nehru's decision to throw his name and influence behind the work. Sir Alec Guinness describes an episode related to him by the film director David Lean.

Nehru had invited him and Cheshire to tea at Government House. At the time, Cheshire was desperate to get hold of a poor piece of land in northern India on which to build one of his homes, but foreigners were forbidden to buy or own land. All his requests were formally dismissed. David said that during tea Cheshire was consumed with shyness and never spoke a word, although he was very aware he was in the presence of the one man in the world who could help him. When it was time for them to leave Nehru asked Cheshire how he was getting back to his hotel. Speaking for the first time he said he would take a bus or tram and then walk. Nehru ordered his own car, saw Cheshire into it (an almost unheard of courtesy) and stood waving until the car was out of sight. Then, with tears in his eyes, he turned to an aide and said, 'That is the greatest man I have met since Gandhi. Give him the land he wants.'*[13]

With Sue Ryder, he was no longer thinking of the international unit as a single home, but as a kind of colony, a constellation of projects, with a hospital as part of it. They would name it after Raphael, the archangel of healing.

Loneragan wrote dispiritedly from Sydney. She had been auditioned for a job in television, thus far without result.

. . . my whole life seems very unsatisfactory at the moment. I have gradually realized that I don't really fit in anywhere. I can't go on leading the life of lunches, bridge parties, cocktails and the like, all my friends are married with their own homes and families, and I just don't seem to be able to settle down to anything . . .

I have finally decided to ask advice from a Passionist father, who is very good in helping mixed up people like me who feel that they might have a vocation, but are too muddled and confused to think it out for themselves. So please pray very hard for me will you, I must get myself straightened out and find out what is God's will for me.

Take care of yourself [will write to your mother and father]. Don't forget the prayers.[14]

In late summer Cheshire snatched a few days with Sue Ryder in Poland, and again in Germany during September. Their shared hopes deepened.

He wrote a long, almost passionate letter to Alan Green in Singapore. Green was about to visit China, and China, Cheshire told him, 'is a place on which I have long set my heart'.[15]

In November he returned to India, to be greeted by a welcome party and speeches on the doorstep of 16 Pritnam Road. They had missed him. He flew on to Singapore, where a flurry of letters from Sue Ryder reached him. He replied on the instant.

---

* The incident is chronologically problematic. According to Cheshire he first met David Lean late in 1958 or early in 1959, whereas Lean's meeting with Nehru took place earlier. That Nehru had already met Cheshire is attested in his testimonial of 22 June 1958.

Phew! What a welcome surprise – a letter from you; the first since Nov. 11th. I'd almost given up hope of seeing your handwriting again. Anyway there it was waiting on my desk at Singapore this morning; still is morning. Dec 2, 3 4th from Warsaw. And all the good news of progress too. Most exciting and encouraging; I'm so pleased, and you certainly sound on top of it all in spite of the rushing about. I wasn't expecting a second home quite so soon . . .[16]

The letter was entirely about projects, but in its rush there was new urgency.

Of projects, there were at least three. One was that Raphael should also become home for a community of displaced Poles. Cheshire was in correspondence with Indira Gandhi about the possibility of arranging entry for up to 250. 'Raphael would then become a very large settlement, with Indian patients as well and helpers from all over the world. The Poles would come to contribute their spirit and example, in addition to any practical help they could give. We would shame the Germans into paying their fares and compensation.'

Compensation was the subject of a second project. In 1958 there were still some 200,000 stateless persons living in Germany, all of whom had been uprooted during the war and who for various reasons were unable to return to their home countries. They lived in camps and barracks without rights of nationality. Debarred from work other than labouring, lonely, frustrated and often unwell,* to all intents and purposes they underwent continuing punishment for the offence of having already been ill-treated. Sue Ryder had been doing what she could to uphold their cause, driving about in a battered Austin A35, sometimes covering upwards of a thousand miles in a week, to visit hospitals, camps and barracks which housed them. Alongside this ran a worldwide campaign to obtain compensation for the stateless victims of Nazi persecution, which just then was moving into high gear, with the imminent lobbying of British and Indian churchmen and media about what was, in truth, an international scandal. When the Foreign Office got wind of this plan Cheshire was urged to drop it, for fear of its effects on Anglo-German relations.[17]

---

* Many suffered from disability or illness, a result of earlier ill-treatment and conditions in concentration camps.

The third project concerned the configuration of Raphael itself. A site was in view, some thirty acres of virgin forest and scrub beside the Rispana river, beyond Dehra Dun's boundary. But the shape of the enterprise would be influenced by whether or not the Poles joined it. 'Actually I would still like you to choose the site for them with me – or rather confirm it – because it is fairly irrevocable. It either means a huge Raphael of 600 patients plus subsidiary homes round about (up to ten miles), or putting the Poles completely on their own – which I don't really like so much.'[18] Sue Ryder would be joining him in January. He poured his diary into the letter to clarify dates.

At Christmas, Cheshire sent news of the work to Phil Loneragan. He had called at the cathedral and said a prayer for her.

In September Cheshire had announced plans to open two homes for the incurably ill in Poland, which would run under a new Ryder–Cheshire Foundation[19] – although in a characteristic confusion it was at first unclear whether this was to result from a merger between the two existing foundations, or a separate body standing alongside both. Merger had certainly been under discussion, and a statement had announced that 'an amalgamation' had been made between the two bodies.[20] But this was premature, and early in 1959 Geoffrey Cheshire told his son that he foresaw problems. When Sue reached Dehra Dun, could he and she put their heads together to 'knock out some new plan'?[21]

They had already put their heads together. The Ryder–Cheshire Foundation was to be an entirely new body. Indeed, it already existed. Cheshire said later:

We would have been happier still if our respective foundations . . . had been able to merge. But they had each been in existence too long, each with their specific terms of reference and their own separate body of supporters, to make that possible . . . Only at Dehra Dun, and later in one or two other projects, were we to have the happiness and challenge of working together in full harness.[22]

And on to Dehra Dun Sue Ryder now came.

A little beforehand – probably a few days, it is hard to pinpoint – Cheshire found a new confidant. David Lean, the director of *Brief Encounter*, *Oliver Twist* and *The Bridge over the River Kwai*, had earlier been in India with scriptwriter Emeric Pressburger to explore prospects for a film about the life of Mahatma Gandhi. Lean's mistress had a son at Dun school, and Lean drove her up from Delhi to visit him. Hearing that Cheshire was at work somewhere outside the city, Lean went to find him. Over thirty years later, Cheshire remembered the day.

We walked across the dry river to this thirty-acre jungle site – no water, no electricity – and I told him I had plans for a little place for leprosy patients, the mentally retarded and others. He looked around and said, 'Hmm . . . I just wouldn't have the faintest idea how to begin.' I said, 'But David, I wouldn't have the faintest idea how to begin a film.' He drove me down to Delhi in his Rolls-Royce and he transported the tents and tent poles back to Dehra Dun.[23]

So began a friendship.

The lepers were one of Raphael's shaping influences.

I am not quite sure how or by whom I was first told of the Dip, for one could well live in Dehra Dun half a lifetime and not really know that it existed. It was an unsavoury place on the south-western edge of the town that must once upon a time have been a largish quarry. An open drain ran through the middle of it and at the far end was a city refuse dump . . . From the road itself the Dip was out of sight. Indeed one would have to walk up to its edge and peer into it before realizing that it contained a cluster of little mud houses with beaten-out milk-powder tins for roofing, and that a hundred or more people actually lived in them.[24]

Leprosy was rife in the hills, and a leprosarium in the city attracted victims in hope of cure. The majority, however, were not cured and, 'with little prospect of being received back into their villages, they remained in Dehra Dun'.

I shall never forget my first impression of this little community, barricaded, as it were, from the rest of the town and yet in essence just another section of the city itself, whose inhabitants were owed the same rights and privileges as everybody else . . . the sheer poverty of the tiny houses in which they lived was not very different from other shanty towns I had seen . . . But somehow the combination of such a degree of poverty with the fact of being ostracized had the effect of creating a common solidarity. Certainly I was not prepared for the extraordinary and spontaneous warmth of their welcome . . .

From out of nowhere two or three simple garlands of marigolds were produced. Someone brought out the best available chair, dusted it with a handkerchief and in the process gave it a sharp but discreet knock, presumably to evict any bugs that might have settled into its joints. When this process was over I was asked to sit down, and a simple ceremony followed, with appropriate but short speeches on both sides.[25]

The dwellers in the Dip set the seal on Cheshire's determination to colonize the land beyond the Rispana Rao. There was no water, no electricity and no accommodation except the tents. But they would do it. 'I hope,' said Cheshire, 'that it will become a sort of international island.'

A team gathered. Some members were old hands, like Barty from Staunton Harold, and Chippy and his wife from Singapore. Others were new. One was Ava Dhar, a serene, shy, reserved lady, the widow of an Indian civil servant, who offered her services as secretary-administrator. Graceful herself, and compassionate, she also brought beauty to her surroundings. Early risers would see her returning with wild flowers to decorate the office.

Another newcomer was Laurence Shirley, a young builder who volunteered to come out from England.

The Raphael hospital project started alright; we felled trees and cleared the site to start building. Marked out the position of the various wards and buildings . . . Then things started to slow. There was difficulty in obtaining construction drawings from the design engineers in England . . . A worse problem was lack of funds. For a time this brought the work to a halt.

It was decided to put the building materials on site to good use . . . a number of small houses were put up to accommodate lepers who were outcasts and living on the city rubbish dump. The most difficult and distressing thing was to choose just two or three people at a time out of many to live in the houses we had built. People would hang on to us and our legs asking to be taken in. But we only had enough materials and money to build no more than six simple little houses.[26]

Discontinuous funding was a problem. But it was a start. As more help arrived, they built more houses.

In Singapore, Cheshire had acquired a second-hand ambulance which had been shipped back to Calcutta, reconditioned by the

Indian Army and christened Ezekiel. With Ezekiel, he met Sue Ryder. Taking it in turns to drive, they covered several thousand miles to Jamshedpur, Burnpur, Allahabad, Lucknow, Agra, Delhi and finally Dehra Dun.[27]

Cheshire's account book for those days survives. Its stark list of simple things (breakfast – 1:75 rupees; a telegram – 6:40 rupees; a bus fare – 7:80 rupees) confirms how little he spent on himself, and how far and often he travelled. His journeying recalls John Wesley. Before Sue Ryder's arrival in late January, he had traversed the subcontinent several times since New Year's Day.

Somewhere along the way, they became engaged. They had been talking about this possibility for a good while, and much agonizing preceded it. Sue Ryder explains:

The work had meant my life, and nothing I felt should or could change this. How in the future could one combine both marriage and work? . . . Moreover, even in normal circumstances, marriage inevitably brings great responsibilities – I had always felt that it was a gamble. Furthermore, the implications are so serious that it is wiser to remain single and work than to run the risk of an unhappy marriage. Comparatively few people prepare themselves for or are equal to sharing literally everything.[28]

But they decided to do it. Early in February they wrote to tell friends, supporters and helpers, and to ask their blessings. A little sadly, the news leaked into the *Daily Express* before all the letters arrived. Another tabloid piled in with the vapid headline 'Cheshire VC – My Romance Secrets. He plans £14,000 humanitarian empire with his bride.'[29]

Primrose was elated. 'I'm so *v. v.* glad that you have found happiness in love is *the* great thing.'[30] Geoffrey thought so too.

Dearest Pots, this is wonderful news and I'm simply delighted and am already looking forward to welcoming you both in May, which is not too far off now. You are both eminently suited to each other, having the same interests and ideals, so that it cannot be one of those marriages which dies of starvation. The only thing is that the bad Sue must not communicate to you her bad ideas about sleep and grub, otherwise we shall have you back in Midhurst.

Geoffrey offered to 'do the job of disclosing the news' but asked for briefing about 'reconciling your remarriage with the Catholic views on divorce. That flummoxes me, unless perhaps it is that your marriage to the divorced Constance was no marriage in Catholic eyes. I've no doubt you must have discussed the matter with some bishop.' (Which he had: the Church had never recognized his first marriage, because Constance was divorced with a husband still living.) 'So, dear Pots, it's a vast joy to realize that you won't have a lonely life, which is what I feared.'[31]

Frances Jeram said, 'It completed him, in a way.'[32]

Hélène was pleased too – she 'felt that Leonard needed a wife' – although Cheshire asked a relative to write to her with the news on his behalf.

Cheshire wrote to Keith Astbury, 'Aspro', his 617 bomb-aimer, announcing the 'recent plunge'. Astbury was now back in Australia, to which Cheshire and Sue Ryder planned to come soon after their wedding to enlist help for their work, 'especially Sue's in Poland, where there is a desperate need and she has been asked for 50 homes, but also to see you and your family while we are all still ticking over, thank God. I'm not after a gay time or anything like that – except in spirit of course. Wouldn't be much fun walking about with long faces!' The letter bubbled. 'Can hardly believe that I'll really be seeing you.'[33]

The day before the wedding, Cheshire posted the manuscript of *The Face of Victory* to George Greenfield. 'At long last, here is the manuscript finished. I have had to rewrite it practically from the beginning, and feel that it is now more as I would like it.' Any money from the serialization rights would 'go to building the first children's home at Raphael, so please get as much as possible and as quickly as possible. The building is halfway up and I need £1,700 to pay for it. Not very much for twenty-eight children.'[34]

Cardinal Valeria Gracias married them on 5 April in a private chapel in Bombay's Catholic cathedral before a handful of close friends. Afterwards they went out to Bethlehem House, and then boarded a train for the thirty-six-hour journey to Raphael, where they were garlanded and there was further gentle celebration. Before leaving for Australia they sought a few days' solitude at a bungalow in the hills. Obstructed by a landslide, they camped instead in a corrugated iron hut[35] near the river Jamna, 'cooking over a campfire and drawing water from the river, seeing the everyday life of India continuing in the distance . . . hearing at night the beat of drums in the neighbouring village'.[36] On the second day an outing of three hundred children arrived, followed by an Indian family who joined them in the hut.

Together, before the wedding, they had composed a prayer.

Thou, O My God,
Who art infinite love,
Yet who hast called us to be perfect
Even as Thou art perfect,
Who so loved the world
That Thou hast given us Thine only begotten son,
And hast thereby given us Thine all, Thine everything.
Who emptied Thyself of Thy Glory,
And was made obedient unto death,
Even the death of the Cross
For us.
To Thee
We offer our all, our everything
To be consumed in the unquenchable fire of Thy love.
We desire to love Thee even as Thy own Mother loved Thee
To be generous as Thou Thyself was generous,
To give our all to Thee even as Thou hast given Thine to us.
Thou hast called us, O Lord, and we have found Thee,
In the sick, the unwanted and the dying,
And there we will serve Thee,
Unto death.

And so it was.

PART EIGHT: CHOSEN VESSEL, 1959–1992

22. Flames from a Candle

In a sense, the story is told.

Like new flames lit from the single taper of Arthur Dykes's life, the movement spread. When Cheshire left for India in 1955 there were six homes. In 1959, the year of his marriage, the figure had risen to fifteen in the United Kingdom and eight abroad, and Raphael. By the last year of his life there were 270 homes in forty-nine countries, and Raphael is what they hoped it would become. Raphael sparkles. There are children there, rescued from all kinds of sadnesses, who race about, and play, and their laughter is hope.

Other projects followed. They must be reckoned not simply in terms of numbers, but also in range and in awareness. The foundations broadened their work to tackle other forms of need and exclusion in new ways, while the climate of attitudes in which they pioneer has itself changed. All three foundations have played their part in the continuing emancipation of the disabled, countering the ignorance and indifference which not so long ago tolerated denial of their civil rights and disallowed their individuality.[1] Disappearing, too, is the notion that addressing disability is simply a matter of victims being cared for by the well-intended fit. In *The Hidden World*, a slender book of fathomless simplicity which Cheshire published in 1981, we are shown that it is often the other way round.

In pointing to landmarks such as the 1975 UN Declaration of Rights of Disabled Persons, the 1981 International Year of the Disabled Person, the Brandt Report[2] and successive domestic legislation – upon much of which Cheshire had some effect – it is not suggested that all wrongs have been righted. Far more remains to be accomplished than has yet been done. The propensities for different parts of the world to slide into autolytic barbarism, for new diseases to appear like jack-in-the-boxes, and for old ones, supposedly vanquished, to climb back out of the oblivion to which antibiotics were thought to have banished them, for poisoning the planet and laying waste its resources, are all about us. But in places it is possible to point to the bettering of a scene which, when Cheshire first came upon it in 1948, was tragically backward. As he often told us, all journeys begin with a first step. If there are times when it seems that history, like polar ice, is afloat on currents which flow contrary to progress, we can nevertheless see that Leonard Cheshire and Sue Ryder have together helped humanity forward for a measurable distance. There are few figures in history of which this can be said.

And yet, although it is only half over, in a sense the story is told. Much followed, but by 1959 the main elements were in place. After a decade of physical, intellectual and spiritual struggle, false starts, bruising collisions and rueful diversions, a theory of human action had taken final shape in Cheshire's mind and heart. By the time of his marriage – and perhaps it is no coincidence that it *was* around the time of his marriage – the seeds of everything else, like the thematic material for a symphony, were all there. From now on the ideas ripen, but they do not fundamentally change. His remaining work was to help their development.

How did the work spread?[3] Initially it travelled through Cheshire's personal example and influence. We have seen the process accelerating. Le Court took two or three years – in some respects, four or five – to find itself. By the time we reach Singapore, eight years later, there is a method, a body of experience. Singapore also marked the boundary between the founding phase, when Cheshire's presence was necessary to set things going, and the later period when others took over. One of the most moving aspects of the foundation's expansion is the almost apostolic process whereby a succession of others stepped forward to carry it on. Some, like Margot Mason, who took the work into the Middle East and west Africa, and Wilfrid Russell, were already involved. Others, like Pamela Farrell, who pioneered in Canada, joined later. Those stories would be worth telling in full.

A second factor was what might be called the foundation myth: 'myth' used here in the sense of an embodiment of underlying realities. By some instinct, in the early 1950s Cheshire knew that a book had to be written about what had happened. To be on the safe side he made it two, Braddon's journalistic, Boyle's more earnest, and then added a third by writing *The Face of Victory* himself. All three cover broadly the same ground, albeit in different ways, like a cross-ploughed field. In later books like *The Hidden World* and *The Light of Many Suns* he travelled some of the ground again. Cheshire was near-incapable of writing in the abstract, finding it necessary to explore spirituality and theory in terms of concrete experience. Even today, the story of Arthur Dykes is told in foundation literature, and on my own first visit to Le Court it was the spirit of what had happened at the beginning that was regarded as the propellant for all that had happened since.

To an extent, Cheshire himself has become a mythological figure, all the more powerful for the fact that the narrative is true. It is thus odd that the film was never made. There have been scores of films and TV programmes about him, but the biopic which might stand alongside *Gandhi* or *Reach for the Sky* remains unvisualized. On the other hand, film is a medium of limited span. There cannot be many scenes in a two-hour script. Perhaps there is too much to tell.

In the background, there were practical assets. In Britain and across the Commonwealth, Cheshire's war record gave the work a platform and public prominence. Because of his reputation in war, people were prepared to listen to what he had to say about peace, just as the secularity of his youth strengthened his advocacy of Catholicism. Later, as younger generations stepped forward, these assets lessened. Today, it is not difficult to find a young person who has never heard of Leonard Cheshire. In the 1950s and 1960s it would have been virtually impossible.

Yet, more practically, there were several overlapping networks which he cultivated and, with gentle diffidence, cheerfully exploited. One was provided by the armed services, particularly the RAF, which in the 1950s and decolonizing 1960s was more far-flung than it is today. Many senior officers knew Cheshire personally, and any who didn't knew him by repute. Senior airmen and soldiers were recruited as trustees or chairmen, or enlisted to spearhead projects when they retired, while local commanders willingly lent equipment and men, advised on sites, engineered introductions and provided spare seats in aircraft travelling the globe. So large was his reputation that similar help was offered by the forces of many other countries.

Then there was the diplomatic service. Britain's ambassadors and the staffs of High Commissions could provide briefing on internal affairs, special sensitivities, personalities, introductions to key figures, occasionally even warnings, as in the case of a fund-raiser for a home in Ireland who was suspected of gun-running. Whether or not to seek such help was a matter of judgement. 'My general policy is not to, because I don't want to be a nuisance. On the other hand, sometimes you need advice or feel it's right and proper to put them in the picture.'[4] At least three homes were started on the initiative of local ambassadors, and others helped in their retirement.[5]

Cheshire toured annually and widely, and, being generally *persona grata*, after the award of the Order of Merit universally so, he was quite often invited to stay at an embassy, absorbing insights in the process. He discovered other cultural traits by himself. In Japan, for instance, 'you get very good marks for persistence'.[6] In China, 'If you are old, that gives you a stronger position; they respect age. There was a lot of protocol, a lot of VIP treatment. You've got to observe the protocol and respond in a dignified way.'[7] The protocol included three gargantuan banquets, each of twenty courses, with speeches between each, to which Cheshire – in later life accustomed to the simplest food and little of it – did not find it easy to do justice. In Moscow 'I was . . . told by Russians that somebody in a wheelchair in the street would be treated with hostility. They might even say, "What have you done to get that disability?" So that was the first thing, the very great need.'[8]

Creative as it generally was, Cheshire's relationship with the Foreign Office was not always straightforward. There were some issues, like the plight of post-war stateless people, upon which his determination to speak made him unpopular. There were also times when his refusal to allow the foundation to be drawn into political antagonisms which themselves turned on issues of human justice earned unpopularity at home. His dislike of apartheid was intense, but that did not mean that all who enforced it were incapable of all good, and when it came to the question of working in South Africa or not, the considered answer was 'obviously yes', because:

we are solely concerned with helping disabled people towards greater freedom and independence. The fact that there's an unjust or repressive regime at the top . . . cannot be a reason for not helping the disabled person living under that regime. In fact, in a certain way, there's all the more reason to help them, because, if the regime is oppressive, then their condition is likely to be even worse than in a freer society . . .[9]

Cheshire's humane impartiality, his growing stature as a kind of one-man United Nations, enabled him to treat directly with heads of state and sometimes overcome barriers as phantoms walk through walls. His contact with Nehru has been mentioned. There were similar encounters, as for example with Julius Nyerere of Tanzania. Or Deng Pufang:

the son of Deng Xiaoping, the Chinese leader – a controversial figure now. But Deng Pufang . . . was in a wheelchair. He had opposed the Cultural Revolution as an undergraduate . . . and he was tortured and thrown out of a window. I had met him three times before and we had been very polite . . . This time, I came into the reception room, with the television cameras and glaring lights and there was Deng Pufang in his chair looking at me, and he had such a lovely welcoming look and warmth and happiness in his eyes because the project had come about . . . before I knew what was happening, we were embracing each other.[10]

China was Cheshire's Everest. On this visit in 1990 to the opening of its first home, alongside the banquets and inspirational dancing by disabled people, he passed long silence, in a twilit room.

Although in Israel and elsewhere he was often walking upon political eggshells, only once, it seems, was Cheshire's impartiality put at real risk. This was over Biafra, the name that the eastern region of the Nigerian Federation gave itself when it seceded from Nigeria in 1967. A tragic civil war followed, in which one Cheshire

Home was engulfed by fighting and another was bombed. Cheshire was indifferent to Nigerian politics, but most concerned for the safety of those in the homes. Inquiries brought him into contact with members of Biafra's judiciary – some of whom were already connected with the homes – and made him a *de facto* channel for Anglo-Biafran contact. As the UK government had little or no access to Col. Ojukwu, the Biafran leader, Cheshire was sounded out by the Foreign Office as a possible go-between.

What followed might have been invented by John Le Carré. It involved a hazardous flight into Biafra (the aircraft landed on a road, in the dark, with approach lights available for only twenty seconds), and an attempt at synchronized diplomacy in Lagos, where it was intended that Harold Wilson should broker a peace settlement on the basis of information about the Biafran position received from Cheshire. Tragically, while Cheshire's part of the mission succeeded, the UK's follow-through diplomacy did not. The ramifications ran on for months. The story went live in the British media, Cheshire appeared on television, at one point refuting disingenuous explanations given by the government, and one of Ojukwu's emissaries in Europe turned out to have been acting in bad faith. It was a war story, a spy story, a humanitarian story, a story of political confusion and betrayal rolled into one. Happily, those in the homes were safe, but having seen the catastrophic conditions inside Biafra for himself – the country was under siege – Cheshire eventually called for an international humanitarian airlift. This attracted widespread support and was considered by some to have brought world opinion to a head. The killing stopped soon afterwards, although Cheshire's general sense of the affair was that he had failed.

Further networks were provided by the Church and the law. Across the world ran ready-made channels along which new initiatives could flow and new friends be found. Cheshire used religious communities, seminaries, the episcopate and pastoral structures as stepping stones from one place or project to another, and as sources of guidance. As for the law, between them, Alfred Denning, the foundation's first chairman, and Cheshire's father provided a far-flung web of suitable connections. Members of judiciaries everywhere either knew of Professor Cheshire because of his books or had actually been taught by him. Quite a few pupils went on to become public figures and politicians, while in different parts of Britain it was often someone with a legal background who was instrumental in taking an early step.

All these assets, however, would have stood for nothing in the absence of an underlying dynamic – Cheshire considered it a principle – of local involvement. Ultimately, homes were founded and run not because of Cheshire's connections or anyone else's, but because local people believed in them, understood the particular needs of their communities, raised the funds and did the work.

Local sovereignty also made changing demands. As the homes multiplied, regular direct contact between them and Cheshire became less and less easy to sustain. Already by 1960 the UK structure had outgrown the mechanisms which had first been used to make it work, and as the number of homes increased so did the number of local committee members and residents who expected a voice in the foundation's affairs. For the same reason, the penalties of inadequate communication increased as well.[11]

In the later 1950s and early 1960s expansion led to calls for membership of the foundation to be extended to elected representatives – a proposal resisted by Cheshire on the grounds that it would diminish the role of the trustee body. Nevertheless, there was obviously a case for strengthening the relationship between individual homes and the centre. A model constitution was drawn up to bring each home into formal relation with the foundation, trustees were assigned as links with particular homes, regional committees were established and alongside Family Days and the Spring Conference other types of representative meeting were introduced.[12] National topic-specific advisory committees were formed to counsel the trustee body. Internationally, cognate steps were taken. For Cheshire, this added up to a lot of work. As time passed he withdrew from all but the most important meetings, but with so much in progress a large load remained.

A widely spread organization which combines national accountability with local responsibility contains propensities for stress. Unless communication is continuously first-rate, such structures can breed grouses, feuds, charges that one part of the system does not understand another, suppositions of high-handedness, and misunderstandings. Within devolved bodies there are nearly always one or two constituent parts which regard it as their proper business to annoy the centre, while those at the centre often underestimate needs at the grass roots. With all such problems, and more, the foundation, and Cheshire, had to contend. A debit side of Cheshire's celebrity was that when strikes, allegations of abuse or disciplinary issues arose in particular homes, they attracted disproportionate media attention because of who he was.[13]

By the early 1970s, the frequency of new starts had been so great that the foundation awoke to the fact that a number of homes were simultaneously in need of repair – that in the first flush of founding, they had overlooked some of the basics of continuation. The solution was to commission a survey of all home fabrics, and thereafter to build cyclical maintenance into everyone's thinking. Structurally, some of the first homes were already elderly when first occupied – 'a lot of manor houses', as someone put it – and in time merited replacement or relocation. Today, even homes which were purpose-built twenty or thirty years ago have sometimes reached a point at which their fitness for the next quarter century must be reviewed, and the concept of residential care is itself now debated. When the homes began, such needs or issues were little discussed, although it is interesting that they were already exemplified at Le Court and St Teresa's.

For Cheshire himself, the greatest challenges lay not at home but in developing countries. It saddened him that so much of western influence was reinvested in western self-advancement. The mission of his last decades was to develop the foundation's international work. Its pattern of little steps, each taken to confront some particular need in a modest, practical way, spanned the planet. This was where his heart was, and where most of his pioneering energy went. Typically, when Rotarians declared Cheshire to be their International Man of the Year, a colleague accepted the award on his behalf. He was abroad.

For someone whose ultimate faith lay in immutable things, Cheshire's outlook on change may seem odd. Back in the days of

617 Squadron he had presided over a continuous technical and tactical revolution, and while he had little interest in process for its own sake, he could be very interested in it indeed if it could be improved to serve others' needs. His testament, *Thoughts for the Future*, a spellbinding video shot in 1975 but not released until after his death, would stand showing in any business school (in any film school too, as it follows the unlikely format of a thirty-minute monologue to camera, fleetingly diverted only twice, when we realize that he is talking to his daughter). Its themes are those things which gave the foundation its unique personality – the paramount importance of the individual, delegation, a radical attitude to money and funding, and lay participation – and from those, its characteristics as a family. Cheshire simultaneously celebrated localism and globalism, and saw both as the enemies of insularity.

Cheshire visualized a cycle which begins with zeal, progresses through struggle, overcomes difficulties, arrives at a *floruit* and by then should already be restarting, as new kinds of need are identified and better ways of handling existing tasks are found.[14] Even stability involves change. The cycle is thus never entirely in repose or, if it is, there is probably something wrong with it. A word which Cheshire himself might have used for this is renewal: a perpetual creative refashioning. During his lifetime, the foundation embarked upon successive episodes of renewal, both in its governance and operations (where Cheshire generally favoured devolutionary innovations) and the types of need it tackled – building outward from traditional homes into projects of medical and educational rehabilitation, vocational training, brain injury, life skills at home for the blind – the list goes on. Alongside were the further projects of the Ryder–Cheshire Foundation.[15]

To this extent he was progressive, a radical. He became cautious – 'resistant' or 'conservative' wouldn't be quite the right words – only in circumstances where change seemed to be too precipitate, usually under the influence of fashion or an external environment which was itself in change, and running ahead of verifiable outcome. The Community Care Act 1990, NHS reforms and growing challenges to the principle of residential care all exercised him, not because he was unreceptive to community-based approaches (he had been suggesting them back in 1954), but because at base he was mistrustful of designer futures.

Despite the large degree of local autonomy, ultimate responsibility for each home rested with the trustee body of The Cheshire Foundation Homes for the Sick. The trust, a registered charity, is the body in which all property is vested, and which guarantees to the public that the individual homes are being properly managed in conformity with the general aims of the Cheshire Homes.[16] In what might be called the middle period, roughly speaking the later 1950s to the early 1970s, the trustee body was small – between seven and fifteen members, each of whom kept close contact with three or four specific homes. The central staff was small, too, reflecting Cheshire's resolve to ensure that the foundation's ethos, and the spirit of the individual homes, would not be smothered by excessive professionalism. In 1975 he spoke about this:

... fundamental to us is this fact that we are a layman's organization, that we, so to speak, take over where the doctors have finished. That's not to say we don't need doctors, that we don't need highly professional nurses and therapists – we do. But basically it is ordinary people, who may be business people, professional people, managing it in their spare time.[17]

Nevertheless, as time passed professionalism advanced, and trustee numbers rose. In 1985 the trustees debated proposals which in Cheshire's eyes 'seemed to be based on the assumption that the foundation was moving towards being run by full-time professional staff, with the trustees responsible only for broad policy'. He opposed this, predicting that it would lead to 'a radical change in the foundation's way of working'. There would be less local involvement, diminished local fund-raising and a decline in voluntary help. Against this, core costs would rise, and the foundation 'would become more and more like the NHS or the social services'. One of the foundation's unique features, he said, had been its insistence upon maximum local responsibility. It had been this which had enabled it to extend so rapidly, in such diverse ways, without high overheads.

A good marriage was needed between professionals and non-professionals – that he accepted. However, whereas a professional is a specialist in a limited field, 'it is impossible to treat the individual part successfully without reference to the greater whole to which it belongs. In modern, highly sophisticated society, the problem is to know how to have an adequate understanding of both the part and the whole.'[18] Of course, much can turn on how the word 'professional' is used. A professional standard, for instance, is perfectly susceptible to amateur delivery, as so many of the local management committees have themselves demonstrated down the years. On another level, Cheshire certainly, and in some eyes mistakenly, came to conflate two things – responsibility and management – which nowadays most would assert are distinct. Any trustee body is accountable for what a charity does and should determine the structure and policy within which a charity's paid staff work. In the foundation's earlier days, however, the trustees themselves had been more 'hands on', in some cases combining the responsibilities of trusteeship with what nowadays would be considered as operations or management. As the foundation grew, the trustees, and Cheshire himself, were thus peculiarly vulnerable to sensitivities arising from the evolution or erosion of traditional roles.

What of his style? In meetings he was seldom voluble, unafraid of leading off but often holding back until others had declared themselves, his eventual intervention the more effective for the earlier restraint. In earlier chapters we have seen that his instinct was the opposite, he was naturally impulsive, but he had studied the psychology of committees and trained himself to read their moods. Face to face he had no time to waste, although an unexpected visitor who interrupted something else, someone next to him in the lunch queue at a home or even an unwelcome telephone caller, might suppose that for them he had all the time in the world. In a sense, he did.

Colleagues might hear from him only when there was something to say. One chairman reckoned to be in touch with him on points of detail perhaps three times a week, on slightly lengthier matters maybe a few times each month, but to hold a lengthy conversation perhaps once in six months.[19] As the work grew, so did the habit of holding trustees' residential weekends, at which themes could be explored, innovations aired, ideas debated. Expansion also required new premises. After the move to Market Mews in 1958 it relocated to Maunsel Street at the end of 1979. Today, it is in Millbank, and there are ten regional offices.

It was, however, at the grass roots where in Cheshire's mind 'the Foundation' really existed and where his influence may have been most powerful. Each year he toured groups of homes in Britain, and others abroad, taking infinite pains to prepare himself for each one. Before departure he would consider the order in which they would best be visited; the backgrounds of patients, staff and committee members; the history of the home and its dynamics. He would ask for briefing on problems – for instance, whether there was any feeling of alienation, a committee not abreast of things or a chairman who should be counselled out. During a visit he would sometimes demonstrate that he had, so to speak, 'been there', with an aside such as 'keep an eye on the muscular dystrophy boy in Room 7'. But his forte lay more in listening than speaking, and at times he would stand for hours at social functions to do it. Afterwards, back at the home of a committee member, he would cheerfully dry dishes, talk to the children about their hamsters, remember the hamsters in his thank-you letters (of which no two appear to have been the same) and remember the names of the children when he next wrote. Although in many other respects his memory was a sieve of very broad mesh, with some categories of people it was different. A member of Le Court who had not spoken to him for some years recalled the day when he came up to her and 'knew who I was' (see p. 100). For many, moments like this counted for everything.

Although possessed of infinite patience and tact, he could be startlingly blunt towards trustees or committee members who he felt had outstayed their terms or whose abilities he had overestimated. In such cases, things said unwarily or for effect – 'Well, then perhaps I should resign' – might be laconically answered, 'Yes, I think you should.' Such episodes were rare, but when they occurred the victims could be broken-hearted. Contrariwise, he could be extraordinarily accommodating of those who were awkward, bungling or even rude, valuing them for their strengths as much as mourning their drawbacks. Despite the tendency of one colleague to 'outbursts of temper of a frequency and violence that I have not known before', Cheshire continued to work with him, recognizing particular gifts which no one else possessed. Curiously, even colleagues from whose company he parted, like Cuthbert Fitzherbert, would often continue to work with him on some other basis.

He hated extravagance. 'Leonard has rapped Le Court over the knuckles about those two bungalows for which they wanted to spend eight or nine thousand pounds,' wrote Margot Mason to a trustee.[20] His reaction to something as small as the unnecessary use of a first-class stamp could be as stern. On one occasion he urged a senior staff member to take a 'hard look' at issues of economy, for he had noticed the circulation of memos on a two-colour letterhead, the use of unnecessarily large envelopes and burning lights in rooms where no one was working. Second-class post was to be the norm, and envelopes were to stay open for weekly posting.

Until the 1980s Cheshire's voice in the selection of new chairmen, and some others, was decisive. His recruiting methods were sometimes so subtle that a candidate might be unaware that enlistment was in process. In a short conversation he might size someone up, meditate for up to several years, perhaps making discreet inquiries of mutual friends, and then invite them to join the work. In 1972 Air Chief Marshal Sir Christopher Foxley-Norris was on the point of retirement from the RAF. Cheshire and Foxley-Norris had known one another since pre-war Oxford, although recent acquaintance had been slight. Cheshire invited him to lunch. They talked about this and that, Cheshire mentioning that he was on the lookout for a new chairman and inquiring about Foxley-Norris's plans. Foxley-Norris replied that he needed a paid job. But he knew little about what the foundation did and the thought ran through his mind that he might be too frivolous for such serious work. The subject lapsed until the lunch ended, whereupon Cheshire smiled and said, 'Good – I'm so glad.'[21]

His ways with treasurers were notorious. Broadly, he divided them into those who were rigorously prudent, seeking to amass reserves and engage in safe housekeeping, and those who shared his belief that 'money isn't really the key . . . the basic key is people', and supported him accordingly. Treasurers of the latter kind are fairly rare. In the earlier days, when his influence was strong, any who displayed the former tendencies were often eased out to make way for them.

Cheshire's influence upon the trustee body became more circumscribed as time passed. In the earliest days, the combined efforts of his father and Lord Denning, and the experience of figures like Cherry Morris, had kept his wilder ideas contained, while furnishing the trust with reliable procedures to underpin schemes which everyone agreed should be taken forward. This combination was formidable. Inevitably, however, the chemistry changed. Lord Denning departed in 1962, following his appointment as Master of the Rolls, and in some respects the next few years have a slightly doldrum air: there was a tendency for trustees to remain into old age, an atmosphere of paternalism and little contact with other organizations. In 1969 Cheshire notified the trustees of his wish to withdraw from administration to refocus on communicating the underlying ideals to a wider, younger audience. He was particularly interested in the medium of film, and for some years funds were committed to a film unit, a caravan, staff and specialist equipment.[22]

If there was a watershed in Cheshire's relationship with the foundation, it was arguably around 1980/81, when his nomination for a new chairman was rejected. How and why this happened will be matters for the foundation's historian; our concern here lies in Cheshire's reaction.

In the autumn of 1980 Cheshire sounded out Sir Peter Ramsbotham, former UK ambassador to Washington and lately retired. As usual, he also canvassed opinion among the trustees. In October he told Ramsbotham that he had put his name forward, and had 'received the warmest response I could have hoped for from the trustees'.

In reality, it was not so straightforward, and in the decorous language with which counter-strokes are made by members of the British establishment – 'inopportune', 'limited knowledge of the foundation', 'in view of his other commitments' – a case was subsequently constructed for departing from the original position. On 7 July 1981 Cheshire told the trustees that it was 'with regret' that he was withdrawing his nomination for chairman elect of the UK foundation. 'This brings to an end the era when, in the absence of an agreed electoral procedure, it was I who nominated each successive chairman.' Regarding what would follow, he would 'prefer not to be involved' in that discussion.

> I confess to a sense of disappointment that the trustees as a body do not feel able to trust me in this all-important matter, at any rate just this one more time . . . Behind my disappointment lies a growing feeling that Providence is once more guiding the foundation, and myself personally, into new fields.

Towards the end of his life, the foundation's professional staff grew in size and role, increasing further with the appointment of a director general as the 'fountainhead of executive authority', a reformed committee structure and more explicit provision for training.[23] After his death, the foundation's public-affairs department characterized the organization as 'professional but with voluntary commitment' (a description at which the founder might have bridled, in which the 'but' speaks volumes)★ and as a body with 'local roots, national voice, international experience' (which he might have liked).[24]

Many aspects of Cheshire's developing work have been left unmentioned. There were some fascinating might-have-beens. One concerned linkage with the work of Mother Teresa, of whom Cheshire saw quite a lot during his Calcutta days, and with whom both he and Sue Ryder remained friendly. There was recurrent talk of amalgamation, and by 1963 there was a proposal, in some documents a decision, that Mother Teresa would become a third party to the Ryder–Cheshire Foundation. For various reasons, however, this did not proceed.

Of lesser enterprises, some – like the idea of converting an ocean liner into a floating home – were rather quirky; others, like a volunteer corps, fell by the wayside, and yet more, like a voluntary air service, to help in air ambulance work, traffic spotting and the

---

★ A key Cheshire principle was the co-valuation of different contributions. While there was necessarily a hierarchy in weight of responsibility, volunteer helpers, members of local management committees, trustees, residents and professional staff all had a part to play which should be valued alike.

chaperoning of yacht races,[25] had nothing to do with the homes at all. But one stands out. It was for a new kind of monastery.

For Cheshire, to be a 'good Catholic' was not enough. In 1952 he came close to joining the Cistercian Order, and his yearning to invest a succession of projects with formal Catholic identity was like an unerupted wisdom tooth which periodically tried to break through. Several of the early homes were conceived with a strong religious tinge. At Midhurst and in India he devised Rules for laypeople. Some of his work in the mid-1950s, visible in the symmetry of Walsingham and the Holy Shroud, symbols of Christ's birth and death, were grounded in a desire to trigger a counter-Reformation which would eventually restore Catholicism.

Since the mid-1950s – the exact beginning is hard to pinpoint – Cheshire had been thinking of combining his two greatest loves – care for the sick and Catholicism – to make a third – a religious community for disabled people. At the start, this led to all kinds of ideas which were temporarily explored and then dropped. It might have been an institute or a religious congregation, and disability might have been social rather than physical – ex-convicts, for instance.

By April 1960 the idea had stabilized as a house of contemplation, aiming at the most perfect possible rendering of the Divine Office, wherein members offered the rest of their lives on behalf of the dying. The Holy Face, 'whose reflection is to be found in the dying', would be their great devotion. However, attempts to start by establishing two or three priests in a small property had failed.[26]

He looked at sites in England, the Holy Land and India. 'How very exciting for a monastery,' wrote Gwen Forrestier-Walker[27] when told of a site at Chakrata – 'a good site visually' – at 15,000 feet (quite normal for a Buddhist monastery), where snow lay for three months of the year. But that would have drawbacks for the disabled, and he discarded it, or any Indian setting, electing instead for Bethlehem, where he felt 'a cradle is waiting for it'.

Cheshire's mind raced on all kinds of aspects – its architecture, layout, floor levels (which would have to be different from those of conventional churches), the ergonomics of its conventual buildings, how the *opus Dei* might function in a context of disability, how to integrate medical care (a new kind of lay-brother?), whether the offices should be recited in the vernacular or Latin. He talked to architects, wrote countless letters to members of religious communities in Britain begging all kinds of advice and studied the directions of the Holy See – or as he put it in a note, 'the drill' – in starting new religious congregations.

In 1962 a site was purchased outside the village of Beit Jala in Jordan, overlooking Bethlehem and Jerusalem. Cheshire appealed to the Knights of the Holy Sepulchre for help, but when the project came to the ears of the Patriarch of Jerusalem he pointed out that 'urgently needed schools and churches' came first.[28] There may have been other reasons why the project did not proceed.

In its developed form, outlined on the last day of 1963, the house would have been a community of men who suffered from some sickness or disability which precluded their entry to a religious order but yet had a vocation for the contemplative life, happily and self-effacingly caring for one another, dedicated to prayer for the dying throughout the world.[29] Had this come to pass, it would have been called Penuel, the place where Jacob wrestled through the night and saw God face to face.*

* Genesis xxxii, 24–31.

23. At Home and Abroad

Cavendish lies in the Stour Valley, where Suffolk and Essex meet. Weatherboarded and colour-washed houses lie along a main street, parting around a sloping green which is overlooked by the parish church of St Mary. After Sue Ryder and Cheshire married in 1959, this was home.

They lived in a corner of the former farmhouse which Sue Ryder had bought from her mother in 1953. Sharing the house was a community of physically disabled residents, nurses, assistants, volunteers and helpers in the headquarters. Alongside them, as often as not, there were visitors.

In the earliest days meals had been taken communally in shifts, in a fashion cheerfully described by a secretary as 'gobble and go'. Down the years campaigns of new building spread across the kitchen gardens. Whatever new space was added to it, however, more went on at Cavendish than there was room for. Incoming mail was colossal, sackfuls of clothing and other items destined for Sue Ryder shops arrived daily, as did the volunteers who helped to sort, wash, iron, repair, re-sort and re-bag their contents. Everyone shared the work, Cheshire's speciality being the laundering of delicate items in the family washing machine.

Space was always at a premium, and in their early years together the Cheshires lived and worked in one room. It was here that their first child, Jeromy, was born in 1960, followed by Elizabeth in 1962. Sue Ryder's concessions to impending motherhood were modest. She was 'able, and anyway preferred, to keep working normally until a few hours before the children were born', and returned to it almost immediately afterwards.[1] The weeks before Jeromy's birth, indeed, found her driving an unheated truck across snow-bound Europe.

Just as the home and headquarters were commingled, so the children grew up as members of the extended Cavendish family. For seven years the children were brought up with the help of Kitty McGrath, an Irish nurse, who did what she could to minimize the resemblance between their one-room home and a main-line railway station.² She had her work cut out, for the Cheshires were a family divided by absences. The two foundations took nearly all their time, and journeys abroad meant that one or the other was often away, one sometimes departing as the other returned. 'We were fortunate enough to have a whole week together at Christmas,' Cheshire told a friend in February 1962. Cheshire himself was frequently abroad, usually for months at a time. Even when he was theoretically at home, there were engagements all over the country, and part of each month was passed at Market Mews or (subsequently) Maunsel Street, where there was a small flat which he used as a London base.

As the children grew there was a modest expansion of accommodation, with a bedroom each for Jeromy and Elizabeth, and a small study-cum-sitting room where Cheshire kept his books and wrote. When the children reached their teens Cheshire became more stalwart in refusing engagements which clashed with things like half-term holidays, but there were limits to his success.

Grandparents are often good standbys for busy families. Until her death in 1974 Mabel Ryder continued to live near by, latterly in a bungalow across the garden. Jeromy was only two when Primrose died in 1962, but Geoffrey lived on for another seventeen years, cultivating his garden and remarrying along the way. Laundry Cottage remained a family retreat. After his divorce Christopher remarried, but he and his family lived abroad, Christopher eventually retiring to Spain, and the brothers saw little of one another.

Cheshire remained faithful to his decision to live on his RAF pension and give everything else to his work. After Geoffrey Cheshire's death in 1979 the pension was augmented by income from his father's books, although at the time this seemed a mixed blessing because the Inland Revenue issued a Capital Transfer Tax demand for a sum equivalent to eight years' royalties. Hence, in terms of disposable income he lived in near-poverty. Some costs were met elsewhere. From the 1960s, when the second-hand car given to him by his mother wore out, the foundation provided a car, which was periodically renewed, and a driver. The costs of foundation-related telephone calls, and a tape recorder for the dictation of correspondence, were also underwritten by the foundation. In matters of work-related technology Cheshire was progressive, encouraging the foundation's acquisition of a microcomputer as early as 1981, and what was described as a 'car telephone' in the following year.

In most families there is a clear split between work and home, the job and family being in different places with hours belonging to each. In the Cheshires' case it wasn't like this at all. Work was wherever they were, and they lived less over the shop than actually in it. Even conversation at meals – which in later life were eaten from a tiny table on the landing – was interrupted by telephone calls. At home the sound of the telephone would sometimes cause him to groan, but whoever the caller was – and some were intrusive, or would ring shortly before midnight – he almost invariably gave his time to them. Face to face, on the other hand, an experienced Cheshire watcher would know if time had been outrun. If time was available, or whatever was being talked about was interesting, Cheshire would accept or make a cup of coffee. If it wasn't, glances at his watch would signal that something more important awaited him. After he stopped smoking in 1952, instant coffee was the nearest he came to indulging in a vice.

Relaxation, therefore, was a near-alien condition for which little opportunity existed. 'I don't have a social life, because once you have a social life, where do you stop?' There were few exceptions. When the children were young there were occasional family holidays, and TV programmes like *Dad's Army* were viewed as a family. As the children grew older television was seldom watched by their parents, although *Upstairs, Downstairs* was a Ryder–Cheshire favourite; Cheshire appreciated programmes about the natural world, Sue Ryder liked *Face the Music* and Joseph Cooper's silent keyboard. Along with most of the rest of the nation, they watched the 1966 World Cup, and became uninhibitedly frantic towards its end. Sue Ryder's love of music, inherited from her mother, was not much shared by her husband, although he retained his youthful passion for 1930s dance bands and swing, and Solesmes had introduced him to Gregorian chant. In later years he began to compile tapes of different kinds of music for Sue Ryder to play during long journeys, and widened his own tastes in the process. The rhythms of their days did not quite coincide. Sue Ryder is an early riser, as she says, a lark. Cheshire was more nocturnal, the owl.

His main relaxation was tennis, which he played partly because it was in his family's blood and he enjoyed it, and partly to exercise his chest muscles. In 1979 he entered himself for the over-fifty-fives tennis tournament at Queen's, and remained a strong player to within a few months of his last illness. On the court he liked competition, and among the welcome guests at Cavendish was the tennis international Ken Fletcher, who provided it.

His other hobby was photography, which he adopted after Sue Ryder bought him a box Brownie as a birthday present. He became good at it. A darkroom was fitted up at Cavendish, and into this, his 'black hole', he would retreat when other things allowed. On successive trips abroad he took thousands of pictures, a fair number of them striking and of publication standard. Although not technically minded in a practical engineering sense, he had an abiding fascination with gadgets, and would discuss their potentialities with an enthusiasm that led Sue Ryder to think that he would have made a good salesman. Other pursuits linked with work. For a time, he tried to teach himself Chinese – a project which reflected his hopes for the eventual extension of the foundation into China. His French remained fluent; German was not so well retained.

Most literature passed him by, although in theology he was widely read. His bookcases are interesting. One is chiefly filled with reference works about the strategic air offensive, the other with religious history, spiritual texts and theology. He seldom read novels, and never seems to have engaged with authors like Dostoevsky, with whom he might have discovered some kinship. Poetry he 'professed not to understand'. Among the religious works are primary sources (with an English–Greek lexicon to support them), mystics, explorations of death, spirituality and prayer. The collected works of St Teresa of Avila, St Ignatius' *Spiritual Exercises*, Gérard Rossé's *The Cry of Jesus on the Cross, On the Theology of Death* by Karl Rahner, Cardinal Newman's *Meditations and Devotions*, the Vulgate, the complete works of St John of the Cross, Kierkegaard, and O'Collins's *Fundamental Theology* are a sample. Alongside stand several works on human origins and anthropology, and Teilhard de Chardin's *Milieu Divin*. On another wall he compiled a time-line of human evolution – the human family again, in its chronological dimension.

Cheshire's thinking about evolution looked forwards as well as back, culturally as well as genetically. While his wife thinks that too much money is spent on space exploration, he considered it was not enough: that it was important for humanity to explore, and find out what goes on on other planets.

A sizeable library relates to the Turin Shroud, to which Cheshire's devotion remained undiminished when Oxford scientists reported radiocarbon determinations indicating a date in the range 1260–1390. The Shroud was one of the strongest influences in his life, uniting all about which he cared.

His days were framed by prayer. Of all the books, his breviary was the one from which he would not be parted. When he rose he would pass at least half an hour in silent meditation, in summer perhaps walking in the garden, in colder months in the chapel. When events of the day allowed it he read the divine offices. He returned to the chapel for an hour at evening. When Sue Ryder and Cheshire were both at Cavendish, they prayed together. If he could, he passed six days in retreat each year in the Carthusian house at Parkminster.

In the company of others his devoutness was invisible, at least in the sense that it did not resemble the kind of maudlin piety that non-believers or agnostics often associate with the Church. He was difficult, probably impossible, to dislike. With close colleagues he 'had a way of getting at you, so that you'd work twice as hard, without getting the whip out'.[3] As aircrew had noted, he 'suggested' rather than ordered. However, although he became an exceptionally wise student of management, aspects of its actual practice eluded him. For much of the time he seemed oblivious to the pressures under which others worked, and was prone to make requests which broke concentration at inopportune moments. He took it for granted that others would wish to share his own long and indefinite hours. Very often they did, but after a while the expectations which went with the assumption could become wearing. Although he was an enemy to disorder, piling papers in tidy stacks, making lists and ticking things off, tasks were often left until the last minute and the lists themselves might be lost. Stories about minor Cheshire crises – key documents forgotten, slides knocked over before a lecture, lights fused when a photographic lamp was switched on in an hotel room – are legion. In cars, his inclination to give advice from the back seat – 'What speed are we doing?' 'Not six lengths from that car in front!' – was well known to those who chauffeured him, as was the likelihood that an instruction to take a particular turn would not take them to the place to which they wanted to go. At such moments Cheshire would then disarmingly agree that he was completely wrong. As far as organization went, there was a kind of unworldliness which led him to assume that if, for instance, he removed his shoes for a barefoot ascent at Lourdes, they would somehow be waiting for him when he reached the top. Others around him compensated with good humour and loyalty. Better than most, they also knew his strengths, and those such as Ron Travers and Wally Sullivan, who worked closely with him in later years, were as loyal and committed as figures like Frances Jeram and Phil Loneragan at the beginning. Moreover, when it mattered, as it had in a bomber with six lives behind him, or when giving a sermon, or in prayer, or writing a book – which he never found easy – he was collected, focused and disciplined.

As he grew older, a last-minute alteration to his programme, an unanticipated visitor, confusion at an airport, could leave him flustered. To outsiders, however, this was seldom apparent. When several former RAF colleagues called upon him without warning at Maunsel Street, he left an important meeting, offered them sherry, passed what seemed to be a leisurely half hour as if there was nothing else in the world that might be distracting him and then returned to the meeting. Annoyances faded rapidly, and on occasions when he felt that he might have expressed them too strongly he would return to apologize, sometimes going to great lengths to do so.

Towards others, he remained so equable that they were seldom
aware of his real feelings. Idolizing admirers troubled him, for by
seeking his acquaintance they missed the point – which was the
work. There were some who supposed themselves to be more
warmly favoured than they actually were. Whoever he was with,
in conversation he looked them in the eye, and it was upon strangers
that he often seems to have had greatest effect, perhaps because
with them he was less inhibited. Conversation about theology he
loved best of all, and when a priest or member of a religious order
was staying at Cavendish he could talk for hours. An Anglican
clergyman seated next to Cheshire at a formal dinner found him
virtually mute, until conversation turned to theology.

In dealings with those he did not know, Cheshire was easy-going,
informal and quickly on Christian-name terms – unlike his wife,
who inclines more to the eastern European tradition which expects
a number of years' acquaintance before familiarity is reached. His
sense of humour remained strong, and his eye for the absurd keen,
although as he grew older the laugh became an almost soundless
chuckle. There were limits to his humour. He was not a joke-teller
or mimic, and a risqué joke repeated in his hearing would be met
by a grimace. Careful about his own appearance, he was disappointed
by scruffy dress in others, but would seldom show it.

In public, lecturing or giving sermons, the ordered, connected
quality of his speaking belied his prior nervousness. As before
take-off on air raids, he liked time alone beforehand to collect his
thoughts, and then usually spoke without notes, having memorized
the overall framework. His sermons were powerful, delivered
with simplicity, fluency and directness. They sometimes drew
tears.

Although Cheshire's circle of acquaintance was vast – by the late
1980s the Ryder–Cheshire Christmas card list ran to over four
thousand addresses and the writing of the cards began in September
– he had few close friends. One, possibly the only one, was the
film-maker David Lean, whom he had met at Dehra Dun. Cheshire
spoke, movingly and spontaneously, at Lean's funeral in 1991.
Afterwards he told Kevin Brownlow: 'I think David was almost
my best friend . . . I can't tell you how much I miss him. I keep

thinking, "I must talk to David about that," and then realize I can't.'[4] The two men saw each other once or twice a year. At Lean's invitation, and usually at his expense, Cheshire visited a number of films in the making, combining visits to homes with trips to locations in Jordan for *Lawrence of Arabia*, Madrid for *Doctor Zhivago*, and Fiji for *Mutiny on the Bounty*.

The relationship between Lean, the vehement atheist and veteran of six marriages; and Cheshire, the devout, frugal Catholic, looks strange. Yet there were affinities and similarities, and a mutual fascination. Lean was competitive, good with young people, a boy at heart who 'never grew up'. Some of the things said of him could be, or actually were, said of Cheshire as well. Lean, for instance, 'had this style of making you feel that when you were with him you were the only one who really mattered' (see p. 61). He did this with everybody, 'so it was quite hard to tell who he really liked'.[5] Lean was 'amazed and fascinated by [Cheshire's] goodness . . . He and Leonard were crazy about each other.'[6] They also shared a linearity of mind in relation to the important things they did.[7] Both had an early love of the cinema and took delight in photography – its equipment, feel and touch, as well as results – and both were largely itinerant, lived out of suitcases and devoted to their work. Lean's atheism did not preclude an interest in religion, and they held long theological sparring matches, which Cheshire may have enjoyed as a means of honing his own thinking. Lean was generous to Cheshire's work, taking on the direction of several videos, including *Chance Encounter* and *A Hidden World*.

He was extremely generous. When he directed those three films, he said, 'How much has this cost, Leonard?' I said, 'In the region of six thousand pounds.' Immediately he paid for it.

And when I needed some money for a film on a leprosy boy that I was making, I wrote to him. Was there any possibility of his signing a letter for me to a funding agency? He rang up my secretary and said that it would be much easier for him just to give her the money. I couldn't believe it. I mean, it was three or four thousand pounds in the early sixties and for me that was huge money.[7a]

Although Cheshire rather enjoyed mingling with the great and the famous, he found it difficult to regard himself as either. He disliked being paraded as a hero, shrank from adulation which he did not feel he merited, and often doubted that there was much about himself that anyone would find interesting. In some ways, he may have looked back at his young self with a sense of shame. He accepted several honorary degrees and humanitarian awards, but did not nominate colleagues for state honours (and declined them himself) because under his principle of co-equality he considered that no one had done more than anyone else. The peerage was offered at least once before his eventual acceptance in 1991, when he took advice from Jack Ashley and agreed, on the grounds that it would provide a platform from which to talk back to government on matters about which he cared.

The Order of Merit was different. Of all that happened to him in any public sense, it was this for which he cared most. Membership of the order, which at any one time is twenty-four strong, is in the personal gift of the monarch, and as an ardent royalist it was with deep appreciation that he accepted the invitation to join the group in 1981. Thereafter, if he was in the country he would attend its annual receptions, which in 1987, for instance, brought together such figures as the crystallographer Dorothy Hodgkin, Dame Veronica Wedgwood, Owen Chadwick, Sir Isaiah Berlin, Yehudi Menuhin, Sir Frank Whittle and Graham Greene. Another who attended had been his companion on the flight to Nagasaki: William, now Lord Penney.[8] The last engagement of his life was a gathering of the Order of Merit.

Although Cheshire was intensely patriotic, he drew a sharp distinction between patriotism and nationalism, regarding the former as culturally and emotionally wholesome, and the latter as inimical to progress. He saw the United Nations, for all its imperfections, as essential to the world's future.

When he reached it, the House of Lords fascinated him. In domestic politics he took positions on moral issues such as abortion and euthanasia, to both of which he was opposed, but had no party alignment. If he voted in 1945 it is not clear for whom, although in letters to friends around that time he expressed doubts about the Attlee government, just as he later departed from an initial neutrality towards Mrs Thatcher. He considered the poll tax a mistake, and deplored the relaxation of restrictions on Sunday trading. He took a keen interest in ecological and sustainability issues, causing investigation to be made of the potential of wind energy for the homes as early as 1979.[9] At base, however, it was issues that touched the relief of suffering and the emancipation of sufferers that concerned him most, and for those purposes he would work with any MPs, ministers or peers who showed like concern. In 1970 he had much contact with Alf Morris during the formulation of Labour's landmark disability legislation, and he had a special regard for the advice of those with direct experience, like Jack Ashley.

Wherever Cheshire was, whatever he was doing, there were letters to answer. The homes alone generated a huge correspondence, but hundreds of other letters arrived each week, sometimes each day. They came from schools, religious orders, ex–servicemen and women, ex–TB sufferers, children, lonely people, troubled people, generous people, pompous people, readers of the books by Braddon and Boyle. Some accompanied gifts. More wanted something: his autograph, his views, his advice, his name, favour, money, a job. Would he contribute to a *Complete Limerick Book*? Name his favourite poem? Open a jumble sale? Be patron of a new nursing home? Write an article? Put in a word for a former RAF officer? Advise a schoolmaster on whether he had a monastic vocation? To all he replied with care, often at length, and usually within a few days. Sometimes he wrote more than once, adding further thoughts to those already given.

There were reasons for this. One was his compassionate interest in people, and his uncanny affinity with strangers. Behind that lay his faith. 'Christ,' wrote Cheshire, 'goes about this world as a beggar, in disguise, stretching out His hand for alms. He comes in the guise of a bereaved child, a widow, one who is lonely or homeless or sick, or unpopular; He is there in the consummate bore, the convicted thief or liar, the sensual and worldly, the frivolous modern pagan . . . ever asking for our love and gentleness and *reverence*, our courtesy and sympathy.'

He therefore believed that his first response to any fellow human should be reverent humility, for it is Christ whom I am meeting . . . All true love is founded on humility, and unless we look with humility on every man we meet, we shall not begin to love him. Someone said that democracy does not consist in saying 'I'm as good as you', but 'You're as good as me'; and Christian charity begins by saying, not 'You're better than me' (for only God knows which is better), but 'You are the apple of God's eye.'

Christ therefore lived in letters which many would dismiss as rude, nutty or pointless. He didn't find this easy.

My Father used to say: 'When you've got a pile of work you think you'll never get through, pick up each letter and do it as if it's the only letter you're going to do that day. Don't let your mind worry about the ones ahead.' Father Prior at Parkminster added, 'Yes, but don't let it escalate!'

Pacing such work was taxing.

You can easily give a letter disproportionate time, which means you haven't got time left for the others beneath it. Once they get beyond a certain point, they depress me and I feel I'll never catch up. They keep coming in every day and I need to reduce them, otherwise they're a sort of hidden load on my mind and I keep thinking, 'That in-tray!' So I think you should discipline yourself to keep nibbling away at them.[10]

The archive shows that he was being extremely modest when he said this. Crassness was met with docility, mean-spiritedness with generosity, impatience with calm, doubt with hope. Letter-writing was almost a kind of ministry.

. . . I like to write a personal answer, but at times it takes a huge amount of effort. There are very few letters I can just dash off. I find I've got to think how to compose them properly, but recently I've begun to worry less about style. I don't judge the time I give to letters or people by their position in life, but by what the content of the letter is. If I'm mentally tired, I pick out the ones that don't need a lot of thought. Unless it's a little boy or a student working on a thesis, I'm not going to give as much time to a person who just writes idly and says, 'Please send me a couple of pages on your war experiences,' as I would to somebody who says, 'My wife has died and I've got no purpose to my life – can you suggest something?'[11]

Some letters told of tragedies or troubles, where, if he could help, he did. When he heard that a former aircrew colleague was dying of cancer and about to be turned out of his home for failing to keep up with the mortgage, he immediately found money to stave off repossession, and wrote to the building society to plead the man's case. To anyone who gave anything to the work – and down the years tens of thousands did – he replied. Cheshire measured gifts according to the means of the giver, and letters like this moved him: 'A small appreciation of your courage in danger and affliction and a trifle to help in your work for the suffering. An old-age pensioner and a widow. See Numbers, Chapter 6, vv. 24–26.'★

Naturally, a lot of letters concerned the war. And there was the bomb. Always the bomb.

War never really left Cheshire, nor he it. Conflict was a subject about which historians consulted him, members of the public wrote, publishers asked for books, editors for articles, the electronic media invited him to broadcast, institutions and staff colleges asked him to lecture. His part in the bomber offensive against Germany meant that he was often invited to account for its conduct, while his position as one of only two Britons to have taken part in an atomic attack, and a Christian, marked him as a unique figure in the debate about nuclear weapons. The fraternity of former aircrew was important. He attended their reunions and travelled widely to address anniversary ceremonies. Inevitably, he was asked to hold office in several veterans' associations. Just as inevitably, he accepted. Even had the homes not existed, his life would have been full.

Cheshire's continuing involvement with war was not simply a result of others' invitations. Until the end of his life he laboured under self-imposed obligations to remembrance, warning and explanation. Although pacific, he was not a pacifist. In pursuit of justice he did not disavow his fighting. As a witness of the atomic bomb, he strove to elucidate the paradox whereby nuclear weapons were morally faulted but could not be relinquished in isolation from the context in which they were held. He kept abreast of war's

---

★ The Lord bless thee, and keep thee:
The Lord make his face shine upon thee, and be gracious unto thee:
The Lord lift up his countenance upon thee, and give thee thy peace.

development, reading widely and studying hard. Overseas work took him perilously close to new wars. Sue Ryder introduced him to the Holocaust, causing him to contemplate a Creation which his friend David Lean bleakly suggested had been forsaken by its maker. He became an ardent champion of international military intervention for peacekeeping, and urged the use of military skills for humanitarian purposes. He foresaw NATO's intervention in the Balkans. His last great project was conceived as a living memorial to war's victims.

Cheshire's overall attitude to war is summed up in a reply he gave to some children who wrote to him from a school in Seaford. 'What the war taught me,' he told them, 'is that we don't do enough in peacetime to remove the causes of war.'[12] Or as he explained in an article for the *Baptist Times*:

Peace is not merely the absence of war . . . Peace is the result, the priceless fruit, of justice. Without real justice and freedom – freedom under law – there is no peace. Justice, then, is the gateway to peace, and injustice, itself the first violence, is the dangerous slope that ends in confrontation and war.

He wrote many articles like this. He wished to see the abolition of war and the disarmament of nations, but parted from pacifists over the question of means. Unlike them, he did not see disarmament as an issue to be pursued aside from the chronic injustices which make wars likely. While he admired the peace movement for the emphasis it brought, it seemed to him that its campaign against weapons alone missed the point. A missile or a bomb is no more than an instrument of human intentions. In the absence of such intentions it is so much junk.[13] Cheshire's project was to change the intentions. He wanted to pull war up by the roots rather than lop its branches.

This is why disarmament and his humanitarian work went hand in hand. They were aspects of each other, and his eagerness to develop the work in totalitarian countries drew from a faith that demonstrations of love would become sources of energy for more fundamental change. He knew that neither he nor the foundations would light the world's darknesses alone, or come anywhere near doing so. But in a black cavern, even the smallest flame is precious.

In April 1982, while staying at the Venerable English College in

Rome, he attempted an essay which explained why the repudiation of nuclear weapons must form part of a wider agenda for human progress. 'The greatest affront to man's dignity, greater even than that of the world's nuclear armouries, is our failure to act decisively against the poverty of developing nations.' To go to the rescue of the poor, Cheshire wrote, 'would be to create an entirely new political climate within the family of nations'. The near future would bring new generations of weapons, more lethal, easier to build and more readily obtainable. Ought we not to see this threat 'as a timely, perhaps merciful, warning that all is not well in the heart of man'? Money alone was not the answer, which lay rather in the need for an 'urgent and informed inner commitment'. This was also practical. 'Whereas nuclear weapons present us with a most perplexing dilemma, no dilemma is involved in the relief of poverty, neither do we lack the necessary means, only the collective will and a sense of sacrifice.'[14]

In the 1970s and 1980s, after decades of incessant work for the foundation, he took several sabbatical years. Two of his books were written during these periods, which in practice turned out to be almost as busy as any others. Another book, 'For Your Tomorrow', an anthology of wartime experiences, was begun and abandoned. The letters, of course, did not respect sabbaticals.

For much of their time both Sue Ryder and Cheshire lived as international gypsies. Cheshire considered it essential to maintain personal contact with homes and projects across the world, and put huge effort into overseas tours which would take in as many centres as possible. In 1979, for instance, he was contemplating requests for visits from fifty homes across Asia on a tour involving stops in thirty different places, while the tour he had undertaken to India, Pakistan, Nepal and Bangladesh in the previous year, when he was away from mid-October to early December, involved twenty-one flights in twenty-nine days. On that trip, he estimated that he had given an average of two speeches, one major, one minor, on each day. On return, he would write a lengthy report for circulation to foundation colleagues, giving his impressions and opinions about the calibre and commitment of local management committees, politicians, the general culture of individual homes.

Although briefed to allow clear periods, local organizers frequently did the opposite, packing in extra visits, meetings and
receptions. Lengthy social gatherings were a physical torment. Long
periods of standing induced acute back pain, and discomfort from
varicose veins, yet he was not good at resisting pressure to stay
longer than was good for him. Organizers of such events never
knew that his eventual departure was often followed by a physical
collapse on the hotel room floor. Restaurant food held little interest
for him and he hated pointless noise. If piped music were played
in a restaurant, he left it.

When arriving somewhere new, if time allowed he would find
a priest to say mass, and liked to meditate about the place, to absorb
its mood. He travelled with his tennis kit, and would play if the
chance arose. If eminent companions, such as foundation chairmen,
journeyed with him, they learned to anticipate the likelihood that
at some point he would hide their suitcases.

The grind of moving from place to place could be ameliorated
when international airlines provided discounted or free first-class
travel, accommodation in their hotels or transport on the ground.
But overall it was a pitiless existence. On a thirty- or forty-day trip
he would be lucky to have three or four days to himself. Even then
he was isolated. The happiest times were when he and Sue Ryder
managed to tour together, and there was the spectacular occasion*
in 1983 when Family Week was held in Rome, an international
gathering of over 650 friends and colleagues which coincided with
their silver wedding anniversary, each and all receiving the blessing
of the Pope.

It says much about the pressures under which they worked
that some of their most contented hours together were spent in
aeroplanes, where there were no letters, documents or meetings,
and no phones rang. Latterly, they took no holidays. After so much
travel, the closest thing to a break was to be at home. More often,
in any case, Sue Ryder was out on her own, not infrequently in
places of danger or extreme suffering. In 1968 she was in Poland

---

* Despite careful reconnaissance, the hotel turned out to be double booked, apparently
by other visitors whom the hotel felt it would be unwise to disappoint.

Top: Wild Goose on its
launch trolley

Middle: Cheshire on
Wild Goose control rig

Bottom: Procession at
Predannack, Good
Friday 1952

Phil Loneragan

Margot Mason

Staunton Harold

Bethlehem House, Andheri, Bombay, December 1955

Govind Bhavan, Dehra Dun, August 1956

Opposite, top: Raphael at the beginning, 1959

Opposite, bottom: Raphael: the leprosy colony

Top: Wedding celebration: Sue Ryder and Cheshire with patients and staff at Dehra Dun, April 1959

Middle: Geoffrey Cheshire and his grandson, Jeromy, in the garden at Laundry Cottage, 1964

Bottom: Geoffrey Cheshire and Christopher at Laundry Cottage, July 1964

The family at Cavendish, 1967, a few days before Cheshire's fiftieth birthday

Cheshire and his daughter, Elizabeth, during International Week, June 1981

Members of the Cheshire home for polio victims at Bo, Sierra Leone, 1990

Raphael children

Above left: Resident of the Cheshire Village,
Jamaica, competing in the 1986 World
Paraplegic Games

Above right: Kunming, China, March 1990: 'We
could just sit together in a little circle and hold
hands, or put arms round each other'

Right: Kunming, 1990: dancing by the disabled
at the official opening

Below: Last pilgrimage: Raphael, May 1992

during serious disturbances at Poznan – these are merely examples – and August that year found her in Czechoslovakia amid the Russian invasion. Cheshire fielded anxious calls from the Foreign Office, politely explaining that he was not responsible for Sue Ryder's safety.

He was, however, concerned for Sue Ryder, whether she was in Bosnia, Ethiopia or the next room. When one or other of them was going away, he wrote messages, affectionate notes, planting them in places – in a drawer, under a pillow – where they would turn up hours or days later. As the children grew up and the last parents died, these two very private, ultimately very shy people turned towards each other with a deepening devotion. Sue Ryder relied on him as a counsellor, pouring out problems and listening to his advice, while Cheshire's quiet humour and gentle demeanour provided her deepest anchorage.

Towards the end of his life Cheshire said that marriage had been his saving. 'It stopped me taking myself too seriously.' There is no hiding place in marriage for self-deception – as Goethe put it, 'Love is an ideal thing, marriage is a real thing' – and Cheshire's marriage countered the public admiration of which he was increasingly wary yet could never escape. Marriage also curbed his impulsiveness. 'I had a tie. I couldn't just do whatever came into my mind.' And it inspired him. Sue Ryder's selflessness almost invariably causes her to put herself second to the task ahead, and then to the task beyond that.

My first meeting with Sue Ryder was in Cheshire's study, on a winter Sunday afternoon, about eighteen months after his death. She talked about him, quietly, and it grew dark. With their children, she was the only person who really knew him.

24. For Your Tomorrow

The Horsemen of the Apocalypse were abroad in the 1980s. They always are, of course, but television now brings them into the living room. Shocked by sights of natural disasters, shaken by mounting evidence for climate change and misuse of the earth's resources, in the 1980s many sat up and asked 'What can I do?'

In September 1988 Cheshire found himself watching television pictures of mass starvation. A day or two later he was in Winnipeg for a reunion of Commonwealth aircrew. His mind connected things which others box separately. How, he wondered, might the spirit of reunion, which stems from the past, be harnessed to the future? The twentieth century had been an age of unprecedented slaughter. Would it not be miraculous if at the end of the century those lost lives could be the means for saving future lives? In October, he developed this on paper.

The unprecedented succession of famine, flood and hurricane of recent weeks coinciding with an ever-increasing number of wartime reunions has put an idea into my mind which will not go away and which I would like to share.

In a nutshell it is that those who have participated in either of the two world wars, irrespective of which side they fought on, create an emergency disaster fund to be given to the Secretary-General of the United Nations. It would stand as a living memorial to the men, women and children who were involved in those two made-made disasters and be their gift to future generations for their times of natural disaster.[1]

$10 contributed for each life lost in the two world wars would create a permanent capital fund of $800,000,000 which could be put at the disposal of the UN. Although at heart a global project, each country could be autonomous in collecting its own funds.

Nothing would be spent on administration. And 3 September 1989
– the fiftieth anniversary of the outbreak of the Second World War
– would be an ideal moment to inaugurate it at the United Nations.
The paper was headed 'World War Memorial Fund for Disaster
Relief'. The idea blazed like an electric storm: 'with a kind of inner
compulsion and I knew I had to react to it'.[2]

Cheshire was due to give a televised Remembrance Day address
at Christ's Hospital, and he spoke of the concept. In his original
paper he had urged that the appeal be left to spread naturally by
word of mouth, with no high-profile publicity or paid fund-raisers.
Unless it had the inner momentum to run on its own, he reasoned,
it could not conceivably reach its target.[3] Spontaneous development
is exactly what now seemed to happen. The *Daily Telegraph* published an article which followed up the address at Christ's Hospital.[4]
The reaction staggered him. Saatchi and Saatchi pledged their
advertising services. A bank offered financial advice. Mrs Thatcher
announced her support. Laurence van der Post and Robert Maxwell
asked Cheshire for meetings. The *Daily Telegraph* provided a leaflet.
Donations totalled £100,000 in six months. Although not much
in relation to a target of £480 million, it felt a lot. It had all come
in of its own accord.

Within months, the scheme was being independently adopted
abroad. Australia launched it from the new parliament building in
Canberra on Anzac Day.[5] The Prime Minister of Italy backed it.
An inaugural ceremony in Delhi later in 1989 was attended by eight
hundred people. In New Zealand, Canada, Japan and in several
European countries, the fund took off.

Cheshire chose a whistle for the fund's identifying symbol,
because on 1 July 1916 a chorus of whistles had signalled the start
of that most awful cull of human life, the first day on the Somme.
Early in 1989 plans were laid for a sponsored national 'Whistle
Walk' during the week in which the anniversary of the battle's
opening fell. Cheshire wrote to schools across the country asking
them to organize courses of sixteen miles, a distance corresponding
with the length of front along which the Somme assault had taken
place. The elderly or infirm were encouraged to join in for lesser
distances – say, a hundred yards, which on that hot day seventy-three

years before was about as far as many soldiers managed to get.

Cheshire originally seems to have entertained the target as quickly attainable, as the concept went, so to speak, supercritical in the public mind. He was still thinking this way the following spring, when he told building societies and several high street banks that a million walkers, each raising, say, £10, would yield £10 million.[6] Would they help with administration or publicity? The building societies agreed, the banks were cagey. Barclays' Head of Community Enterprises considered the target over-optimistic.[7] In any case, the banks were already contributing through something called the Disaster Emergency Committee, which included Oxfam, the Save the Children Fund, Christian Aid and the British Red Cross.[8] How did the WWMF differ?

From the start Cheshire had seen that inter-charity turf wars were to be avoided, and that the fund should complement, not undermine, existing ex-Service and disaster relief appeals.[9] This meant projecting the fund's unique identity as a living form of remembrance, without which, as he often said, it would be 'just another disaster relief fund'.[10] It also required consultation with others.[11] Six months on, it is not clear how far such coordination had proceeded. But then, it was still early days.

In May 1989 a UK management committee was formed which enlisted such talents as the financial director of Morgan Grenfell, the creative director of Saatchi and Saatchi, David Puttnam, a partner from Beer Davis Publicity, Sir Peter Ramsbotham and Wendy Robinson, who had previously headed fund-raising for Comic Relief. To judge from its minutes, the first meeting was upbeat.[12] Cheshire reiterated the concept, summarized progress and looked ahead to a ceremony at the beginning of September, when the WWMF's first-fruits would be handed to the Secretary-General of the United Nations. The tape of a specially composed song[13] was so well received that members asked to hear it again, wondering if Cliff Richard would adopt it, or if an orchestral arrangement could be played at the Proms. There was talk of a promotional film. Saatchis unveiled two eye-catching posters. It was heady stuff.

There was also some hard thinking. PR experts advised that

public support was not inexhaustible. What was needed, they said, was a new approach to disaster relief, something with 'sweep awareness' which would transcend differences of age, class and nationality. The way to counter first-world compassion fatigue might be to raise the capital fund in a single concentrated campaign. If fund-raising were to start in earnest, say, in September 1989 and finish in 1995, its duration would correspond with that of the Second World War itself, with anniversaries like the Battle of Britain and D-Day to sustain public awareness along the way. The target was upped to £500 million.

Planning and press coverage[14] continued through the summer. The sum raised by the Whistle Walk was relatively modest, but individual walks attracted local media attention, which helped to spread the fund's message. At the end of August an international council of twelve participating nations was launched in Paris,[15] in a week which began with a volley of letters to the UK press, each urging support for the fund's aims over the signatures of Bob Geldof, Bobby Charlton, Paul McCartney, Sir David Lean, Sir Alec Guinness, Dan Maskell, Lord Penney, Henry Cooper, Sir Matt Busby, the Archbishop of Canterbury, Cardinal Hume and the Chief Rabbi[16] – a list for sweep awareness if ever there was one. On 28 August Péres de Cuéllar, the UN Secretary-General, met Cheshire in Paris for the symbolic ceremony. Back in Britain four days later, flanked by two Vietnamese boat children, Cheshire laid a wreath upon the grave of the Unknown Soldier in Westminster Abbey.

This takes us to September 1989. Thus far the memorial fund had run under the auspices of the Ryder–Cheshire Mission for the Relief of Suffering. However, the Charity Commission advised that the charitable objects of the mission were not wide enough to embrace those of the fund,[17] and it was therefore decided to establish the Memorial Fund as an independent charity. A trust deed was drafted and approved.[18] The new trustees would be Sir Peter Ramsbotham, Lady Ryder, David Puttnam and Cheshire himself. Ramsbotham briefly formed an impression that Cheshire wished him to chair the trustee body, but Cheshire told him:

I am afraid that unintentionally I left this a little unclear. When I referred to your being chairman, I meant chairman of the mission. To ask you to be chairman of the UK section of the WWMF would not be realistic. For one thing it would involve you in a huge amount of work and meetings, and for another I am anxious to keep this under my own control . . . Things happen with great speed and decisions have to be taken quickly.[19]

As if to make his point, on 9 November the Berlin Wall came down. Its fall seemed to epitomize what Cheshire had been saying since 1945: the world was improvable if ordinary people acted together in goodwill. Twentieth-century Berlin, successively a metaphor for war and peace, division and reconciliation, now offered inspiration to span national and demographic boundaries and kindle the imagination of youth. 'Events *this week* in Berlin,' Cheshire noted, 'have altered perspectives.'

Cheshire and the management committee had already been thinking about 'a major international Bob Geldof type concert' to raise funds,[20] and it was only a small step from this to the idea of a rock concert astride the line of the Berlin Wall. An advisory committee was formed of people 'with extensive experience in the promotion of major charity fund-raising events'. This body predicted 'huge profits for the fund' if the concert succeeded, and no financial risk to the fund if it didn't. Talk of failure was in any case hypothetical. When Cheshire asked each member of the committee in turn whether there was any conceivable possibility that the concert might miscarry, all said 'no'.[21]

Cheshire reflected. His entire life had been a negotiation between impetuosity and reflection. At some times he had acted spontaneously. At others he had becalmed himself, listening for the wind of Providence. His normal method when starting something new was to avoid grandiose strategy and move gradually, making each step proportional to means and circumstance. He was therefore wary of those who urged the appointment of professional highflyers. Yes, they should listen to and be grateful for expert advice, and of course a time would come when formal business planning would be needed. But his instinct at this point was not to try to mastermind the future. Only through openness did it seem possible that the Holy Spirit might orient the project in the longer term.

Paradoxically, this is what convinced him to go ahead. Had the Berlin Wall opportunity not arrived out of a clear sky? It was self-contained. Organization would be no burden because it would be out-sourced. Money was not a problem either, because everyone said the concert was going to be self-financing. All that was being asked just then was a little seed money, 'to promote interest and attract commercial backers'. Assured that the concert would help and could not hinder, Cheshire agreed. They should go ahead. A date was set.

One idea led to another. In reply to Cheshire's natural desire for Soviet involvement in the concert, Moscow volunteered a consignment of metal from scrapped SS20 nuclear missiles, suggesting that the metal be recycled into something which would advance the fund's aims – medallions, for instance – with attendant publicity that linked to the concert. If the Americans did likewise, the symbolism would be powerful.

Welcome in itself, this proposal was additionally heartening because it offered new means to engage American public interest. The United States was essential to the fund's success, not least because its wealth and organizing power exceeded those of all the other participating nations put together. Yet headway there had been slow. Early approaches to public figures had been inconclusive,[22] and the main veterans' associations had been unresponsive.[23] Cheshire also discovered, or was reminded, that many Americans take a poor view of the United Nations.*[24] The idea of recycling metal from decommissioned missiles was thus timely.

Cheshire put the idea to Casper Weinberger,†[25] and Sir Antony Acland, the UK's ambassador in Washington, was asked for advice about organizing a joint ceremony at which materials from both superpowers could be handed over. A scheme to turn the metal into pens was evolved with the pen-makers Parker, prompting headlines

---

* Ironically (or perhaps most appropriately) some of the strongest encouragement had come from veterans of the 509TH Composite Group. Chuck Sweeney, who had delivered the bomb to Nagasaki, was enthusiastic, and another member, now a distinguished lawyer, gave extensive help in bringing the US fund into existence.

† Former US Secretary of State, then working for *Forbes Magazine*.

like 'Charity pens mightier than missiles' and 'Swords into Plow-shares'.[26] Dick Cheney, the US Defence Secretary, applauded.[27] In parallel, famous names were being canvassed as trustees for a US fund,[28] and the search was on for a flag-bearer among 'well known, publicly credible American figureheads'.[29] Everything, it seemed, was moving in the right direction. The fact that it was seemed to confirm Cheshire's faith in letting things unfold of their own accord.

Nevertheless, as the project grew, so did a tension between Cheshire's frugality and the demands of an enterprise aiming to raise £500 million in six years. In some minds the size of the target, and the brevity of the time allowed to achieve it, called for a high-profile campaign. In the United States alone, set-up costs for an office, staff, furniture, equipment and travel were estimated at $512,000. This was unaffordable, but Cheshire was temporarily under a misapprehension that the costs would be borne elsewhere. In the event a bill for half of the US coordinator's salary was presented to the Leonard Cheshire International Committee, with Cheshire himself responsible for finding the rest.

The US coordinator herself[30] kept Cheshire busy with questions and suggestions. Could they afford to spend $30,000–50,000 on a specialist organizer of fund-raising events? On his next visit, an appearance on *Good Morning America* might be possible. Courtney Kennedy was being canvassed, because it's 'always useful to have a Kennedy on board'. And what about Mother Teresa – as an 'adviser, as a name, as anything? It spells immediate credibility in the States.'[31] This was moving away from the spirit of a movement meant to 'spread naturally by word of mouth and as opportunity presents'.

Cheshire was caught in a maelstrom of work, much of it unfamiliar yet highly specialized, and as the concert neared he was asked for decisions he had not expected to have to take. One was to find a new date – for various reasons the planned date had to be abandoned and the event was put back. Then there was the matter of money. Responsibility for finding sponsorship to offset production costs rested with the concert's producer, who had suggested that the merchant bankers Morgan Grenfell (who were already helping in other ways) be asked to underwrite them against a contract with a concert sponsor. Morgan Grenfell were sympathetic, but lack of time defeated the search for the amount of sponsorship that was required. This left a hard choice. Either the fund itself could underwrite the production costs, or they must cancel.

The figures looked daunting, but financial forecasts provided by reputable accountants indicated little actual risk. Cheshire accordingly agreed that the fund should advance £400,000 to the concert via Operation Dinghy Ltd, a company which had been set up as the fund's trading arm.[32]

The event appeared to be in the best of hands. Two of the foremost set designers of global events were invited to design and produce the set. World-famous bands and soloists agreed to perform. Live Aid's commercial activity coordinator was involved. A writer was commissioned, a site found. The media warmed to it with headlines like 'Cheshire Backs Huge Berlin Concert to Boost Disaster Fund' and 'Cheshire's £500m Dream a Stage Closer'.[33] On the concert's eve, the figures still looked reassuring. It would be the largest rock concert Europe had ever seen.

Which it was. Some 350,000 people attended what the *Frankfurter Allgemeine Zeitung* described as '*Die Rockshow der Rockshows*'.[34] First indications next day were that it had run to budget and would be in surplus. Others close to Cheshire breathed a sigh of relief. Cheshire conceded that he might have done more to keep his fellow trustees informed during the run-up, but explained that this would have been impractical because of the speed at which decisions had been needed. Nevertheless, he had known in his bones that it would come right, and so it had. Royalties from the album and video were expected to run into millions. The concert had put the fund in a strong position.

Except that it hadn't. Production costs had been forecast at around $8.5 million, $9 million at the outside. When the bills arrived and the effects of the exchange rate were factored in, the actual costs were close to $13 million. By September 1990 Operation Dinghy Ltd was in debt to the tune of approximately £1.5 million. This included the £400,000 which had been advanced by the fund.

At the end of the year, Morgan Grenfell withdrew its annual covenant.

A lesser spirit might have sagged. For Cheshire, however, two setbacks did not invalidate the concept. If the cause was right, the means would follow, and this cause was undoubtedly right. Moreover, the royalties were still to come and other revenue-generating initiatives – like the Parker pen project (upon which large hopes were pinned) – were in the pipeline. Without the concert, indeed, there would have been no World Memorial Pen project, and he was therefore reluctant to see the concert in isolation from the continuum of the fund's development. The appointment of a full-time appeals director[35] promised much and would spread some of the load. Given a little time and a fair wind they could turn things round.

And for a while, it looked as though they could. Over the next twelve months, some good things happened. David Puttnam dedicated the world premiere of *The Memphis Belle* to the fund.[36] The video went to number one in the United States. There was an inspiring performance of Mozart's *Requiem* in Oxford's Christ Church cathedral,[37] and talk of a concert in Westminster Abbey which Simon Rattle might be asked to conduct. John Major agreed to launch Crickathon, a fund-raising initiative by the cricketing world which was expected to raise £10 million in three years.[38] Cheshire's life peerage in the 1991 Birthday Honours reawakened public interest in the fund. Plans were laid for the first World Memorial Day on 1 January 1992.

The fund itself, meanwhile, was renamed as the Memorial Fund for Disaster Relief. With that came a shift of focus. The fund was taking shape against a background which included the disintegration of the Soviet empire, wars in Ethiopia, Somalia and Kashmir, and ominous discord in the Balkans. Emphasis was accordingly broadened from natural catastrophe to embrace disasters of conflict. The fund was not to be an operating body in itself. It aimed rather to commit its income to those front-line agencies best placed to provide relief, and to relieve disasters which were not well publicized. The underlying concept, however, remained the same. For every life lost, a life saved.[39]

Yet the underlying position was bad. By early 1992 there were still creditors awaiting payment. Royalties, though substantial, had not recouped the deficit,[40] and despite some slow improvement the company was technically insolvent. The World Memorial Pen had yet to meet expectations.[41] Crickathon's launch had been washed out by bad weather, and its organizing company was in liquidation.

Beyond all this, Morgan Grenfell's cancellation of its covenant at the end of 1990 had denied income upon which the fund had relied to meet operating costs and develop new projects. Since that time, and in the absence of revenue from the World Memorial Pen project, the fund had drawn on its reserves. It was now existing from month to month.

World Memorial Day 1992 exemplified many of these difficulties. Cheshire saw it as an occasion for individual inner observance, when people the world over would pause at the start of a new year to reflect that human progress required their personal contribution.[42] He hoped that the day would establish itself in the world's calendar, bring charities together for common purposes and further the general aims of the fund. Although primarily intended as a spiritual occasion, it obviously required some material embodiment, at least at the start. Hence, alongside the circulation of information and press publicity, 300,000 badges had been struck out of missile metal.

During January the project's coordinator, Tom Beaumont, compiled a report on how the first World Memorial Day had gone.[43] For a start, only 25,000 badges had been sold. No research as to costs or quantity had preceded their manufacture, and inflexible pricing had discouraged many potential sales outlets. The badges themselves had been disliked, and the provenance of the metal caused some to take them back, in fear that they might be radioactive. Press coverage had been 'modest', and the responses of fund branches which had been written to beforehand had mostly been 'pitiful'. Research among young people disclosed low awareness of the fund and World Memorial Day – which was a worry, as the young were a target audience. Few undergraduates had heard of either, the significance of the whistle logo was a mystery to them, and the fund's £500 million target was considered 'faintly ridiculous'. The fund's concept was not getting through.

Beaumont traced many weaknesses to the short time which had been allowed for preparation. The proper lead time for such an event would be eighteen months, with all essential planning, research, sponsorship and marketing decisions in place one year ahead. Their actual run-in had been seven weeks.

Robert Kandt, the fund's appeals director, passed Beaumont's report to Cheshire in February 1992. Cheshire appears not to have acknowledged it, nor to have given much guidance for World Memorial Day 1993 beyond voicing a wish that it should take place.[44] Yet the fund was now barely able to meet its own operating costs, let alone mount another major event. Kandt was still wondering what to do with 275,000 badges left over from 1992. Cheshire's non-reaction to the report might have concealed a sense of hurt, for Beaumont had been forthright, and some of his observations related to Cheshire's own decisions. But Cheshire normally welcomed well-intended straight talking, and for all its prickly home truths the report was sympathetic to World Memorial Day's impulse. A simpler explanation is that in mid-February 1992 Cheshire had other things on his mind.

Throughout 1991 Cheshire had continued to champion the fund, coaxing forth donations, encouraging events and travelling to canvass the backing of heads of state and public figures. This ceaseless effort had included two visits to the United Nations. Cheshire believed that the disappearance of the Soviet veto from the Security Council could open the way to more active UN involvement in curbing wars and guaranteeing the safety of the insecure. In this respect, the fund linked with his larger vision of a world in which the UN would confront injustice rather than simply alleviate its consequences. By 1992 Cheshire had come to believe that the Memorial Fund's primary efforts should be to encourage the establishment of a United Nations disaster relief corps, and to assist 'improved cooperation and integration amongst international aid and relief agencies'.[45]

Cheshire saw formation of the relief corps as a project for countries willing to place elements of their armed forces – already trained for emergencies and rapid mobilization – under UN direction. The corp's function would be rapid response, the provision of necessities in the first hours after an earthquake, a flood, a typhoon. Its establishment would require powerful political advocacy, and one of the tasks he set himself early in 1992 was the lobbying of British and US statesmen to bring this about.

For the other aspect, coordination, Cheshire was thinking of something which might be called 'Pathfinders', an umbrella body for the numerous small, often specialized, charities which existed in the humanitarian field, whose collective efforts seemed not always to mesh as well as he thought they might.

This, then, was the UK fund's agenda at the end of a meeting of its trustee body on 25 March 1992. The trustees agreed to convene again in August. Earlier that afternoon Cheshire had indicated that, for health reasons, he would be reducing his future involvement, doing so gradually over the next twelve months. No one then foresaw that when the trustees did reassemble, he would not be with them.

A detailed account of subsequent events lies outside the scope of this book, which is about Cheshire rather than about the institutions he founded. Even so, most readers will ask two questions about the fund which should not be shirked: what went wrong, and what happened to it?

Taking the second question first, after Cheshire's death the idea of raising £500 million faded. The UK fund was subsequently wound up, its assets being assigned to the establishment of the Leonard Cheshire Chair of Conflict Recovery at University College London, and a National Memorial Arboretum within the National Forest at Alrewas, near Lichfield.* The Chair is intended to advance Cheshire's wish to encourage a more coherent and rapid response to disaster and conflict. The arboretum, launched with its own appeal by John Major in November 1994, symbolizes commemoration.

As to what went wrong, it is tempting to discern a kind of Sophoclean drama in which a final enterprise miscarries, or the protagonist falls victim to a long-buried flaw which returns to haunt him. Time and again, for instance, Cheshire had cautioned himself

---

* Respectively, under the auspices of the Leonard Cheshire International Committee and the Ryder–Cheshire Mission. The funds in several other countries have been reassigned to cognate purposes; that in India, considered by Cheshire in 1992 to be 'probably the strongest anywhere', lives on.

against the notion of personal indispensability,[46] yet in 1989 he was 'anxious to keep this under my own control'. Or again, 'Everything that has started small seems to be expanding. The few things that started big have all vanished.'[47] The Memorial Fund started as a very big idea. We might also wonder if there were fair-weather friends who deserted when the going got tough, or recall his mother's comment that money management had never been her son's strong suit. Looking at his many ventures down the years, some might say that a debacle like this had been waiting to happen all along. In all such musing, however, we would probably be on the wrong track.

There was no flaw in the fund's underlying vision, in which past individual and collective tragedy would be redeemed by future hope, and no hint of hubris in Cheshire's effort to attain it. Proportional to the world's need £500 million was a modest target. Cheshire often said that he never chose to do anything on his own initiative, but rather responded to a need, and then only on the basis that there was no alternative. Evidence of need was mounting by the day, and does so still. Four or five of the world's richest nations could have written the cheque on the spot, but since they didn't, the Memorial Fund met all those tests. With effective underpinning it could have worked.

The underlying issue was structural, and yet relates to Cheshire's spirituality. Most of the structures supporting his projects had evolved over many years, adapting as circumstances changed. Gradual growth had allowed him time to foster the ethos of his work among those who took it forward, so attaining the mysteriously enviable fusion of head and heart outlined in *Thoughts for the Future*. In the case of the fund, however, the tree needed to be full-grown almost overnight. This is why in 1989–90 Cheshire refused to let go, fearing that the project's essence might be throttled by uncomprehending managerialism, and why in 1991 he was still resisting advice to introduce a three-year plan. Even then he remained apprehensive, lest over-organizing strategy should obstruct Providence. So often his projects had taken unforeseen turns, which nevertheless made perfect sense when viewed in retrospect, and cumulatively. Imposed strategies limited the context in which such things could happen. His most recent experience of the fund – its birth, the cascade of help, the scrapped missiles – convinced him that they were happening then. He was trying, as it were, to hold the door open for a little while longer.

Yet in extrapolating from experience, taking one step at a time, reacting to events as they unfolded, he may have underestimated the extent to which the fund did *not* equate with previous lessons. Most notably, from 1990 the main events to which he was reacting do not now look like providential innovations so much as the compounding consequences of earlier over-optimism, which inexorably narrowed space for manoeuvre.

This was harrowing, not least because Cheshire regarded the fund as one of the three most important steps of his life. To one friend, he confided that nothing else had mattered more. Nothing else had worked him more, either. The sketch above conveys no inkling of the emotional and intellectual energy which he brought to it, the distances he travelled, the multitude of further problems with which he wrestled, or the exhausting effort which supported his patience in dealings with others who had strong views of their own. More labour went into some memos than would have been needed to write his finest book.

Above all, in this project as in no other, Cheshire had striven to open his heart and mind to the will of the Holy Spirit, and it is difficult not to wonder whether towards the end he did not feel some bewilderment, perhaps even desolation in consequence of what had happened. Yet if he did, there is no trace of it. While he was at times racked by concern, and his responsibilities to creditors caused him much personal anguish, he never wrote or said anything which implied reproach about the predicament in which he found himself. In faith, he may have supposed that the fact that the concert had not turned out as expected would have meaning which God's good time would illuminate. Thirty years before, looking back at the collapse of VIP, he had said: 'Who could tell what it might lead to? Everything works out for the best. Even failure.'[48]

Late in 1991 Cheshire asked Father Fuller to supper at Maunsel Street. Down the years the two had kept in touch, although after that intense companionship in the mid-1950s their meetings had not been so many. Father Fuller wondered what lay behind the invitation, half expecting it to be something to do with the homes. Instead, Cheshire produced a small book, and asked if he had read it.

I had. The title is *The Cry of Jesus on the Cross* ('My God, my God, why have you forsaken me' [Matthew xxvii, 46; Mark xv, 34]). This cry, says the author, expresses the greatest loneliness imaginable, the experience of the absence of God. Not something, one might think, that the Son of God could undergo. Nevertheless, he chose to be tempted [Hebrews iv, 15] in *every* way that we are, though without sin. Leonard was greatly moved by this thought . . . Our response, he said, must be to give nothing less than everything in return.[49]

Cheshire talked about the book with intense enthusiasm, saying that 'he wanted to hold nothing back from the Lord'.[50] Or as Father Fuller later considered, 'Leonard's discovery of this little book can be regarded as a timely preparation, in God's providence, for his final illness.'

25. Going Forth

Down the years Cheshire's body and health had taken a battering. Midhurst's surgeons had removed a lung and sections of four ribs. Malaria and dysentery had done him no good. Coeliac disease demanded a gluten-free diet. Years of sitting hatless in the sun may have contributed to skin cancer in later life. Relentless work taxed him.

Overall, however, despite the wear and tear, he remained fit. At the age of seventy he could sprint about on a tennis court for an hour and a quarter, provided there was someone on the other side of the net to challenge him. His eating was frugal. Smoking had long been abandoned, and although he never came to disapprove of alcohol, he lost interest in it and became teetotal by default. He knew the importance of sleep, and his ability not to worry about problems he could not solve had protected him from destructive stresses. As for the work, new ideas rejuvenated his spirit.

Even so, from 1988 he began to lose weight, and from time to time he noticed odd sensations. Sometimes his feet felt cold. He became prone to dehydration and fumbled when tying shoelaces. Holding a pen to write four thousand Christmas cards no longer seemed easy.

After a long African tour in 1988 he became so tired that he cancelled several engagements. His doctor cleared him of any serious complaint, but warned against overwork, ordered a month's complete rest and a cut in workload of 25 per cent thereafter.[1] Then the idea of the Memorial Fund flared up. The month off was scrapped, and into this new project Cheshire plunged. Thus it was that at the age of seventy-three, eight years after most men have retired from one job, Cheshire found himself working at two. He worked all day, every day. 'So long as I can run,' he said cheerfully a year later, 'I shall run.' For a time he did, and burned more brightly because of it. But gradually, fatigue returned.

Early 1992 found Sue Ryder in Poland, Cheshire at Laundry Cottage. One evening he turned in, having unplugged the telephone to avoid disturbance. He reawakened in a roomful of smoke. Something was on fire. Feeling along the wall he managed to reconnect the telephone and called for help. By now scarcely able to breathe, and pausing only to retrieve his breviary, he climbed outside on to the window ledge. The drop seemed too great to jump, at any rate in the dark, so there he waited in his pyjamas until the emergency services arrived. When they did, he was whisked off to hospital. An assistant telephoned Sue Ryder in Warsaw. Sue Ryder offered to cancel her trip and come home. No, said Cheshire, all things considered, he was fine. But there was damage to the house, and soot damage to family possessions it contained. Cheshire put his best face on things, later saying that the house would be 'a far better building' following the repairs.[2] There was, nevertheless, some cost to his spirit. Laundry Cottage was his bolt-hole, a place which linked with his parents and the early days of Le Court. He was not to stay there again.

There was a cost to his spirit, too, in the continuing trials of the Memorial Fund. Writing in early 1992 about the calamitous debts he said, 'Nothing in my forty-two years of working in the field of charity has worried me as much as this.'[3]

A few days later Cheshire went to see a neurologist in Cambridge and another in London. In mid-February he was told that he was suffering from motor neurone disease. He telephoned the news to Sue Ryder from the House of Lords. She had already noticed the symptoms and suspected their meaning. Quietly, they talked about what would follow. Weight loss would continue until he shrank to a husk. There would be racking cramps. Breathing would become harder. So would swallowing, to the point where he might choke on his own saliva. A new tennis court was planned at Cavendish. A little plaintively, he asked 'Will I play tennis again?' Gently, Sue Ryder said no. Decline might be slow or it might be swift, but whichever it was there wouldn't be any more tennis.

Sue Ryder telephoned the diagnosis to Sir Geoffrey Howlett, chairman of the foundation. On 25 February the foundation informed the Queen and the Prime Minister.

Cheshire had often watched death. Not its result (although he knew that too) but as a personal encounter, an intimacy, during the many times he had accompanied others to death's threshold. Vigils with others had taught him that everyone's death is 'all of its own, different from anybody else's'.[4]

Death is the final and crucial consummation of that lifelong process of self-determination and struggle for perfection. It is the bringing to maturity of all that a man has made himself during his lifetime, the taking possession without possibility of self-deception or ambiguity of his own personality as it has been developed through the conduct of his life, and most particularly in the domain of his freely expressed moral acts. As such it is an act of the profoundest meaning and consequence, which gives an irrevocable direction to our life for all eternity.[5]

Cheshire believed that we are born to live a particular life and die a particular death. Death was the hour to be lived as no other. Or, as he put it four months later, 'It's no use running the race brilliantly and then stopping one yard short. You have to cross that tape.' Yet just then he had no idea how far ahead the tape was stretched.

For some weeks he worked normally. His letters and memoranda – a number of them upon extremely thorny subjects – were as focused and painstaking as ever, and on 25 March he chaired the inaugural meeting of the board of trustees of the Memorial Fund. Not liking to disappoint others, he fulfilled as many outside engagements as he could. Forthcoming trips to India, Moscow and Australia were held open. His diary continued to accumulate commitments into 1993.

Early in April he wrote to his cousin Michael Barstow: 'Yes, it would help if the diagnosis were wrong, but the last ten days or so have seen quite a substantial wastage of muscles. All the same . . . it's just one of those things that happen in life and may well turn out a blessing in disguise . . . I see it . . . as a little challenge, though the thought of being a nuisance to those close to me is perhaps the one setback.'[6] He greeted accelerating weight loss and ebbing strength with a kind of elation, as if motor neurone disease was a pool in which God had gently dipped him. Hitherto, he told Wally Sullivan, he'd been 'on the outside looking in. Now I'm one of them.'

> . . . if you find yourself inside a disability, there must be ways in which you can work (I don't like to say 'for') disabled people; ways which you can't actually describe or see; working in a more profound way than you could as a very fit man on the outside.[7]

> That gives me great joy; a kind of joy that wants to well up inside me. I say that with hesitation because when my family look at me and obviously see me slipping away I must respond to their need and be careful not to sound unkind. But if it is joy within me, then in some way that I don't understand, it's going to be shared by those I'm close to. That is the most significant part of this disability to me.[8]

Again and again he returned to the idea of the illness as a blessing.[9]

It was, nevertheless, a blessing with growing practical limitations. By mid-April he was visibly wasting and the trip to India and Moscow which had been scheduled for September looked impossible. Yet he yearned to see India. India, where they had been married; Dehra Dun, where so much of their work had begun. With Sue Ryder, he longed to go back to Raphael.

The Indian journey was brought forward to mid-May.[10] Lord King, the then Chairman of British Airways, stepped in with two first-class return tickets to Delhi. Jeromy and Elizabeth would go too. Before they left, Christopher came to visit, and the brothers reminisced as they had not done in years. On the day of the departure a press release announced Cheshire's illness. The news was in Britain's papers next morning.[11]

Cheshire was now capable of walking only short distances. Maj. General K. M. Dhody, Chairman of the India Memorial Fund, helped with the arrangements, which included a pause in Delhi for several days' rest, a farewell visit to the Delhi home, and meetings of the Eastern Region committee and the fund. The army laid on a helicopter to fly them up to Dehra Dun.

Millions will have seen something of this journey, for Paul Freeman of Anglia TV rearranged his diary to make a film about it. *An Indian Summer: Leonard Cheshire's Final Pilgrimage* is lit with smiles, coloured by garlands, perhaps above all warmed by uninhibited touch. If he could not speak for long, he could hold. Lepers, helpers, children, friends and colleagues from other parts of India who had come up to Raphael all embraced him, and he them. He was asked a question about death, and replied in a kind of poem.[12]

> Heaven is a place of peace;
> This world, by contrast, is a battlefield.
> I just want to remain on this battlefield.
> I want to remain with my family
> and those I love and do what
> little I can to help those in need.

As he left, he suddenly sank to his knees and kissed the ground.[13]

On 29 May, immediately after the return from Raphael, the foundation held a reception at the Tower of London. With Wally Sullivan's support, Cheshire insisted on walking down the steps into the hall.

. . . I am he sure he knew [that] would be his final farewell to his trustees. He asked me to stand near him with a glass of orange juice. As he had no saliva, he needed to moisten his mouth now and again. Because I was standing so close to him I saw the emotion that flowed between him and some very old friends. I was choked with emotion, as was everyone there, so Heaven alone knows what he was going through.[14]

Two days later the Queen Mother unveiled a statue of Sir Arthur Harris beside the RAF church of St Clement Danes in London's Strand. This was a highly charged occasion, at which members of the Bomber Command Association listened with pensive dignity while the Queen Mother spoke against a background of heckling and scuffles. Cheshire attended against medical advice, afterwards saying, 'I would have gone even if I had to be carried on a stretcher.' Then, above the shouts, the voice of an approaching Lancaster. Sitting in his wheelchair, flanked by companions of fifty years before, Cheshire looked skyward. It was his last public appearance.

Back at Cavendish, he tried to write.

. . . my mind is woolly. It is difficult to hold it down on to something. Even dictating a letter, I now have great difficulty focusing my mind on the letter although it is quite specific and held in front of me. This also happens at Mass. My hour of prayer in the morning, the time I used really to love, is now just sitting and finding I'm all over the place. As my complaint takes greater hold on me I get forgetful. The fact that I can't remember Carney's name – Christian name – is astonishing.[15]

He embarked on a series of reflections about things that finally mattered: acceptance of his illness, the homes, the role of the UN, the Memorial Fund, the task of death, the Family of the Cross, his own family, prayer. Above all, prayer. Some thoughts he dictated, others were taken down during conversations.[16] At first sight the ideas are a jumble. They meander, repeat, digress, start and stop randomly, like bars shuffled from an incomplete music. That does not matter, for they can be read as they were created, in no particular order. The fragments glow, and record a struggle. As Father Fuller puts it. 'He had not yet reached perfection, but with St Paul he pressed on, "hoping to take hold of that for which Christ once took hold of me".'*

Pressing on wasn't easy.

There is a great danger that we automatically say what we know we ought to say. Forty years ago the Church was always telling you – if anything disastrous happens – to say 'I accept it' or 'I offer it up'. And so it's quite easy to make that an automatic response which isn't really in your heart. Let me look at my own case. In the four or five months since I've known the diagnosis I've been going down more or less steadily and I do find new things I wasn't expecting. Things that limit your privacy, your ability to manage on your own. I have no doubt that some of those things are going to be difficult to accept. All the same, in your heart, you know perfectly well that it's uniting you a little more closely with the sufferings of our Lord. It's bringing you closer to other disabled people. They are going through it but we look at them and I don't think we really always appreciate what some of the things they have to put up with mean to them as people.[17]

Or again:

* Philippians iii, 12.

A small point about motor neurone. I said that it was difficult to sleep. The reason is you get peculiar cramps which at night are hard to bear . . . I find it impossible to lie at ease in bed due to the fact that I have only one lung and that I have no flesh on my body. But the basic problem with it to me is the fatigue. There is just this weight of heaviness and tiredness, both mental and physical, so sleep makes a big difference. Obviously eating is important but it's difficult to eat as I can't tolerate too much and now have swallowing problems. Then you must exercise within your limits as much as you can but you can't go beyond the limits. Doing letters, seeing people and talking is tiring, so it's very difficult to work out the right balance of what you should do to remain at your optimum. In a way it's quite a challenge; I find it exhilarating in one sense but nobody can give you a straight answer. You have to work it out yourself.[18]

He continued to mull over the question about death which had been put to him at Raphael.

I think they were really saying 'Are you looking forward to it?' Well I had to say that . . . the thought of what God is giving us is so overwhelming that you just can't face it. It's too unbelievable. Then immediately it induces the thought that if this is what God is giving us, out of His sheer goodness and not for any merit at all of mine, then 'Please give me a little more time to do better than I have done.'[19]

There were still things he wanted to do. One of them was to hammer the spiritual appeal behind World Memorial Day into language which would outlast him, and so 'help people understand that if we want a better world each of us must make a contribution to bring it about'.[20]

On Thursday 9 July the Queen gave her annual reception for members of the Order of Merit. Although down to the weight of a child he was determined to attend, at least some of his resolve stemming from a hope that he would be able to broach the subject of World Memorial Day.[21] Sue Ryder went with him to Buckingham Palace. The Queen remembered the occasion in her Christmas message that year. Cheshire had borne illness 'with all the fortitude and cheerfulness to be expected of a holder of the Victoria Cross'. However, what struck her more forcibly than his physical courage was the fact that he made no reference to the illness at all. He spoke only of 'his hopes and plans to make life better for others'.

After this there were no more engagements.

The truth is that I have to withdraw from active participation in all my ventures. I have to do this as quickly as possible but remain consistent in doing it properly. In other words I have to see that the right people are in place with the right instructions, or, according to which is appropriate, the correct vision of what we are going for. But that does not mean that my involvement diminishes – it just alters.[22]

Sue Ryder nursed him. A common feature of advanced motor neurone is the over-production of saliva, to the point at which a sufferer is at risk of drowning. In Cheshire's case it went the other way – saliva dried up, and his mouth and throat became permanently sore. Sue Ryder scoured local pharmacies for a saliva-inducing preparation, but none were able to make it up. There remained a risk of choking, for his muscles were now so wasted that he was unable to cough. Unable to chew, he drank through a straw. Cramps hindered sleep. Pressure on his bones through emaciated flesh denied even the limited comfort of finding a restful position in which to sit or lie. Dance music of the 1930s, a recreational standby since his twenties, was now too poignant to play.

Until the last days he continued to work, seated in an electrically operated chair, using what very little was left of his voice to dictate memos and letters. At other times he rested as best he could, propped on the window seat of his study, looking into the garden. As at Midhurst, there were birds on the window sill.

A journalist rang from the *Evening Standard*. He invited her to Cavendish. Was he frightened by death?

Oh no, how could I be? I've worked all these years with disabled people and, really, it's a kind of confirmation of my vocation. Before, it was always a case of me and them but I can now say, 'We disabled'.

I mustn't be presumptuous – I may find that the physical difficulties get me down – but it has given me a kind of inner joy. If you're a Christian, then you have to believe that the Christian way is the way of the Cross. I've had a good life. This is just something to be got round – a bit of flak on the way to the target.[23]

A bit of flak. The words would be better heard than read, for his knack of tackling subjects which might be awkward or profound in a voice which combined simplicity and impishness was one of the things that made him irresistible.

Priest friends were among those who kept him company. A member of the Royal Family visited incognito. On hot days, Sue Ryder cooled him with ice cubes in muslin bags. The illness had conferred a strange benediction on the marriage, and she dearly wanted to talk. But he was not able to talk much now. At intervals of a few hours she read out lines from his breviary.[24] On 24 July he dictated some last instructions.

The following Wednesday, 29 July, he rang Wally Sullivan.

I asked him how he was, and immediately felt awful for asking such a daft question, but one does this sort of thing sometimes without thinking. He said he was all right, but had had a bad night's sleep. He said that because he had almost no flesh on him, he could not get comfortable. I said I was so sorry, and wished that I could do something to help. He simply said, 'Oh, don't worry Wally – it's just a passing phase.'[25]

The fluctuating consciousness of the little that was left of him had itself became a kind of prayer – no longer something he did, but something he was.* He struggled to explain.

. . . nearly everybody, all the priests and the modern spiritual writers, say that when you are ill all your energies are focused on coping with your illness and getting better. So you cannot pray. But I dispute that. I know it's true but I refuse to accept that we should just merely resign ourselves to that. We should find a way of making our time prayerful.

He was still thinking forwards.

I find that the beginning of the day as you wake up is important . . . Picture in your mind a whole world waking up to a new day. People are getting organized to go out to their work: some of them are leaders of government, others are going to sweep the streets, others ill or disabled and at home. But there in that moment you have the whole world waking up, we hope to put the day to the best advantage.

The morning light is brushing aside the night's darkness. That also symbolizes

---

* After this was written I read something which Cheshire himself said in 1990: 'A man of prayer is the man whose work becomes a prayer.'

the fact that we are all in a state of becoming and evolving, so God is at work all the time, recreating the present earth and heaven into the new heaven and the new earth. So that process is also going on: *identify* with it. Don't try to be clever and think it out — just have that thought in your mind. Beauty is springing out of darkness . . . Somebody once said: 'the things that we see help us understand the unseen things'. I like the linking of what we do and what we see with a prayer aimed at the spiritual counterpart:

> *The shining sun looks down on all things*
> *and the work of the Lord is full of his glory.*
>
> Ecclesiasticus, 42:16[26]

This was one of the last things he said. On Friday 31 July, in the night, a heart attack finished him, and the light of a new sunrise swept aside all darkness.

26. Chosen Vessel

Among the papers which Andrew Boyle filed away when he finished *No Passing Glory* was a tribute to Sir Edmund Hillary. It came from a British ambassador to Paris after the war, and spoke of 'an uncompromising search into the deeper meaning of things'. One passage caught Boyle's eye. 'Men of an extreme sensibility – possessing in fact the sensibility of the artist – forced nevertheless by an interior power to choose action, yet were men of action incapable of finding a happy oblivion in action alone because they were tormented by a sense of responsibility and the need to try to understand.' 'This,' wrote Boyle in a note to himself, 'is made to apply to Hillary and to Saint-Exupéry but applies equally I think to Leonard.' Now the struggle to understand was done, and as Sue Ryder surrounded his body with candles and flowers, its end stirred the nation. *The Times*'s obituary occupied a full page. On the following Monday the *Evening Standard* published the last interview, describing him as 'The most outstanding Englishman of his generation.'[1] Letters, cards, faxes and telephone messages poured into Cavendish. There were tributes from the Royal Family, the Prime Minister, Mother Teresa, Lord Callaghan, those who knew him and many who didn't. Over three thousand of them, each to be answered individually. Cheshire's Requiem was celebrated ten days later in the chapel at Cavendish, a simple ceremony which at his own request was restricted to members of the family. Otherwise, he had said, 'where would one stop?' He was buried in the village cemetery, across the green from the home.

Later, on 25 September, a memorial mass was held in Westminster Cathedral in the presence of the late Cardinal Hume, Bishop Alan Clark, eleven priests and a congregation of seventeen hundred people. Cardinal Hume delivered a homily. He listed Cheshire's qualities, and continued: 'But there was something else. It was simply this. He had allowed God into his life and this transformed him. He had said "yes" to God, not half-heartedly, not with reluctance but, characteristically, in a manner that was total and even radical.' Total and even radical said it very well.

What other words can finish such a story? The chapter title may help. 'Chosen vessel' occurs in Chapter 9 of the Acts of the Apostles, that famous passage where Saul, on a persecutory mission against Jesus's followers in Damascus, is blinded by 'light from heaven'. Three days later the Lord appears in a vision to Ananias, one of Saul's prospective victims, asking him to go to Saul to restore his sight. Ananias bridles. Is not Saul an enemy? 'But the Lord said unto him, Go thy way: for he is a chosen vessel unto me, to bear my name before the Gentiles, and kings, and the children of Israel.'★ For some reason the phrase 'a chosen vessel' was written into the flyleaf of the Bible which was given by my godfather at my own baptism in 1947. I often wondered about its relevance, for as I grew up it never seemed likely to apply to me. But it does have an uncanny resonance for Leonard Cheshire.

Let us lastly listen to some who knew him. Sir Christopher Foxley-Norris:

When he had nothing to be proud of, there was conceit; when everything, humility.[2]

His voice was always quiet and low-pitched, but somehow almost hypnotic. Certainly inspirational, and never defeatist. 'If the cause is right, the means will be found somehow.'

He was undoubtedly the greatest stock of his generation, perhaps of all time. So far.[3]

★ Acts ix, 15. Father Fuller explains to me that the phrase 'chosen vessel' occurs in the Authorized Version (which took it from Tyndale), but apparently in no other version. The Greek can be rendered variously. The Latin Vulgate's *vas electionis* influenced the Catholic (Rheims) translation of 1582, which gives 'vessel of election'. Bishop Challoner's eighteenth-century edition follows the Rheims.

Lord Denning:

He has done more good for more people than anyone else in the country.[4]

Sir Alec Guinness:★

I ran into him briefly a few times, here in Petersfield, in London and Bangalore. His modesty, simplicity and sheer ordinariness were awe-inspiring; he also had a quiet charm. We never got much beyond the annual exchange of Christmas cards but I always felt better for having encountered him. In good time I suppose the process will start which will lead to him being called Blessed; and eventually, I hope, his canonization. That should be a proud day for Petersfield, even if the local paper fails to notice it.[5]

Wilfrid Russell:

I think what struck me most forcibly in those early days was the improbability of the whole thing and Cheshire's insouciance in taking on those extraordinary ventures.[6]

Frances Jeram:

Le Court in 1949. It was a halcyon summer. In my memory the sun shone every day . . . It was just as well it was hot because we couldn't afford any fuel . . . GC insisted that it was to be a *home* in the very best sense of the word. We were a *family* and everyone had to do something to help . . . GC insisted that everyone ought to have a little more to do than they could manage – and that was one way he got the best out of us all. So long as he was with us all went well. He was a very quiet sort of person and one was never aware of him throwing his weight about. You seldom heard him coming. Just by being there he made it work. There were no proper arrangements about finance. Somehow, though, whenever it became crucial I found GC and he had just got some money from somewhere – enough to meet the emergency . . .

GC had insisted on sending for everyone on the waiting list (Sister Olive was away!) and told me to put them up somehow. This day, the last two were coming . . . We . . . were short on bedclothes. I had already been round the house taking a blanket off a bed here and a pillow there . . . It was unthinkable to fail, but this time I had to say to GC that we had only three hours to go before the men

★ Like Cheshire, Sir Alec Guinness was received into the Catholic Church at Petersfield by Father Henry Clarke.

arrived and I just hadn't any blankets. He laughed and said it would be all right.
Then he suggested I unpack a large thing that had just come by rail, all done up
in sacking . . . Sure enough . . . packed inside were just enough blankets for my
two beds! . . . Ted passed through the hall . . . He knew my predicament about
the beds and I said to him, 'Ted, how about this for Faith?' He grunted and said:
'They do say the Devil looks after his own.'[7]

Wally Sullivan:

My very first week at Market Mews, I answered the telephone one lunchtime
when everyone was out except myself and the young girl receptionist. It was a
man who said he wanted to speak to someone important. I told him that everyone
was out and asked if I could help him. He asked, 'Are you important enough?'
I said, 'I doubt it, as I've only been here a short while, but can I get someone
to call you back?' 'Well,' he said, 'you can help me, but only if you are important
enough.' I started to get angry and he sensed this in my voice, so he said 'It's all
right, Wally, this is Leonard Cheshire. I'm just teasing.'[8]

Father Fuller:

One is struck forcefully by the contrast between the action-packed life he had
led and the constraints of the fatal motor neurone disease which steadily deprived
him of his physical abilities. Such a situation would be traumatic in any age but
perhaps most of all in the present-day world where physical health and material
possessions are commonly regarded as essential to a worthwhile life. This was
the challenge that Leonard had often to meet since the Second World War but
now urgently on his 'last long journey', to use Freya Stark's graphic phrase. He
met it, as always, head-on, accepting in advance all that it implied.[9]

Wilfrid Bickley, his front gunner:

He was just a gentleman. He stuck up for his men.[10]

Christopher, his brother, in 1994:

I don't know how he did all that. If you find out, let me know.[11]

Sue, his wife:

Whenever I look I see him and whoever I am with he is there.[12]

And Cheshire himself:

The effect of all that I have witnessed, during the Second World War as well as since, has been to impress ever more deeply upon me the solidarity and interdependence of the entire human family. Leaders there have to be, and these may appear to rise above their fellow men, but in their hearts they know only too well that what has been attributed to them is in fact the achievement of the team to which they belong.

> . . . *It means we are all involved, all needed, all organically part of the one human family as a leaf is of a tree. It means that every single thing we do, provided it has a good and constructive purpose, is helping our world grow towards its common goal.*[13]

Down on the page (and the italics are mine) his words seems so simple, because they are, yet they subsist in a haze of complexity which resists paraphrase. A tree, for instance, is easily recognized, yet not so simple. Leonard Cheshire was a visionary in love with every one of his fellow human beings. The uncompromising, sometimes perplexed, choices about what could usefully be done about that in a few mortal years gave us the story I have tried to tell.

I began by toying with his name. Leonard, let me remind you, is patron saint of the oppressed and marginalized, a dedication favoured by travellers. Lives are journeys. Few lives have been travelled so valiantly, with greater faith, more hope and deeper charity than this one. The journey is unfinished, because the earthly fulfilment of this Leonard's life is now for us, in every single thing we do.

Epilogue

The writing of a biography inevitably leaves hanging threads – the incomplete stories of people who appear, perhaps loom large for a time, and then recede or vanish. Such discontinuities cannot be made good here – where would one stop? – but a word or two may be said in a handful of cases. Christopher Cheshire, who retired to the Costa Blanca after a successful career in the oil industry, died a few months before this book was finished. Andrew Boyle went on to become a prominent broadcaster and author, his best-known book probably being *The Climate of Treason*. He kept in touch with Cheshire until his death. Hélène married in 1955, and today lives quietly in France, rejoicing in her grandchildren. Josie Woollam grew up, married and had a family. Father Fuller is an alert and fit ninety-one.

What of the Leonard Cheshire Foundation itself? Today it calls itself Leonard Cheshire, and goes from strength to strength. It is Britain's leading disability care charity, operating 140 homes, respite units, care at home services, day centres and other projects which help over 10,000 disabled people to live lives of their own choosing. Overseas, through its International Committee, Leonard Cheshire provides a framework, training and support for a further 240 services in fifty-one countries. This great family is a thriving, growing reality.

And Sue Ryder? In 1999 the Sue Ryder Foundation, which now works in twenty different countries, announced upbeat plans for expansion. In 1998, on her seventy-fifth birthday, Sue Ryder retired as a trustee of the foundation which she established, and since then has had no formal authority in relation to the foundation's work. The retirement was against her wishes.

Abbreviations and Acronyms

AA	Anti-aircraft
AAEE	Aircraft and Armament Experimental Establishment
AASF	Advanced Air Striking Force
a/c	aircraft
ACAS	Assistant Chief of Air Staff
ACM	Air Chief Marshal
ACSEA	Air Command South-East Asia
ADGB	Air Defence of Great Britain
ADIEU	Any definite target in enemy use
AFC	Air Force Cross
Air Cdre	Air Commodore
AM	Air Marshal
AOC	Air Officer Commanding
ATFERO	Atlantic Ferry Organization
AVM	Air Vice-Marshal
Avro	A. V. Roe & Co. Ltd
BEF	British Expeditionary Force
B&G	Bombing and gunnery
C-in-C	Commander-in-Chief
CMS	Catholic Mission Society
CO	Commanding Officer
Col.	Colonel
COS	Chief(s) of Staff
CR42	Italian biplane fighter
CSC	Course Setting Calculator
CTS	Catholic Truth Society
CU	Conversion Unit
DArm D	Director of Armament Development
DArm R	Director of Armament Research
DB Ops	Director of Bomber Operations
DBST	Double British Summer Time

DDArm D	Deputy Director of Armament Development
DF	Direction finding
DFC	Distinguished Flying Cross
DFM	Distinguished Flying Medal
DSO	Distinguished Service Order
EAC	Eastern Air Command
E-boat	British term for German high-speed torpedo boat
ETA	Estimated time of arrival
FANY	First Aid Nursing Yeomanry
Fg Off.	Flying Officer
Flak	*Fliegerabwehrkanonen*: anti-aircraft artillery
Flt Lt	Flight Lieutenant
Flt Sgt	Flight Sergeant
G	Acceleration due to gravity
GMT	Greenwich Mean Time
Gp Capt.	Group Captain
HCU	Heavy Conversion Unit
H-hour	Start time for attack
HQBC	Headquarters Bomber Command
Ju	Junkers
KG	*Kampfgeschwader*: bomber wing
LAC	Leading Aircraftman
LCT	Landing craft, tank
Lt	Lieutenant
Lt Col.	Lieutenant Colonel
MAP	Ministry of Aircraft Production
MEW	Ministry of Economic Warfare
MoI	Ministry of Information
MTB	Motor torpedo boat
MV	Motor Vessel
NCO	Non-commissioned officer
NFS	National Fire Service
OC	Officer Commanding
Ops	Operations
ORB	Operations Record Book
OT	Organisation Todt

OTC	Officers' Training Corps
OTU	Operational Training Unit
OUAS	Oxford University Air Squadron
PFF	pathfinder force
Plt Off.	Pilot Officer
PRU	Photographic Reconnaissance Unit
RAE	Royal Aeronautical Establishment
RAFVR	Royal Air Force Volunteer Reserve
R-boat	*Räumboot* – small German coastal vessel
RCM	Radio counter-measures
R/T	Radio-telephony
SABS	Stabilized Automatic Bomb Sight
SASO	Senior Air Staff Officer
S-boat	*Schnellboot* – small, fast, German naval vessel – E-boat
SEAC	South East Asia Command
Sgt	Sergeant
SHAEF	Supreme Headquarters Allied Expeditionary Force
SHQ	Station headquarters
SOE	Special Operations Executive
Sqn	Squadron
Sqn Ldr	Squadron Leader
T-boat	German torpedo boat, in 900–1,200 ton range
TI	Target Indicator
TRE	Telecommunications Research Establishment
U-boat	*Unterseeboot*: German submarine
u/s	unserviceable
USAAF	United States Army Air Force
VAD	Voluntary Aid Detachment
VC	Victoria Cross
VHF	Very High Frequency
WAAF	Women's Auxiliary Air Force
Wg Cdr	Wing Commander
w/op	wireless operator
WRAC	Women's Royal Army Corps
W/T	Wireless-telegraphy

Codewords

Centreboard	Operation by 509th Composite Group following tactical format of atomic strike
Chubb	Mannheim
Coronet	Projected invasion of Honshu
Crossbow	Aerial operation against V-weapon site
Downfall	Projected invasion of Japan
Dumbo	Air-sea rescue flying boat
Fat Man	Atomic bomb with plutonium core, working by implosion
Fortitude	Deception operation in support of Overlord
Gee	Radio-based navigation aid
G-H	Radio-based navigation aid, air-ground-air
Glimmer	Operation simulating convoy by airborne transmission of signals on frequencies used by German Freya radar. Companion operation to Taxable
Heyday	Type of high-speed submarine
Highball	Bouncing mine to be used against capital ships
H2S	Ground-scanning radar used as bombing aid
Kipper	Kiel
Little Boy	Atomic bomb with components of uranium 235
Mandrel	Electronic radar jamming device
Manhattan	US programme for production of atomic bomb
Millennium	Attack on Cologne by 1,000+ aircraft of Bomber Command (augmented), 30 May 1942

Moonshine	Surface vessels supporting Glimmer and Taxable
Neptune	Maritime operation in support of Overlord
Newhaven	Ground marking of an aiming point by visual identification
Noball	V-weapon target
Oboe	Radio-based navigation aid, ground-air-ground
Olympic	Projected US operation for invasion of Kyushu
Overlord	Invasion of northern France, June 1944
Pumpkin	Casing of Fat Man atomic bomb filled with high explosive
Shark	Genoa
Silverplate	USAAF programme for operational implementation of Manhattan
Superdumbo	B-29 equipped for coordination of air-sea rescue
Swallow	Type of tailless variable-geometry aircraft
Tallboy L(arge)	22,0000 lb bomb designed for deep penetration, later known as Grand Slam
Tallboy M(edium)	12,000 lb medium-capacity bomb designed for deep penetration of the ground and subterranean detonation following release from high altitude and spin-stabilized fall
Taxable	Operation simulating a convoy by airborne release of Window
Upkeep	Bouncing mine, used against Ruhr dams in May 1943
V-1	*Vergeltungswaffe 1*: Reprisal Weapon No. 1, the Fieseler 103 flying bomb ('doodle-bug')
V-2	*Vergeltungswaffe 2*: Reprisal Weapon No. 2, the A-4 ground-to-ground rocket

V-3	*Vergeltungswaffe 3*: Reprisal Weapon No. 3, long-range gun
Whitebait	Berlin
Wild Goose	Type of tailless variable-geometry aircraft
Window	Short metallized strips dropped to confuse enemy radar
Zebra	Greenwich Time (US usage)
Zulu	Greenwich Time (UK usage)

NOTES

ABBREVIATIONS USED IN THE NOTES

AIR   Lettercode for classes of Air Ministry record held by the Public
Record office

BC   Boyle Collection

BP   Leonard Cheshire, *Bomber Pilot*

CHR   *Chatham House Remembered*

CL   Leonard Cheshire, *Crossing the Finishing Line*

CML   Sue Ryder, *Child of My Love*

FP   Fuller Papers

FV   Leonard Cheshire, *The Face of Victory*

FYT   Leonard Cheshire, 'For Your Tomorrow' (draft)

HW   Leonard Cheshire, *The Hidden World*

IWM   Imperial War Museum

LCA   Leonard Cheshire Archive

LMS   Leonard Cheshire, *The Light of Many Suns*

Log book   Pilot's Flying Log Book, vol. 2, Imperial War Museum

NPG   Andrew Boyle, *No Passing Glory*

ORB   Operations Record Book

PRO   Public Record Office

TG   R. C. Rivaz, *Tail Gunner*

W   Peggy Worthington, unpublished memoir (1956)

WG   *Where is God in All This?* (conversations with Alenka Lawrence)

Principal archive sources have been the Public Record Office, Kew, and
the Leonard Cheshire Archive and Library at Staunton Harold.

The Cheshire Archive was set up in 1990. It houses his papers, films,
tapes and photographs, as well as the increasing records of the voluntary
organization which Cheshire inspired. The Boyle Collection (a body of
correspondence and original sources assembled by Andrew Boyle in the
course of writing *No Passing Glory*) and Fuller Papers (Cheshire-related
correspondence of the mid-1950s) have been deposited there. The

Leonard Cheshire Archive is open to researchers by appointment during office hours at Staunton Harold Hall, Ashby-de-la-Zouch, Leicestershire LE65 1RT (01332 863660).

Documents referenced 'Eleanor Boyle' remain in the private hands of Andrew Boyle's widow.

Details of published works are given in the bibliography.

PROLOGUE

1 Letter, 5 Nov. 1916, Barstow Collection.
2 Letter, 12 Dec. 1916.
3 Letter, 15 Jan. 1917.
4 Letter, 28 Jan. 1917.
5 G. C. Cheshire, 'Ballooning, 1916', *J. Soc. Friends of the Royal Air Force Museum*, vol. 13, no. 3, pp.19–27.

1. LINES FROM OTHER DAYS

1 Cheshire, speech at Steenbergen, 7 May 1990.
2 Cheshire, 'Thoughts for the Future', April 1975.
3 Unless otherwise referenced, quotations in this chapter come from G. C. Cheshire, 'The Origins of the Cheshire Family', unpublished MS, 1974–5.
4 Andrew Boyle in interview with Edith Dichter (3 Dec. 1953) and Primrose Cheshire (21 Jan. 1954): LCA BC 53.
5 Christopher Cheshire, conversations with author, 20 Aug. 1994, 28 May 1995.
6 Christopher Cheshire, conversations with author, 26–8 May 1995.
7 Christopher Cheshire, conversation with author, 26 May 1995.
8 Christopher Cheshire, conversation with author, 28 May 1995.
9 Michael Barstow, conversations with author, 19 Sept. 1995 and 23 Feb. 1996.
10 A characteristic of some Barstow women was their 'admiration for strong men': Michael Barstow, conversation with author, 23 Feb. 1996.
11 Cited in Lawson, 1979, p.626; cf. p.612.

2. STOWE

1 A. E. Lynam, letter to J. F. Roxburgh, 22 May 1931: Stowe Archive.
2 A. E. Lynam, letter, 22 May 1931: Stowe Archive.
3 Annan, 1965, pp.6–15.
4 ibid.
5 ibid., p.62.
6 ibid., p.95; cf. pp.8–12.
7 Cited in Croom-Johnson, 1953, p.27.
8 Cited in Annan, 1966, p.65.
9 Christopher Cheshire, conversation with author, 28 May 1995.
10 Annan, 1965, p.64.
11 Peter Anstey, reminiscence, *CHR*, p.34.
12 Christopher Cheshire, conversation with author, 28 May 1995.
13 Peter Anstey, reminiscence, *CHR*, p.33.
14 ibid.
15 *The Times Saturday Review*. 'A Childhood', 21 July 1990.
16 Annan, 1965, pp.71–2.
17 Warner, S.T., 1989, p.77.
18 Cited in Warner, S.T., 1989, p.64.
19 ibid., p.65.
20 Patrick Hunter, letter: LCA BC 53.
21 Stowe School, personal record: Stowe Archive.
22 T. H. White, letter, 20 March 1954: LCA BC 53.
23 Cheshire, dictated reminiscence (transcript), June 1954: LCA BC 53.
24 Stowe School Debating Society Minute Book 1930–1939, 1 July 1932: Stowe Archive.
25 ibid., 16 Nov. 1932.
26 ibid., 22 Feb. 1932.
27 ibid., 8 March 1933.
28 *The Stoic*, VI, p.88.
29 *LMS*, p.9.
30 ibid.
31 T. H. White, letter, 20 March 1954: LCA BC 53.
32 Cheshire, dictated reminiscence (transcript), 17 April 1954: LCA BC 53.
33 Letter, 20 March 1954: LCA BC 53.

34 *LMS*, p.10.

35 Philip Tweedale, letter to author, March 1997.

36 Cheshire, dictated reminiscence (transcript), 17 April 1954: LCA BC 53.

37 Patrick Ashton, reminiscence, *CHR*, p.28.

38 Annan, 1965, pp.108–15.

39 Stephen Whitwell (Chatham, 1934–9), reminiscence, *CHR*, p.31; Richard McDougall (Chatham, 1931–5), letter to author, 27 Jan. 1997.

40 T. H. White, letter, 21 April 1954: LCA BC 53.

41 Cheshire, dictated reminiscence (transcript), June 1954: RCA BC 53.

42 Philip Tweedale, letter to author, March 1997.

43 '. . . when I joined Chatham in May 1930 we had one cup in the House Common Room – the School Singing Cup! When I left in July 1933 we had won every cup in the School *except* the Singing Cup', Philip Tweedale, letter to author, March 1997.

44 J. F. Roxburgh, letter, 17 Jan. 1954: LCA BC 53.

45 *LMS*, p.9.

46 Letter, 17 Jan. 1954: LCA BC 53.

47 Letter, 17 Oct. 1935: Stowe Archive.

3. OXFORD AND BEYOND

1 Cf. Adolf Hitler, *Der Angriff*, 5 Dec. 1930.

2 Leonard Cheshire, taped reminiscence (transcript), June 1954: LCA BC 53; cf. *The Times Weekend Magazine*, 'A Childhood', 21 July 1990.

3 Geoffrey Cheshire in interview with Andrew Boyle: LCA BC 53.

4 Cheshire, taped reminscence (transcript), June 1954: LCA BC 53; Christopher Cheshire, conversation with author, 20 Aug. 1994.

5 Primrose and Geoffrey Cheshire in interview with Andrew Boyle: LCA BC 53.

6 Geoffrey Cheshire in interview with Andrew Boyle, 15 Jan. 1954: LCA BC 53.

7 Christopher Cheshire, conversation with author, 20 Aug. 1994.

8 See for example Boyle, 1955, p.64, pp.81–2.

9 Leslie Bibby to Christopher Cheshire, 14 Nov. 1954: LCA BC 53.

10 F. M. Lawson in interview with Andrew Boyle, 4 Feb. 1954: LCA BC 53.

11 *WG*, p.18.

12 ibid.

13 Andrew Boyle in conversation with Primrose and Geoffrey Cheshire, 8 April 1954: LCA BC 53.

14 *Oxford Mail*, 17 Sept. 1938.

15 Cheshire, *Sunday Telegraph Magazine*, 24 May 1981, pp.26–7.

16 Sir Christopher Foxley-Norris, conversation with author, 14 Oct. 1994.

17 Christopher Cheshire, conversation with author, 20 Aug. 1994.

18 Cheshire, dictated reminiscence (transcript), 5 April 1954: LCA BC 53.

19 Christopher Cheshire, conversation with author, 20 Aug. 1994.

20 Boyle, 1955, p.70.

21 *WG*, p.106.

22 *Sunday Times*, 16 Oct. 1955, p.4.

23 Mrs Edith Stowell, letter, 16 Oct. 1955: LCA GLC 7:17/3.

24 *WG*, p.19.

25 J. N. Whitworth in interview with Andrew Boyle, 15 April 1954: LCA BC 53.

26 *WG*, p.20.

27 Boyle, 1955, p.80.

28 Cheshire, taped reminiscence (transcript), June 1954: LCA BC 53.

29 Abingdon ORB: AIR 28/8.

30 *LMS*, p.11.

31 Cheshire, taped reminiscence (transcript), June 1954: LCA BC 53.

32 *LMS*, p.11.

33 Faulkes, 1996, p.113; Dickson, 1950, pp.138–9.

34 Faulkes, 1996, pp.121, 127.

35 Others have made much of this. For contemporary accounts see the *Oxford Mail*, 3 Aug. 1939, 8 Aug. 1939.

36 *FV*, p.9.

37 Cheshire, reminiscence (transcript), 5 April 1954: LCA BC 53.

38 Sir Christopher Foxley-Norris, conversation with author, 14 Oct. 1994.

39 9 SFTS ORB: AIR 29/559.

40 Log book, 6 April 1940.

41 Harris, 1947, p.62.

42 No. 5 B&G School, Jurby: AIR 29/545.

4. WONDERFUL LIFE

1 FYT, 12 Feb. 1973: LCA GLC 21/5.

2 *BP*, p.7.

3 Mahaddie, 1989, p.68.

4 FYT, 5 March 1973: LCA GLC 21/5.

5 ibid.

6 ibid.

7 FYT, 1 Feb. 1973: LCA GLC 21/3.

8 *BP*, p.7.

9 15 May 1940, Confidential Annexe to Minutes of the War Cabinet
   No.123: PRO CAB 65/13.

10 *BP*, pp.9–10.

11 Driffield ORB, Appendices: PRO AIR 28/223.

12 *BP*, p.11.

13 ibid.

14 ibid., p.14.

15 ibid., p.16.

16 ibid., p.17.

17 ibid., p.20.

18 Log book, 9 June 1940.

19 *BP*, p.21.

20 Mahaddie, 1989, p.69.

21 Letter (transcript), 12 June 1940: LCA BC 51.

22 Letter (transcript), 15 June 1940: LCA BC 51.

23 Terraine, 1988, p.158.

24 Letter (transcript), 18 June 1940: LCA BC 51.

25 Driffield ORB: AIR 28/221.

26 *BP*, p.26.

27 ibid., p.28.

28 FYT, 1 Feb. 1973: LCA GLC 21/5.

29 *BP*, pp.29–30.

30 FYT, 13 Feb. 1973: LCA GLC 21/5.

31 Letter (transcript), 20 June 1940: LCA BC 51.

32 ibid.

33 FYT, 5 March 1973: LCA GLC 21/5.

34 *BP*, p.27.

35 ibid.

36 Douglas Mourton, 102 Squadron, letter to author.

37 *BP*, p.48.

38 Letter (transcript), 23 July 1940: LCA BC 51.

39 *TG*, p.8.

40 FYT, 5 March 1973: LCA GLC 21/5.

41 *BP*, p.26.

42 *TG*, p.13.

43 Letter (transcript), 12 Aug. 1940: LCA BC 51.

44 Letter (transcript), 16 Aug. 1940: LCA BC 51.

45 *BP*, p.52.

46 *TG*, p.10.

47 John Grimstone, letter to author, 8 June 1996.

48 *TG*, p.11.

49 ibid.

50 ibid.

51 Letter, 16 Aug. 1940: LCA BC 51.

52 Boyle, 1955, p.103.

53 Letter (transcript), 26 Aug. 1940: LCA BC 51.

54 Driffield ORB, 19 Aug. 1940; 25 Aug. 1940: AIR 28/221.

55 Leeming ORB, 27 Aug. 1940; 29–30 Aug. 1940: AIR 28/450.

56 Letter, 2 × 7 Sept. 1940: LCA BC 51.

57 Letter (transcript), 4 Sept. 1940: LCA BC 51.

58 Letter (transcript), 11 Sept. 1940: LCA BC 51.

59 *BP*, pp.58–9.

60 Terraine, 1988, p.234.

61 Harold Chapman, letter to author, 24 April 1996.

62 Recollections of Gp Capt. O. A. Morris, RAF Museum, Hendon, B2079.

63 AIR 27/149.

64 Letter (transcript), 25 Sept. 1940: LCA BC 51.

65 Letter (transcript), n.d. (Sept. 1940): LCA BC 51.

66 *BP*, p.61.

67 Letter (transcript), 6 Oct. 1940: LCA BC 51.

68 Letter, LCA BC 51.

69 Linton ORB, 4 Nov. 1940: AIR 28/484.

70 Linton ORB, 20 Oct. 1940: AIR 28/481. Linton was attacked by three Ju 88s in the early evening of 27 October 1940. Further raids took place on 28 October, 11 and 14 November.

71 Cheshire's sorties to Pretzsch on 6/7 November (when the primary target was Nuremberg) and Ruhland on 10/11 November were flown from Tholthorpe.

72 Douglas Mourton, 102 Squadron, letter to author.

73 George Roberts to Andrew Boyle, letter, 21 June 1954: Eleanor Boyle.

74 FYT: LCA GLC 21/5.

75 ibid.

76 George Roberts, letter: LCA GLC 27:99/6–7.

77 *TG*, p.12.

78 ibid, p.17.

79 *TG*, p.19.

80 *BP*, p.80.

81 *TG*, p.19.

82 *BP*, p.81.

83 Letter, 28 Feb. 1973: LCA GLC 21/3.

84 *TG*, p.20.

85 ibid.

86 ibid., pp.20–21.

87 George Roberts to Andrew Boyle, letter, 21 June 1954: Eleanor Boyle.

88 Harold Chapman, 102 Squadron, letter to author, 16 April 1996.

89 Douglas Mourton, 'Lucky Doug' (MS), p.35.

90 Letter, 18 Nov. 1940: LCA BC 51.

91 AIR 29/602.

92 Letter, n.d. (Dec. 1940): LCA BC 51.

93 *BP*, pp.91–2.

94 *BP*, pp.93–4; AIR 28/851.

95 Christopher Cheshire, conversation with author, 28 May 1995.

96 Letter, 18 Dec. 1940: LCA BC 51.

97 Douglas Mourton, 'Lucky Doug' MS, p.35.

98 Letter, 18 Dec. 1940: LCA BC 51.

99 LCA GLC 3:30/18.

100 AIR 28/854.

101 *BP*, p.101.

102 Douglas Mourton, letter to author.

5. EVERY WISE MAN'S SON

1 LCA GLC 21/5.

2 *BP*, p.101.

3 ibid.

4 R. A. Read, 1995.

5 ibid.

6 ibid.

7 *BP*, p.101.

8 *BP*, p.102–3.

9 *FV*, p.15.

10 35 Sqn ORB: AIR 27/379.

11 Sqn Ldr Gilchrist and his flight engineer escaped by parachute. The rest of the crew were killed: 35 Sqn ORB, AIR 27/379.

12 FYT, 5 March 1973, p.3: LCA GLC 21/5.

13 *BP*, p.102.

14 ibid.

15 *FV*, p.12.

16 R. A. Read, 1995.

17 Linton ORB, 21 March 1941: AIR 28/482.

18 *BP*, p.103.

19 ibid.

20 George Roberts to Andrew Boyle, letter, 21 June 1954: Eleanor Boyle.

21 *BP*, p.106.

22 Richard Rivaz described this episode in his book *Tail Gunner*, pp.40–55.

23 Linton ORB: AIR 28/482.

24 *BP*, p.107.

25 AIR 27/379.

26 *WG*, p.113.

27 *BP*, p.108.

28 AVM Donald Bennett in interview with Andrew Boyle, 19 May 1954: LCA BC 51.

29 *FV*, p.13.

30 *BP*, p.111.

31 ibid.

32 ibid.

33 ibid., pp.111–13.

34 ibid., p.133.

35 ibid., pp.112–13.

36 ibid.

37 William Shakespeare, *Twelfth Night*, II, iii.

38 *BP*, p.115.

39 *TG*, p.55.

40 *FV*, p.14.

41 ibid., pp.13–14.

42 Peter Y. Stead, *Intercomm* (Aircrew Association Magazine), Spring 1993, p.51.

43 R. A. Read, letter to author, 20 Jan. 1997.

44 ibid.

45 *FV*, p.15.

46 ibid.

47 Christopher Cheshire, conversations with author, 20 Aug. 1994 and 27 May 1995.

48 Peter Y. Stead, diary, 12 Aug. 1941.

49 Leonard Cheshire, letter to W. R. Chorley, 4 Dec. 1979: LCA.

50 Peter Y. Stead, diary, 14 Aug. 1941.

51 *BP*, p.129.

52 Peter Stead, diary, 14 Aug. 1941.

53 ibid.

54 R. A. Read, 1995.

55 *BP*, p.132.

56 ibid., pp.132–3.

57 Terraine (1988, p.522; cf. Memorandum, 16 Nov. 1942: AIR 20/2859) suggests that the calculation was based on a 50:50 chance of survival and quotes Webster and Frankland in support of it. However, Webster and Frankland did not quote Peirse's letter of 10 November 1942 to the effect that he claims.

58 *BP*, p.133.

59 ibid., p.131.

60 *FV*, p.16.

61 *BP*, p.116.

62 Christopher Cheshire, conversation with author, 28 May 1995.

63 Letter, n.d. (July 1941?), cited in Boyle, 1955, p.126.

64 Letter, n.d. (July 1941?), cited in Boyle, ibid.

65 *FV*, p.13.

66 Memorandum of Agreement between Leonard Cheshire and Hutchinson, Dec. 1941: LCA BC 51.

6. PLACES YOU MIGHT NOT COME BACK FROM

1 'Marston Moor opened in November 1941 and from early 1942 was home to 1652 Heavy Conversion Unit. 1652 HCU's work was to convert pilots of twin-engined aircraft to the four-engined Halifax. During the two-week course, pilots flew, navigators, wireless operators and bomb aimers familiarized themselves with Halifax equipment, and rear and mid-upper gunners practised in their respective turrets both in ground school and during fighter affiliation exercises in the air. Crews arriving at the HCU were joined by two new members, a flight engineer and a mid-upper gunner, to make a total of seven' (Ken McDonald, MS memoir, p.1).

2 ibid.

3 *FV*, pp.16–17.

4 ibid., p.17.

5 R. A. Read, 1995.

6 ibid.

7 ibid.

8 While flying on two engines the Halifax dropped a wing and spiralled into the ground near Wetherby: 1652 CU ORB, AIR 29/612.

9 Harris, *Despatch*, p.13.

10 ibid.

11 Harris, 1947, p.110–11.

12 Webster and Frankland, 1961, i, p.404.

13 1652 HCU ORB: AIR 29/612.

14 Marston Moor ORB: AIR 28/524.

15 Two returned early, one because of engine trouble, the other 'due to the carelessness of the navigator': 1652 CU ORB, AIR 29/612.

16 MS, LCA BC 51.

17 Joan Ling to Cheshire, 18 June 1942: LCA BC 51.

18 Terraine, 1985, pp.489–91.

19 Harris to Portal, 20 June 1942, cited in Webster and Frankland, 1961, i, p.413.

20 The rough surfaces damaged tyres: 1652 CU ORB, AIR 29/612.

21 4 Group ORB, Appendix: AIR 25/100.

22 Log book; 1652 CU ORB, AIR 29/612.

23 H. Hilton to Cheshire, 6 July 1942: LCA BC 51.

24 Joan Ling to Cheshire, 11 Aug. 1942: LCA BC 51.

25 Irene Josephy to Cheshire, 10 Aug. 1942: LCA BC 51.

26 Joan Ling to Cheshire, 28 Aug. 1942: LCA BC 51.

27 Irene Josephy to Cheshire, 3 Sept. 1942: LCA BC 51.

28 Irene Josephy to Cheshire, 6 Nov. 1942: LCA BC 51.

29 Ken McDonald, MS memoir, p.2.

30 R. A. Read, 1995.

31 ibid.

32 Ken McDonald, letter to author, 27 Jan. 1997.

33 Murray Peden, via Ken McDonald, 27 Jan. 1997.

34 Ken McDonald, letter to author, 27 Jan. 1997.

35 R. A. Read, 1995.

36 Early in the war 'there was very little mixing of the officers and the rest when off duty unless by accident you happened to be in the same public house, dance hall, etc.': G. Robson, 102 Squadron, letter to author, 18 April 1996.

37 Hastings, 1981, p.258.

38 R. A. Read, 1995.

39 ibid.

40 ibid.

41 G. E. Woods, conversation with author, 11 Aug. 1996.

42 4 Group ORB, Appendix: AIR 25/100.

43 ibid.

44 *Daily Telegraph*, 9 March 1943.

45 R. A. Read, 1995.

46 4 Group ORB, Appendix: AIR 25/101.

47 Basil Jones to Andrew Boyle, letter, 30 Dec. 1954: LCA BC 51.

48 Ken McDonald, letter to author, 9 Dec. 1996.

49 ibid.

50 4 Group ORB, Appendix: AIR 25/101.

51 Ken McDonald, letter to author, 9 Dec. 1996.

52 Hastings, 1981, p.257.

53 MS, LCA GLC BC 51.

54 76 Squadron ORB: AIR 27/650.

55 Cited in A. Revie, *The Lost Command*, Corgi, London, 1972, pp.247–9.

56 All on board were killed: 76 Squadron ORB, 18 Aug. 1942: AIR 27/650.

57 *FV*, p.27.

58 4 Group ORB, Appendix: AIR 25/100.

59 Sir F. Handley Page, letter, 15 Nov. 1954: LCA BC 51.

60 4 Group ORB, Appendix, Nov. 1942, para. 102: AIR 25/100.

61 ibid., para. 106.

62 Ken McDonald, letter to author, 9 Dec. 1996. AVM Carr considered that 'the real menace is the unseen fighter', and that a high standard of crew cooperation was needed to defeat it. Following trials with several 76 Sqn aircraft 4 Group introduced an additional lookout, a navigation blister in the bottom of the fuselage, as a measure against interception from below.

63 Sir F. Handley Page to Andrew Boyle, 15 Nov. 1954: LCA BC 51.

64 R. A. Read, 1995.

65 The broadcast to children was made on 7 October 1942. Other broadcasts included 'Planning a large raid' (6 Sept. 1942), and a transmission to China (12 July 1943).

66 Air Ministry P.R.3 to Cheshire, 26 Jan. 1943: LCA BC 51.

67 R. A. Read, 1995.

68 ibid.

69 Serialization had begun in June 1942.

70 Cheshire to Douglas Baxter, letter, 1 Jan. 1943: LCA BC 51.

71 Ken McDonald, MS memoir, p.4.

72 MS note, 28 March 1943: Stowe Archive.

73 Edith Kup, letter to author, 9 April 1996.

74 76 Sqn ORB: AIR 27/651.

75 Flt Lt Bill Day in A.M. Bridson, *From Needles-sewing to Irons-soldering*, Merlin Books, Braunton (Devon), 1989, p.38.

76 J. F. Roxburgh, MS note, 28 March 1943: Stowe Archive.

77 Cheshire's appointment coincided with the introduction of the base system, whereby the administration and servicing of six heavy bomber squadrons or three HCUs were accommodated on three separate but associated airfields. This permitted the centralization of many functions previously undertaken on individual stations, and enabled 'the Group Commander and his staff to limit their normal contacts to five instead of fifteen lower formations' (A. T. Harris, internal report, 1945, published 1995, pp. 152–3). Marston Moor was designated a base, with dependent stations at Riccall (which housed 1658 HCU) and Rufforth (1663 HCU). Cheshire became deputy base commander, in addition to his duties as station commander of Marston Moor itself.

78 *FV*, p.20.

79 Letter, October 1943, cited in Boyle, 1955, pp.170–71.

80 Bill Webb, cited in Geoffrey Jones, *Raider. The Halifax and Its Flyers*, William Kimber, 1978.

81 *FV*, p.21.

82 Ken McDonald, MS memoir, p.3.

83 Air Commodore J. N. Whitworth in interview with Andrew Boyle, 1954: LCA BC 51.

84 Cited in Boyle, 1955, p.165.

85 *FV*, p.21.

86 On 29 May 1652 CU's diarist noted: 'A total of 8.40 hrs brought total flying for the month to 1750.05 and Stn Cdr . . . gave permission for flying to cease until 1 June': AIR 29/612.

87 *Ossett Observer*, 22 May 1943.

88 *North Berks Herald & Didcot Advertiser*, 28 May 1943.

89 *Sunday Graphic*, 20 June 1943.

90 e.g. J. R. Campbell, letter, 6 May 1943; Nurse N. Davidson, letter, 25 April 1943: LCA BC 51.

91 In 1943 commando attacks were anticipated as a possible German reaction to Bomber Command's growing offensive.

92 Cheshire to Douglas Baxter, letter, 1 Jan. 1944.

93 *Sunday Graphic*, 20 June 1943.
94 *FV*, p.20.
95 Ken McDonald, MS memoir, p.3.
96 John Kirby in interview with Andrew Boyle, n.d. (1953 × 1954), MS: LCA BC 53.
97 ibid.
98 Bryne Knight, letter to author, 10 Jan. 1997.
99 *FV*, p.22.
100 Letter: LCA GLC 21/3.
101 AVM Donald Bennett in interview with Andrew Boyle, 19 April 1954: LCA BC 51.
102 Mahaddie, 1989, p.69.
103 J. N. Whitworth, recollected in interview with Andrew Boyle, 1954: LCA BC 51.
104 Letter, 1 Feb. 1944: LCA BC 51.
105 In September Cheshire visited Air Commodore Charles Symonds, a specialist in study of flying stress, and co-author of *Psychological Disorders in Flying Personnel* (1942), in the hope of securing Symonds's agreement to the ingenious proposal that psychiatric breakdown might be occasioned by too little operational flying rather than too much.
106 *FV*, p.24; Boyle, 1955, pp.177–8.
107 *FV*, p.24.
108 Letter, October 1943, cited in Boyle, 1955, p.171.
109 *FV*, pp.24–5.
110 ibid., p.25.
111 Ken McDonald, MS memoir, p.4.
112 R. A. Read, letter to author, 20 Jan. 1997.
113 *FV*, pp.26–7.
114 Lord Cheshire VC, conversation with author, 9 July 1991.
115 Sqn Ldr Louis Gunter, letter to author, 8 April 1996.

7. NIGHT SCENES

1 From July 1944 some crews joined 617 Sqn direct from Lancaster Finishing School without any previous Bomber Command experience.
2 *FV*, p.29.

3 Nick Ross, conversation with author, 11 April 1996.

4 Leonard Cheshire, address at St Clement Danes, 4 Jan. 1989.

5 David Shannon, conversation with author, 3 July 1989.

6 Nick Ross, conversation with author, 11 April 1996.

7 David Shannon, conversation with author, 3 July 1989. 'Mick got a raw deal by the RAF . . . if anybody should have been made commander of 617 Squadron on a permanent basis it should have been Martin' (Simpson, 1995, p.118).

8 David Shannon, conversation with author, 3 July 1989; Lord Cheshire VC, conversation with author, 9 July 1991; *FV*, p.27.

9 5 Group ORB, Appendix: AIR 25/120.

10 For discussion of the Pointblank directive, issued on 10 June 1943, and the 'Eaker Plan', both of which aimed at the destruction of selected segments of German industry, see Webster and Frankland, 1961, ii, p.20.

11 Report from Coningsby's CO to AOC 5 Group, MAP, RAE and HQ Bomber Command on bombing with SABS Mk IIA at Braid Fell, 6 Nov. 1943: AIR 14/977. Bombs were plotted to within 2 yards, and seventy bombs assessed showed a crew average of 77.5 yards.

12 *FV*, p.27.

13 *FV*, pp.25–6.

14 Tom Bennett, letter to author, 8 Dec. 1998.

15 Report submitted to Gp Capt. McKenchie, copied to HQ 5 Group: AIR 14/2052, Document 1b.

16 AIR 14/2052, Document 1a.

17 *FV*, p.27.

18 SABS training report for November: AIR 2/2031, Document 75a.

19 Operations were detailed and then cancelled on 25 November and 2 December: Coningsby ORB, Form 540, AIR 28/171.

20 Bomber Command to 1,3,4,5,6,8 Groups, Crossbow Targets: AIR 14/2040, Document 1a, 8 Dec. 1943.

21 Cheshire to Pickard, Form 96 Message, 8 Dec. 1943: LCA BC 51.

22 Pickard had previously flown for SOE, and was widely known as the hero of the drama-documentary film *Target for Tonight*. He was killed two months later while leading Operation Jericho – the raid to breach the walls of Amiens prison.

23 617 Sqn ORB: AIR 27/2128.

24 Coningsby ORB, Form 540 report: AIR 28/171.

25 Night Raid Report No. 489: AIR 14/3411.

26 105 Squadron ORB: AIR 27/827.

27 In November 1943 work to model the destruction of the Rothensee ship lift's underground shafts was undertaken by the Road Research Laboratory: Barnes Wallis Papers D6/2.

28 Cochrane to HQ Bomber Command on high-level bombing of GH673, 18 Dec. 1943: AIR 14/2008.

29 105 Squadron ORB: AIR 27/827.

30 Operation Order, 5 Group ORB, Appendix: AIR 25/120.

31 High-level bombing by night: AIR 14/2008.

32 High-level bombing by night of small targets, 29 Dec. 1943: AIR 14/2008.

33 Target signal, 5 Group ORB, Appendix: AIR 25/121.

34 Night Raid Report No. 503: AIR 14/3411.

35 Cochrane to HQ Bomber Command: AIR/2000, Document 67b, 5 Jan. 1944.

36 Coningsby ORB, Form 540: AIR 28/171.

37 Minutes: AIR 14/2008, Document 15a.

38 Harris, 1947, p.130.

39 LCA GLC 21/3.

40 AIR 14/717, Document 43a, 20 Jan. 1944.

41 AIR 14/2008, Document 14a, 21 Jan. 1944.

42 *FV*, p.29.

43 Sqn Ldr E. P. G. Moyna, No. 1 Film Production Unit, letter, 21 Jan. 1944: LCA BC 51.

44 Cheshire to Messrs William Lawson Ltd, letter, 16 Jan. 1944: LCA BC 51.

45 Barnes Wallis Papers, File 97N.

46 MoD, Air Historical Branch, Accident Card, Lancaster F.

47 5 Group ORB, Appendix, 21 Jan. 1944: AIR 25/121.

48 Bomber Command Night Raid Report No. 512.

49 Warning Order signal, 5 Group ORB, Appendix, 25 Jan. 1944: AIR 25/121.

50 AIR 14/2040, Crossbow, Document 3a.

51 Log book, 25 Jan. 1944.

52 Taped recollection, transcript, 4 May 1953: LCA BC 53.

53 PRO AIR 14/2062, Document 14b.

54 Evans Evans to Satterly (SASO, 5 Grp), 1 Feb. 1944: ibid., Document 14a.

55 Letter, 1 Feb. 1944: LCA BC 51.

56 Air Ministry Director of Accounts, letter, 13 Jan. 1944; Cheshire, letter, 3 Feb. 1944: LCA BC 51.

57 AIR 14/2101, Document 3a.

58 AIR 14/2008, Document 16a.

59 Wallis to Wg Cdr Verity, 3 Feb. 1944: Wallis Papers, D2/10 File 97H.

60 AIR 14/2011, Document 2a, 3 Feb. 1944.

61 AIR 25/121.

62 Night Raid Report No. 525.

63 AIR 14/1067, Minute 13.

64 Nick Ross, conversation with author, 11 April 1996.

65 The Target Signal detailed a force of ten aircraft to carry 12,000 lb bombs, plus a leader (Cheshire), to be armed with two 1,000 lb bombs and six TIs (red spotfires), and a deputy leader (Martin) with one 4,000 lb high capacity bomb, one green TI and four red spotfires. Z hour was set for 01.00: AIR 25/121.

66 Larry Curtis, conversation with author, 28 Nov. 1995.

67 Larry Curtis, conversation with author, 28 Nov. 1995.

68 Joan Lloyd, letter, 20 Feb. 1944: LCA BC 51.

69 M. L. Hamilton, *So Many*, p.146.

70 SABS, AIR 14/2032, Document 15a.

71 Tom Bennett, MS: Owen Collection.

72 Cheshire: LCA.

73 Wilf Bickley, conversation with author, 27 Feb. 1998.

74 Larry Curtis, conversation with author, 28 Nov. 1995.

75 Nick Ross, conversation with author, 11 April 1996.

76 Albert Hepworth, letter, 31 Jan. 1990: Owen Collection.

77 Nick Ross, conversation with author, 11 April 1996.

78 David Shannon, MS note: LCA BC 53.

79 Letter, 12 March 1944: LCA BC 51.

80 Memorandum, 9 March 1944: Owen Collection: WS/MS.25/AIR.

81 Sharp to HQ 5 Group, 16 March 1944: AIR 14/2062, Document 16a.

82 HQBC to 5 Group, 26 March 1944: AIR 14/2062.

83 These aircraft, ML 975 and ML 976, were on loan from 109 Sqn for one month. On or around 11 April they were replaced by two FB VIs (NS 992 and NS 993). Two more FB VIs, equipped with rocket fittings, were received the following month.

84 26 March 1944: AIR 14/2062, Document 24b; No. 5 Group target marking procedure, 21 April 1944: AIR 14/868.

85 Cochrane to HQBC, 18 March 1944: AIR 14/987, Document 1a.

86 Wallis to Bufton, letters, 9 and 17 March 1944: Wallis Papers, D2/21.

87 Terraine, 1985, p.562.

88 Minutes, 26 March 1944 (of meeting on 22 March): AIR 14/2008, Document 22a.

8. NO EASY RUN

1 Barnes Wallis, letter, 17 April 1944: LCA BC 51.

2 Letter, 14 April 1944: Harris Archive, File H89.

3 5 Group ORB, Appendix, 4/44–6/44, 22 April 1944: AIR 25/122; Night Raid Report No. 584, AIR 14/3411.

4 Nick Ross, conversation with author, 11 April 1996.

5 *FV*, p.35.

6 *WG*, p.43.

7 Nick Ross, conversation with author, 11 April 1996.

8 *WG*, p.43.

9 Frankland, *History at War*, 1998, pp.25–6.

10 Bennett, 1988, p.178.

11 Tom Bennett, letter to author, 8 Dec. 1998.

12 Charles Owen: IWM Archive, 109489.

13 Tom Bennett, letter to author, 8 Dec. 1998.

14 For a personal account of Taxable's planning, training and execution, consult T. Bennett, 'Operation Taxable', *Flypast*, Nov. 1984, pp.58–62.

15 Around this time Barnes Wallis proposed that 617 should revisit the Sorpe Dam. The Sorpe had escaped serious damage in the Dams Raid the year before. Now, Wallis pointed out, there was every chance of breaching it with Tallboy M (Wallis to Sidney Bufton, DB Ops, 6 May 1944: Barnes Wallis Papers, D2/21, File 97R). Unbeknown to

Wallis, however, Bomber Command now insisted that 617 Squadron was 'not, repeat not, to be employed upon operational duties until further notice' (Radio countermeasures role of 617 for Overlord: AIR 14/1357).

16 627 Squadron was not yet fully trained in low-level marking. 627 Sqn did, however, take part, contributing Mosquitoes for flak suppression and to gain familiarity with marking technique.

17 617 ORB, Form 540, Appendix: AIR 28/2129.

18 Bennett, 'Operation Taxable', p.59.

19 The meeting at HQBC on 8 May was chaired by Air Commodore L. Dalton-Morris: AIR 14/1373, Document 4b. On tests of eastern Gee chain: AIR 14/1373, Document 6a, 15 May 1944. Taxable/ Glimmer review meeting at HQBC, 17 May: AIR 14/1375, Document 7a, and Minutes, AIR 14/1373, Document 8a. Operational plan: AIR 14/3173.

20 On the construction of RP target markers: HQBC, AIR 14/2062, Document 33a; on AAEE (Boscombe Down) firing trials on Enford Range (from Mosquito and Mustang aircraft): AIR 14/987, Document 6.

21 AIR 14/2011, Document 14c. For thinking in May about the employment of Tallboy M against E- and U-boat pens: AIR 14/2011; a decision to test Tallboy M against such a target 'as soon as 617 is released from present commitment' (= Taxable): HQBC to HQ 5 Group, high-level bombing of small target at night, 30 May 1944, AIR 14/2008, Document 26a. For discussion of special crane and handling equipment: AIR 14/2180, Document 1b, 24 May 1944.

22 Lord Cheshire VC, conversation with author, 9 July 1991.

23 Albert Hepworth, diary: Owen Collection.

24 On 4 May Cochrane wrote to HQ Bomber Command about 617's establishment of aircraft, recommending that the squadron be augmented by 4 Mosquitoes and 6 H2S Lancasters on a permanent basis (AIR 14/2062, Document 31a). Cochrane's arguments about the squadron's establishment were appreciated, but contested (AIR 14/ 2062, Document 37a); debate ensued about the fundamentals of 617's function in relation to the new provision at 54 Base (HQ 5 Group to 54 Base, 20 May 1944, AIR 14/2062, Document 37a).

25 *FV*, p.42; Tom Bennett to Robert Owen, letter, 17 Nov. 1985: Owen Collection.

26 617 Establishment: AIR 14/2062, Document 40b.

27 Flg Off. A. Hickman, letter, 2 April 1944: LCA BC 51.

28 Flg Off. F. Lawrence, letter, 24 Jan. 1944: LCA BC 51.

29 Cheshire to Sharp, letter, 20 May 1944; Gp Capt. D. D. Christie to Air Commodore Sharp, letter, 2 June 1944; Sharp to Cheshire, letter, 3 June 1944: LCA BC 51.

30 617 Establishment: AIR 14/2062, Document 40a.

31 Bennett to Harris, letter, 29 May 1944: Harris Archive.

32 Bennett also seems to have overlooked the fact that the marking technique pioneered by 617 and handed on to 627 Squadron was being exported to other groups. In mid-April a Special Duty Flight consisting of six crews was formed in 1 Group for marking. The flight was part of 12 Base Headquarters at Binbrook, and on 22 April *1 Group News* (AIR 25/12) gave special thanks 'to the CO of No. 617 Squadron for unstinted advice and valuable hints on the marking technique we employed. Our success was due, by no small extent, to this wholehearted assistance.'

33 Nick Ross, conversation with author, 11 April 1996.

34 Bennett, 'Operation Taxable', p.60.

35 There was a corresponding contingency plan for 5 Group to use gas bombs in retaliation: 5 Group ORB, 5 June 1944, Appendix: AIR 25/122.

9. SECOND TO NONE

1 T. Davies, letter, 17 May 1987: Owen Collection.

2 Cochrane's announcement had already been discussed with, and ratified by, Harris.

3 Cochrane to 54 Base, establishment of aircraft, 6 June 1944: AIR 14/2062, Document 41a.

4 Woodhall Spa's medical officer noted that 'morale was extremely high' at this time: Woodhall Spa ORB, Appendix 88, Medical Officer's Reports, June 1944: AIR 28/956.

5 5 Group ORB, Appendix: AIR 25/122.

6 5 Group ORB: AIR 25/110; Saumur attack report: AIR 14/2057.

7 Letter, 9 June 1944: Harris Archive, H59.

8 Night Raid Report No. 628, Saumur: AIR 14/3412.

9 On 9 January 1944 Gp Capts. Winter Morgan and Molesworth, AVM Cochrane and Air Cdr Patch had met Wallis to discuss methods of destroying E- and U-boat pens. Wallis then estimated that such pens would be vulnerable to near misses by Tallboy, and that Tallboy M would be capable of penetrating their roofs: Tallboy Development Trials and G–S, AIR 14/2011, Document 1a.

10 Tallboy: AIR 14/2008, Document 29a.

11 Tent, 1996, p.141.

12 Reconnaissance of Le Havre was undertaken by a Spitfire of 542 Squadron, which left Benson at 12.45 and returned 90 minutes later: 542 Sqn ORB, AIR 27/2017.

13 Action Sheet signal, Le Havre (Z536), 5 Group ORB, Appendix, 14 June 1944: AIR 25/122.

14 *Boulogne, 15 June* – E-boat pens: 5 Group ORB, Appendix, AIR 25/122; 5 Group ORB, AIR 25/110; Bomber Command Operational Film No. 165. *Watten, 19 June* – V-weapon site: 5 Group ORB, AIR 25/110. *Wizernes, 20 June* – V-weapon site. *Wizernes, 22 June*; *Wizernes, 24 June*; *Siracourt, 25 June* – V-weapon site. *St Leu d'Esserent, 4 July* – V-1 installation site: 5 Group ORB, AIR 25/110; Appendix, AIR 25/123; Night Raid Report No. 651, AIR 14/3412.

15 For example, AAEE report MAP, 21 June: Tallboy handling, AIR 14/2180.

16 The attack met difficulties, including bomb-release and bombsight failures, the indistinctness of TIs in bright daylight, and much flak: 5 Group ORB, Appendix, AIR 25/123.

17 Letter, 8 June 1944: Harris Archive, H59.

18 Recommendation for immediate honours and awards, 10 July 1944.

19 Letter, 8 June 1944: Harris Archive, H59.

20 Letter, 10 June 1944: Harris Archive, H59.

21 As soon as Cheshire departed, crews began to be assimilated to 617 Sqn direct from Lancaster Finishing School, without any previous Bomber Command experience. Tom Bennett believes that this policy was Cochrane's, that it 'diluted the overall effect of the squadron's efforts', and that the change of policy influenced the decision to screen

Cheshire, who would otherwise have objected (letter to author, 8
Dec. 1998).

22 Cheshire to Douglas Baxter, letter, 12 July 1944: LCA BC 51.

23 Taped recollection, transcript, 4 May 1953: LCA BC 53.

24 Sir Ralph Cochrane, 21 May 1954: LCA BC 53.

25 Dobson, 9 Sept. 1944; Handley Page, 13 Sept.; Evill, 8 Sept.; Sinclair,
7 Sept.; 'Man in Street', 8 Sept.; William Teeling MP, 11 Sept.; J. H.
Barnes, 9 Sept.; Carr (by telegram to India), 14 Sept.: LCA BC 51.

26 Guy Gibson, letter, 12 Sept. 1944: LCA BC 51.

10. ASIA AND WASHINGTON

1 Boyle, 1955, pp.241–50; *FV*, pp.45–7.

2 Anderson, 1991, p.312.

3 Richards and Saunders, 1975, iii, p.312.

4 P. Warner, 1981, p.184.

5 Sqn Ldr Hole to Cheshire, letter, 20 Dec. 1944: LCA BC 51.

6 Richards and Saunders, 1975, iii, p.343.

7 'Special bombing force for attacks on precision targets': AIR 23/
2608.

8 Luedecke to Stratemeyer, 11 Oct. 1944: AIR 23/2608.

9 Nick Ross, conversation with author, 11 April 1996.

10 Cheshire to N. Ross, letter, 16 Oct. 1944.

11 Mountbatten to Leigh-Mallory, 2 Nov. 1944, Top Secret SC4/1771/
1: AIR 23/2869.

12 DAC 379: AIR 23/2608.

13 Letter, 18 Nov. 1944: LCA BC 51.

14 Signal, ACSEA to HQ EAC, 21 Nov. 1944: LCA BC 51.

15 Letter Order 976, HQ AAF, India-Burma Sector, 23 Nov. 1944:
LCA BC 51.

16 LCA BC 53.

17 Boyle, 1955, p.248.

18 ibid.

19 Service records, 'Movements', 22 Dec. 1944.

20 Service records, 'Movements', 15 Jan. 1945.

21 Cheshire to Air Commodore W. A. D. Brook. Director of Plans,
HQ ACSEA, 16 Jan. 1945: LCA BC 51.

22 Cheshire regularly lectured to the RCAF staff course at Toronto: e.g. 23 March 1945, RAF Target Marking; 7th War Course, April 1945: LCA BC 51.

23 V. H. Tait (Dg of S) to S. O. Bufton (DB Ops), 24 May 1945; Bufton to Tait, 25 May 1945: AIR 20/4060.

24 *FV*, p.45.

25 Cheshire to Harris, 6 March 1945: LCA BC 51.

26 cf. *FV*, p.46.

27 Gotthelf to Cheshire, letter, 18 July 1945: LCA BC 51. For this commission Cheshire was due to be paid $1,000.

28 Dorrie Peace to Cheshire, 5 Nov. 1945, delivered in Washington: LCA BC 51.

29 e.g. Cheshire to Mrs James Loughland, 8 May 1945: LCA BC 51.

30 H. A. Unwin to Cheshire, 20 June 1945: LCA BC 51.

31 Christopher Cheshire, conversation with author, 26 May 1995.

32 *FV*, p.47.

33 *FV*, p.48.

34 Boyle, 1955, p.276.

35 ibid., p.277.

36 *Face of Victory*, draft: LCA 7:1/17.

37 John Bunyan, *The Pilgrim's Progress*.

38 Cheshire gave conflicting accounts of the date at which he received instructions to travel to the Pacific. In *The Face of Victory* he wrote that the orders were given a few days after his return from England, and that there followed 'three difficult weeks of marking time, of being briefed more closely on what was expected of me' (pp.48–9). Letters written at the time indicate that he was aware of a forthcoming journey at least a week before the Trinity test at Alamogordo, New Mexico. However, in *The Light of Many Suns* and some other later sources Cheshire recorded that his orders were given on the day after the Trinity test, which would have been 17 July.

39 Cheshire (writing from Los Angeles) to Gotthelf, AC Spark Plug Division, 11 July 1945; to H. A. Unwin, 20 July 1945: LCA BC 51.

11. POTSDAM AND TINIAN

1 Cheshire, MS note, August 1945: LCA BC 51.
2 J. Chadwick, 'The Atom Bomb', *Liverpool Daily Post*, 4 March 1946. Chadwick's account drew extensively from that of another Manhattan scientist, Otto Frisch.
3 Thomas Farrell, impressions, contained within Memorandum from Groves to Marshall, 18 July 1945; Otto Frisch, eyewitness account, reproduced in Szasz, 1992, Appendix IV, p.153; Groves, 1962 (1983), pp.433–4.
4 *FV*, p.48.
5 *LMS*, pp.6–7.
6 ibid.
7 Szasz, 1992, p.xvii.
8 Gowing, 1964, p.236; cf. Brown, 1997.
9 Alperovitz, 1996, p.602.
10 USAEC, *In the Matter of J. Robert Oppenheimer*, p.175.
11 *LMS*, p.7.
12 *FV*, p.50; *LMS*, pp.7–8.
13 Ehrman, 1953, p.279.
14 L. R. Groves, Memorandum for the Secretary of War, 18 July 1945.
15 Henry Stimson, diary, 22 July 1945.
16 Sir Alan Brooke, CIGS, diary, 23 July 1945; Churchill: 'Moreover, we should not need the Russians', *Triumph and Tragedy*, 1954, p.553.
17 ibid., pp.552–3. Writing nine years later, Churchill misdated the arrival of Groves's full report to 18 July.
18 Proclamation to Japan, Article 10.
19 *LMS*, p.8.
20 ibid.
21 Truman, journal, 25 July 1945.
22 Gowing, 1964, p.373.
23 Cited in Groves, 1962 (1983 reprint), pp.308–9.
24 *LMS*, p.21.
25 Cheshire to Lt S. F. Stowe, US Navy Department, 1 Sept. 1945: LCA BC 51.
26 *LMS*, p.22.

27 Proclamation to Japan, Article 1.

28 Proclamation, Article 5.

12. CENTREBOARD

1 Cited in Boyle, 1955, p.256.

2 *LMS*, p.56.

3 Report of the Activities of 509th Composite Group during July and August 1945, d(2), Bombardier's Plan, HE Twentieth Air Force APO 234.

4 ibid., paras 2, 3.

5 General Arnold, diary of Pacific trip, 13 June 1945, Box 272, Arnold Papers, LC.

6 LeMay believed that Japan's surrender was already inevitable. The US Strategic Bombing Survey afterwards concurred, estimating categorically that Japan's government 'would have surrendered prior to 1st November and certainly before the end of the year, whether or not the atomic bombs had been dropped and Russia had entered the war': *Pacific Report No. 14; The Effects of Strategic Bombing on Japanese Morale.*

7 Boyle, 1955, p.255.

8 *LMS*, pp.25–6.

9 ibid., p.36.

10 ibid., p.37.

11 Taped recollection, transcript, 4 May 1953: LCA BC 53.

12 For the atmosphere and details of this briefing, recorded by one crew member in his diary, consult Thomas and Morgan-Witts, 1995, pp.167–9.

13 Sgt Abe Spitzer, diary, 4 Aug. 1945, cited in Thomas and Morgan-Witts, 1995, p.169.

14 ibid., p.182.

15 'The idea of a Britisher flying over Japan in a US bomber whatever it carried was looked on with disfavour. One was handicapped by the supra-secrecy and most of the individuals in the Pentagon not in the know', Lord Wilson to Andrew Boyle, letter, 16 Jan. 1955: LCA BC 51.

16 Reported by Boyle (1955, p.259) in direct speech. The source for the words attributed to Spaatz does not appear among Boyle's papers.

17 On 25 July, in Washington, Spaatz had received the authorization order for use of the bomb. It provided only for 'military and civilian scientific personnel from the War Department to observe and record the effects of the explosion'. Hence, while the order did not expressly forbid UK observers to take part, neither did it say that they could. As the only formal instruction in existence, it left Spaatz and LeMay with no latitude. Of course, if Cheshire was right in suspecting that LeMay was the problem, then the wording of the directive would have assisted LeMay's purpose. However, the directive was drafted by Groves.

18 Groves, 1962 (1983 reprint), p.314.

19 ibid.

20 *LMS*, p.38.

21 Cheshire, tactical report, 18 Aug. 1945.

22 Taped recollection, transcript, 4 May 1953: LCA BC 53.

23 Maitland Wilson to Andrew Boyle, letter, 16 Jan. 1955: LCA BC 51.

24 Telegram from JSM Washington to AMSSO, JSM 993, 8 Aug. 1945, 081850Z: CAB 105/50.

25 Szasz, 1992, p.xiii.

26 *LMS*, p.53.

27 *LMS*, p.54.

28 Leonard Cheshire, *Sunday Times*, 4 Aug. 1985.

29 *LMS*, pp.54–5.

30 Cheshire, tactical report, 18 Aug. 1945.

31 Hopkins's distance from Nagasaki at the moment of explosion has been various recorded as a hundred miles (Groves, 1962 (1983), p.346), 'about fifty miles' (*LMS*, p.58), and 'about forty miles' (Penney, cited in Boyle, 1955, p.261). Cheshire's report made nine days after the attack specified 'some eighty miles'.

32 *LMS*, p.57.

33 Cheshire, extracts from BBC telediphone recording, Manchester, 12 Nov. 1945: LCA BC 51.

Notes

13. SMITTEN CITIES

1 M. S. Attlee: Box 23, JSM Washington to AMSSO, 15 Sept. 1945.
2 'Group Captain Cheshire, V.C. Tells the First British Eyewitness Story of Nagasaki', *News Chronicle*, 18 Sept. 1945, p.2.
3 *Washington Mail*, 5 Sept. 1945.
4 *FV*, p.52.
5 Gowing, 1964, p.386.
6 Outline, 5 Dec. 1945: LCA BC 55.
7 *FV*, p.54.
8 17 Oct. 1945.
9 *FV*, p.54.
10 e.g on *Quiz Team*, recorded 15 Jan. 1946.
11 'Future of The Bomb', *Sunday Graphic*, 4 Nov. 1945, p.4.
12 Hennessy, 1993, pp.119–23.
13 Andrew Boyle suggested that Cheshire's departure from Washington was engineered 'by a mixture of bluff and special pleading' in the course of an interview with 'an official psychiatrist' (1955, p.265). The record of his medical board in London on 18 September 1945 leaves no doubt that the RAF's doctors reached an independent conclusion when they pronounced him unfit for continued service.
14 *Star*, 30 Jan. 1946; *Evening Standard*, 31 Jan. 1946.
15 *FV*, pp.52–3; *LMS*, p.68.
16 *FV*, p.53.
17 Gowing, 1964, p.381.
18 When, a year later, delivery systems were considered, Britain took exactly the conventional path against which Cheshire warned. The path led to the V-bombers: Wynn, 1994, p.6.
19 Hennessy, 1993, p.89.
20 LCA BC 55.
21 *FV*, pp.54–5.
22 Cheshire declined a second meeting: letter to Winn, 30 March 1946: LCA BC 55.
23 Letter to Sir Roy Dobson, A. V. Roe, 14 Dec. 1945: LCA BC 55.
24 Gaumont-British to Cheshire, 11 Feb. 1946: LCA BC 55.
25 'Speed. What is the Air Limit?' *Sunday Graphic*, 1 Jan. 1946.

26 'My Day with the Fastest Men on Earth', *Sunday Graphic*, 11 Aug. 1946.

27 'Why I Have Become a Flying Reporter', *Sunday Graphic*, 27 Oct. 1946.

28 *FV*, p.54.

29 MS draft, Feb./March 1946: LCA BC 54.

30 Boyle, 1955, p.275.

31 Letter, 31 March 1946: LCA BC 55.

32 Thomas Eggar & Sons to Cheshire, 27 June 1946: LCA BC 55.

33 Other distractions around this time included arrangements for shipping Constance's possessions back to America, and an unfulfilled plan to transplant the railway bungalow to the garden at Grey Walls.

34 Winstone, 1994, pp.97–8.

35 Tom Bennett wrote about Operation Taxable, enclosing a list of the thirty-two navigators who had made it possible, for consideration of awards: 'I can only appeal to you to see that justice is done' (Sqn Ldr T. Bennett, letter, 10 Dec. 1945). Cheshire replied, 'I agree entirely.' He would try, although since he had already taken the matter up 'most strenuously' he had little hope of success (letter, 12 Dec. 1945): LCA BC 55.

36 Letter from L. Ellwood, 11 June 1946: LCA BC 55.

37 Mrs Doreen Money to Cheshire, 1 May 1944: LCA BC 55.

38 *Sunday Graphic*, 3 Feb. 1946, p.11.

39 Richard Rivaz had survived the war, only to die on 13 October 1945 when a Liberator of RAF Transport Command in which he was travelling crashed at Meelsbrock near Brussels. C. Rivaz to Cheshire, 6 Feb. 1946: LCA BC 55.

40 'Letter about Demobilization', *Sunday Graphic*, 25 Nov. 1945, p.11.

41 *Daily Herald*, 23 Jan. 1946.

42 'A Raw Deal?', *Sunday Graphic*, 17 March 1946, p.6.

43 Taylor, 1992, p.600.

44 *Sunday Graphic*, 25 Nov. 1945, p.11.

45 'The Gibsons, the Martins and the Knights', *Sunday Graphic*, 9 Dec. 1945, p.11.

46 Cheshire to T. G. Redfearn, 19 July 1946: LCA BC 52.

47 *R. H. Tawney's Commonplace Book*, ed. J. M. Winter and D. M.

Joslin, 28 Dec. 1914, p.83. Cheshire wrote in similar terms in the Epilogue of *The Hidden World*.

48 Lionel Curtis, *Civitas Dei*, Vol.1 (1934), Vols.2, 3 (1937).

49 Lionel Curtis to Lord Perry, letter, 19 March 1946: LCA BC 52.

50 *Round Table*, March 1956.

51 'A Raw Deal?', *Sunday Graphic*, 17 March 1946, p.6.

52 W. G. Saunders to Cheshire, 18 March 1946: LCA BC 52.

53 'I Offer a Challenge', *Sunday Graphic*, 31 March 1946, p.6.

54 Lionel Curtis to Lord Perry, letter, 19 March 1946: LCA BC 52.

55 Cheshire to Lady Macrobert, letter, 23 March 1946: LCA BC 52.

56 Lionel Curtis, letter, 1 March 1946: LCA BC 52.

57 Lord Perry, letters, 28 March and 9 April 1946; Sir Percy Malcolm Stewart, annotated reply, 10 May 1946: LCA BC 52.

58 David Shannon, conversation with author, 3 July 1989.

59 Christopher Cheshire, conversation with author, 28 May 1995.

60 Letter, 4 April 1946: LCA BC 52.

61 'My Experiment', *Sunday Graphic*, 21 April 1946, p.4.

62 Letter, 22 April 1946: LCA BC 53.

63 H. H. B. Lund to Cheshire, 13 May 1946: LCA BC 54.

64 Lionel Curtis, letter, 1 May 1946: LCA BC 52.

65 VIP Association, Report of the Second General Meeting, 19 May 1946: LCA BC 52.

66 VIP Association Ltd, First Quarterly Report, 5 Sept. 1946: LCA BC 52.

67 BBC to Cheshire, 19 March 1946: LCA BC 54.

68 VIP Report of Progress, 30 June 1946.

69 Letter, 28 June 1946: LCA BC 52.

70 Letter, 30 July 1946: LCA BC 52.

71 Raymond Broad, MoI, to Cheshire, 4 July 1946: LCA BC 54.

72 P. B. Joubert to AM Sir P. Wigglesworth, AOC-in-C British Forces of Occupation, Germany, 28 Aug. 1946: LCA BC 55.

73 Letter, 18 Oct. 1946: LCA BC 55.

74 19 July 1946.

75 E. Howard-Williams to Cheshire, 23 July 1946: LCA BC 55.

76 VIP Association Ltd, First Quarterly Report by Group Captain Cheshire, 5 Sept. 1946; 'My Colony Today', *Sunday Graphic*, 18 Aug. 1946, p.4.

77 *Leicester Evening Mail*, 2 Sept. 1946.

78 Mrs Nancy Barstow, letter, 15 Sept. 1946: LCA BC 52.

79 Thomas Eggar and Sons to Cheshire, 28 Oct. 1946: LCA BC 52.

80 These were two ex-RAF Mosquitoes PR XVI. Cheshire acquired them through Marshalls of Cambridge, who told him on 23 October that they were ready for collection from 44 MU at Edzell in Scotland.

81 'Why I Have Become a Flying Reporter', *Sunday Graphic*, 27 Oct. 1946, p.6.

82 Letter, 2 Nov. 1946: LCA BC 52.

83 Letter, 28 Oct. 1946: LCA BC 52.

84 Letter, 28 Oct. 1946: LCA BC 52.

85 'Germany: the Truth', *Sunday Graphic*, 10 Nov. 1946, p.6.

86 *Daily Graphic*, 8 Nov. 1946.

87 *Evening Standard*, 8 Nov. 1946.

88 20 Nov. 1946.

89 Letter, 18 Nov. 1946: LCA BC 55.

90 *FV*, p.82.

91 ibid.

92 Or possibly Munich: there is a break in his log book entries between 12 January (when he records himself as arriving in Munich) and 1 February, when he departed. However, the log book in this period was unusually inaccurate.

93 *FV*, p.81.

94 Marguerite Cowey to Andrew Boyle, 15 July 1954: LCA BC 53.

95 Boyle, 1955, p.294.

96 *FV*, p.83.

97 Cheshire to Sqn Ldr W. Young-Robinson, War Office, 27 Feb. 1947: LCA BC 52.

98 Cheshire, MS fragment, n.d. (1947): LCA BC 52.

99 Cheshire to Sir John Slessor, 25 March 1947: LCA BC 52.

100 *Evening Standard*, 28 April 1947.

101 In March 1947 Whitney Straight expressed interest in one of the machines. Both were eventually sold, and then illicitly flown to join the makeshift Israeli air force. One crashed en route.

102 Robinson, manager, Barclays Bank, Oxford, to Cheshire, 15 April 1947: LCA BC 55.

103 Cheshire to Barclays Bank, 28 April 1947: LCA BC 55.

104 VIP Association accounts, year to 31 Dec. 1947; *FV*, p.100.

105 *FV*, p.108.

106 Portsmouth Group Hospital Management Committee, 15 March 1955.

14. LE COURT

1 Letter, 22 Aug. 1948: LCA BC 55.

2 Boyle, 1955, p.320.

3 *FV*, p.135.

4 Leonard Cheshire, 'Mission for the Relief of Suffering', MS, Feb. 1957.

5 *FV*, p.121–2.

6 Cited in *FV*, p.123.

7 *FV*, p.123.

8 *FV*, p.125.

9 *FV*, p.115.

10 John iii, 8.

11 Leonard Cheshire, 'Mission for the Relief of Suffering', MS, 1957.

12 Cheshire to Harry Rae, letter, 1 Nov. 1948: LCA BC 56.

13 'Yes, nominally I was brought up as an Anglican, but Father and Mother weren't really believers . . . it was a social convention': *WG*, p.20.

14 *FV*, p.140.

15 *FV*, p.141.

16 *WG*, p.202.

17 *Second Readings*, 'Out of the Blue', p.7: Stowe Archive.

18 *WG*, pp.85–6.

19 *FV*, pp.155–6.

20 Frances Jeram to Cheshire, letter, 13 April 1949: LCA BC 57.

21 Cheshire to Frances Jeram, letter, 14 April 1949: LCA BC 57.

22 Cheshire to Frances Jeram, letter, 6 May 1949: LCA BC 57.

23 Frances Jeram to Cheshire, letter, 8×15 May 1949: LCA BC 57.

24 Cheshire to Frances Jeram, letter, 6 June 1949: LCA BC 57.

25 Cheshire to Frances Jeram, letter, 26 June 1949: LCA BC 57.

26 Christopher Cheshire, conversation with author, 28 May 1995.

27 Bill Roberts, conversation with author, 9 June 1995.
28 Frances Jeram, conversation with author, 7 May 1996.
29 'Friendless Find an Open Door', *News Chronicle*, 24 Dec. 1949.
30 Frances Jeram, conversation with author, 7 May 1996.
31 Cheshire to Frances Jeram, letter, 14 Feb. 1950: LCA BC 57.
32 Cheshire to Frances Jeram, letter, 6 March 1950: LCA BC 57.
33 F. Jeram, 'Le Court', *The Almoner*, Vol. 4, No. 4, July 1951.
34 Cheshire to Frances Jeram, letter, 6 March 1950: LCA BC 57.
35 Conversation with author, 28 May 1996.
36 Cheshire to Frances Jeram, letter, 29 June 1950: LCA BC 57.

15. NEAR ENGLAND'S END

1 See p.400
2 B. N. Wallis, cited in Rabbets, p.18.
3 Wallis's earlier work on airships, and aircraft like the Wellesley, had fallen into this pattern: Norman Boorer, *Barnes Wallis, Designer: A Memorial Lecture*, Royal Aeronautical Society, 4 March 1981.
4 Norman Boorer, conversation with author, 3 July 1996.
5 Morpurgo, 1981, p.312.
6 Andrew Boyle, interview with B. N. Wallis, 1954: LCA BC 53.
7 *Sunday Pictorial*, 3 Feb. 1952, p.5.
8 Cheshire to Andrew Boyle, letter, n.d. (Oct. 1950): Eleanor Boyle.
9 Cf. Andrew Boyle, 'The Bomber and the Theologian', *Catholic Herald*, 17 Aug. 1951.
10 Cheshire to Boyle, letter, 24 Oct. 1950: Eleanor Boyle.
11 Cheshire to Boyle, letter, 27 Nov. 1950: Eleanor Boyle.
12 MS, 23 Nov. 1950: Eleanor Boyle.
13 MS, n.d. (Nov. 1950): Eleanor Boyle.
14 'Concentrated and Immovable Targets. A Method of Attacking the Axis Powers', B. N. Wallis, 1940.
15 'The Atom Bomb', MS, n.d. (November/December 1950): Eleanor Boyle.
16 Cheshire to Boyle, letter, 11 Dec. 1950: Eleanor Boyle.
17 Cheshire to Boyle, letter, 17 Dec. 1950: Eleanor Boyle.
18 *Catholic Herald*, 22 Dec. 1950, p.1.
19 *FV*, p.162.

20 *HW*, p.37.

21 An uncontested divorce hearing was held in New London on 12 January 1951 and ratified twelve days later.

22 Andrew Boyle in interview with John Kirby, n.d. (1953 × 1954), MS notes: LCA BC 53.

23 *HW*, p.38.

24 Cheshire to Boyle, letter, 2 Feb. 1951: Eleanor Boyle.

25 'V.C. Begins a New Venture for the Sick', *Catholic Herald*, 16 March 1951.

26 Although the King Edward's Hospital Fund gave £1,500 to Le Court in December 1950, the year's out-turn still showed a deficit of £500.

27 'Our possible target date is August 4th', Cheshire to Boyle, letter, 13 April 1951: LCA GLC 26:7/3.

28 St Teresa's and Holy Cross account book, 2 May 1952–1953: LCA.

29 Cheshire to Boyle, letter, 13 April 1951: LCA GLC 26:7/3.

30 Margaret Masters, conversation with author, 28 Aug. 1994.

31 The correspondence centred on Wallis's Gaussian distribution plots of the fall of 617 Sqn's bombs.

32 Cheshire to Boyle, letter, 18 May 1951: Eleanor Boyle.

33 *Hants and Sussex News*, 18 July 1951, p.6.

34 'Le Court, Cheshire Foundation Home for the Sick, Liss, Hants', *The Almoner*, Vol.4, No.4, July 1951.

35 Cheshire to Boyle, 5 Sept. 1951: Eleanor Boyle.

36 'War Hero's Home for Handicapped', *Western Sunday Independent*, 25 Nov. 1951.

37 Frances Jeram, letter to author, 16 May 1996.

38 Cheshire to Shelagh Howe, letter, 18 Feb. 1952: LCA.

39 Eirene Andrews via Frances Jeram, letter to author, 16 May 1996.

40 Cheshire to Boyle, letter, 9 Oct. 1951: Eleanor Boyle.

41 Cheshire to Frances Jeram, 10 Jan. 1952: LCA BC 55.

42 Cheshire to Boyle, letter, 4 April 1952: Eleanor Boyle.

43 Fr Ripley to Boyle, letter, 4 June 1954: LCA BC 53.

44 Revd Austen W. Delaney OSB to Andrew Boyle, n.d., 1954: Eleanor Boyle.

45 Cheshire to Shelagh Howe, letter, 23 Aug. 1952: LCA.

16. CONTEMPLATION AND ACTION

1 'Profile – Cheshire, V.C.', *Observer*, 19 Dec. 1954.
2 *Thoughts for the Future* (video), 1975.
3 W, pp.10–11.
4 Cheshire to Father Fuller, letter, 12 Aug. 1954: LCA FP.
5 Tony Mahon to Cheshire, letter, 16 March 1954: LCA LCF: UK 4, St Bridget's and St Cecilia's (1).
6 Cheshire to Andrew Boyle, letter, 28 Dec. 1954: Eleanor Boyle.
7 E. Anne Layton, letter to author, 4 April 1997.
8 Primrose Cheshire to Shelagh Howe, letter, 16 × 20 March 1953: LCA Howe.
9 *FV*, p.166.
10 Primrose Cheshire to Shelagh Howe, letter, 28 March 1953: LCA Howe.
11 Primrose Cheshire to Shelagh Howe, 8 April 1954: LCA Howe.
12 Primrose Cheshire to Shelagh Howe, letter, 24 May 1953: LCA Howe.
13 *HW*, p.108.
14 *HW*, p.111.
15 The two homes had been separated administratively, but not managerially, since September 1952: 'St Teresa's/Holy Cross Account Book 2 May 1952–1953': LCA LCF: UK.
16 W. Russell, *New Lives for Old*, p.68.
17 The switch of authority took effect from 29 June 1953: Cheshire to C. Tilson Chowne, letter, 8 Oct. 1953: LCA LCF: UK 4.
18 Cheshire to Shelagh Howe, letter, 7 Sept. 1953: LCA Howe.
19 A note drafted in November 1953 shows that Cheshire was thinking of vocational staff as Third Order members.
20 C. Tilson Chowne to Cheshire, letter, 10 Oct. 1953: LCA LCF: UK 4.
21 Cheshire to Tucker, Turner & Co., letter, 7 Nov. 1953: LCA LCF: UK 4.
22 Cheshire to Shelagh Howe, letter, 18 Sept. 1953: LCA Howe.
23 Cheshire to C. Tilson Chowne, letter, 8 Oct. 1953: LCA LCF: UK 4.

24 Cheshire to C. Tilson Chowne, letter, 2 Oct. 1953: LCA LCF: UK 4.

25 Cheshire to Tucker, Turner & Co., letters, 8 and 27 Oct. 1953: LCA LCF: UK 4.

26 Cheshire to Francis Grimshaw (Bishop of Plymouth), letter, 14 Oct. 1953; cf. memo of 10 Oct. 1953 for Trustees' meeting of emerging St Cecilia's Trust on 14 Oct. 1953: LCA LCF: UK 4.

27 Peter Meade to Cheshire, letter, 29 Oct. 1953.

28 Cheshire to Tucker, Turner & Co., letter, 7 Nov. 1953; Tucker, Turner & Co. to Cheshire, letter, 4 Nov. 1953: LCA LCF: UK 4.

29 W, pp.2–3.

30 Primrose Cheshire to Shelagh Howe, 2 Sept. 1953: LCA Howe.

31 W, p.11.

32 W, p.12.

33 ibid.

34 Cheshire's letter of 25 November was incorrectly addressed to the Rector of Farm Street, which was not then parochial. The letter was forwarded to Father Fuller at Warwick Street: LCA FP.

35 Cheshire to Father Fuller, letter, 28 Nov. 1953: LCA FP.

36 W, p.13.

37 W, p.14.

38 This was to have been crewed by the aristocratic team of Lady Winifred Tryon and Lady Phipps.

39 *Reynolds*, 3 Jan. 1954.

40 A memorandum of 10 Oct. 1953 indicates that Cheshire's first thought was an autobiography.

41 Andrew Boyle to Dr and Mrs Cheshire, letter, 1 Dec. 1953: Eleanor Boyle.

42 Evans to Boyle, letter, 12 Nov. 1953: LCA GLC BC 53.

43 Cheshire to Boyle, letter, 1 Dec. 1953: Eleanor Boyle.

44 J. Browning (Evans Bros.) to Cheshire, letter, 4 Dec. 1953: LCA GLC BC 53.

45 Cheshire to Evans, 6 Dec. 1954; Evans to Boyle, 10 Dec. 1954; Boyle to Evans, 29 Dec. 1954: LCA GLC BC 53.

46 Cheshire to Shelagh Howe, letter, 2 Jan. 1954: LCA Howe.

47 Cheshire to Francis Grimshaw (Bishop of Plymouth), letter, 16 Nov.

1953; Tozers to Cheshire, letter, 3 Feb. 1954; Tucker, Turner & Co. to Cheshire, letter, 4 Feb. 1954: LCA LCF: UK 4.

48 Cheshire to Tucker, Turner & Co., letter, 7 Nov. 1953: LCA LCF: UK 4.

49 Dr D. R. Marley to Cheshire, letter, 20 Jan. 1954: LCA LCF: UK 4.

50 R. Worthington to Father Fuller, letter, 25 Jan. 1954: LCA FP.

51 Cheshire to Shelagh Howe, letter, 25 Jan. 1954: LCA Howe.

52 Cheshire to Shelagh Howe, letter, 7 Feb. 1954: LCA Howe.

53 This was part of the difference between the £1,750 received from Chowne the previous June and the £1,500 returned to him in September 1953.

54 Cheshire to Andrew Boyle, letter, 20 Feb. 1954: Eleanor Boyle.

55 Cheshire to Boyle, letter, 11 March 1954: Eleanor Boyle.

56 W, p.57.

57 ibid., p.58.

58 Cheshire to Father Fuller, letter, 24 Feb. 1954: LCA FP.

59 W, pp.58–9.

60 Cheshire to Shelagh Howe, letter, 8 Feb. 1954: LCA Howe.

61 Primrose Cheshire to Shelagh Howe, letter, 6 March 1954: LCA Howe.

62 Primrose Cheshire to Boyle, letter, 20 Jan. 1954: LCA BC 53. Some considered the buses to be 'a rather pointless sideline': W, p.31.

63 F. Addington Symonds to Cheshire, letter, 8 April 1954: Eleanor Boyle.

64 Cheshire to Boyle, taped message (transcript), 17 April 1954: Eleanor Boyle.

65 Boyle to Collins, letter, 30 April 1954: LCA GLC BC 53.

17. LOURDES AND BROMLEY

1 W, p.36.

2 W, p.40.

3 Father Reginald Fuller, conversation with author, 24 April 1996.

4 Writing to Shelagh Howe, Cheshire was at pains to stress that a cure had not been the 'primary purpose of the visit': letter, 5 May 1954: LCA Howe.

5 *Picture Post*, 8 May 1954, p.13.

6 Letter, 13 May 1954: Eleanor Boyle.

7 MS note, 15 May 1954: Eleanor Boyle.

8 T. H. White to Boyle, 25 May 1954: Eleanor Boyle.

9 Cheshire to Father Fuller, letter, 16 May 1954: LCA FP.

10 Father Fuller, conversation with author, 24 April 1996.

11 Letter, 17 May 1954: Eleanor Boyle.

12 Letter, 18 May 1954: Eleanor Boyle.

13 W, p.50.

14 W, p.51.

15 W, p.52.

16 ibid.

17 Cheshire to Shelagh Howe, letter, 18 May 1954: LCA Howe.

18 Pilgrimage to Lourdes 'For the Relief of Suffering', leaflet, May 1954.

19 Cheshire to Father Fuller, letter, 20 May 1954: LCA FP.

20 W, p.53.

21 On 6 June 1954 Cheshire wrote to Boyle, enclosing a letter to Collins which confirmed Boyle as his official biographer. Boyle commented: 'It certainly promises to cramp and stifle any intention Evans may have had of misleading the press and publishing world': LCA BC 53.

22 Letter, 1 June 1954: LCA FP.

23 LCA: Howe.

24 Primrose Cheshire to Shelagh Howe, 22 June 1954: LCA Howe.

25 Cheshire to Father Fuller, letter and draft, 22 June 1954: LCA FP.

26 Alan Finch to Boyle, letter, 7 May 1954: LCA BC 53.

27 Cheshire Foundation Homes for the Sick, Minute 2 of meeting held 23 July 1954.

28 Cheshire to Cuthbert Fitzherbert, cited by Fitzherbert to Cheshire, letter, 3 Sept. 1954: LCA FP.

29 The Carnegie Foundation's grant required a charitable body to which it could be conveyed.

30 Cheshire to Sir Cuthbert Fitzherbert, letter, 29 July 1954: LCA FP.

31 W, p.18.

32 W, p.19.

33 Valued at £1,500 and £250, respectively.

34 R. Worthington to J. B. Finnie, letter, 30 July 1954: LCA FP.

35 Jamieson handed over a personal cheque for £1,000 when the trustees

met for the first time on 3 August 1954: Minutes of the first meeting of the St Cecilia's Cheshire Trust: LCA FP.

36 R. Worthington to Father Fuller, letter, 17 Aug. 1954: LCA FP.

37 W, p.57.

38 Cheshire was now in close contact with Vera Barclay, the UK representative of Commendatore Enrie, in whom authority over photographs of the Shroud was vested. On 15 August Vera Barclay told Father Fuller that Cheshire had been asked to write a booklet about the Shroud 'for the man in the street', while Cheshire had asked her to write a book for children. Barclay wondered if her own book should be anonymous; her opposition to evolutionary theory had made her suspect in the Catholic intellectual world; it might be bad for 'a crank' to be associated in print with either the Shroud or Cheshire. 'On the other hand, this would be capitulating to the devil – the Enemy.'

39 Author of *Journey's End* and the screenplay of *The Dam Busters*.

40 Strictly, a sodality.

41 On 17 September Vera Barclay told Father Fuller, 'The Shroud is now Leonard's greatest interest . . . it makes him more active than he should be . . . It is not I egg him on: quite the opposite.'

42 Cheshire to Father Fuller, letter, 13 Sept. 1955: LCA FP.

43 On 11 September Frank Layton briefed Cheshire on progress made with the bus. It had been overhauled, a committee had been formed to run it and they would soon be recruiting drivers and speakers. The rector of Wimbledon College had provided space for repair and parking, and would arrange talks to children at Sacred Heart Schools: LCA GLC 39:7/1–2.

44 W, p.20.

45 Cheshire to Shelagh Howe, letter, 9 Aug. 1954: LCA Howe.

46 Cheshire to Shelagh Howe, 18 Sept. 1954: LCA Howe.

47 Mrs Chowne was a Catholic. Cheshire saw the estate, as distinct from the shrine and mansion, as a business proposition for which he sought investors to provide £30,000 at interest of 3 per cent. Father Fuller was asked to stress that it would contribute to an event of 'permanent historical significance'. Cheshire hoped to raise the deposit money from 'other sources': Cheshire to Father Fuller, letter, 12 Aug. 1954: LCA FP.

48 Cheshire asked Father Fuller to ask the trustees if they would appoint him as one of their number: Cheshire to Father Fuller, letter, 12 Aug. 1954: LCA FP.

49 Letter, 13 Sept. 1954: LCA FP.

50 Later in October Cheshire submitted this as a formal proposal to a meeting of the foundation's trustees. The trustees 'had no up-to-date information concerning this home although it was reported that the local governors had resigned. It was felt that the trust could not accept any home unless it appeared to be reasonably able to carry on, and that this home be asked to accept a period of one year's probation before the trustees gave a final decision' (Minute 6 of meeting held 20 Oct. 1954).

51 Cheshire to Father Fuller, letter, 27 Sept. 1954: LCA FP.

52 Letter, 30 Sept. 1954: LCA FP.

52a Fitzherbert to Fr Fuller, letter, 8 Oct. 1954: LCA FP.

53 Father Fuller, letter to author, 8 Oct. 1997.

54 Cheshire to Father Fuller, letter, 21 Oct. 1954: LCA FP.

55 MS from Eleanor Boyle.

56 Boyle to Cheshire, letter, 18 Oct. 1954: LCA BC 53.

57 Boyle to Geoffrey Harmsworth, letter, 25 Oct. 1954: LCA BC 53.

58 Boyle to Christopher Cheshire, 11 Nov. 1954: LCA BC 53.

59 Cheshire's first recording was made on 16 November 1954.

60 Katherine Webb to Cheshire, letter, 18 Nov. 1954: LCA GLC 7:26/ 2; Cheshire to Webb, telegram, 19 Nov. 1954.

61 'Profile – Cheshire, V.C.', *Observer*, 19 Dec. 1954.

62 Andrew Boyle to Mollie Miles (director of the *Catholic Herald*), letter, 25 Nov. 1954: Eleanor Boyle.

63 Letter, 29 Nov. 1954: Eleanor Boyle.

64 Letter, 30 Nov. 1954: Eleanor Boyle.

65 LCA FP.

18. CLOSELY OBSERVED

1 Cheshire told Boyle that he had 'never had so much mail in my life': letter, 27 Dec. 1954: Eleanor Boyle.

2 Contracts were exchanged with Hutchinsons on 22 February 1955.

Cheshire was to have editorial control, and would pay Scott out of an advance on account of royalties.

3 The first draft was dated 3 October 1954. Following comment and criticism a second draft was completed on 11 November, followed by a 'working draft' on St Teresa's Day, and another revision on 10 January 1955.

4 The association's aims were to (i) sanctify the lives of its members; (ii) intercede for the dying; (iii) assist and further the work of mission by prayer, sacrifice, and by helping people to a better understanding of the meaning of suffering.

5 Cheshire considered that much of the trouble had been caused by 'tactless' and 'unauthorized handling of the staff': letter, 19 Dec. 1954: LCA GLC 31:22/4.

6 LCA GLC 40:33/1

7 Cheshire to Father Fuller, letter, 19 Feb. 1955: LCA FP.

8 In May 1952 the owners of Staunton Harold, Lord and Lady Ferrers, visited St Teresa's at Predannack. There was subsequent contact while Cheshire was in Midhurst.

9 The church passed to the National Trust in 1953.

10 Father Fuller to Cheshire, letter, Feb. 1955: LCA GLC 31:22/5–6.

11 Formerly Bishop of Plymouth, now Archbishop of Birmingham.

12 Letter, 1 March 1955: LCA FP.

13 In 1954 the mission published a leaflet which described Le Court, St Teresa's, St Cecilia's and the forthcoming St Bridget's (but not Holy Cross) all as 'Cheshire Homes', but explained that only Le Court and St Teresa's were established under the Cheshire Foundation Homes for the Sick. The foundation's trustees had recently discussed 'the desirability of separating in the public mind the Trust's own works from those of others less stable' (Minutes, 20 Oct. 1954).

14 'I Saw the Face of Christ', *Daily Sketch*, 7 March 1955, pp.4–5.

15 Cheshire to Shelagh Howe, letter, 26 March 1955.

16 Cheshire, 'How Christ was Crucified', *Picture Post*, 9 April 1955, pp.11–12, 16–17, 54.

17 Letters, 14 and 15 March 1955: LCA GLC 3:25/1, 2.

18 W, pp.40–41.

19 23 March 1955.

20 Dr Geoffrey Cheshire to Boyle, letter, 8 April 1955: LCA BC 53.

21 Margot Mason, quoted in Russell, 1963, p.76.

22 W, p.47.

23 ibid.

24 Frances Jeram, letter to author, 16 May 1996.

25 Letter, 25 March 1955: Eleanor Boyle.

26 Cheshire to Andrew Boyle, letter (PS), 11 Feb. 1955: Eleanor Boyle.

27 Letter, 25 March 1955: Eleanor Boyle.

28 Letter, 6 April 1955: Eleanor Boyle.

29 Cheshire to Boyle, letter, 26 April 1955: LCA, GLC: 27:112/3.

30 Greenfield to Cheshire, letter, 4 May 1955: LCA GLC 11:37/2.

31 Cheshire to Greenfield, letter, 5 May 1955: LCA GLC 11:37/1.

32 Boyle to Cheshire, letter, 13 May 1955: Eleanor Boyle.

33 Cheshire saw the need for an academic book. Early in May he raised the idea with Father Langton Fox, and tried it out on Ronald Mann, a doctor at Midhurst. Mann agreed that much written on the Shroud was scientifically 'very poor', and floated the idea of bringing 'real scholarship' to bear in a multi-author volume which could include essays by a biblical scholar, historian, chemist, physicist, and physician. Cheshire jumped at this: 'I am now in the process of forming the initial editorial board,' he told Mann on 13 May. Like the film, the project went unfulfilled, but occupied much of Cheshire's time.

34 On 10 May Cheshire told Shelagh Howe that for the time being Holy Cross could be one of his homes for the sick, but on a personal basis because it could not 'really be part of the mission' nor did it come under the trust. They would review this in three months time. 'In the meantime I will pay all the bills.'

35 Letter, 14 May 1955: Eleanor Boyle.

36 Andrew Boyle to Cheshire, letter, 18 May 1955. The Korda and Rank Organizations showed little interest, and Boyle's approach to R. C. Sherriff (letter, 21 May 1955) led nowhere: Eleanor Boyle.

37 Mrs Woollam to Dan Griffiths, letter, 14 May: LCA FP.

38 Margot Mason to Father Fuller, letter, 10 June 1955: LCA FP.

39 Primrose Cheshire to Shelagh Howe, letter, 19 June 1955: LCA Howe.

40 Cheshire to Sir Geoffrey Todd, letter, 23 June 1955.

41 W, p.50.

42 W, p.58.

43 After a delay at Nice the party divided, one group flying back to England, the other hiring a bus to complete the journey by road. The bus reached Turin after the ceremony.

44 Francis Grimshaw to Cheshire, letter, 18 July 1955: LCA FP.

45 Cheshire to Collins, letter: LCA GLC: PA DO-4, File 26.

46 William Collins to Cheshire, letter: LCA GLC: PA DO-4, File 26.

47 Letter, 18 July 1955: Eleanor Boyle.

48 Cheshire to William Collins, letter: LCA GLC: PA DO-4, File 26.

49 W, p.95.

50 Letter, 22 July 1955: Eleanor Boyle.

51 W, pp.96–9.

52 R. J. O'Connell to Cheshire, letter, 9 Aug. 1955.

53 RCA GLC 7:22/14.

54 BBC Home Service, 8.25 p.m., Sunday, 14 Aug. 1955.

55 Cheshire to Reginald Simpson, letter, 1 Sept. 1955: LCA GLC 7:22/12.

56 Reginald Simpson to Cheshire, letter, 3 Sept. 1955: LCA GLC 7:22/11.

57 Greenfield to Cheshire, letter, 20 Sept. 1955.

58 Shelagh Howe to Cheshire, letter, 19 Sept. 1955: LCA GLC 12/3:2.

59 Primrose Cheshire to Shelagh Howe, letter, 22 Sept. 1955.

60 Philomena Loneragan to Margot Mason, letter.

61 Sqn Ldr J. Hill, 'Cheshire Mission to India', 10 Oct. 1955: LCA GLC 38:56/1–3.

62 Mission for the Relief of Suffering, *Newsletter No. 1*, October 1955.

63 While the Air Council agreed to release Hill for the expedition, it appears that the Treasury refused to allow him to draw his pay during his absence: *Eastern Daily Press*, 'Squeezed Out', 7 Nov. 1955.

64 Passages were booked for Margot Mason, Sydney Whissen and Roy Sugden only on 26 October.

65 Letter, 25 Oct. 1955: LCA GLC 39:18/1–2.

19. TOUCH AND GO

1 Neither the six homes nor the foundation's trustees 'thought highly' of the expedition: *HW*, p.44.

2 W, p.152.

3 W, p.151.

4 *HW*, p.47.

5 On 3 November the AA told Phil Loneragan that the Office of the High Commission for India had not yet received a reply from the Indian authorities about the importation of the vehicles.

6 The import duty exceeded the vehicles' combined value. On top of this were demurrage charges, which rose by the day.

7 *HW*, pp.46–7.

8 This may have added to the pressure during the first days in India. Christopher told Cheshire that their parents were 'very upset mentally', the cause being 'not so much the divorce' itself as Christopher's 'friendship for someone else': Christopher Cheshire to Cheshire, letter, 9 Dec. 1955.

9 *FV*, pp.170–71.

10 *HW*, pp.46–7.

11 *FV*, p.170.

12 Russell was or had been other things too: an airman during the war and an author.

13 Margot Mason described Cheshire at this time as 'imperturbable' and very fit, although he was 'doing more than he should': letters to Robina White and Revd Christopher McNulty OSR, Reading, 18 Dec. 1955 and 4 Jan. 1956: LCA GLC 38:58/1–2, 39:41/1.

14 Russell, 1963, pp.98–101.

15 ibid., pp.101–3.

16 ibid., pp.108–9.

17 ibid; cf. *FV*, p.173.

18 Russell, p.109.

19 ibid.

20 Shanti Rani House, on Upper Strand Road, Serampore, in West Bengal.

21 *HW*, p.157.

22 Tape recording for wardens' meeting held 22 Feb. 1958.

23 See p.329; cf. Russell, 1963, p.93.

24 Geoffrey Cheshire to Andrew Boyle, letter, 10 Nov. 1955.

25 Primrose Cheshire to Shelagh Howe, letter, 6 Nov. 1955.

26 Primrose Cheshire to Andrew Boyle, letter, 17 Nov. 1955: Eleanor Boyle.

27 Shelagh Howe to Andrew Boyle, letter, 16 Nov. 1955: Eleanor Boyle.

28 Robert Worthington to Andrew Boyle, letter, 29 Oct. 1955: Eleanor Boyle.

29 Barnes Wallis to Andrew Boyle, letter, 21 Oct. 1955: Eleanor Boyle.

30 May O'Rourke to Cheshire, letter, 17 Oct. 1955: LCA GLC 40: 72/4.

31 'My feeling is that you are more interested in me as a person than the work itself' (Cheshire to Andrew Boyle, letter, 15 Nov. 1957: Eleanor Boyle). Cheshire was still under medical supervision, and in November 1955 Sir Geoffrey Todd conveniently imposed a three-month moratorium on all public appearances.

32 At this point not all the homes had been formally adopted by the foundation. Several were undergoing a term of probation, to test their viability with a view to adoption later in 1956.

33 Cited in Russell, 1963, p.95.

34 Sir Archibald Jamieson, for instance, wrote to Cheshire on 20 Dec. 1955, reporting on recent visits to Staunton Harold and St Bridget's: 'They are, of course, two very different propositions, but I believe that both will become effective members of the Cheshire Foundation within six months to a year.' An anonymous friend had just contributed £5,000 for a new wing at Bromley.

35 Philomena Loneragan to Cheshire, letter, 29 Nov. 1955.

36 Cheshire to Shelagh Howe, letter, 24 Nov. 1955: LCA Howe.

37 Russell, 1963, p.81.

38 The trustees resolved, in his absence, that Wilding should receive an ex gratia payment (Cheshire Foundation Trust for the Sick, Minutes, 26 Jan. 1956). On 27 January Cheshire's father explained that the trustees had 'sent him off today to Austria for at least a fortnight'.

39 Geoffrey Cheshire to Cheshire, letter, 27 Jan. 1956: LCA GLC 31:6/ 1–2, cf. Minute of Trustees' meeting held on 26 Jan. 1956.

40 Shelagh Howe to Andrew Boyle, letter, 16 Nov. 1955: Eleanor Boyle.

41 Primrose Cheshire to Shelagh Howe, letter, 10 Feb. 1956: LCA Howe.

42 Philomena Loneragan to Cheshire, letter, 2 Feb. 1956.

43 Freda Wilson to Philomena Loneragan, letter, 21 Feb. 1956.

44 Cheshire to Loneragan, letter, 16 Feb. 1956. In earlier letters Cheshire admitted that the care of mentally handicapped children called for special skills which the mission was unable to provide, and that at St Uriel's they had overreached themselves. However, a home for mentally handicapped children was subsequently started at Duntish Court, Buckland Newton, in Dorset, which later relocated to the Cheshire Home at Hawthorn Lodge, Dorchester.

45 Memorandum and Articles of Association, 3 Aug. 1955.

46 Russell, p.89.

47 One such project was at Wardour Castle (p.339, 347–8). Another, at this point still active, was Walsingham, to which for a time Cheshire considered relocating Holy Cross, and where his purchase of the village hall became national news: *News Chronicle*, 26 Jan. 1956.

48 Geoffrey Cheshire to Cheshire, letter, 27 Jan. 1956.

49 Again, Cheshire's pre-departure instructions may have contributed to the hiatus. In November 1955 Boyle wrote to Cheshire's father seeking advice on how to pay over half the first royalties from *No Passing Glory* to the mission. Dr Cheshire replied that it was 'essential' for Boyle to contact John Wilding, 'as he knows all about it' (Geoffrey Cheshire to Boyle, letter, 17 Nov. 1955: Eleanor Boyle).

50 Philomena Loneragan to Cheshire, letters, 25 Feb. 1956, 12 March 1956.

51 Cheshire had completed the book in November 1955, and sent it to Phil Loneragan for typing and circulation to George Greenfield, Francis Grimshaw and several other churchmen for criticism and comment. The eventual title *Pilgrimage to the Shroud* was a compromise. Cheshire wanted *Miracle in Turin*, but Grimshaw had misgivings about 'miracle' and proposed *Turin Pilgrimage*. Greenfield countered with *Little Josie*, and then just *Josie*. Cheshire didn't like that either. On 31 January Greenfield offered *Pilgrimage to the Shroud*. Cheshire couldn't improve on it.

52 Vera Barclay to Father Fuller, letter, 7 Feb. 1956: LCA FP.

53 Vera Barclay to Father Fuller, letter, 20 Feb. 1956: LCA FP.

54 Cheshire had asked Andrew Boyle to write this.

55 The *Literary Review*, journal of the Rationalist Press Association.

56 An anonymous well-wisher paid his air fare.

57 Phil Loneragan to Cheshire, letter, 30 March 1956.

58 Patients were transferred from the old home to the new in March 1956. In addition to Family Day on 20 April, the local committee organized an official opening, in two stages, on 5 May and 12 May.

59 For example in Bedford, on behalf of the Friends of Ampthill Park House: *Bedfordshire Times*, 20 July 1956.

60 28 May 1956.

61 'All went well in Rome . . . we were privileged enough to have a private audience at which we received the Holy Father's blessing': Cheshire to Andrew Boyle, letter, 10 May 1956: Eleanor Boyle.

62 The dispute involved a conflict of view on the management of the home, and was the first real test of the foundation's authority. When the trustees acted upon Cheshire's advice and asked the chairman to step down, the committee passed a resolution of non-compliance. Lord Justice Denning, chairman of the foundation, found the differences between the two principal figures in the dispute to be so acute that 'one or other must cease to have any part in running the home': 'Note on the Position at St Cecilia's, 24 August 1956'.

63 25 June 1956.

64 The trustees were doubtful about this project, which did not proceed: Minutes, 22 June 1956.

65 Cited in S. T. Warner, 1989, p.264.

66 *Daily Mail*, 17 July; *Daily Sketch*, 18 July; *Evening Standard*, 19 July 1956.

67 The Kangaroo Hop was composed for the occasion.

68 The earlier part of this letter concerned the mission's Land Rover. Despite the apparently conclusive intervention of the Indian Air Force, it appears that import negotiations remained unconcluded: Philomena Loneragan to Margot Mason, letter, 18 July 1956.

69 *Daily Sketch*, 18 July 1956.

70 ibid.

20. GATEWAY

1 Russell, 1963, p.107.

2 One of them was Russell Braddon.

3 LCA GLC.

4 *HW*, p.48.

5 The trustees insisted that the Walsingham proposal be 'thoroughly investigated', and that in the meantime the Cornwall County Council 'be left to take such action as they might think fit in removing the present patients from Holy Cross': Cheshire Foundation Trust, Minutes, 22 June 1956; Wilfrid Russell to Shelagh Howe, letter, 19 July 1956: LCA LCF: UK Wilfrid Russell.

6 Andrew Boyle to Cheshire, letter, 3 Feb. 1957: Eleanor Boyle.

7 Cheshire to Father Fuller, letter, 3 Dec. 1956: LCA FP.

8 Mr G. A. Worth and his family offered the house either as an outright gift, or for discounted purchase coupled with a covenant in favour of the foundation for seven years: Russell, 1963, pp.130–31.

9 e.g. Newcastle branch of the RAFA: *Newcastle Sunday Sun*, 19 May 1957.

10 e.g. Nottingham branch of Friends of Staunton Harold, 28 April 1957.

11 'Bomber VC Plans Home for Tyneside', *Newcastle Journal*, 25 May 1957; 'Cheshire Home for Tyneside?' *Newcastle Chronicle*, 25 May 1957.

12 Cheshire to Andrew Boyle, letter, 15 Nov. 1957: Eleanor Boyle.

13 *HW*, p.58.

14 *HW*, pp.60–68.

14a Letter, LCA FP.

15 *HW*, p.68.

16 ibid.

17 Primrose Cheshire to Cheshire, letter, 22 Feb. 1958.

18 Geoffrey Cheshire to Cheshire, 23 Feb. 1958.

19 Cheshire to Fr Fuller, letter, 29 March 1958: LCA FP.

20 Letter, 6 March 1958: LCA GLC 26.

21 Letter, 19 March 1958: LCA GLC 26.

21. RAPHAEL

1 *CL*, p.23.

2 Letter to Mabel Ryder, cited in *CL*, p.37.

3 *CL*, p.64.

4 cf. George Steiner, 'Postscript', *Language and Silence*, Penguin Books, 1969, p.192.

5 *CML*, p.192.

6 *CML*, p.231.

7 Primrose Cheshire to Cheshire, letter, 22 March 1958: LCA.

8 Phil Loneragan to Cheshire, 21 March 1958: LCA.

9 Cheshire to Phil Loneragan, 15 April 1958: LCA.

10 Letter, 9 May 1958: LCA.

11 Cheshire to George Greenfield, letter, 7 May 1958: LCA.

12 Russell, 1963, p.186.

13 Guinness, 1996, p.136.

14 Phil Loneragan to Cheshire, 27 Oct. 1958: LCA.

15 Cheshire to Alan Green, letter, 9 Sept. 1958: LCA.

16 Cheshire to Sue Ryder, letter, 14 Dec. 1958: LCA.

17 Cheshire to Sue Ryder, letter, 28 Nov. 1958: LCA.

18 Cheshire to Sue Ryder, letter, 14 Dec. 1958: LCA.

19 *The Times*, 9 Sept. 1958.

20 n.d. (1958).

21 Geoffrey Cheshire to Cheshire, letter, 31 Jan. 1959: LCA.

22 *HW*, pp.76–7.

23 Leonard Cheshire, interview with Kevin Brownlow, 21 Aug. 1991: Brownlow, 1996, p.739.

24 *HW*, p.71.

25 ibid.

26 Laurence Shirley, letter to author, 28 Dec. 1996.

27 *CML*, p.269.

28 ibid.

29 8 March 1959.

30 Primrose Cheshire to Cheshire, letter, 18 Feb. 1959: LCA GLC 33:9.

31 Geoffrey Cheshire to Cheshire, letter, 18 Feb. 1959: LCA GLC 33:10/2.

32 Frances Jeram, conversation with author.

33 Cheshire to Keith Astbury, letter, 6 March 1959.
34 Cheshire to George Greenfield, letter, 3/4 April 1959.
35 Lady Ryder of Warsaw, conversation with author, 1 Nov. 1995.
36 *CML*, p.270.

22. FLAMES FROM A CANDLE

1 The work of the Ryder Foundation, and much of that of the Ryder–Cheshire Foundation, is chronicled in Sue Ryder's autobiography, *Child of My Love*.
2 cf. Cheshire, 'Help for the Third World', *Times* letter, 7 Aug. 1980.
3 No systematic history of the foundation has yet been written. Russell (1963) and Spath (1977) give accounts of the early years which are, respectively, personal and anecdotal. A book by Dr Roland Farrell, begun *c.* 1960, was left unfinished at his death in 1966. Developments since the 1970s await a chronicler.
4 *WG*, p.174.
5 *WG*, p.175.
6 In 1979 the Japanese press accused Cheshire of setting up three new homes in Japan as an act of contrition or reparation for his part as an observer in the atomic bombing of Nagaski.
7 *WG*, p.178.
8 *WG*, p.186.
9 *WG*, p.180.
10 *WG*, pp.178–9.
11 In December 1954 Le Court's residents produced the first issue of a periodical, *The Cheshire Smile*, which has since become the homes' house magazine, progressing from a cyclostyled home-made publication bearing the face of a grinning cat (also a pun on Cheshire's own enigmatic smile) to the glossy publication it is today.
12 In 1963 the foundation's Memorandum of Association was modified with the additional object 'To promote organize arrange and participate in conferences and meetings on subjects touching the problems of the disabled and chronic sick and those who are or have been mentally handicapped.'
13 'Cheshire, VC, Sacking: Eleven Quit', *Daily Mirror*, 10 July 1963;

'Cheshire Accuses Staff', *Daily Telegraph*, 14 Dec. 1978 (allegations of the ill-treatment of patients).

14 Cheshire, recording for wardens' meeting held 22 Feb. 1958.

15 At the time of Cheshire's death these included, in various parts of the world, a home for children born with terminal AIDS, several homes for young disabled people, schemes for rehabilitation, programmes to combat TB and training for leprosy sufferers.

16 Memorandum & Articles of Association, The Cheshire Foundation Homes for the Sick, 1955; Foundation leaflet, 1961.

17 *Thoughts for the Future* (video made in 1975).

18 Minute of the Founder's talk to trustees at meeting on 13 July 1985: TRJUL85, Annexe A: LCA GLC UK.

19 Sir Christopher Foxley-Norris, conversation with author, 14 Oct. 1994.

20 Margot Mason to Wilfrid Russell, letter, 16 April 1962: LCA LCF: UK Wilfrid Russell.

21 Sir Christopher Foxley-Norris, conversation with author, 14 Oct. 1994.

22 Finance Committee, minutes of meeting held 9 Dec. 1969: LCA GLC UK 73/12.

23 Report of Study Weekend, November 1990: LCA LCF: UK: CO 74/1.

24 Brief for the Leonard Cheshire Foundation Name Review, 1996.

25 Cheshire to Winston Churchill, letter, 25 March 1974.

26 Cheshire, letter, 20 April 1960. During the preceding eight months houses had been considered and rejected at Aynho (near Oxford), Shepton Mallet and Stone, Staffordshire.

27 Gwen Forrestier-Walker to Cheshire, letter, 9 April 1960.

28 Revd Monsignor Namel Simaan, Vicar General in Amman, to Cheshire, 26 March 1963.

29 Cheshire to Revd G. Volery, Council of Major Religious Superiors, 31 Dec. 1963.

23. AT HOME AND ABROAD

1 *CML*, p.271.
2 ibid.
3 Wally Sullivan, conversation with author, 10 Oct. 1995.
4 Quoted in Brownlow, 1996, pp.738–9.
5 Sara Lean, quoted in Brownlow, 1996, p.593.
6 Lady Sandra Lean, interview with Kevin Brownlow, quoted in Brownlow, 1996, p.784, n. 82.
7 Quoted in Brownlow, 1996, p.740.
7a ibid.
8 23 June 1987.
9 Cheshire to Wally Sullivan, memo, 10 Sept. 1979.
10 *WG*, p.199.
11 *WG*, pp.199–200.
12 Letter, 22 Oct. 1979: RCA GLC DO-35, 195:14.
13 'A weapon is not immoral in itself, it's the use to which it's put': *WG*, p.71.
14 'The Church in the Nuclear Age', draft, 28 April 1982.

24. FOR YOUR TOMORROW

1 'World War Memorial Fund for Disaster Relief', inaugural paper, 11 Oct. 1988.
2 *WG*, p.200.
3 Paper, 11 Oct. 1988.
4 9 Nov. 1998.
5 25 April 1989.
6 Cheshire to the Chairman of Barclays Bank, letter, 3 Feb. 1989; Cheshire to Mr B. Carr, Head of Barclays Community Enterprises, letter, 23 Feb. 1989: LCA GLC RP, D100 46/12.
7 Mr B. Carr to Cheshire, letters, 15 Feb., 8 March 1989.
8 ibid.
9 'World War Memorial Fund for Disaster Relief', inaugural paper, 11 Oct. 1988.
10 There were other differences. The fund was a one-off appeal; 'no one is asked to contribute a second time': inaugural paper, 11 Oct. 1988.

11 ibid.

12 Advisory Committee, Minutes of First Meeting, 16 May 1989.

13 Composed by Vivian Ellis.

14 e.g. *The Times*, 26 June 1989; *Sunday Times*, 23 July 1989.

15 28/29 August 1989.

16 e.g. *Guardian, Independent*. Cf. *The Times*, 23 Aug. 1989.

17 Charity Commission to Cheshire, letter, 1 Sept. 1989: LCA GLC: PA DO/96.

18 Charity Commission to Cheshire, letter, 15 Sept. 1989. However, the trust deed was not engrossed until 15 Feb. 1990: LCA GLC D100 46/12.

19 Cheshire to Sir Peter Ramsbotham, memo, n.d. (1989): LCA GLC PA DO/96.

20 Cheshire to Maurice Price, letter, 29 Sept. 1989: LCA GLC RP, D100 46/12.

21 Minutes of the inaugural meeting of the Board of Trustees, Memorial Fund for Disaster Relief, 25 March 1992.

22 These included Mrs Barbara Bush, Patron of the Cheshire Homes in the US, and Mrs Marilyn Quayle, wife of the vice-president.

23 The associations had said that their main concerns centred upon US national security and the welfare of their own members: Cheshire to Mrs Marilyn Quayle, letter, 25 May 1989: LCA GLC RP, D100 46/12.

24 John A. King to Cheshire, letter, 2 Nov. 1989; Cheshire to Capt. Alan Stuart, letter, 25 May 1989; LCA GLC RP, D100 46/12.

25 Cheshire to Casper Weinberger, letter, 13 Dec. 1989: LCA GLC RP, D100 46/12.

26 *Daily Telegraph*, 17 Jan. 1990; *International Herald Tribune*, 20/21 Jan. 1990.

27 Dick Cheney, letter, 12 April 1990.

28 Winston Lord, Tom Pownall and Jane Fonda were among those mentioned.

29 These included Tom Cruise, ex-President Ford, Admiral William J. Crowe (the newly-retired Chair of the US Joint Chiefs of Staff) and Senator Bill Bradley, just then popularly slated as the next President of the United States.

30 Katerina Thome, a Norwegian, had worked successfully in Japan and

in the US on behalf of the Leonard Cheshire Foundation and Ryder–
Cheshire Mission, and was described at this time as the 'Founder's
Personal International Representative'.

31 Katerina Thome to Cheshire, fax, 24 April 1990.

32 Minute 3/92 of Minutes of the Board of Trustees, 25 March 1992.
At this meeting the trustees unanimously agreed that the making of
the loan had been 'reasonable and prudent and in the best interests
of the fund at that time'.

33 *The Times*, 20 April 1990.

34 23 July 1990.

35 Robert Kandt, who was appointed at the end of 1990.

36 5 Sept. 1990.

37 2 Feb. 1991.

38 Memorial Fund for Disaster Relief, *Newsletter*, 1, autumn 1991.

39 *The Memorial Fund for Disaster Relief*, leaflet, n.d. (*c.* 1991 × 1992).

40 By March 1992 royalties received on the album/video amounted to
£290,000, with a further £60,000 imminently expected.

41 'World Memorial Pen Project. Briefing Paper', April 1992; Robert
Kandt to John Poppleton, memo, 24 April 1992: LCA GLC RP,
D100 46/12.

42 Cheshire, 'World Memorial Day', memo, n.d. (1991?): LCA GLC
RP, D100 46/12.

43 'The Successes and Failures of World Memorial Day 1992', Feb. 1992:
LCA GLC RP, D100 46/12.

44 Robert Kandt to Sir Peter Ramsbotham and David Puttnam, memo,
10 July 1992: LCA GLC RP, D100 46/12.

45 Minute 11/92 of Minutes of the Board of Trustees, 25 March 1992.

46 'Even the thought: "I am the one person equipped to deal with this
problem" may be dangerous': *HW*, p.54.

47 *HW*, p.57.

48 *FV*, p.107.

49 *CL*, 'Epilogue', p.80.

50 Fr R. C. Fuller, conversation with author, 24 April 1996.

25. GOING FORTH

1 Leonard Cheshire Foundation, Executive Committee Minutes, July 1988: LCA GLC 73/12, Box 9; cf. *WG*, p.201.

2 Cheshire to Michael and Pat Barstow, letter, 8 April 1992.

3 Cheshire to Herr E. Meschede, letter, 16 Jan. 1992: LCA GLC RP.

4 *HW*, p.143.

5 *HW*, p.137.

6 Cheshire to Michael and Pat Barstow, letter, 8 April 1992.

7 *CL*, p.20.

8 *CL*, pp.20–21.

9 Lord Puttnam, conversation with author, 2 July 1999.

10 Cheshire to Sir Peter Ramsbotham, letter, 5 May 1992. Moscow and the main Indian itinerary were dropped, leaving this a journey to Delhi and Dehra Dun: LCA GLC RP.

11 e.g. *Sunday Express*, 'War Hero Cheshire Ill', 17 May 1992.

12 The words were used as a voiceover near the beginning of the film.

13 Writing to General Dhody afterwards, Cheshire told him: 'perhaps of all the visits that I made to India since 1955 this last one has given me the greatest inspiration of all': letter, 4 June 1992.

14 Wally Sullivan, recording, 23 Aug. 1994: LCA, and conversation with author.

15 *CL*, pp.38–9.

16 The pages were edited by Fr Fuller and published in 1998: *Crossing the Finishing Line. Last Thoughts of Leonard Cheshire, VC*.

17 *CL*, pp.47–8.

18 *CL*, p.55.

19 *CL*, p.56.

20 Cheshire to Robert Kandt, memo, 6 July 1992: LCA GLC Ramsbotham Papers, D100 46/12.

21 Beforehand Cheshire asked Robert Kandt for a briefing paper, to help focus his thoughts.

22 *CL*, pp.75–6.

23 Anne de Courcey, published in the *Evening Standard*, 3 Aug. 1992.

24 Sue Ryder, conversation with author.

500

Notes

25 Wally Sullivan, recording, 23 Aug. 1994: LCA, and conversation with author.

26 *CL*, pp.78–9.

26. CHOSEN VESSEL

1 3 Aug. 1992.
2 Conversation with author, 14 Oct. 1994.
3 Lecture, Stowe School, 18 Nov. 1994.
4 *An Indian Summer*, Anglia TV.
5 Guinness, 1996, p.136.
6 Wilfrid Russell, letter to author, 18 Nov. 1996.
7 Frances Jeram, lecture, 10 June 1993.
8 Wally Sullivan, conversation with author, and recording, 23 Aug. 1994: LCA.
9 *CL*, p.13.
10 Wilfrid Bickley, conversation with author, 27 Feb. 1998.
11 Christopher Cheshire, conversation with author, 20 Aug. 1994.
12 *CL*, p.291.
13 *HW*, pp.98–9.

BIBLIOGRAPHY

Alperovitz, G., *The Decision to Use the Atomic Bomb*, Fontana, London, 1996 (first published HarperCollins, 1995).

Alvarez, L. W., *Alvarez: Adventures of a Physicist*, Basic Books, New York, 1987.

Anderson, C. F., *History of the Connection with India of the Family of Findlay Anderson*, privately printed (at Edinburgh University Press), 1927.

Anderson, D., 'Slim', in Keegan, J., ed., *Churchill's Generals*, Warner Books, London, 1992 (first published Weidenfeld & Nicolson, 1991), pp.298–322.

Annan, N., *Roxburgh of Stowe. The Life of J. F. Roxburgh and His Influence in the Public Schools*, The Thurloe Press, London, 1973 (originally published 1965).

Anon., *The Cheshire Homes. A Pictorial Record*, The Cheshire Smile, Liss, n.d.

Barclay, V., *The Face of a King. Group Captain Cheshire VC Champions the Holy Shroud*, Century Art Press, Bognor Regis, 1955.
'The Holy Shroud. A Divine Message for Our Day – through Photography', *Pathfinder*, Autumn 1956.

Bennett, D. C. T., *Pathfinder*, Goodall, London and St Albans, 1988 (originally published 1958).

Bennett, T., 'Operation Taxable', *Flypast*, November 1984, pp. 58–62.
'617: The Cheshire Era', Parts 1–5, *Flypast*, November 1993, pp. 15–16; January 1994, p. 43; March 1994, pp. 59–61; May 1994, pp. 60–62; July 1994, p.57.

Bevington, M., *Stowe. A Guide to the House*, Capability Books, Stowe, Buckingham, 1990.

Blanchett, C., *From Hull, Hell and Halifax. An Illustrated History of No. 4 Group 1937–1948*, Midland Counties Publications, 1992.

Boorer, N. W., *Barnes Wallis, Designer (1887–1979). A Memorial*

Lecture, Royal Aeronautical Society, delivered at British Aero-
space, Weybridge, 4 March 1981.

Boyle, A., *No Passing Glory. The Full and Authentic Biography of
Group Captain Cheshire VC, DSO, DFC,* Collins, London,
1955.

Braddon, R., *Cheshire VC. A Story of War and Peace,* Evans Brothers,
London, 1954.

Brown, A., *The Neutron and the Bomb. A Biography of Sir James
Chadwick,* Oxford University Press, 1997.

Brownlow, K., *David Lean,* Richard Cohen Books, London, 1996.

Cheshire, G. C., 'Ballooning, 1916', *The Flying M* (Journal of the
Society of Friends of the Royal Air Force Museum), vol. 13,
no. 3, pp. 19–27.

Cheshire, L., *Bomber Pilot,* Hutchinson, London, 1943.

    The Holy Face. An Account of the Oldest Photograph in the World,
    R. H. Johns, Newport, 1954.

    Pilgrimage to the Shroud, Hutchinson, London, 1956.

    The Face of Victory, Hutchinson, London, 1961.

    The Story of the Holy Shroud, ATV Library, London, 1958.

    The Hidden World, Collins, London and Glasgow, 1981.

    The Light of Many Suns. The Meaning of The Bomb, Methuen,
    London, 1985.

    Where is God in All This? Interview by Alenka Lawrence, St Paul
    Publications, Slough, 1991.

    Crossing the Finishing Line. Last Thoughts of Leonard Cheshire, VC,
    ed. Reginald C. Fuller, St Pauls, London and Maynooth, 1998.

Chorley, W. R., 'The Raid on Mailly-le-Camp', *Aviation News,*
3–16 October 1986, pp.506–12.

Chorley, W. R., *To See the Dawn Breaking. 76 Squadron History
Operations,* Compaid Graphics, Warrington, 1996 (first published
1981).

Churchill, W. S., *Triumph and Tragedy. The Second World War,* Vol.
VI, Cassell, London, 1954 (2nd edn, September 1954)

Cornwell, J., *Powers of Darkness, Powers of Light,* Viking, London,
1991.

Croom-Johnson, R. P., *The Origin of Stowe School,* Ipswich, 1953.

Dickson, L., *Richard Hillary,* Macmillan, London, 1950.

Donelly, L., *The Whitley Boys. No. 4 Group Operations 1939–42*, Air Research, 1991.

Doyle, W. H., 'Lost Players: Constance and Faire Binney', *Classic Images*, no. 214, April 1993, p.16.

Ehrman, J., *The Atomic Bomb. An Account of British Policy in the Second World War*, Cabinet Office, 1953.

Faulkes, S., *The Fatal Englishman. Three Short Lives*, Hutchinson, London, 1996.

Frankland, N., *History at War*, Giles de la Mare, London, 1998.

Gilbert, M., *Second World War*, Phoenix/Orion Books, 1995.
The Day the War Ended, Harper Collins, London, 1995.

Goss, C., *It's Suicide but It's Fun. The Story of 102 (Ceylon) Squadron 1917–1956*, Crécy Books, Bristol, 1995.

Gowing, M., *Britain and Atomic Energy 1939–1945*, Macmillan, London, 1964.

Groves, L. R., *Now It Can Be Told: The Story of the Manhattan Project*, Da Capo Press, New York, 1962 (reprinted 1983).

Guinness, A., *My Name Escapes Me: The Diary of a Retiring Actor*, Hamish Hamilton, London, 1996.

Harris, A. T., *Despatch on War Operations* (October 1945), with a Preface and Introduction by S. Cox, and *Harris – a German View* by H. Boog, Frank Cass, Ilford, 1995.
Bomber Offensive, Collins, London, 1947.

Hastings, M., *Bomber Command*, Pan, London, 1981 (first published Michael Joseph, 1979).

Hennessy, P., *Never Again. Britain 1945–1951*, Vintage, London, 1993 (first published Jonathan Cape, 1992).

Hersey, J., *Hiroshima*, Alfred A. Knopf, Inc., New York, 1946.

Hinsley, F. H., with Thomas, E. E., Ransom, C. F. G., and Knight, R. C., *British Intelligence in the Second World War*, Vol. 3, Part 1, HMSO, London, 1984.

Hutchinson, M., *The Story of St Bridget's Cheshire Home 1955–1995*, St Bridget's Cheshire Home, Rustington, 1995.

Inskip, H., *Leonard Cheshire Foundation Handbook of Care. 1: Residential Homes for the Physically Handicapped*, Leonard Cheshire Foundation/Bedford Square Press/NCVO, 1981.

Jary, C., *Portrait of a Bomber Pilot*, Sydney Jary, Bristol, 1990.

Jeram, F., 'Le Court, Cheshire Foundation Home for the Sick, Liss, Hants', *The Almoner*, vol.4, no.4, July 1951.

Johnson, B., and Heffernan, T., *A Most Secret Place*, Janes, London, 1982.

Lawrence, W. J., *No. 5 Bomber Group RAF*, Faber & Faber, London, 1951.

Lawson, F. H., 'Geoffrey Chevalier Cheshire 1886–1978', *Proceedings of the British Academy*, Vol. LXV, 1979, pp.611–32.

Mahaddie, T. G., *Hamish. The Memoirs of Group Captain T. G. Mahaddie DSO, DFC, AFC, CZMC, CENG, FRAeS*, Ian Allen, London, 1989.

Marshall, K., *The Pendulum and the Scythe. A History of the Operations Undertaken by No. 4 Group Bomber Command between 1939 and 1945*, Air Research Publications, Walton-on-Thames, 1996.

Mason, F. K., *The Avro Lancaster*, Aston Publications, Bourne End, Buckinghamshire, 1989.

Middlebrook, M., with Everitt, C., *The Bomber Command War Diaries: An Operational Reference Book, 1939–45*, Penguin Books, London, 1990.

Morpurgo, J. E., *Barnes Wallis: A Biography*, Ian Allen, London, 1981 (first published 1972).

Morris, R., with Dobinson, C., *Guy Gibson*, Penguin Books, London, 1995.

Niebuhr, R., *The Nature and Destiny of Man*, Nisbet, London, 1945 (first published 1941).

Norman, Bill, *Luftwaffe over the North. Episodes in an Air War 1939–1943*, Leo Cooper, London, 1993.

Rabbets, J. B., *Barnes Wallis. A Brief Historical Note*, Barnes Wallis Memorial Trust/Yorkshire Air Museum, n.d.

Ray, J., 'Not Made by Hands', *The Times Literary Supplement*, 18 October 1996, pp. 3–4.

Rhodes, R., *The Making of the Atomic Bomb*, Simon & Schuster, New York, 1986.

Richards, D., and Saunders, H., *The Royal Air Force 1939–1945*, Vol. 1 (Denis Richards), Vol. 2 (Denis Richards and Hilary Saunders), Vol. 3 (Hilary Saunders), HMSO, 1975.

Rivaz, R. C., *Tail Gunner*, Jarrolds, London, 1943.

Russell, W., *New Lives for Old. The Story of the Cheshire Homes*, Victor Gollancz, London, 1963.

Ryder, S., *Child of My Love*, Harvill, London, 1998.

Saward, D., *'Bomber' Harris*, first published 1984, Sphere Books, London, 1985.

Scott, J. D., *Vickers. A History*, Weidenfeld & Nicolson, London, 1962.

Sebba, A., *Mother Teresa. Beyond the Image*, Orion, London, 1997.

Simpson, T., *Lower than Low*, Libra, Tasmania, 1995.

Smith, D. J., 'The RAF and the North Atlantic Ferry Route', *Aviation News Magazine*, vol. 14, no. 22, 21 March to 3 April 1986, pp. 1096–105.

Spath, F., *How the Cheshire Homes Started*, Leonard Cheshire Foundation, 1977.

Symonds, C. P., 'The Human Response to Flying Stress', *British Medical Journal*, 4 and 11 December 1943, vol. ii, pp. 703 and 740.
'Anxiety Neurosis in Combatants', *Lancet*, 25 December 1943, p. 785.

Szasz, F. M., *The Day the Sun Rose Twice: The Story of the Trinity Site Nuclear Explosion, July 16, 1945*, University of New Mexico Press, Albuquerque, 1984.
British Scientists and the Manhattan Project. The Los Alamos Years, Macmillan, London, 1992.

Taylor, A. J. P., *English History 1914–1945*, OUP, 1992 (first published 1965).

Tent, J. F., *E-Boat Alert. Defending the Normandy Invasion Fleet*, Airlife, Shrewsbury, 1996.

Terraine, J., *The Right of the Line. The Royal Air Force in the European War 1939–1945*, Sceptre, 1988 (first published Hodder & Stoughton, 1985).

Thomas, G., and Morgan-Witts, M., *Enola Gay – Mission to Hiroshima*, White Owl Press, Loughborough, 1995.

Tibbets, P. W., *The Tibbets Story*, Stein & Day, New York, 1978.

Trower, W. P., ed., *Discovering Alvarez: Selected Works of Luis W. Alvarez, with Commentary by his Students and Colleagues*, University of Chicago Press, Chicago, 1987.

Warner, P., *Auchinleck: The Lonely Soldier*, Buchan & Enright, London, 1981.

Warner, S. T., *T. H. White. A Biography*, Oxford University Press, 1989.

Webster, C., and Frankland, N., *The Strategic Air Offensive against Germany, 1939–45*, 4 vols., HMSO, 1961.

Winstone, R., ed., *Tony Benn. Years of Hope. Diaries, Letters and Papers 1940–1962*, Hutchinson, London, 1994.

Wynn, H., *The RAF Strategic Nuclear Deterrent Forces: Their Origins, Roles and Deployment 1946–1969*, HMSO, London, 1994.

INDEX

Numbers in bold type refer to illustrations